The Dollarization Debate▲

EDITED BY

Dominick Salvatore

James W. Dean

Thomas D. Willett

OXFORD
UNIVERSITY PRESS

2003

OXFORD
UNIVERSITY PRESS

Oxford   New York
Auckland   Bangkok   Buenos Aires   Cape Town   Chennai
Dar es Salaam   Delhi   Hong Kong   Istanbul   Karachi   Kolkata
Kuala Lumpur   Madrid   Melbourne   Mexico City   Mumbai   Nairobi
São Paulo   Shanghai   Taipei   Tokyo   Toronto

Copyright © 2003 by Oxford University Press, Inc.

Published by Oxford University Press, Inc.
198 Madison Avenue, New York, New York 10016

www.oup.com   *au*

Oxford is a registered trademark of Oxford University Press

Library of Congress Cataloging-in-Publication Data
Salvatore, Dominick.
    The dollarization debate / Dominick Salvatore, James W. Dean, Thomas
Willett.
        p. cm.
Includes bibliographical references and index.
    ISBN 0-19-515535-1; 0-19-515536-X (pbk.)
    1. Money.   2. Dollar, American.   3. Foreign exchange.   4. Currency
question.   5. International finance.   I. Dean, James W.   II. Willett,
Thomas D.   III. Title.
    HG221 .S2564 2003
    332.4'564—dc21   2002011754

9 8 7 6 5 4 3 2 1

Printed in the United States of America
on acid-free paper

As my former colleague Bob Mundell likes to say, "Money is a bubble." In other words, it is terribly overpriced. Money as such—especially fiat money—has no inherent value. Its value is derived from social convention and, above all, *trust*—trust that an inherently worthless note will be accepted as a medium of exchange, and that the monetary authority will keep its supply under control. Without trust, the medium of exchange role of money is seriously undermined, with grave consequences for stability and growth. Unfortunately, few moneys have acquired the necessary trust to stand on their own. The U.S. dollar is, of course, an outstanding example. Most other currencies, however, need to find an anchor to reinforce the public's trust. Thus, it is very common to encounter monetary regimes that are anchored to another currency (e.g., through fixed exchange rates) or to goods and services (e.g., through inflation targeting).

A shortcut to achieving trust in the medium of exchange is *dollarization,* that is, adopting a globally trustworthy currency. This is a radical solution that supersedes, in principle, fixed exchange rates, because the latter can be changed at the stroke of a pen (although, as the case of Liberia shows, dedollarization is possible in extreme circumstances). Trust without tears? Not quite. Dollarization implies discarding one's own monetary policy. The central bank would at best become a financial supervisory agency. No longer could monetary policy be used to reactivate the economy during slumps, or prevent overheating during booms. Is this price worth paying? This is a key question that the essays in this book help to answer.

The essays are penned by some of the most prominent thinkers in the field, showing, among other things, that dollarization is beginning to acquire the respectability it lost following the demise of the gold standard. Until a few years ago, the dominant view in the profession was highly influenced by the optimal currency area (OCA) literature. The exchange rate system was judged against its ability to correct real exchange rate misalignment or to provide full-employment liquidity. Thus, within this narrow perspective, dollarization appears as a primitive system unworthy of serious consideration. However, OCA ignores the financial sector. Issues like de facto dollarization, the prevalence of foreign-exchange-denominated debt, incomplete financial contracts, and so on, are not even mentioned in the standard literature. These financial aspects have risen to prominence thanks to the financial globalization that has occurred since 1989 and have caused large capital inflows and outflows in many developing countries. Today, no serious discussion of the exchange rate system can ignore these financial issues. Once they are considered, dollarization becomes more attractive, which explains why the proposal was salvaged from the heap of discarded ideas.

Does dollarization come out the winner? Of course not. No group of economists worth its salt will emerge with a unified view on such a complex issue. However, the reader will be enriched with new vistas and valuable insights unavailable elsewhere in book format. As a bonus, the chapters are highly readable and display a keen policy orientation, adding pleasure to substance. *Bon appétit!*

Guillermo A. Calvo

Nancy Neiman Auerback is Associate Professor of International Political Economy at Scripps College where she holds a joint appointment in the Departments of Politics and Economics. She is author of *States, Banks, and Markets: Mexico's Path to Financial Liberalization in Comparative Perspective.*

Andrew Berg is Deputy Chief of the Financial Studies Division in the International Monetary Fund Research Department. He has a Ph.D. in Economics from MIT and an undergraduate degree from Harvard University. He has also worked at the U.S. Treasury, including as Deputy Assistant Secretary for East Asia and Latin America.

Eduardo R. Borensztein is Chief of the Strategic Issues Division of the Research Department of the International Monetary Fund. He received his Ph.D. in economics from MIT and his undergraduate degree from Universidad de Buenos Aires. He has also worked at the Central Bank of Argentina and at FIEL, a private research institute in Buenos Aires.

Guillermo Calvo is Chief Economist of the Inter-American Development Bank, Director of the Center for International Economics and Distinguished University Professor at the University of Maryland, and Research Associate at the NBER. His main field of expertise is macroeconomics of emerging market and transition economies. He has published several books and more than 100 articles in leading economics journals.

Benjamin J. Cohen is Louis G. Lancaster Professor on International Political Economy at the University of California, Santa Barbara. Educated at Columbia University, he previously taught at Princeton University and the Fletcher School of Law and Diplomacy at Tufts University. His most recent book, *The Geography of Money,* was published in 1998.

Vittorio Corbo is Professor of Economics at Pontificia Universidad Católica de Chile. He holds a Ph.D. in Economics from MIT. He is the Vice-President of the International Economic Association and has served as a researcher and adviser for the World Bank, the IMF, and several Latin American governments. His current research focuses on monetary policy in open economies and economic reforms in Latin America.

Thomas J. Courchene is Jarislowsky-Deutch Professor of Economic Policy at Queen's University and Senior Scholar at the Institute for Research on Public Policy in Montreal, Canada.

James W. Dean holds his Ph.D. from Harvard University and is Professor of International Finance at Simon Fraser University in Vancouver, British Columbia, Canada. His research focuses on debt, currency, and banking crises and their resolution. He frequently consults and lectures internationally, and has published over 100 books and articles.

Sebastian Edwards is Henry Ford II Professor of International Business Economics at the Anderson Graduate School of Management at UCLA. He received his M.A. and Ph.D. from the University of Chicago. He has been a consultant to a number of multilateral institutions, including the Inter-American Development Bank, the World Bank, the IMF, and the OECD. He is a columnist for the *Wall Street Journal* and is the author of more than 200 scientific articles. His latest book is *Preventing Currency Crises* (co-edited with Jeffrey Frankel).

Barry Eichengreen is the George C. Pardee and Helen N. Pardee Professor of Economics and Professor of Political Science at the University of California, Berkeley, and Director of Berkeley's Institute for European Studies. He is also Research Associate of the National Bureau of Economic Research in Cambridge, Massachusetts, and Research Fellow of the Centre for Economic Policy Research in London, England. In 1997-98, he was Senior Policy Advisor at the International Monetary Fund. He is a Fellow of the American Academy of Arts and Sciences. He is a member of the Bellagio Group of academics and economic officials. He has held Guggenheim and Fulbright Fellowships and has been a Fellow of the Center for Advanced Study in the Behavioral Sciences in Palo Alto, California, and the Institute for Advanced Study in Berlin, Germany. He has published widely on the history and current operation of the international monetary and financial system. His books include *Toward a New International Financial Architecture, Globalizing Capital: A History of the International Monetary System, European Monetary Unification,* and *Golden Fetters: The Gold Standard and the Great Depression, 1919–1939.*

José María Fanelli holds a Ph.D. in economics, specializing in macroeconomics and monetary economics. He is currently senior professor of macroeconomics and was the former director of the economics department at the University of Buenos Aires. Since 1984 he has been senior researcher at CEDES (the Center for the Study of State and Society) and Conicet (the National Research Council) in Buenos Aires.

Michael Faulend is an Economist at the Research Department of the Croatian National Bank.

Edgar L. Feige is Professor of Economics (Emeritus) at the University of Wisconsin-Madison and has served as consultant to the Federal Reserve, U.S. Treasury Department, Agency for International Development, International Monetary Fund, and the Central Banks of Croatia and Albania. He is a leading authority on underground economics.

Aldo Flores-Quiroga is Assistant Professor of Political Science at Claremont Graduate University and holds a Ph.D. in Political Science from UCLA.

Herbert G. Grubel occupies the David Somerville Chair in Taxation and Finance at the Fraser Institute and is Professor of Economics (Emeritus) at Simon Fraser University in Vancouver, British Columbia, Canada. He has a B.A. from Rutgers University and a Ph.D. in economics from Yale University.

Steven H. Hanke is a Professor of Applied Economics at the Johns Hopkins University in Baltimore, Maryland, and a Senior Fellow at the Cato Institute in Washington, D.C. He is a Distinguished Associate of the International Atlantic Economic Society and in 1998 was named one of the twenty-five most influential people in the world by *World Trade Magazine*.

Richard G. Harris is the Telus Professor of Economics at Simon Fraser University, British Columbia, Canada. His major area of specialization is international economics, and in particular the economics of integration. He has published extensively on regional trade integration, economic growth, and the economics of North American monetary union.

Ronald I. McKinnon is the William D. Eberle Professor of International Economics at Stanford University.

Robert Mundell is a Professor of Economics at Columbia University. He studied at the University of British Columbia and the London School of Economics before receiving his Ph.D. from MIT. In 1997 he became a Distinguished Fellow of the American Economic Association; in 1998, he was made a Fellow of the American Academy of Arts and Science; and in 1999, he received the Nobel Memorial Prize in Economic Science. He has been an adviser to a number of international agencies and organizations including the United Nations, the IMF, the World Bank, the Government of Canada, several governments in Latin America and Europe, the Federal Reserve Board, and the U.S. Treasury. The author of numerous works and articles on economic theory of international economics, he is known as the father of the theory of optimum currency areas.

John D. Murray is an Adviser to the Governor of the Bank of Canada. His articles have appeared in numerous professional journals, and he has taught at a number of Canadian and U.S. universities, including the University of British Columbia, the University of North Carolina, and Princeton University.

Archibald R. M. Ritter is a Professor of Economics and International Affairs at Carleton University, Ottawa, Canada. He received his Ph.D. from the University of Texas. He has written extensively on Latin American development issues. His works on Cuba include *The Economic Development of Revolutionary Cuba: Strategy and Performance* and *Cuba in the International System: Integration and Normalization.* He was initiator and coordinator of the Carleton-University of Havana Economics Masters program from 1994 to 1999.

Liliana Rojas-Suarez is a Visiting Fellow at the Institute for International Economics. From March 1998 to October 2000, she served as Managing Director and Chief Economist for Latin America at Deutsche Bank. She has also worked at the Inter-American Development Bank and the IMF. She has published widely in the areas of macroeconomic policy, international economics, and financial markets. She holds a Ph.D. in Economics from the University of Western Ontario.

Nicholas P. Rowe is a professor in the Department of Economics at Carleton University, Ottawa, Canada, where he has worked since 1981, teaching mostly macroeconomics. He has taught in the Carlton-University of Havana Economics Masters program numerous times from 1993 to 2001. He received his Ph.D. from the University of Western Ontario. His research interests focus on monetary policy, emphasizing the choice between fixed exchange rates and inflation targeting, and on the econometric analysis of inflation targeting regimes.

Dominick Salvatore is Distinguished Professor at Fordham University in New York. He is a Fellow of the New York Academy of Sciences and Chairman of its Economics Section. He was President of the International Trade and Finance association and is a Research Fellow at the University of Vienna. He has published extensively in the field of international trade and finance.

Jürgen Schuldt is a Peruvian citizen and is Professor of Macroeconomics and Vice-Rector of the Universidad del Pacífico, Lima. He has published extensively on economic policy and development.

Kurt Schuler lives in Arlington, Virginia. He is the Economist of the U.S. Senate. He has worked in a number of developing countries and has written extensively on their monetary problems.

Velimir Šonje is a board member of the Raiffeisenbank in Zagreb and a former director for research and statistics at the Croatian National Bank.

Vedran Šošić is an Economist at the Research Department of the Croatian National Bank.

George S. Tavlas is a director with the Bank of Greece. He was previously Chief of the General Resources and SDR Policy Division of the International Monetary Fund. He has also worked at the U.S. Department of State and has been a consultant for the Organization for Economic Cooperation and Development and a Guest Scholar with the Brookings Institution. He is Vice President of the Center for Economics Planning and Research (DEPE) in Athens, an Affiliated Scholar with the Center for the Study of Central Banks (New York University School of Law), and a Research Associate of the Athens Institute of Economic Policy Studies (IMOP).

George M. von Furstenberg, a Rudy Professor of Economics at Indiana University, is the inaugural holder of the Robert Bendheim Chair in Economic and Financial Policy at Fordham University. He worked at the International Monetary Fund as Division Chief from 1978 to 1983 and at U.S. government agencies, such as the President's Council of Economic Advisors, from 1973 to 1976 and the Department of State from 1989 to 1990. His current work focuses on monetary and financial integration processes.

Thomas D. Willett is Horton Professor of Economics at Claremont Graduate University and Claremont McKenna College and Director of the Claremont Institute for Economic Policy Studies. He has served as Deputy Assistant Secretary for International Research at the U.S. Treasury and has written widely in the fields of political economy and international money and finance.

John Williamson is currently a Senior Fellow at the Institute for International Economics.

The Dollarization Debate

Dominick Salvatore, James W. Dean, and Thomas D. Willett

Introduction

Questions of which exchange rate regimes might be appropriate for countries and regions larger than countries have long been central to the concerns of internationally oriented economists, politicians, and policymakers. Although the issue seemed to be settled after 1945, when most free-market countries signed on to the Bretton Woods regime of fixed exchange rates, by 1953 the wisdom of that regime was being challenged in a now-classic essay by Milton Friedman. By 1973 the Bretton Woods regime had collapsed and major countries were using flexible rates more or less by default. But by 1979, the core countries of Western Europe had adopted fixed rates between one another, and in 1999, despite widespread skepticism among economists, they went one step further and adopted a common currency.

Meanwhile, debate and experiment in countries outside Western Europe intensified. By the mid-1980s, a consensus had formed at the International Monetary Fund (IMF) and other Washington institutions that emerging economies were best served by fixed, or at least "managed," exchange rates, primarily because this would serve to discipline their central banks and keep inflation at single digit levels. By the mid-1990s, this "Washington Consensus" had been terminally undermined, notably by the Mexican currency crisis of late 1994. A new and radically different consensus began to evolve. The new consensus was that in a post–Bretton Woods world of highly mobile capital, only "automaticity" could avert currency crisis. By this was meant regimes that adjusted automatically to market forces, without government intervention: either fully flexible exchange rate regimes, or fixed-rate regimes that are constitutionally bound by so-called currency boards.

Hence by 1999, after the Asian, Russian, and Brazilian crises of 1997, 1998, and 1999, several eminent economists were advocating fully flexible exchange rates for major emerging economies such as Indonesia, Russia, and Brazil, whereas other, equally eminent economists were recommending fully fixed rates, "guaranteed" by currency boards, for the same emerging economies. Even more dramatically, a growing group of analysts and advisors now propose common currencies, modeled loosely on the European euro, for regions as diverse as Belarus and Russia, and Canada and the United States. Moreover in Latin America and elsewhere, proponents of "dollarization" are advocating outright adoption of the U.S. dollar, with implications for both Latin America and the United Sates that run well beyond even a common currency. In fact several prominent economists have

3

begun to argue that essentially all developing countries should dollarize. And now that Argentina's currency board, the world's most highly touted, has teetered and tumbled in early 2002, the dollarization debate is more intense than ever: could Argentina have averted crisis by moving "to the right" on the regime spectrum and dollarizing, or should it have moved "to the left" by adopting fully flexible rates?

This book is based primarily, although not exclusively, on contributions to two conferences and a session at annual meetings of the Allied Social Science Association. The first conference, organized by James W. Dean and Steven Globerman, was held in March 1999 at Western Washington University and focused primarily on whether Canada should dollarize, or at least adopt a common currency with the United States. The second, organized by the North-South Institute in Ottawa, was held in October 2000 and focused on currency choices for Latin America. Dollarization was also the focus of a session organized by Dominick Salvatore for the American Economics Association meetings in New Orleans in January 2001.

With the dissolution of the Soviet Union, the formation of a common currency in Europe, and a rash of currency crises internationally—three economic watersheds of the 1990s—countries throughout the world have been moved to reevaluate their exchange rate regimes. There is widespread agreement that in a world of high capital mobility the old postwar formula of adjustably pegged exchange is a recipe for crisis. But what alternatives countries should adopt has become the subject of heated debate. While most countries have moved, at least temporarily, toward more flexible exchange rates, some have moved toward more genuinely fixed exchange rates—in a variety of forms. These include a common currency (the euro), currency boards (in Argentina, Bosnia, Bulgaria, Estonia, and Lithuania), and, most drastically of all, adoption of a foreign currency. In the latter camp, the most notable developments have been the recent so-called dollarizations of three Latin American countries—Ecuador, El Salvadore, and Guatemala—with more, it is rumored, waiting (or at least debating) in the wings. Indeed, the former chief economist of the Inter-American Development Bank has proposed that virtually all of Latin America should dollarize, and several prominent Canadian economists are urging adoption of the American dollar, or even a new common currency, for Canada, the United States, and Mexico.

Putative abandonment of minor local in favor of major foreign currencies is unlikely to stop with Latin America. In several countries on the periphery of Western Europe academics are already debating the merits and feasibility of unilaterally adopting the euro (that is, without permission from Frankfurt or Brussels!), and there is talk in some quarters of a yen zone in East Asia. The academic literature generally terms all such proposals "dollarization."

The proposals have not gone unchallenged. Many economists maintain that the advocates of dollarization have exaggerated its economic benefits and downplayed its economic costs. Arguments for and against dollarization have also been advanced on political grounds—both on positive grounds of feasibility and normative grounds of desirability. In fact in international macroeconomics, "dollarization" has become perhaps the leading theoretical and policy debate of the past three years.

This book brings together contributions from several leading participants in the debate. Some advocate dollarization, some fixed exchange rates, some flexible. Many adopt the view that all exchange rate regimes have costs as well as benefits and that cost-benefit ratios will vary across countries. Thus flexible exchange rates may be best for one country and fixed rates for another. Where all of the authors agree is that in the modern world of international financial integration, the post–World War II consensus about the Bretton Woods compromise—an adjustable peg within a narrow band— no longer holds. High capital mobility forces the choice of sustainable exchange rate regimes away from the middle toward the extremes.

Just how far countries must move from the middle in order to avoid recurring currency crisis is still a matter of some dispute. Some economists believe it is necessary to move all the way to the extremes, while others believe there is still some scope for intermediate regimes based, for example, on crawling pegs within wider bands. All agree that this is a crucial time for countries to reevaluate their currency policies. Most countries that recently experienced currency crises responded by floating their currencies, but for many that is likely to be just an interim measure.

An important contribution of this book is the explicit recognition that choices about exchange rate regimes are often influenced by political as well as economic considerations. These political considerations become particularly important where countries are considering giving up their national currencies to dollarize or join a currency union. As with their economic analysis, the contributors to this book do not all agree on political analysis. Thus readers hoping for simple answers are likely to be disappointed. But then one really shouldn't expect simple answers in our current world of substantial international financial integration, integration that is increasingly relevant for developing as well as developed countries. What this book does do is give the reader an excellent picture of the key issues involved in this important debate.

The dollarization debate essentially calls for a reevaluation of countries' exchange rate policies. As the literature on exchange rate theory and policy has developed over the postwar period, it has become clear that the choice of optimal exchange rate regimes is one of the most complicated issues addressed by economists. It embodies almost all facets of debate among different schools of thought about domestic macroeconomic policy, and adds the complications of open economy considerations, as well as the trade-offs that may occur between microeconomic efficiency and macroeconomic stability.

As a consequence, it is not surprising that there are such differences in analyses and recommendations among experts. Indeed the traditional split between monetarists and Keynesians is no guide to dispute where exchange rate regimes are concerned. For example, Milton Friedman, the godfather of monetarism, generally advocates flexible exchange rates while Robert Mundell, the godfather of open economy monetarism, is a leading advocate of fixed rates and common currencies. Such differences stem not from differences in priorities or beliefs about how the domestic economy operates but rather from differences in view about the extent to which the world economy is integrated and the consequent effectiveness of exchange rate changes in promoting economic adjustment.

Many of us who are economists would agree that as our knowledge about exchange rate analysis has grown, our confidence about optimal policy recommendations has declined. This is because the thrust of research has been to add more and more factors to the list relevant to optimal policy. Since for many countries not all criteria point in the same direction, good theory is not enough to guide our decisions. We need quantitative magnitudes as well. Many of the considerations emphasized in modern exchange rate analysis are notoriously difficult to measure.

Some economists have reacted to this situation by stressing the need for humility in evaluating currency issues. Others have reacted by ignoring many considerations and emphasizing only one or two factors, those they consider of primary importance. This is clearly the appropriate strategy for incorporating new considerations—for example, currency substitution or liability dollarization—into the analysis. Focus on only a few factors also makes it easier to draw unambiguous policy conclusions. However, such a strategy can generate a spurious impression of certainty. It often degenerates into advocacy rather than unbiased policy analysis.

Advocacy can make a valuable contribution to ongoing policy debates if it is appropriately labeled as putting a case for this or that policy, but if not, it can be highly misleading. In this regard, current writing about exchange rate issues differs little from that of the 1960s and 1970s, when debate was stimulated by the demise of the Bretton Woods system. Advocates of fixed rates still emphasize discipline against domestic inflation, while advocates of flexible rates still emphasize their buffer role against exogenous shocks such as foreign inflation.

One thing that we do understand much better today is that the costs and benefits of alternative exchange rate regimes vary greatly across countries. Hence a universally optimal compromise between fixed and flexible exchange rates is not possible. Nor is the narrow-band, adjustable peg system adopted at Bretton Woods sustainable in a world of high capital mobility. Thus today more economists make their recommendations contingent on the circumstances of particular countries.

Given the complexity involved in analyzing optimal exchange rate regimes for countries with different characteristics, a number of economists have taken to emphasizing the need for consistency between exchange rate regimes and domestic macroeconomic policy. On this need for consistency, there is considerable agreement among economists. While we often disagree on what regime would be best for a particular country, we can agree on particular regimes that will not work on a sustained basis.

At first glance this might not seem like a very substantial intellectual advance. But in fact it holds considerable promise for reducing the incidence of currency crises. Governments have frequently failed to pay attention to these consistency constraints, often summarized as the "unholy trinity": a country cannot simultaneously have freedom of capital flows, fixed exchange rates, and independent monetary policy. Perhaps a major reason governments try to ignore the unholy trinity is that it operates only in the medium or long term. In the short run there is scope for inconsistency without crises as long as international reserves are adequate. Political pressures on governments often lead them to actions that increase short-run political benefits at the cost of heightened risk of future crisis. We may hope that the costly rash of currency crises during the 1990s will prompt governments to pay closer attention to long-run considerations.

Indeed, one role that the past decade's currency crises have already played is in helping to engender the view that the only stable options for currency regimes are at one of two extremes: either highly flexible or genuinely fixed. Almost all economists today agree with the "unstable middle" hypothesis: the traditional, narrow-band adjustable peg exchange rate regime is likely to be unstable in a world of high capital mobility. Since governments tend to persist with such pegs longer than is sustainable, they produce one-way bets for speculators and are therefore highly prone to crisis.

There is much less agreement, however, about how far from dead center countries must go to avoid being prone to crises. The key here is, again, consistency constraints. The unholy trinity analysis does not logically imply that midrange exchange rate arrangements must be unstable, but it does require that systems of limited exchange rate flexibility are operated in a manner that pays attention to consistency constraints. Limited flexibility can be stable to the extent that exchange rate and monetary policies are mutually consistent. This approach gives countries a wide range of options for stable exchange rate regimes but requires a fundamental rethinking at the policy level of the interrelationships between exchange rates and monetary policy.

Dollarization and freely flexible exchange rates are end-point regimes that both meet consistency constraints. They are more than this, however, for these pure forms eliminate the role of short-run discretionary government policies that can give rise to policy inconsistencies. For intermediate regimes, the political requirements for avoiding inconsistent policies are as important as strictly economic considerations.

A prime motive for dollarization—or, more commonly, the adoption of currency boards, which are a close substitute—has been to stop high inflation. In this respect, the track record of such regimes has been excellent. But their record in providing fiscal discipline, and in promoting more flexible labor markets, has been less clear-cut. Recent optimal currency area (OCA) theory focuses on policies, market structures, and even institutions that will hold after a particular regime is adopted and suggests that these may be endogenous to the choice of regime. Thus, for example, a genuinely fixed exchange rate—or a currency board or dollarization—should induce greater domestic wage and price flexibility.

Recent Argentine experience highlights both the strengths and weaknesses of this "endogenous OCA" approach. Argentina's currency board has indeed led to increased labor market flexibility. But the magnitude of increased flexibility has been insufficient to avoid a deep and prolonged recession. And, certainly, the currency board was not sufficient to enforce fiscal discipline. Thus we have a clear counterexample to the optimistic scenario that clear commitment to a fixed exchange rate guarantees that the rest of the economy will adjust painlessly. On the other hand, the aftermath of the Asian crisis clearly showed that the adoption of flexible exchange rates was no panacea. A theme of many of the contributors to this book is that hard choices must be made. While the reader will find considerable disagreement, collectively the contributors convey both the flavor of current debate and a certain consensus about relevant considerations in light of recent research.

▶ Part I: General Analysis

A Visionary's View

Robert Mundell of Columbia University, who received the Nobel Prize for Economics in 1999, begins the book with a characteristically wide-ranging article that is at once historically grounded and visionary about the future. He begins by arguing that the dollar replaced the pound sterling as the world's preeminent currency as early as 1915. He then builds a case for currency unions: first by advocating monetary rules (and "fixed" as opposed to "pegged" exchange rate regimes!), next by suggesting that currency and free trade areas reinforce each other, and finally by disputing the common criticism that "one-size-fits-all" monetary policy won't work across countries with differential growth rates. Mundell then discusses at some length the merits of a single-currency area for the world and suggests how this might be implemented.

De Facto Dollarization

A problem that has long plagued the so-called currency substitution literature, and that continues to complicate our analysis of dollarization, is the absence of data on stocks of foreign cash abroad. In recent years Edgar L. Feige, professor emeritus at the University of Wisconsin in Madison, has begun to remedy this lacuna by meticulously cumulating data from the U.S. Customs Service on net flows of U.S. dollars to foreign countries. His chapter, written with Michael Faulend, Velimir Sonje, and Vedran Sosic of the National Bank of Croatia, uses these data to estimate foreign currency holdings in 13 Latin American countries, and then to develop currency substitution indices. The upshot is that these differ substantially from asset substitution indices based on dollar-denominated bank deposits. Feige and his coauthors then use currency and asset substitution to analyze network externalities in foreign currency usage. Finally, they employ time series data and a "hysteresis" model to estimate the dynamics of Argentina's dollarization process, incorporating two levels of equilibria: low and high. The model tracks reversals following temporary periods of inflation stabilization in the 1980s but concludes that by 1990, "high-level" dollarization had become for practical purposes irreversible.

Pros and Cons

Andrew Berg and Eduardo Borensztein, both at the IMF, tackle the pros and cons of dollarization by comparing it with its closest relative, a currency board. First on their list of pros is lower interest rates. They analyze whether lower rates would result primarily from reduced currency risk or reduced default risk, and they conclude that (as Liliana Suarez-Rojas contends later) at least some default risk would survive dollarization. A second, less immediate, and less measurable set of gains from dollarization might come in the long run from "stability and integration." For developing countries this would mean fewer currency crises, as well as closer economic integration with the United States. On the con side, loss of seigniorage is likely, though not necessary if the United States is willing to share it with dollarizing countries. Berg and Borensztein also discuss other downsides of dollarization: notably, loss of autonomous monetary policy, loss of an "exit option," and reduced scope for lender-of-last-resort benefits, particularly under systemic circumstances. Finally, like José Fanelli, they look at the putative relationship between dollarization and the Mercosur customs union.

Like Berg and Borensztein, Vittorio Corbo of the Pontificia Universidad Catolica de Chile concludes that for countries with a poor record of financial stability, and whose economic relations are mostly with the United States, dollarization can be very advantageous. But for countries with a decent record of financial stability and a diversified trading sector by country, the combination of prudent monetary policy and exchange rate flexibility seems superior to dollarization.

Sebastian Edwards, of the University of California at Los Angeles, points out that dollarization is being recommended as the way for emerging market economies to achieve credibility, growth, and prosperity. Countries that give up their currencies, we are told, would be unable to engage in macroeconomic mismanagement. Their public finances would stay in order, their external accounts would remain sustainable, and all this would mean lower interest rates, higher investments, and superior economic performance. Edwards concludes, however, that we actually know very little about the cost and benefits of dollarization, and that based on the limited experience available dollarization does not seem as positive a policy as some analysts would want us to believe.

Barry Eichengreen, of the University of California at Berkeley, points out that whether dollarization is a good or a bad depends on whether it will significantly speed the pace of fiscal, financial, and labor market reform in the dollarizing country—but that we do not have clear and precise answers to these questions. Nations with malfunctioning banking systems, budgets, and labor markets will perform miserably whether they retain their own currency or dollarize, and we cannot say a priori whether dollarization is desirable or not. Theory alone simply provides little guidance.

Probably the most persuasive argument against dollarization—to economists and noneconomists alike—is that it would undermine monetary sovereignty. Kurt Schuler, economist at the U.S. Senate, challenges the core of this contention by questioning the inherent usefulness of such sovereignty. Whereas it is logically correct that any monetary policy "rule" constrains monetary sovereignty, it is nevertheless important to distinguish between externally imposed and self-imposed rules. Schuler argues that external "rules" that derive from globalization, as well as new technology, infringe on monetary sovereignty less severely than is commonly claimed. Moreover, economic benefits do not necessarily follow from monetary sovereignty: he cites evidence that since the 1970s, when the Bretton Woods system of pegged rates broke down, developing countries with central banks have had much lower growth, higher inflation, and more extensive exchange controls than those without central banks. Schuler closes by distinguishing between political sovereignty, monetary sovereignty, and consumers' sovereignty. He concludes that neither the first nor the last require monetary sovereignty, and that if most national central banks were eliminated and citizens were allowed to use any currency they wished, consumers' sovereignty would be enhanced.

One Regime for All Countries?

While some of the chapters in this book argue particular points of view or stress particular considerations, others seek to provide frameworks for evaluating conflicting considerations. The standard economists' approach to the analysis of exchange rate issues is the theory of optimum currency areas pioneered by Robert Mundell. Thomas Willett, of the Claremont Colleges, also a contributor to OCA theory, explains the basic concept—that there are costs and benefits to all exchange rate regimes and that the ratio of costs to benefits will vary systematically across countries based on a number of factors. His chapter discusses recent developments in OCA theory as additional considerations continue to be added, and emphasizes that OCA criteria are relevant for the analysis of all types of exchange rate regimes, not just the choice of whether to join a common currency.

This theme, that different exchange rate regimes will be optimal for different countries, is continued in the chapter by John Williamson of the Institute for International Economics. He presents data demonstrating vast differences across countries on key OCA criteria and argues that while dollarization may make sense for some countries in Latin America, it definitely does not make sense for all.

Ronald McKinnon, of Stanford University, begins with the observation that although many claim that only dollarization (including euroization) or full exchange flexibility is sustainable for emerging market economies, on close examination most such economies' regimes lie between these extremes. For these economies, a common monetary standard based on the dollar may still be feasible. Moreover, countries where regional trade is important but a regional common currency politically infeasible would do well to stabilize their dollar exchange rate over the long run.

Dominick Salvatore, of Fordham University, concludes that good candidates for dollarization are small open economies for which the United States is the dominant economic partner, and which have a history of poor monetary performance and hence poor economic-policy credibility. Most of the small countries of Latin America, especially those in Central America, fit this description very well and have indeed either dollarized already or are seriously considering it. For Argentina and Mexico, on the other hand, dollarization would be useful only if they were not capable of managing their economic and financial affairs efficiently and with discipline. For Canada and Brazil, dollarization would be neither politically feasible nor economically useful.

George von Furstenberg, also of Fordham University, extends the analysis to all small, open emerging-market economies by pointing out the declining usefulness of their currencies and questioning whether many of them will survive in the new world of global trade and finance. Even currency boards are likely to prove unsustainable in today's world. Currency boards may, however, be a stepping-stone toward the more complete and sustainable form of currency consolidation provided by monetary union.

▶ *Part II: Political Economy*

A very positive development in recent years has been increased recognition
by both economists and political scientists of the need to take political
considerations explicitly into account when analyzing economic policy. International monetary policy has been one of the areas in which this resurgence of interest in political economy has been most apparent. After all,
giving up a national currency has important implications for national identity and sovereignty, not just for economics. Furthermore, adopting another
country's currency is politically quite different from joining a common currency based on collective decision making.

While our contributors agree on the importance of politics, we find,
not surprisingly, as much difference of opinion about politics as about economics. Benjamin J. Cohen was educated as an economist but has been a
pioneer of the new international political economy and now holds a chair
in political science at the University of California in Santa Barbara. Cohen
provides a broad-ranging overview of political considerations relevant to
dollarization and monetary union. He does not see an American version of
the euro as likely, nor does he foresee widespread dollarization in the Americas.

On the other hand, Jürgen Schuldt, of the Universidad del Pacifico,
Lima, Peru, sees the spread of dollarization as almost inevitable. Interestingly, his differences with Cohen rest heavily on judgments about how the
United States sees its economic and political interests in encouraging dollarization. The official U.S. position appears to be roughly neutral at present, but the views of the various policymakers are sufficiently disparate that
it is understandable that such divergent readings emerge.

Whereas Cohen's primary emphasis was on perceptions of national interest and the distribution of international power, reflecting the realist perspective in international relations theory, Nancy Neiman Auerbach, of
Scripps College and Claremont Graduate University, and Aldo Flores-
Quiroga, of Claremont Graduate University and the Ministry of Foreign
Affairs of Mexico, take a more micro approach. They analyze the debate
about dollarization in Mexico. In addition to the parts played by state
actors, they stress the roles of redistributive politics and of private sector
interests. While President Fox's support for the continuation of Mexico's
flexible exchange-rate policy has muted domestic debate for the moment,
they predict that it is likely to reemerge in the future. Harris Dallas and
George Tavlas argue that whereas political-economy factors were of paramount importance in the euro experiment, with the political benefits out-
weighing the political costs, for Latin American countries considering dollarization, the calculus of political costs and benefits is reversed. Floating
exchange rates or a currency board arrangement appear to entail fewer political costs for these countries than dollarization.

► Part III: North America

Our chapters on Canada illustrate a wide range of disagreement. Thomas Courchene of Queen's University and Richard Harris of Simon Fraser University argue that Canada's flexible exchange rate has served it poorly, and that fixed rates, dollarization, or, best of all, a North American Monetary Union (NAMU), would bring Canada enormous benefits.

During the 1980s, well before the dollarization debate was under way, the first person to propose a common currency for North America (the "amero") was Herbert Grubel of the Fraser Institute, who is also a former member of the Canadian Parliament and professor emeritus at Simon Fraser University. Grubel's analysis is consistent with Harris and Courchene's. He discusses some of the important institutional features that NAMU would entail.

John Murray, of the Bank of Canada, offers a very different perspective on the performance of Canada's flexible exchange rates. While granting that flexible rates can work imperfectly, he concludes that overall they have served Canada well. Given the types of shocks that have hit the Canadian economy—mostly terms of trade shocks associated with declining relative prices for natural resources—adjustment under fixed exchange rates would have been more costly than it has been under the long-standing flexible regime.

► Part IV: Latin America

James Dean, of Simon Fraser University, introduces our Latin American section by suggesting that the case for dollarization there may be much stronger than in Canada. In recent years several prominent economists who specialize in Latin America have made the case that Latin America's extensive de facto adoption of the U.S. dollar should be made de jure: that is, local currency should be withdrawn and the dollar declared legal tender. Dean identifies six interrelated facts of Latin American economic life that support this case: dangers of liability dollarization, currency and default premiums on interest rates, slippage in monetary control, vulnerability to exogenous monetary shocks, irreversibility of informal dollarization, and impotence of exchange rate policy. He concludes by arguing, on the same grounds, that although much of Latin America is ripe for dollarization, Canada is not.

While sympathetic to the case for Latin American dollarization, Liliana Rojas-Suarez, of the Institute for International Economics, argues that for the moment, and under current conditions, increased exchange rate flexibility combined with inflation targeting would be far preferable. Latin America, she suggests, primarily faces default risk, not currency risk per se. Although the two interact, causality runs from default risk to currency risk rather than the reverse as maintained by proponents of dollarization. Default risk in turn originates with policy inconsistencies: to wit, "large and increasing stocks of short-term debt fueled by large and increasing fiscal deficits ... that raise ... doubts about the capacity ... to service ... debt." It is this, and not flexible currency regimes, that has generated huge risk premiums on Latin America's borrowing rates. Hence dollarization would not eliminate such premiums. She illustrates this phenomenon with data on domestic real interest rates: since yields on domestic and foreign-currency-denominated debt tend to converge, she concludes that the spreads over U.S. Treasury rates are explicable primarily by default rather than currency risk. Dollarization would not address default risk unless accompanied by reform of domestic fiscal policy.

By contrast, Steve Hanke, of Johns Hopkins University, argues that "the case for dollarization [in Argentina] is stronger today than ever ... [but] there is more than one way for Argentina to use the dollar." Hanke harks back to the days of competitive note issue by banks. He suggests, persuasively, that a country can reap all the advantages of dollarization and, in addition, capture seigniorage, by permitting its commercial banks to issue dollar-denominated paper money. He points out that in Argentina there are no constitutional barriers to such note issuance, but he notes that it would be crucial to repeal the central bank's power to issue pesos.

José Maria Fanelli, of (CEDES) in Buenos Aires, considers Argentina's decade-long experience with a currency board in the context of the fledgling Mercosur customs union. He begins with a substantial, 10-year review of the performance of the so-called convertibility regime. He then addresses macroeconomic policy coordination within Mercosur. He suggests that although OCA criteria might dictate flexible regimes for both Argentina and Brazil, Argentina's history of hyperinflation led, perforce, to a currency board and hence, since 1999, to accentuated asymmetry with Brazil's flexible rate regime. He suggests further that for OCA reasons, calls for a common currency are premature. However, macroeconomic coordination would be wise. Fanelli concludes by advancing a politically radical proposal: a common compensatory fiscal policy.

Archibald Ritter and Nicholas Rowe, both of Carleton University, have written a fascinating essay on dollarization in Cuba. They examine the causes of this process, its economic and social effects, and the official policy response so far. They then analyze the desirability of substituting the euro for the dollar, a proposal that has been widely debated in Cuba. They argue that a forced switch to the euro from the dollar would probably generate more problems than it would resolve, regardless of its political attractiveness to the Cuban leadership. A preferable objective, they suggest, would be to reestablish the preeminent position of a fully convertible peso.

Contents

General Analysis

I

1 Robert Mundell

Currency Areas, Exchange Rate Systems, and International Monetary Reform

Charles Rist, French economist and central banker, once said that "democracy killed the gold standard." A nice phrase—he was a very good economist. What I think he meant was that democracy results in an increase in social demands and redistribution programs that governments have to supply or else be ejected at the next election. In the effort to finance the new programs governments raise taxes to the limit and then engage in borrowing and deficit financing from the central bank, leading to a breakdown of convertibility and the collapse of the gold standard. The gold standard will no longer act as the "golden brake." Rist's idea was very prophetic, but I think it does not provide the right clue as to what destroyed the gold standard. We have to look elsewhere.

Strong currencies are the children of empires and great powers. The dollar became the greatest currency of the twentieth century because it was comparatively stable and America became the superpower. As the United States came to dominate the international monetary system, the dollar elbowed out gold as the principal asset of the system. When General de Gaulle in the 1960s wanted to attack the United States and its "dollar imperialism," he served up a demand for a return to the gold standard, the only conceivable rival to a dollar-based system. The United States, of course, wouldn't hear of it, and, after it was taken off gold in 1971, the dollar, instead of sinking into oblivion, had no rivals. What killed the gold standard was the financial supremacy of the United States and its delivery system, the dollar.

Currency power configurations, however, are never static. They evolve along predictable lines with the growth and decline of nations. Looking at the international monetary system as a constantly evolving oligopoly, it seems inevitable that a countervailing power would develop to challenge the dollar. Now, at the close of the "American century," the euro has appeared as a potential rival, the countervailing power, to the dollar.

The euro may turn out to be more of an important change in the international monetary system than the breakdown of the Bretton Woods arrangements in 1971. If it fulfils its promise as an alternative to the dollar, the euro can change the power configuration of the system. The breakdown of Bretton Woods changed its veneer but not its fundamentals. Before and after the collapse, the dollar remained unchallenged as the de facto monarch, the most important currency used in reserves, in denominating values, settling contracts, and effecting payments in the international monetary system. The advent of the euro may therefore turn out to be the most important development in international monetary arrangements since the emergence of the dollar as the dominant currency shortly after the creation of the U.S. central bank, the Federal Reserve System, in 1913.

International monetary arrangements make a big difference to the success or failure of the world economy. Bimetallism in the first part and the gold standard in the second part of the nineteenth century were important catalysts in the "century of peace" under the "pax Britannica," and the reign of the dollar has been at least a concomitant of the general (and comparative) peace and prosperity of the last part of the twentieth century. Globalization has been facilitated by the dollar just as it was facilitated in the twentieth century by the pound and the gold standard. The modern trend toward globalization has been accelerated by systematic tariff reductions, free trade areas, enhanced capital mobility, and revolutions in transportation, communications, and information technology.

It needs to be emphasized, however, that globalization is much less efficient now because of some telling defects in our international monetary system. The inefficiency of our current "system" is reflected in the hundreds of trillions of dollars of waste capital movements that cross international borders every year solely as a consequence of uncertainty over exchange rates. In this respect we should look with more respect at the international monetary system at the beginning of the century when the gold standard provided a highly efficient international monetary system. If we cannot recreate that system, we should at least be able to duplicate it with a more modern alternative.

▶ *The Preeminence of the Dollar*

In my Nobel Prize lecture (Mundell, 1999, 2000), I argued that the international monetary system of the twentieth century had played a fundamental role as a determinant of political events. Its breakdown in World War I, restoration in the 1920s, and subsequent breakdown in the 1930s played a major causal role in the Great Depression and World War II, and these great events in turn had a feedback effect on the international monetary system, altering its power configuration. The U.S. economy and the U.S. dollar played a determining role in this story.

The U.S. economy was the star performer of the nineteenth and twentieth centuries. It started the twentieth century as the biggest economy in the world. In a speech presented at Cambridge University in 1906, Whitelaw Reid, the U.S. ambassador to Britain, discussed the subject "The Greatest Fact in Modern History," which he took to be the rise of the United States!

Bismarck said that the greatest fact of the nineteenth century was that Britain and the United States spoke the same language. That prescient comment acknowledged the growing might and domination of the Anglo-Saxon powers. By 1914, the U.S. economy was three times as large as its British or German counterparts, respectively the second and third largest economies in the world. By the 1920s the United States was five times as large as its next rival. The United States had already become the superpower in the 1920s.

At the end of World War II—amid the wreckage of Europe and much of the Far East—the United States had become the supereconomy. It was at this time that the Bretton Woods agreements set the course of the international monetary system for the next generation. But as the postwar period evolved, the U.S. economy lost some of its luster; it became sluggish and lagged in growth, while the European economies spurted ahead. In the meantime, Sputnik showed that the United States had a technological rival.

The seeds of this relative decline had been sown as early as World War I when tax rates soared to punitive levels. It took a decade after the end of the war before marginal tax rates at the highest level were lowered to 25 percent. What confirmed the slump of 1930–31 as a great depression was the rise in marginal tax rates in June 1932 to 60 percent, the first manifestation of the spread of the class conflict that had already infected much of Europe and would penalize production in favor of redistribution. Rist's predictions (mentioned earlier) were coming true! With World War II, tax rates were pushed up even higher to levels above 90 percent, and they stayed that way after the war. While the economies of Europe and Japan were soaring, the U.S. economy began to stagnate.

Americans looked with envy on the growth rates and low unemployment in Europe and Japan in the 1950s and, to a lesser extent, the 1960s. Then came the breakdown of the international monetary system in the 1970s, which ended the discipline of fixed exchange rates anchored to gold. The result was lax monetary and fiscal discipline all over the world and an outbreak of inflation and stagnation. It will astonish some to learn that the increase in the U.S. price level in the 1970s exceeded the increases in all the American wars since the War of Independence. In 1979–81, the United States had three years of back-to-back two-digit inflation, flanking an inflation rate of 13 percent in 1980. The tide turned only with the advent of supply-side economics during the Reagan administration, which implemented a policy mix of tight money to control the inflation and sweeping tax cuts to expand the economy. After a sharp but short recession, the U.S. economy moved into a long expansion in which employment revived and inflation subsided. In a book entitled *The Seven Fat Years,* Robert Bartley, editor of the *Wall Street Journal,* describes in detail the sequence that led to the creation of no less than 19 million new jobs between 1982 and 1990. Between 1980, the last year of the Carter administration, and 1988, when President Ronald Reagan left office, marginal federal income tax rates at the highest brackets had been lowered from 70 percent in 1980 to 28 percent, and corporate tax rates from 48 percent to 34 percent, a supply-side revolution that, in a more limited form, spread to the rest of the world.

Except for a nine-month recession in 1990–91, the U.S. economy has been expanding now for 18 years. The result has been an increase in employment of about two million people per year, 38 million new jobs since 1982, almost as much as the entire labor force of the third largest economy in the world, Germany. It is fair to say that in the last two decades the U.S. economy has been the mainspring of growth in the world economy.

There was some backsliding on tax rates after Ronald Reagan left office. Top marginal income tax rates were increased to 33 percent under President George H. W. Bush and to 39.6 percent under President Bill Clinton. When account is taken of state and local taxes, the aggregate top marginal income tax rate is again well over 50 percent—despite the fact that the national budget has recently moved into surplus. Nevertheless, the U.S. economy, under the impetus of the information technology (IT) revolution and the "New Economy" has continued to expand. A new round of supply-side tax cuts will be needed when the economy slows down.

▶ *The Fate of the Gold Standard*

In the 1920s, in his book *A Tract on Monetary Reform,* John Maynard Keynes had already pointed out that the gold standard after World War I was nothing like the gold standard of earlier years. It was in this context that Keynes made his famous (and much misquoted) remark: "already the gold standard is a barbarous relic." Keynes was the first to point out that gold was no longer operating efficiently as a mechanism in the old-fashioned decentralized way and that the stability of gold now depended increasingly on the policies of a few central banks—mainly the Federal Reserve System, the Bank of England, and the Bank of France. His statement was precocious and correct but it did not go far enough. In understanding the twentieth century, it is necessary to understand the overwhelming importance of the Federal Reserve System.

The importance of the United States in the international monetary system would have been recognized much earlier had the United States possessed a central bank in the nineteenth century. Upon its creation in 1913, it was instantly the most powerful central bank in the world—this despite the much-vaunted prestige of the Bank of England, the acknowledged importance of sterling, and the London financial market. The creation of the Federal Reserve System in 1913 was one of the most important events of the twentieth century. It was the Federal Reserve System that enabled the paper dollar to become the most important currency in the world. The primacy of the dollar can be said to have begun in 1915, the second year of World War I, when the dollar took over from the pound sterling the role of most important currency in the world.

The whole future of the gold standard came to depend on the policy of the United States with regard to gold. During World War I, the value of gold had fallen by a half as the U.S. dollar, which remained more or less on the gold standard, experienced a doubling of its price level between 1914 and 1920. In 1921 the Federal Reserve liquidated assets and tightened credit. Prices then fell precipitously, from an index of 200 (1914 = 100) in 1920 to 140 in 1921. The Federal Reserve then shifted to a policy of stabilizing the price level, and it remained more or less constant until 1919. Thus, during the 1920s, the U.S. price level was about 40 percent above the prewar gold-standard equilibrium.

All other countries gradually got rid of gold from their monetary systems, and then the status of gold became just a question of U.S. economic policy. After World War II came the Bretton Woods arrangements. Gold was still an important part of the international monetary system as the official denominator of currency values in the system, even if it ceased to be a really effective anchor. But the dollar was increasingly filling the functions of a world currency.

▶ *Currency Areas and Currency Unions*

The growing importance of the dollar was a little-noticed event at the start of the twentieth century. The advent of the euro is the big news at the close. It has led to a redrawing of the map of currency areas. When the euro was created it instantly became the second most important currency in the world.

Monetary mass is important. Judging by its monetary mass, the euro is more important than the yen but less important than the dollar. The 11 countries of the European Union (EU) that went into monetary union have a gross domestic product (GDP) of something like 7 trillion dollars, which compares to a U.S. GDP of 9 trillion and Japan's GDP of 5 trillion dollars.

These currency areas are of course evolving. The euro area—and possibly the dollar area—are getting bigger. The euro area has 11 countries now, and Greece is already on board. In a few years we can expect the EU-12 to be joined by Britain, Sweden, and Denmark. By the end of the decade, the EU will contain several more of the 13 countries that have been invited to apply for membership. Though meeting the requirements poses a significant challenge, entry into the EU and EMU represents the best chance they have to lift their standards of living toward EU levels, and most of the countries are working very hard toward meeting them.[1]

In 10 years, therefore, there could be as many as 28 member countries in the EU. In addition, 13 CFA franc countries in West and Central Africa, since 1946 tied to the French franc, are also tied to this euro area. If, as seems plausible, a few countries in North Africa and the Middle East also choose to fix their currencies to the euro, the euro area could easily contain as many as 50 countries with a population exceeding 500 million and a GDP substantially larger than the United States within a decade.

Turning to Asia, what about the chances of a currency area forming in that burgeoning continent? There has been some discussion of a kind of APEC Monetary Fund, and even a currency area based on the yen. But the European model of single currency would not fit at the present time in Asia. The stumbling block is not economics but politics. The single-currency project of the EU became possible because Europe became a security area, that is, an area within which war could be, in all probability, ruled out; the long-standing Franco-German enmity was laid to rest. An Asian currency area would be possible in the future only if a formula could be found for correcting the political disequilibrium. An Asian Monetary Fund could, however, be a catalyst for constructive political developments and might pave the way eventually to a viable Asian currency area.

We mustn't forget the dollar! The dollar area will also expand over the next 10 years. Some countries in Latin America and elsewhere will be inclined to follow the path pioneered by Argentina in 1991. They will be using the dollar as an anchor for their currency, just as countries in Africa and elsewhere will be using the euro as an anchor for their currencies. The dollar area is likely to expand. New currency areas may form. A currency area has been talked about for Brazil, Argentina, Uruguay, and Paraguay, the countries that form the Mercosur Free Trade Area. It might even be possible to establish some kind of currency union for all the Americas, a kind of Latin dollar.

There are many models for currency areas. The tightest form is a single-currency monetary union. Dollarization represents a hegemonic approach to a single-currency monetary union. The alternative of a new currency created by political agreement (such as the euro, or Herbert Grubel's plan for an "amero" in North America) involves a high degree of political co-operation and sharing of sovereignty. Multiple-currency monetary unions could include currency board arrangements, as well as a parallel currency system, both of which could be looked at or not as stages toward a more complete single-currency monetary union. The less tight monetary unions depend for their success on credibility.

When one fixes exchange rates to a currency area, there are many ways to buy credibility for the exchange rate commitments. One way is to build up reserves. After nine years with a currency board—an enormously important step toward monetary stability—Argentina still has credibility problems, especially in times of crisis. These problems are reflected in high interest rates in dollars. But I doubt Argentina would have any problems with the credibility of its exchange rate if it had the foreign exchange reserves of Taiwan. Taiwan has more than U.S.$100 billion in foreign exchange reserves. That is a very high rate for a country of 22 million people, and it has to be high partly because of the political isolation and vulnerability of Taiwan. Nevertheless, larger rather than smaller currency reserves are a big plus, and that's one alternative. By and large, I believe most countries' currency reserves are too small.[2]

Convertibility is a unilateral fix. Another way to achieve credibility is through a bilateral approach. Would a monetary agreement with the United States help? The answer is yes, certainly. If the Federal Reserve or Treasury guaranteed the peso rate whenever there was a run on the peso it would be unnecessary for interest rates to rise. There is a problem (or worry), though, about moral hazard. Instead of building up reserves or keeping to the strict requirements of a currency board, the country might rely on the guarantee to do the job! The United States might be more willing to give Mexico a guarantee, because Mexico is part of the North American Free Trade Agreement (NAFTA) and Mexico's problem is thus the United States' problem too. There might be more willingness if Mexico had a currency board with the United States. I could well imagine the Federal Reserve being willing to guarantee this in a time of crisis, and to avoid the need for a complete dollarization of the economy with which that was associated.

◤ The Importance of Monetary Rules

At the Davos meeting of the World Economic Forum this year, the governor of the central bank of a Latin American economy said that one thing we have learned from the recent currency crises is that fixed exchange rates are no good! I think nothing could be more opposite from the truth. I'm sure that he was thinking of pegged rates.

It is essential to make a distinction between "pegged" and "fixed" rates. The difference lies in the adjustment system. A fixed rate is one where intervention in the exchange market is allowed to affect the money supply. If a country has a surplus, the central bank has to intervene to prevent its currency from appreciating; it buys foreign exchange in return for domestic currency. The increased supply of domestic currency increases the reserves of the banking system and increases domestic expenditure, automatically correcting the surplus. Similarly, a deficit requires intervention in the opposite direction. The central bank sells foreign exchange to support the domestic currency and gets back domestic currency, which reduces the reserves of the banking system, the money supply, and domestic expenditure, and thereby corrects the deficit. A fixed exchange rate system is a monetary rule that contains a self-adjusting equilibrating mechanism of the balance of payments.

By contrast, a pegged rate is an arrangement whereby the central bank intervenes in the exchange market to peg the exchange rate but still keeps an independent monetary policy. To maintain an independent monetary policy the central bank may offset the monetary effects of intervention in the exchange market by sterilization operations. For example, when a country has a surplus, the central bank must intervene to prevent the pegged rate from appreciating; it buys foreign exchange and supplies in return domestic currency, increasing reserves as before. But now, to neutralize the monetary effects of intervention, the central bank sells an equal quantity of domestic assets (say government bonds), canceling the effects on the money supply. It then makes a separate decision to expand or contract the money supply, increase or lower interest rates. The result is that there is no mechanism of adjustment for ensuring balance-of-payments equilibrium. This is in fact the automatic practice of the U.S. and British central banks (in the event of intervention in the exchange market), which adhere to flexible rates. A pegged exchange rate may be defended as a temporary expedient in certain situations, but as a general rule, because it matches an international system with a domestic monetary policy, it involves conflicts that lead to crises and breakdowns. Pegged exchange rates sooner or later always collapse.

The gold standard was a good example of fixed rates. Countries defined their currencies in terms of weights of gold, and exchange rates represented the ratios of the weights. When gold left the country (a balance-of-payments deficit) the money supply shrank, domestic expenditure (total spending) was cut, and the deficit was corrected; when it arrived, the money supply increased, expenditure rose, and the surplus was eliminated. The system got into trouble only rarely, when, as during war, countries turned to deficit finance. Success of the gold standard depended of course on fiscal prudence.

Panama is a contemporary example of a country that has a fixed exchange rate. Its currency is the balboa, which is a metallic currency equivalent to and freely convertible into the U.S. dollar. Upon its creation as a country, in a treaty with the United States, the government committed itself not to create a paper currency. As a consequence, Panama is "dollarized," and the paper dollar circulates freely in Panama and is equivalent as legal tender and unit of account. Panama could of course at any time abrogate this "self-denying ordinance" but has chosen not to because the dollar anchor has given it a degree of monetary stability that is quite unique in Latin America. The balance of payments is kept automatically in equilibrium by the unhindered exports and imports of dollars, shrinking and expanding the money supply in the process, and Panama gets the same core inflation rate as the United States.

A currency board represents a rigorous form of a fixed exchange rate system. A country fixes the exchange rate between its currency and an important foreign currency. Intervention to keep the rate fixed automatically affects the money base of the system. When a central bank buys (say) dollars, it pays for them with national currency, and that expands the reserves in the monetary system; similarly, a sale of dollars contracts reserves. A currency board lets this intervention determine monetary policy, and it works automatically to preserve equilibrium in the balance of payments: a deficit, for example, leads to a contraction of the money supply, which lowers expenditure and corrects the deficit. Currency boards were commonly used in small countries or colonies of the great European empires of the twentieth century, but they have made a comeback in independent and much more important countries today. Several of the transition countries of central and eastern Europe have used currency boards as an anchor for their monetary policy, and Hong Kong's currency board has been in place since 1983. But the outstanding example in the modern world is, of course, Argentina.

It is worth taking time out to reflect on why "currency boards," as a special case of fixed exchange rates, have come back into fashion. It is mostly because of the common confusion between pegged and fixed exchange rates. Largely because of the way international economics has been mistaught in many of our schools and our international financial institutions, fixed exchange rates have been identified with pegged rates; that is, a system with a built-in mechanism of reequilibration has been confused with a system with no adjustment mechanism at all. The practice is reinforced by the absurd classification of exchange rate arrangements in the *IMF International Financial Statistics,* which lumps together (amid several other confusions) under the same system—"currency pegged to the U.S. dollar"—Panama and Iraq! This misinformation has cast discredit on the phrase "fixed exchange rates," which has become mixed up with "pegged" exchange rates, so that, to avoid confusion, some writers now speak of a "currency board" in order to describe a fixed exchange rate system that lets the balance of payments influence the money supply in an equilibrating way.

Argentina, for example, does not have a currency board in the sense that this term was used before World War I. But it has a fixed exchange rate system with an automatic adjustment mechanism, governed by the convertibility law that every new peso created is backed by one U.S. dollar. Under convertibility, Argentina by and large gets the U.S. inflation rate, modified according to the differences in the Argentine basket of goods in the price index. Currency boards represent one extreme end of the spectrum of fixed exchange rate systems. Other viable fixed exchange rate systems that differ substantially from currency boards are Austria and the Netherlands, two countries that kept their currencies fixed to the deutsche mark.

But to come back to the question that has been posed in much of the literature: Should countries have fixed or flexible exchange rates? To me it is not a good question. First of all it is not clear what "fixed" exchange rates mean in the question, so that economists who debate the issue are often talking about quite different animals. How many times have I heard young (and sometimes old) economists rant on about the superiority of flexible rates over "fixed" exchange rates, proving their case by pronouncing as a theorem that fixed exchange rate systems always break down! The alert student will see this theorem as an oxymoron.

But even if "fixed rates" refers to truly fixed rates, the question is a terrible one. As I defined it, a fixed exchange rate is a monetary rule. It's a rule that gives the country the monetary policy of the partner country. How can you compare a fixed rate, which is a monetary rule, to a flexible rate, which is a noncommittal absence of a monetary rule? Fixed exchange rates imply a precise monetary policy that will give the country the inflation rate of its partner countries. By contrast, a flexible exchange rate is consistent with any monetary policy at all—hyperinflation, hyperdeflation, or price stability! You can only legitimately compare a fixed rate, which is a monetary rule, with other monetary rules.

The proper question is, I think, what is the best monetary rule? What variable should be fixed? Should it be a currency fix? A currency fix would fix the domestic currency to a currency, or a basket of currencies. Should it be a commodity fix? A commodity fix would anchor the domestic currency to a commodity (e.g., gold) or a basket of commodities (inflation targeting). Should it be a monetary fix? That would stabilize the level or growth rate of some definition of the money supply. Which of these three systems is the best? Just asking the question in this way should caution against glib and dogmatic answers. The choice of monetary rule depends on the size configuration of countries. Some countries don't have the option of fixing the exchange rate.

Some countries are too small not to fix, but at least one country is too large to fix! The United States cannot have a fixed exchange rate. What currency would it fix to? You can fix the Canadian dollar or the Mexican peso to the U.S. dollar (not a bad idea), but you can't fix the U.S. dollar to the Canadian or Mexican currencies. If there were a single world currency, you could never have a currency fix! With a single world currency, the only choice is between inflation targeting or monetary targeting.

The choice between inflation and monetary targeting depends on the inflation rate. Monetary targeting comes into its own in cases of hyperinflation and at very high inflation rates, say over 3 percent a month. Very high inflation rates are typically caused by budget deficits financed by the central bank. Stabilization policy depends on getting the rate of monetary expansion down.

After inflation has been brought down below 3 percent a month, inflation targeting becomes a superior rule. Monetary targeting is too heavy-handed a weapon for fine-tuning at low rates of inflation, and it is completely dominated by inflation targeting. Every country that has tried it has found out sooner or later that the ratio between monetary growth and inflation rate fluctuates too much to be relied on. Some leading countries continue to publish monetary "targets"; they have tended to become predictions rather than policy determinants. Quite apart from their use as targets, however, it must always be remembered that monetary aggregates contain important information about the economy.

At low inflation rates the serious choice is between inflation targeting, using a goods-and-services basket, and exchange rate targeting, using a currency basket. With a commodity basket, a country is free to choose its own inflation rate. Its inflation target rate is a matter of national preferences. By and large, however, the major currency areas—the dollar, euro, and yen areas—have adopted 0–2 percent as the inflation target, and there are strong arguments for inflation rates to remain within this range. Alternatives outside this range tend to be arbitrary and readily subject to change.

Stability of the inflation rate is an important policy goal, and low inflation rate targets produce in general more stable inflation rates. But if a country wanted to maintain a higher inflation rate than that which prevailed in one or more of the major currency areas, it would have to rule out the possible alternative of a fixed exchange rate.

Argentina's system can be contrasted with Chile's. Argentina gets the inflation rate of the United States by fixing its peso to the dollar, and it has been successful in that respect for nearly a decade. Chile, by contrast, has managed to use inflation targeting with a considerable degree of success and has achieved a good record on growth, but it has nevertheless had to rely on controls over capital movements. It remains to be seen which method will be more successful in the long run.

Capital controls are not necessary if uncertainty over the exchange rate is eliminated. Remember the 11 European members of EMU that will soon be 12 when Greece comes in. The 11 countries now have an absolute fix of the exchange rate, and they have no need for controls over capital movements. It is the fix that gives you market freedom, if you can find an appropriate currency to fix to!

◣ *Monetary Arrangements in Free Trade Areas and Customs Unions*

What is the relation between free trade areas or customs unions and the exchange rate system? Put somewhat differently, is it possible to achieve the full benefits of a free trade area and at the same time have exchange rates that fluctuate? I will make the argument that free trade areas and currency areas (zones of fixed exchange rates) reinforce one another.

In the postwar world, a great deal of effort was devoted to tariff reduction through the numerous negotiating rounds. Part of the gains in real incomes in the modern world can be attributed to this effort. But the postwar era needs to be divided into two parts. In the first two and a half decades there was an international monetary system that produced fixed exchange rates. This system was destroyed in the early 1970s. Some of the gains made in an open system were wiped out by fluctuating exchange rates.

Uncertainty over exchange rates affects trade directly because it affects profit margins and indirectly because it misdirects investment. Small changes in exchange rates can completely wipe out expected profits. This is no doubt why trade between areas sharing a common currency is several times higher than trade between areas with different currencies. Some empirical studies have demonstrated—subject to all sorts of qualifications, of course—that the trade among or between Canadian provinces is several times greater than trade with the American states south of the border, which use a different currency. This is despite the existence of the free trade area. A very recent study further demonstrated that Britain's trade with the continent would triple if it joined the EMU.

Europe has many impediments to trade that keep it from the ideal of a complete free trade area. Uncertainty over exchange rates was one of the problems. After the 1992 exchange rate mechanism (ERM) crisis, there were all kinds of problems associated with Italy's departure from the exchange rate mechanism. After Italy left the ERM, the lira depreciated by 25 percent as the deutsche mark rose from 800 to almost 1,000 lire. Germans and other nonresidents poured into Italy to buy German cars, the prices of which had been fixed in lire. This was of course illegal under EU rules, and the parent companies were eventually required to rescind their threats. The episode nevertheless illustrates the problems of exchange rate changes in free trade areas.

Argentina has experienced the problem of devaluation by a partner country in a free trade area. Brazil's devaluation threatened for a time to break Mercosur apart. Fortunately, the effects, harmful and damaging as they may be in the short run, do not persist indefinitely. But the incident, which probably affected Argentina's real income in one year more than the tariff reductions, demonstrates the advantages that would be gained by a fixed exchange rate zone among the Mercosur countries and even a common currency. Even the former would be a good instrument for achieving economic convergence.

The next question is this: What kind of fixed exchange rate zone would be desirable? There is a wide spectrum of possibilities, ranging from the deep monetary integration of a single-currency zone to a looser union of separate currencies connected by fixed exchange rates. Provided there is a common and low inflation rate, all the options would be superior to pegged rates or fluctuating rates. But a single-currency monetary union possesses advantages: transparency, saving in information and transactions costs, and sense of permanence that does not exist with separate currencies connected by fixed exchange rates. Is there a chance of creating a single Mercosur currency?

The answer to this question depends on a number of factors that form the basis of strong currency areas. One issue to consider is monetary mass. It is important for a currency area to be large. Think of currencies as ships on a stormy ocean. The most stable ship would be the largest. That is why the dollar today best meets the requirements of a world currency. The monetary mass of the four countries of the Mercosur area would not at the present time rank very high among currency areas in the world economy.

Another issue concerns the potential stability of its monetary policy. The Mercosur countries have recently been approaching monetary stability. In Argentina, stability is approaching its tenth anniversary. Brazil's stability is more recent, but there seems to be a real commitment to maintain the gains already made and bring the inflation down further, to 4 percent as next year's target. These are very encouraging signs, but it is not completely clear how the national commitment to stability would carry over to a multinational enterprise such as a Mercosur central bank.

The European model does not exactly fit Mercosur. No single country in the EMU is dominant in the way Brazil is dominant in Mercosur. It is hard to think of a monetary union of one country with 160 million people, another country of 35 million, and two tiny countries of 3 or 4 million people that would not be dominated by the larger country or at best the two largest countries. A hegemonic pattern seems unavoidable. If this were politically acceptable, it might be possible to go the extra step and build the monetary union around the Brazilian currency, suitably internationalized, controlled by a Mercosur central bank that includes all four countries. An alternative approach would be to converge toward an outside currency—either the dollar or the euro or a basket of the three main currencies. Argentina has already achieved this convergence, though not perfectly, with respect to the dollar. If this approach were adopted, Brazil would need to bring its inflation close to the U.S. level and then fix its real to the dollar. Paraguay and Uruguay would then follow suit. All four countries would have then converged to the dollar and therefore to each other. Given convergence, it would then be comparatively easy to develop a separate Mercosur currency.

What should be said about the choice between the dollar, the euro, or a basket of those currencies and possibly the yen? In a speech I made in Seoul, South Korea, at an APEC forum, I suggested that if APEC was thinking of having a kind of monetary fund, they needed a unit of account. One possibility would be a basket of the three currencies, with 45 percent in dollars, 20 percent in yen, and 35 percent in euros. That would be a pretty good basket for the whole world economy for the next few years. It wouldn't be all that different from the special drawing rights (SDR). The SDR is now based on the euro plus the dollar, the yen, and the pound, because the franc and the mark have been submerged together in the euro. That three-currency basket could be a good unit of account. However, a problem with using a currency basket is that it is usually not a transparent target for monetary policy. In countries that used one in the past, the authorities kept saying yes, we have a basket, but we are not going to tell you what the proportions of currencies in the basket are. This is the opposite of transparency. Clever econometricians working on this topic tried to determine what the basket was. They could figure it out for some time, but they usually caught the authorities changing the basket. As implemented in the past, it has not been a stable basket.

A more basic problem with a multiple-currency basket is that you don't get capital market integration. If a currency is absolutely fixed to the dollar or the euro, then you will get the interest rate of that area. If you have a mechanism that convinces people that you're not going to end up with a budget deficit that will lead to relaxing the convertibility law or the automatic system, then you can get exactly the same interest rate as in the partner currency. That kind of integration is not as straightforward or as transparent with a multiple-currency basket. On the other hand, a multiple-currency basket does not suffer from the possible defect of a single-currency basket, namely, that the currency appreciates (or depreciates) significantly against other currencies.

The only strong argument against a single-currency basket is that the country that produces the currency to which the national currency is fixed might become unstable. Is the United States (or the euro area) likely to be unstable? There were periods in the twentieth century when the U.S. economy was unstable. The most glaring example was in the 1930s, when the United States let itself be dragged into deflation and depression by the gold standard. Forty years later, in the 1970s, the United States let itself in for inflation after it cut the link between the dollar and gold. In both these situations, the United States economy was unstable. Gradually, however, the United States learned from its earlier experiences and reacquired stability. The countries that fixed to the dollar in the 1990s, including Argentina, did very well. Both the dollar and the euro areas can be counted on in the future to have a high degree of stability or at any rate more stability than most other areas in the world.

One argument sometimes made against fixed exchange rates is that a "one-size-fits-all" monetary policy is no good. (This is a popular argument made by euroskeptics opposed to Britain joining the euro area.) One example often pointed out is the situation of fast-growing countries. Are differential growth rates an argument for flexible, rather than fixed, exchange rates? One must ask, first of all, about the implications of differential growth rates on the real exchange rate. If productivity growth is biased toward domestic goods, the real exchange rate must depreciate; if it is biased toward traded goods, it must appreciate; and if it is neutral, the real exchange rate remains unchanged. But none of these instances is a convincing case for flexible exchange rates. Relative prices can change without difficulty under differential growth rates, and the faster increase in money and real wage rates, which is bound to raise the prices of labor-intensive goods, is not a problem.

Hong Kong and Japan in the 1980s were good examples of two very rapidly growing economies that were both probably having very rapid growth in their international traded goods sectors. Hong Kong had a fixed exchange rate currency board with the United States after 1983, while Japan left its exchange rate flexible. Both countries had to have an appreciation of the real exchange rate. Japan took its real appreciation through an appreciation of the nominal exchange rate, as the dollar went from 250 yen down toward 100. Hong Kong took its real appreciation through an increase in the rate of inflation as measured by their national price index. People kept asking, "Oh, Hong Kong's inflation rate is 6 or 7 percent. America's inflation is 2 or 3 percent. Does it mean that Hong Kong's currency is getting overvalued?" No, it just meant that Hong Kong's domestic factors of production (e.g., barber services) were getting richer and that land and rents were rising. This reflected the appreciation of the real exchange rate, which every country in a common monetary area would have. A similar example in the 1990s would be the case of Ireland, the fastest-growing country in Europe, which has benefited by becoming a member of the euro area.

Under fixed exchange rates, most of the time nobody bothers about the adjustment process between two areas of a common currency area because there are no problems. The adjustment is effortless.[3] Of course, the problems of slow-growing and poor countries are greater than the problems of fast-growing and rich countries. The slow-growing country lacks the prospect of improving itself as rapidly as the rapidly growing country. Rapid growth is good, and slow growth or negative growth is bad. Why add salt to the wound by imposing an unstable monetary or fiscal system?

◤ Central Banks, Dollarization, and the Maastricht Conditions

While the Europeans are completing their transition to a currency union, recent discussion in the Americas has been about the benefits of dollarizing. Dollarization and its alternatives provide an option open not only to Latin America but to other countries with substantial trade and connections to the United States, such as Canada. The same arguments have been applied to Canada, and thus my examination of the merits and costs of dollarization in Canada will generally apply to most nations in Latin America.

The interest in dollarization stems at root from the belief that the central bank movement has been a failure. People need to be reminded that central banks are in most countries a comparatively recent phenomenon, a product of the 1920s or 1930s. It is true that the Riksbank in Sweden and the Bank of England were created as early as the late seventeenth century. But most central banks in the world were creatures of the twentieth century and, specifically, the period after World War I when the international gold standard had broken down. Even the largest economy (by far) in the world did not have a central bank until the Federal Reserve System was created in 1913. Most colonial countries had currency boards or allowed their commercial banks to manage the gold standard.

Central banks were introduced to fulfill a deeply felt need. Even under the gold standard, periodic crises had created a demand for a more "elastic" monetary system, and the central bank became an instrument of that elasticity. In time of crisis, when gold was flowing out, the central bank could mitigate the harsh effects of contraction by the provision of domestic credit, sterilizing the effects of gold outflows. There was of course a danger: if carried too far, sterilization would undermine the adjustment process and confidence in the gold parity. The Federal Reserve System was created to eliminate defects in the U.S. banking system, but during the process the "solution" created new problems with which the Fed was ill prepared to cope.

With the instability of gold during World War I and its aftermath, new arguments appeared for central banks. Rather than submit to imported price fluctuations under the gold standard, a country could set up its own central bank and use it to create a managed currency. In an age where colonialism was beginning to be unpopular, a central bank as well as a national currency could be looked upon as a badge and confirmation of sovereignty. It was not realized until much later that these central banks would become instruments of inflationary finance under the thumb of the finance or treasury administration.

The Bank of Canada is a comparatively young central bank, created only in 1935. A quick glance at its subsequent history will set the stage for a discussion of dollarization. During World War II, the Bank of Canada served as a handmaiden of the Ministry of Finance, assisting in the war effort by providing credit to the government that doubled the price level. (In this respect the bank was no better and no worse than its peers, the Federal Reserve and the Bank of England.) The traditional parity of the Canadian dollar with the American dollar was maintained by exchange controls and "austerity" in the postwar period. After September 1949, following the great 30 percent devaluation of sterling, Canada devalued by 10 percent. However, after the opening of hostilities in Korea, capital inflows swamped the monetary authorities, and they reacted, not by returning to parity (it would have focused attention on what could be called the mistake of 1949) but by moving on to floating exchange rates. This was in violation of the IMF charter, but Canada was given permission to float pending its determination of a new parity. By accident, therefore, Canada—for what would become a G-7 country—pioneered in the development of floating exchange rates.

The Canadian dollar was kept strong, at a premium over the U.S. dollar, by the Bank of Canada's tight monetary policy, but it proved to be at the expense of growth and caused excess unemployment. In the early 1960s, the Canadian authorities came to believe that the Canadian dollar was overvalued, and the Ministry of Finance announced its determination to use the resources of the Bank of Canada to depreciate the rate. This action proved to be a mistake, as the bottom fell out of the market. In a panic, the authorities reacted by supporting the rate at U.S.$0.92, fixing the rate at that level and drawing on the IMF. The Canadian dollar was then kept fixed throughout the rest of the decade, and during this period Canada experienced the U.S. inflation rate and the great growth boom of the United States. In 1970, however, in the midst of the U.S. recession of 1970–71, the Canadian dollar was again set loose, and it promptly appreciated. Since that time Canada has had a floating exchange rate. The experience from 1970 until the present therefore constitutes a useful test case of the efficiency and effectiveness of flexible rates. In 14 of the 20 years between 1972 and 1991, Canada had a higher inflation rate than the United States, but in the 1990s, the Canadian inflation rate was in general lower than the American. The Canadian dollar, however, which had once in the 1970s been as high as U.S.$1.07, fell to an all-time low (so far) of U.S. $0.62 in 1998. A fixed exchange rate would obviously have given Canada a lower rate of inflation over the period. At the same time, Canada's employment rate and growth rate were in general significantly lower than those in the United States. Canada, contrary to the long-term pattern, did not participate in the magnificent boom that got its start in the early 1980s. The prima facie evidence is that Canada has paid a price for its flexible exchange rate in the form of a poorer economy.

Now to consider dollarization. One quick and brutal way to accomplish it would be to abolish the Bank of Canada. If you abolished the Bank of Canada, and destroyed all the Canadian dollars in existence, what would Canadians do? First of all, they would have suffered a capital loss and would feel poorer. They would need a new money, and it would be natural for them to turn to importing the currency south of the border, the most important currency in the world. Of course Canadians would have to earn U.S. dollars by generating an export surplus or by going into debt. This would involve a real cost, which is a factor that on balance must be taken into account. Putting that issue aside for the moment, Canada would have the same money as the United States, the same price level and inflation rate, and the same interest rates. Trade between Canada and the United States would soar, and Canada's standard of living would converge toward that of the United States. The two countries would become much more closely integrated economically. Instead of having a purely local currency, Canadians would now participate in the benefits of a world currency.

The case for dollarization rests not just on the gains from monetary integration but also on the fact that American monetary policy is better than Canada's. As already mentioned, in the early 1970s, the Canadian dollar was as high as U.S.$1.07, but it fell in 1998 to a low of U.S.$0.62 cents. In this respect the Canadian currency was more like the Australian dollar, which depreciated from U.S.$1.5 in 1974 to around U.S.$0.65. Both central banks arrogantly thought they could improve on United States performance when the United States inflation rate increased, but both subsequently did much worse.

The gains from dollarization are substantial if, as can generally be assumed, it implies a better monetary policy in addition to gain of world-class currency. But what about the costs, which have to be balanced against the benefits? There are three costs. One is the loss of seigniorage. The second is the loss of a national symbol. The third is the loss of sovereignty arising partly from the fact that the United States would not adjust its inflation rate to take into account the policy interests of Canada. The importance of these costs are likely to differ between countries but would have to be weighed against the advantages of a monetary policy that, I am assuming, would be superior, as well as the benefits from using a world-class currency.

What would happen if suddenly the whole hemisphere became dollarized? It would surely result in a great increase in the gains from trade and investment and probably economic growth. The gains would be greater the more countries participated. Whatever gains Argentina might capture due to dollarization would be much enhanced if Chile and Brazil and other countries joined. Similarly, Brazil would gain additionally if Argentina and Chile were dollarized. Dollarization of the hemisphere would represent a considerable gain to all the countries in the hemisphere, including the United States.

Of course it is necessary to anticipate objections. A clever economist might say: "We don't need complete dollarization. Why not create a central bank and create some of our own money and have 50 percent dollarization? Every country could have its national dollar, convertible into U.S. dollars, saving both seigniorage and national face!" A Latin American dollar freely convertible into U.S. dollars would give Latin America the best of both worlds.

Theoretically, this alternative is an attractive one. The problem arises from the vicissitudes of human nature, always hoping to get something for nothing. Back in the 1920s, when Edwin W. Kemmerer, professor of international finance at Princeton University, was helping to create central banks all over Latin America, no one anticipated that they would be transmogrified into instruments of inflation, handmaidens of the fiscal authorities. If central banks were created to produced national dollars, what would prevent them from exceeding the limits of prudence and rendering the national currency inconvertible? How can we prevent history from repeating itself? It would be necessary to impose some statutory limit on the fiduciary component of the backing for domestic money.

If there existed a single world currency (say gold, for example, as in the past), countries would always have an incentive to economize on the expense of gold payments by bank money or national currencies, the pattern historically since the seventeenth century. Even if countries agreed to prohibit national currencies they would take steps to economize on the use of foreign currency and find money substitutes at home, creating an inflationary bias in the world economy. You would get a gradual decline—or more exactly a slower rate of growth—in the demand for money that would, if not taken into account, create more inflation than otherwise.[4]

If dollarization were good for Latin America, would it not be even better for the entire world? Suppose that the whole world were dollarized! Essentially, then, the world would have a common currency and a world central bank called the Federal Reserve System. As long as the Federal Reserve kept to its policy of stabilizing the American basket of goods—representing between a fifth and a quarter of world output—it would have the merit of being a very stable currency, more stable even than the gold standard or its bimetallic predecessors.

There is, of course, always a danger that Federal Reserve policy might lapse into the inflationary pattern of the 1970s or (much less likely) the deflationary pattern of the 1930s. But these historical episodes have produced their lessons and are not likely to be repeated. In the discussion hereafter, I shall assume that U.S. monetary policy continues to be as exemplary as it has in the recent past.

The benefits from a world currency would be enormous. Prices all over the world would be denominated in the same unit and would be kept equal in different parts of the world to the extent that the law of one price was allowed to work itself out. Apart from tariffs and controls, trade between countries would be as easy as it is between states of the United States. It would lead to an enormous increase in the gains from trade and real incomes of all countries, including the United States.

Another dimension of the benefits from a world currency would be a great improvement in the monetary policies of perhaps two-thirds of the countries of the world. The benefits to each country from a stable currency that is also a universal currency would be enormous. If the whole world were dollarized, there would be a common inflation rate and similar interest rates and an increase in trade, productivity, and financial integration, all of which would produce a considerable increase in economic growth and well-being.

Two arguments against dollarization relate to the transfer of seigniorage and the political barrier or "cost." Global dollarization would involve a transfer of seigniorage to the United States, greater than the already substantial seigniorage gained from the use of the dollar as an international reserve asset and money. The seigniorage transfer could be substantial, perhaps amounting to more than $100 billion per year.[5] But the seigniorage issue is not insuperable. The bill proposed in the U.S. Senate by Senator Connie Mack represents one way the seigniorage issue could be handled.[6] An alternative approach would be to set aside the seigniorage profits for international public uses.

The political issue or cost is more difficult to quantify. Countries would have transferred monetary sovereignty to the United States in return for a better money and (probably) monetary policy without receiving any share of a global sovereignty. Unlike members of the euro area, which have a share in the ownership and control of the central bank, members of the dollarized world simply transfer sovereignty to another country.

An analogy may help to make this issue clear. Many countries in the world are poorly managed. By contrast, the United States is well managed. Why not turn over the tasks of government to the United States? By internalizing the problem of foreign relations, military conflict would be eliminated and the gains from disarmament put toward an improvement in welfare. The U.S. government as the world government would be a force for stability and peace! But whatever the potential gains, how much of the rest of the world would be willing to scrap their sovereignty for membership in an American empire?

The costs and benefits of dollarization are not independent of the number of countries that participate. With economies of size the gains are larger when more countries participate, and thus economic gains would be greatest if the entire world were dollarized. But in the other direction, consider costs that arise when only a part of the world is dollarized. If major countries stay outside the dollarized zone, exchange rate volatility appears as a new problem. When there are two or more blocs, as in the present there are dollar, euro, and yen currency areas, getting locked into a dollar area that is appreciating (or depreciating) strongly against the other currencies would impose substantial adjustment problems.

Taken from the starting point of a barter economy, dollarizing is easy. In the absence of an existing currency, people would be quite willing to import a foreign currency to fill their monetary requirements. History is replete with examples of countries that have used a foreign currency. Most of the colonies in the Americas used Spanish, Portuguese, English, or French currencies—in some cases all of them—over that period. There is no need for Maastricht-type conditions in a barter economy, because if you have a barter economy the government has no means of creating an unbalanced budget or an erring monetary policy. Once the economy is dollarized and people start to use dollars, the new monetary economy makes it possible for the government to make mistakes. But because the government can't print any money, it can't have an unbalanced budget. It can borrow and run a deficit, but it can't run an inflationary deficit. It can run deficits up to the limit of its borrowing capacity, but discipline is assured without any Maastricht-type conditions.

But in our actual economies, the problem is different. The experience of Europe is instructive. Monetary union would have been easy immediately after the Hague summit in December 1969 because the European currencies were fixed to the dollar and had converged to dollar variables and therefore one another's; under the Bretton Woods arrangements, countries knew that it was dangerous to run budget deficits that would threaten convertibility. But monetary union was not politically possible in the first years, and by the time the international monetary system had broken down, in two steps in 1971 and 1973, countries lost their convergence around the dollar. As a consequence of flexible exchange rates, the European countries went their own way, and coordinated policy became much more difficult. The Maastricht conditions were imposed as a result of the undisciplined policies of the 1970s and 1980s and the commendably stern insistence of the Bundesbank on fiscal and monetary rectitude. Gradually, they worked their way back to monetary stability. Take the case of Italy. Italy had a fixed exchange rate from the postwar period until 1971, and throughout this period recognized that it had to maintain fiscal balance as well as pursue a monetary policy that would keep the balance of payments in equilibrium. The exchange rate was 620 lire to the dollar, and Italy had one of the fastest-growing economies in the world, with a stable price level and a low level of unemployment. Flexible exchange rates, however, led to the breakdown of discipline. Monetary inflation was the result. By the end of the decade, Italy decided it had enough inflation, so it joined the ERM. Its monetary stability was improved, but Italy then succumbed to fiscal instability, running up its debt/GDP ratio to over 100 percent of GDP.

The Maastricht conditions were needed to strap down ministers of finance. Like naughty children, they kept running deficits and forcing the central banks to buy government bonds when the market no longer wanted them.

In my Nobel Lecture (Mundell, 1999), delivered in Stockholm on December 6, 1999, I called the first and last decades of the twentieth century "bookends" of the century, in the sense that they were decades of monetary stability separated by a long period of instability. In both decades there was monetary and fiscal discipline. The gold standard imposed it automatically in the first decade of the twentieth century. In the last decade, when almost all the OECD countries had inflation rates below 3–4 percent a year, many of the countries achieved stability not automatically but by self-discipline or, in the case of Europe, the Maastricht conditions. The creation of the euro zone in fact prepared countries for the kind of gold standard mechanism that would be automatically imposed on them when their currencies were locked to the euro. It was a kind of replay—an automatic programming of the conditions that existed under the gold standard. The 11 countries of Europe are now following a gold standard type of mechanism that gives these countries automaticity.

▶ Exchange Rate Volatility and Internal versus External Stability

The dollar, euro, and yen areas make up nearly 60 percent of the world economy. Because there is a high degree of price stability in each area, they can be seen as three islands of stability. Despite the stability, however, exchange rates are very volatile. The dollar-yen rate has in the past been very unstable. The dollar-euro rate may be in the future equally unstable—we do not know yet.

If we judge the future of the dollar-euro rate by the history of the mark (the backbone of the ecu, which became the euro), we'd have to be pessimistic about volatility. As for the deutsche mark–dollar rate, in 1975 the dollar was about DM3.5. Five years later, in 1980, the dollar was worth half that, DM1.7. Five years later, by February 1985, the dollar had doubled to DM3.4. By 1992, the dollar had plummeted below DM1.4—a fall to 40 percent of its value—and now the dollar is up around DM2. It is hard to believe this extreme volatility isn't a very serious problem. Think of the problems at the time of the 1992 ERM crisis in Europe. A doubling or halving of the rate would be devastating for Europe. If the euro went down to 50 cents that would be awful for inflation, and if it doubled to U.S.\$2 that would be terrible for unemployment.

How much flexibility is good? How much can a country stand? Well, flexibility of the kind that existed between the dollar and the mark rate over the past 25 years would crack euro-land apart. And when the dollar-euro rate changes, it creates hard problems for the countries on the periphery of Europe that are doing business with both currency areas. It's disturbing to developing countries and to the rest of the world.[7]

The same difficulty exists for Asia. Look at the volatility of the dollar-yen rate: in 1985 the dollar was 250 yen. Ten years later, in April 1995, it was 79 yen (one-third the value). In June 1998, the dollar had soared from 79 yen to 148 yen, and speculators were saying it was going to go up to 200 yen. Instead it came down to about 105 yen. This volatility is terrible for countries that are closely involved with the Japanese and American markets. This volatility played a big role in the so-called Asian crisis.

Why "so-called"? Because the crisis hit only a few countries in Asia.[8] It was a crisis for four countries: Thailand, Malaysia, Indonesia, and Korea. Their currencies were pegged, not very efficiently, to the dollar, which was strongly appreciating against the yen, and currencies that stayed pegged had also to appreciate. They lost markets in Japan.[9] Many had debts fixed in dollars, which exacerbated their debt burdens. To understand the crisis better, however, one must also look at the countries that did not have a crisis—to see why Singapore, China, Hong Kong, Taiwan, and Japan were able to avoid it. What were these economies doing differently from the others? The differences were remarkable. Each of these countries had a very explicit target for their monetary policy. Their targets were transparent and automatic, and everybody knew they were. Singapore, Taiwan, and Japan had commodity basket targets (inflation targeting), China had a fixed exchange rate with the dollar with capital controls, and Hong Kong had a currency board fix against the dollar. They had a successful track record in following that policy, and everybody knew what they were going to do when important things were happening such as changes in the exchange rate elsewhere. They also had huge amounts of international reserves, so they didn't have to draw on the IMF or listen to advice, whether bad or good. They could follow their own policies, which in the past had been successful.

Keynes, in his book *A Tract on Monetary Reform* (Keynes, 1923), made the crucial distinction between "internal stability" and "external stability." Internal stability refers to a stable price level. External stability refers to a stable exchange rate and equilibrium in the balance of payments. He said it was good to have both. But if you had to make a choice, choose internal stability first and make external stability only a secondary choice.

When Keynes wrote that book, he was looking at the world economy in the economic crisis after the war—and one important event especially: the fluctuation in the U.S. price level and (because the dollar was tied to gold) gold. The price level in the United States had soared from 100 in 1914 to 200 in 1920. At this point, belatedly, the Federal Reserve System shifted to tight money, and the U.S. economy went into a nosedive. The price level came from an index of 200 down to an index of 140. This fall in the dollar price level (and consequent appreciation of gold) posed a great problem for the pound and other currencies.

Keynes clearly recognized the consequences for Britain. If Britain kept the exchange rate stable, it would suffer deflation too. On the other hand, if it kept the price level stable, Britain would have to allow the pound to appreciate against the dollar and gold. Because the dollar, now the dominant currency, was unstable against commodities, Britain could not have both internal and external stability; it would have to choose between them.

Keynes's distinction between internal and external stability and his preference for internal stability are well known. What is often ignored is the importance he attached to external stability, even though it was secondary to internal stability. He was quite explicit in saying it was better to have both, if it were possible. If the United States and gold are stable against commodities, Britain could have both internal and external stability. There is a contemporary lesson for our three islands of stability eight decades later.

If there is price stability within each of the dollar, euro, and yen areas, why should there be exchange rate fluctuations between them? Volatility of the exchange rates aggravates instability of the financial markets and disrupts trade and the efficiency of capital flows. Exchange rate uncertainty is an immediate cause of gross, excessive volatility in financial markets and the massive shifts in crossborder funds today. Capital market transactions in foreign exchange currently amount to something like 2 trillion dollars a day! It's largely capital that is going in and out, in and out, every five or ten minutes. People with their computers are pushing the funds back and forth, and it's nearly all pure waste. Only a tiny part of these shifts represents legitimate and beneficial capital movements.

▶ *Toward a World Currency*

Earlier I discussed the possibility—and the costs and benefits—of dollarizing the world economy. That would be the quickest and most effective way to produce a world currency. The political limitations of that solution, however, would make it difficult if not impossible to negotiate. It would greatly increase the power of the United States and leave the world at the mercy of potentially aggressive unilateralism. The temptation to exploit its monopolistic position and raise the inflation rate to maximize offshore seigniorage would be too great.[10] The power of nationalism continues to rule emotions, and sovereignty[11] is the last asset to be pawned. The idea was in the air at the 1944 Bretton Woods meeting, but it was dropped at the insistence of the United States. A world currency could only have legitimacy within the framework of a new Bretton Woods type of international agreement.[12]

The advent of the euro, however, invites a reconsideration of the need for and possibility of a world currency. Historically, the superpower has been an obstacle to monetary reform[13] because it has the most sovereignty to lose. England, the producer of the dominant currency in the nineteenth century, rejected the efforts of France and the United States to establish a world currency in that century. In the twentieth century, the United States has been the obstacle. The creation of the euro, however, diminishes the monopolistic position of the dollar, and in this respect U.S. power in the international arena will increasingly have to be shared. The United States may therefore find it in its interest to become less of an obstacle to international monetary reform in the future than it has been in the past. At the very least, the need for some guidelines in conflict situations over management of the dollar-euro-yen exchange rates will become increasingly apparent.

It is entirely possible that in the future the United States may adopt a sympathetic approach to international currency management and even a genuine international currency. To experiment with some possibilities: imagine an agreement for the world economy modeled after the monetary union forged by the 11 countries of the euro area. Instead of doing it for 11, do it for two hundred countries. If everyone used the same currency, wouldn't that make a great improvement in the way prices are compared, transactions are effected, and payments are made? There would be no currency crises, and the 2 trillion dollars' worth of cross-border transactions that exist only because of uncertainty over exchange rates would disappear.[14] Good riddance!

Of course there would be problems of management. A governing council, modeled on that of the ESCB, with more than two hundred members, would be much too unwieldy. It would be necessary for the board of governors to designate a few leading countries to manage the new system and the new currency.

Is it realistic to think of international monetary reform along the lines, pioneered by EMU, of a single currency for the world? I myself doubt it. The single-currency option adopted by the EU was a gamble that happened to pay dividends at a time when members of the EU were and still are considering closer political integration. But in the absence of closer political integration, a single-currency monetary union, requiring that national currencies be given up, would probably not be successful on the world stage. Quite apart from the preferences of smaller countries, the United States is not likely to be willing to give up the most successful currency of the twentieth century, and the rest of the world is not going to be content with the dollar as its world currency. Nor would the countries of the euro area be willing to scrap their new currency after decades of negotiations to bring it into being, which in any case they want partly for political reasons. And if Americans and Europeans keep their currencies, the Japanese will not be willing to give up the yen. A single-currency monetary union is not feasible in the present world and could not be negotiated in the absence of greater political integration.

Let's be more modest and consider a multiple-currency monetary union for two or three of our three islands of stability, the dollar, euro, and yen areas, and then consider how this union might be generalized to accommodate the interests of the rest of the world. There are no technical obstacles to a three-currency monetary union among the G-3. It could be patterned on the EMU construction, stopping short of replacing the three currencies by a single currency. Europe has locked its currencies. There is no speculation whatever for or against the franc, lira, mark, peseta, and all the other currencies in the euro area. Even before the new currency has been introduced in tangible form, there is a fixed exchange rate multiple-currency monetary union.

The same approach could work with two or three of the three main currency areas. Given convergence of inflation rates, it would be possible to lock exchange rates and bring interest rates into line with one another.[15] The mechanism for locking exchange rates could be simplified by assigning different tasks to the three central banks. One of the three currencies could be chosen as the pivot currency. It is best to choose the currency with the largest monetary mass—at the moment, the dollar. The other countries could be assigned the task of fixing exchange rates. Japan could fix the yen to the dollar at a rate of 100 (to make use of round numbers), Y100 = 1, so that 1 yen equals 1 cent. The Bank of Japan would stand ready to buy and sell dollars at that rate for all spot and forward offers and cease open market operations in domestic assets. Similarly, the ECB would stand ready to buy and sell dollars at (say) €1 = $1.

The assignment for the Bank of Japan and ECB would be to keep exchange rates fixed while that for the expanded Federal Reserve would be to stabilize the price level. The policy committee of the Federal Reserve (now the Open Market Committee) would incorporate Japanese and European as well as American experts. A nine-member committee might include four Americans, three Europeans, and two Japanese. Members of the committee should be independent of their governments (as are, theoretically, members of the Governing Council of the ESCB).

The expanded Fed would make the decisions about tightening or loosening credit. There would be a common target for monetary policy. The price index would incorporate goods representative of all areas, much like the harmonized index of consumer prices in Europe (Eurostat's HICP). The next step would be to agree on a common target for inflation. Members would then cast votes for tightening or loosening credit just as the three central banks do today.[16] There would also be a formula for redistributing seigniorage, just as in the ECB. The system would be very similar to a single currency monetary union, but it would preserve the individual currencies. The system would work in much the same way as in a single-currency monetary union.[17]

The arrangement would work best if all three areas participated. But it would also be possible with any two of the three areas. Any two of the three areas would become the dominant currency force, the mainstream of the world economy. The costs of being left out might be substantial, however, and an exchange rate fix of the three currencies would be superior to a currency fix of only two.

In the example given, the numbers accidentally work out neatly, with the yen being a cent and the euro and dollar at parity, the currencies are like different denominations and the need for a parallel currency is not so apparent. In general, however, it would be useful to introduce a common *numéraire* for denominating prices. All members would quote prices in this *numéraire* currency in addition to local currencies.

I will now show how the exchange rate stability of the three major currency areas could be used to create a multiple-currency monetary union for the world as a whole. The IMF could be turned into a world central bank and granted the authority to produce a world currency. The three largest currency areas could be designated as agents of the Board of Governors of the IMF. The *numéraire* currency might be equated to a dollar or a euro or 100 yen. We might call this new currency "intor" or "unor." Each participating member in the union would fix its local currency to the world currency, following the adjustment principles of a currency board, and denominate prices in the world currency as well as the local currency. The world currency itself would be backed by the currencies of the three largest central banks. The WCB would stand ready to buy and sell the world currency on demand so that it would not add to or subtract from the world money supply. Some provision could be made for redistributing seigniorage on a global rather than tripartite basis, perhaps with the three designated leaders setting up a special fund that could be used to finance agreed international projects.

Think of the great benefit to the rest of the world, including Latin America, if it never had to worry about changes in the dollar-euro, the dollar-yen, or the euro-yen exchange rates and could link its currencies to a true international currency in the production of which it participates. There would be no currency crises in participating countries as long as they adhered to the rules for fixed exchange rates. A world currency would provide a universal unit of account for transmitting values and be a source of a substantial increase in the gains from trade.

The link between language and currency has often been noted. Language is a medium of communication, and currency is a medium of exchange. National, ethnic, and liturgical languages are here to stay, but a common world language, understood as a second language everywhere, would obviously facilitate international understanding. By the same token, national or regional currencies will be with us for a long time in the next centuries, but a common world currency, understood as the second most important currency in every country, in which values could be communicated and payments made everywhere, would be a magnificent step toward increased prosperity and improved international organization.

◣ Notes

This chapter was presented at Universidad del CEMA, Buenos Aires, Argentina, on April 17, 2000.

1. At the time of the writing of this chapter, I had a discussion with President Kwasniewski of Poland. He said they were absolutely setting their sights on 2004 for the entry of Poland into this market.

2. A country may not want, or may not be able, to invest its resources in building up that large currency reserve over the long run. Like everything else, it's costly, but it's not that much of a cost. A country can invest its currency reserves in treasury bills that earn 5 percent.

3. The same question was frequently asked in Europe about Ireland, which has overtaken the U.K. in economic growth and overtaken Canada in per capita income—an amazing feat for a country that was always one of the poorest in Europe. Ireland has had very rapid economic growth. People kept saying Ireland shouldn't join the monetary union of Europe because it is growing rapidly and countries growing rapidly have to have a higher interest rate than other countries. Of course, that is not true. Ireland now is part of the Union, it has the same nominal interest rate as in the rest of Europe, and it's the same real interest rate in terms of the common basket of goods of the EU. I think the people say the same about the Spanish economy, a very rapidly growing economy. According to its national inflation basket, Spain has an inflation rate that is a couple of percentage points above the European average. This is a natural consequence when countries that are poorer than others start to grow rapidly: wage rates rise, and the prices of services and labor intensive goods have to rise. It may also be partly attributed, as Larry Sjaastad has suggested, to the more rapid pass-through effect of the euro's depreciation against the dollar.

4. I have warned elsewhere (Mundell 2000a) that the money multiplier in Europe might increase because of this phenomenon.

5. Suppose, for example, that reserve money in the world economy amounts to $4 trillion and is held in paper dollars. Something less than one-quarter of this would be held in the United States. Interest on the remainder at 5 percent would be $150 billion.

6. The short title of the bill (S.2101), introduced into the U.S. Senate of February 24, 2000, is the "International Monetary Stability Act of 2000" and its purpose is stated to be "to promote international monetary stability and to share seigniorage with officially dollarized countries."

7. Too much flexibility creates problems for developing countries. For instance, one of Argentina's problems has been that although the dollar has gone down against the yen, the dollar has been appreciating against the euro for the past few years. That means that the Argentine peso appreciates against the euro. Should Argentina think of shifting from a dollar fix to a euro fix? When you start a policy, it is a bad idea to change it if it's been a successful policy. If you do make a permanent shift, you should have very good reasons, and make sure you don't shift into a currency that's going to be appreciating more than you would like. If you shifted over to the euro in what may be the bottom of its cycle, you might shift into a currency that would be further appreciating, making matters worse.

8. A less well-known term used by some is "the Asian-IMF crisis." I think this denomination is more appropriate than to stamp a whole area with a crisis.

9. A related problem was the devaluation of the Chinese yuan on January 1, 1994.

10. I have discussed the "optimum inflation rate" in the context of maximizing offshore seigniorage in Mundell (1971).

11. I have discussed the problem of monetary sovereignty in Mundell (2000c).

12. See Mundell (1995) for a discussion of the Bretton Woods agreement and why the world currency idea, which was contained in both the White and Keynes plans, was dropped.

13. Mundell (1995).

14. A single-currency monetary union would eliminate speculative capital movements. Capital never moves in the wrong direction from New York to California, or Illinois, or Louisiana. It always moves to where it is more profitably employed, because there is no speculation about exchange rates. The same holds for securely fixed exchange rates. Panama and the United States have had a monetary union since 1904, with the passive Panamanian balboa coins maintained at par; Scotland and England have had a monetary union for centuries with the passive Scottish pound still in existence; Luxembourg and Belgium have had a monetary union since the 1920s, with the passive Luxembourg franc still in existence. Nor have the locked exchange rates of the euro area produced any speculative capital movements. There are no bad capital movements; there are only bad exchange systems.

15. Interest differentials arise because of expectations of exchange rate changes. Locking the dollar and the yen would equalize interest rates, mainly through a rise in Japanese rates, which have been traditionally low because of bullish expectations about the future of the yen.

16. There is still a role for gold in the international monetary system. In the development of the three-currency monetary union among the G-3 countries, one of the uses of gold would be as an index of inflation. Almost everyone thinks that if the price of gold suddenly shoots way up, that is an index of inflationary expectations, because in the event of an increase in inflation the expectations of people will shift into gold and gold will rise in price.

17. A multiple-currency monetary union may not, however, impart the same sense of permanence as a single-currency monetary union, and to the extent this was so, interest rates would not fully become equalized.

◣ References

Keynes, John Maynard. (1923). *Tract on Monetary Reform.* London: Macmillan.

Mundell, R. A. (1968, September). *A Plan for a World Currency.* (U.S. Congress, Joint Economic Committee Hearings). Washington, D.C.

Mundell, R. A. (1971). The Optimum Balance of Payments Deficit and the Theory of Empires. In P. Salin and E. Claassen (Eds.), *Stabilization Policies in Interdependent Economies* (pp. 69–86). Amsterdam: North Holland Press.

Mundell, R. A. (1995). The International Monetary System: The Missing Factor. *Journal of Policy Modeling, 17*(5), 479–92.

Mundell, R. A. (1998a, March 24). The Case for the Euro: Part I. *Wall Street Journal.*

Mundell, R. A. (1998b, March 25). The Case for the Euro: Part II. *Wall Street Journal.*

Mundell, R. A. (1998c, April 30). Making the Euro Work. *Wall Street Journal.*

Mundell, R. A. (1999, December 8). *Reconsideration of the Twentieth Century.* (Nobel Memorial Prize Lecture). Video.

Mundell, R. A. (2000a, March 30). Threat to Prosperity. *Wall Street Journal.*

Mundell, R. A. (2000b, June). A Reconsideration of the Twentieth Century. *American Economic Review.*

Mundell, R. A. (2000c). Money and the Sovereignty of the State. *Zagreb Journal of Economics.*

2

Edgar L. Feige, Michael Faulend, Velimir Šonje, and Vedran Šošić

Unofficial Dollarization in Latin America

Currency Substitution, Network Externalities,
and Irreversibility

The current dollarization debate in Latin America (Berg and Borensztein, 2000; Bogetic, 2000; Calvo, 2000; Calvo and Reinhart, 2001) focuses on the normative policy issue of selecting an optimal foreign exchange system for an emerging market economy. At issue is whether or not Latin American countries should officially dollarize, that is, adopt the U.S. dollar de jure as the official legal tender.[1] Advocates suggest that official dollarization enables countries to avoid currency and balance of payment crises by eliminating the temptation of inflationary finance and encourages foreign investment. These effects reduce the level and volatility of interest rates and ultimately stimulate growth. Opponents cite the loss of seigniorage and the loss of an independent monetary policy.[2]

Often overlooked in this normative debate are the positive issues concerning the causes, consequences, and extent to which these countries are already "unofficially" (de facto) dollarized. We need to know the degree to which individuals and firms have voluntarily chosen to use a foreign currency as either a transaction substitute or a store of value substitute for the monetary services of the domestic currency, and the implications of such actions. De facto dollarization, involving both currency substitution and asset substitution, may be widespread, but since foreign currency use rarely leaves a paper trail, measuring its scope is a particularly elusive task. The absence of empirical estimates of unofficial dollarization makes the outcomes of macroeconomic decisions more difficult to predict. The greater the extent and variability of unofficial dollarization, the weaker is the central bank's knowledge and control over the effective money supply. Unofficial dollarization also reduces the monetary authority's ability to earn seigniorage from its own currency issue. Finally, unofficial dollarization reflects citizens' perceptions of the stability of the domestic monetary regime, the credibility of monetary policies, and the perceived stability of the domestic banking system.

This chapter presents new empirical evidence concerning the extent to which the U.S. dollar already serves as the de facto unit of account, store of value, and dominant medium of exchange in Latin America. Asset and currency substitution is induced by past inflations, devaluations, and currency confiscations. Often, unofficial dollarization becomes irreversible, due to network externalities that significantly reduce the cost of using dollars once they exceed a threshold level. When de facto dollarization is widespread, the effective money supply is larger than the domestic money supply and is subject to endogenous behavioral responses reflecting currency substitution on the part of the public. Hausmann et al. (1999) suggest that under such circumstances, expansionary monetary policy can have procyclical instead of countercyclical consequences. Unofficial dollarization will thwart government efforts to employ inflationary finance to impose implicit taxes on domestic monetary assets. Knowledge of the extent of de facto dollarization is therefore an important input into the normative debate since extensive unofficial dollarization is likely to make domestic monetary policy less effective and active exchange rate intervention more dangerous.

Unofficial dollarization also has fiscal consequences. Foreign cash transactions reduce the costs of tax evasion and participation in the unreported (unofficial) economy. This weakens the government's fiscal ability to command real resources from the private sector and deepens fiscal deficits. The shifting of economic activity toward the underground economy distorts macroeconomic information systems (Feige, 1990, 1997), thereby adding to the difficulty of formulating macroeconomic policy. By obscuring financial transactions, de facto dollarization reduces the cost of enterprise theft and may facilitate greater corruption and rent seeking. Given these extensive ramifications, informed policy decision making requires better knowledge of the extent, causes, and consequences of unofficial dollarization, as well as the specific effects of its components, currency substitution and asset substitution.

The major limitation of any analysis of unofficial dollarization is that the amount of foreign currency in circulation (FCC) is typically unknown. Despite the substantive importance of the issues cited, earlier research has provided no reliable empirical information concerning the actual extent of unofficial dollarization. In their review of the key issues concerning currency substitution, Calvo and Végh (1992) observed:

> In the final analysis, the relevance of currency substitution is an empirical issue. . . . At the empirical level, the study of currency substitution faces a fundamental problem: there is usually no data available on foreign currency circulating in an economy. Therefore the importance of currency substitution is basically unobservable. (p. 25)

There is now a growing body of evidence (Feige, 1994, 1996, 1997; Porter and Judson, 1996) suggesting that 40–60 percent of U.S. currency is held abroad. This chapter presents newly collected data on the location of U.S. currency, specifically, estimates of the amount of U.S. dollars in circulation in Latin America. These data enable us to finally circumvent the fundamental problem of "unobservability" that has plagued the currency substitution literature since its inception, permitting a refinement of definitions and measures of the extent of currency substitution, asset substitution, unofficial dollarization, and the credibility of domestic banking institutions.

Once the nature and extent of unofficial dollarization is empirically measurable, it becomes possible to examine the causes of dollarization, and to examine the circumstances under which unofficial dollarization is likely to become persistent and possibly irreversible.[2] Hysteresis and irreversibility will be affected by network externalities associated with the use of foreign currency. We therefore present models of network externalities that seek to determine the conditions under which foreign currency usage is likely to dominate the use of domestic currency by specifying the costs and benefits of the flight from domestic currency. When network externalities in the use of foreign currencies become sufficiently large, countries may decide to officially dollarize their economies, foregoing the flexibility of domestic monetary management in exchange for greater financial stability and an enhanced ability to attract foreign investment. Panama, Ecuador, and most recently El Salvador and Guatemala have chosen to dollarize officially. Argentina attempted to effectively dollarize by pegging the peso to the dollar on a one-for-one basis; however, the most recent crisis has shown this policy to be unsustainable.

Much of the dollarization literature has focused on the experience of those Latin American countries whose hyperinflationary episodes have induced a flight to dollars. With new estimates of the extent of dollar currency holdings in these countries, we also set out to model the dollarization process. Our empirical models are based on the Argentina experience since Argentina appears to be the most heavily de facto dollarized country in Latin America.

The first section of the chapter briefly reviews earlier efforts to measure dollarization by indirect means and defines several new measures of unofficial dollarization that attempt to distinguish between currency and asset substitution. Currency substitution occurs when a foreign currency substitutes as a medium of exchange for the domestic currency, whereas asset substitution refers to the substitution of foreign denominated monetary assets for domestically denominated monetary assets. The next section presents new empirical estimates of the extent of dollarization in Latin America and compares these estimates to earlier proxy measures employed by the IMF. We find that IMF dollarization measures are highly correlated with our measure of asset substitution but appear to be imprecise measures of currency substitution.

The following section extends the network externality model of currency competition originally presented by Dowd and Greenaway (1993). We analyze the factors that influence individual decisions to use services of different moneys showing the motives that lead initially to asset substitution and finally to currency substitution. We show that the choice of exchange rate regime depends on a number of key relationships, such as the extent to which the broad money supply is covered by foreign exchange reserves, the level of the nominal exchange rate and the sensitivity of the number of agents who use the foreign currency to exchange rate changes, and the impact of exogenous monetary shocks on the exchange rate. As the use of a foreign currency increases, network externalities induce a reduction in the transaction costs associated with the use of the foreign currency. Once these transaction costs are lower than the costs of switching back to the local currency, a threshold of dollarization is achieved, after which currency substitution is likely to become irreversible.

In the final section we estimate an empirical network externality model of the dollarization process in Argentina developed by Oomes (2001) based on the discrete choice framework with social interactions of Brock and Durlauf (2001). The estimated model permits us to investigate the dynamic circumstances under which Argentina's de facto dollarization occurred, as well as the necessary conditions that would be required to reverse unofficial dollarization. The model reveals the difficulty of reversing the process of unofficial dollarization once it has reached a threshold level.

▲ Definitions

In an economy with unofficial dollarization, the *effective* broad money supply (EBM) consists of local currency (cash) in circulation outside the banking system (LCC), foreign currency (cash) in circulation outside the banking system (FCC), local checkable deposits (LCD), foreign currency deposits (FCD) held with domestic banks, and local currency time and savings deposits (LTD).[3] Quasi money (QM) consists of FCD and LTD. Thus, the typical definition of broad money (BM) falls short of the EBM by the unknown amount of FCC. The narrow money supply (NM) is typically defined to include only LCC and LCD. However, in a dollarized economy, the effective narrow money supply (ENM) also includes FCC.[4] Thus,

[1] $EBM \equiv LCC + FCC + LCD + QM \equiv BM + FCC$, where:
[2] $QM \equiv FCD + LTD$
[3] $BM \equiv LCC + LCD + QM$
[4] $NM \equiv LCC + LCD$
[5] $ENM \equiv NM + FCC$

In a regime with unofficial dollarization, the recorded money supply falls short of the effective money supply due to the omission of FCC, which is typically unknown and is not directly controllable by the local central bank.

Due to data limitations on measuring the amount of FCC, cited by Calvo and Végh (1992), research on the currency substitution process has been forced to accept as a proxy for dollarization the observable amount of FCD. Studies of currency substitution, often associated with the IMF (Balino, Bennett, and Borensztein, 1999; Canto, 1985; Clements and Schwartz, 1992; Ize and Yeyati 1998; Marquez, 1987; Sahay and Végh, 1995; Ortiz,

1983), employ the ratio of FCD to BM as the means of establishing the extent to which countries are dollarized.[5] We denote this common dollarization index:

[6] $(DI_{IMF}) \equiv FCD/BM.$

Unofficial dollarization, in the Latin America context, was often a response to hyperinflation. Under such circumstances, a foreign currency may first serve as a unit of account and store of value and only later as a circulating medium of exchange. "Currency substitution" suggests that the foreign currency largely displaces the domestic currency as the medium of exchange. If one is primarily concerned with the extent to which a foreign nation's currency has substituted for local currency primarily as the medium of exchange, it is useful to define an explicit currency substitution index (CSI). When the main impact of dollarization takes the form of asset substitution, it is useful to define an asset substitution index (ASI). Finally, when both asset substitution and currency substitution take place, we define a broader unofficial dollarization index (UDI) that reflects the fraction of the broad effective money supply that is composed of foreign currency and foreign deposits. We use the following definitions throughout the chapter.

Currency substitution occurs when foreign currency is partly or entirely used as a unit of account and medium of exchange. Currency substitution can be official or unofficial.[6] While official cases are still rare, unofficial dollarization is widespread. The most sensitive transaction measure of de facto dollarization is represented by the CSI, which shows the fraction of a nation's total currency supply held in the form of foreign currency.[7] Thus,

[7] $CSI \equiv FCC \, / \, (FCC + LCC)$

Since domestic transactions are typically settled by debiting and crediting LCD accounts, when institutional circumstances warrant, it may also be useful to modify the CSI and use instead (CSI_n), defined as the fraction of the effective narrow money supply that is made up of foreign currency.

[8] $CSI_n \equiv FCC \, / \, (ENM)$

Asset substitution involves the use of foreign denominated monetary assets as substitutes for domestic ones, in their capacity as a store of value. It is measured by the ASI, defined as the ratio of foreign denominated monetary assets to domestic denominated monetary assets, excluding cash outside banks.[8]

[9] $ASI \equiv FCD \, / \, (LCD + QM)$

Dollarization is a summary measure of the use of foreign currency in its capacity to produce all types of money services in the domestic economy. When both asset substitution and currency substitution take place, or when FCDs are used by firms to make transactions with international partners, we define a broader UDI, which represents the fraction of a nation's broad effective money supply that is composed of foreign monetary assets. Thus:

[10] $UDI \equiv (FCC + FCD) / EBM$

Bank credibility: The choices individuals make concerning the disposition of monetary assets reflects their perceptions of the credibility of the domestic banking system. Since this perceived credibility is an important factor affecting the ability of the monetary authority to pursue its macroeconomic objectives, it is useful to define a *bank credibility index (BCI)* reflecting the ratio of monetary assets held in the domestic banking system to assets held in the form of currency outside the banking system. Thus,

[11] $BCI \equiv (LCD + FCD + LTD) / (LCC + FCC)$

the higher the BCI, the higher the public's confidence in the domestic banking system.

Each of the foregoing indices depends on a number of economic variables that reflect the relative incentives to hold the different assets described in both the denominator and numerator of each index. These incentives include relative rates of return as reflected by interest rate differentials, inflation differentials, and exchange rate depreciation, as well as the relative costs and benefits associated with network externalities, switching costs, and risks of banking institutions.

The conventional IMF dollarization index (DI_{IMF}) will be an adequate proxy of de facto dollarization when foreign currency holdings are of marginal importance, or when FCC and FCD are highly complementary. However, if significant amounts of foreign currency circulate for transaction purposes or if FCC and FCD are in fact substitutes, then the IMF dollarization measure is likely to perform poorly as an indicator of unofficial dollarization, understating the true extent of dollarization due to its omission of FCC holdings. Moreover, DI_{IMF} does not permit one to distinguish between the dynamic currency substitution and asset substitution processes that our more refined indicators attempt to capture. In order to examine the adequacy of the IMF index, we first turn to a discussion of our efforts to obtain direct estimates of U.S. currency holdings in Latin America.

▲ Measurement

Direct Measurement of FCC

United States currency is widely used outside of the United States. By the end of 2001, 50 percent of the $580 billion of U.S. currency in circulation is believed to have been held abroad.[9] United States currency (cash) has many desirable properties. It has a reputation as a stable currency and is therefore a reliable store of value. It is available in many countries, is widely accepted as a medium of exchange, and protects foreign users against the threat of bank failures, devaluation, and inflation. United States dollar usage preserves anonymity because it leaves no paper trail of the transaction for which it serves as the means of payment. Indeed the very characteristics that make the U.S. dollar a popular medium of exchange also make it difficult to determine the exact amount and location of U.S. notes circulating abroad. Nevertheless, there is a direct source of information that can be used to determine the approximate amounts of U.S. cash in circulation in different countries.

Over the past two decades, the United States Customs Service has been mandated to collect systematic information on cross-border flows of U.S. currency. The Currency and Foreign Transactions Reporting Act (also known as the "Bank Secrecy Act") requires persons or institutions importing or exporting currency or other monetary instruments in amounts exceeding $10,000, to file a Report of International Transportation of Currency or Monetary Instruments. The U.S. Customs Service has collected these reports, commonly known as Currency and Monetary Instrument Reports (CMIRs) since 1977. Although the CMIR data system was established with the aim of recording individual instances of cross-border inflows and outflows of currency and monetary instruments, its micro records can be usefully aggregated to study the size, origin, and destination of cross-border currency flows. The CMIR data system consists of more than 2.5 million inbound filings and more than three hundred thousand outbound filings. The information contained in the millions of accumulated confidential individual CMIR forms has been aggregated in such a way as to fully preserve the confidentiality of individual filers' information. The aggregated data yield time series observations on the gross inflows and outflows of U.S. currency to different destinations. By cumulating the net outflows of U.S. dollars to all destinations, we are able to obtain estimates of the approximate amount of U.S. currency held abroad as well as the location of U.S. currency around the world.[10]

Table 2.1 presents the available evidence on the actual amounts of U.S. currency in circulation in various Latin American countries. Column 1 contains the authors' estimates obtained from aggregated CMIR reports, and column 2 is obtained from informal surveys conducted by a team of representatives of the Federal Reserve and U.S. Treasury Department (United States Treasury Department, 2000). Both measures suggest that Argentina exhibits the highest per capita holding of U.S. dollars in Latin America.

Estimates of dollar FCC holdings are then used to calculate the currency substitution, asset substitution, and dollarization indices described in the previous section. Feige et al. (2002) examined these ratios for a

Table 2.1
Estimates of Per Capita Holdings of U.S. Currency and Domestic Currency in Latin America

Country	(1)[a] Per Capita $FCC CMIR Estimates (1997/98) (Dollars)	(2)[b] Per Capita $FCC U.S. Treasury Informal Survey (Dollars)	(3)[c] Per capita $LCC (Dollars)
Argentina	1478	698	374
Bolivia	144	NA	49
Brazil	15	6	108
Colombia	NA	52	81
Costa Rica	209	NA	130
Dominican Republic	NA	188	98
Mexico	NA	51	124
Nicaragua	135	NA	25
Panama	NA	648	0
Paraguay	NA	18	85
Peru	67	185	50
Uruguay	762	NA	199
Venezuela	104	NA	93

[a]Author's calculations. [b]United States Treasury Department (2000). [c]International financial statistics.

sample of 24 countries for which data were available and found that the widely used IMF dollarization index is highly correlated with the asset substitution index but appears to be an imprecise measure of currency substitution.

Figure 2.1 displays a country-by-country comparison of the conventional IMF dollarization proxy (DI_{IMF}) and our broader dollarization index (UDI), which takes explicit account of the estimated amount of FCC circulation in each nation. The IMF dollarization index understates the true extent of unofficial dollarization due to its omission of FCC. Our estimates suggest that the highest de facto dollarization has occurred in Bolivia, Nicaragua, Uruguay, and Argentina, whereas Mexico and Venezuela are the least dollarized Latin American countries in our sample.

Figure 2.2 presents our estimates of the degree of currency substitution and asset substitution in Latin American countries.

The figure reveals that the patterns of currency substitution and asset substitution are in fact quite different among the countries observed. Bolivia, Peru, and Uruguay are notable because asset substitution dominates currency substitution, whereas the other countries display a pattern in which currency substitution dominates.

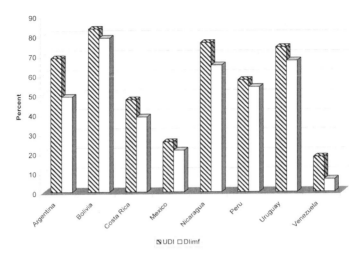

Figure 2.1. Alternative dollarization measures.

▲ Network Externalities: Asset and Currency Substitution

Latin American hyperinflations and severe exchange rate depreciations dramatically reduce the rates of return on local domestic currency relative to U.S. dollars, inducing individuals to flee from weak currencies into stronger ones. Such shifts are initially motivated by asset substitution to avoid the costs of a depreciating store of value. However, currency also represents an

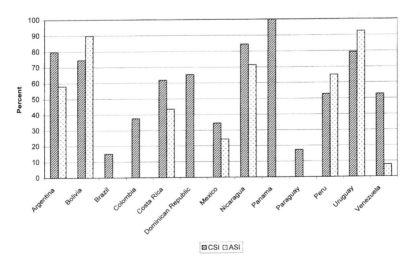

Figure 2.2. Currency and asset substitution indicies.

important medium of exchange, and the extent of currency substitution depends on the relative transaction costs of foreign and local currency. These relative transaction costs are, in turn, determined by the network externalities enjoyed by the users of each alternative medium of exchange and the costs of switching between them. For any expected rate of depreciation of the domestic currency, it is more likely that agents will substitute into a foreign currency if other agents already use it as a cocirculating medium of exchange in the domestic economy. When severe exchange rate depreciation induces unofficial dollarization, network externalities tend to reinforce the rewards of holding the stronger currency. Switching costs inhibit a return to the local currency even after a successful stabilization effort. These well-known incentive effects give rise to the conjecture that once de facto dollarization has reached a threshold, it may well persist, leading to the observation of dollarization hysteresis.

These considerations have been formalized in the models presented by Farrell and Saloner (1986) and Dowd and Greenaway (1993). Building on these foundations, we consider $(N + 1)$ money-using agents with infinite life horizons. They make decisions on the use of currency in time T. Up to time T they used only local currency, but from T onward they can also use a competing foreign currency. Agents' decisions concerning the use of local currency are based on the following utility function:

$$[12] \qquad u(T) = (a + bn)\int_{T}^{\infty} e^{-r(t-T)}dt = (a + bn)/r$$

where $u(T)$ is utility in time T derived from using the local currency from time T to infinity; $t \geq T$ are time periods from now (T) onward; r is the discount factor; n is log of N. If there are no network externalities, the parameter (a) reflects the redemption value of the local currency when no one else uses it, and bn $(b > 0)$ reflects the network externality benefit of others using the currency.

Similar logic applies to the utility of using a foreign currency with or without network externalities, where an^{*} denotes values for the foreign currency. Hence, when all agents use local currency,

$$[13] \qquad u(T) = (a + bn)/r \text{ and } u^{*}(T) = a^{*}/r$$

Conversely, when all agents use competing foreign currency,

$$[14] \qquad u(T) = a/r \text{ and } u^{*}(T) = (a^{*} + b^{*}n^{*})/r$$

All agents will hold local currency even if it is not used for transactions purposes (hypothetical absence of network externalities) if the utility from holding it for purposes other than settling payments is greater than the utility from using competing foreign currency when all agents are using it minus the cost *(s)* of switching between the two currencies. Hence all agents will use local currency when:

[15]   a/r > [(a* + b*n*)/r] − s

Conversely, all agents will switch to competing foreign currency if the utility from using it when no one else switches to its use is higher than the sum of utility derived from use of local currency when everybody uses it including switching costs, that is, when:

[16]   a*/r > [(a + bn)/r] + s

These corner solutions define the conditions under which agents use local currency exclusively or foreign currency exclusively. The more interesting intermediate cases consider the range of circumstances under which asset and currency and substitution behaviors induce both currencies to cocirculate simultaneously. These intermediate cases are indeterminate unless agents have a mechanism for determining the gains from asset substitution and a mechanism for forming expectations of whether other agents will switch to the competing currency. If agents knew the redemption values of the two currencies as well as the extent to which others are likely to switch, they would adopt the foreign currency when:

[17]   [(a* + b*n*)/r] − s ≥ (a + bn)/r,

that is, when the expected present value of asset substitution returns (represented by the parameter *a**) and currency substitution returns (network externality returns represented by *bn**) of the new currency, minus switching costs, exceeds the expected present value of asset and currency substitution returns to the local currency. The limitation of the Dowd-Greenaway model is that it provides no behavioral mechanism for trading off the utility derived from asset substitution with that of currency substitution. This requires additional relationships connecting the asset substitution parameters and the currency substitution parameters to observable variables.

Asset Substitution and the Exchange Rate

Recall that the asset substitution parameter *(a)* depends on the redemption value of the currency. We will assume that this redemption value depends positively on the extent to which the broad domestic money supply is covered by international reserves, that is, by the "coverage ratio" *c*. The coverage ratio (expressed in local currency) is defined as

[18] $c = e_{(BM)}R[BM]^{-1}$

and

[19]   a = a(c), da/dc > 0,

where R represents the central bank's international reserves, e is the nominal exchange rate of domestic currency versus the foreign currency, and BM is the domestic broad money supply ($BM = LCC + LCD + LTD$). As long as the coverage ratio (c) is high, the likelihood of asset substitution is low.

It is interesting to note how this ratio reacts to an exogenous monetary expansion. On one hand, expansionary monetary policy reduces the ratio (c) by increasing the denominator of (18). On the other hand, expansionary monetary policy leads to exchange rate depreciation, which increases the numerator. Since the asset substitution parameter (a) is a positive function of (c), the net effect of exogenous monetary expansion on the redemption value of the local currency is

[20] $\partial a/\partial BM = a'_c c'_{BM} = a'_c[e'_{BM}(R/BM) - eR/(BM)^2]$

Equation (20) reveals that expansionary monetary policy has both positive and negative impacts on utility from the use of money; however, the second term in the brackets converges to zero, so the ratio (R/BM) dominates the outcome. The effect depends on the initial level of coverage, that is, redemption value (R/BM), on the sensitivity of the exchange rate to changes in domestic money supply (e'_{BM}), and on the level of the nominal exchange rate (e). After normalizing e and e'_{BM} to one, we see that the higher the initial coverage, the greater is the impact of domestic monetary expansion on the utility of holding domestic money. Next, higher exchange rate sensitivity increases the utility of holding domestic money (reduces likelihood of asset substitution) because, for a given expansion in BM, higher sensitivity means a greater coverage ratio (c) expressed in domestic currency. For plausible values of reserves, money, and the exchange rate sensitivity, there is nothing in the mechanics of the asset substitution component of the model that can turn the utility of holding domestic money negative. Asset substitution will arise earlier if the initial coverage ratio (redemption value of the local currency) is lower, although higher exchange rate sensitivity to money supply can partly alleviate this impact.

Exchange Rate and Currency Substitution

Dowd and Greenaway (1993) showed that the decision to switch to competing foreign currency depends on expectations about the behavior of other agents. Assume that agents will form expectations about how many other agents will switch on the basis of nominal exchange rate movements. When the exchange rate depreciates, agents expect the others to switch. Therefore,

[21] $n = n(e), dn/de < 0$.

Combining (12), (19), and (21), the utility function under which all agents use local currency is:

[22] $u(T) = [a_{(c)}c_{(BM)} + bn(e_{(BM)})]r^{-1}$

The consequences of a monetary expansion including both currency and asset substitution effects is now represented by

[23] $\partial u/\partial BM = [\partial a/\partial BM + dn/dBM]r^{-1} = \{a'_c[e'_{LM}(R/BM) - eR/(BM)^2] + be'_{LM}n'_e\}r^{-11}$
$dn/dBM < 0$ because: $b > 0$; $e'_{BM} > 0$; $n'_e < 0$.

Since the term added to (23) is negative, the conclusion is that the currency substitution effect shortens the period in which expansionary monetary policy can be effective (where effectiveness is measured by its impact on the utility from holding local currency).

Choice of Exchange Rate Regime

Equation (23) provides a formal elaboration of the choice of exchange rate regime on the desirability of dollarization. As long as $\partial u / \partial BM > 0$, monetary expansion will not induce unofficial dollarization. However, the sign of $\partial u/\partial BM$ is ambiguous, depending on the sensitivity of the exchange rate to money, the extent to which BM is covered by foreign reserves, the absolute level of the nominal exchange rate, and the sensitivity of the number of people using the currency to exchange rate changes. In these circumstances, policymakers must be concerned about the consequences of monetary expansion since policymakers are liable to induce switching out of the local currency, thereby making monetary expansion ineffective.

If the two sensitivities are high and the coverage ratio is low, policymakers need to consider that a prudent course of action may be to officially dollarize, that is, to either peg the exchange rate to the foreign currency or to adopt the competing currency as legal tender. Otherwise, unofficial dollarization may take its course, with an induced loss of seigniorage and reduced potency of any given monetary action. The costs of these hysteresis effects that derive from network externalities increase as the de facto dollarization continues and may lead to an irreversibility that precludes a return to the use of domestic currency. In Latin America, with its legacy of high inflation and wage indexation, flexible exchange rate regimens may be unable to capture the potential benefits of monetary interventions. As real exchange rates become less responsive to monetary manipulation, the need for more extreme depreciations increases the dangers of extensive asset substitution.

Further Extensions of Network Externality Models

Oomes (2001) suggests an alternative means of characterizing the consequences of positive network externalities in the use of foreign currencies. On the basis of the discrete choice framework with social interactions developed by Brock and Durlauf (2001), Oomes demonstrates that network externalities in the demand for currency can explain the hysteresis in the unofficial dollarization observed in Russia.

Our extension of the Dowd–Greenaway model shows that network externalities are useful in specifying the determinants and dynamics of the currency substitution process, but it does not produce a readily testable empirical specification. An innovation of the Oomes framework is the derivation of a reduced form equation that can be directly estimated empirically and that can be used to explain the dynamics of the currency substitution process.[11]

The model belongs to the class of cash-in-advance models with random matching of buyers and sellers. Buyers and sellers have a choice of conducting a transaction in either domestic (m) or foreign currency (m^*). Each agent that is a buyer in one period becomes a seller in the next. The decision problem faced by a given agent i is which currency to hold after receiving currency from a random buyer at the beginning of period t and before being matched with a random seller j at the end of period t. The currency choice of agent i in period t is denoted by $m_{i,t} \in \{m, m^*\}$.

The cost of holding domestic currency one period prior to the transaction is the depreciation of the domestic currency (e_t). There are also varieties of different costs associated with transacting in foreign currency. The first type of cost is the "shoe-leather cost" (σ_t), that is, the cost of searching for and transacting at an exchange office. This cost occurs only if there is a mismatch between the currency the buyer decides to hold and the currency choice of the seller. This type of cost can be classified as a transaction cost, or a switching cost in terms of the Dowd-Greenaway model. To the extent that these costs are used as an explanation for the hysteresis effect, the intuitions guiding the two models are similar.

Since the Oomes model was originally developed for the case of Russia, it also includes a second type of transaction or switching cost, that is, the explicit tax (τ) on the purchase of foreign currency, which was introduced in Russia in 1997. This cost is incurred only if the buyer holds domestic currency and the seller prefers to transact in foreign currency. Finally, there is a variable that captures the institutional barriers to the use of foreign currency for transaction purposes that can be interpreted as the probability of confiscation of the foreign currency involved in the transaction (q).[12] Depending on the actual preferences of the buyer and seller, the costs of alternative choices of agent i acting as a buyer conditional on the choice of seller j are summarized in table 2.2.[13]

The decision of the representative buyer to hold domestic or foreign currency will also depend on its expectations of sellers' preferences. If the probability, expected by i, that any random seller j prefers to hold foreign currency in period $t + 1$ is denoted by $\hat{p}_{t+1}$, it can also be interpreted as the expected proportion of buyers holding foreign currency in that period, that is, $\hat{p}_{t+1}$ represents the dollarization ratio expected in period $t + 1$.

Table 2.2
Cost Matrix for Agent i

	$m_{j,t+1}=m$	$m_{j,t+1}=m^*$
$m_{i,t}=m$	e	$e + \sigma + \tau$
$m_{i,t}=m^*$	σ	q

The expected costs of holding domestic currency $c(m_t)$ and foreign currency $c(m_t^*)$ can then be derived from table 2.2, where

[24] $c(m_t) = \left(1 - \hat{p}_{t+1}\right)\hat{e}_t + \hat{p}_{t+1}\left(\hat{e}_t + \hat{\sigma}_{t+1} + \hat{\tau}_{t+1}\right)$

and

[25] $c(m^*_t) = \left(1 - \hat{p}_{t+1}\right)\hat{\sigma}_{t+1} + \hat{p}_{t+1}\hat{q}_{t+1}$

where (^) denotes expectations. In order to close the model and introduce a stochastic element that allows for noncorner solutions, Oomes introduces the random utility terms $\varepsilon_{i,t}$ and $\varepsilon^*_{i,t}$ (or random disutility terms) that account for unobserved variables affecting the costs or benefits of holding domestic and foreign currency. If φ measures the impact of these terms on the expected total cost, the probability $p_{i,t}$ that a given agent i will hold foreign currency can be written as:

[26] $p_{i,t} = \Pr\{c(m_t^*) + \varphi\varepsilon^*_{i,t} < c(m_t) + \varphi\varepsilon_{i,t}\}$

$= \Pr\left\{\varepsilon^*_{i,t} - \varepsilon_{i,t} < \frac{1}{\varphi}\left[\hat{e}_t - \hat{\sigma}_{t+1} + \left(2\hat{\sigma}_{t+1} + \hat{\tau}_{t+1} - \hat{q}_{t+1}\right)\hat{p}_{t+1}\right]\right\}$

The final reduced form for estimating the model is derived employing the following additional assumptions: (1) confiscation risk is assumed to be constant over the whole period, $q_t = q$; (2) the "shoe-leather" costs are assumed to decrease with the dollarization ratio because as dollarization increases, more exchange offices emerge: $\sigma_t = \gamma_1 - \gamma_2 p_{t-1}$, where $\sigma_t > 1$; (3) agents expect the depreciation rate to remain the same with some probability α, but will equal the maximum past depreciation rate with probability $(1 - \alpha)$. Thus, expectation formation is assumed to be a linear combination of perfect foresight and the ratchet effect (the maximum depreciation from the recent past).

[27] $\hat{e}_t = \alpha e_t + (1 - \alpha)e_t^{\max}$

The structural form of the model is linearized by the means of the logarithmic transformation, and the final reduced form for the model can be written as:

[28] $\ln\left(\dfrac{1 - p_t}{p_t}\right) = \dfrac{\gamma_1}{\varphi} - \dfrac{\alpha}{\varphi}e_t - \dfrac{1 - \alpha}{\varphi}e_t^{\max}$

$$- \dfrac{2\gamma_1 + \gamma_2 + \tau - q}{\varphi}p_{t-1} + \dfrac{2\gamma_2}{\varphi}p_{t-1}^2 + \xi_t$$

and is estimated by OLS as:

[29] $\ln\left(\dfrac{1 - p_t}{p_t}\right) = \delta_0 + \delta_1(e_t - e_t^{\max}) + \delta_2 e_t^{\max} + \delta_3 p_{t-1} +$

$\delta_4 p_{t-1}^2 + \xi_t$

where, $\delta_0 = \dfrac{\gamma_1}{\varphi}; \delta_1 = -\dfrac{\alpha}{\varphi}; \delta_2 = -\dfrac{1}{\varphi}; \delta_3 = -\dfrac{2\gamma_1 + \gamma_2 + \tau - q}{\varphi}; \delta_4 =$

$\dfrac{2\gamma_2}{\varphi}$

▲ Empirical Evidence of Hysteresis and Irreversibility

The Latin American country that has the highest per capita holdings of U.S. dollars is Argentina, as evidenced by available CMIR data. Our new estimates of dollar holdings in Argentina permit us to test the currency substitution and "irreversibility hypothesis" directly, by estimating demand functions for the observed accumulation of dollar holdings in Argentina. Kamin and Ericsson (1993) indirectly examined currency substitution by estimating "the flip side of the demand for dollars: the demand for domestic currency assets."

Our first effort to model the Argentinean currency substitution phenomenon employs the familiar partial adjustment model applied to the dollarization index LUDI, logarithmically transformed so that the fitted dependent variable falls within the interval between 0 and 1.[14]

[32]   LUDI = −Ln[(1 − UDI/UDI)]

The explanatory variables of the dollarization process are those typically employed to specify the demand for money in situations where foreign currency and foreign currency deposits are available substitutes for domestic money. In particular, we employ as regressors the lagged value of the dependent variable, the expected depreciation of the exchange rate (dlex), a banking crisis dummy variable (crisis),[15] and a ratchet variable (Ratchet) to capture the hysteresis effects that have been observed in dollarized countries when network externalities produce incentives for the continued use of a foreign currency even after inflation or exchange depreciation effects have moderated. Specifically, the equation estimated for Argentina is:

Table 2.3
Regression Results

	LUDI
const	−0.5839
	(−4.1018)
LUDI(−1)	0.81197
	(19.0302)
dlex(+1)	0.13781
	(2.23524)
Ratchet	0.25687
	(4.0945)
Crisis	1.67477
	(4.56825)
R-squared	0.97744
Adjusted R-squared	0.97624
Durbin-Watson stat	2.51075

Note: t-statistics are in parentheses.

[33] $LUDI = c(1) + c(2)*LUDI(-1) + c(3)*dlex(+1)$
$$+ c(4)*ratchet + c(5)*crisis$$

The ratchet variable takes the form of the highest previously attained rate of depreciation of the exchange rate.[16] The results of the OLS estimate obtained for Argentina are reported in table 2.3. All of the coefficients have the expected signs, and all are significant at the 5 percent level. Table 2.4 presents the corresponding long-run estimate of the key coefficients of the model presented earlier.

Figure 2.3 displays the actual and simulated values of UDI ratio for Argentina for the period 1978–99 based on the estimated equation presented in table 2.3. Figure 2.3 reveals that dollarization in Argentina began in the early 1980s and then accelerated dramatically during the period 1989–90 as a result of a severe hyperinflation. Despite subsequent successful stabilization efforts, the unofficial dollarization index remained stubbornly around 70 percent. Argentina appears to represent an economy in which

Table 2.4
Estimated Long-Run Coefficients

Dependent Variable	LUDI
dlex(+1)	0.73
Ratchet	1.37
Crisis	8.91

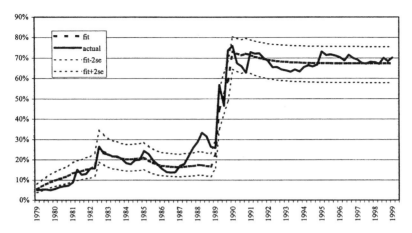

Figure 2.3. Actual and simulated UDI for Argentina.

unofficial dollarization reached a threshold, after which network externalities in the use of the foreign currency made the process of unofficial dollarization irreversible.

The Dynamics of Dollarization

Empirical estimation of the Oomes model presented in figure 2.3 permits a more detailed examination of the dynamics of de facto dollarization. Assuming a zero tax rate, equation (29) was estimated for the Argentina data, and the results are presented in table 2.5 with the Goodness of Fit and Residual Tests presented in table 2.6.

The dynamics of de facto dollarization can be illustrated with the use of the phase diagram derived from the estimated model. Figure 2.4 reveals that intersections of the 45° line with a generic phase diagram (showing the structural dependence of this period's dollarization outcome on the outcome of the last period) represent possible equilibrium points.

A stable equilibrium occurs when the phase diagram cuts the 45° line

Table 2.5
OLS Regression Estimates

Variable	Coefficient	Std. error	t-statistic
δ_0	3.218	0.110	29.20
δ_1	−0.460	0.077	−5.96
δ_2	−0.539	0.084	−6.43
δ_3	−8.891	0.606	−14.67
δ_4	5.003	0.869	5.76

Table 2.6
Goodness of Fit and Residual Tests

R-squared		0.98	Adjusted R-squared	0.98
Jarque-Bera normality test		244.244	Probability	0.000
Serial correlation LM (4) test		2.814	Probability	0.031
Serial correlation LM (8) test		2.714	Probability	0.012
White heteroskedasticity test		32.183	Probability	0.000

from above, and an unstable equilibrium occurs when the phase diagram intersects the 45° line from below. The diagram indicates that stable steady states exist at either very low or very high dollarization ratios.

In order to explain the dynamic adjustment of the dollarization process in Argentina, figure 2.5 displays the unofficial dollarization index and the exchange rate depreciation history. De facto dollarization of Argentina gained momentum during the early 1980s, reaching approximately 25 percent, but declined in the aftermath of the 1985 Austral Stabilization Plan. As depreciation rates rose once again, dollarization also increased, but this trend was again reversed in the immediate aftermath of the Primavera Plan, instituted in August 1988. This experience suggests that there are conditions under which the dollarization process may be reversed. However, as depreciation rates began to rise once again, the dollarization process accelerated

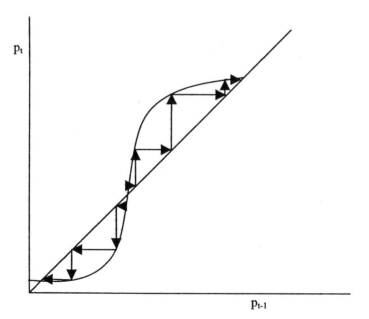

Figure 2.4. Phase diagram.

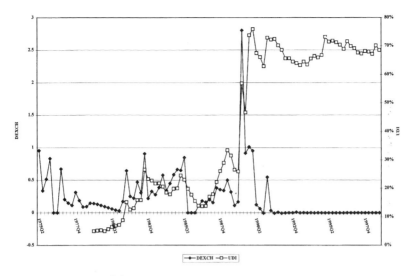

Figure 2.5. UDI and depreciation—Argentina.

in the second quarter of 1989, and then exploded as a consequence of the huge depreciation that occurred in the last half of 1989. By the first quarter of 1990, the unofficial dollarization index reached a high of 76 percent, with 90 percent of the value of the nation's currency supply held in the form of U.S. dollars. Despite the success of the subsequent stabilization programs and the sustained period of exchange rate stability, the dollarization process was never reversed, giving rise to the fundamental question about the Argentina experience, namely, how can one account for the persistence and apparent irreversibility of the dollarization process?

The explanation offered here is the effect of network externalities. Once de facto dollarization had reached a particular threshold, the transactions costs of using dollars had fallen below the costs of switching back to the local currency. The dynamics of this process can be understood by examining the phase diagrams estimated for the preceding model.

Figure 2.6 displays two positions of the phase diagram derived from the estimates of equation (29).

The lower curve's position is specified under the assumption of exchange rate stability and no previous inflationary experience. The equilibrium occurs at the low dollarization equilibrium, which is a stable equilibrium. The higher curve is positioned so as to reflect exchange rate stability in the aftermath of the second quarter 1989 deflation experience, where emax = 2.8. Under these conditions the phase diagram intersects the 45° line at the high equilibrium position, representing steady state equilibrium with the approximately 65 percent dollarization.

The dynamic adjustment to the high steady state equilibrium can be

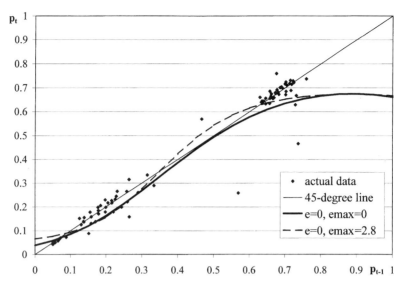

Figure 2.6. Phase diagram before and after a hyperinflation episode.

inferred from figure 2.7, which presents the estimated phase diagram for two historic time periods, December 1984 and September 1989. For a sufficiently high depreciation rate, the lower and middle equilibria disappear and only the high dollarization steady state remains. The estimated functions for those periods reveal that the transition from the low to the high steady state occurred only in late 1989.

It appears that after the 1984 crisis, rapid stabilization reduced the rates of depreciation within two or three quarters, thereby preventing the full adjustment to the higher dollarization level. A similar process occurred in the immediate aftermath of the Primavera Plan. The model suggests that dollarization levels reached the unstable midequilibrium from which they could still return toward the low stable equilibrium. However, with sufficiently high devaluation, the dollarization index jumped to the high stable equilibrium, from which it has not retreated, despite the subsequent long-term stabilization.

The structural parameters estimated from the model imply that $\alpha = \delta_1 / \delta_2 = .85$, suggesting that there is a .85 probability that any given agent correctly predicts the depreciation rate. The confiscation risk parameter $q = .08$ suggests that agents perceived that holding dollars either in the form of cash or foreign currency deposits entailed a risk of 8 percent that either their dollars might be counterfeit or their bank accounts might be confiscated. Although this estimated perceived risk premium appears very high, it has been justified by recent events in Argentina.

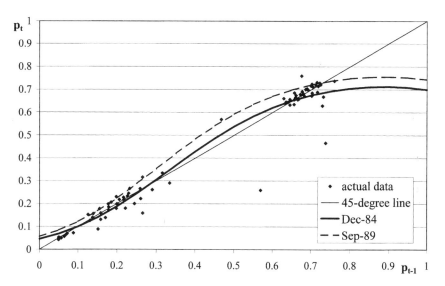

Figure 2.7. Phase diagrams for Argentina: December 1984; September 1989.

Irreversibility

A final issue that can be addressed by the estimated model is to inquire under what conditions, if any, it would be possible to reverse the de facto dollarization process? One way to reduce dollarization would be to appreciate the domestic currency. Appreciation would shift the phase diagram downward until eventually only one stable steady state would emerge, corresponding to the low dollarization equilibrium. However, the requisite downward shift in the phase diagram estimated for Argentina requires the exchange rate to appreciate by 35 percent. The impact of a 35 percent appreciation (given the present value of emax) producing the requisite downward shift is displayed in figure 2.8. The appreciation would have to be sustained for a long enough time to allow the actual level of dollarization to fall below the middle equilibrium, finally coming to rest at the low-equilibrium steady state.

◣ Summary and Conclusions

This chapter addresses the positive issue of determining the extent and implications of de facto dollarization in Latin America. In an effort to overcome the "unobservability" problem that has plagued the currency substitution literature, we present direct estimates of the amounts of U.S. dollar foreign currency in circulation in various Latin American countries. Traditional measures of dollarization employed in earlier literature largely relied

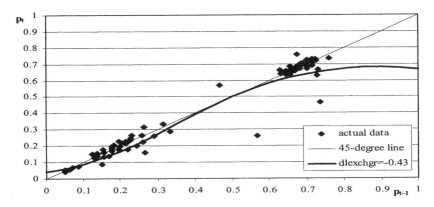

Figure 2.8. Necessary condition for dollarization reversibility.

on foreign currency deposits as an indicator of currency substitution because actual measures of foreign currency in circulation were unavailable. Employing aggregated data derived from Currency and Monetary Instrument Reports on inflows and outflows of dollars to and from the United States, we estimate the amounts of U.S. dollars in circulation in various Latin American countries. These new estimates of the location of U.S. currency held overseas permit a refinement of definitions and indicators of currency and asset substitution, as well as the development of more accurate indices of the extent of unofficial dollarization. We find that traditional measures of dollarization tend to be indicative of asset substitution but perform poorly as measures of currency substitution.

Argentina appears to be the Latin American country with the highest level of de facto dollarization. Moreover, we find that Argentina's residents have maintained high levels of dollar holdings despite almost a decade of successful stabilization efforts. Argentina therefore represents a classic case of hysteresis, suggesting that once a threshold level of dollarization is attained, it may be maintained, producing what is known as dollarization "irreversibility." In order to explain this phenomenon, we present models of network externalities, which suggest that transaction costs associated with dollar usage fall sufficiently beyond some threshold usage of dollars so that switching back to the domestic currency becomes prohibitively expensive.

Estimates of the network externality model reveal that the threshold level of dollarization appears to be in the neighborhood of 35 percent. The dynamics of the model reveals that stable steady states exist at both low and high dollarization levels. The intermediate equilibrium is unstable, suggesting that de facto dollarization can take place rapidly in the aftermath of a monetary crisis, and once attained may be very difficult to reverse. Interestingly, the model also estimates that the perceived risk of confiscation in Argentina remained high, despite a prolonged period of economic stability.

This perception has been borne out by the most recent financial and banking crisis in Argentina.

▲ Notes

The authors wish to thank Nienke Oomes for valuable comments and suggestions.

1. A similar discussion is under way in central and eastern Europe concerning the possible adoption of the euro—the euroization debate.

2. For an elaboration of the irreversibility problem see Guidotti and Rodriguez (1992) and Balino, Benett, and Borensztein (1999).

3. This conceptual framework was developed in Feige et al. (2002).

4. We ignore those rare institutional circumstances in which transfers between foreign currency deposits are employed for transaction purposes.

5. Balino et al. (1999) choose to define highly dollarized countries as those whose ratio of FCD/broad money exceeds 30 percent. The major shortcoming of this definition is that it takes no account of foreign cash in circulation. Further study is required to determine whether there exists a unique value of the dollarization index that represents a threshold effect at which point dollarization is likely to become irreversible because of network externalities. Mongardini and Mueller (1999) define the degree of currency substitution as measured by the ratio of FCD to total deposits.

6. Officially dollarized independent countries include the Marshall Islands, Micronesia, Palau, Panama, Ecuador, and El Salvador.

7. In some countries foreign banknotes may simply be hoarded and treated purely as a store of value. When this part of FCC can be estimated, it should be treated in the capacity of money as the store of value and included in the asset substitution index.

8. Again, a reader should keep in mind that the definition of ASI also depends on the particular institutions of a nation. Its quality is high when the amount of FCD and LTD used for transactions purposes is low in comparison to the amount of those deposits used as income earning assets.

9. This "official" estimate, now published by the Bureau of Economic Analysis and the Federal Reserve Board, is based on an adjusted version of the proxy measure proposed by Feige (1994). The official estimate is based on net shipments of $100 bills from the Federal Reserve offices in New York and Los Angles. A more refined proxy measure (Feige, 1997) also includes data from the Miami and San Francisco Federal Reserve offices. The refined proxy suggests that at the end of 2001, 40.9 percent of U.S. currency was held overseas.

10. Feige (1997) and Feige et al. (2002) present greater detail on the collection and processing of CMIR data.

11. The model does not however provide an unambiguous means of empirically discriminating between network externality effects and other potential causes of hysteresis.

12. Oomes assumes that transacting in dollars is illegal and that the amount of the transaction, which is normalized to unity, can be confiscated with probability q, which then equals the expected total cost associated with confiscation risk.

13. The explicit assumption made in the table is that the costs of transacting in the foreign currency (q) are smaller than the costs of the buyer and seller choosing to convert the currency twice ($2\sigma + \tau$), that is, that $q < 2\sigma + \tau$. This assumption is made so as

to remove the indeterminacy associated with the question of whether the buyer or the seller will bear the transaction costs.

14. Mongardini and Mueller (1999) employ a similar model and the same transformation.

15. Andy Berg of the IMF generously provided the bank crisis variable.

16. A number of ratchet variables were tested, including the past peak inflation rate, depreciation rate, and currency substitution index. All were highly significant, and the past peak depreciation rate was chosen to simplify the simulation.

▲ References

Baliño, T. J. T., A. Bennett, and E. Borensztein. (1999). *Monetary Policy in Dollarized Economies.* (Occasional Paper 171). Washington, D.C.: International Monetary Fund.

Berg, A., and E. Borensztein. (2000). *The Pro's and Cons of Full Dollarization.* (IMF Working Paper). Washington, D.C.: International Monetary Fund.

Brock, W. A., and S. N. Durlauf. (2001). Discrete Choice with Social Interactions. *Review of Economic Studies, 68*(2), 235–60.

Bogetic, Z. (2000). Official Dollarization: Current Experiences and Issues. *Cato Journal, 20*(2), 179–213.

Calvo, G. A., and C. A. Végh. (1992). *Currency Substitution in Developing Countries: An Introduction.* (IMF Working Paper WP/92/40). Washington, D.C.: International Monetary Fund.

Calvo, G. A. (2000, June 22). Testimony on dollarization presented before the Senate Subcommittee on Domestic and Monetary Policy. Committee on Banking and Financial Services. Washington, D.C.

Calvo, G., and C. Reinhart. (2001). *Reflections on Dollarization.* In A. Alesina and R. Barro (Eds.), *Currency Unions.* Stanford: Hoover Institute Press.

Canto, V. (1985). Monetary Policy, Dollarization and Parallel Market Exchange Rates: The Case of the Dominican Republic. *Journal of International Money and Finance, 4*(4), 507–21.

Clements, B., and G. Schwartz. (1992). *Currency Substitution: The Recent Experience of Bolivia.* (Working Paper 92/65). International Monetary Fund.

Dowd, K., and D. Greenaway. (1993). Currency Competition, Network Externalities and Switching Costs: Towards an Alternative View of Optimum Currency Areas. *Economic Journal, 103,* 1180–89.

Farrell, J., and G. Saloner. (1986). Installed Base and Compatibility: Product Preannouncements and Predation. *American Economic Review, 76,* 940–55.

Feige, E. L. (1990). Defining and Estimating Underground and Informal Economies: The New Institutional Economics Approach. *World Development, 18*(7), 989–1002.

Feige, E. L. (1994). The Underground Economy and the Currency Enigma. Supplement to *Public Finance/Finances Publiques, 49,* 119–39. Reprinted in Gianluca Fiorentini and Stephano Zamagni (Eds.). (1999). *The Economics of Corruption and Illegal Markets* (pp. 23–40). International Library of Critical Writings in Economics. Cheltenham, U.K.: Elgar.

Feige, E. L. (1996). Overseas Holdings of U.S. Currency and the Underground Economy. In S. Pozo (Ed.), *Exploring the Underground Economy* (pp. 5–60). Kalamazoo, Mich.: W. E Upjohn Institute for Employment Research.

Feige, E. L. (1997). Revised Estimates of the Size of the U.S. Underground Economy: The Implications of U.S. Currency Held Abroad. In Owen Lippert and Michael Walker (Eds.), *The Underground Economy: Global Evidence of Its Size and Impact* (pp. 151–208). Vancouver, British Columbia: Fraser Institute.

Feige, E. L., and M. Faulend, V. Šonje, and V. Šošić. (2002). Currency Substitution, Unoffical Dollarization and Estimates of Foreign Currency Held Abroad: The Case of Croatia. In Mario Blejer and Marko Skreb (Eds.), *Financial Policies in Emerging Markets and the Exchange Rate Regime.* Cambridge, Mass.: MIT Press.

Guidotti, P. E., and C. A. Rodriguez. (1992). Dollarization in Latin America: Gresham's Law in Reverse? *International Monetary Fund Staff Papers, 39*(3), 518–44.

Hausmann, R., M. Gavin, C. Pages-Serra, and E. Stein. (1999). *Financial Turmoil and the Choice of the Exchange Rate Regime.* (Working Paper No. 400). Inter-American Development Bank.

Ize, A., and E. L. Yeyati. (1998). *Dollarization of Financial Intermediation: Causes and Policy Implications.* (IMF Working Paper WP/98/28). Washington, D.C.: International Monetary Fund.

Kamin, S. B., and N. R. Ericsson. (1993). *Dollarization in Argentina* (International Finance Discussion Paper, No. 460). Board of Governors of the Federal Reserve System.

Marquez, J. (1987). Money Demand in Open Economies: A Currency Substitution Model for Venezuela. *Journal of International Money and Finance, 6*(2), 167–78.

Mongardini, J., and J. Mueller. (1999). *Ratchet Effects in Currency Substitution: An Application to the Kyrgyz Republic* (IMF Working Paper WP/99/102). Washington, D.C.: International Monetary Fund.

Oomes, N. (2001). Essays on Network Externalities and Aggregate Persistence. Unpublished doctoral dissertation. University of Wisconsin, Madison.

Ortiz, G. (1983). Currency Substitution in Mexico: The Dollarization Problem. *Journal of Money, Credit and Banking, 15*(2), 174–85.

Porter, R., and R. Judson. (1996). The Location of U.S. Currency: How Much Is Abroad? *Federal Reserve Bulletin, 82,* 883–903.

Sahay, R., and C. A. Végh. (1995). Dollarization in Transition Economies: Evidence and Policy Implications. (IMF Working Paper WP/95/96). Washington, D.C.: International Monetary Fund.

Seitz, F. (1995). The Circulation of Deutsche Mark Abroad. (Discussion Paper 1/95). Economic Research Group of the Deutsche Bundesbank, Frankfurt, Germany.

United States Treasury Department. (2000). *The Use and Counterfeiting of United States Currency Abroad.* (A Report to the Congress by the Secretary of the Treasury, in consultation with the Advanced Counterfeit Deterrence Steering Committee, pursuant to section 807 of PL 104–132).

3 Andrew Berg and Eduardo R. Borensztein

The Pros and Cons of Full Dollarization

There is an old joke that says that the exam questions in economics remain the same every year—only the answers change. Certainly, the debate about the best exchange rate regime has been with us forever, but new answers keep appearing. The newest answer to the question of what exchange rate regime countries should choose is "none." That is, countries should forgo using their own currency entirely and adopt as legal tender a stable foreign currency, most commonly the U.S. dollar. Then-president Carlos Menem of Argentina suggested last year that Argentina should adopt the U.S. dollar—that is, "dollarize"—as the ultimate solution to its long history of difficulties with monetary and exchange rate policy. More recently, Ecuador has announced its intention to adopt the dollar, in the context of a deep economic and political crisis. Prominent economists have begun to argue that essentially all developing countries should also dollarize (see Calvo and Reinhart, 1999). Not only developing countries, however, are considering dollarization. Partly prompted by the example of the adoption of the euro this year, some have suggested that Canada should adopt the U.S. dollar as well.

New answers to the exchange rate question appear because the world continually presents new problems to policymakers, while old ones sometimes recede. During the 1980s, much of the debate about exchange rate regimes for developing countries centered on the role of exchange rate pegs in inflation stabilization programs. Two distinguishing features of the 1990s have changed the terms of the discussion. First, the inflation problem has abated notably. Second, as the degree of capital mobility and scale of capital flows have increased sharply, so has the apparent frequency and severity of currency crises. And many of the victims of these fierce speculative attacks were maintaining some sort of pegged exchange rate regime. Because of those crises, the idea of dollarization has elicited considerable interest. The view has emerged that in a world of high capital mobility, exchange rate pegs are an invitation to speculative attacks and that only extreme choices—a firm peg such as a currency board or a free float—are viable. Advocates of dollarization have gone on to attack both of these alternatives. Free floats, they argue, are not viable for many countries because they result in excessive exchange rate volatility or a de facto "soft peg" if the authorities resist exchange rate movements. Meanwhile, it has become clear that even currency boards are not immune to costly speculative attacks. Argentina and Hong Kong suffered from contagion episodes in recent years that resulted in both sharp increases in interest rates and recessions.

Dollarization promises a way of avoiding currency and balance of payments crises. Without a domestic currency there is no possibility of a sharp depreciation, and sudden capital outflows motivated by fears of devaluation are ruled out. Dollarization may also bring other benefits. A closer integration with both the United States and global economies would be promoted by lower transaction costs and an assured stability of prices in dollar terms. By definitively rejecting the possibility of inflationary finance, dollarization might also strengthen institutions and create positive sentiment toward investment.

Yet countries may be reluctant to abandon their own currencies. For one thing, the currency is a national symbol, and proposals to join a monetary union (or directly adopt the U.S. dollar) may draw questions and criticism from some political quarters. From an economic point of view, the right to issue a country's currency provides its government with seigniorage revenues, because currency, and sometimes all of base money (the central bank's monetary liabilities), is non-interest-bearing debt. These seigniorage revenues show up as central bank profits and are transferred to the government. They would be lost to countries that dollarized their economies, unless the United States decided to share part of the extra seigniorage it would obtain. In addition, a dollarizing country would be relinquishing any possibility of having an autonomous monetary and exchange rate policy, including the use of central bank credit to provide liquidity support to its banking system.

Is dollarization, then, a better exchange rate regime for developing countries? Two considerations make this a difficult question to answer. First is the virtual absence of historical experiences to draw on. Panama is the only sizable country now using a foreign currency as legal tender—the others that have done so are mostly tiny economies. And even Panama is a fairly small economy with very close historical, political, and economic links to the United States. Second, the difficulty of reversing dollarization dictates that the analysis should consider a much longer horizon than is usual for evaluating monetary and exchange rate options.

To simplify the discussion, we compare the merits of dollarization to those of its nearest "competitor"—the currency board. Such a focus is more tractable and captures the main implications of dollarization and how its effects differ from those of adopting a firm peg rather than the more general question of choice of exchange rate regime. Furthermore, if we were to conclude that a currency board is at least equivalent to dollarization, in terms of the balance of costs and benefits, then a currency board should be the alternative for countries seeking a firmly pegged exchange regime, as it preserves seigniorage and it is simpler to establish.

Currency board and dollarization arrangements are quite similar, but a comparison is nonetheless revealing. To begin with, dollarization implies the loss of seigniorage revenue for the government. But dollarization's key distinguishing feature is that it would be permanent, or nearly so. It would presumably be much more difficult to reverse dollarization than to modify or abandon a currency board arrangement. With few recent exceptions, countries introducing their own currencies have done so in the context of newly gained national independence, as with the countries of the former Soviet Union. These currencies have, moreover, almost always replaced a weak and inconvertible currency. In fact, the largest benefits from dollarization derive from the credibility attached to it, precisely *because* it is nearly irreversible. We now take a closer look at the benefits and costs of full dollarization.

▶ Main Benefits and Costs of Dollarization

Why Dollarize?

The main attraction of full dollarization is the expectation that the elimination of the risk of sharp exchange rate adjustments will bring about significantly more stable international capital movements. A higher level of confidence by international investors would also lead to lower spreads on international borrowing, which would lower fiscal costs and promote investment and growth. Moreover, dollarization would promote a closer economic and financial integration with the United States and the global economy, which would contribute to accelerate the convergence to the income levels of the advanced economies. The actual impact of these factors is difficult to quantify, however, particularly for those effects that would depend on institutional changes resulting from greater financial integration.

The Risk Premium

An immediate benefit from the elimination of the risk of currency crisis would be a reduction of country risk premiums and a consequent lowering of interest rates. Lower interest rates and more stability in international capital movements would result in a significantly lower fiscal cost of servicing the public debt, as well as in a higher level of investment and economic growth.

It is difficult to estimate the magnitude of this potential gain. In Argentina, the persistence of a differential between peso interest rates and dollar interest rates is evidence of a residual risk of abandonment of the exchange rate peg. Yet interest rates on dollar-denominated Argentine government (and private) securities also exceed those on advanced countries' debt, reflecting "sovereign" or default risk on those securities. With dollarization, the interest premiums owing to devaluation risk would disappear, but sovereign risk would not. Moreover, whether governments or the private sector borrow in foreign or domestic currency is largely a matter of choice in an economy already as heavily dollarized as Argentina. This means that borrowers can already eliminate the direct effect of devaluation risk from their borrowing costs, and that the key question is the effect of dollarization on the cost of dollar-denominated borrowing.

In Argentina, both peso- and dollar-denominated interest rates have tended to come down since the convertibility plan (currency board) was implemented in 1991. Both peso- and dollar-denominated interest rates have shot up at times of market turbulence, however. In figure 3.1, which shows the yields on otherwise identical dollar-denominated and peso-denominated Argentine government bonds issued in the domestic markets, spikes are visible at the time of the "tequila" crisis (end of 1994 to early 1995), the Russian default (August 1998), and the Brazilian crisis (January 1999), with a smaller one at the time of the failed attack on the Hong Kong dollar of October 1997. Increases in interest rates have tended to be smaller and briefer in the more recent episodes than in the "tequila," however.

The key question is whether full dollarization, by eliminating currency risk, would substantially reduce the risk premium on dollar-denominated debt. Yields on bonds with different features can help disentangle sovereign and devaluation risk, as perceived by markets. Sovereign risk can be measured by the spread on dollar-denominated Argentinean government bonds over U.S. Treasuries. This spread has tended to come down with time but has still averaged 3.3 percentage points during 1997/1998. Devaluation risk

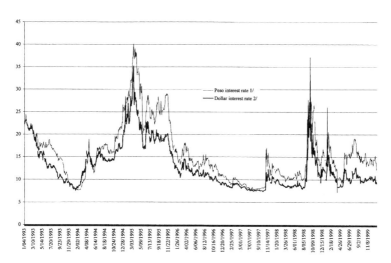

Figure 3.1. Argentina: Dollar and Peso Interest Rates. *Source*: Bloomberg and IMF staff estimates. 1/ Annual interest rate on Argentinean domestic peso-denominated bond "Pre 1". 2/ Annual interest rate on Argentinean domestic dollar-denominated bond "Pre 2".

76

Brady Bonds

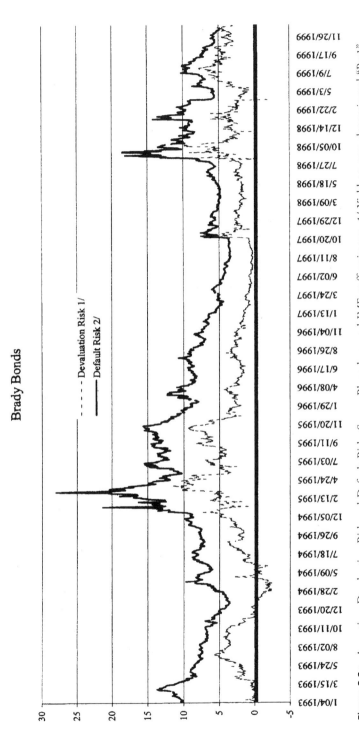

Figure 3.2a. Argentina: Devaluation Risk and Default Risk. *Source*: Bloomberg and IMF staff estimates. 1/ Yield on peso-denominated "Pre1" bond less yield on dollar-denominated "Pre2" bond. 2/ Spread (stripped of value of collateral) of Argentinean Brady bond over comparable U.S. Treasury bond. 3/ Spread of Argentinean dollar-denominated Eurobond '03 over comparable U.S. Treasury Bond.

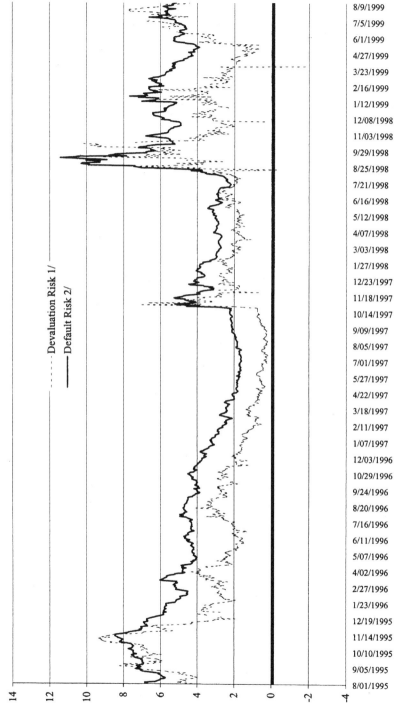

Eurobonds

------- Devaluation Risk 1/

——— Default Risk 2/

Figure 3.2b. Argentina: Devaluation Risk and Default Risk. Source: Bloomberg and IMF staff estimates. 1/ Yield on peso-denominated "Pre1" bond less yield on dollar-denominated "Pre2" bond. 2/ Spread of Argentinean dollar-denominated Eurobond '03 over comparable U.S. Treasury Bond.

can be measured by the spread between the peso- and dollar-denominated Eurobonds, which averaged 2.5 percent over the same period. (Figure 3.2 shows these yields since 1994.)

A surprising feature revealed in figure 3.2 is the much higher yields on Brady bonds than on Eurobonds. This poses the question of what the relevant cost of borrowing is for Argentina. The discrepancy seems to be somewhat of a puzzle; after all, both are bonds owed by the same borrower, the Argentine state.[1] This apparent anomaly is due to the perception that countries would assign implicit seniority to Eurobonds over Brady bonds in order to strengthen market access. The former are a new source of finance to which they may wish to resort again in the future, while the Bradies are the result of a debt restructuring agreement after debt service had been missed (Petas and Rahman, 1999).[2] In fact, the yields on Brady bonds are broadly similar to the yields on other Argentine dollar-denominated bonds, the Bonos de Consolidacion (BOCONs), that were also issued in the context of a debt restructuring agreement, in this case to settle arrears to domestic suppliers and pensioners (Kiguel, 1998). In any event, as the Eurobond market is the source of new financing for emerging markets, it would be appropriate to take the yield on this type of bond as representative of the marginal cost of borrowing currently faced by Argentina.

Currency Risk and Country Risk

Devaluation risk might increase sovereign risk for several reasons. First, governments attempting to avoid currency crises may take actions that increase the risk of default. For example, an attempt to defend the currency may cause the government to issue too many dollar-denominated bonds or dollar-indexed bonds, as in Mexico in 1994. A government may also impose capital controls in the interests of defending the currency, thereby causing other debtors to default on dollar-denominated debt. Russia chose in 1998 to impose currency controls essentially to prevent Russian private debtors in foreign currency from getting access to the foreign currency with which to service their obligations.

Default risks could rise with devaluation risk due to fiscal losses stemming from the devaluation. Government revenues are largely related to domestic prices, so a government borrowing in dollars is exposing itself to exchange rate risk. A large devaluation would compromise the financial strength of a government that is heavily indebted in dollars, especially if it faces large short-term debt payments.

The stress that a devaluation can place on the financial sector provides a further link from devaluation to default. As discussed hereafter, it is difficult for banks to insulate themselves from devaluation risk in highly (de facto) dollarized economies. Governments in turn may bear the burden of supporting the distressed banking systems, raising the risk of devaluation on other obligations.

Not all default risks emerge from the risk of currency crises, however. Sovereign defaults may result from an unsustainable fiscal position or political turmoil. Investors may flee from domestic assets, from government obligations, or from the country as a whole, such that the government would have problems servicing its debt. Certainly, dollarization cannot prevent the occurrence of this sort of crisis.

Moreover, a devaluation of the exchange rate may improve the domestic economy and the fiscal position and thus *reduce* default risk. Indeed, this has been the case with some of the currency devaluations in the European Monetary System. Even devaluations that have initially contractionary effects may improve longer-term prospects and thus reduce the risk of sovereign default. The importance or even existence of this effect would vary strongly from country to country.[3] The abandonment of a currency board under heavy market pressure would, surely, however, badly hurt the domestic economy.

There are thus arguments on both sides of the question of how much of the default risk to attribute to devaluation risk. Although sovereign risk and devaluation risk move closely together (fig. 3.2), this does not establish a causal link from devaluation risk to sovereign risk (or vice versa).[4] In fact, a plausible explanation is that the observed correlation between spreads on dollar-denominated interest rates and spread differentials owes to common factors that affect both peso and dollar spreads. For example, a global "flight to quality" would raise both the measured risk of default and risk of devaluation. In this case, dollarization would not help reduce dollar spreads very much.

In illustration of this possibility, figure 3.3 shows the relationship between the spreads over Treasuries of Argentine and Panamanian Brady bonds.[5] The figure suggests that yields on these two bonds are, in large measure, driven by common factors, despite the widening of the differential in recent months. The absence of currency risk in Panama does not isolate that country from swings in the prevailing market sentiment toward emerging markets. Moreover, since movements in dollarized Panama's spreads cannot reflect devaluation risk, the implication is that at least a part of Argentina's spread also cannot be explained by currency risk alone.[6]

Estimating the Remaining Default Risk in the Absence of Currency Risk

We are interested in getting some sense of the reduction in the risk premium or, more precisely, the spread over U.S. Treasuries applied to Argentine foreign debt, in the event of dollarization. We can exploit market information on default premiums and expected exchange rate changes as measured by various interest rate spreads, complemented with some assumptions, to infer what markets assess as the probability of default on Argentinean foreign debt in the absence of currency crisis risk.

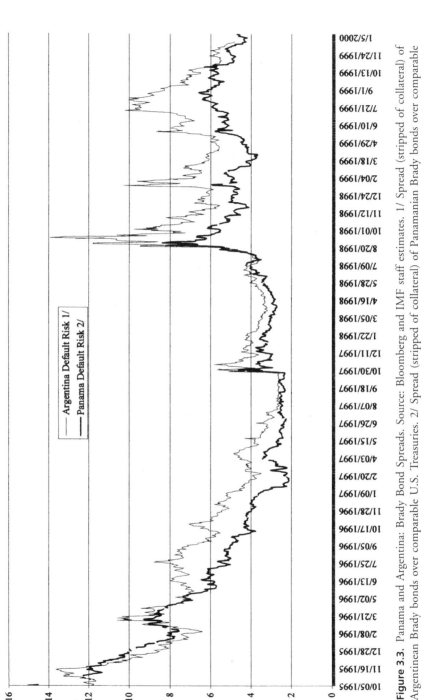

Figure 3.3. Panama and Argentina: Brady Bond Spreads. Source: Bloomberg and IMF staff estimates. 1/ Spread (stripped of collateral) of Argentinean Brady bonds over comparable U.S. Treasuries. 2/ Spread (stripped of collateral) of Panamanian Brady bonds over comparable U.S. Treasuries.

The perceived probability of default on Argentinean dollar-denominated bonds, that accounts for the interest premium on those securities, can be decomposed, by definition, into a component associated with currency crisis and a pure default component:

$$d = p(d \mid cc)^* p(cc) + p(d \mid ncc)^* [1 - p(cc)]$$

Currency crisis term   Pure default term

where:

d is the (total) probability of default

$p(d \mid cc)$ is the probability of a default given that there is a currency crisis,

$p(cc)$ is the probability of a currency crisis, and

$p(d \mid ncc)$ is the probability of default given that there is no currency crisis.

We are interested in estimating $p(d \mid ncc)$. This probability, which measures the remaining default risk if the risk of currency crisis disappears, is equal to:

$$p(d \mid ncc) = \frac{d - p(d \mid cc)\, p(cc)}{[1 - p(cc)]}$$

We can infer the value of the total default probability, d, and of the probability of currency crisis, $p(cc)$, from the pricing of various bonds, although this necessitates adopting some assumptions. Conditional on those assumptions, we can calculate the reduction in the interest rate spread that could be achieved by dollarization.

A measure of the total default probability, d, can be inferred from the interest rate spread between dollar-denominated Argentinean bonds and comparable U.S. Treasury bonds. Thus:

$$(1 - \alpha)d = \frac{i_A^{\$} - i_{US}^{\$}}{1 + i_A^{\$}}$$

where α is the assumed expected (fraction) recovery value of the bond in case of default. The idea is that defaults are almost never complete; even the Russian czarist bonds preserved some positive value.

A direct estimate of the probability of currency crisis $p(cc)$ can be obtained from the differential between dollar and peso interest rates on Argentinean bonds of similar characteristics. Assuming that the interest differential is equal to the expected exchange rate change, we have:

$$(1 + i_A^{peso})(1 - \Delta e\, p(cc)) \qquad = 1 + i_A^{\$}$$

Expected return to peso asset in dollars   Expected return to dollar asset

where Δe is the expected size of devaluation (measured as a discount) in the event of a currency crisis.

We can directly measure the interest rate differential and make an assumption about the expected size of devaluation in the event of a currency crisis, allowing us to estimate $p(cc)$ as:

$$p(cc) = \frac{\left(i_A^{peso} - i_A^{\$}\right)}{\Delta e(1 + i_A^{peso})}$$

We need to make one more assumption, about the probability of default in the event of a currency crisis, $p(d|cc)$. Having made this last assumption and calculated the probability of default in the absence of a currency crisis, $p(d|ncc)$, from the preceding formula, we can calculate what would be the spread on dollar-denominated bonds in the absence of currency crisis risk for Argentina.

The risk premium on Argentinean dollar-denominated Eurobonds averaged 3.3 percentage points during 1997 and 1998. How much of this might be attributed to devaluation risk? Table 3.1 shows how variations in assumption 1(Δe, the size of devaluation in the event of a currency crisis) and assumption 2 ($p(d|cc)$, the probability of default in the event of a currency crisis) affect the estimate of the interest rate spread that would remain after the elimination of currency crisis risk. If, for example, a currency crisis would result in a 20 percent probability that Argentina defaults on its Eurobonds, while a currency crisis would result in a 30 percent devaluation, then the elimination of currency crisis risk would reduce spreads by 138 basis points spread, and the resulting spread would be 182 basis points.[7]

Stability and Integration

Important as risk spreads are, dollarization may offer other gains that, although not immediately observable, may provide larger benefits over time. For developing countries, the main attraction of full dollarization is the prospect of eliminating currency crises. To begin with, currency crises are costly not just because their possible emergence widens risk premiums but

Table 3.1
Argentina: Reduction in Dollar Spread after Elimination of Currency Risk

		Assumption 1: Size of devaluation in the event of a currency crisis (percent)			
		20	30	40	50
Assumption 2: Probability of	10	103	85	77	72
default in the event of a	20	186	138	116	103
currency crisis (percent)	30	271	182	155	133

Note: Based on average Eurobond spread of 330 basis points during 1997–98. Assumes a recovery fraction after default of 25 percent.

because of the dire consequences to the domestic economy.[8] In Mexico, GDP fell by 7 percent in 1995, and the Asian countries affected by currency crises witnessed recessions in the range of 7 to 15 percent of GDP in 1998. Most of the severely affected countries in recent crises devalued and floated their exchange rate, but even countries with currency boards such as Hong Kong and Argentina suffered fierce speculative attacks that, although unsuccessful, still had serious consequences for their economies.

It should be stressed again that dollarization would not eliminate the risk of external crises, as investors may flee because of problems of sustainability of the fiscal position or the soundness of the financial system, and such a "debt crisis" could be just as damaging.[9] Nevertheless, dollarization holds the promise of a steadier market sentiment, as the elimination of exchange rate risk would tend to limit the incidence and magnitude of crisis and contagion episodes. Moreover, large swings in international capital flows cause sharp business cycle fluctuations in emerging economies even when they do not involve balance of payments crises.

Another powerful but somewhat hypothetical argument for full, legal dollarization is that the change in monetary regime may establish a firm basis for a sound financial sector, which would provide the basis for strong and steady economic growth. The argument here is that dollarization would signal more than the adoption of a foreign currency; it may be perceived as an irreversible institutional change toward low inflation, fiscal responsibility, and transparency. This perception would be reinforced, in particular, if legal dollarization is instituted not as a unilateral action but through some sort of monetary agreement with the United States.

Furthermore, dollarization may contribute to economic integration with the United States to an extent not possible otherwise. A number of studies have found evidence that Canadian provinces tend to be more integrated (in terms of trade volume and price level differences) among themselves than with U.S. states that are closer geographically. Canadian provinces trade more than 20 times more among themselves than with U.S. states after correcting for other variables that explain trade across provinces or states (McCallum, 1995). The prices of similar goods exhibit 50 percent more variability for cities across the U.S.-Canadian border than for cities within a country (Engel and Rogers, 1996).

The use of a common currency may be an important factor explaining this pattern of national market integration, given the fairly low transaction costs and restrictions to trade across the U.S.-Canada border. The difference in prices across the border, for example, may be due to "sticky" prices (or wages) in the domestic currency, so that fluctuations in the nominal exchange rate result in changes in the relative prices of (nontraded) goods in cities across the border. A similar hypothesis was advanced by Mussa (1986), who noted the higher variance of the real exchange rate between different Canadian and American cities (using the local price levels in the calculation) when there are floating exchange rates between the United States and Canada. In short, the adoption of a common currency could thus bring about a closer economic integration in goods markets.

Dollarization could also bring about a closer integration in financial markets. One of the most profound effects attributed to dollarization in Panama is the close integration of its banking system with that of the United States and indeed with the rest of the world, particularly since a major liberalization in 1969–70. Currency risk can be an important source of vulnerability in financial systems, particularly when there are large volumes of dollar-denominated assets and liabilities. The elimination of that source of vulnerability may contribute to build a stronger system that can more easily be an active part of international financial markets. Dollarization also would make the imposition of capital controls more difficult as it would be possible to convert all assets to dollar cash. Thus, dollarization makes integration easier and insulation of the domestic financial system more difficult.

Seigniorage

A country adopting a foreign currency as the legal tender would forgo its seigniorage rights. Seigniorage is the profits accruing to the monetary authorities from its right to issue legal tender currency. Currency can be thought of as non-interest-bearing debt; the ability to issue this non-interest-bearing debt is a source of revenue for the monetary authorities. In addition, legal reserve requirements on banks may also be non-interest-bearing (or be remunerated well below market rates levels) and thus contribute to seigniorage. Thus the annual flow of seigniorage is frequently measured as the increase in base money (the sum of currency plus bank reserves). The monetary authorities can use seigniorage to purchase assets (foreign currency reserves, government securities, and loans to the banking sector, typically) or to "consume" the seigniorage by financing a fiscal deficit. The measurement of seigniorage is explained in more detail in the box.

There are two components to the seigniorage loss implied by dollarization. First, there is an immediate "stock" cost. To adopt the dollar and withdraw the domestic currency from circulation exchanging it for U.S. dollar currency, the monetary authorities would have to "purchase" the stock of domestic currency held by the public (and banks), effectively returning to them the accumulated seigniorage that had accrued over time. Second, the monetary authorities would give up future seigniorage earnings stemming from the flow of new currency printed every year to satisfy the increase in money demand. Note that, even with dollarization, the central bank (or its successor institution) will still preserve the ability to impose reserve requirements on banks.[10] Therefore, the unavoidable loss of seigniorage comprises only currency.

Measurement of Seigniorage

The annual flow of seigniorage is simply the increase in the volume of domestic currency, assuming that there are no unremunerated reserve requirements on banks. As counterpart of the issue of currency, the central bank acquires assets that do pay interest, such as foreign currency reserves, government securities, and loans to private banks. In a currency board system, for example, the central banks must acquire foreign reserves in an amount equal to the domestic currency issue. As a result of issuing non-interest-bearing debt (currency) and holding interest-earning assets (foreign reserves, etc.) the central bank earns a (gross) profit, which is often also called seigniorage by central banks.

The relationship between seigniorage (the increase in volume of domestic currency) and the resulting central bank profits may create some confusion. It is useful to show, then, that these two quantities are equivalent in present discounted value. For the currency board case, this can be done in the following way. First, the present value of the annual increases in currency is equal to:

$$S_1 = M_t - M_{t-1} + \frac{M_{t+1} - M_t}{(1 + i)} + \frac{M_{t+2} - M_{t+1}}{(1 + i)^2} + \dots$$

Second, (gross) profits of the central bank are the interest earned on reserves (equivalently, on currency), which in present value are equal to:

$$S_2 = \frac{iM_t}{1 + i} + \frac{iM_{t+1}}{(1 + i)^2} + \frac{iM_{t+2}}{(1 + i)^3} + \dots$$

Rearranging the right-hand side of the first equation gives:

$$S_1 = - M_{t-1} + \frac{iM_t}{1 + i} + \frac{iM_{t+1}}{(1 + i)^2}$$
$$+ \frac{iM_{t+2}}{(1 + i)^3} + \dots = S_2 - M_{t-1}$$

which shows that the two measures are equivalent in present value sense, except for the initial stock of money, M_{t-1}. (Or that they are fully equivalent if the computation starts from the beginning of the economy, when money was first issued.)

In the case of Argentina, the first, or stock, cost of dollarization would be the redemption of about $15 billion in domestic currency held outside the central bank. In addition, one should consider the flow of additional seigniorage that comes from the increase in currency over time. This annual increase in currency averaged $1.0 billion, or about 0.35 percent of GDP, in 1993–98, although it was seriously affected by the tequila crisis.[11] Looking forward, even in the absence of crisis, the annual increase in currency is likely to decline as technological progress permits an increasing use of alternative means of payment.

For G7 countries, average annual increase in currency was equivalent to 0.3 percent of GDP over the last 10 years. Making the assumption that the annual increase in currency for Argentina will also amount to 0.3 percent of GDP over the next few years, the loss of seigniorage on account of the increase in currency demand would amount to an additional $1.0 billion approximately. Thus, the seigniorage cost would be an initial $15 billion plus the annual loss of $1 billion on account of the increase in currency demand. Equivalently, one can estimate the potential loss of seigniorage from dollarization as the interest currently earned on reserves that will be forgone as those reserves will circulate as currency. (This measure is akin to the central bank profits measure described in the box.) The annual interest earnings accruing on the stock of international reserves that is the counterpart of the stock of domestic currency is estimated at some 700 million dollars per year, or 0.2 percent of GDP.[12] These interest earnings would grow over time on account of the increase in currency demand; under the preceding assumptions, the flow of interest profits would double the original amount in about 10 years.

For countries that do not already have enough foreign reserves to buy up their domestic currency and thereby dollarize, the acquisition of the initial stock may bring with it some indirect costs.[13] If the country is credit constrained and cannot borrow the reserves, it would be forced to run current account surpluses to accumulate them. This might represent a substantial cost in terms of forgone investment if, as is likely for many developing countries, the optimal policy would otherwise involve some current account deficits. Even if the country can borrow the required backing, the resulting increase in external government debt might increase the risk premium faced by the country and hence domestic interest rates, and more generally may increase the risk of debt crisis down the road.

The United States would get more seigniorage from dollarization in other countries. There is, therefore, a case for the U.S. authorities to share part or all of these additional seigniorage revenues with other economies that adopt the U.S. dollar. There is a precedent for this in the arrangements between South Africa and three other states that use the rand (Lesotho, Namibia, and Swaziland). The United States does not have a sharing arrangement with Panama or any other legally dollarized economy, though the U.S. authorities have so far not rejected this possibility in connection with new countries in the Western Hemisphere willing to adopt the U.S. dollar.

Monetary Policy Autonomy and the "Exit Option"

Full dollarization implies the complete relinquishing of monetary and exchange rate policy. It may seem that there is no difference in this regard between currency board arrangements and full dollarization, since a country with a currency board arrangement cannot devalue. A currency board does, however, imply some scope for exit of the pegged exchange rate, if only under extreme circumstances. Indeed, the elimination of the risk of such an adjustment is the main purpose of full dollarization. While it is, in principle, possible to reintroduce a domestic currency, this would probably be a lengthy and complex process, particularly as the new currency might be presumed weaker than the dollar it would be attempting to replace. With few recent exceptions, countries introducing their own currencies have done so during exceptional political circumstances, notably in the context of newly gained national independence. They have, moreover, almost always replaced a weak and inconvertible currency.[14] If dollarization is instituted through an accord with the United States, it would be even more difficult to terminate the legal tender status of the U.S. dollar. Thus, full dollarization is much like a currency board with no exit option.

Large shocks may require sizable adjustments of the real exchange rate. Without exchange rate flexibility, the adjustment to such shocks may require lowering nominal wages and certain prices, which may not be feasible without a substantial recession, particularly for economies with less flexible labor markets.[15] It is worth remembering, also, that a prolonged deflation (fall in the price level) that a required fall in the real exchange rate would entail may have other problems. Such a deflation, if unexpected, would result in high real interest rates and large transfers from debtors to creditors. At the same time, the deflation would limit the extent to which real interest rates could fall to mitigate the output decline. This set of circumstances could be as stressful for the financial system as a sharp devaluation.[16]

Experiences such as departures from the gold standard and the devaluation of the Colonies Francaise d'Afrique (CFA) franc, suggests that an exit option may in fact have some real value in the presence of extreme shocks. The Great Depression is perhaps the most important example in this century of an extreme negative shock that justified an exit from the fixed exchange regime of the time, the gold standard. Indeed, Argentina started to follow an active monetary policy that sterilized the monetary impact of capital outflows after 1931 (after abandoning convertibility a couple of years earlier), and this policy has been considered instrumental for the relatively minor impact of the depression on Argentina (della Paolera and Taylor, 1999). There is also a consensus that advanced countries that had an early exit from the gold standard fared better during the Great Depression (Eichengreen and Sachs, 1985; Eichengreen and Temin, 1997).[17]

The countries of the CFA franc zone of West and Central Africa represent recent examples of firmly pegged countries choosing to devalue in the face of severe external shocks and poor growth performance. The regime resembles in some respects a currency board, with a fully convertible currency and a fixed exchange rate with the French franc maintained from 1948 until 1994. Convertibility was guaranteed by provisions for overdrafts at the French treasury and a requirement that a percentage of local monetary liabilities be backed by foreign reserves deposited at the French treasury.[18] During the second half of the 1980s and in the early 1990s, a prolonged worsening of the terms of trade and a steep rise in labor costs, combined with a nominal appreciation of the French franc against the U.S. dollar, led to a considerable real effective exchange rate appreciation of the CFA franc and contributed to a stagnation of real output. In 1994, the 14 countries of the zone ceased to rely exclusively on measures of internal adjustment and devalued their common currency by 50 percent. This exchange rate realignment led to a significant turnaround in economic activity in the zone, with output, exports, and investment increasing rapidly during 1994–97 and little inflation pass-through.[19]

These examples suggest that forgoing the option to exit from a fixed exchange rate arrangement in the face of large shocks could imply a substantial cost, particularly for countries that are in a better position to benefit from a devaluation. For example, some countries are more likely to face large shocks that require a real exchange rate adjustment. In addition, countries that have highly inflexible domestic labor and goods markets will find it especially hard to engineer a real devaluation without a nominal devaluation. Finally, highly credible policymakers would be in a more favorable position to take advantage of the option to devalue, as the negative effects of the devaluation on inflationary expectations would be lower.

Under different conditions, it would be difficult for countries to use the devaluation option successfully. To the extent that monetary policy has been poorly managed and inflationary expectations are highly sensitive to the exchange rate, a devaluation is likely to have a high degree of pass-through to domestic prices, making it hard to achieve changes in the real exchange rate by this means. Similarly, countries that are highly dollarized, so that the dollar is often the de facto unit of account, would tend to find rapid pass-through of devaluation into domestic prices, limiting the effectiveness of devaluations. In fact, these were central reasons why Argentina adopted a currency board.[20]

A high degree of dollarization of financial assets and liabilities provides another reason why some economies may not benefit from devaluations. If a country receives substantial inflows in the form of dollar-denominated lending to banks or corporations, a devaluation sharply worsens the balance sheet of these domestic banks and firms. Even if banks on-lend to domestic firms in dollars, and thus have matched risks in terms of currency on their books, they will still carry a substantial currency risk. If there was a sharp depreciation of the domestic currency, some of the banks' clients would experience a sharp fall in the value of their revenues in dollar terms, and would not be able to service dollar debts. That is, for highly (de facto) dollarized economies, it is ultimately difficult for banks to insulate themselves from devaluation risk. Thus, a devaluation may result in major disruptions in the financial sector. As observed in a variety of recent currency crises, from Mexico in 1994 to the East Asian crises of 1997, devaluations in a context of weak banking systems and large foreign exchange exposure in the private sector can damage the financial health of banks and firms, sharply disrupting real activity.[21] This implies that devaluation as a policy option may be prohibitively costly for highly dollarized economies, and that moving to full dollarization would not entail the loss of an important policy tool.[22]

Finally, it is noteworthy that, while now the United States enjoys a strong reputation for monetary stability and the U.S. dollar is globally accepted and desired, this situation could eventually change. Two or three decades ago, the U.S. dollar was perceived as weaker than the deutsche mark, for example, although this did not affect the global demand for dollars significantly. Therefore, one exit option from a currency board system is to change the currency to which the domestic currency is pegged. While the desirability of the U.S. dollar is likely to continue in the foreseeable future, the nearly permanent nature of a decision like dollarization through a bilateral or multinational agreement makes it worthy of consideration.

Lender of Last Resort Function and Financial System Stability

This chapter has already argued that one potential benefit of full dollarization is the elimination of currency mismatch throughout the entire economy, so that sharp devaluations cannot cause or aggravate a banking crisis, as was the case in many recent currency crises.[23] However, full dollarization could impair the lender of last resort (LLR) function and hence the central bank response to financial system emergencies.

It is important here to distinguish the role of the central bank operating a discount window to provide short-term liquidity from its role as the ultimate guarantor of the stability of the financial system and the payments system in the event of a systemic bank run. Dollarization should not greatly impede the ability of the authorities to provide short-term liquidity to the system or assistance to (small) individual banks in distress. The central bank (or its replacement) needs to "save" the necessary funds in advance or perhaps secure lines of credit with international banks.

In contrast, the authorities would lose some ability to respond to a sudden run on bank deposits throughout the entire system. In the case of a generalized loss of confidence, the authorities would be unable to guarantee the whole payments system or to fully back bank deposits. Ultimately, the ability to print money as needed is what allows a central bank to guarantee beyond any doubt that all claims (in domestic currency) will be fully met under any circumstances. Once the ability to print money ceases to exist, limits to the LLR function appear.

The ability to respond to a bank run in a dollarized economy would also depend on the nature of the disturbance. If the run involved a flight to quality within the domestic banking system, it could be accommodated by action of the monetary authorities to withdraw liquidity from strong banks and provide it to the weaker institutions. However, if the emergency involved a run from the whole domestic banking system and into dollar assets held abroad, it would require that the authorities held large liquid dollar assets relative to the total banking system liabilities. In the latter case, a fully dollarized economy would have less flexibility to respond if it operates with less international reserves (as would be the case, other things equal, if foreign exchange reserves have been "spent" to redeem the stock of domestic currency).

Currency boards can create base money only to the extent that they accumulate reserves, so they are almost as tightly constrained as would be the monetary authorities in a dollarized economy. It is significant, however, that in important currency board cases the authorities have allowed themselves some flexibility to create money that is not fully backed on the margin, in part so as to be able to deal with banking crises. This creates the ability to relax liquidity conditions in situations where pressures may be high and the normal adjustment channels of a currency board (through the external sector) may operate relatively slowly. Even though the margin for this type of operations by a central bank would be necessarily limited, they can be helpful in a situation of stress in financial markets. In the case of the run on the Argentinean peso during the 1995 tequila crisis, for example, the Argentinean monetary authorities were able to partially accommodate the run out of peso deposits into dollars held abroad as well as dollar cash.[24] By temporarily reducing their reserve coverage of the money base, they could increase the issuance of dollar cash and provide the dollar credits the banks needed to stay afloat. In the wake of the 1997 attack on the Hong Kong dollar, the Hong Kong Monetary Authority (HKMA) introduced in September 1998 a discount window to provide short-term liquidity to banks in a more flexible way and at lower cost than under previous arrangements. The new system is expected to reduce the volatility in short-term domestic interest rates. The maximum volume of rediscounts is bounded, however, and the HKMA fully backs rediscounts with foreign exchange.

The scope for accommodation to financial crises in a currency board is inevitably restricted. Indeed, even without the restrictions imposed by a currency board system, the ability of a central bank to find a way out of a financial crisis by resorting to printing money alone is limited. The injection of liquidity into the banking system to keep it from defaulting on depositors may only lead to greater pressure on foreign reserves or the exchange rate.

Foreign exchange reserves will generally not be large enough to finance a large move out of deposits.

Dollarization may, moreover, make a bank run less likely. With all monetary assets already dollarized and without significant currency mismatches in the banks' positions, depositors may be more confident in the domestic banking system. A dominant role of large and solid foreign banks in the banking system, which presumably would be encouraged by dollarization, would also reduce the danger of a weakened LLR, both because those banks could indirectly bring support from foreign central banks, and because depositors' confidence on the financial backing of those institutions would be significantly higher. These effects may be stronger than the more limited ability to perform LLR functions under certain circumstances.

Certain measures could be taken to strengthen the banking system and make it more resilient to runs.[25] For example, setting higher liquidity requirements and securing contingent credit may help improve the ability to respond to a drawdown of deposits. The banking system in Argentina has very high liquidity levels nowadays; it could withstand the loss of 27 percent of deposits out of its readily available financial resources, and more if liquidity requirements were lowered.[26]

There are costs to this type of measure, however. Imposing high liquidity requirements raises the cost of financial intermediation and ulti-

Table 3.2
Argentina—Liquid Resources in the Financial System

	December 1994		June 1999	
	In billions of U.S. dollars	As percent of deposits	In billions of U.S. dollars	As percent of deposits
Total resources	13.4	29.0	33.9	42.5
Liquidity requirements	7.7	16.7	16.5	20.7
Cash in banks in pesos and dollars (A)	3.0	6.5	2.9	3.7
Central bank rediscounts (B)[a]	2.7	5.9	7.8	9.7
REPO agreement with international banks (C)	0.0	0.0	6.7[b]	8.4
Maximum loss of deposits covered[c]	6.8	14.8	21.8	27.2
Memorandum Items:				
Total deposits	46.2		79.9	
In pesos	22.8		34.3	
In dollars	23.5		45.6	
Deposits in foreign banks	7.54	16.3	39.6	49.6

Source: IMF staff estimates and Estudio Broda.

[a]Assuming the full use of 33 percent of the monetary base, which can be backed with government dollar-denominated bonds.

[b]Including World Bank and IDB loans of $1.0 billion for "margin calls."

[c]Calculated as (A + B + C)/(1-liquidity requirements rate)

mately reduces the amount of credit available for use. Moreover, credit lines from international banks could probably play only a small role in the event of an unfolding crisis. The experience so far with this type of financing has been limited but suggests that commitments will have short maturities and banks will have alternative means to reduce their exposure during the crisis periods when the lines would be activated.[27]

It seems inherent to the nature of banking crises that only public support would be consistently available where support is needed. This suggests that some form of official assistance with the LLR function could help mitigate this type of risk. This could be provided by international organizations or even the United States. One suggestion has been to establish a mechanism to apply the return of seigniorage by the United States to the creation of a fund that provides LLR functions.

▶ *Dollarization and Mercosur*

The development of regional trade arrangements like Mercosur adds another dimension to the dollarization question and to the choice of exchange rate regime more generally. In particular, a question that has been posed is whether dollarization by Argentina would be compatible with deepening economic integration through Mercosur when the largest Mercosur partner, Brazil, maintains a floating exchange rate. The disparity of exchange rate systems leads to volatility in the bilateral real exchange rates of member countries that may be problematic both on political and economic grounds.

The real bilateral exchange rate of Argentina and Brazil, by far the largest partners of Mercosur, has displayed a varying degree of volatility in recent years (fig. 3.4).[28] The widest misalignments were related to episodes of high inflation and stabilization in both countries, and to the more recent currency crisis that forced the flotation of the *real*. During 1994–98, the bilateral real exchange rate was quite stable. During that period, which comprises most of the Mercosur years, the currencies of both countries were, to a larger or lesser extent, pegged to the U.S. dollar. While it is difficult to anticipate the volatility of this bilateral rate after the floating of the *real,* one would expect the volatility to be higher than in the period when both countries were pegging to the U.S. dollar but much lower than during the periods of highest volatility that occurred in the context of hyperinflations or currency crises (fig. 3.5). Some degree of flexibility in real bilateral exchange rates is desirable to achieve changes in relative prices and macroeconomic balance. Exchange rates respond to macroeconomic conditions, and if business cycles are not synchronized in two countries, the real exchange rate between their currencies should be expected to show a fair degree of variability. It is possible to shed some empirical light on this question for a given set of countries by generating estimates of supply and demand shocks in each country and asking to what extent these shocks are

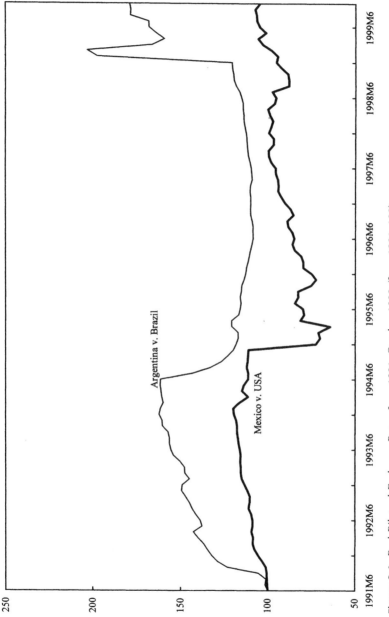

Figure 3.4. Real Bilateral Exchange Rates, June 1991–October 1999 (June 1991–100).

Source: International Monetary Fund, International Financial Statistics.

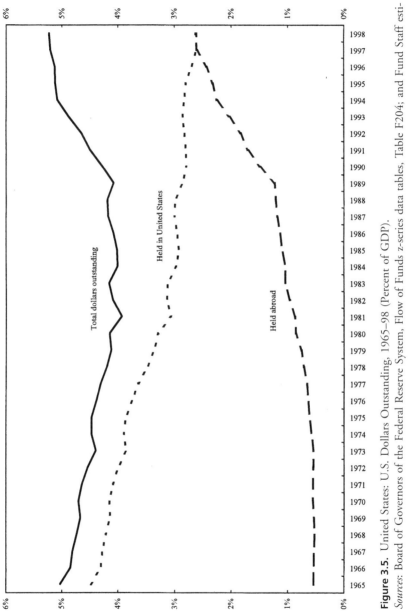

Figure 3.5. United States: U.S. Dollars Outstanding, 1965–98 (Percent of GDP).
Sources: Board of Governors of the Federal Reserve System, Flow of Funds z-series data tables, Table F204; and Fund Staff estimates.

correlated across countries. If the shocks are highly correlated, little adjustment of the bilateral real exchange rate is called for on their account. We have shown that much of the Argentina-Brazil bilateral real exchange rate volatility in recent years seems to be associated with anti-inflationary programs, a type of demand shock. It can be expected that a unified exchange rate policy would eliminate most of these types of shocks and hence this justification for bilateral real exchange rate fluctuations. The pattern of supply shocks, however, is more likely to be the same under different exchange rate regimes and so is of more interest. The evidence suggests that neither demand nor supply shocks are positively correlated across Mercosur countries. This implies that changes in intra-Mercosur exchange rates may be appropriate responses to shocks.[29] Alternatively, the implication is that fixing these exchange rates could increase real output volatility.[30]

Highly volatile bilateral real exchange rates may nonetheless be problematic for economies that are closely integrated in the context of a regional trade agreement, both for economic and political reasons. The impact of bilateral real exchange volatility depends on how extensive the trade links between the economies are. While Mercosur economies were once fairly closed, this has been changing rapidly in the last decade. Yet the tendency toward "regionalization" of international trade in this region is not as strong as commonly believed, especially if one takes 1995 as the starting date for Mercosur. While exports by Mercosur countries to the region have expanded considerably since the launching of the agreement, there has not been a significant increase in market penetration in the import markets of member countries.[31] In other words, exports within the agreement region have grown largely in line with the growth of imports by member countries, but the share of Mercosur countries in the imports of Mercosur countries has increased only moderately (table 3.3). The increase in import penetration is much more significant, however, if an earlier date is considered as the starting point, partly reflecting the fact that some tariff reductions were agreed prior to the customs union. Even from that longer perspective, however, the process can be seen as slowing down significantly in recent years.

The impact of bilateral exchange rate fluctuations also depends on the structure of the trade between the countries. If trade largely comprises commodities or other homogeneous products with a well-integrated world market, fluctuations in the bilateral exchange rates would not have much of an impact. But if bilateral trade takes place in sectors producing similar products and competing for market share in the domestic markets of both countries (intraindustry trade), large changes in the real exchange rate would have a quick impact on the profitability and performance of the affected producers. This volatility would affect investment and growth in the affected sectors and might also give rise to protectionist pressures. Even if the fluctuations in the bilateral real exchange rate represent an adjustment to changing macroeconomic conditions in the respective countries, the close integration in the context of a trade agreement may still give rise to

Table 3.3
Share of Trade within Mercosur, 1980–1998 (Selected Years) (in Percent of the Country's Total Trade)

	1980			1985			1990			1995			1998		
	Exports	Imports	Total	Exports	Imports	Total	Exports	Imports	Total	Exports	Imports	Total	Exports	Imports	Total
Argentina	18.6	17.2	17.8	10.1	30.6	16.5	19.1	30	21.8	40	25.6	33	43.7	28	35.1
Bolivia	31.8	21.6	27.3	57.4	40.9	49.1	38.2	40.8	39.3	16.2	28.7	23.2	16.2	50.2	39.7
Brazil	12.1	6.6	8.9	5.5	6.6	5.9	6.3	13.2	9.4	16.9	16.1	16.5	20.7	17.8	19.1
Chile	16.9	11.9	14.3	8.4	12.7	10.3	9.1	15.7	12.3	11.9	17.5	14.6	11.6	15.6	13.8
Paraguay	44	51	48.6	29.3	54.6	44.6	38.9	32.3	35.2	61.2	43.1	47.1	58.9	52	53.6
Uruguay	35.2	30.3	32.2	25.3	32.5	28.6	35.4	42.5	38.5	48.9	47.9	48.3	55.3	41	46.5

From International Monetary Fund, Direction of Trade Statistics, Washington, D.C.

political tensions. Indeed, trade frictions between Argentina and Brazil have increased considerably following the depreciation of the real in early 1999.

As regards the compatibility of Mercosur arrangements with dollarization, two issues must be underscored. First, dollarization would not significantly alter the current situation, with Argentina maintaining a firm peg to the U.S. dollar and Brazil having a floating exchange rate. Perhaps the main difference would be in terms of the near irreversibility of dollarization compared to the currency board arrangement. Second, the degree of integration between the economies of Argentina and Brazil may increase considerably in the future. While the agreement is currently a customs union (with a number of special exemptions), there are plans to extend it toward forming a single market economy, much in the European Union style. If the region does reach that level of economic integration, the question of the necessity of a common currency would need to be considered.[32]

◤ *Conclusions*

What is the balance of costs and benefits of full dollarization? Our analysis has been perhaps frustratingly two-handed. In our view, this is inevitable, given the complexity of the issue and the current state of knowledge about it. We can at least estimate the potential benefits of lower interest rates and the cost of forgone seigniorage revenues. But many of the most important considerations, such as the value of keeping an exit option, are the least quantifiable.

Which countries are likely to benefit from dollarization? The first group of candidates is formed by countries that are highly integrated with the United States in trade and financial relations (and are candidates to form what the economics literature calls an OCA). Yet most countries in Latin America are quite different from the United States in their economic structure and would probably not benefit greatly from dollarization unless it took place in the context of a deep market integration (in EU style). The current discussion (and this chapter) centers on a different group of candidates: emerging market economies exposed to volatile capital flows but not necessarily close, in an economic sense, to the United States. For this group, the more the U.S. dollar is already used in their domestic goods and financial markets, the smaller the advantage of keeping a national currency. For an economy that is already extremely dollarized, seigniorage revenues would be small (and the cost of purchasing the remaining stock of domestic currency also would be small), the exposures of banks and businesses would make devaluation financially risky, and the exchange rate would not serve as a policy instrument because prices would be "sticky" in dollar terms. In such cases, dollarization may offer more benefits than costs.

▶ *Notes*

1. The same discrepancy exists for other countries that have issued Brady bonds.

2. The longer maturity of the Bradies and the effect of the existing collateral on the "stripped" part of the return may also explain part of this yield difference.

3. We return to this issue later.

4. The ERM crisis provides an example where the direction of causality was plausibly from devaluation to default. For Italy, the spread of long-term lira bonds over German government (deutsche mark) bonds rose by roughly 200 basis points in 1992, while the spread on dollar-denominated Italian Republic bonds (not affected by a potential devaluation of the lira) also rose by some 60 basis points.

5. Both are "stripped" of the value of U.S. Treasury collateral.

6. Similarly, spreads on U.S. high-yield (junk) bonds over Treasuries are highly correlated with both Panamanian and Argentinean dollar spreads, with correlation coefficients of 0.39 and 0.70, respectively, over the period October 1995 through March 1999.

7. A few shortcuts have been taken in performing these calculations. In particular, we are inferring annual default risk probabilities on the basis of spreads that apply to multiannual bonds with the implicit assumption that those probabilities will stay constant over time.

8. See IMF (1999b) for estimates of the cost of currency crashes.

9. Indeed Panama has had several crises, and a high number of Fund programs.

10. Currently, liquidity requirements deposited at the central bank of Argentina earn an interest rate comparable to market levels. But the decision to maintain or change that policy is independent from dollarization.

11. Argentina perceived much higher seigniorage, an average of 2.2 percent of GDP, over the past 20 years, which resulted in high inflation.

12. Under the rules of the currency board the government is required to hold sufficient foreign reserves to back the domestic currency, and thus cannot "consume" the annual issue of currency by financing public spending, for example.

13. On these points see Fischer (1982). For Argentina, the stock of reserves on hand is sufficient to purchase the outstanding monetary base.

14. The main exception to the rule that new currencies replace weak ones is Slovakia after the breakup of the Czech and Slovak Federal Republic in 1993, while Botswana's introduction of its own currency in 1976, first circulating at par with the rand then following a basket peg, is an exception to both generalizations.

15. An alternative adjustment mechanism, typical across U.S. states during recessions, is labor migration. See Blanchard and Katz (1992).

16. Calvo (1999) makes this point. Note that adjustment via devaluation also generates sharp capital gains and losses for agents that have different positions on foreign exchange.

17. Departures from the gold standard by Argentina at other times, during financial crises for example, did not suffice to avoid serious recessionary consequences.

18. For a description of the workings of the CFA franc zone, see Clement et al. (1996).

19. This account draws heavily on Hernández-Catá et al. (1998).

20. Note, however, that Cavallo (1999) has suggested that currency boards may just be the first stage in the development of sound currencies, and that a multinational

regional currency (a la the euro) could be the next stage once institutions and credibility have reached the necessary degree of maturity.

21. See Lane et al. (1999) for a review of the Asian crises.

22. This is pointed out in Calvo (1999). See also Hausmann et al. (1999) for other arguments against the use of exchange rate policy in the Latin America case.

23. Banking crises may of course be a cause of currency crises, but in general the causality runs in both directions. On these "twin crises," see Kaminsky and Reinhart (1999).

24. See Baliño, Bennett, and Borensztein (1999).

25. Of course, improving supervision and regulation would help to strengthen the banking system, but those are initiatives that should be followed whether the economy is dollarized or not.

26. During the "tequila," bank deposits declined by less than 20 percent.

27. See IMF (1999a).

28. The customs union of the Mercosur countries started on January 1, 1995. The lifting of trade barriers within the region, however, started as early as 1986, with a significant acceleration after the Treaty of Asunción in 1991.

29. The methodology is that of Bayoumi and Eichengreen (1994), updated with data through 1998 by Arora (1999).

30. The same analysis suggests that there is also a weak basis for an OCA comprising the United States and other countries in the hemisphere.

31. See, for example, Levy Yeyati and Sturzenegger (2000).

32. This point is made by Eichengreen (1998).

◤ References

Arora, Vivek. (1999). *Exchange Rate Arrangements for Selected Western Hemisphere Countries.* Unpublished manuscript. International Monetary Fund.

Baliño, Tomás J., Adam Bennett, and Eduardo Borensztein. (1999). *Monetary Policy in Dollarized Economies.* (Occasional Paper 171). Washington, D.C.: International Monetary Fund.

Bayoumi, Tamim, and Barry Eichengreen. (1994). *One Money or Many?* (Princeton Studies in International Finance, No. 76). Princeton, N.J.: Princeton University.

Blanchard, Olivier Jean, and Lawrence Katz. (1992). Regional Evolutions. *Brookings Papers on Economic Activity (U.S.), 10*(1), 1–61.

Bogetic, Zeljko. (1999, June). *Official or "Full" Dollarization: Current Experiences and Issues.* Mimeograph. International Monetary Fund.

Calvo, Guillermo A. (1999, April). *On Dollarization.* Mimeograph. University of Maryland.

Calvo, Guillermo A., and Carmen M. Reinhart. (1999). Capital Flow Reversals, the Exchange Rate Debate, and Dollarization, *Finance and Development, 36*(3), 13–15.

Cavallo, Domingo F. (1999). La qualité de la monnaie, *Economie Internationale.* La revue de Centre d'études prospectives et d'informations internationales (France), *80,* 103–18.

Clement, Jean A. P., J. Mueller, S. Cosse, and J. Le Dem. (1996). *Aftermath of the*

CFA Franc Devaluation. (IMF Occasional Paper No. 138). Washington, D.C.: International Monetary Fund.

Collings, F. d'A. (1983). *The Rand Monetary Area.* (IMF Paper DM/83/6). Washington, D.C.: International Monetary Fund.

Courchene, Thomas H., and Richard G. Harris. (1999). Canada and a North American Monetary Union, *Canadian Business Economics, 7* (Dec.), 5–14.

Engel, Charles, and John H. Rogers. (1996). How Wide Is the Border? *American Economic Review, 86,* 1112–25.

Eichengreen, Barry, and Peter Temin. (1997). *The Gold Standard and the Great Depression.* (NBER Working Paper No. 6060). Cambridge, Mass.: National Bureau of Economic Research.

Eichengreen, Barry. (1998). *Does Mercosur Need a Single Currency?* (NBER Working Paper No. 6821). Cambridge, Mass.: National Bureau of Economic Research.

Eichengreen, Barry, and Jeffrey Sachs. (1985). Exchange Rates and Economic Recovery in the 1930s. *Journal of Economic History, 45,* 925–46.

Fischer, Stanley. (1982). Seigniorage and the Case for a National Money. *Journal of Political Economy, 90,* 295–313.

Fischer, Stanley. (1993). Seigniorage and Official Dollarization. In Nissan Liviatan (Ed.), *Proceedings of a Conference on Currency Substitution and Currency Boards* (pp. 6–10). (World Bank Discussion Paper 207). Washington, D.C.: World Bank.

Frankel, Jeffrey. (1999, April 20). *No Single Currency Regime Is Right for All Countries or at All Times.* Graham Lecture. Princeton University.

Ghosh, Atish R., Anne-Marie Gulde, Jonathan D. Ostry, and Holger C. Wolf. (1998). Does the Nominal Exchange Rate Regime Matter? (NBER Working Paper No. 5874). Cambridge, Mass.: National Bureau of Economic Research.

Hausmann, Ricardo, Michael Gavin, Carmen Pages-Serra, and Ernesto Stein. (1999). Financial Turmoil and the Choice of Exchange Rate Regime. (Working Paper). Washington, D.C.: Inter-American Development Bank.

Hernández-Catá, Ernesto, et al. (1998). *The West African Economic and Monetary Union: Recent Developments and Policy Issues.* (IMF Occasional Paper No. 170). Washington, D.C.: International Monetary Fund.

International Monetary Fund. (1999a, September). *International Capital Markets Report.* Washington, D.C.: Author.

International Monetary Fund. (1999b, October). *World Economic Outlook.* Washington, D.C.: Author.

Kaminsky, Graciela L., and Carmen M. Reinhart. (1999). The Twin Crises: The Causes of Banking and Balance of Payments Problems. *American Economic Review, 89,* 473–500.

Kiguel, Miguel. (1998). *Debt Management: Some Reflections Based on Argentina, Inter-American Development Bank.* (Office of the Chief Economist, Working Paper No. 364). Washington, D.C.: Inter-American Development Bank.

Lane, Timothy, Atish Ghosh, Javier Hamann, Steven Phillips, Marianne Schulze-Ghattas, and Tsidi Tsikata. (1999). *IMF-Supported Programs in Indonesia, Korea and Thailand.* (IMF Occasional Paper No. 178). Washington, D.C.: International Monetary Fund.

McCallum, John. (1995). National Borders Matter: Regional Trade Patterns in North America. *American Economic Review, 853,* 615–23.

Moreno-Villalaz, Juan Luis. (1999). Lessons from the Monetary Experience of Panama: A Dollar Economy with Financial Integration. *Cato Journal, 18*(3), 421–39.

Mussa, Michael. (1986). Nominal Exchange Rate Regimes and the Behavior of Real Exchange Rates: Evidence and Implication. *Carnegie Rochester Conference Series on Public Policy, 25,* 117–214.

Paolera, Gerardo della, and Alan Taylor. (1999). *Economic Recovery from the Argentine Great Depression: Institutions, Expectations and the Change of Macroeconomic Regime.* (NBER Working Paper No. 6767). Cambridge, Mass.: National Bureau of Economic Research.

Petas, Peter, and Rashique Rahman. (1999). Sovereign Bonds: Legal Aspects That Affect Default and Recovery. *Global Emerging Markets, Deutsche Bank, 2*(3).

Yeyati, Eduardo Levy, and Federico Sturzenegger. (2000, April). Is Emu a Blueprint for Mercosur? *Cuadernos de Economia, 37*(110), 63–99.

4 Vittorio Corbo

Is It Time for a Common Currency for the Americas?

The series of crises that have affected emerging markets in recent years have reopened the debate on the most appropriate exchange regime for an emergent economy.[1] It is no coincidence that all countries that suffered severe crises in the 1990s had some sort of fixed exchange rate. This is not surprising because the exchange rate system and the structural characteristics of an economy, particularly with regard to prices and wage flexibility, affect its ability to make adjustments in the face of shocks. These factors acquire special relevance in light of the fact that countries are always exposed to real and nominal shocks. (Real shocks are such as changes in the terms of trade, the discovery of a new ore lode, drought, earthquakes, or political change with positive or negative impact on aggregate demand; nominal shocks are changes in the international interest rate and sudden changes in the demand for money.) Finally, exchange rate systems also have a bearing on the volatility of the real exchange rate and on the efficacy of monetary policy, with final effects on the level and variability of output and unemployment. The rest of this paper is organized as follows. The second section briefly compares the cost and benefits of fixed and flexible exchange rate systems; the third sections reviews the arguments in favor of full dollarization in Latin America; and the fourth section presents concluding remarks.

◣ *Fixed versus Flexible Rates: A Look at the Costs and Benefits*

Fixed exchange rates have the advantage of reducing volatility in the real exchange rate, thus contributing to better allocation of resources and the expansion of foreign trade and, ultimately, to higher growth.[2] They also provide a nominal anchor for conducting monetary policy and allow for more efficient adjustments when shocks are of a nominal nature; they also may serve as a rule for policies in situations with poor track records on monetary policy. In the latter case, a fixed rate provides a clear commitment that can be monitored by private agents. Their main costs lie in the fact that, in the presence of nominal rigidities, real depreciations are difficult to make. Thus when, due to real shocks, a real depreciation is required and nominal wages are downwardly rigid—for example, when wages are indexed to past inflation—adjustment with a fixed exchange rate, generally, results in a sharp increase in unemployment. Another not insignificant cost of fixed exchange rates is that they facilitate an overexpansion of foreign indebtedness, as the risk of an exchange rate adjustment is underestimated, which may be very costly in economies with weak financial systems.

A fixed exchange rate also requires prescinding from the use of monetary policy to stabilize output. This is not a minor cost because, for a central bank to be credible, monetary policy is the most effective stabilization tool. On the other hand, some of the benefits of a less rigid system are significant. Indeed, a consensus is emerging that the countries that suffered least from the Great Depression were those that abandoned the rigid gold standard early on.[3]

In contrast to fixed rates, flexible exchange rate systems facilitate adjustments of the real exchange rate when real shocks make those adjustments necessary. They also make it possible to use an active monetary policy for purposes of stabilization. Another advantage of those schemes is that they force agents to internalize the cost of a depreciation of the local currency when they decide to take on open foreign currency positions. However, one significant cost of flexible regimes is that they introduce high volatility in the nominal and real exchange rates. How high volatility may rise is well illustrated by the exchange rate between the yen and the dollar, which went from 147 yen per dollar in August 1998 to 115 in October of that same year. Another significant cost of this system obtains in economies with a severe mismatch between assets and liabilities in the financial system, that is, in situations in which the liabilities of private agents are dollarized while their assets or income-generating capacity are in local currency. In that case, a drastic exchange rate adjustment could result in generalized bankruptcy. This point has been made forcefully by Calvo and Reinhart (2000). However, currency mismatch can be dealt with by appropriate regulation and supervision of the financial system, and therefore should be an integral part of the institutional framework for an economy that operates with a flexible exchange rate system.

It is occasionally claimed that countries are afraid of floating and, consequently, countries with flexible exchange rate systems do not use the flexibility entailed by those systems. Fear of floating could be due to the high pass-through effect of devaluation on inflation or to the commercial risks associated with an exchange rate adjustment in an economy where agents have a mismatch between the currency composition of their assets and liabilities (Calvo and Reinhart, 2000). However, recent analytical and empirical work shows convincingly that pass-through effects are much weaker than initially thought (Obstfeld and Rogoff, 2000). In addition, Corbo and Schmidt-Hebbel (2001) show that Latin American countries that are listed as floaters are indeed floating. This is especially so for countries that have a well-established monetary framework of the inflation targeting type.

However, one should keep in mind, as a reference, that in the absence of market friction, there is no gain from exchange rate flexibility, independent monetary policy, or providing lender-of-last-resort services, when adopting a domestic currency and choosing a degree of exchange rate flexibility—the only residual issue is a minor one, related to the international distribution of seigniorage revenue. At the same time, nothing is gained by giving up the domestic currency, as currency transaction costs are nil, and perfect financial markets hedge the currency risk premiums and currency mismatch.

Another point to keep in mind, which is also one of the main lessons to be learned from the recent crises, is that with free capital movement and high levels of worker remittances, fixed—but adjustable without too high a cost—exchange rates are very vulnerable to speculative attacks. That vulnerability gives rise to both potential conflicts in domestic monetary policy and distrust in economic agents with regard to the authorities' ability to maintain fixed parity. The distrust arises in situations in which it is believed that the increases in interest rates required to maintain interest rate parity in the face of a rise in foreign interest rates, or the expected rate of depreciation, will lead to sharp rises in unemployment, an excessive increase in risk to financial loans, and/or an increase in the fiscal cost of public debt expressed in domestic currency.

To avoid these problems, the main options are to establish a credibly fixed exchange rate system or to employ a more flexible exchange rate system, developing, at the same time, instruments to cover exchange rate risks. This is the emerging consensus among economists today.

Can one achieve a combination of a fixed exchange rate regime and a flexible regime? At their heyday a decade ago, adjustable pegs seemed to provide a perfect compromise between credibility (due to the nominal anchor provided by the exchange rate peg or band) and flexibility (allowance for limited and gradual adjustments of the real exchange rate in response to shocks). After a decade of growing disappointment with intermediate arrangements, the current consensus has shifted in favor of the two pure cases: credible fixed or fully flexible regimes (Edwards and Savastano, 2000; Mussa et al., 2000; Obstfeld and Rogoff, 1995; Summers, 2000).[4]

A third option, generated in certain cases to avoid exchange rate crises, is to introduce controls on capital flows. However, it must be kept in mind that, given lower communication and information costs and advances in information technology, the world is an ever more integrated market, so that capital controls are very difficult to implement and, at best, are only temporarily effective (until the private sector finds ways to avoid them).[5]

Credible fixed exchange rate systems are currency boards (for example, Hong Kong, since 1983, or Argentina since 1991) or the more extreme case of replacing the domestic currency with that of a large country. Currency boards (as well as dollarization) have certain prerequisites and introduce significant rigidities. First, a country needs sufficient foreign reserves to finance the short-term monetary liabilities of the monetary system, or it will not be credible. The financial system must also be sufficiently strong to be able to survive without a lender of last resort. If this is not possible, a provision must be made for emergency loans from foreign commercial banks—as is the case in Argentina—or from a financial institution, probably the Fed or the ECB. Wage flexibility and labor mobility must also be sufficiently great to facilitate real exchange rate changes, when a change in macroeconomic fundamentals makes a real depreciation necessary. Nevertheless, the discipline inherent to a currency board means that a government must be ready, and must have the political support, to live with the high interest rates (and high unemployment) that are an integral part of an adjustment to a drop in foreign reserves.

Currency boards are not fully protected from the effects of financial contagion either. Financial turmoil and contagion in open economies that have adopted currency boards (e.g., Argentina and Hong Kong) and protracted high exchange rate risk premiums, as is the case after nine years for Argentina's currency board (reflected both directly and indirectly through large country-risk premiums; see Powell and Sturzenegger, 2000), have given rise recently to a degree of disillusion with currency boards.

Thus some believe that in order to reduce the cost associated with distrust with regard to the authorities' ability to maintain a currency board it is necessary to renounce one's domestic currency and adopt that of a larger country with a history of monetary discipline, such as the dollar. Obviously, abandoning the domestic currency eliminates the risk of a devaluation, but the country also completely renounces the use of monetary policy and/or adjustments of the exchange rate to face real shocks to the economy, as is the case in currency boards. In fact, aware of this, the central banks in the main industrial countries use monetary policy for stabilization purposes.

All this is in theory. However, in the choice of exchange rate regime, strong path dependence is the rule. Thus, in countries with poor records of monetary stability resulting in widespread currency substitution, the domestic currency is rarely used as a medium of exchange or as an accounting unit, and therefore there is not much room for monetary policy. Furthermore, in these cases, an exchange rate adjustment could have substantial economic costs due to balance sheet effects (Calvo and Reinhart, 2000). For that type of country, the benefits of adopting a rigid exchange rate system could outweigh the costs involved. In contrast, in countries that have built a reputation for financial prudence, the benefits of exchange rate flexibility and of having the option to use monetary policy for stabilization purposes could be an important asset.

Countries with a decent track record of financial prudence can choose which exchange rate regime to use. Both systems—a credibly fixed exchange rate and a flexible exchange rate—have both costs and benefits, but given that credibly fixed exchange rates tend to link recessions to real negative shocks, they are not to be recommended for countries in which shocks are important given the relative size of their economies and when the shocks are mainly idiosyncratic. Flexible exchange rates, given the real costs of volatility in the real exchange rate, must be accompanied by mechanisms that provide coverage for exchange risks and commitments to elements of macro policy and intervention, which will tend to keep volatility under control. Moreover, as a prerequisite, they require a solid and appropriately regulated and supervised financial system, in which exchange risks can be estimated correctly.

▶ *Dollarization in Latin America*

There has been renewed interest in dollarization in Latin America in recent years. Dollarization has been introduced in Ecuador, and El Salvador is making preparations to adopt that regime. The eventual dollarization of El Salvador will force the rest of the countries in Central America to follow suit (indeed, at present, there is some discussion on the convenience of dollarization in Guatemala and Nicaragua). In the case of Ecuador, the country's poor record with its crawling peg regime and with independent monetary policy in general has prompted the movement toward dollarization. But Ecuador still has many problems and weaknesses to face (a bankrupt financial system, rigid nominal wages in the formal sector, a severe structural fiscal problem, etc.) that could make the dollarization a complete failure. In the case of Central American countries, where the financial and real crises of the 1980s resulted in high dollarization, room for independent monetary policy is severely curtailed. Furthermore, given that their labor markets are highly flexible and a substantial part of their trade and capital flows are with the United States (including worker remittances), the benefits of dollarization could outweigh the costs. Here the main justification is found in the OCA literature (Mundell, 1961). However, for these countries the adoption of the U.S. dollar does not resolve the problem of their fragile fiscal situation, or of their weak financial systems.

The potential benefits of a monetary union or dollarization (or a 100 percent credible currency board) accrue from the implicit constraints on monetary policy and low (lower) inflation, the elimination of currency risk and its associated premium, the elimination of currency transaction costs, lower variability in relative prices of tradable goods among member countries, and the elimination of currency mismatch in foreign assets and liabilities.

In contrast, for some of the large countries in the region, dollarization has been suggested as a way of giving up on the perennial misuse of monetary policy. In this direction, dollarization has been suggested for some of the large countries (Argentina, Brazil, and now Mexico). I will discuss each of these cases separately.

In the case of Argentina, after almost a full decade of adapting institutions and policies to work with a currency board system, the option to move back to a flexible system could be too costly, so that it may be beneficial to go the extra mile and dollarize. The only residual issue is the loss of seigniorage revenue, which is estimated at ¼ of 1 percent of GDP per annum. This issue could be a matter of negotiation with the U.S Treasury. For the other large countries in the region, the choice is not so clear-cut. Indeed, given the diversification of their trade among countries, their pervasive nominal rigidities, and the potential important stabilization role that well-run monetary policy could play, the option to dollarize implies greatly reduced scope for policy measures. Furthermore, as country after country masters the technicalities of inflation targeting, abandoning the use of monetary policy as a stabilization tool could be a cost difficult to ignore. In the particular case of Mexico, a country that has gone far to recover the credibility of its central bank and its monetary policy and has reduced its inflation to an annual rate below 10 percent, there is no need to tie itself to the rigid structure inherent to the dollarization of its economy. This is especially so given the high dependence of its economy on the price of oil. In this case, as in the case of Canada, a more flexible exchange rate system may be preferable. However, in the long run, it could be attractive for Mexico to become a member of a larger currency area within NAFTA or an eventual Free Trade Area of the Americas (FTAA).

In Brazil, the flexible exchange rate system played a key role—together with fiscal and monetary policy—in the surprising recovery from the crisis of early 1999. Furthermore, given the diversity of Brazil's trading partners and capital flows and the size of its economy, OCA arguments are much less relevant.[6]

An open question is the type of monetary arrangement that would be more appropriate for Mercosur as a whole. Here the idea of having a common currency as a means of deepening integration will have to wait until substantial progress is made on macroeconomic policy coordination within the area. There is, moreover, still much room for the reduction of more typical barriers to trade in goods and services.

However, with time, as Europe and the rest of the world benefit from the experience of the euro, interest on moving toward currency areas will increase, the natural early candidate for a common currency area in Latin America being Central America.

▲ Concluding Remarks

For countries with poor records on financial stability, in which currency substitution is high, dollarization may be advantageous. It could also be beneficial for countries a substantial part of whose trade in goods and capital flows occurs with the United States. For both types of countries, dollarization would be even more advantageous if labor markets are flexible and the appropriate institutions are in place to support the financial system in the event of a sudden crisis. However, for open economies with a decent record of financial stability and large tradable sectors, in which exports are not very diversified by country and where nominal rigidities are widespread, dollarization could be a major hindrance to the adjustment process. For this type of country, a real depreciation—when a change in fundamentals requires one—could be too costly, given that it depends on the downward flexibility of nontradable prices. In this case, a more flexible exchange rate regime would be preferable. Indeed, the combination of prudent monetary policy and exchange rate flexibility has facilitated adjustment in most countries in the region. With capital mobility, exchange rate flexibility also leaves the door open to the use of discretionary monetary policy in response to unexpected domestic and external shocks.

Given that few countries are willing to go down the road to dollarization, one observes that most are moving toward the use of more flexible systems. However, more flexible systems must be accompanied by the development of future exchange rate markets, to enable market participants to buy protection against exchange rate volatility. Otherwise the real costs of real exchange rate variability would be high. In any event, as countries move to the use of more flexible exchange rate regimes, they will need to make the selection of their monetary anchor more explicit.

◣ Notes

1. Among recent work on exchange rate regimes are Obstfeld and Rogoff (1995), Ghosh, Gulde, Ostry, and Wolf (1997), Edwards and Savastano (2000), Frankel (1999), and Mussa, Mason, Swoboda, Jadresic, Mauro, and Berg (2000).

2. Empirical work on Latin America shows that the variability of the real exchange rate has a detrimental effect on growth (Corbo and Rojas, 1993).

3. See Eichengreen and Sachs (1985), Eichengreen (1992), and Bernanke (1995) for industrial countries and Díaz-Alejandro (1982), Corbo (1988), and Campa (1990) for Latin America.

4. For minority views in favor of exchange rate bands, see Williamson (1996) and Frankel (1999).

5. For a recent survey on the effectiveness of capital controls, see Edwards (1999).

6. In the case of Chile, in a recent article Morandé and Schmidt-Hebbel (2000) conclude that, among various Southern Hemisphere countries, Chile would gain the least (or lose the most) if it gave up its currency. Subject to large idiosyncratic shocks and significant temporary wage and price rigidity, and a conservative monetary policy, it is argued, Chile has the most to gain from a floating exchange rate and an independent monetary policy.

◣ **References**

Bernanke, B. (1995). The Macroeconomics of the Great Depression: A Comparative Approach. *Journal of Money, Credit, and Banking, 27*(1), 1–28.

Calvo, G., and C. Reinhart. (2000, September). *Fear of Floating.* Mimeograph. University of Maryland.

Campa, J. M. (1990). Exchange Rates and Economic Recovery in the 1930s: An Extension to Latin America. *Journal of Economic History, 50,* 677–82.

Corbo, V. (1988). Problems, Development Theory and Strategies of Latin America. In *The State of Development Economics: Progress and Perspectives,* edited by G. Ranis and T. P. Schultz. London: Blackwell.

Corbo, V., and P. Rojas. (1993). Investment, Macroeconomic Stability and Growth: The Latin American Experience. *Revista de Análisis Económico, 8*(1), 19–35.

Corbo, V., and K. Schmidt-Hebbel. (2001, November). Inflation Targeting in Latin America. (Paper presented at the Latin America Conference on Fiscal and Financial Reforms). Center for Research on Economic Development and Policy Reform, Stanford University.

Díaz-Alejandro, C. (1982). Latin America in Depression, 1929–39. In *The Theory and Experience of Economic Development,* edited by M. Gersovitz, C. Díaz-Alejandro, G. Ranis, and M. Rosenzweig. London: Allen and Unwin.

Edwards, S. (1999). How Effective Are Capital Controls? *Journal of Economic Perspectives, 13*(4), 65–84.

Edwards, S., and M. Savastano. (2000). Exchange Rates in Emerging Economies: What Do We Know? What Do We Need to Know? In *Economic Policy Reform: The Second Stage,* edited by Anne O. Krueger. Chicago: University of Chicago Press.

Eichengreen, B. (1992). *Golden Fetters: The Gold Standard and the Great Depression, 1919–1939.* New York: Oxford University Press.

Eichengreen, B., and J. Sachs. (1985). Exchange Rates and Economic Recovery in the 1930s. *Journal of Economic History, 45,* 925–46.

Frankel, J. (1999, September). *No Single Currency Regime Is Right for All Countries or at All Times.* (NBER Working Paper 7338). National Bureau of Economic Research.

Ghosh, A., A. Gulde, J. Ostry, and H. Wolf. (1997). *Does the Nominal Exchange Rate Regime Matter?* (NBER Working Paper 5874). National Bureau of Economic Research.

Morandé, F., and K. Schmidt-Hebbel. (2000). Chile's Peso: Better Than (Just) Living with the Dollar? *Cuadernos de Economía, 37*(110), 177–226.

Mundell, R. (1961). A Theory of Optimum Currency Areas. *American Economic Review, 51*(4), 657–665.

Mussa, M., P. Masson, A. Swoboda, E. Jadresic, P. Mauro, and A. Berg. (2000). *Exchange Rate Regimes in an Increasingly Integrated World Economy.* (IMF Occasional Paper 193). International Monetary Fund.

Obstfeld, M., and K. Rogoff. (1995). The Mirage of Fixed Exchange Rates. *Journal of Economic Perspectives, 9,* 73–96.

Obstfeld, M., and K. Rogoff. (2000, August). *Perspectives on OECD Economic Integration: Implications for US Current Account Adjustment.* (Paper presented at the symposium "Global Economic Integration: Opportunities and Challenges"). Sponsored by the Federal Reserve Bank of Kansas City.

Powell, A., and F. Sturzenegger. (2000). *Dollarization: The Link between Devaluation and Risk Default.* Mimeograph. Universidad Torcuato di Tella, Buenos Aires.

Summers, L. (2000). International Financial Crises, Causes, Prevention and Cures. *American Economic Review, 90*(2), 1–16.

Williamson, J. (1996). *The Crawling Band as an Exchange Rate Regime: Lessons from Chile, Colombia and Israel.* Washington, D.C.: Institute for International Economics.

5 Sebastian Edwards

Dollarization

Myths and Realities

A number of proposals for reforming the "international financial architecture" have recently been advanced by academics, policymakers, and pundits of various types. These reform blueprints have included the imposition of controls on capital inflows, abolishing the IMF, and the creation of a global lender of last resort. But perhaps the most intriguing reform proposal is that emerging countries should completely give up their currencies and adopt an advanced nation's currency as legal tender.

This proposal has come to be known as "dollarization" and is being pushed with increased vigor by a small but increasingly influential group of economists.[1] What started as an intellectual but mostly impractical idea has recently become a real policy option. During the past few years some countries have either dollarized or have announced that they are moving in that direction. In 2000, and in the midst of a major crisis, Ecuador abolished its national currency, the sucre, and adopted the U.S. dollar as legal tender. El Salvador adopted the dollar during 2001, and Guatemala and Nicaragua are considering the option seriously.

At a general level, dollarization is being presented as the ultimate way for achieving credibility, growth, and prosperity. Countries that give up their currencies, we are told, will be unable to engage in macroeconomic mismanagement. Thus public finances will stay in balance, and the external accounts will move within reasonable bounds. Dollarization-imposed macroeconomic stability, the story goes, will mean lower interest rates, higher investment, and superior economic performance. Current arguments in favor of dollarization have gone beyond traditional discussions on optimal currency areas. Indeed, dollarization proponents have recently argued that giving up the national currency is the right option for the vast majority— if not all—of the emerging nations.

What is remarkable, however, is that this rather drastic piece of advice—giving up the national currency—is being dispensed on the bases of very limited empirical and historical evidence. Dollarization supporters seldom expand on the historical record of those few countries that have been dollarized for some time. Moreover, they rarely spell out the policies that should be implemented alongside this reform, nor do they refer in detail to the potential costs of adopting this monetary regime. This is equivalent to a physician prescribing a drug without making clear what other steps the patient must take (stay in bed, abstain from drinking alcohol, say) and without explaining the drug's side effects or its rate of success in clinical trials.[2]

The purpose of this article is to remedy, at least partially, this situation, and to investigate the historical record of countries that have lived under a "dollarized" monetary system. As it turns out, this is a very small group of countries, most of which have operated under very special circumstances, and for which there are very limited data. In spite of the poverty of the data, I believe that it is possible to address some important historical questions regarding performance under dollarization. These include the following. (1) Historically, has dollarization provided an effective way for tying policymakers' hands, and for achieving "credibility"? Another way of posing this question is: Have dollarized nations indeed enjoyed fiscal and external balance? (2) Have dollarized countries experienced faster growth and lower inflation than nondollarized ones? And (3) how costly has macroeconomic adjustment been in dollarized countries? In standard macroeconomic models, economies with superfixed exchange rate regimes and nominal price rigidities will have difficulties accommodating (real) external shocks.

Since Panama is the dollarized country with better and more complete data, much of this article deals with the Panamanian economy. When the data permit it, however, I deal with the experiences of other dollarized nations. The article is organized as follows. This section is the introduction. In the second section I present some basic data on economic performance in dollarized nations, and I ask whether there have been significant differences in the behavior of dollarized and nondollarized economies. In the third section I concentrate on the case of Panama, the largest country with a prolonged dollarization experience. The fourth section is devoted to analyzing the way dollarized countries have been affected by external shocks. In particular, I inquire whether external shocks have tended to affect dollarized countries in a different way from other nations. In the final section I make some brief concluding remarks.

▶ *Dollarization Experiences in Comparative Perspective*

It should be said at the outset that my interest—and the relevant policy question, I may add—is to understand how *independent* nations have performed under a dollarized monetary system. This means that in this article I am not interested in analyzing the performances of provinces or states within a national entity. The reason for this should be obvious: countries contemplating dollarization are independent nations looking for an efficient monetary arrangement; they are *not* countries looking to be annexed by larger and more advanced ones.[3] Table 5.1 contains a list of independent countries that have had an official dollarized system during the 1970–98

Table 5.1
Fully Dollarized Independent Nations, in 1970–98

Country	Population	Currency Used	Since
Andorra	73,000	French franc, Spanish peseta/euro	1278
Kiribati	82,000	Australian dollar and own coins	1943
Liberia	2,900,000	U.S. dollar	1847–1982
Liechtenstein	31,000	Swiss franc	1921
Marshall Islands	61,000	U.S. dollar	1944
Micronesia	130,000	U.S. dollar	1944
Monaco	32,000	French franc/euro	1865
Nauru	10,000	Australian dollar	1914
Palau	17,000	U.S. dollar	1944
Panama	2,700,000	U.S. dollar	1904
San Marino	26,000	Italian lira/euro, own coins	1897
Tuvalu	11,000	Australian dollar, own coins	1892

Sources: Bogetic (2000) and *The Statesman's Yearbook* (several eds.). A few other, very small territories, colonies, and self-governing regions use foreign currencies, such as Niue (New Zealand dollar), Norfolk Islands, Cocos (Keeling) Islands (Australian dollar), Pitcairn Island (New Zealand dollar and U.S. dollar), Tokelau (New Zealand dollar), Turks and Caicos Islands (U.S. dollar), Cook Island (New Zealand dollar), Northern Cyprus (Turkish lira), Greenland (Danish krone), Guam (U.S. dollar), Montenegro (German mark/euro), Northern Mariana Islands (U.S. dollar), Puerto Rico (U.S. dollar), Saint Helena (pound sterling), American Samoa (U.S. dollar), UK's Virgin Islands (U.S. dollar), and U.S.'s Virgin Islands (U.S. dollar).

period.[4] As may be seen, these are very small countries indeed. Many are, in fact, city-states fully integrated into their neighbors' economies—Monaco, Liechtenstein, and Andorra are good examples. The largest dollarized countries in table 5.1 are Liberia and Panama. Only the latter, however, remains dollarized today; Liberia abandoned the system in the 1980s, when the government of President Samuel Doe decided to issue local currency as a way of avoiding the constraints imposed on the public sector by the dollarized system.[5]

Analyzing performance in small city-states has traditionally represented a challenge for economists. Data are usually not available, and when they are, they are of poor quality and cover selected variables only. In this case the problem is particularly serious, since data for Liberia—one of only two countries with population over a million—are of extremely low quality. Panama is the only dollarized country with a reasonably complete data set.

In this study I focus on the 1970–98 period, and I use the best data available for as many of the countries in table 1 as possible. In collecting the data I first turned to the World Bank data files. If the World Bank had no information—or if the data quality was deemed to be suspect—I turned to the IMF and the United Nations. Overall, I was able to collect data on GDP per capita growth for 11 countries in table 5.1 (a total of 286 country-year data points). Data on other variables of interest—inflation, fiscal deficit, the current account, investment and terms of trade—are only available for a much smaller number of countries.[6] In the rest of this section I analyze the economic performance of the dollarized economies in table 5.1. In order to provide a comparative perspective I also present data on two comparison groups: (1) a group of all emerging and advanced countries for which there are data, and (2) a group of all emerging countries where data are available. I excluded from both of these groups countries that have had a "superfixed" exchange rate regime—dollarized or currency board. This means that my comparison groups comprise countries with a variety of exchange rate regimes, going from floating, to crawling, to pegged-but-adjustable. That is, I do not perform a "horse race" between dollarized countries and specific alternative regimes.

Table 5.2 contains summary data on (1) GDP per capita growth;

Table 5.2
Economic Performance in Dollarized and Nondollarized Economies (1970–97)

	Dollarized	All Nonsuper-fixed Countries	Emerging Markets (Non-superfixed)	Panama
A. Annual Per Capita GDP Growth (%)				
1st quartile	−2.28	−1.10	−1.70	−0.44
Median	0.49	1.87	1.71	1.80
3rd Quartile	2.74	4.37	4.61	3.46
Mean	0.16	1.38	1.20	1.31
Standard deviation	8.00	6.55	7.13	4.56
B. Yearly Inflation (%)				
1st quartile	1.26	3.99	4.49	1.00
Median	3.92	8.54	9.58	1.82
3rd Quartile	7.30	16.17	18.39	4.59
Mean	5.28	46.37	56.32	3.49
C. Annual Fiscal Deficit (as % of GDP)				
1st quartile	0.14	0.69	0.59	−0.58
Median	4.62	2.98	2.93	4.62
3rd Quartile	7.51	5.96	6.01	4.59
Mean	4.00	3.66	3.65	3.64
D. Current Account Deficit (as % of GDP, yearly)				
1st quartile	−3.56	−0.01	0.53	1.76
Median	4.33	3.20	4.07	4.34
3rd Quartile	8.62	7.21	8.28	8.40
Mean	2.22	4.09	4.82	4.26

Sources: World Bank, IMF, and United Nations.

(2) inflation; (3) fiscal deficit; and (4) current account deficit. For each variable I present information on the first quartile, the median, the third quartile, and the mean. For GDP per capita growth I also present data on the standard deviation. Simple inspection of the data suggests that, when compared with either of the two nondollarized groups, dollarized countries have had: (1) lower GDP per capita growth; (2) lower inflation; (3) similar or slightly higher fiscal deficits; and (4) a higher median and lower mean current account deficit. In addition, GDP growth has been more volatile in dollarized countries.[7]

In order to test formally whether these four variables have behaved differently across groups of countries, I estimated a series of tests for the equality of means and medians. I also computed a nonparametric Kruskal-Wallis χ^2 test on the equality of distributions. The Kruskal-Wallis χ^2 test is computed as:

[1] $K = \{ [12/ n(n + 1)] \sum (R_j^2/n_j) \} - 3(n + 1),$

where n_j is the sample size for the j group ($j = 1, \ldots m$), n is the sum of the $n_j s$, R_j is the sum of the ranks j group, and the sum $\sum$ runs from $j = 1$ to $j = m$.

The results obtained from these tests are reported in tables 5.3 and 5.4. They show formally that: (1) GDP growth has been significantly lower in the dollarized countries than in nondollarized ones. (2) Inflation has been statistically lower under dollarization. (3) There are no statistical differences in the behavior of fiscal deficits or current account balances across dollarized and nondollarized nations. These results also show that inflation has been significantly lower in Panama. There are no significant differences between growth behavior in Panama and the other groups. Interestingly, the median fiscal deficit has been statistically higher in Panama than in the rest of the Latin American nations. I discuss this puzzling result in the third section.

The GDP growth comparisons in table 5.2 refer to unconditional statistics. An interesting question is whether dollarized countries perform differently from nondollarized ones, after controlling by the fundamental determinants of growth. Results obtained from a panel regression using a (very) small number of data points for the dollarized economies suggest the conditional rate of growth of per capita GDP is lower for dollarized than nondollarized nations.[8] In these regressions—not reported here—the coefficient of the dollarized dummy is negative; its p-values, however, were rather high, ranging from 0.16 to 0.11.

The results reported in this section, then, can be summarized as follows: (1) There is evidence that dollarized countries as a group have statistically grown at a significantly lower rate than nondollarized nations. (2) Dollarized countries have experienced a significantly lower rate of inflation. (3) There is no evidence that dollarized countries have run more prudent fiscal policies than nondollarized nations. In fact, the formal tests show that, statistically speaking, it is not possible to make a distinction between dollarized and

Table 5.3
Tests for Equality of Means and Medians in Dollarized and Nondollarized Economies (1970–97)

	Dollarized vs. All Countries	Dollarized vs. Emerging Countries	Panama vs. Latin America
A. GDP per Capita Growth			
Means (t)	2.91	2.20	−0.68
	(0.04)	(0.03)	(0.49)
Medians (χ^2)	27.56	17.49	0.16
	(0.00)	(0.00)	(0.69)
B. Inflation			
Means (t)	4.35	4.27	4.52
	(0.00)	(0.00)	(0.00)
Medians (χ^2)	17.10	17.13	17.05
	(0.00)	(0.00)	(0.00)
C. Fiscal Deficit			
Means (t)	0.37	0.38	1.37
	(0.71)	(0.70)	(0.17)
Medians (χ^2)	0.51	0.52	3.63
	(0.47)	(0.48)	(0.05)
D. Current Account Deficit			
Means (t)	0.97	1.37	0.03
	(0.34)	(0.18)	(0.98)
Medians (χ^2)	2.62	0.22	2.44
	(0.11)	(0.75)	(0.12)

Note: p-values in parentheses

nondollarized countries. And (4) in terms of current account balances, dollarized nations' behavior has been no different from that of nondollarized ones. Given the very small number of observations for the dollarized group, and the low quality of the data, these results are subject to stronger caveats than usual and should be interpreted with care.[9]

▶ *Panama's Experience with Dollarization*

Supporters of "dollarization" have pointed to Panama's experience as proof of the merits of that system. Low inflation, macroeconomic stability, and low interest rates—including the existence of long-term credit in nominal terms—are mentioned as some of Panama's most remarkable accomplishments (Moreno-Villalaz, 1999; Bogetic, 2000). In this section I provide a

Table 5.4
χ^2 Tests for Dollarized and Nondollarized Economies (1970–97)

	Dollarized vs All Countries	Dollarized vs. Emerging Countries	Panama vs. Emerging Countries
	A. GDP per Capita Growth		
χ^2	24.82	15.82	0.11
	(0.00)	(0.00)	(0.92)
	B. Inflation		
χ^2	20.99	24.74	23.42
	(0.00)	(0.00)	(0.00)
	C. Fiscal Deficit		
χ^2	0.79	0.84	0.84
	(0.37)	(0.36)	(0.36)
	D. Current Account Deficit		
χ^2	0.16	0.09	0.09
	(0.69)	(0.78)	(0.78)

Note: p-values in parentheses

brief analysis of Panama's experience, and I argue that, in spite of some very important achievements, its record has been embellished.

A fundamental omission in virtually every recent account of Panama's economic experience refers to the country's heavy reliance on the IMF during the last 35 years or so. With the exception of a brief interregnum during the Noriega years, Panama has been almost permanently under the tutelage of the Fund. Since 1973 Panama has had 17 IMF programs, the most recent of which was signed in late 2000 and is expected to run until late 2002. According to Mussa and Savastano (2000), during the last quarter of a century Panama has been the most assiduous user of IMF resources in the Western Hemisphere; since 1973, only Pakistan has had a larger number of IMF programs. The main factor behind this proliferation of IMF programs has been Panama's inability, until very recently, to control its public finances. Between 1973 and 1998 the fiscal deficit averaged 4 percent of GDP, and during 1973–1987—a period of continuous IMF programs—it exceeded a remarkable 7 percent of GDP. In fact, it has only been in the last few years that Panama has been able to put its fiscal accounts somewhat in order.[10]

In 1904 Panama adopted the dollar as legal tender. Although there is a national currency—the balboa—its role is largely symbolic. There is no central bank and the monetary authorities cannot issue balboa-denominate notes. Since 1970 Panama has had no controls on capital mobility and has been financially integrated to the rest of the world. For decades Panama has been an important center for offshore banking, with a large number of international banks operating in the country. A number of authors have argued that in Panama foreign banks play the role of "lender of last resort," a function usually performed by the national central bank. It should be noted, however, that in spite of dollarization and of the massive presence of international banks, Panama has been recently subject, as many other countries in Latin America, to massive banking crises. Indeed, in 1988–89 Panama suffered a major systemic banking crisis, where as a result of the weak "financial position of most state-owned and private commercial banks . . . 15 banks ceased operations" (Beim and Calomiris, 2000, p. 282).[11]

As may be seen from table 5.2, Panama's most remarkable achievement is its very low rate of inflation. Between 1955 and 1998, it averaged 2.4 percent per annum, and during the 1990s it barely exceeded 1 percent per year. In addition to low inflation, Panama has posted a healthy rate of growth during the last four decades. Between 1958 and 1998, Panama's real GDP expanded at 5.3 percent per year. Although Panama's rate of growth has exceeded that of other dollarized economies, it has not been statistically different from that of nondollarized countries. This is true independently of whether the nondollarized comparison group is composed of all nations, emerging countries, or only Latin American countries (see the nonparametric tests in table 5.3).

Behind these achievements, however, hides Panama's serious addiction to IMF programs. In spite of not having a central bank, or a currency of its own, for years Panama failed to maintain fiscal discipline. Initially, these large fiscal deficits were financed through borrowing from abroad. And when the foreign debt became too high, the IMF stepped in with fresh resources. And when this was not enough, Panama restructured its foreign debt. This was the case in 1983, 1985, and more recently 1996, when Panama finalized its Brady-deal negotiations.[12] Panama had its first IMF program in 1965. A year later the fiscal deficit was brought into check. In 1968, however, the fiscal accounts were again out of hand, and the IMF was called in once more. A remarkable 19-year period of uninterrupted IMF programs was thus initiated. Although in some of the early programs there were no withdrawals, the sheer presence of the IMF signaled that the monies would indeed be there when needed.

Year after year, a new IMF program called for the strengthening of public finances. And, invariably, year after year, Panama failed to take serious action. After all, the authorities knew that the IMF was there, ready to bail them out. This continuous IMF presence was only broken in 1987, when as a result of General Noriega's confrontational policies, Panama was subject to severe United States–led economic sanctions. The IMF returned to Panama in September 1990, with a monitored program. This was followed by lending programs in 1992 (22 months), 1995 (16 months), 1997 (36 months), and 2000 (22 months). Significantly, in the last few years the authorities have finally acknowledged the need for maintaining a solid fiscal position. Between 1990 and 1996 the country posted small public sector surpluses. By 1998, however, the public sector deficit had grown to almost 3 percent of GDP, and the IMF has estimated that during 2000 the deficit had declined to a more modest 1 percent of GDP. Why has the IMF been so willing to accommodate Panama's repeated macroeconomic transgressions? A full analysis of this issue is well beyond the scope of this paper, but political economy considerations—including the U.S. interest in maintaining the Canal Zone free of political turmoil—are surely part of the answer.

In contrast with Argentina, a country with a superfixed currency-board type of monetary regime, Panama has been largely successful in eliminating devaluation risk. This has been reflected in a relatively low cost of capital in international financial markets. Between 1997 and 1998, for example, the average daily spread on Panamanian par bonds was 464 basis points, lower than that of Argentine par Brady bonds, which averaged 710 basis points. Contrary to what dollarization supporters usually claim, however, Panama's cost of capital in international markets has *not* been the lowest in Latin America. In fact, as is illustrated in figure 5.1, the spread over Panamanian bonds has been systematically and significantly higher than that over Chile's sovereign bonds of similar maturity.[13] Interestingly, Chile is a country that during the period under discussion experienced an overall increase in its degree of exchange rate flexibility. The comparison between Chile and Panama underscores the important point—not always acknowl-

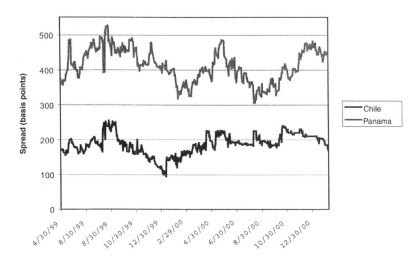

Figure 5.1. Sovereign Bonds Spreads: Chile and Panama, 1999–2001

edged—that dollarization does not by itself reduce country risk. In fact, during the last few years, and in spite of its improved fiscal performance, Panama has experienced a sizable country risk premium and has been subject to "contagion."

Recent discussions on dollarization have focused on the loss of seignorage that would result from unilaterally adopting a foreign currency. Supporters of dollarization have argued that this loss could be reduced if a monetary treatise is signed with the advanced country whose currency is adopted. This is not a new idea. In fact, it was proposed in 1972 by Harry Johnson within the context of the Panamanian experience.[14]

▶ Accommodating External Disturbances under Dollarization

Macroeconomic models of open economies have traditionally emphasized the role of the exchange rate regime during the adjustment process. In principle, under superfixed regimes a required depreciation of the equilibrium real exchange rate will have to take place through deflation. In the presence of nominal price and wage rigidities, this will lead to unemployment and slower growth (Dornbusch, 1980). The actual quantitative importance of these deflationary forces is an empirical issue. In this section I use data from the dollarized nations to address this issue. In particular I ask the following two questions: First, what has been the effect of terms of trade shocks on dollarized nations' performance? More specifically, I ask whether these shocks affect dollarized countries differently than other (nondollarized) countries. Second, I investigate whether macroeconomic adjustment episodes—and in particular major current account reversals—have been more costly in dollarized than in nondollarized nations. Originally I intended to use data from a large number of dollarized countries; unfortunately, only Panama has data for all the variables of interest.

Current Account Reversals and Terms of Trade Shocks

Table 5.4 contains data on terms of trade volatility and on current account reversals for Panama and three comparison groups during 1970–98. Terms-of-trade volatility is defined as the standard deviation of the log of the relative price of exports to imports. I have defined a "current account reversal" as a situation where the current account deficit has declined by at least 3 percent of GDP in one year.[15] The data in this table show that the frequency of current account reversals has been similar in Panama, in all the emerging markets in the sample, and in the (rest of the) Latin American nations. The mean current account reversal has also been similar in Panama and the other Latin American nations—7.7 percent of GDP in Panama and 8.1 percent of GDP in Latin American Countries. Finally, terms-of-trade volatility has been somewhat lower in Panama than in the comparison groups.

Adjustment and Growth: Panama's Experience in a Comparative Perspective

In this subsection I use panel data for 1970–98 to investigate whether terms-of-trade shocks and current account reversals have been more "costly" in Panama than in other (nondollarized) countries. The starting point is the following growth equation:

$$[2] \quad \text{GROWTH}_{tj} = \beta \, \text{INVGDP}_{tj} + \varphi \, \text{EDU}_{tj} + \delta \, \text{GOVCONS}_{tj}$$
$$+ \, \phi \, \text{OPENNESS}_{tj} + \theta \, \text{LOGGDPO}_{j}$$
$$+ \, \gamma \, \text{REVERSAL}_{tj} + \lambda \, \text{LOGTOT}_{tj} + \xi_{tj}$$

where GROWTH_{tj} is growth of GDP per capita in country j during year t; INVGDP is the investment to GDP ratio; and EDU is a proxy for human capital, measured as secondary education attainement. GOVCONS is the ratio of government consumption to GDP, and OPENNESS is an index of the degree of openness (imports plus exports over GDP). REVERSAL is a variable that takes the value of one if the country in question has been subject to a current account reversal. LOGTOT is the log of the terms of trade. Finally, LOGGDPO_{j} is the initial level of GDP (1970) for country j. The main interest of this analysis is the coefficients of REVERSAL and LOGTOT. The coefficient of the former will be negative if reversals are costly; the coefficient of LOGTOT is expected to be positive. In order to analyze whether these coefficients are different for Panama, I also interacted LOGTOT and REVERSAL with a Panama dummy. The error ξ_{tj} is assumed to be heteroscedastic, with a different variance for each of the k countries (panels).

$$[3] \quad \text{E}[\xi\xi'] = \begin{pmatrix} \sigma_1^2 \, \mathbf{I} & 0 & \ldots & 0 \\ 0 & \sigma_2^2 \, \mathbf{I} & \ldots & 0 \\ . & . & . & . \\ . & . & . & . \\ . & . & . & . \\ 0 & 0 & \ldots & \sigma_k^2 \, \mathbf{I} \end{pmatrix}$$

Equation (2) was estimated using the feasible generalized least squares (FGLS) procedure suggested by Beck and Katz (1995) for unbalanced panels. The samples in the different estimations were determined by data availability. For details, see Edwards (2001a).

Since current account reversals are not drawn from a random experiment, the REVERSAL_{jt} dummy is possibly correlated with the error term. In order to deal with this problem I follow the procedure recently suggested by Heckman, Ichimura, and Todd (1997) for estimating "treatment interventions" models. This procedure consists of estimating the equation in question using observations that have a common support for both the treated and the nontreated samples. In the case at hand, countries that experience a reversal are considered to be subject to the "treatment intervention."[16]

In table 5.5 I present the results obtained from the estimation of various versions of equation (2), after making the correction suggested by Heckman, Ichimura, and Todd (1997). Estimates are presented for the complete panel, for the emerging countries only, and for the Latin American and Caribbean nations. The results for the complete panel (including Panama), reported in column 1, are highly satisfactory. All the coefficients have the expected signs and are significant at conventional levels. These results suggest that current account reversals are costly and de-accelerate the rate of growth in the country in question.[17] The coefficient of LOGTOT indicates that negative (positive) terms of trade shocks have a negative (positive) effect on growth. The results obtained when Panama interactive dummies are introduced are in columns 2–4. The coefficients for the Panama variable are always significant at conventional levels. According to the χ^2 tests, the hypothesis that the Panama coefficients are jointly zero is rejected. More important, Panama's terms-of-trade coefficient is significantly *positive*, and Panama's current account reversals coefficient is significantly *negative*. These results indicate that external shocks in the form of terms-of-trade disturbances and current account reversals have had larger (negative) effects on Panama than in nondollarized countries. This result holds independently of the group of nondollarized nations used as a comparison.[18]

In an effort to understand better the results reported in table 5.5, I used the estimation from the complete panel (including Panama) reported in column 1 to compute Panama's residuals. I then analyzed the value of

Table 5.5
Terms-of-Trade Volatility and Current Account Reversals: Panama's Experience in Comparative Perspective (1970–1998)

	Panama	All Countries	All Emerging Countries	Latin America and Caribbean
Variability of (log of) terms of trade	0.133	0.248	0.267	0.236
Incidence of CA reversals (% of years)	24.1	20.4	23.3	22.9
Average magnitude of CA reversals (% of GDP)	5.6	4.2	10.4	11.2

these residuals during the years when Panama experienced current account reversals and large negative terms-of-trade disturbances. By pursuing this strategy I was particularly interested in analyzing whether the results in table 5.5 were driven by the Noriega crisis years (1988–90). This exercise shows that the finding that external shocks have been particularly costly in Panama are not driven by the Noriega crisis years.

The results in table 5.6. have been obtained assuming that the other variables in equation (2) remain constant. In reality, however, other things do change. In particular, terms-of-trade shocks and current account reversals are likely to result in a decline in investment.[19] In Edwards (2001a) I use a dynamic panel to estimate investment equations, and I find that this is indeed the case. Moreover, according to these results, terms-of-trade shocks and current account reversals have had a greater (negative) effect on Panama's investment ratios than on nondollarized countries' investment. Overall, then, the results in table 5.6, as well as those on investment ratios, indicate that during the period under consideration external shocks have generated higher costs—in the form of lower investment and slower GDP growth—in dollarized Panama than in the nondollarized nations.

◤ Concluding Remarks

The purpose of this article has been to analyze the economic record of dollarized countries. In doing this I have made an effort to give dollarization the benefit of the doubt; when judgment calls had to be made, I deliberately tried to "favor" the dollarization position. For instance, I did not use the IMF's data on Liberia's GDP; I report extensive results for Panama, the best-performing dollarizer; and in many Panama calculations I excluded the Noriega crisis years. It should be emphasized once again, however, that because of serious data limitations, this study's conclusions should be interpreted with care. In some cases they are based on data for one or two countries only.

My main conclusion from this analysis is that the recent push for dollarization is a typical case of misleading advertisement. Most dollarization supporters have either ignored the record or have embellished it. The reality is that the historical record is very limited and concentrated on tiny countries. The largest one (Panama) has a population of less than three million people! As I wrote in the introduction, advocating dollarization is like recommending a new drug that has been subject to very limited clinical trials. Worse yet, the results of these trials are not particularly positive or encouraging, and they generate a number of serious questions. In terms of this medical analogy, a physician may still prescribe the untried drug to a terminally ill patient but would not prescribe it to a rather healthy individual who has access to other treatment options.

In a nutshell, the analysis reported here suggests that, when compared

Table 5.6
Growth and External Disturbances (Feasible Least Squares with Heteroskedastic Panels, 1970–1998)

Sample	All	All	Emerging Markets	LAC
INVGDP	0.171	0.169	0.207	0.174
	(11.89)	(11.80)	(11.51)	(4.24)
EDU	0.023	0.023	0.049	0.070
	(3.40)	(3.40)	(4.32)	(2.27)
GOVCON	−0.082	−0.081	−0.118	−0.150
	(−5.52)	(−5.45)	(−6.40)	(−2.74)
OPEN	0.005	0.005	−0.001	−0.017
	(2.13)	(2.07)	(−0.60)	(−1.28)
LOGGDPO	−0.146	−0.135	−0.382	−0.269
	(−1.22)	(−1.16)	(−2.05)	(−0.60)
REVERSAL	−1.085	−1.028	−0.602	−1.882
	(−4.69)	(−4.43)	(−2.15)	(−3.50)
REVERSAL$_{-1}$	−0.419	−0.372	−0.209	0.037
	(−1.82)	(−1.61)	(−0.75)	(0.07)
LOGTOT	0.996	0.986	0.717	0.906
	(2.27)	(2.25)	(1.44)	(1.03)
PANAMA* REVERSAL	—	−4.273	−4.606	−3.421
		(−1.99)	(−2.13)	(−1.75)
PANAMA* REVERSAL$_{-1}$	—	−3.910	−3.73	−4.396
		(−1.82)	(−1.73)	(−2.01)
PANAMA* LOGTOT	—	0.504	0.531	0.617
		(1.83)	(1.90)	(2.13)
Panels	88	88	68	21
No. of observations	1686	1686	1253	415
Log likelihood	−4501	−4497	−3558	−1166
χ^2	—	8.56	8.80	7.79
		(0.03)	(0.03)	(0.05)

Note: Assymptotic t-statistics in parentheses. Constants are not reported. The χ^2 statistic corresponds to the log-likelihood test for the joint exclusion of the variables interacting with the PANAMA dummy; the null hypothesis is rejected in all cases.

to other countries,*the dollarized nations (1) have grown at a significantly lower rate; (2) have had a similar fiscal record; (3) have not been spared from major current account reversals; and (4) have had significantly lower inflation. In addition, my analysis of Panama's case suggests that external shocks result in greater costs—in terms of lower investment and growth—in dollarized than in nondollarized countries.[20]

A particularly puzzling result is that dollarizers have not had a better fiscal performance than nondollarizers. How did they manage to be equally "irresponsible" on the fiscal side and yet maintain their monetary regime and have very low rates of inflation? The answer to this query comes in two parts. First, the record shows that not all the dollarized countries maintained the system. For instance, when the fiscal constraint became too tight, Liberia abandoned dollarization. It is true that this development took place in the midst of a civil conflict, but political upheaval is a reality of life among the poorer nations. Second, and as shown in the third section, Panama has been able to run large fiscal deficits by accumulating a large stock of debt—that it occasionally restructured—and by maintaining a very special relationship with the IMF. It is not obvious that the IMF will be so friendly to future dollarizers that do not have Panama's geopolitical importance.

It is important to clarify what this study does not say. It does not say that dollarization is a policy option that all emerging markets should avoid. It does say, however, that empirically we know very little about the costs and benefits of dollarization. It further says that when the limited record is investigated, it does not appear to be as positive as some analysts want us to believe. In that regard, the recent experiences of Ecuador and El Salvador should provide important information that will help us assess more fully the merits of dollarization in larger and somewhat more complex settings.

Overall, Mundell's (1961) OCAs analysis continues to be the right approach for dealing with the dollarization question. There are good reasons to think that countries that are highly integrated in terms of factor mobility and trade will benefit from having a common currency.[21] The benefits from such a policy could more than compensate for the costs, including the loss of seignorage if the country dollarizes unilaterally. Countries with a high degree of unofficial dollarization and foreign currency–denominated liabilities are also likely to benefit from dollarization. It is unlikely, however, that dollarization will be the most adequate option for all countries. Large countries that face volatile terms of trade, that are not deeply integrated to major economies, and whose financial sector operate mostly in terms of domestic currency are likely to incur net costs if they dollarize. They will have difficulties in accommodating external shocks while, as suggested by the results in this article, the alleged benefits in terms of low costs of capital, fiscal discipline, and stability may, indeed, continue to be elusive.

◣ Notes

I thank Igal Magendzo for his assistance. I have benefited from discussions with John Cochrane and Ed Leamer.

1. Sometimes this policy is called "official dollarization" as a way of distinguishing it from currency substitution, or "unofficial dollarization." See Savastano (1992).

2. Recent articles by Moreno-Villalaz (1999) and Bogetic (2000) discuss some im-

portant characteristics of dollarized economies. For a lucid conceptual treatment of dollarization see Calvo (1999). See also the useful piece by Schuler (2000). For a debate on the merits of dollarization, see Edwards and Hausmann (2001). Ricardo Hausmann, the former chief economist of the Interamerican Development Bank, has been a vocal supporter of dollarization. Interestingly, and in contrast with the case of dollarization, there are now a number of studies on currency boards. See, for example, Baliño, Enoch, Ize, Santiparbhob, and Stella (1997), Schuler (1992), and Ghosh, Gulde, and Wolf (2000).

3. The focus on independent nations raises the question of whether we should concentrate on the period since independence or on the complete period under analysis. The results reported in this article refer to countries that have been independent for at least five years. If, however, different criteria are used, the results obtained are very similar to those reported here.

4. By dollarized countries I mean countries that use another nation's currency. I have excluded countries that use a common supranational currency, such as the euro.

5. It is not easy to date unequivocally Liberia's abandonment of the dollarized system. In July 1974 the National Bank of Liberia (NBL) was opened. In 1982 the NBL began issuing five-dollar coins, and in 1989 it began issuing five-dollar notes. On Liberia's dollarization experience, see Barret (1995) and Berkeley (1993).

6. See Edwards (2001a) for a detailed discussion of the data available and of data sources.

7. There are 4,272 observations for GDP growth in all nonsuperfixed countries; 3,378 observations for emerging countries; 750 observations for Latin American countries; and 286 observations for dollarized countries. See Edwards (2001a) for more details on the data set.

8. The lack of data makes this exercise difficult, however: while there are 286 observations for growth in dollarized countries, there are only 56 for investment, 58 for openness, and 58 for government expenditure. In the estimation I used random effects and GLS methods.

9. The power of my nonparametric tests is reduced when the number of observations in the two groups are very different.

10. During some years Panama did not make actual withdrawals from the IMF funds. However, even during those years, the IMF had a fundamental role in overseeing the Panamanian economy.

11. Bogetic (2000), in an interesting article, incorrectly writes that in Panama "there have been no systematic banking crises" (p. 192).

12. According to Beim and Calomiris (2000) Panama also restructured its debt in 1932.

13. Bogetic (2000, p. 193) has claimed that "Panama's sovereign spreads have been consistently lower than in other Latin American countries." As figure 5.1 shows, this is not so. The spreads in figure 5.1 correspond to daily data for Panama's 8½ percent sovereign bond due in 2008, and Chile's 6⅞ percent sovereign bond due in 2009.

14. In 1999–2000 a bill that would have allowed for the sharing of seignorage was introduced to the U.S. Senate. Without support by Congress or the administration, however, the bill did not go anywhere.

15. When I used alternative definitions the results were similar to those reported here. On current account reversals, see Milesi-Ferreti and Razin (2000).

16. From a practical point of view, a two-step procedure is used. (1) The conditional

probability of countries facing a reversal—the *propensity score*—is first estimated using a probit regression. Equation (2) is estimated using only observations whose estimated probability of reversal falls within the interval of estimated probabilities for countries with actual reversals.

17. When the first differences of LOGTOT are introduced instead of the levels, the results are qualitatively similar.

18. The results in table 5.5. were obtained using a dummy variable for current account reversal. I also estimated the growth equations replacing REVERSAL with the reversals dummy interacted with the actual magnitude of the reversal. These results confirm those presented in table 5.5.

19. See Edwards (2001b).

20. In a recent article Levy-Yeyati and Sturzenegger (2001) find that countries with flexible exchange rate regimes have grown faster than countries with fixed exchange rates.

21. Recent interesting work by Frankel and Rose (2000) suggests that belonging to a monetary union increases a country's trade significantly. Whether this (potential) effect will be enough to offset the costs of dollarization is still an open question.

◣ References

Baliño, T. C, Enoch, A. Ize, V. Santiparbhob, and P. Stella. (1997). *Currency Board Arrangements.* IMF Occasional Paper No. 151. International Monetary Fund.

Barret, L. (1995). "The Economic Trials of Liberia." *West Africa,* 461–63.

Beck, N., and J. N. Katz. (1995). "What to Do (and Not to Do) with Time-Series Cross-Section Data." *American Political Science Review, 89* (3), 634–647.

Beim, D., and C. Calomiris. (2000). *Emerging Financial Markets.* McGraw-Hill.

Berkeley, B. (1993). "Liberia's Warring Currencies." *Institutional Investor.*

Bogetic, Z. (2000). "Official Dollarization: Current Experiences and Issues." *CATO Journal, 20*(2), 179–213.

Calvo, G. A. (1999). *On Dollarization.* Department of Economics, University of Maryland.

Dornbusch, R. (1980). *Open Economy Macroeconomics.* New York: Basic Books.

Edwards, S. (2001a). *Dollarization: Myths and Realities.* (NBER Working Paper). National Bureau of Economic Research.

Edwards, S. (2001b). Does the Current Account Matter? (NBER Working Paper). National Bureau of Economic Research.

Edwards, S., and R. Hausmann. (2001, February 7). "The Peg Rift on the Chair Lift." *JP Morgan's Emerging Markets Today.*

Frankel, J., and A. Rose. (2002, May). "An Estimate of the Effect of Common Currencies on Trade and Income." *Quarterly Journal of Economics 117*(2), 437–66.

Ghosh, A. T., A. M. Gulde, and H. C. Wolf. (2000). "Currency Boards: More Than a Quick Fix?" *Economic Policy, 31*(1), 269–321.

Heckman, J. J., H. Ichimura, and P. Todd. (1997). "Matching as an Econometric Evaluation Estimator: Evidence from Evaluating a Job Training Programme." *Review of Economic Studies, 64*(4), 605–54.

International Monetary Fund. (2000). IMF Approves Stand-by Credit for Panama. Press Release 00/39.

Levy-Yeyati, E., and F. Sturzenegger. (2001). To Float or to Trail: Evidence on the Impact of Exchange Rate Regimes. Universidad Torcuato di Tella, Buenos Aires.

Milesi-Ferretti, G., and A. Razin. (2000). "Current Account Reversals and Currency Crises: Empirical Regularities." In *Currency Crises,* edited by P. Krugman. Chicago: University of Chicago Press.

Moreno-Villalaz, J. L. (1999). "Lessons from the Monetary Experience of Panama: A Dollarized Economy with Financial Integration." *CATO Journal, 18*(3), 421–39.

Mundell, R. A. (1961). "A Theory of Optimum Currency Areas." *American Economic Review, 51,* 509–17.

Mussa, M., and M. A. Savastano. (2000). "The IMF Approach to Economic Stabilization. In *NBER Macroeconomics Annual 1999,* Ben S. Bernanke and Julio Rotemberg. Cambridge, Mass.: MIT Press.

Savastano, M. A. (1992). "The Pattern of Currency Substitution in Latin America: An Overview." *Revista de Analisis Economico, 7* (1), 37–48.

Schuler, K. (1992). *Currency Boards.* Ph.D. dissertation, George Mason University.

Schuler, K. 2000. *The Basics of Dollarization.* Joint Economic Committee Staff Report, U.S. Congress.

6   Barry Eichengreen

What Problems Can Dollarization Solve?

Those of us who are skeptical about the viability of intermediate exchange rate arrangements find ourselves tempted to climb aboard the dollarization bandwagon. I may be the most extreme and unreformed proponent in this room of the view that high capital mobility has made it exceedingly diffi-cult—and in any case undesirable—to operate pegged-but-adjustable exchange rates, target zones, crawling pegs, and other arrangements that specify explicit limits on how far the exchange rate can move but that do not entail the commitment of a currency board or dollarization. Interme-diate regimes are fragile. Operating them is tantamount to painting a bull's eye on the forehead of the central bank governor and telling speculators to "shoot here." History shows that intermediate regimes collapse sooner or later.[1] And when they do they heighten the severity of subsequent crisis, because the implicit ex ante insurance against exchange risk they provide encourages banks and corporates to accumulate unhedged exposures, height-ening financial dislocations when the denouement comes. For an exchange rate economist, this may be the most important lesson of the Asian crisis.[2]

It follows that only two alternatives remain: a more freely floating cur-rency, whose management does not involve an explicit range or target for the rate, or a hard peg in the form of a currency board or dollarization.[3]

Given that countries must move to these extremes, we can presumably invoke standard OCA considerations to determine who should float and who should dollarize. These criteria suggest that El Salvador is a candidate for dollarization: it is small, open, and tightly linked to the United States both commercially and financially. Brazil should float because it is larger and more open and because its trade and finances are more diversified. Argentina is a disputed case because it is in the middle: it is neither as small as El Salvador nor as large as Brazil. This is how authors like John Wil-liamson (2000) see the cases for and against dollarization.[4]

In fact, this approach is almost completely orthogonal to the issues at the heart of the dollarization debate. That debate is about financial stability and whether dollarization is a means of enhancing it. It is about fiscal stability and whether budget balance is easier to attain after dollarization. It is about economic reform and whether dollarization is an effective means of encouraging it. These are issues about which the theory of optimum currency areas has little to say.

To be clear, I am not asking whether reforms of the banking sector, the financial sector, the fiscal accounts, and the labor market are prerequisites for dollarization. While there is a large literature on this subject, the question it addresses is analytically distinct.[5] My own reading is that this debate is over. There is by now an overwhelming body of evidence that countries can effectively solve the exchange rate problem—that is to say, they can effectively eliminate exchange rate instability—by dollarizing or installing a currency board without first having to satisfy a long list of economic preconditions like strengthening their banking systems, balancing their budgets, funding their public debts, and removing labor market rigidities. The economies that have dollarized or adopted currency boards in the last decade—from Ecuador to Estonia, from Bulgaria to El Salvador—have done so without first eliminating these problems. Indeed, countries like Ecuador and Argentina have dollarized or installed currency boards not because they succeeded in pushing through other reforms but precisely because their economic and financial problems have proven so intractable. They have done so precisely in order to prevent those problems from spilling over into the currency market. And the fact that dollarization and currency boards, once adopted, have stuck confirms that this is a perfectly feasible way of insulating the currency market from these other problems. My reading of the scholarly discourse is that the economics profession is now in broad agreement with this view.

But, to repeat, this is not the question I am asking. I am not challenging the now conventional wisdom that dollarization is feasible prior to economic reform. Rather, I am asking whether dollarization is more likely to speed or slow economic and financial reform generally. This is what we should care about. Countries with screwed-up banking systems, budgets, and labor markets will perform miserably when the exchange rate is collapsing and inflation is running out of control, but they will perform just as miserably if the national currency is replaced by the dollar and these other problems remain unsolved. Their economic performance will be dismal whether they use someone else's currency or their own. Is dollarization the answer? It is if and only if it delivers solutions to these other problems.

What do we know about the effect of dollarization on the pace of fiscal, financial, and labor-market reform? While there exist a few theoretical models linking the exchange rate regime to fiscal, financial, and labor-market outcomes, and while we use evidence from countries with pegged and floating rates to argue by analogy, the honest answer is "not much."

◣ *Financial Sector Reform*

There are two versions of the argument that dollarization will encourage reform of the banking system. One is that by constraining the ability of the monetary authority (and perhaps also the fiscal authorities) to lend in the last resort, dollarization will compel bank owner-managers to acknowledge that they are no longer protected by the financial safety net. The realization that the authorities regard them as too big and important to fail encourages banks to engage in imprudent behavior, and only a hard constraint on the ability of the central bank to aid ailing banks by injecting domestic credit into the financial system can compel them to shape up. This is how some advocates of dollarization interpret Turkey's crisis: Turkish banks were encouraged to take short-term open foreign currency positions, exposing them to excessive and ultimately unmanageable exchange risk, by the knowledge that the Turkish central bank was operating a soft peg, which could be let go if it became necessary to bail out the banking system. Dollarization would have been a better alternative for the country.[6]

But if it is implicit ex ante insurance against exchange risk (that is, the government's promise that the exchange rate will not be allowed to change unexpectedly) that encourages the accumulation of unhedged foreign-currency exposures, then greater exchange rate flexibility can be as effective as dollarization in discouraging this form of excessive risk taking.[7] Dollarization may be a solution, but so too may greater exchange rate flexibility. Which currency regime is more conducive to reform—dollarization or floating—depends on which form of moral hazard—the financial safety net or the exchange rate guarantee—is more serious.

Ultimately, this issue can only be resolved empirically. I have examined it by extending a model of banking crises estimated previously in joint work with Andy Rose.[8] I find that it is intermediate exchange rate regimes (neither hard pegs nor floats) that are most strongly associated with crises; this is support for the view that these encourage the accumulation of unhedged foreign exposures that cause financial distress when the exchange rate regime is placed at risk. When I distinguish currency boards and dollarized economies from other fixed rate arrangements, it turns out that the hard pegs are associated with an unusually great incidence of banking crises. I hesitate to interpret this as suggesting that currency boards and dollarization undermine financial stability, given the small number of observations we have for currency board and dollarized economies and the possibility of reverse causality.[9] But these results shift the burden of proof.

The other argument, prominently associated with Ricardo Hausmann, is that dollarization enhances financial stability not by discouraging excessive risk taking but by promoting the development of domestic financial markets.[10] The prevalence of currency and maturity mismatches in emerging financial markets, and the consequent fragility of the latter, reflect distrust of the national currency. Banks and firms funding themselves abroad are unable to borrow in the domestic currency. Since this leaves them saddled with mismatched dollar liabilities and domestic-currency-denominated assets, they get smashed whenever the currency depreciates. And so long as currency depreciation remains a possibility, foreigners will be reluctant to lend and domestics to borrow, given the danger of bankruptcy and default. The domestic financial system will remain shallow and crisis-prone.

Similarly, where there is a legacy of distrust in the currency, firms with long-term investment projects will be unable to fund them using long-term loans. Domestic intermediation will be skewed to the short end, saddling balance sheets with maturity mismatches. If the exchange rate is attacked, requiring the authorities to raise short-term interest rates, debt-servicing costs will rise relative to revenues, creating the danger of cascading bankruptcies. Given these dangers, the level of intermediation will be less. Again, the financial system will be narrow, fragile, and likely to require lending in the last resort.

Eliminating the domestic currency solves these problems in a stroke. Currency risk disappears, making it easier for firms with long-term projects to borrow long term at home as well as abroad. (It is assumed, in other words, that it was currency risk that previously impeded the emergence of a long-term market.) Currency mismatches having been eliminated and maturity mismatches having been attenuated, the main threats to banking stability will be removed.

The dramatic impact of European monetary unification on the growth and development of European financial markets is supportive of this view. By eliminating Europe's second-tier currencies and generating economies of scale and scope, the EMU has led to a dramatic rise in the liquidity of European financial markets. It has allowed European corporations to fund long-term investment projects by floating long-term loans to a much greater extent than was possible so long as each of the members of the monetary union issued its own national currency.[11] Recent work by Hausmann et al. (2000) suggests more generally that countries with pegged exchange rates are able to issue more of their external debt long term and denominate more of their debt in the domestic currency.

There are reasons to pause before accepting these findings. These are inconsistent with the large literature on financial deepening, in which it is not the exchange rate regime per se that is associated with financial deepening but whether inflation and currency depreciation are rapid, uncertain, and disruptive.[12] For countries like Canada and Australia, floating and deep domestic financial markets are entirely compatible. Only if one believes that stable floating is an oxymoron is the case for dollarization strong.

◣ *Fiscal Reform*

Similarly, there are two arguments that dollarization will produce quick consolidation of the public finances. First, by eliminating inflation dollarization will bring interest rates down to world levels, reducing debt-servicing costs. Second, by removing the inflation tax as a revenue source of last resort, it will force governments to live within their means.

It is of course the second mechanism that is key. The way to understand it is in terms of Sargent and Wallace's game of "chicken" (Sargent, 1986).[13]

The central bank asserts that it will not engage in inflationary monetization under any circumstances in the hope of forcing the fiscal authorities to reduce the budget deficit. The fiscal authorities counter that they will not reduce the budget deficit under any circumstances, hoping to induce the central bank to monetize the excess to prevent a steep rise in interest rates, a debt default, or some other unacceptable consequence. If the monetary authority retains the option of backing down and monetizing, then the fiscal authority may prevail. But if the commitment not to monetize is fully credible, as it will be if the economy is dollarized, then the fiscal authority, if it regards the costs of default as prohibitive, will back down. Fiscal consolidation will result.

But, in most countries, fiscal policy is not made by a single centralized authority. Municipal, state, and central fiscal authorities have to agree on how to share the cuts. Introduce a little bit of uncertainty into the model (for example, uncertainty about the discount rates of the different fiscal authorities, as in Alesina and Drazen's model [1991] of the war of attrition), and eliminating the inflation tax could precipitate debt default rather than fiscal consolidation, leaving the country worse rather than better off, under the assumption that default is more costly than inflation.[14] This suggests that dollarization makes the most sense in countries where the fisc is centralized or there exist mechanisms for assuring coordination among the various fiscal authorities.[15]

European experience is consistent with this view. The fear that fiscal profligacy could precipitate debt-servicing difficulties with serious cross-border repercussions in a fiscally decentralized Europe explains why the Maastricht Treaty features a set of procedures designed to avert excessive debts and deficits along with penalties for countries failing to comply. Even a European Central Bank firmly committed to price stability may be tempted to renege on that commitment if faced with a fiscally induced financial crisis. The Maastricht Treaty and the Stability Pact negotiated subsequently are designed to limit this danger.[16]

▶ *Labor Market Reform*

The intuition for the belief that dollarization will hasten labor market reform is as follows. Unions negotiate a path for nominal wages extending into the future. The authorities can then use monetary policy to partially offset any resulting unemployment. Unions will be aware of the ability of the monetary authorities to respond in this way and have an incentive to anticipate that response when negotiating wages; this will partly limit the capacity of an inflation-averse monetary authority to respond to unemployment with expansionary monetary policy. But only partly: under discretionary monetary policy there will be a lower variance of unemployment, as well as a higher average rate of inflation.[17] Hardening the exchange rate constraint thus will increase the variability of unemployment, other things being equal. If unions regard more variable unemployment unfavorably, dollarization will provide additional incentive for reform.

Or will it? Drawing on work by Lars Calmfors, I have analyzed the consequences of extending the Barro-Gordon model to include in the government's loss function not just inflation and unemployment but also the amount of (costly) labor market reform, where equilibrium unemployment is declining in the level of reform.[18] In the standard one-shot game, there is an optimal amount of labor-market reform whose costs are just matched by the benefits in terms of the reduction in equilibrium unemployment (and hence expected unemployment) plus the benefits of the reduction in inflation (because lower equilibrium unemployment reduces inflationary bias). With dollarization, labor market reform no longer results in a lower average rate of inflation. Hence labor market reform following dollarization is less, not more. Other results can be obtained by modifying the specification slightly. But this result should disturb the advocates of dollarization.

What about the evidence? Observers of Argentine convertibility will be skeptical that a hard exchange rate constraint accelerates the process of labor market reform. But perhaps Argentina has not seen more labor market reform because convertibility remains less than credible. This is why it is argued that it is necessary to take the additional step of dollarizing. This makes it useful to also consider Europe, where the commitment to exchange rate stability is long-standing and monetary union is essentially irreversible. As in Argentina, there is some evidence of reform, and unemployment is beginning to come down. The question, though, is whether this is a cyclical or a structural phenomenon. It is suggestive that some of the countries undertaking the most extensive reforms—the Netherlands, for example— have also had the longest hard exchange rate commitment. But there are also counterexamples—countries like the United Kingdom, which have neither participated in the ERM for any period of time nor committed to the monetary union, where labor markets have been rendered significantly more flexible since the late 1970s. If one constructs an index of the extent of labor market reform from the reforms tabulated by the OECD (1999), then a simple t-test for differences suggests no difference in the extent of reform between countries with or without hard exchange rate constraint.

What are the implications for dollarization? Theory cannot tell us whether dollarization will speed or slow labor market reform. There are conditions under which reform of the labor market will accelerate, and many people's intuition will tell them that these are the plausible conditions. There is some anecdotal evidence that a hardening exchange rate commitment and monetary union are encouraging efficiency-enhancing reforms in Argentina and Europe, but systematic analysis suggests that reform remains partial and incomplete.

What lessons can we draw from this discussion? Let me suggest four.

- The first lesson is humbling for an exchange rate economist. In our preoccupation with the exchange rate, we pay too much attention to the choice between pegging and floating and between retaining the national currency versus adopting that of someone else. It is not the color of the currency in one's wallet but the level of living standards and the rate of economic growth that we should care about. The literature on the link between the exchange rate regime and economic growth is inconclusive; one can find in it an almost uniform distribution of significant and insignificant results. But even those studies that conclude in favor of a positive link acknowledge that the effect is small.[19] Other variables, be they the development of markets and institutions or the accumulation of human capital, are more important determinants of economic growth. We are interested in the exchange rate regime and alternatives like dollarization only insofar as there is a plausible case that they can play a role in putting in place these fundamental prerequisites for growth. But the fact that countries have succeeded in sustaining growth under a variety of exchange rate regimes and currency arrangements suggests that, for those interested in the mainsprings of growth, this is not the first place to look for such prerequisites.
- Second, since the exchange rate is a financial variable, the most plausible link is between dollarization and the development of financial markets. Thus, I find quite provocative recent work suggesting that countries that peg their exchange rates have deeper and more liquid financial markets.[20] But I am not sure whether the association between financial development and currency stability reflects the causal impact of the latter on the former or simply the ability of some governments to make credible commitment—in other words, it may reflect an omitted factor that creates a spurious correlation between the two variables of interest. I regard this as an important issue for research.
- Third, the key issue for crisis countries is whether dollarization will accelerate or retard economic reform. If dollarization accelerates fiscal, financial, and labor market reform, then it is a way out of the crisis. If it slows reform, then it is part of the problem, not part of the solution. And if it has no first-order effect on the pace of reform, then it is largely irrelevant.
- Fourth and finally, these are issues on which theory provides little guidance. Results from analytical models of whether reform is more or less likely under a particular currency and exchange rate regime are sensitive to small changes in specification. As usual, it is possible for clever theorists to build models that point in both directions. What is

needed is systematic empirical work on the links from the exchange rate regime to the pace, scope, and credibility of economic reform. Until we have it, we will be unable to say with confidence whether dollarization is a good or bad idea.

▲ Notes

Prepared for an ASSA panel on dollarization chaired by Dominick Salvatore, and forthcoming in *Journal of Policy Modeling*. This chapter draws on my article "When to Dollarize," forthcoming in *Journal of Money, Credit and Banking*.

1. As documented by the work of Klein and Marion (1997).
2. See for example Goldstein's (1998) analysis of the problem.
3. The conclusion that they should exhibit zeal for the extremes applies to countries that are integrated into international financial markets; for those prepared to retain capital controls, other (intermediate) arrangements are of course possible. To be clear, the implication is not that countries are left with the options of floating freely versus dollarizing but that intervention should not be framed as an explicit target for the exchange rate. Such targets set the authorities up as sitting ducks for speculators, and they encourage the misapprehension on the part of banks and corporates that they will be protected against exchange rate movements, encouraging the accumulation of unhedged exposures. The greater uncertainty created by the absence of explicit ex ante limits on how far the exchange rate is allowed to move is better from these points of view both because it creates more of a two-way bet for speculators and because it provides a continuous reminder to banks and corporates that they should take exchange risk into account when formulating their financial plans. Guillermo Calvo and Carmen Reinhart (2000) have provided convincing evidence that many emerging markets which have abandoned official exchange rate targeting regimes continue to intervene in the foreign exchange market to limit currency movements. But precisely because that intervention is not framed in terms of an explicit exchange rate target, their observation is by no means inconsistent with my view.
4. It is ironic that Williamson is himself the leading defender of the view that intermediate exchange rate arrangements are still viable, which from this point of view makes the issue of dollarization less pressing.
5. See for example Hanke (2000b).
6. See Hanke (2000a,b) on the Turkish case. More generally, George Kaufman (1996) has noted the tendency for U.S. banks to hold larger amounts of capital and liquidity prior to the inauguration of the financial safety net. Gary Gorton (1984) similarly emphasizes the greater tendency for banks to engage in peer monitoring, thereby limiting the moral hazard from mutual assistance, prior to the founding of the Fed.
7. Burnside, Eichenbaum, and Rebello (1999) model the determinants of open foreign-currency positions and their dependence on the exchange rate regime.
8. See Eichengreen and Rose (1998). The results I discuss here are reported in full in Eichengreen (2002).
9. The fact that I lag the exchange rate/currency regime in my banking crisis equations reduces the danger of reverse causality, but there is still the possibility that what

we are observing in the data is the tendency for countries with chronic financial problems to opt for a currency board or to dollarize.

10. See for example Hausmann (1999).

11. A thorough analysis of these effects can be found in Danthine, Giavazzi, and von Thaden (2000).

12. I return to this point later.

13. This is of course a familiar scenario from the literature on European monetary unification; see Buiter and Kletzer (1990), on which I draw.

14. See Alesina and Drazen (1991).

15. Elsewhere, I have adapted Tornell and Velasco's (1995, 1998) model of exchange rate policy and fiscal consolidation to analyze this problem. This model lays bare the assumptions behind the premise that dollarization encourages fiscal consolidation. This result rests on the assumption that dollarization is more credible and permanent than a simple exchange rate peg. Because the fiscal authority in a dollarized economy knows that there is no prospect of additional inflationary finance, not just now but also in the future (this is where the greater permanence of this monetary regime comes in), it has a stronger incentive to cut spending now and to more efficiently distribute it across periods. Eliminating the inflation tax will require other taxes to be increased, *ceteris paribus.* If distortions are increasing in the level of taxation, then this will strengthen the incentive to cut spending now as a way of balancing the budget. However, this result also rests on the assumption of no Ponzi finance—that the government is not permitted to default on its debt. If it is assumed that politicians have to live within their means—that the intertemporal budget constraint holds—then of course the model will deliver the result that eliminating the inflation tax once and for all produces an intertemporally balanced budget. Similarly, if politicians still derive private benefits from additional government outlays and have a higher discount rate than other agents (for example, because they may no longer be in office in future periods), they will still be tempted to undertake excess spending now and let someone else deal with the consequences later. How their successors will then deal with those consequences is unclear. To be sure, if the costs of default are even higher than the costs of inflation, then dollarization will increase the pressure for higher taxes and spending cuts to deal with the consequences down the road. But if the parties involved are not willing collectively to bear the burden, the result could be a messy and costly default rather than the hoped-for fiscal consolidation.

16. A Latin American dollarizer that experienced a debt crisis would probably be left by the Fed to stew in its own juices; a dollar bloc would lack the political solidarity that could impel the European Central Bank to run to rescue a European country in this plight. A crisis that led to an inflationary debt bailout in Europe would instead precipitate a default in Latin America. Hence the United States would not demand Maastricht-like provisions of a Mexico or Argentina that chose to dollarize unilaterally. The reason, however, would not be because dollarization removes the danger of default. It does not.

17. This is the prediction of the Barro-Gordon model.

18. See Calmfors (1998).

19. A notable exception is Frankel and Rose (2000). Because these authors find a very large effect of a common currency on the volume of trade, even a moderate positive impact of trade on growth means that dollarizing will have an economically significant impact on living standards in the medium term. But I for one remain unconvinced that

their dummy variable for countries sharing a currency is really picking up the effect of currency unification on trade, as distinct from the effects of other economic, social, military, and political links that encourage countries to adopt the same currency but also lead them to engage in additional trade. The point applies equally to the EU (where currency unification is part of a larger economic and political bargain stretching back over a period of decades) and trade between the major powers and the microstates that use their currencies, the two of which account for the bulk of common currency cases in the Frankel-Rose data set.

20. See Hausmann et al. (2000) and Levine and Carkovic (1999). Note that Hausmann et al. and Levine and Carkovic advance rather different interpretations of the link from the exchange rate to growth. Hausmann et al. argue that it is the stability of the exchange rate per se that is conducive to financial deepening and development. Levine and Carkovic find no evidence that the volatility of the exchange rate is related to development, financial or otherwise. But they do confirm the findings of other work to the effect that the rate of inflation is positively associated with financial development. And the rate of inflation is presumably something that an inflation-prone country can affect by adopting the currency of a neighbor more deeply committed to price stability.

► References

Alesina, Alberto, and Allan Drazen (1991). Why Are Stabilizations Delayed? *American Economic Review, 81,* 1170–88.

Burnside, Craig, Martin Eichenbaum, and Sergio Rebello. (1999, May). *Hedging and Financial Fragility in Fixed Exchange Rate Regimes.* (NBER Working Paper No. 7143). National Bureau of Economic Research.

Buiter, Willem, and Kenneth Kletzer. (1990, May). *Reflections on the Fiscal Implications of a Common Currency.* (Centre for Economic Policy Research [CEPR] Discussion Paper No. 418).

Calmfors, Lars. (1998). *Unemployment, Labour-Market Reform, and Monetary Policy.* Unpublished manuscript. Institute for International Economic Studies, Stockholm University.

Calvo, Guillermo, and Carmen Reinhart. (2000, November). *Fear of Floating.* (NBER Working Paper No. 7993). National Bureau of Economic Research.

Danthine, Jean-Pierre, Francisco Giavazzi, and Ernst-Ludwig von Thaden. (2000, December). *European Financial Markets after EMU: A First Assessment.* (NBER Working Paper No. 8044). National Bureau of Economic Research.

Eichengreen, Barry. (2002). When to Dollarize. *Journal of Money, Credit and Banking, 34.*

Eichengreen, Barry, and Andrew Rose. (1998, January). *Staying Afloat When the Wind Shifts: External Factors and Emerging-Market Banking Crises.* (NBER Working Paper No. 6370). National Bureau of Economic Research.

Frankel, Jeffrey A., and Andrew K. Rose. (2000, August). *Estimating the Effect of Currency Unions on Trade and Output.* (NBER Working Paper No. 7857). National Bureau of Economic Research.

Goldstein, Morris. (1998). *The Asian Financial Crisis.* Washington, D.C.: Institute for International Economics.

Gorton, Gary B. (1984). Private Clearinghouses and the Origins of Central Banking. *Business Review of the Federal Reserve Bank of Atlanta, 79,* 3–12.

Hanke, Steve H. (2000a). The Disregard for Currency Board Realities. *Cato Journal, 20,* 49–59.

Hanke, Steve H. (2000b, 12 December). How to Forestall International Rescue: Currency Boards in Turkey and Argentina Could Have Saved the IMF from Having to Bail Them Out Again. *Financial Times,* p. 15.

Hanke, Steve H. (2000c, 19 December). Letter to the Editor. *Financial Times,* p. 14.

Hausmann, Ricardo. (1999). Should There Be Five Currencies or One Hundred and Five? *Foreign Policy, 116,* 65–79.

Hausmann, Ricardo, Michael Gavin, Carmen Pages-Serra, and Ernesto Stein. (2000). *Financial Turmoil and the Choice of Exchange Rate Regime.* Unpublished manuscript. Inter-American Development Bank.

Kaufman, George G. (1996, September). *Bank Fragility: Perception and Historical Evidence.* (Issues in Financial Regulation Working Paper 96–18). Federal Reserve Bank of Chicago.

Klein, Michael, and Nancy Marion. (1997). Explaining the Duration of Exchange Rate Pegs. *Journal of Development Economics, 54,* 387–404.

Levine, Ross, and Maria Carkovic. (1999). *How Much Bang for the Buck? Mexico and Dollarization.* Unpublished manuscript. University of Minnesota.

Organisation for Economic Cooperation and Development. (1999). *Implementing the OECD Jobs Strategy: Assessing Performance and Policy.* Paris: Author.

Sargent, Thomas. (1986). *Rational Expectations and Inflation.* New York: Harper and Row.

Tornell, Aaron, and Andres Velasco. (1995). Fiscal Discipline and the Choice of Exchange Rate Regime. *European Economic Review, 39,* 759–70.

Tornell, Aaron, and Andres Velasco. (1998). Fiscal Discipline and the Choice of a Nominal Anchor in Stabilization. *Journal of International Economics, 46,* 1–30.

Williamson, John. (2000). *Dollarization Does Not Make Sense Everywhere.* Revised outline of remarks delivered to the North-South Institute, Ottawa, Canada. Available online at www.iie.comz/testimony/jwdollar.htm.

7 Kurt Schuler

What Use Is Monetary Sovereignty?

A key issue in recent debates about official dollarization, currency boards, and monetary unions is monetary sovereignty. A frequent objection to replacing a national central bank with any of these rival monetary systems is that doing so would reduce national monetary sovereignty and, by extension, national political sovereignty. Surprisingly, though, the idea of monetary sovereignty has rarely received careful examination. The great majority of writers who invoke it simply assume it is desirable. For example, in a discussion of exchange rate policies, the Nobel Prize–winning economist James Tobin (1998, p. 7) remarks that "while globalization of financial markets . . . has contributed importantly to the economic progress of developing and emerging economies and can continue to do so, these trends also threaten the monetary sovereignty of those countries." Tobin and others never define what they mean by monetary sovereignty, nor do they examine the possibility that for many countries, less monetary sovereignty may bring more economic progress.

▶ *What People Mean by "Monetary Sovereignty"*

The idea of monetary sovereignty involves elements of economics, law, and politics. Perhaps because of the difficulties of untangling the elements, those who discuss monetary sovereignty almost never define it explicitly, though they often talk around the subject informatively. A number of books and essays by economists containing the phrase "monetary sovereignty" in their titles never define it (including Aliber, 1968; Clark and Grubel, 1972; Goodman, 1992). Nor do legal scholars who discuss the scope of the sovereign's power over the monetary systems (Mann, 1992, pp. 461–78; Nussbaum, 1939, pp. 23–36). Nor do political scientists (though Kirshner [1995, p. 8] and Cohen [1998, p. 17] hint at definitions). Writings that use terms that might be considered synonyms for monetary sovereignty, such as "monetary autonomy" and "monetary policy independence," are generally not relevant. They focus on aspects of the debate over fixed versus floating exchange rates or the degree to which central banks are insulated from political pressures—issues that are only peripheral to discussion of monetary sovereignty.

My wide-ranging though not exhaustive search for discussions of monetary sovereignty found only four authors who have defined what they mean by monetary sovereignty. The American economist Kenneth Kurihara (1949, p. 165) wrote: *"Monetary sovereignty is an attempt to insulate the domestic economy from the adverse repercussions of a depression elsewhere."*[1] Kurihara's definition was suited to his specific purpose—a review of national monetary policies and international monetary cooperation from the 1920s to the 1940s—but it seems too narrow to be a general definition. People think of monetary sovereignty as having economic and political benefits outside of periods of depression. The Dutch lawyer and government official Rutsel Martha (1993, p. 752) gives a broader definition:

> Monetary sovereignty refers to a State's undeniable power, recognized by international law, to regulate its own currency, i.e. the power to issue or designate money with legal tender character, to impose exchange control and exchange restrictions and to select the mechanisms through which the internal and external value of the money is determined and maintained.

The Yugoslav economist and government official Dorde Dukic (1995, p. 226) similarly writes:

> Monetary sovereignty in its contemporary sense signifies a sovereign right of a state to regulate all matters dealing with money issue and the conduct of monetary policy by the central bank with the purpose of achieving the projected economic policy targets.

Finally, the Nobel Prize–winning Canadian economist Robert Mundell (1997, p. 14) says:

> Monetary sovereignty can be broken into three parts: (a) the right to determine what constitutes the unit of account—the commodity or token in which price lists are specified; (b) the right to determine the means of payment—legal tender for purposes of the discharge of debt; and (c) the right to produce money—or else determine the conditions under which it is produced by others.

These last three definitions capture what most people seem to mean by monetary sovereignty. Important elements of the definitions are as follows.

Monetary sovereignty is a legitimate exercise of authority by the national government, not an illegitimate exercise of raw power that must merely be endured. Monetary sovereignty is recognized as legitimate internally and externally. If people thought of a national currency as a matter of indifference or as illegitimate, losing monetary sovereignty would not be controversial.

Monetary sovereignty belongs with the national government rather than any higher or lower level of government, or any body other than government. (Benjamin Cohen [1998, pp. 27–34] discusses the origins of this idea, which he calls the "One Nation/One Money myth.") The national government has for a few centuries been and is still the most important source of political power. Subnational governments derive their powers from national governments, while international arrangements exist by the consent of the national governments involved. One reason for the primacy of national governments is precisely that they have monopolized the power to issue currencies.

People think of monetary sovereignty as resting with national governments rather than individuals. According to this viewpoint, which is well entrenched in national and international law, individuals have no particular rights in the sphere of money that they can assert to block the government's pursuit of its goals. For example, freedom in foreign exchange dealings may be desirable, but it is not a right comparable to the right to freedom of religion or freedom of the press. Assets denominated in national currency are in some sense government property, not entirely the property of individuals. Devaluation, exchange controls, and other measures that impose losses on people who hold assets in or are paid in the national currency may be undesirable to many citizens, but they are within the rightful power of the national government (Mann, 1992, pp. 461–78).

People usually think of a national central bank as embodying monetary sovereignty in the highest degree, because a central bank has more room for discretionary monetary policy than, say, a currency board. Proposals for replacing central banks with currency boards have been characterized as reducing monetary sovereignty even though they would leave national currencies intact (Williamson, 1995, p. 42). So monetary sovereignty involves more than just having a separate national currency; it involves exercising, or at least being able to exercise, a discretionary monetary policy independently of other nations.

Many people also think of a floating exchange rate as embodying monetary sovereignty to a higher degree than a pegged or fixed exchange rate, and they consider that international monetary agreements such as the Bretton Woods system reduce monetary sovereignty by restricting freedom of action in monetary policy. Carried to an extreme, this line of thought suggests that any rules for monetary policy infringe on monetary sovereignty. However, few people go so far; most are willing to distinguish between externally imposed rules and self-imposed rules. Municipal governments lack monetary sovereignty because of externally imposed rules: their national governments prevent them from issuing currency. International agreements entered into without coercion, in contrast, are self-imposed rules that nations agree to impose on themselves presumably to promote national interests more effectively within an international framework. Self-imposed rules do not necessarily reduce monetary sovereignty, particularly if a nation can exit from them at relatively low cost.

A nation always retains the legitimate right to change its monetary arrangements in whatever fashion its government sees fit. Monetary sovereignty trumps all appeals to long-established custom. Thus if the United States were to prohibit private ownership of gold, which was legal until 1933 and has been legal again since the end of 1974, it would be a perfectly legitimate exercise of monetary sovereignty.

Even under official dollarization, where a nation dispenses with locally issued currency and uses foreign currency instead, it retains the ability to reintroduce a national currency. As a practical matter, a truly irrevocable surrender of monetary sovereignty is almost impossible for a nation: a nation can break even a monetary arrangement established by an international treaty, though the cost may be high. The charter of the European Central Bank contains no provision for nations that wish to quit, but observers have been aware from the beginning that what the member nations have formed, they can dissolve. One of the characteristics of a sovereign nation is that even when it yields considerable monetary sovereignty by acts of self-limitation, it retains the potential to abrogate those acts and reassert monetary sovereignty to the fullest extent.

External circumstances can limit the effective degree of monetary sovereignty. External circumstances, particularly the state of technology, impose some limits to the practical freedom of action of national governments in monetary policy. Large countries are usually considered to have more freedom of action in monetary policy than small countries have because they tend to be more self-sufficient; the exchange rate tends to be correspondingly less significant in the economic decisions of the private sector and the government, and a wider range of economic policies is thought to be feasible without harming economic growth.

▲ *The Purpose of Monetary Sovereignty*

What benefits does a country supposedly receive from exercising monetary sovereignty? Because most people consider a strictly national currency issued by a national central bank to be the monetary arrangement with the highest potential for monetary sovereignty, I will concentrate on it. People typically think of a multinational central bank as allowing less scope for monetary sovereignty than a national central bank, an orthodox currency board still less scope, and official dollarization almost no scope.

One benefit of monetary sovereignty is the potential for policy independence. A national central bank gives a country the widest range of choice about what type of monetary policy to have. A central bank can practice a wide range of policies: it can target the exchange rate or the money supply or interest rates, and it can impose exchange controls or not. Not all of these policies are mutually compatible, but a central bank can switch from one combination of policies to another if necessary. In contrast, an orthodox currency board or official dollarization commit a country to a single, well-defined monetary policy: a fixed exchange rate, full convertibility into the anchor currency, and no attempt to target the money supply or interest rates.

Another benefit of monetary sovereignty is that it generates seigniorage revenue from issuing the monetary base. Arrangements for sharing seigniorage across national borders exist (Bogetic, 2000), but they involve international agreements that limit the potential for policy independence. With a national central bank, the national government has the ability to change the rate of inflation and thus the amount of seigniorage collected, whereas without a national central bank somebody outside the country decides on the policies that determine what the rate of inflation will be. Inflation can be considered a kind of tax. It also affects other taxes, especially if they are not indexed. The mixture of taxes that is most appropriate varies from country to country, and in some countries the inflation tax may be the easiest tax to collect (Cooper, 1991, pp. 49, 55–56). A national central bank supposedly allows a country the greatest freedom to design the optimal tax policy. The flexibility that a national central bank allows may be especially important in wartime. As John Maynard Keynes (1971 [1923], p. 37) wrote of seigniorage, "a government can live by this means when it can live by no other."

A national central bank can act as a lender of last resort to commercial banks. In other monetary systems it is possible to establish deposit insurance funds or other arrangements to lend to banks in times of trouble, but a national central bank has the greatest flexibility because it can print money to cover the domestic currency debts of commercial banks.

Finally, a national currency can be an expression of national identity and national pride. A currency, like a language, flag, and government, can foster the cohesion among a group of people that melds them into a nation. A national currency is both a symbol and a tool of national identity (Cohen, 2000).

The Scope for Monetary Sovereignty

It is often thought that a floating exchange rate allows more monetary sovereignty than a rigid exchange rate. However, experience indicates that monetary policy can have wide freedom of action even in a country with a highly rigid exchange rate. Exchange controls can create barriers that prevent arbitrage with the rest of the world. The more effectively the controls can be enforced, the more they separate the national economy from world financial markets. A pertinent recent example is China, which has run a highly independent monetary policy even though the yuan is pegged to the U.S. dollar. China used exchange controls to prevent the yuan from being devalued against the dollar during the Asian currency crisis of 1997–98.

What about the extreme case of a rigid exchange rate, official dollarization? The case of Panama in 1988–89 is sometimes cited as an example of the perils of lack of monetary sovereignty (Kirshner, 1995, pp. 159–65).

The United States imposed trade sanctions, stopped passing along revenue from the Panama Canal, froze Panamanian bank deposits in the United States, and ceased shipping U.S. currency to Panama. Panama's economy suffered a severe recession, and a shortage of currency occurred. However, Panama was vulnerable to U.S. pressure not because of dollarization but because of the importance of the U.S.-controlled Canal Zone, which would have affected it no matter what monetary system it had. Panama potentially had considerable freedom of action despite being dollarized. It could have avoided the freeze on bank deposits by holding them in an offshore financial center such as the Bahamas. It could have avoided the shortage of currency by authorizing banks to issue notes on the same basis as deposits-free banking, a system with a long historical experience (Dowd, 1992), though one that is unfamiliar today and apparently was never considered by the Panamanian government as an option. The dollar would have remained as a unit of account, but greenbacks would not have circulated as a medium of exchange; their role would at most have been confined to interbank clearings. The financial system would then have been beyond the reach of the United States, and Panama would have had as much insulation from U.S. political pressure as a central bank could have provided in the same circumstances. For a country worried about encountering similar pressure from the United States under official dollarization today, the existence of the euro as a serious rival to the dollar offers further potential relief. A switch from the dollar to the euro would boost the euro's international standing and correspondingly reduce the standing of the dollar.

An argument that dates back at least to the 1960s says that no matter what the exchange rate arrangement, as international trade and international flows of capital increase in importance, the ability to have a truly independent monetary policy diminishes. (Llewellyn [1980, p. 198] calls this the difference between "constitutional" and "effective" sovereignty.) According to the argument, no matter what the type of exchange rate, if capital is highly mobile, flows of speculative capital will quickly offset the effects on the "real" economy that the central bank hopes to achieve. In its extreme form the argument claims that effective monetary sovereignty no longer exists because flows of capital, particularly in foreign exchange markets, are so big that they overwhelm whatever national central banks can do.

A related recent argument is that electronic money, in untraceable "smart cards" and other forms, will soon give many people the opportunity to use any currency. Since there is no reason people should want to use bad currencies, they will cease to use the currencies of many developing countries. The governments of those countries will then be unable to control the local supply of money (Frezza, 1997).

In my opinion, these arguments are more useful as stimuli for thought than as analyses of the situation that actually exists today and is likely to exist in the near future. Much capital does flow across borders, but capital flows more easily within national borders than across them. The existence of separate national currencies is in itself a powerful obstacle to trade in goods and financial assets alike, which is why, other things being equal, countries that have a common currency trade with one another more than those that do not (Rose, 1999). Especially under floating exchange rates, separate currencies create exchange risk, which tends to keep domestic savings in and foreign investment out. National borders and national currencies are still very important in affecting economic relations. If that were not so, there would be no point in trying to influence or reform monetary policy.

There is also reason to be skeptical that electronic money will eliminate many national currencies. People who talk about electronic technology making money harder to trace neglect that the same technology also makes it easier than ever to gather personal and financial information. In the United States, with legal or illegal access to the right databases, it is possible to find out within minutes the value of a person's house, car, bank accounts, retirement fund, even how much he spends on groceries. Electronic technology offers the possibility of greater surveillance as well as greater freedom, and further developments may make surveillance cheaper and more attractive than it is now. If so, it will be possible for governments to enforce the use of national currency in electronic transactions with at least as much success as they now have. Despite trends that reduce the scope for an independent monetary policy compared to 20 or 30 years ago, considerable scope will remain. Globalization and electronic technology have not yet reduced monetary sovereignty to the point of ineffectiveness.

Has Monetary Sovereignty Produced the Expected Benefits?

I have reviewed the arguments, largely theoretical, for monetary sovereignty. If monetary sovereignty is generally beneficial, it should yield broadly based and readily discernible economic or political benefits. In countries with central banks, economic growth should be higher or less variable, the financial system should be more stable, the currency should perhaps be more stable (measured by changes in purchasing power, not by exchange rates), or governments should be more durable than in countries with currency boards or official dollarization. The benefits of monetary sovereignty must be broadly based because otherwise it is hard to justify monetary sovereignty as a legitimate exercise of authority. A national central bank always benefits some people by giving them positions, prestige, or privileged access to credit that would not exist under other monetary arrangements. Unless a much wider group also benefits, however, monetary sovereignty is just camouflage for redistributing wealth from the public at large to a special-interest group that is often substantially richer.

What is the actual record of central banks, particularly in developing countries, whose people presumably have the most to gain if monetary sovereignty is economically beneficial? Until recently, economists had not bothered to compare systematically the performance of central banking to the performance of other monetary systems, because they assumed that almost every country should have a central bank. Research comparing the performance of central banking to other monetary systems, such as currency boards and official dollarization, is still scarce but indicates that most developing countries have received no discernable benefit from having their own currencies, issued by their own central banks. The long-term record of central banking compared to other monetary systems in developing countries is poor (Ghosh, Goulde, and Wolf, 1998; Hanke, 1999; Schuler, 1996). Developing countries with central banks have not grown faster than those without them; outside of East Asia, many developing countries have even lost ground relative to developed countries in the last generation. National currencies in developing countries from Albania to Zimbabwe have suffered currency crises and massive depreciation against the major international currencies in the past decade. National currencies do not seem to have made financial systems more stable; rather, currency crises resulting from bad monetary policy have often preceded wider financial crises (Kaminsky and Reinhart, 1999). Banking crises have generally been more costly in monetary systems with central banks than in those without them (for data, see Frydl, 1999). Nor have national currencies and national central banks promoted confidence in many national governments: there have frequently been cases when keeping U.S. dollars in a jar in the ground would have preserved people's wealth better than keeping national currency on deposit in a bank.

Table 7.1 updates data from my own study of monetary performance (Schuler, 1996). Since the breakdown of the Bretton Woods system in the early 1970s, the performance of monetary policy in developing countries *without* central banks has been roughly as good as the performance of monetary policy in developed countries, all of which have had central banks during the period. Monetary policy in developing countries *with* central banks, on the other hand, has been poor, with lower economic growth, high inflation, and far more extensive exchange controls than in the other two groups. The same pattern also existed in less pronounced fashion under the Bretton Woods.

Has monetary sovereignty produced any political benefits that might offset its lack of obvious economic benefits? Here the standards for measurement are vague. It has been argued that a national currency contributes to political unity by being a symbol of national identity and an object of national pride. But are national currencies issued by central banks objects of national pride in most developing countries? Judging by what people actually do rather than what they say, no. From Southeast Asia to Russia to Latin America, hundreds of millions of people mistrust their national currencies so much that they prefer the major international currencies. Researchers at the Federal Reserve System estimate that foreigners hold 55 to 70 percent of U.S. dollar notes, mainly as $100 bills (Porter and Judson, 1996, p. 899). A study by the Deutsche Bundesbank estimated that for-

Table 7.1
Performance of Central Banking versus Other Monetary Systems, 1971–2000

	Developed countries with central banking	Developing countries with central banking	Countries with other monetary systems
Average annual inflation (consumer prices), 1971–98(%)			
Mean	8.9	79.7	11.8
Median	5.4	10.8	8.7
Standard deviation	19.7	702.4	17.4
Countries ever having a system that suffered inflation over 20% a year, 1971–2000	16% (8 of 36)	59% (86 of 145)	13% (8 of 64)
Ever had inflation over 100% a year, 1971–2000	0% (0 of 36)	22% (32 of 145)	0% (0 of 64)
IMF member countries with restrictions on current-account transactions, end of 2000	19% (7 of 36)	78% (105 of 135)	27% (4 of 15)
Exchange rate depreciated against U.S. dollar or official anchor currency, start of 1971 or date of first issue versus end of 2000	72% (26 of 36)	94% (133 of 141)	3% (1 of 31)
Average annual GNP growth/person, 1971–98 (%)			
Mean	2.1	1.1	1.8
Median	2.3	1.6	1.9
Standard deviation	6.1	7.0	6.6

Note: The United States is counted among countries whose currency has depreciated because the dollar has depreciated against gold. "Countries with other monetary systems" excludes former Soviet republics that briefly used the Russian ruble in 1991 and 1992 before issuing their own currencies. Data are from World Bank, *World Development Indicators* CD-ROM, 2000 (Washington: World Bank), except for exchange restrictions, which are from International Monetary Fund, *Annual Report on Exchange Arrangements and Exchange Restrictions, 2001* (Washington: International Monetary Fund, 2001), and some supplementary exchange rate information from newspapers. There are some significant omissions in coverage, especially in earlier years.

eigners held 40 percent of German mark notes (Seitz, 1995). (These have now been replaced by euro notes.) A survey by the IMF of unofficial dollarization found 18 developing countries where foreign currency deposits exceeded 30 percent of a broad measure of the money supply as of 1995 and another 34 developing countries where foreign currency deposits averaged 16.4 percent of a broad measure of the money supply (Baliño, Bennett, and Borensztein, 1999, pp. 2–3). (A number of developing countries forbid or strongly discourage foreign currency deposits, so these numbers might be considerably higher absent such barriers. Moreover, the survey examined only foreign currency deposits, not use of foreign currency notes.) Widespread unofficial dollarization in so many countries suggests that rather than being sources of national unity, many national currencies aggravate social tensions by causing economic problems.

Political Sovereignty, Monetary Sovereignty, and Consumers' Sovereignty

An important reason monetary sovereignty has been harmful for most developing countries is that the rhetoric of sovereignty fails to distinguish among three types of sovereignty: national political sovereignty, consumers' sovereignty, and monetary sovereignty.

National political sovereignty exists when a state has a permanent population, a defined territory, a government, and the capacity to enter into relations with other states. (This definition comes from the 1933 Montevideo Convention on Rights and Duties of States, article 1.) When a nation is sovereign, no other state has legal authority over it. A state may yield some of its legal authority in international agreements, such as NAFTA or the IMF's Articles of Agreement, but it yields authority by its own consent. A national government has the right to withdraw from international agreements and regain the legal authority it has yielded, if it is willing to suffer the cost of doing so. The same is not true of, say, a municipal government, which is not sovereign because it lacks the right to withdraw from the nation by seceding.

"Consumers' sovereignty" is a term devised by the South African economist William Harold Hutt (1936, pp. 257–72, 1940). It expresses the idea that in a market economy, the preferences of consumers rather than those of producers or a central planner ultimately determine what is produced. The consumer in a sense is king. As it applies to monetary matters, the idea of consumers' sovereignty implies that people should have an unrestricted choice of what currency they wish to use. Governments should not impose exchange controls, should not force people to accept national currency in preference to foreign currencies, and should allow people to use any currency they wish for making contracts.

The idea of consumers' sovereignty places choice at the level of the individual person. In contrast, the idea of monetary sovereignty places choice at the level of the nation, by giving the government monopoly power to decide what currency will be used and under what conditions it will be used. For other goods, most people now implicitly or explicitly agree that consumers' sovereignty is the appropriate standard both from the standpoint of economic efficiency and the standpoint of justice. There is no compelling case for governments to monopolize the production of shoes, sausages, or steel. The experience of the centrally planned economies showed that monopoly decision making in economic affairs obstructs the creation of wealth, not just for a few but for all. Why should monopoly decision making in money be an exception?

People think of monetary choice occurring at the level of the nation rather than at the level of the individual because today's monetary arrangements originate from the political history of nation-states rather than from considerations of consumers' sovereignty. For centuries, many princes monopolized the minting of coins within their principalities because it was a way for them to literally make money. The monopoly of minting coins was one of the many powers that they had over their subjects. Many also created monopolies or granted special privileges in banking, trade, and other activities. (Notable examples from the 1600s and 1700s include the Bank of England; the British and Dutch East India Companies; and France's Compagnie de la Louisiane ou d'Occident, the "Mississippi scheme.") Today, the principle of government monopoly is dead or dying except in money. It is a logical extension of the principle of competition that a government should not have the power to force people to use a particular currency or to restrict their use of other currencies.

As more people come to understand the inconsistency between competition in other economic spheres and monopoly in money, it is likely that the focus in monetary policy will shift from asking how a policy would affect monetary sovereignty to the more appropriate question of how it would affect consumers' sovereignty. In most developing countries, historical experience indicates that renouncing monetary sovereignty would substantially improve consumers' sovereignty. Linking monetary policy to a good external currency through official dollarization, a currency board, or monetary union would eliminate any perceived need to impose exchange controls, give people a currency superior to their present national currency, and be compatible with allowing complete freedom of choice in deciding which currency they wish to use for making contracts.[2] The experience of currency board and dollarized systems has been that they have no need for the restrictions that many developing countries impose to prevent foreign currencies from competing freely with the national currency.

Perhaps government officials in countries where many observers judge monetary policy to be poor will claim that the government knows what is best for the people, and that the national central bank is already giving the people what they desire. There is a simple way to test such claims. The government can offer its own employees a choice of being paid during the next year either in national currency or in U.S. dollars or euros at today's exchange rate for the national currency.

Official dollarization, a currency board, or a monetary union diminish the economic power a government can exercise over citizens by eliminating its power to create inflation. However, they do not reduce national political sovereignty—the power of the government to enter into relations with the governments of other states. Estonia, which has a currency-board-like system, or Panama, which has official dollarization, are as politically sovereign as Poland or Brazil, which have central banks. In the same way, an effective constitutional declaration of the rights of citizens diminishes the political power of the national government over citizens by forbidding the government to practice certain kinds of behavior, such as restricting the freedom of worship, but it does not diminish national political sovereignty.

Political sovereignty does not require a national central bank or even a separate national currency. *Consumers'* sovereignty in most developing countries would be enhanced by eliminating national central banks and allowing people to use any currency without restriction. *Monetary* sovereignty is a concept that has too often been used to excuse the poor performance with which so many national central banks have saddled their citizens; it deserves a quick and lasting burial.

◤ Notes

This chapter is based on a speech at the Twentieth International Symposium of Economics at the Instituto Tecnológico y de Estudias Superiores de Monterrey, Monterrey, Mexico, April 10, 1999.

1. Italics in original.

2. The complement to giving consumers freedom of choice in deciding which currency to use would be giving potential issuers freedom of choice in offering various credit instruments and units of account. The result would be a free banking system, which, as I mentioned, has historical precedents. In principle, government-issued currency could compete on an equal basis with bank-issued currency, but in practice governments have rarely been impartial when they have been both referees and players in issuing currency.

A possible criticism of allowing competition in the use and issue of currency is that it may reduce the benefits ("network externalities") that arise when everyone in a country uses the same currency. One response is that people can use different currencies denominated in a common unit of account. A deposit at the Chase Manhattan Bank and a deposit at Citibank in U.S. dollars are different "currencies" that use a common unit of account, though we rarely think of them as such. People do not claim that every country should have only one bank that accepts deposits; why should every country have only one issuer of notes and coins? Another response is that if the benefits of using a currency increase as the number of users increases, the national currency should be able to sustain its dominance without legal restrictions on the use of other currencies. There is no way other than competition to determine the costs and benefits from using one currency as opposed to another. The U.S. dollar, for example, offers users access to a larger and potentially more important network of users than the national currency of most countries. (For more on competition in currency, see Selgin [1984] and White [1999].)

◤ References

Aliber, Robert Z. (1968). National Monetary Sovereignty and International Financial Order. Santa Monica, CA: Rand Corporation.

Baliño, Tomás J., Adam Bennett, and Eduardo Borensztein. (1999). *Monetary Policy in Dollarized Economies.* (Occasional Paper 171). Washington, D.C.: International Monetary Fund.

Blanc, Jérôme. (2000, February). Invariants et variantes de la souvrainté monétaire: Reflexions sur un cadre conceptuel compréhensif. *Economies et Sociétés,* 193–213.

Bogetic, Zeljko. (2000). Seigniorage Sharing under Dollarisation. *Central Banking, 10* (4), 77–87.

Clark, P. B., and H. G. Grubel. (1972). National Monetary Sovereignty under Different Exchange Rate Regimes. *Bulletin* (New York University Graduate School of Business Administration, Institute of Finance), *78–79.*

Cohen, Benjamin J. (1998). *The Geography of Money.* Ithaca, N.Y.: Cornell University Press.

Cohen, Benjamin J. (2000, June 7). *Monetary Union: The Political Dimension.* Paper presented at Federal Reserve Bank of Dallas conference, Dallas, Dollarization: A Common Currency for the Americas? Published in French as: Dollarisation: la dimension politique. *L'économie politique, 5.*

Cooper, Richard. (1991). *Economic Stabilization in Developing Countries.* (Occasional Papers No. 14). San Francisco: International Center for Economic Growth.

Dowd, Kevin. (Ed.). (1992). *The Experience of Free Banking.* London: Routledge.

Dukic, Dorde. (1995). Monetary Sovereignty: Some Theoretical and Empirical Considerations. *Development and International Cooperation, 11,* 225–48.

Frezza, Bill A. (1997). The Internet and the End of Monetary Sovereignty. In James A. Dorn (Ed.), *The Future of Money in the Information Age* (pp. 29–33). Washington, D.C.: Cato Institute.

Frydl, Edward. (1999, March). *The Length and Cost of Banking Crises.* (IMF Working Paper 99/30). International Monetary Fund. Available online at www.imf.org.

Ghosh, Atish R., Anne-Marie Gulde, and Holger Wolf. (1998, January). *Currency Boards: The Ultimate Fix?* (IMF Working Paper 98/8). International Monetary Fund. Available online at www.imf.org.

Goodman, John B. (1992). *Monetary Sovereignty: The Politics of Central Banking in Western Europe.* Ithaca, N.Y.: Cornell University Press.

Hanke, Steve H. (1999). Some Thoughts about Currency Boards. In Mario I. Blejer and Marko Skreb (Eds.), *Balance of Payments, Exchange Rates and Competitiveness in Transition Economics* (pp. 341–66). Norwell, Mass.: Kluwer Academic.

Hutt, W. H. (1936). *Economists and the Public: A Study of Competition and Opinion.* London: Cape.

Hutt, W. H. (1940). The Concept of Consumers' Sovereignty. *Economic Journal, 50* (197), 66–77.

Kaminsky, Graciela L., and Carmen M. Reinhart. (1999). The Twin Crises: The Causes of Banking and Balance-of-Payments Problems. *American Economic Review, 89* (3), 473–500.

Keynes, John Maynard. (1971[1923]). *A Tract on Monetary Reform.* In *Collected Writings of John Maynard Keynes* (Vol. 4.) London: Macmillan.

Kirshner, Jonathan. (1995). *Currency and Coercion: The Political Economy of International Monetary Power.* Princeton: Princeton University Press.

Kurihara, Kenneth K. (1949). Toward a New Theory of Monetary Sovereignty. *Journal of Political Economy, 57* (2), 162–70.

Llewellyn, David T. (1980). *International Financial Integration: The Limits of Sovereignty.* New York: Wiley.

Mann, F. A. (1992). *The Legal Aspect of Money* (5th ed). Oxford: Clarendon Press.

Martha, Rutsel Silvestre J. (1993). The Fund Agreement and the Surrender of Monetary Sovereignty to the European Community. *Common Market Law Review, 30* (4), 359–86.

Mundell, Robert. (1997, September 4–7). *Money and the Sovereign State.* Unpublished paper prepared for International Economic Association Conference, Trento, Italy.

Nussbaum, Arthur. (1939). *Money in the Law.* Chicago: Foundation Press.

Porter, Richard, and Ruth Judson. (1996). The Location of U.S. Currency: How Much Is Abroad? *Federal Reserve Bulletin, 82* (10), 883–903.

Rose, Andrew K. (1999). *One Money, One Market: Estimating the Effect of Common Currencies on Trade.* (NBER Working Paper W7432). National Bureau of Economic Research.

Schuler, Kurt. (1996). *Should Developing Countries Have Central Banks? Currency Quality and Monetary Systems in 155 Countries.* London: Institute of Economic Affairs.

Seitz, F. (1995). *The Circulation of the Deutsche Mark Abroad.* (Discussion Paper). Deutsche Bundesbank.

Selgin, George. (1984). *The Theory of Free Banking: Money Supply under Competitive Note Issue.* Totowa, N.J.: Rowman and Littlefield.

Tobin, James. (1998, April 20–21). *Financial Globalization: Can National Currencies Survive?* Paper prepared for Annual World Bank Conference on Development Economics. Available online at www.worldbank.org.

White, Lawrence H. (1999). *The Theory of Monetary Institutions.* Malden, Mass.: Blackwell.

Williamson, John. (1995). *What Role for Currency Boards?* (Policy Studies in International Economics No. 40). Washington, D.C.: Institute for International Economics.

8 Thomas D. Willett

The OCA Approach to Exchange Rate Regimes

A Perspective on Recent Developments

The basic insight of the theory of OCAs is that there is not one best exchange rate regime for all countries. Thus the traditional debate about fixed versus flexible exchange rates should not be conducted in the abstract. All regimes have both costs and benefits, and the balance of these varies systematically across countries based on the factors identified in OCA theory. Thus the relevant question is what regime is best for a particular country, not in general.

Interest in OCA theory has waxed and waned over the years since Robert Mundell's (1961) pioneering contribution.[1] In recent years the rash of global currency crises and the formation of the EMU have helped stimulate a tremendous resurgence of interest in using OCA theory to analyze exchange rate issues. Unless one believes that the recent financial crises were caused primarily by destabilizing speculation,[2] these crises have little relevance for the choices that should be made between fixed and flexible rates. What they do highlight, however, is that high international capital mobility has made it increasingly difficult to run compromise systems based on adjustably pegged exchange rate regimes. Thus countries face increased pressure to move toward one or the other end of the fixed versus flexible rate spectrum. This in turn greatly increases the relevance of traditional OCA analysis for policy decisions.

Less well recognized is the usefulness of OCA theory for analysis of the degree to which exchange rate development should influence monetary policy for countries following regimes of limited exchange rate flexibility. Recent years have seen considerable theoretical development of OCA analysis, especially in terms of the expansion of the number of considerations that have become recognized as relevant to OCA theory. These include the influences of currency substitution, seigniorage, foreign currency debt, and political economy considerations. Interestingly, at the same time, some economists have argued that OCA theory has become obsolete. For example, Bofinger, Svindland, and Thanner conclude that "the traditional literature on optimum currency areas has to be regarded as a relic from the Keynesian paradigm" (1993, p. 15), while Goldberg, Ickes, and Ryterman "question the relevance of using optimum currency area arguments for considering the adoption of independent currencies in the FSU [Former Soviet Union]" (1994, p. 295). Another criticism that has been raised against OCA theory is that it reflects a central planning rather than a market competition approach. This is misleading, however, unless one is willing to go all the way to the advocacy of only private monies. As long as there is publicly supplied money there must be formal or informal rules for the creation of money, and for this issue OCA theory is relevant since genuinely fixed exchange rates imply a particular role for money creation. There is nothing in basic OCA theory that argues that international currency competition should be restricted by governments.

This chapter reviews the recent developments in OCA theory, both positive and critical, and attempts to put them in perspective. It argues that the recent criticisms do not undermine the OCA approach but, as with the positive contributions, add to the number of considerations that are relevant and in some cases influence the relative weights that should be given to the traditional criteria. As a result, the OCA criteria do not always give clear and unambiguous signals about what exchange rate regime a country should adopt. But this should not be any more surprising than that economists continue to disagree about optimal macroeconomic policies. Even where we cannot reach agreement about policy recommendations, OCA theory helps us understand better why we disagree.

◣ A Perspective on OCA Analysis

Some economists such as Charles Goodhart (1995) have challenged the practical relevance of any economic criteria at all. Currency area formation, they argue, is dominated by political considerations. A prime example is the recent creation of the EMU. While it was sold in part on the questionable assertion that monetary union was a necessary step to complete the single market, it was motivated overwhelmingly by political considerations.[3] It is arguable that monetary union might be economically efficient for an inner group of the EU on OCA grounds, but many members of the large EMU clearly do not come close to meeting OCA criteria.[4] Rather, joining the EMU came to be seen by politicians as the distinction between first- and second-class European citizenship.

Political considerations certainly impose important constraints on the relevance of applications of OCA analysis. For example, in his original contribution Mundell (1961) suggested that on economic grounds it might be desirable to replace the Canadian dollar and the U.S. dollar with two new currencies, one for the Eastern regimes of Canada and the United States and one for their Western regimes. Recent statistical work by Bayoumi and Eichengreen (1994a,b) has supported Mundell's conjecture. However, Mundell recognized that this is not a practical suggestion on political grounds. While many countries allow foreign currencies to circulate in their economies, it is difficult today to imagine a national government allowing the creation of multiple domestic currencies. It is true that common currency areas are sometimes split apart as nations split apart, as has occurred recently with Czechoslovakia and Yugoslavia, but there is little reason to think that OCA considerations played any role in these dissolutions. Likewise, I am not aware of any emphasis on OCA considerations in Canadian discussion of secession by Quebec.

Thus, for practical purposes, we should pursue OCA analysis primarily from an outward perspective with respect to national political units. Practical political considerations will also often limit a country's options with respect to the terms of joining currency areas. An issue of obvious importance is who determines monetary policy within a common currency area. When Austria decided to fix the schilling to the German mark and become a part of the deutsche mark area, it would obviously have preferred the creation of a new joint currency in whose management it had some say. For this, however, Austria had to await the formation of the much broader currency area of the euro, which in turn required a very unusual set of political circumstances. The situation in North America is quite different. In the near future there is little possibility that the United States would agree to combine with Canada and Mexico to form a new common currency to complement NAFTA. Thus for the foreseeable future the only relevant option for Canada, Mexico, and the countries of Central and South America is the unilateral joining of the U.S. dollar area through adoption of a hard peg, as in Austria with the deutsche mark, a currency board, as in Argentina, or dollarization, as in Ecuador and El Salvador. For the potential entrants to the EU, the adoption of a common currency is a feasible option, although the new entrants would probably have only a small say in joint monetary policy making.

Despite the importance of politics in determining the formation of regional currency areas, OCA analysis retains strong relevance both for normative analysis of the costs of monetary unions[5] and for both positive and normative analysis of the choices of exchange rate regimes by individual countries. The analytic core of OCA theory is its focus on the factors that influence the relative costs and benefits of fixed versus flexible exchange rates. This makes OCA theory relevant for the choice of exchange rate regimes by countries with independent currencies, and for this purpose the economic criteria of OCA theory have considerable positive explanatory power as well as normative value.[6]

Another type of criticism is that OCA theory does not lead to a single quantifiable criterion. As the literature developed and more considerations were shown to be relevant, some concluded that the OCA approach was a dead end.[7] At the same time other economists, such as Tower and Willett (1976), suggested that the incorporation of additional considerations showed the power of OCA analysis, not as specific theory but as an approach for thinking about exchange rate issues. In this view the greatest value of the OCA approach is that it demonstrates the fallacy of debating the virtues of fixed versus flexible exchange rates in the abstract and focuses attention instead on the factors that influence the relative costs and benefits of alternative exchange rate regimes for different countries. From this perspective one should never have expected OCA theory to lead to a single quantifiable criterion any more than that macro economic theory would lead to unambiguous strategies for optimal monetary and fiscal policies. Indeed, in his original contribution to the OCA literature, Robert Mundell (1961) was careful to note that "the idea of optimality ... is complex and difficult to quantify precisely" (p. 717).

◣ *The Basic OCA Trade-Off*

Traditional analysis of OCA theory has typically been conceived in terms of balancing the micro benefits to be gained by enhancing the usefulness of money by expanding the effective domains of individual currencies through currency unification or fixed exchange rates against the macroeconomic costs of giving up the exchange rate as an instrument of balance of payments adjustment and therefore subjecting domestic macroeconomic policies to a binding balance of payments constraint. As Robert Mundell put it in his original development of OCA theory,

> a system of flexible exchange rates is usually presented, by its proponents, as advice whereby depreciation can take the place of unemployment when the external balance is in deficit, and appreciation can replace inflation when it is in surplus. (1961, p. 657)

Against this must be balanced not only the diminution of the usefulness of money implied by a greater number of currencies but also the lower effectiveness of exchange rate adjustments in highly open economies. In modern parlance, the latter consideration is usually discussed in terms of whether changes in nominal exchange rates can have more than fleeting effects on real exchange rates. If not, then the only loss from giving up the freedom to make exchange rate adjustments is the possibility of protection from price inflation or deflation abroad.

In their survey of the OCA literature, Masson and Taylor put the basic trade-off succinctly:

> The value of [monetary] unions clearly derives from the wider circulation of a stable currency; major benefits include reducing transaction costs, lowering price and exchange rate variability, and enhancing the anti-inflationary credibility of monetary policy ... the costs of currency union for a given country involve the loss of exchange-rate flexibility, which can be seen as providing an instrument to cushion "shocks" to the economy. The traditional literature on optimum currency areas considers the circumstances in which the loss of this instrument is least costly: within currency unions exhibiting high factor mobility and wage

price flexibility, for economies that are relatively open, and for countries with a high degree of industrial diversification. (1993, p. 38)

As Krugman (1992, 1995) has emphasized, most of the OCA literature has focused on the costs of balance of payments adjustments under alternative exchange rate regimes. We know relatively little about the value of the microeconomic benefits from broader currency areas other than that the marginal value of expanding currency domain will decline as the size of the domain increases.

Given the difficulties in quantitatively determining optimality in terms of OCA criteria, it is perhaps best to begin analysis with the question of whether a currency domain is large enough to be viable. Where an economy is small and highly open, there will be little liquidity value to the currency. There would be few nontraded goods and services, so a depreciation would result primarily in a rise in domestic currency prices—undercutting the effectiveness of exchange rate changes in promoting balance of payments adjustment (except through the resulting decline in the value of real money balances, which could be better accomplished through reducing the nominal money supply directly). With high domestic price variability resulting from exchange rate changes, the value of the services provided by domestic currency would be sharply reduced. If there is a high level of international currency substitution (which a low degree of usefulness of the domestic currency would be likely to produce) then a flexible rate would be subject to greater fluctuations, and the value of domestic currency would be further reduced. The main factors undercutting the viability of a currency are high and variable inflation, high trade ratios, and high degree of dollarization or other forms of international currency substitution.[8]

Recently economists such as Hausmann (1999) and Calvo and Reinhart (2000) have stressed the effects of the dollarization of countries' financial liabilities as well as their currencies. Such dollarization increases the case for fixed rates, but in many cases such liability dollarization may have been artificially high because of the adoption of pegged exchange rates and implicit or explicit government guarantees (see Willett, 2001). While the qualitative effects of greater currency substitution and liability dollarization on the case for fixed rates are clear, as yet there have been no good estimates of the quantitative magnitudes of these effects. Nor do we have a formal research literature on how small a viable currency area can be. Global monetarists such as Ron McKinnon and Robert Mundell believe that the minimum size for OCAs is quite large, but the relatively successful experiments of tiny economies such as Latvia and Slovenia with managed floats suggest that minimum viable sizes may be quite small.[9]

Advocates of exchange rate flexibility such as Friedman (1953) and Yeager (1966) were quite clear that exchange rate flexibility can only act as a second (or nth) best substitute for factor mobility and wage-price flexibility for adjustment to many types of shocks.[10] They believed, however, that there were often sufficient rigidities in economies for this second-best policy to be useful. In other words, while under ideal conditions the optimal currency area was a single world currency, under actual conditions, the optimal number of currency areas was much greater.

In such a world of rigidities in domestic factor mobility and wage and price behavior, economic size and openness become a major influence on the costs and benefits of alternative exchange rate regimes. As both Mundell (1961) and McKinnon (1963) emphasized, the smaller and more open an economy, the less useful its domestic currency will be, and, because of the high ratio of traded to nontraded goods, the less a given change in the nominal exchange rate will affect the real exchange rate.[11] On the other hand, the higher a country's marginal propensity to import, the smaller the domestic real income decline required to achieve any given required improvement in the trade balance. Thus, the smaller and more open an economy is, the more attractive the cost-benefit ratio of fixed exchange rates will be.

This is easy to see intuitively. Consider the question of whether in the case of a conflict between internal (domestic macroeconomics) and external (balance of payments) equilibrium, the domestic sector should be adjusted to the external sector, as would have to occur under fixed exchange rates, or the external sector should be forced to adjust to the domestic sector, as would occur with exchange rate adjustments. Obviously an important part of the answer lies in the relative size of the two sectors, that is, the openness of the economy. Thus it makes considerable sense for small countries like Estonia to fix their exchange rates and for large economies like the United States and Japan to adopt flexible rates. In the North American context, this implies that the prospective benefits for fixing exchange rates are much greater for Canada and Mexico than for the United States. Thus, while the United States would probably have no objection to policies by Canada and Mexico to fix their currencies to the U.S. dollar, the United States would be unlikely to favor the creation of a new common currency for all three countries.

The importance of a third consideration, industrial structure, was pointed to by Kenen (1969), who argued that if economies were highly diversified, they were less likely to be subject to shocks that would require major adjustments and hence would have less need for exchange rate adjustment. This has lead to a broad body of literature that I will discuss hereafter.

◤ *Expansion of the Criteria*

Over time the list of considerations analyzed in the OCA literature has continued to grow. In an important survey article, Tavlas (1994) listed nine characteristics from the traditional literature: similarity of inflation rates, the degree of factor mobility, the openness and size of the economy, the degree of commodity diversification, price and wage flexibility, the degree of goods market integration, fiscal integration, real exchange rate variability, and political factors—before going to discuss a number of additional considerations that have been raised in the "new" OCA theory. And this list omitted the range of shocks analyzed by Tower and Willett (1976) and Aghelvi, Khan, and Montiel (1991) and emphasized in the surveys by Masson and Taylor (1993, 1994).

Looking only at the surveys of the previous decades by Bofinger (1994), Masson and Taylor (1993, 1994), Tavlas (1994), and Wihlborg and Willett (1991), one finds added to the list of considerations factors such as optimal public finance, the degree of international currency substitution, the new classical view of policy ineffectiveness, the informativeness of price and quantity signals from the money and financial markets, controllability of the money supply, time inconsistency problems and credibility issues, and the case for using institutional arrangements to discipline national monetary and fiscal policies.[12]

Given this proliferation of considerations, attempts to simplify the analysis down to one or a few key criteria are quite understandable. Unfortunately, they have not been successful. Arguments initially presented in strong terms as to what is relevant and irrelevant generally end up in more modest terms as arguments about shifts in the relative weights that should be given to different criteria or the addition of criteria that were originally meant to be replacements of other criteria. A good example is Vaubel's (1976) intriguing argument that the crucial criterion is the variability of a country's real exchange rate, since "real exchange rate changes are clearly measurable and automatically give the appropriate weights to the economic forces of which they are the result" (p. 440). While this is clearly an important variable to consider, Vaubel did not convincingly demonstrate that real exchange rate variability captured all relevant considerations or that it necessarily weighted optimally those that it does capture.[13] Thus it has become an addition to the other OCA criteria, not a replacement for them.

Consider two more examples. In their opening critique of traditional OCA theory as a "Keynesian relic," Bofinger, Svindland, and Thanner (1993) give the impression that it should be totally scrapped in favor of their proposed monetarist approach to OCA theory. Yet by the end of their article they quite sensibly refer to the monetary analysis they provide as offering "important additional criteria" (p. 29) for OCA theory. In a similar vein, early on in his discussion of Mundell's factor mobilization criterion, Jacques Melitz (1995b) argues that "Mundell's view belongs to the era of long-run Phillip's curves and should have been abandoned when this notion fell into disrepute in the early seventies" (p. 293). Within the following two paragraphs, this criticism is appropriately softened to the argument that while "labor mobility will unambiguously improve the merits of a fixed rate" because of "the flexibility of prices in the long run, Mundell's criterion of labor mobility loses much plausibility," and "there is little reason to place labor mobility on a special pedestal in analyzing the OCA" (p. 293).[14]

In a similar vein, Masson and Taylor (1994) argue that

> there is no single overriding criterion. . . . Increasingly analytical attention has therefore turned to analysis of shocks affecting economies since shock absorption combines the net influence of several of the traditional criteria. (p. 35)[15]

This search, however, has not succeeded in developing more easily operationalized criteria. While a shock absorption criterion like the narrower real exchange rate variability criterion does capture the net effect of several of the traditional criteria, just how it does so is not explicitly discussed by Masson and Taylor, nor is this analyzed systematically elsewhere in the OCA literature. Thus how this composite criterion relates to the full range of OCA criteria is not yet well understood.

As Pilbeam [1992, p. 36] has aptly put it, the conclusions of the now vast literature on automatic stabilization under alternative exchange rate regimes and policy targets "have proved to be quite complex and . . . very sensitive to the model specification."

As Masson and Taylor (1993, 1994) observe, one must distinguish whether shocks are real or nominal, permanent or temporary, and domestic or foreign. Furthermore, there is the question of whether financial market shocks occur primarily with respect to demands for money, domestic interest-bearing assets, or for foreign assets. Despite the complicated nature of this analysis, if countries were persistently hit with only the same single type of shock, then the literature could provide a powerful criteria for choosing a particular exchange rate regime, that is, a genuinely fixed or freely flexible exchange rate. However, as Bofinger (1994) stresses in his critique of Vaubel's real exchange rate variability criteria, the pattern of past disturbances will not always be a good guide to the pattern of future disturbances. As Guitian (1994) argues, "all economies confront both nominal and real shocks. Yet a shift in exchange rate regime in response to the nature of shocks is clearly an unworkable proposition" (p. 19).

Recent discussions of the importance of patterns of shocks have sometimes failed to distinguish between evaluations on grounds of automatic stabilization and of balance of payments adjustment. Thus, for example, according to standard stabilization analysis, countries that were out of phase cyclically would make good partners, helping to dampen each other's cycles. Thus temporary asymmetrical shocks would enhance the attractiveness of a currency union. On the other hand, where internal adjustment mechanisms worked poorly (due to wage and price stickiness and factor immobility), a permanent asymmetric shock would force internal macroeconomic adjustments and could be quite costly.[16]

In some cases structural characteristics may give us good clues to patterns of shocks. For example, countries where exports are heavily concentrated in agricultural products or raw materials are likely to be subject to above-average variability in export earnings and thus are likely to have greater need for both higher holdings of international reserves and the use of exchange rate adjustments. Likewise, countries with extremely weak domestic political institutions and a consequent tendency toward high inflation are likely to have a strong need for exchange rate adjustments. While there are possibilities of using fixed exchange rates to promote domestic discipline, this will only work if there is already considerable domestic support for stabilization. Otherwise, efforts at fixed rates will break down and worsen the economic situation.[17]

Simple statistical tests of past patterns of shocks, despite their recent popularity in the literature, are unlikely by themselves to offer good guidance to future patterns of shocks. In some cases, the combination of such statistical analysis with careful political and economic analysis of the causes of these patterns can give good clues to the future, but this is likely to be much more relevant to issues of the need for balance of payments adjustment than to the automatic stabilization properties of alternative exchange rate regimes.

In the early days of the new classical macroeconomics revolution, the strong policy ineffectiveness conclusions from the flexible price rational expectations models undercut the traditional rationale for being concerned with using macro policy to correct the balance of payments. This in turn removed the need for exchange rate adjustments as a mechanism to remove balance of payments constraints and hence allow discretionary domestic macroeconomic policy. Subsequent theoretical and empirical research has strongly suggested that while in the long run one cannot trade off higher inflation for more rapid growth and lower unemployment (indeed, higher inflation will hurt growth over the long run), in the short run trade-offs still exist, and thus there is still a plausible (if controversial) case for using macro policy instruments to help soften the effects of shocks to the economy. Thus current macroeconomic analysis suggests the prospective gains from independent macroeconomic policies are less than implied by traditional Keynesian models but are still positive.

Against this must be balanced the increased recognition of the incentives for governments to pursue macroeconomic policies that destabilize the economy in order to reap political gains (or avoid political losses). Furthermore, even in an economy where the strong policy ineffectiveness conclusion held so that price level stability was the only short-run, as well as long-run, macroeconomic objective, it would not always follow that a fixed exchange-rate-based monetary rule would be the best one to follow. Only if there were price level stability abroad and no changes in equilibrium real exchange rates would this be the case. Otherwise, using the exchange rate as the economic nominal anchor could lead to imported inflation or deflation.[18] Indeed, while it has become common for younger writers to think of traditional OCA theory as dealing only with Keynesian unemployment and output stability issues, from early on, many of the contributions such as Mundell (1961), McKinnon (1963), and Tower and Willett (1976) were concerned with price level stability as well.

▶ Are Exchange Rate Adjustments Ever Effective?

While one major line of attack on traditional OCA theory has challenged its Keynesian macroeconomic origins, another has challenged the effectiveness of exchange rate changes as an instrument of policy. In the early postwar period there was considerable elasticity pessimism—there were concerns that the responsiveness of quantities to changes in exchange rates were so low that the proportional changes in trade volumes would be less than the proportional changes in price, and as a result depreciation would lead to a worsening rather than an improvement in the trade balance. The empirical research of the last several decades has suggested that this possibility is generally limited to short-run J curve effects. As Goldberg, Ickles, and Ryternan (1994) argue, this can reduce the effectiveness of exchange rate changes for short-run macroeconomic stabilization policy, but as Willett and Wihlborg (1999) point out, this does not undercut the usefulness of exchange rate changes for insulation against foreign inflation or as an instrument for longer-term balance of payment adjustment.

Elasticities analysis is based on responses to changes in real exchange rates. Another type of critique of the effectiveness of exchange rate adjustments is the view that changes in nominal exchange rates will have only quite temporary effects on real exchange rates. Analysis of such price feedback effects has been an important component of OCA theory from the very beginning. As stressed by both Mundell (1961) and McKinnon (1963), the more open the economy, the greater the effects of a devaluation on the domestic price level and the greater in turn are the likely induced effects on domestic wages. For a highly open economy, the exchange rate is typically not an effective instrument because there will be little scope for nominal exchange rate changes to have a substantial impact on the real exchange rate. Likewise, as has been emphasized in the literature on the vicious circle, the more likely initial domestic wage and price increases are to be supported by accommodative monetary policy, the less effective will be exchange rate changes in promoting real adjustment.

All this analysis has been standard for decades. What is new is that there are now arguments that such considerations apply to relatively large countries such as Britain, France, Germany, and Italy. Since the 1970s, the global monetarists such as Ronald McKinnon, Robert Mundell, and Arthur Laffer have argued that global integration has reached a point where all countries, no matter their size, are functionally small open economies. This view is highly controversial and has won only a limited number of converts (myself not included). Over the past decade, however, the increasing eco-

nomic integration within Europe has contributed to the frequent espousal
of this view by advocates of European monetary union. If exchange rate
adjustments are no longer effective anyway, then the costs of joining a
monetary union are substantially reduced, they argue.

This view has been greatly oversold, however. The substantial devaluations and depreciations of the British pound, the Italian lira, and the Swed-
ish krona following the 1992–93 European monetary crisis led to substantial
sustained changes in real exchange rates. An important reason was that these
depreciations were not accompanied by monetary accommodation, but this
merely makes the point that exchange rate changes are not a substitute for
sound domestic policies.

The recent empirical literature has found mixed results for some western European countries, but overall it suggests that nominal exchange rate
changes will have a substantial impact on real exchange rates for policy-
relevant time periods for most European countries.[19] Likewise, there appears
to be considerable scope for nominal exchange rate changes to meaningfully
affect the real exchange rate in many developing countries. The evidence
seems clear that in general there is still scope for the exchange rate to be a
useful policy instrument and that its effectiveness needs to be evaluated on
a case-by-case basis along the lines suggested by OCA theory, that is, the
smaller and more open is the economy, the stronger is the case for adopting
a fixed exchange rate.

History can also be important. The more depreciation is associated with
inflation in the minds of the public, the less effective and more costly
exchange rates changes are likely to be. Even where public perceptions are
due to false guilt by association, these perceptions can affect the short-term
effects of depreciation on inflationary expectations and the degree of sense
of crisis. These in turn can greatly complicate the tasks of currency and
macroeconomic stabilization. Thus on these grounds exchange rate adjustments are likely to be more effective for some countries than for others.
For example, throughout much of Latin America historical tendencies toward high inflation have increased the effects of depreciations on inflationary expectations above what one would expect on the basis of trade openness
alone. On the other hand, despite this adverse history, the shifts to low
inflation policies during the 1990s and the strong monetary and fiscal policy
actions that accompanied them kept both Mexico's depreciation in 1995
and Brazil's depreciation in 1999 from being undermined by induced inflation.

◣ Conclusion

Optimum currency area theory shows that many considerations are relevant
to the costs and benefits of alternative exchange rate regimes. To those

seeking simple answers, this is a severe drawback, but ignoring relevant factors does not make them go away. It just makes for bad thinking and poor decisions.

In this concluding section, I briefly highlight two aspects of OCA analysis that are only now beginning to receive the attention they deserve. One is that many small open economies may not have good options for a currency to fix their exchange rate to. A second is the need to estimate how criteria will look ex post. I conclude by arguing that OCA analysis can be quite relevant for the large number of countries that score in the intermediate range on OCA criteria and are thus good candidates for neither fixed nor freely floating exchange rates.

One problem that is receiving increased attention is that of appropriate partners for countries that want to fix their exchange rates. Ideally one would like to choose a partner or set of partners with which one has a high proportion of trade and which is likely to be relatively stable. Sometimes these criteria conflict, however. Consider, for example, the recent experiences of the Russian ruble and the Baltic states. All three of the Baltic states—Estonia, Latvia, and Lithuania—are small open economies that had Russia as their dominant trading partner. With rampant inflation in Russia, however, it would have been economic folly for these countries to fix their currencies to the ruble, even apart from their strong political disincentives to do so.[20] Many countries, such as New Zealand, have no dominant trading partner. Often in developing countries, countries with geographic proximity do not have high levels of trade with each other, making adoption of a regional currency less attractive. This was the case with the Baltic states. Both Argentina and Thailand present vivid recent examples of the problems that can be generated by fixing your exchange rate to a currency (the dollar) with which trade was relatively limited. Thus Austria was quite fortunate to have Germany as a close trading partner.

On these criteria, both Canada and Mexico score well above average, having a high proportion of their trade with the United States, a country that has had one of the most stable macroeconomies in the postwar period. There are still substantial problems on this score, however, because the United States has had huge fluctuations in the dollar against both the yen and the European currencies. Thus, while stabilizing for a large proportion of trade, fixing to the U.S. dollar by Canada, Mexico, or the countries of Central and South America could be quite destabilizing for a nontrivial portion of trade and investment.

Another point emphasized in recent OCA literature is that the initiation of currency areas may itself affect such factors as the level of trade openness, the country and product composition of international trade, the discipline of monetary and fiscal policies, and the flexibility of wages and prices. In other words, the OCA criteria are endogenous.[21] In most cases these will move countries closer to meeting OCA criteria. Thus if a country is close to meeting the OCA criteria for fixed rates ex ante, it may be wise to go ahead on the basis of the prediction that the criteria will indeed be met ex post.

It would be dangerous to assume substantial rapid changes in all variables, however.[22] For example, some economists have argued that because fixed exchange rates would increase the costs of wage and price rigidities, the creation of the EMU will generate strong pressures to increase wage and price flexibility. This ignores, however, the public choice insight that politically powerful groups usually benefit from these rigidities and will be loath to give them up. In the operation of this political process, such rent-seeking by particular groups will often dominate the effects of aggregate economic inefficiencies. Thus, for example, while Argentina's currency board did lead to an increase in wage and price flexibility, this increase was not sufficient to eliminate high unemployment. Thus I am quite skeptical about how much increased wage and price flexibility the joining of a currency area will produce. Likewise, as the recent Argentine crisis illustrates, we cannot safely assume that the adoption of fixed exchange rates will always provide sufficient discipline over fiscal policy.[23]

A third point I would like to emphasize is that it is often not recognized that the OCA framework is relevant not just to the choice of exchange rate regime but also the management of macroeconomic policies under flexible exchange rates.[24] Specifically, the more open is the economy, the greater is the weight that should be given to developments in the foreign exchange market in setting domestic monetary and fiscal policies. It would probably be wise under uncertainty to adopt a risk-adverse bias against adopting permanently fixed exchange rates or a common currency.

◤ Notes

1. It is interesting that Mundell's thinking has evolved considerably since his original contribution and he now sometimes argues that the whole world is an OCA. On this evolution see McKinnon (2000) and Mundell (1997).

2. For a view that this was not the case, see Willett (2000). With destabilizing speculation genuinely fixed, as opposed to adjustably pegged, rates would eliminate the disturbance.

3. See, for example, Andrews and Willett (1997), Eichengreen and Frieden (1994), and Willett (1994, 2000).

4. See De Grauwe (1993).

5. To many economists it seems likely that the EMU's strategy may backfire, with the economic costs of inappropriate memberships in EMU generating more political friction than cohesion. See, for example, Feldstein (1997) and Willett (1994). For a useful recent symposium on EMU, see the May 2000 issue of the *Journal of Policy Modeling*.

6. See, for example, Bayoumi and Eichengreen (1997; 1998) and von Hagen and Zhou (2001).

7. See, for example, Ishiyama (1975). For valuable reviews of this and other criticisms of OCA theory, see DeGrauwe (1993) and Tavlas (1994).

8. Note that high openness to international financial flows per se does not have a clear effect on the case for fixed or flexible exchange rate. See Isard (1995) and Tower and Willett (1976). What it does unambiguously do, however, is make compromise systems more difficult to operate.

9. After several years of flexible rates, Latvia did adopt a pegged rate, implying that its government did not consider flexible rates to be optimal. Latvia was, however, able to achieve considerable disinflation during its flexible rate period. Likewise, Slovenia anticipates adopting the euro.

10. For recent discussions of the limits of exchange rate adjustment as a substitute for factor and wage-price flexibility see Bofinger (1994) and Melitz (1995a, b). Note that while Friedman (1953) has often been criticized on the assumption that he advocated flexible exchange rates for all countries, no matter how small; this was in fact not the case. For references to precursors of OCA theory, see Tower and Willett (1976).

11. While Mundell has become generally associated with the labor mobility criterion and McKinnon (1963) with this openness criterion, Mundell also explicitly discussed openness, and this is appropriately noted in McKinnon's contribution.

12. Overviews of the issues surrounding the use of the exchange rate as a nominal anchor for monetary policy are presented in Willett and Westbrook (1999) and Willett (1998).

13. See Bofinger (1994).

14. There has also been recent criticism of the labor mobility criterion on the grounds that high labor mobility may impose substantial social costs. See Melitz (1995a, b).

15. One of the major purposes of Tower and Willett (1976) was to integrate more systematically the literature on patterns of shocks and optimal exchange rate management into the framework of the OCA approach.

16. See Wihlborg and Willett (1991).

17. See Willett (1998) and Willett and Westbrook (1999).

18. On the other hand, with monetary stability abroad and international currency substitution as the only disturbance, a fixed exchange rate would be an optimal monetary rule. See McKinnon (1982).

19. See the analysis and references in Mast (1996) and Pappell (1994). For the United States the evidence is overwhelming.

20. At first glance it might seem that the Baltic states were logical candidates to form a currency area among themselves. This was not the case, however. Apart from political differences that made such bonding unattractive, they had surprisingly small amounts of trade with one another. In this case, close geographic proximity was not accompanied by substantial economic integration. On these issues see the contributions in Sweeney, Wihlborg, and Willett (1999).

21. See Frankel and Rose (1998).

22. Changes in some variables such as trade patterns can also be large under flexible exchange rates. Both Canada and Mexico have recorded substantial increases in their trade ratios in recent years. From 1990 to 1997 Canada's average ratio of exports and imports to GDP rose from a little over 25 percent to almost 40 percent. Over the same period Mexico's ratios rose from a little over 19 percent to over 30 percent. Exports of both countries are highly concentrated on the United States, running about 80 percent for Canada and a few percentage points higher for Mexico. Imports are a little more diversified, with about two-thirds of Canada's imports coming from the United States

and about three-fourths for Mexico. Direct trade between Canada and Mexico is quite small.

23. For systematic empirical evidence on this point see Edwards (2000) (chapter 5 herein), Fatás and Rose (2001), and Tornell and Velasco (2000).

24. See Willett (2002).

◣ References

Aghelvi, B. B., M. S. Khan, and P. J. Montiel. (1991). *Exchange Rate Policy in Developing Countries: Some Analytical Issues.* (IMF Occasional Paper No. 78). International Monetary Fund.

Al-Marhubi, Fahim, and Thomas Willett. (1998). *Determinants of Exchange Rate Regime Choice.* (Claremont Working Paper). Claremont Graduate University.

Andrews, David, and Thomas D. Willett. (1997). Financial Interdependence and the State. *International Organization, 51* (3), 429–511.

Bayoumi, Tamim. (1994). A Formal Theory of Optimum Currency Areas. *IMF Staff Papers, 41*(4), 537–54.

Bayoumi, Tamim, and Barry Eichengreen. (1994a). Monetary and Exchange Rate Arrangements for NAFTA. *Journal of Development Economics, 43,* 125–65.

Bayoumi, Tamim, and Barry Eichengreen. (1994b). *One Money or Many? Analyzing the Prospects for Monetary Unification in Various Parts of the World.* (Princeton Studies in International Finance No. 76). Princeton: Princeton University Press.

Bayoumi, Tamim, and Barry Eichengreen. (1997). Optimum Currency Area and Exchange Rate Volatility. In Benjamin J. Cohen (Ed.), *International Trade and Finance* (pp. 194–215). Cambridge: Cambridge University Press.

Bayoumi, Tamim, and Barry Eichengreen. (1998). Exchange Rate Volatility and Intervention: Implications of the Theory of Optimum Currency Areas. *Journal of International Economics, 45,* 191–209.

Bean, Charles R. (1992, Autumn). Economic and Monetary Union in Europe. *Journal of Economic Perspectives, 6*(4), 31–52.

Bofinger, Peter. (1994). Is Europe an Optimum Currency Area? In Alfred Steinherr (Ed.), *Thirty Years of European Monetary Integration* (pp. 38–56). London: Longman.

Bofinger, Peter, Eirik Svindland, and Benedikt Thanner. (1993). Prospects of the Monetary Order in the Republics of the FSU. In Bofinger et al., *The Economics of New Currencies* (pp. 10–33). London: Centre for Economic Policy Research.

Bofinger, Peter et al. (1993). *The Economics of New Currencies.* London: Centre for Economic Policy Research.

Calvo, Guillermo, and Carmen M. Reinhart. (2000). *Fear of Floating.* (NBER Working Paper No. 7993). National Bureau of Economic Research.

Cesarano, Filippo. (1997). Currency Area and Equilibrium. *Open Economies Review 8,* 51–59.

Cohen, Benjamin J. (1998). *The Geography of Money.* Ithaca, N.Y.: Cornell University Press.

DeGrauwe, Paul. (1993). The Political Economy of Monetary Union in Europe. *World Economy 16*, 653–61.

Eichengreen, Barry. (1992). *Should the Maastricht Treaty Be Saved?* (Princeton Studies in International Finance No. 74). Princeton: Princeton University Press.

Eichengreen, Barry, and Jeffry Frieden (Eds.). (1994). *The Political Economy of European Monetary Unification.* Boulder, Colo.: Westview Press.

Fatás, Antonio, and Andrew K. Rose. (2001). Do Monetary Handcuffs Restrain Leviathan? *IMF Staff Papers 47,* 40–61.

Feldstein, Martin. (1997). EMU and International Conflict. *Foreign Affairs, 76*(6), 60–73.

Frankel, Jeffrey A., and Andrew K. Rose. (1998). The Endogeneity of the Optimum Currency Area Criteria. *Economic Journal, 108,* 1009–25.

Friedman, Milton. (1953). The Case for Flexible Exchange Rates. In *Essays in Positive Economics.* Chicago: University of Chicago Press.

Goldberg, Linda S., Barry W. Ickes, and Randi Ryterman. (1994). Departures from the Ruble Zone: The Implications of Adopting Independent Currencies. *World Economy, 8*(1), 293–322.

Goodhart, Charles. (1995). The Political Economy of Monetary Union. In Peter B. Kenen (Ed.), *Understanding Interdependence: The Macroeconomics of the Open Economy* (pp. 450–505). Princeton: Princeton University Press.

Guitian, Manuel. (1994). "The Choice of an Exchange Rate Regime." In Richard D. Barth and Chong-Huey Wong (Eds.), *Approaches to Exchange Rate Policy: Choices for Developing and Transition Economies* (pp. 13–36). Washington, D.C.: International Monetary Fund.

Hausmann, Ricardo. (1999). Should There Be Five Currencies or One Hundred and Five? *Foreign Policy, 116,* 65–78.

Isard, Peter. (1995). *Exchange Rate Economics.* Cambridge: Cambridge University Press.

Kenen, Peter. (1969). The Theory of Optimum Currency Areas: An Eclectic View. In Robert A. Mundell and Alexander K. Swoboda (Eds.), *Monetary Problems of the International Economy* (pp. 41–60). Chicago: University of Chicago Press.

Krugman, Paul. (1995). What Do We Need to Know About the International Monetary System? In Peter B. Kenen (Ed.), *Understanding Interdependence* (pp. 509–30). Princeton: Princeton University Press.

Krugman, Paul. (1992). Second Thoughts on EMU. *Japan and the World Economy, 4,* 3.

Mahdavi, Mahnaz, and Hossein Kazemi. (1996). Indeterminancy and Volatility of Exchange Rates under Imperfect Currency Substitution. *Economic Inquiry, 34*(1), 168–81.

Masson, Paul, and Mark P. Taylor. (1994). Optimal Currency Areas: A Fresh Look at the Traditional Criteria. In Pierre Siklos (Ed.), *Varieties of Monetary Reform* (pp. 23–44). Boston: Kluwer.

Masson, Paul, and Mark P. Taylor. (1993). Currency Unions: A Survey of the Issues. In Paul Masson and Mark P. Taylor (Eds.), *Policy Issues in the Operation of Currency Unions* (pp. 3–5). Cambridge: Cambridge University Press.

Mast, Tamara. (1996). *The Impact and Feedback Effects of Nominal Exchange Rates on Real Exchange Rates: New Evidence from the European Monetary System.* Unpublished doctoral dissertion, Claremont Graduate School.

McKinnon, Ronald I. (2000). Mundell, the Euro, and the World Dollar Standard. *Journal of Policy Modeling, 22*(3), 311–24.

McKinnon, Ronald I. (1982). Currency Substitution and Instability in the World Dollar Standard. *American Economic Review, 72*(3), 320–33.

McKinnon, Ronald I. (1963). Optimum Currency Areas. *American Economic Review, 53,* 717–25.

Melitz, Jacques. (1995a). The Current Impasse in Research on Optimum Currency Areas. *European Economic Review, 39,* 492–500.

Melitz, Jacques. (1995b). A Suggested Reformulation of the Theory of Optimum Currency Areas. *Open Economies Review, 6*(3), 281–98.

Minford, Patrick. (1995). Other People's Money: Cash-in-Advance Microfoundations for Optimal Currency Areas. *Journal of International Money and Finance, 14*(3), 427–40.

Mundell, Robert A. (1997). Updating the Agenda for Monetary Union. In Mario Blejer et al. (Eds). *Optimum Currency Areas* (pp. 29–48). Washington D.C.: International Monetary Fund.

Mundell, Robert A. (1961). A Theory of Optimum Currency Areas. *American Economic Review, 51,* 657–65.

Papell, David. (1994). Exchange Rates and Prices: An Empirical Analysis. *International Economic Review, 35*(2), 397–410.

Pilbeam, Keith. (1992). *International Finance.* London: Macmillan.

Sweeney, Richard J., Clas G. Wihlborg, and Thomas D. Willet, eds. (1999). *Exchange-Rate Policies for Emerging Market Economies.* Boulder, CO: Westview Press.

Tavlas, George S. (1994). The Theory of Monetary Integration. *Open Economies Review, 5*(2), 211–30.

Tavlas, George S. (1993). The New Theory of Optimum Currency Areas. *The World Economy, 16*(6), 663–85.

Tornell, Aaron, and Andres Valasco. (2000). Fixed Versus Flexible Exchange Rates: Which Provides More Fiscal Discipline? *Journal of Monetary Economics, 45,* 399–436.

Tower, Edward, and Thomas D. Willett. (1976). *The Theory of Optimum Currency Areas and Exchange Rate Flexibility.* (Special Papers in International Economics No. 11). International Finance Section, Department of Economics, Princeton University.

Vaubel, Roland. (1976). Real Exchange-Rate Changes in the European Community: The Empirical Evidence and Its Implications for European Currency Unification, *Weltwirtschaftliches Archiv, 112*(3), 429–70.

Von Furstenberg, George and David Tevlis. (1993). Growth and Income Distribution Benefits of North American Monetary Union for Mexico. *North American Journal of Economics and Finance, 4*(1), 127–43.

Von Hagen, Jürgen, and Jizhong Zhou. (2001). The Choice of Exchange Rate Regimes. (Ms. ZEI). University of Bonn.

Wihlborg, Clas. 1996. *Searching for the Gains from a Monetary Union.* (Yrjö Jahnsson European Integration Lectures No. 9). Helsinki: Gothenburg University Working Paper.

Wihlborg, Clas, and Thomas D. Willett. (1991). Optimal Currency Areas Revisited. In Clas Wihlborg, Michele Fratianni, and Thomas D. Willett (Eds.), *Financial Regulation and Monetary Arrangements After 1992* (pp. 279–97). Amsterdam: North Holland.

Willett, Thomas D. (2002). Fear of Floating Need Not Imply Fixed Exchange Rates. Prepared for the Fordham Conference on Euro and Dollarization, Centers for Economic and Policy Research.

Willett, Thomas D. (2001). Truth in Advertising and the Great Dollarization Scam. *Journal of Policy Modeling, 23*(3), 279–89.

Willett, Thomas D. (2000). International Financial Markets as Sources of Crisis or Discipline: The Too Much, Too Late Hypothesis. *Princeton Essays in International Finance No. 218.*

Willett, Thomas D. (1998). Credibility and Discipline Effects of Exchange Rates as Nominal Anchors: The Need to Distiguish Temporary from Permanent Pegs. *World Economy, 21*(6), 803–26.

Willett, Thomas D., and Jilleen R. Westbrook. (1999). Exchange Rates as nominal Anchors: An Overview of the Issues. In Richard J. Sweeney, Clas G. Wihlborg, and Thomas D. Willett (Eds.), *Exchange-Rate Policies for Emerging Market Economies* (pp. 83–112). Boulder, Colo.: Westview Press.

Willett, Thomas D., and Clas G. Wihlborg. (1999). The Relevance of the Optimum Currency Area Approach for Exchange Rate Policies in Emerging Market Economies. In Richard J. Sweeney, Clas G. Wihlborg, and Thomas D. Willett (Eds.). *Exchange-Rate Policies for Emerging Market Economies* (pp. 61–79). Boulder, Colo.: Westview Press.

Willett, Thomas D. (1994). Some Often Neglected Aspects of the Political Economy of European Monetary Integration. In B. Abeyaz et al. (Eds.), *The Challenge of European Integration* (pp. 205–18). Boulder, Colo.: Westview Press.

Yeager, Leland. (1966). *International Monetary Relations.* New York: Harper and Row.

9 John Williamson

Dollarization Does Not Make Sense Everywhere

My title reflects a conviction that it is profoundly mistaken to debate the merits or otherwise of dollarization in the abstract, assuming that the advantages are the same everywhere, or even everywhere in the Western Hemisphere. Exchange rate flexibility may well make sense in some parts of the region, but in other parts it does not. In this chapter I endeavor to explain the reasons for that conclusion and the criteria that led me to judge some places to be much stronger candidates for dollarization than others.

▶ Intellectual Framework

I propose to compare fixed-rate systems against flexible-rate systems, using a battery of five criteria drawn from the optimum currency area (OCA) literature for that purpose. The first is size: small size points to fixed rates. The second is openness: an open economy points to fixed rates. The third is trade concentration: trade focused on the dollar bloc points to a fixed rate to the dollar. The fourth is similarity of shocks: similar shocks suggest fixed rates. The fifth is liability dollarization: the more extensive this is, the more difficult and dangerous it becomes to devalue.[1]

There are also at least three different fixed-rate systems under discussion at this conference: currency boards, dollarization, and monetary union. (I might have added a fixed exchange rate maintained by a central bank, which we have learned that Barbados still succeeds in making work, with the aid of capital controls.) These differ in terms of seigniorage, the interest premium a country has to pay, financial depth, access to a lender of last resort, and influence on decision making. A comparison of these five characteristics across the three regimes is offered in table 9.1.

The second and third rows accept the claim of the proponents of dollarization that adoption of the dollar would eliminate currency risk and thereby reduce interest rates and also that it would offer a shortcut to deepening the financial system. The final column also shows normal preferences over those five characteristics. This makes it clear that monetary union would be the preferred regime: if it were on offer, one would expect any country, for which the OCA criteria are reasonably favorable to fixity to choose this option.[2] However, since the chance of the Fed offering a seat

Table 9.1
Criteria for Choosing among Fixed-Rate Regimes

	Currency Board	Dollarization	Monetary Union	"Ideal"
Seignorage	Yes	No	Yes	Yes
Interest premium	High	Low	None with rest of monetary union	None
Financial depth	No	Yes	Yes	Yes
Lender of last resort	No[a]	No[a]	Yes	Yes
Decision role	No	No	Yes	Yes

[a]Except to the extent that a bailout authority commands resources, which can provide a lender of next-to-last resort
Source: John Williamson

on the Open Market Committee to Canada (let alone Argentina or Mexico) would seem to be minimal, even a favorable outcome on the OCA criteria has to be weighed against the disadvantages of dollarization vis-à-vis monetary union. (There is also a case for a country to dollarize as a counsel of despair if it has decided it is incapable of governing itself, but I do not regard that as a general problem.)

◣ Regional Disaggregation

Excluding the United States for obvious reasons and Cuba as sui generis, the remainder of the Western Hemisphere may be divided into the following country groupings:

• Canada
• Central America and the Caribbean
• Mexico
• Brazil
• Argentina
• The rest of Mercosur: Bolivia, Chile, Paraguay, and Uruguay
• The Andean group: Colombia, Ecuador, Peru, and Venezuela

Table 9.2 shows how these different groupings match up on the five criteria drawn from the OCA literature. The entries for the first three criteria are objective and quantitative; those for similarity of shocks are impressionistic and qualitative.

◣ Conclusions

Although Canadians customarily think of *Canada* as a small economy, it is in fact the ninth-largest economy in the world, which makes it large by my

Table 9.2
The Optimum Currency Area Criteria for Different Country Groupings

	Canada	Central America/ Caribbean	Mexico	Brazil	Argentina	Rest of Mercosur	Andean Group
Size relative to U.S. (*GNP as percent of US GNP*)	7.7	0.2 max	4.8	9.6	4.1	0.9 max	1.3 max
Openness (*Imports plus exports as percent of GNP*)	67.1	89.1	63.7	14.3	17.7	52.8	32.5
Trade concentration (As percent of *total trade*)							
U.S.	77.5	37.9	81.0	21.6	14.2	18.0	38.0
Western Hemisphere	80.4	63.9	86.2	47.9	54.9	53.9	66.8
Rest of Mercosur	n.a.	n.a.	n.a.	19.1	35.1	26.2	n.a.
Similar shocks (*Relative to U.S.*)	Not all	Yes?	Not all	No	No	No	?
Liability dollarization	No	Yes in some	Yes	No	Yes	Yes in some	Yes

Source: GNP figures are taken from the 1999/2000 World Bank World Development Report. Trade concentration for each area is computed using the IMF Direction of Trade Statistics, December 1999. All figures indicate 1998 levels.

standards. The openness and trade concentration criteria suggest that Canada would be quite a good candidate for a fixed dollar exchange rate, but John Murray (this volume) has pointed out that Canada still receives very different shocks to the United States because of the importance of its resource-based exports. In addition, it has no problem of liability dollarization; floating is unproblematic; its interest rates are actually lower than those in the United States; it already has deep financial markets; it would lose a lender of last resort capacity under dollarization; and it would have no seat at the policy table. These factors lead me to regard Canada as an unlikely candidate for dollarization.

The small countries of Central America and the Caribbean have all the characteristics of being part of a dollar OCA. They would lose seigniorage, but for most of them, at least, that is probably outweighed by the saving in interest costs that they could expect. They are too small to exert any influence on U.S. policy, whatever the rule book says. Most of their shocks seem likely to parallel those in the United States, with the exception of natural disasters, to which devaluation seems a poor policy response in any event. The only other disadvantage of dollarization is that they would lack a lender of last resort, but one suspects that use of the central bank to bail out banks in countries as small as these would be a disaster anyway. This implies that dollarization would be virtually all gain and almost no loss, at least in economic terms.

Mexico's position is fairly similar to that of Canada. It is somewhat smaller and slightly less open, but more important are the facts that it has an interest premium, more liability dollarization, and less developed capital markets. Its shocks also differ from U.S. shocks: even today oil and interest rates are significant factors in the Mexican economy, with impacts very different to those on the United States.

Brazil is clearly a much less compelling candidate than Canada for dollarization. Its economy is larger and much less open and has a far more diversified trade pattern. Its exports still contain an important component of primary commodities (much of it partly processed and therefore statistically counted among manufactures), leading to a presumption that its shocks are unlikely to match those in the United States. It is large enough to develop its own financial markets now that it has stabilized inflation. It has made use of the lender of last resort facility in recent years. It does not have much of a problem of liability dollarization. It increasingly expects to have a place at the table. Perhaps the major disadvantage of not dollarizing is that interest rates could not be expected to fall close to those in the United States. Thus there is not much of an economic case for dollarization, while politically there is no constituency for it. I judge it inconceivable that Brazil will dollarize.

If, contrary to that prognostication, Brazil were to dollarize, then that might be a reasonable policy for *Argentina* as well. Since Brazil will not dollarize, however, it looks like a terrible policy choice. Argentina has a pretty large economy; it is almost as closed as Brazil; its trade is highly diversified, with trade with Brazil alone almost double that with the United States (and growing more rapidly); and its shocks are more likely to be similar to those faced by Brazil than to U.S. shocks. The only real argument for dollarization is the extent of liability dollarization already. Despite that, I would have thought that a monetary union with Brazil would be a more interesting long-run possibility for Argentina, especially if one believes that the architects of the EU were right in arguing that a common market would be unable to strengthen and thrive in an environment of exchange-rate instability. It is doubtless true that interest rates would not converge to a level as low as dollar interest rates in a Mercosur monetary union, and it would take longer to build deep financial markets. Nevertheless, rather than contemplate dollarization, Argentina would seem better advised to research the possibilities of a Mercosur monetary union (which would certainly face formidable transitional problems in both dedollarizing the Argentinean private sector and aligning exchange rates).

The *other countries of Mercosur* are stronger candidates for monetary union than Argentina on grounds of size and openness. Their direction of trade and probably their pattern of shocks would suggest that they might have more to gain from a Mercosur monetary union than from dollarization. On the other hand, interest rates would not fall as much, financial development would not be as rapid, and some of them already suffer from a high level of liability dollarization. One could probably make an economic case for whichever course seemed politically more attractive.

The *Andean countries* (Colombia, Ecuador, Peru, and Venezuela) are in an intermediate situation: smaller economies, fairly open, a substantial concentration of trade on North America, though all with important commodity exports that make it unlikely that they will experience a benign coincidence of shocks with the United States. They probably all have a significant level of liability dollarization. Perhaps the rest would be best advised to wait and see how dollarization works in Ecuador before they make a move.

▶ Concluding Comments

Dollarization is not something that should be debated in the abstract, as though the issues are the same for Antigua and Argentina, for Barbados and Brazil, for Canada and Costa Rica. Circumstances differ, and policy should therefore differ accordingly. In particular, I see a stronger case for Mercosur to start thinking of creating its own monetary union rather than for some of its members to adopt the currency of a faraway country that shows not the slightest willingness to share its monetary sovereignty.

▶ Notes

This chapter is a revised outline of remarks delivered to the Conference of the North-South Institute entitled *To Dollarize or Not to Dollarize: Exchange-Rate Choices for the Western Hemisphere,* Ottawa, October 4–5, 2000. This revised version has benefited from the discussions at the conference, as well as helpful comments from Marcel Fratzscher and highly competent research assistance from Katherine Russ. Copyright © Institute for International Economics.

1. I neglect the issue of labor mobility, because I have concluded that Robert Mundell is right in thinking this issue is less central than his original analysis suggested.

2. I acknowledge that the Danish electorate defied this expectation.

10 Ronald I. McKinnon

The Problem of Dollar Encroachment in Emerging Markets

The U.S. dollar dominates international finance throughout most of the world—the major exception being Europe and its periphery of small countries that struggle to maintain exchange stability against the euro. Otherwise, the U.S. dollar is king. In a world of 150-plus national currencies, the efficiency of international exchange, including the settling of international payments, is greatly enhanced by having one dominate as international money.

But peripheral economies respond to this dollar dominance quite differently. At one extreme, some countries opt to give up monetary independence altogether by "dollarizing," as in Ecuador and Panama, or by adopting a strong form of a currency board based on the dollar, as in Argentina and Hong Kong. At the other extreme, some countries opt to assert domestic monetary independence by floating freely. But appearances are deceiving. The number of currencies that float "freely" against the dollar is also now very small—perhaps only the euro and the yen (Calvo and Reinhart, 2000)—and only then when measured on a very short-term basis, that is, by daily, weekly, or monthly fluctuations in exchange rates. So the polar extremes are thinly inhabited.

In between these extremes, the great majority of countries accommodate themselves more or less rationally to the pervasive use of the dollar in international finance. With unfavorable circumstances and poor policies, the dollar may *encroach* severely on the natural domain of the domestic currency, worsening monetary instability and losing seigniorage.

Even with a good domestic monetary policy toward the dollar for any one country, how well it works could well depend on how regional trading partners and competitors determine their dollar exchange rates. Unfortunately, a common regional currency among closely integrated economies is seldom politically feasible—with the outstanding exception of the success of the euro within the EU. However, a *common monetary standard based on the dollar* may still be feasible—as I will show for East Asia and for Canada, albeit in a somewhat less stringent format.

But a common monetary standard is robust only if domestic monetary policy is so constrained that exchange rate expectations are *regressive*. That is, if the domestic currency depreciates—either sharply and suddenly, as with the crisis of 1997–98 in East Asia, or gently, as with the downward

177

float of the Canadian dollar from 1991 to 2000—markets believe that the rate will come back to a more normal level.

To simplify the analytics, I shall consider three quite different—but highly stylized—classes of economies called "Canada," "Latin America," and "East Asia" (without Japan), respectively. How is, and how best should, monetary and exchange rate policies toward the dollar be conducted within each class? What then are the parallel implications for regulating their domestic financial systems—particularly banks—in intermediating international capital flows? The answers depend on the level of domestic financial development in general, and on the term to maturity of domestic finance in particular.

But first I will review the dollar's general role in monetizing and facilitating international exchange in the world economy.

◣ *The Dollar as Facilitator of International Exchange*

Apart from the large size of the American economy, why should the U.S. dollar now be so important in international finance?

The reasons are partly historical. In the aftermath of World War II, the United States provided the essential funding for the IMF, the Marshall Plan, and the Dodge Plan, which jointly restored exchange and price-level stability among the industrial countries while replenishing official exchange reserves. The world's only capital market without exchange controls was the American. Thus, the U.S. dollar, under the legal cover of the IMF's requirement that member countries declare a par value for their currencies, became the official *reserve* and *intervention* currency to which governments in other industrial, as well as developing, economies pegged their exchange rates. As long as the United States kept its own price level stable (as was more or less true in the 1950s and 1960s), these dollar pegs served to anchor the domestic price levels of participating countries (McKinnon, 1996).

Even when America's money manager, the Federal Reserve System, was controlling inflation rather badly—through the 1970s into the early 1980s—the dollar-based modes of international exchange proved surprisingly resilient. Although many other industrial countries had by then opened their financial markets and floated their exchange rates, the dollar was not significantly displaced as the international vehicle, invoice, and reserve currency in the foreign exchange markets. I will now go into more depth on the dollar's benign role of facilitating international exchange.

If postwar history had not been biased in favor of dollar supremacy, a "natural" asymmetry across different countries' currencies would have developed anyway. First consider a world of N national currencies without official interventions or foreign exchange targeting by governments. In organizing *private* interbank markets for foreign exchange, great savings in transactions costs can be had if just one national currency, the Nth, is chosen as the vehicle currency. Then all foreign exchange quotations—bids and offers—at all terms to maturity can take place against this one vehicle currency. The number of active markets can be reduced from $N(N-1)/2$ to just N-1. In a world of more than 150 national currencies, this is a tremendous economy of markets for the large commercial banks that make the foreign exchange market. The dollar's interbank role as the *vehicle* currency (being on one side of almost 90 percent of interbank transactions outside of Europe) allows banks to cover both their forward exchange and options exposures in much more liquid markets.

At longer term, international bond markets gain liquidity if just one, or no more than a small number, of fully convertible currencies denominate private or sovereign bond issues. Here, the U.S. dollar remains the most important currency but with diminished status because America is a net borrower with ongoing current account deficits. In contrast, the EU as a whole is a large net creditor to the world economy, with ongoing current-account surpluses. Thus, without diminishing the dollar's role in short-term international finance, the euro could become more important for new issues of international bonds.

However, trade in primary commodities shows a stronger pattern of using one national money as the main currency of *invoice*. Exports of homogeneous primary products such as oil, wheat, and copper all tend to be invoiced in dollars, with worldwide price formation in a centralized exchange. Spot trading, but particularly forward contracting, is concentrated at these centralized exchanges—which are usually in American cities such as Chicago and New York, although dollar-denominated commodity exchanges do exist in London and elsewhere. In periods of reasonable confidence in American monetary policy, these dollar commodity prices are relatively invariant to fluctuations in the dollar's exchange rate. In contrast, if any other country allows its exchange rate to fluctuate against the dollar, its domestic currency prices of primary commodities will vary in proportion—unless its trade is restricted.

Invoicing patterns for exports of manufactured goods are more complex. Major industrial countries with strong currencies tend to invoice their exports in their home currencies (Grasssman, 1973; McKinnon, 1979). Before the EMU, more than 75 percent of German exports had been invoiced in marks, more than 50 percent of French exports invoiced in francs, and so on. But these illustrative ratios were dominated by intra-European trade. With the advent of the EMU, continental European countries will begin invoicing much of their net exports outside the EU in euros. However, because intra–Latin American and intra-East Asian trade is mainly invoiced in U.S. dollars, a substantial but as yet unknown fraction of EU industrial exports to these areas will also be dollar invoiced.

Latin American exports to Europe are dollar invoiced if only because such a high proportion is primary products. Countries like Canada and Australia also find that the great bulk of their imports and exports are invoiced in U.S. dollars. In East Asia, another strong dollar area, the great bulk of foreign trade is invoiced in U.S. dollars even though Japan is the principal exporter to the region (McKinnon, 2000b). (The central role of the euro for trade on the European periphery is similarly dominant.)

So, in the absence of a purely international medium of exchange—such as gold in the nineteenth century—to facilitate a region's trade, one national money or regional one (if it exists) naturally tends to intermediate among a multitude of national moneys. If the U.S. dollar wasn't already playing this role, another (major) currency would replace it. But once established, the economies of scale for reducing transactions costs are so great in having most participants in international commerce using the same intermediary currency that only some cataclysmic financial event could displace it (Krugman, 1984).

The upper panel in table 10.1 summarizes my paradigm of the dollar's central role as the benign facilitator of international exchange in the absence of single world money. For both the private sector and for governments, the upper panel classifies how the dollar performs as medium of exchange, store of value, unit of account, and standard of deferred payment for purely international transacting on current and capital accounts. It is a slight generalization of a similar table presented in Kenen (1983), and applies as much

Table 10.1
The U.S. Dollar's Role as International Money

1. Facilitates international exchange: All countries

	Private	Official
Medium of exchange	Vehicle	Intervention
Store of value	Banking	Reserve
Unit of account	Invoice	Peg or target
Standard of deferred payment	Private bonds	Sovereign bonds

2. Encroaches on national money in domestic uses: Strongly in Latin America, less so in other LDCs

Medium of exchange: dollar circulates domestically in parallel with national money.
Safe haven (store of value): domestic currency assets only held at higher real interest rates than those on dollar assets.
Unit of account: money-wage and other short-term domestic contracts linked to dollar exchange rate.
Standard of deferred payment: longer-term domestic private debt contracts in dollars. But finance is generally short term.
Nominal anchor: Fiscal conditions permitting, the national central bank naturally gears monetary policy toward stabilizing its dollar exchange rate—if only on a downward crawl. Directly targeting domestic price inflation is not feasible.

to countries like Canada and Australia (with the European exception to be discussed) as to most of the developing world.

As long as the rules of the game—that is, the conventions of international exchange for using the dollar as the facilitating currency (see McKinnon [1996] for a deeper discussion of the evolution of these rules)—are well understood by all the participating countries, then international trade can be monetized and multilateral. However, if the rules and conventions for converting one national money into another break down, as they did in the 1930s, international trade becomes more bartered and bilateral.

▲ Dollar Encroachment on National Moneys?

But this central role of the dollar in international finance today also has a darker side: the potential displacement of national moneys for domestic uses—displacement that is particularly marked in the Latin American context. The lower panel of table 10.1 displays the various textbook roles of *domestic* money—medium of exchange, safe haven (store of value), unit of account, and standard of deferred payment—and summarizes how the U.S. dollar might encroach (has encroached, in the Latin American case) in each of these dimensions.

To be sure this dollar encroachment is not now a problem in the industrial economies, although it was a potential problem in the aftermath of World War II when European and Japanese currencies suffered from a complete loss of confidence. Most countries in western Europe, as well as Japan, retained capital controls well into the 1970s—in large part to protect the domains of their domestic currencies. But step-by-step European unification, culminating in the late 1990s with the adoption of the euro, ended any lingering problem of dollar encroachment in Europe. This huge new, but highly credible, euro-based regime can operate on a stand-alone basis with perhaps the world's largest market for long-term bonds.

The Canadian Case

Similarly, in Canada the U.S. dollar does not circulate domestically in parallel with the Canadian dollar, even though foreign trade with the U.S. is huge: all but two of the Canadian provinces export more to the United States than to other Canadian provinces (Courchene and Harris, 1999). And the term to maturity of Canadian bond and mortgage finance is fairly long. Canadians can, on occasion, sell bonds to foreigners denominated in Canadian dollars. Unlike most developing countries, Canada does not suffer from "original sin" (Eichengreen and Hausmann, 1999), that is, where all domestic finance is short term and borrowing from foreigners is always denominated in foreign exchange. Nevertheless, the relationship between the Canadian and American dollars remains unbalanced because of the special role of the U.S. dollar in the world economy.

Thus "optimum" monetary cum exchange rate policy for Canada should recognize that Canada, much more than Europe, is part of a *common monetary standard* dominated by the United States. The Canadian authorities have little scope for departing significantly from this standard, which can be approximated by a credible rule for targeting Canadian domestic inflation similar to the rule used by the U.S. Federal Reserve for targeting price inflation in the United States. And this rule is credible if fiscal deficits by the Canadian federal and provincial governments remain under control, and the Bank of Canada has elbow room for hitting its inflation targets through open-market operations in Canada's well-developed financial markets.

As long as the value of the Canadian dollar in terms of the American is thereby pinned down in the longer run, expectations in the foreign exchange markets remain regressive. Because the markets view any downward drift to be temporary, the Canadian dollar can then float "gently," that is, without being attacked in the Latin mode. These regressive exchange rate expectations create a virtuous circle: the long-term domestic bond market, with foreign participation in Canadian provincial and private corporate debt issues, is enhanced.

However, the Bank of Canada still has little discretionary monetary authority to offset macroeconomic shocks that are asymmetric to those occurring in the United States. Attempts by the Bank to undertake a vigorous countercyclical monetary policy out of phase with the U.S. Federal Reserve would result in excess exchange rate volatility and soon undermine the regressive exchange rate expectations that are so important for the health of Canada's financial markets. Whence the success of the Bank of Canada's neutral policy of targeting price inflation similar to that followed by the U.S. Federal Reserve, coupled with a policy of fiscal retrenchment by Canada's federal and provincial governments after 1995, in virtually eliminating risk premiums from Canadian long- and short-term interest rates relative to their American counterparts.

Even under a "gentle" float where the Bank of Canada sticks to its long-term inflation target, the range of variation in the Canadian dollar may still be uncomfortably wide in the medium term—sometimes helping to absorb macroeconomic shocks but other times aggravating them (Courchene and Harris, 1999). Thus, in circumstances where the Canadian dollar seems clearly misvalued (either too high or too low by a PPP standard) and is moving in the wrong direction, occasional official stabilizing intervention—perhaps joint with the U.S. government—is warranted.

Latin America and East Asia

However, for developing economies suffering from original sin, that is, domestic finance is naturally very short term and external liabilities are denominated in foreign exchange, encroachment is more of a problem, and "gentle" floats are not an option. In Latin America, we see widespread dollar encroachment on all the functions of domestic money listed in the lower panel of table 10.1. I will consider each in turn.

◣ Medium of Exchange

As a medium of exchange, the dollar now circulates widely as hand-to-hand currency throughout Latin America—and dollar bank accounts (interest-bearing and some checking) have been legalized within several countries. This parallel circulation means that comprehensive capital controls, designed to prevent switching between the domestic money and dollars, are impossible to enforce. (But mild reserve requirements or taxes on foreign borrowing, as in Chile until recently, may still be feasible.)

Why have Latin American monetary authorities allowed such invasive parallel circulation in dollars, where the demand for the domestic monetary base erodes and becomes quite unstable, to develop? First, many governments, with short time horizons of their own, want to attract emigrant remittances to the home country. So they offer domestic dollar deposits to nationals returning money to the country. (Even if Mexico's banking system does not now offer dollar-linked bank accounts, Mexico's long border with the United States with heavy two-way migration makes holding of interest-bearing dollar bank accounts just across the border very easy.) Second, where records of illegal export earnings don't exist for very important export products, such as narcotics, the national government can neither tax them nor force conversion of dollar export proceeds back into its domestic currency. Better to keep at least some of the dollar proceeds in banks within the country by offering attractive domestic deposit facilities in dollars.

Last, but not least, is the long history in almost all Latin American countries of persistent financial instability: high inflation, temporary stabilizations, currency crashes, renewed inflation, and so on. Holders of naked cash balances in the domestic currency have been heavily taxed in the past. Thus, the precautionary motive for holding at least some dollar balances, at home or abroad, is strong. Similar relatively large dollar holdings are commonplace in much of Africa and in the disintegrated fragments of the old Soviet Union—including Russia itself.

However, the internal circulation of dollars in parallel to domestic currencies is not a general phenomenon. Virtually all the economies of East Asia provide counterexamples. Even in those economies—Indonesia, Korea, Malaysia, Philippines, and Thailand—whose currencies were attacked in the great crisis of 1997–98, the internal circulation of U.S. dollars was negligible before the attacks began. These crisis economies—as well as the noncrisis ones of China, Hong Kong, Singapore, and Taiwan—all had what looked like sustainable, if informal, fixes for their dollar exchange rates before 1997

(McKinnon, 2000b). By and large, they did not have the same turbulent history of inflation and currency attacks so common in Latin America in the postwar. Indeed, with the possible exception of Indonesia, after the 1997–98 crisis all the emerging markets of East Asia appear to be returning to informal dollar pegging (McKinnon, 2000a). Their domestic rates of inflation remain surprisingly muted.

▶ Store of Value

However, as a *safe haven* store of value, interest-bearing dollar assets dominate domestic assets of the same term to maturity in Asia and Latin America as well as in other developing countries—all those parts of the world not dominated by the subsystem of European trade based on the euro. In the 1990s, the Federal Reserve System again succeeded in stabilizing the American price level (as measured by the U.S. producer price index). A political or economic crisis in any one of the developing countries on this periphery of the dollar standard generates pressure from domestic nationals to fly into dollars (unless restrained by capital controls)—including interest-bearing dollar assets.

Even on the East Asian periphery of the world dollar standard, U.S. Treasury bonds and certificates of deposit in American banks are viewed as the "risk-free" asset in the international bond markets. In the absence of exchange controls, domestic-currency bonds will only be willingly held if they bear a real rate of return higher than those on dollar bonds at an equivalent term to maturity. In effect, a substantial risk premium must be paid on term deposits (or bonds) in domestic currency compared to term deposits (or bonds) denominated in dollars—and this risk premium is typically much greater at long term than at short term. Indeed, the risk premium on long-term bonds denominated in domestic currency may be so great that an open market at the long end of the maturity spectrum usually doesn't exist.

How to measure this risk premium, that is, distinguish it from the expected annualized depreciation (or appreciation) of the domestic currency, is a tricky econometric problem. Moreover, within developing economies, interest rates are highly variable—both in time series and across countries. Before the 1997 currency attacks began in Thailand, the relevant risk premiums on three-month deposits in the East Asian debtor economies averaged about 4 percentage points, whereas in Latin America they averaged closer to 5 to 6 percentage points, above those on benchmark dollar assets.[1]

When finance is very short term, having such marked asymmetry between the center's and the periphery's interest rates poses severe problems for regulating banks and other domestic financial institutions—particularly in the peripheral countries themselves. Because of deposit insurance, whether formal or informal, and other bailout provisions for the banking system in a general crisis, there is always latent moral hazard. Thus if interest spreads between accepting domestic-currency and dollar deposits are high, domestic banks may prefer to gamble by accepting low-interest dollar deposits to finance high-interest loans in the domestic currency and not hedge the foreign exchange risk. The resulting "overborrowing" syndrome has been analyzed by McKinnon and Pill (1999).

This interest rate gap between the center and the periphery, coupled with weak regulation of domestic banks, helps explain excessive capital inflows into Chile in the late 1970s, into Mexico in the early 1990s, and into the East Asian crisis economies before 1997. Even when the U.S. dollar does not encroach directly on domestic monetary circulation, the problem of regulating banks to hedge their foreign exchange risks is more difficult for debtor countries on the periphery of the dollar standard. Importers and banks see the cost of forward cover, that is, the interest differential, to be too high. In contrast, in the United States itself, virtually all short-term claims on, and liabilities to, foreigners are dollar denominated—so that chronic foreign exchange exposure is generally not a problem for the world's biggest debtor economy. In this important respect, the regulation of banks at the center is much easier than it is on the periphery.

▶ *Unit of Account*

Unit of account and standard of deferred payment are closely related concepts and refer to money's role as a *numéraire* in domestic contracts: the former is more of a short-term concept whereas the latter is longer term. For longer-term private debt contracts within Latin American countries, the dollar is commonly used as the standard of deferred payment even when the domestic currency is used as the means of settlement. The presumption is that the dollar keeps its real purchasing value through time better, and that one can get instantaneous exchange rate quotes on the value of the dollar in domestic currency when the contract matures. Correspondingly, private debt contracts are seldom linked to domestic price indexes—such as the wholesale price index (WPI) or consumer price index (CPI)—in part because of doubts over the statistical reliability of such indexes and because of lags in collecting price data. Even with the dollar as *numéraire* for domestic bond issues, such contracts are usually short term—or have a floating interest rate set according to the yield on short-term (30-day) assets.

More subtle is the dollar's role as a unit of account in other short-term contracts—such as the setting of money wages, and its impact on the flexibility of real wages. In Latin America, it seems that real wages may be more rigid under flexible exchange rates than if the exchange rate is fixed.

Consider the problem faced by a trade union representative of the widget industry that is negotiating a collective contract. He is asked to sign a contract that is implicitly denominated in dollars in the fixed exchange rate regime but is denominated in an erratic and unpredictable unit in a flexible regime. It is reasonable to assume that under the flexible-rate regime the representative would bargain for a shorter life to the contract (to provide more rapid renegotiations) or for some form of indexation (to denominate the contract in a more stable unit). Under these conditions, nominal wages tend to react more swiftly to price shocks under flexible regimes than under fixed, leading to more de facto indexation (Hausmann et al., 1999, p. 13).

Hausmann et al. (1999) provide empirical evidence that real wages are more rigid in response to, say, terms of trade shocks for Latin American countries with flexible exchange rates than for those with fixed rates. This finding is quite contrary to what had been the accepted theory (Friedman, 1953; Mundell, 1961) of flexible exchange rates' leading to greater real wage flexibility for easing adjustment to real economic shocks. These problems in domestic labor and capital markets, with the very short term of both domestic and international payments, help explain why we do not observe "pure" floats in emerging market economies (Calvo and Reinhart, 2000).

To see this better, suppose ongoing inflation requires some downward drift in the dollar value of the domestic currency measured at low frequencies, that is, monthly or quarterly, as with the fairly predictable downward crawl of 4 to 5 percent per year in the Indonesian rupiah before 1997 or Brazil before the currency attack in 1999. This predictable crawl is then reflected in commensurately higher domestic nominal (but not real) interest rates and in ongoing nominal wage adjustments—perhaps built into longish domestic wage contracts—of 4 to 5 percent per year. Even then, governments find it optimal to peg closely to the dollar at high frequencies, that is, on a weekly or even daily basis, in order to reduce (short-term) payments risk—thus further reducing the risk premium in the short-term interest differential.

Before the 1997–98 crisis, *all* the emerging market economies in East Asia pegged remarkably tightly to the dollar on a daily basis in comparison to the much greater daily fluctuations in the yen/dollar or euro/dollar rates (McKinnon, 2000a). Like the United States itself, Europe and Japan have robust longer-term bond markets—as do Canada and Australia. Their better-developed capital markets without exchange controls make hedging short-term exchange risk by importers and banks relatively easy. Thus the euro and the yen float "freely" against the U.S dollar in the short term. Subject to the longer-term restraints on Canadian monetary policy described earlier, so does the Canadian dollar float freely on a daily or weekly basis. In contrast, after the 1997–98 crisis, all the emerging markets in East Asia have returned to very tight high-frequency pegging against the dollar into the year 2000 (McKinnon, 2000a). In Latin America, the same kind of high-frequency exchange rate pegging is observed in noncrisis periods.

◣ *Exchange Rate Policy and Bank Regulation*

Can we relate this general tendency for high-frequency exchange rate peg-ging to different bank and foreign exchange regulatory regimes in devel-oping countries on the periphery? If the regulatory authorities strictly limit any net direct or indirect foreign exchange exposure on the part of banks, this would drive them out of the business of accepting low-cost foreign exchange deposits to finance higher-yield domestic currency loans. The in-flow of *short-term* foreign capital into the economy would be reduced. But such strict regulation would not impair the banks' role of servicing and facilitating foreign exchange transactions by domestic merchants and man-ufacturers.

However, strict regulation against foreign exchange exposure could se-verely limit the ability of the banks to act collectively as dealer-speculators to "make" the foreign exchange market. "Stabilizing" speculation by banks, the most natural foreign exchange traders and dealers, would not be pos-sible.

Consider the implications for optimal short-term foreign exchange management, first when capital controls are absent, and second when they are effectively applied.

Case 1: No capital controls, imperfect bank regulation. Either because regulatory weakness leaves too many banks (and possibly importers) with exposed foreign exchange positions, or because the government doesn't want to impose draconian rules against institutions assuming *any* open foreign exchange position, an informal hedge is provided by keeping the exchange rate steady in the short term. The short time frame over which foreign currency debts—largely in dollars—are incurred and then repaid on a day-to-day or even a week-to-week basis, defines the same time frame over which the dollar exchange rate is (and should be) kept stable in noncrisis periods.

Case 2: Direct capital controls. Suppose the government prevents banks, other financial institutions, and individuals from holding any foreign exchange assets or liabilities. Nonbank firms engaged in foreign trade cannot take positions in foreign exchange except for the minimum necessary in their particular trade. Importers are prevented from building up undue for-eign currency debts except for ordinary trade credit, and exporters are re-quired to repatriate their dollar earnings quickly. In particular, banks cannot accept foreign currency deposits or hold foreign currency deposits abroad or make foreign currency loans. Then private agents in general, and banks in particular, cannot act as dealer-speculators to determine the level of the exchange rate (McKinnon, 1979, ch. 6). The exchange rate will become indeterminate (highly volatile) unless the government steps in as a dealer to clear international transactions. Thus, the government must take open po-sitions, which determine the level of the exchange rate, and assume the exchange risk. So if the government is determining the exchange rate day-to-day anyway, why not keep it stable?

China and Malaysia more or less correspond to case 2 in imposing capital controls (although not as rigidly as just described). Thus their governments have wisely fixed their dollar exchange rates—certainly in the short run and maybe longer. Because Korea and Thailand have now pretty well rid themselves of the last vestiges of the capital controls they once had, they correspond more to case 1. And the Korean and Thai governments are indeed reducing exchange risk in their economies by keeping their rates virtually pegged in the short run, even if they cannot prevent some medium- and longer-term movement—particularly in the unsettled aftermath of the 1997–98 crisis.

However, while such soft short-term pegs reduce foreign exchange risk for "well-behaved" merchant traders and financial institutions, this regime may be exploited by financial institutions (and some traders) with moral hazard. Poorly regulated and undercapitalized banks with deposit insurance may be more willing to gamble by accepting short-term foreign currency deposits to finance their domestic loan portfolios if they know the exchange is stable in the short run.

What might we conclude? *With* or *without* capital controls, high-frequency pegging is optimal when the term structure of finance is very short and domestic capital markets are underdeveloped. Beyond the nominal anchor argument for stabilizing exchange rates in the medium and longer terms, there is a risk-reducing argument for very short-term pegging.

But, except in a crisis, pervasive direct capital controls on the gross foreign exchange positions of banks (as under case 2) are unlikely to be the best way of controlling exchange risk when private financial markets are incomplete.

First, preventing banks from accepting any foreign currency deposits, or making any foreign currency loan, disrupts banks' traditional role of clearing foreign payments and settling accounts. On any trading day, the enormous flow of foreign payments would have to be cleared directly by the central bank.

Second, such capital controls make it impossible for banks to do the covered interest arbitrage necessary to make the forward market in foreign exchange, that is, determine the forward rate relative to the spot rate (McKinnon, 1979, ch. 5). Either the private sector is left with no mechanism for hedging international transactions, or the government (central bank) is dragged willy-nilly into writing forward exchange contracts for private traders—a process that has been open to abuse around the world.

So, on the periphery, the best way of controlling risk in the foreign exchanges is case 3.

Case 3: Net foreign exchange exposure of banks is regulated to be zero. The domestic banking authorities let authorized commercial banks acquire foreign exchange assets and liabilities gross, but their net position, perhaps defined at the end of each trading day, must be zero. And, in making this calculation, the regulators also consider indirect as well as direct foreign exchange liabilities. For example, if a bank accepts dollar deposits to lend to domestic firms in dollars, its balance sheet may look square. But the nonbank domestic borrower may now be exposed to currency risk and could default if the domestic currency is devalued. Exchange risk is translated into default risk into banking risk. Similarly, banks may undertake off-balance-sheet transactions in derivatives, which increase their foreign exchange exposure and are hard to detect.

While necessarily only approximate in practice, forcing banks to (near) zero net foreign exchange exposure is nevertheless a valuable regulatory principle. It counters the various margins of temptation not to hedge—as described earlier. In particular, it prevents banks from accepting foreign currency deposits to make domestic currency loans. But even if applied quite strictly, this regulatory principle leaves enough flexibility for the commercial banking system as a whole to perform its normal facilitating role in the foreign exchanges. For any given spot exchange rate, the clearing of international payments and settling accounts can devolve from the central bank. The commercial banks can still undertake covered interest arbitrage and so create a market in forward exchange to service the hedging needs of their nonbank "retail" customers.

That said, however, imposing the rule of no net foreign exchange exposure (case 3) means that the banks still cannot act as (stabilizing) speculators to determine the level of the exchange rate. In this one important respect, case 3 is similar to case 2. With either capital controls or a rule of no net foreign exchange exposure, the exchange rate would be indeterminate, that is, highly volatile, unless the government itself enters the market to act as a stabilizing speculator. So even with "first-best" bank regulation for controlling risk in place, that is, case 3, the government is still forced to determine the equilibrium exchange rate on a daily basis.

Because Latin American countries have a much longer history of currency attacks and internal bank failures than those of East Asia, most now (as they did during the 1997–98 Asian crisis) aspire to regulate banks toward no net foreign exchange exposure. Of course, there are other dimensions of domestic finance—such as fiscal deficits, ongoing inflation, and huge bad loan portfolios in commercial banks, as well as regulatory weakness—that increase macroeconomic volatility and limit growth in Latin America.

With these cases, I have examined three quite different foreign exchange regimes for "emerging market" economies. All three were found to be consistent with the high-frequency pegging to the dollar observed in East Asia. But the argument applies quite generally to other developing countries in Latin America, South Asia, and so on.

For Canada, by contrast, such draconian regulatory stringency as is embodied in case 3 is unnecessary and unwarranted. Long-term finance is available for intermediating international capital flows, and banks are better supervised, with effective capital requirements to limit the moral hazard arising out of deposit insurance. Most important, the interest differential between deposits denominated in Canadian dollars and U.S. dollars is negligible. Thus Canadian banks and merchant importers have little or no incentive not to hedge their exchange risks.

◣ Lengthening the Term Structure of Finance in Emerging Markets

For the peripheral countries, how can the regulatory and foreign exchange regimes be reformed so as to encourage the development of longer-term bond markets, both domestically and for foreign capital inflows? In short, how can they escape from original sin?

First, in the face of fiscal deficits, inflation, and ongoing depreciations, the term structure of domestic finance cannot be lengthened. Redemption is not possible. Domestic finance will remain short-term—with the risks somewhat ameliorated by the high-frequency exchange rate pegging described earlier. But measured on a low-frequency basis, that is, monthly or quarterly, the domestic currency inevitably depreciates—whether by a comparatively gentle downward crawl or by a series of discrete devaluations. The result is that nobody will willingly hold longer-term unindexed financial instruments denominated in the domestic currency.

Because Latin America has been associated the most strongly with this syndrome, many see the solution to be one of eliminating domestic monetary independence altogether. Currency boards based on the dollar, as in Argentina[2] and Panama, or outright dollarization, as in Ecuador, are draconian schemes for reducing the monetary distinction between the periphery and the center. At the same time, they solve the time consistency problem in domestic macroeconomic decision making. And the net loss of seigniorage is minimal because many of these economies start from a position of being largely dollarized anyway.

However, out-of-control fiscal policies remain a serious loose end, so that the interest rate differential in Argentina and Panama with the United States remains surprisingly large at various terms to maturity. Moreover, capital inflows into these dollar-based countries remain ultrasensitive to shocks in the world capital market, as with the 1998 Russian crisis and the 1999 Brazilian crisis (Hausmann, 2000). Indeed, the depreciation of the Brazilian real against the dollar created a double whammy for Argentina: a sudden loss of competitiveness against a major trading partner and the increased spread over London Interbank Offer Rate (LIBOR) of all dollar-based borrowing in the area. Clearly, it is risky for one country to adopt a currency board when close trading partners do not.

Nevertheless, because of the tumultuous financial history of countries such as Argentina and Ecuador, using a currency board to become part of the monetary regime of the center country may still be worthwhile in the longer term. Macroeconomic stability is more easily maintained, and greater credibility in the international capital markets may eventually allow lengthening the term to maturity of both domestic finance and foreign borrowing. The key is to give investors long-term assurance that 10 to 20 years from now the peripheral country's nominal exchange rate will be the same as it is today. Then both private firms and the government can issue 10- to 20-year fixed interest rate bonds on terms not too much less favorable than those on "risk-free" U.S. Treasury bonds of the same maturities.

But what may be best for Latin America's already largely dollarized economies need not be a good choice for East Asian debtor economies. In East Asia, dollars don't impinge on domestic monetary circulation, and ongoing inflation has not been a problem (except for Indonesia), as government budgets often showed surpluses. During their "miracle" growth phases before 1997, the East Asian economies successfully pegged to the dollar as the nominal anchor for their domestic price levels (McKinnon, 2000b). With the benefit of hindsight, however, we now know that this policy was seriously incomplete. First, and most obviously, was the failure to properly regulate the financial system—including the central bank itself in some cases—against undue risk taking, including short-term foreign exchange exposure.

Second, and more subtly, the East Asian debtor economies had not committed themselves to a long-term exchange rate parity in the mode of the nineteenth-century gold standard (Goodhart and Delargy, 1998)—even though they seemed to be securely pegged in the short and medium terms. Because of the short-term structure of finance, each was vulnerable to a speculative attack on its currency; but none had a long-run exchange rate strategy in place to mitigate the worst consequences of any such attack. Postcrisis, there was no well-defined tradition of returning to the precrisis exchange rate. In contrast, under the classical gold standard, if a government was forced to suspend its gold parity in a crisis, it was obligated to return to its precrisis parity (McKinnon, 1996, chs. 2 and 4). This restoration rule kept exchange rate expectations regressive.

The problem was aggravated because the pre-1997 East Asian dollar standard was informal rather than formal. With the exception of Hong Kong, none of the countries involved had formally declared a dollar parity—and each had been classified by the IMF as following some variety of managed floating rather than being pegged to the dollar. Thus, with the forced suspension of these dollar pegs in the 1997–98 crisis, there was no traditional dollar parity (gold parity in the nineteenth-century sense) to which the government was bound to return. In the crisis, the absence of regressive expectations led to a very inefficient trade-off: the East Asian five suffered from both deep (albeit temporary) devaluations and very high (short-term) interest rates (McKinnon, 2000b).

Thus, emerging economies whose macroeconomic fundamentals are sound so as to permit a "good fix" for their exchange rates (McKinnon and Pill, 1999) should extend the maturity of that commitment to the distant

future. If the East Asian Five had, before the 1997 crisis, adopted a restoration rule explicitly—and, ideally, collectively—they could have moderated
the high interest rates and deep devaluations that bankrupted so much of
their economies once the attacks began. (Of course, countries that must
rely on the inflation tax, and cannot credibly commit to long-run exchange
rate stability, should not try it.) The benefits from having the exchange rate
pinned down in the long run exceed those from having a hard short-term
fix.

Only with long-term confidence in the purchasing power of domestic
money (against the center country's) would exchange rate expectations be
naturally regressive, and are long-term bond and mortgage markets possible
to organize—both domestically and for commercial (nonsovereign) international borrowing. An appropriate accounting framework with full disclo-
sure for bond issuers, and a legal framework to secure the rights of bond
holders, and so on, now become more relevant.

Barry Eichengreen and Ricardo Hausmann (1999) discuss, very per-
ceptively, the need to lengthen the term to maturity of domestic markets
for bonds and bank loans. However, their approach is the inverse of what
I am suggesting here. They want to start encouraging longer-term bond
finance by domestic institutional and legal changes and hope that this would
lead to greater (long-term) exchange rate stability. I would start with a long-
run exchange rate commitment, that is, the restoration rule, to create a
friendlier environment for strengthening the institutions governing bond
markets. The emphasis of the two approaches is different, but they are not
in conflict.

There is a virtuous circle. When long-term bond issues in the
nineteenth-century mode begin to displace short-term bank finance, the
government's commitment to long-term exchange rate stability is naturally
reinforced. On the one hand, lengthening the term structure of finance
makes the economy less vulnerable to currency attacks in the foreign exchanges; and, on the other hand, the domestic banking system becomes less
vulnerable to internal runs. And the empirical evidence suggests that currency attacks and commercial bank runs are strongly correlated (Kaminsky
and Reinhart, 1999). Finally, with a more vigorous domestic bond market,
the central bank can better conduct domestic open-market operations to
defend the currency and secure the domestic price level over the longer run.

▲ Common Monetary Standards among Neighboring Countries: A Concluding Note

Although Canada's bond and mortgage markets are already long term, with
minimal risk premiums in interest rates at all terms to maturity, I argued
earlier that the Bank of Canada must (should) still consider itself on a
common monetary standard with the United States. A truly independent

Canadian monetary policy is simply not feasible without upsetting the regressive expectations that make the Canadian dollar's "gentle" float possible. And, because of Canada's massive and growing trade integration with the United States, the acceptable range of variability Can\$/U.S.\$ rate is narrowing, and there is a case for evolving back into a fixed exchange rate with the United States (Courchene and Harris, 1999). However, Canada's financial system seems healthy in other dimensions. Thus the additional economic gains from taking this last politically difficult step of fixing the Canadian dollar against the American are moderate.

Canada also has the advantage of being able to decide on its "optimal" monetary and exchange rates policies against the United States without much regard for economic events in the rest of the world. An astonishingly high proportion of Canadian exports, over 80 percent, now flow to the United States, so that the importance of other trading partners pales in comparison. True, the Canadian authorities must still worry whether or not the U.S. Federal Reserve is succeeding in anchoring the virtually common price level. However, they need not worry about exchange rate and monetary changes in other countries.

Such is not the case in East Asia or in Latin America.

For any one member country of the East Asian dollar standard, the stability of its nominal anchor depends more on having all or most of East Asian countries jointly stabilizing their dollar exchange rates—and not just on the American price level itself. The 1997–98 crisis throws strong light on the issue. The sharp currency devaluations of Indonesia, Korea, Malaysia, Philippines, and Thailand—and the collapse in their demand for imports—imposed severe deflationary pressure on those countries that did not devalue or that devalued by considerably less than did these crisis economies. The *dollar*-invoiced prices of most goods traded in the region fell (McKinnon, 2000a). This fall in the region's dollar price level then muted the increases in the internal price levels of the devaluing economies, while contributing to the serious absolute deflationary pressure in China and Hong Kong, which did not devalue at all.

What is the lesson from this regional deflation? East Asian countries are now highly integrated in their trading relationships with each other. Indeed, C. H. Kwan (2000) shows that, for the last two decades, intra-Asian trade (including Japan) has risen much faster than trade with the United States. Now about 50 percent of gross East Asian exports goes to other East Asian countries, and only 25 percent goes to the United States. The 1997–98 crisis revealed how the success of any one country pegging to the dollar as a nominal anchor depends heavily on also having its trading partners and competitors securely anchored as well. From this collective "nominal anchor" perspective, East Asia has become a natural currency area over which one wants exchange rates to be stable.

In Latin America, the spillover effects from neighboring countries being knocked off their dollar pegs can be similarly devastating. Within Mercosur, the southern Latin American free trade area, the 1999 devaluation of the Brazilian real had a devastating effect on Argentina. To end expectations of ongoing inflation and to lengthen the term structure of Argentinian finance, there was a strong case for Argentina unilaterally adopting a currency board—with a "permanently" fixed exchange rate against the dollar. However, other close trading partners should be, should have been, on the same standard.

So in rationalizing national exchange rate cum monetary policy against the world's dominant international money, only Canada and a few other countries can safely act unilaterally. In other parts of the world where regional trade is important but a regional common currency is not politically feasible, establishing an efficient common monetary standard is much more a matter of collective choice. Policymakers in a region with integrated trade should expend their political capital to ensure that countries in the region have similar commitments to stabilize their dollar exchange rates over the long term.

▲ Notes

1. Measured against the absurdly low nominal interest rates on yen assets in the 1990s, these spreads would have been much higher. But one can show that the low-interest-rate trap in Japan in the 1990s was also an indirect effect of the operation of the world dollar standard. See McKinnon and Ohno (1997) and Goyal and McKinnon (2002).
2. Written before Argentina's currency board collapsed in January 2002.

▲ References

Calvo, Guillermo, and Carmen Reinhart. (2000, May). Fear of Floating. Mimeograph. University of Maryland.

Courchene, Thomas, and Richard Harris. (1999). From Fixing to Monetary Union: Options for North American Currency Integration. C. D. Howe Institute *Commentary*, June. Toronto, Canada.

Eichengreen, Barry, and Ricardo Hausmann. (1999). *Exchange Rates and Financial Fragility*. 1999 Pacific Basin Conference: Financial Crises in Emerging Markets, San Francisco.

Friedman, Milton. (1953). The Case for Flexible Exchange Rates. In *Essays in Positive Economics* (pp. 157–203). Chicago: University of Chicago Press.

Goyal, Rishi, and Ronald McKinnon. (2002). Japan's Negative Risk Premium in Interest Rates and Fall in Bank Lending, *World Economy.*

Goodhart, Charles, and P. J. R. Delargy. (1998). Financial crises: Plus ça change, plus c'est la même chose, *International Finance, 1*(2), 261-88.

Grassman, Sven. (1973). *Exchange Reserves and the Financial Structure of Foreign Trade*. London: Saxon House.

Hausmann, Ricardo. (2000). Latin America: No Fireworks, No Crisis? In J. Bisignano, W. Hunter, and G. Kaufman (Eds.), *Global Financial Crises: Lessons from Recent Events* (pp. 27–48). Chicago: Kluwer Academic Publishers.

Hausmann, R., G. Gavin, C. Pages-Serra, and E. Stein. (1999). *Financial Turmoil and the Choice of an Exchange Rate Regime* (Working Paper #400). Inter-American Development Bank.

Kaminsky, G., and C. Reinhart. (1999). The Twin Crises: Balance of Payments and Banking Crises in Developing Countries. *American Economics Review, 89*(3), 473–500.

Kenen, Peter. (1983). *The Role of the Dollar as International Currency* (Occasional Paper No.13). Group of Thirty, New York.

Krugman, Paul. (1984). The International Role of the Dollar: Theory and Prospect. In J. Bilson and R. Marston (Eds.), *Exchange Rate Theory and Practice* (pp. 261–78). Chicago: University of Chicago Press.

Kwan, C. H. (2000). *The Economics of a Yen Bloc.* Brookings Institution and Nomura Research Institute, Washington.

McKinnon, Ronald I. (1993). *The Order of Economic Liberalization: Financial Control in the Transition to a Market Economy.* Baltimore: Johns Hopkins University Press.

McKinnon, Ronald I. (1979). *Money in International Exchange: The Convertible Currency System.* New York: Oxford University Press.

McKinnon, Ronald I. (1996). *The Rules of the Game: International Money and Exchange Rates.* Cambridge: MIT Press.

McKinnon, Ronald I. (2000a). After the Crisis, the East Asian Dollar Standard Resurrected: An Interpretation of High Frequency Pegging. (Working Paper, Stanford Economics Department). Available online at *http://www-econ.stanford.edu/faculty/workp/index.html.*

McKinnon, Ronald I. (2000b). The East Asian Dollar Standard: Life After Death? (World Bank workshop on "Rethinking the East Asian Miracle"). *Economic Notes, 29*(1). Earlier version available online at http://www-econ.stanford.edu/faculty/workp/index.html.

McKinnon, Ronald I., and Kenichi Ohno. (1997). *Dollar and Yen: Resolving Economic Conflict Between the United States and Japan.* Cambridge, Mass.: MIT Press. (Japanese translation published by Nihon Keizai Shimbun, 1998).

McKinnon, Ronald I., and Kenichi Ohno. (in press). *The Foreign Exchange Origins of Japan's Economic Slump and Low Interest Liquidity Trap.* Available online at http://www-econ.stanford.edu/faculty/workp/index.html.

McKinnon, Ronald I., and Huw Pill. (1999). Exchange Rate Regimes for Emerging Markets: Moral Hazard, and International Overborrowing. *Oxford Review of Economic Policy, 15*(3), 19–38. Earlier version available online at http://www-econ.stanford.edu/faculty/workp/index.html.

Mundell, Robert A., (1961). A Theory of Optimum Currency Areas. *American Economic Review, 51,* 509–17.

11 Dominick Salvatore

Which Countries in the Americas Should Dollarize?

During the past two years a great debate has taken place in the Americas on the feasibility and benefits of official or full dollarization, where the dollar acquires the exclusive or predominant status of full legal tender in a country. If the domestic currency is retained, it is clearly confined to a secondary role, such as circulating only in the form of coins having small denominations and value, as, for example, in Panama today. Under full dollarization, the nation gives up control over the nation's money supply and hence its ability to conduct an independent monetary policy.

The reason for concentrating on full or official dollarization is that partial or unofficial dollarization—where people hold a significant amount of dollars in cash, or even as dollar deposits, but the national currency remains the money in use for most everyday transactions and the nation retains control over its money supply and the ability to conduct an independent monetary policy—is already widespread in most Latin American countries and requires no official action, except allowing it to take place. It is also clear that the reason for its occurrence is the desire on the part of many Latin Americans to protect themselves against devaluations of the national currency and high domestic inflation.

Berg and Borensztein (chapter 3 of this book) found that six Latin American countries (Argentina, Bolivia, Costa Rica, Nicaragua, Peru, and Uruguay) were already "highly dollarized" as of 1995, in the sense that dollar deposits in the nation's banking system exceeded 30 percent. They classified another eight Latin American countries (Dominica, Ecuador, El Salvador, Guinea, Honduras, Jamaica, Mexico, and Trinidad and Tobago) as "moderately dollarized," with dollar deposits averaging 16.4 percent of total deposits in the domestic banking system.

Occupying an intermediate position is a currency board (as Argentina had from 1991 until the beginning of 2002) under which the national currency circulates alongside the dollar but remains predominant in everyday usage but the national central bank relinquishes control over the nation's money supply and its ability to conduct an independent monetary policy. By retaining its own currency, however, the currency board still leaves the nation vulnerable to exchange rate and financial crises arising out of the fear of a devaluation of the national currency vis-à-vis the dollar. The currency risk forces the nation to pay a significant interest-rate premium on its international borrowing. This is the reason that Argentina began to consider full or official dollarization at the beginning of 1999 when it came under heavy pressure after Brazil (its major economic partner in and the dominant economic power in Mercosur) sharply devalued its currency. With the financial crisis actually deteriorating in the fall of 2001, Argentina again faced the choice of either devaluing the peso or fully dollarizing.

Besides the Commonwealth of Puerto Rico and the U.S. Virgin Islands in the Americas, Panama has had full or official dollarization since 1904 (i.e., since a few years after it gained its independence from Colombia). Ecuador fully dollarized in 2000, and El Salvador and Guatemala in 2001. Several other Latin American countries are also strongly considering full dollarization. Many businesspeople in Mexico, Canada, and even Brazil are advocating the full dollarization of the entire American continent. Thus it is important to examine the benefits and costs of full dollarization as compared with having a currency board or simply a fixed exchange rate.

▶ Benefits and Costs of Dollarization

There are several important benefits that a country would receive by fully dollarizing. These are as follows.

1. *Lower Transaction Costs.* With the adoption of the dollar as the currency of the nation, its citizens and businesspeople avoid the cost of exchanging the domestic currency for dollars and the need to hedge foreign exchange risks. This tends to facilitate and increase international trade and investments in the nation. Banks in the nation are also able to hold lower reserves with full dollarization. A study by Moreno-Villalaz (1999), for example, estimated that Panamanian banks held 5 percent fewer reserves than they would have without dollarization.

2. *Lower Inflation and Interest Rates.* By adopting the dollar, the nation will face an inflation rate and thus an interest rate similar to that of the United States. This encourages savings and investments (both domestic and foreign) and stimulates the nation's growth. For example, fully dollarized Panama had a much lower interest rate than Argentina (which was only partially dollarized, with a currency board rigidly tying the pesos to the dollar) and still lower than Brazil (the least dollarized of the three countries). Although the interest-rate spread of dollar-denominated bonds over comparable U.S. Treasury securities increased by an average of 800 basis points for all of Latin America during the Russian crisis in summer 1998, the increase was only 200 basis points for fully dollarized Panama.

The reason that a dollarized country will have an inflation rate similar to that of the United States is, of course, because of commodity arbitrage. This does not allow the price of internationally traded goods to exceed U.S. prices by more than the costs of transportation and whatever trade restriction the nation might have (which, however, tends to be much lower with

dollarization than without it). Similarly, interest rates in the dollarized country tend to fall to the U.S. level, except for any remaining country risk (i.e.,
political factors that affect security and property rights in the nation). That
is, dollarization removes the currency but not the country risk, but this can
still be very beneficial to the nation and may even lead to a reduction in
the country risk.

3. *Greater Openness, Transparency, and International Financial Integration.* By eliminating foreign exchange crises, dollarization reduces or eliminates the need for foreign exchange and trade controls. In addition, by
giving up the ability to create money and inflationary financing, dollarization also fosters budgetary discipline, whereby fiscal deficits must be financed by higher taxes rather than by the less transparent method of printing money. Furthermore, full or official dollarization encourages more rapid
and full international financial integration by providing foreign financial
institutions the same treatment as domestic ones. Dollarization per se does
not create international financial integration, but it does facilitate and encourage it. International financial integration then facilitates the inflow of
foreign capital (in the form of financial and direct investments), which
stimulates growth.

Although (as pointed out by Eichengreen in chapter 6 of this book) a
direct way is not available for measuring quantitatively the benefits of full
dollarization, a good indirect way is to estimate how much the growth and
the international financial integration of the nation would be increased by
dollarization. While hard numbers are not available, the softer evidence that
is available all seems to point out that dollarization can greatly stimulate
growth and significantly improve the economic performance of the nation.
For example, the government of Argentina estimated that during the past
decade the rate of national growth would have been 2 percentage points
higher with dollarization than without it. Furthermore, since the collapse
of the Bretton Woods system, only Panama (a fully dollarized country)
among all developing countries did not have a single year with inflation
exceeding 20 percent, and only Panama never imposed any restriction on
the purchase or sale of dollars in the nation.

◣ *Costs of Dollarization*

Dollarization does, however, impose some costs on the dollarizing nation,
as follows.

1. *Lost Seigniorage.* This is the cost that a dollarizing country sustains
from replacing the domestic currency with the dollar. There are two different methods of measuring this cost: a stock method and a flow method.
The stock cost of dollarization is the cost of obtaining sufficient dollars to
replace the domestic currency in circulation. This has been estimated to be
about 4 to 5 percent of GDP for the average Latin American country. The

flow cost of dollarization, on the other hand, is the loss of interest on the central bank's holdings of foreign bonds or other interest-earning assets in the dollarizing country.

A low-end flow cost estimate of dollarization can be obtained by multiplying the dollarizing country's currency in circulation by the interest rate on foreign assets. In Latin American countries this amounts to about 0.2 percent of GDP per year. A high-end flow cost estimate can be obtained by multiplying the dollarizing country's monetary base (which is greater than its currency in circulation) by the domestic inflation rate or by some domestic interest rate (which is usually higher than the interest rate on foreign assets). For Latin American countries, this high-end flow cost ranges from 0.5 percent of GDP per year for Argentina to 7.4 percent of GDP per year for Ecuador (it is 0.8 percent of GDP per year for Mexico and 1.3 percent of GDP per year for Brazil; see U.S. Senate [2000]).

2. *Loss of Independence of Monetary and Exchange Rate Policies.* A dollarized country cannot eliminate or moderate a recession with an expansionary monetary policy or a currency devaluation (and do the opposite to correct inflation) because it no longer has a domestic currency. As a result, a dollarized country essentially faces the same monetary and exchange rate policy of the United States, regardless of its cyclical situation. For example, if the U.S. interest rate rises and the dollar appreciates, it will worsen a recession in a dollarized country. A dollarized country, however, is likely to be closely integrated with the United States and become more synchronized with the U.S. business cycle over time (and thus have less need for an independent monetary policy). Even if this were not the case, it must be remembered (as pointed out by McKinnon in chapter 10) that in a world of large capital flows and integrated capital markets, the effectiveness of an independent monetary policy by a developing country is very limited indeed, unless the nation restricts international capital flows—but this can seriously dampen its growth.

The same is generally true for the exchange rate policy. That is, the ability of a developing country to correct a balance of trade deficit or deal with an oil shock by devaluing or allowing its currency to depreciate is very limited by the high inflation that usually results from it and which nullifies the effectiveness of the devaluation or depreciation. Thus, the real cost of giving up an independent monetary or exchange rate policy on the part of a dollarizing country is usually, for the most part, rather small. Specifically, a "real" economic shock usually requires real economic adjustment and pain, which an exchange rate change can only temporarily soften rather than eliminate.

3. *Loss of Lender of Last Resort.* By dollarizing, a country loses its central bank as a lender of last resort to bail out a domestic bank or a number of banks or other financial institutions that may be near collapse. However, the lender-of-last-resort capability of an emerging-market central bank is largely illusory without inordinately large international reserves, which are

beyond the reach of most emerging market economies. Furthermore, nothing prevents a dollarizing country from setting aside liquid funds to lend to domestic banks in a crisis and/or arranging lines of credit with foreign banks (as Argentina has done) or for foreign banks to provide credit to domestic banks (as it actually happened in Panama). These can operate as substitutes for the central bank serving as the lender of last resort in a dollarized country. We must also keep in mind that a system-wide banking problem is less likely to occur in a fully dollarized country that is moving toward international financial integration (a condition necessary for fully exploiting the benefits of dollarization and stimulating domestic growth).

What dollarization cannot do is solve the other serious economic problems that the nation might face. Specifically, if the dollarized country is living beyond its means and faces an unsustainable budget deficit or debt burden, the country will face an economic and financial crisis, which dollarization cannot prevent. A good example of this was Argentina in the fall of 2001. Dollarization does, however, expose the problem sooner and impose a discipline that a nondollarized country does not face.

◣ Candidates for Dollarization

So which countries should dollarize? Those countries for which the benefits of full dollarization exceed the costs. The problem is that, as I have shown, while the costs of dollarization can be measured fairly accurately, the benefits are much more difficult to measure (except for the lower interest that usually results in a dollarized country) and depend crucially on how much the nation also restructures its financial sector and integrates it with that of the United States and the world economy.

A good candidate for dollarization is a small open economy for which the United States is the dominant economic partner and which has a history of poor monetary performance and hence very little economic policy credibility. The ability of such a country to conduct an independent monetary and exchange rate policies to address domestic real and monetary shocks is only imaginary. At the same time, such a country is very likely to face much higher interest rates (to compensate for the higher risk it exhibits) than the rate that prevails in the United States and is very vulnerable to speculative attacks (unless it insulates itself from the world economy)—but this, again, would severely reduce capital inflows and the country's growth rate (Antinolfi and Keister, 2001; Balino and Enoch, 1997; Calvo, 2001; Calvo and Reinhart, 2000; LeBaron and McCullock, 2000; Posner, 2000).

Most of the small countries of Latin America—especially those in Central America—as well as the Caribbean nations, fit this description very well and are, therefore, the best candidates for full dollarization. In fact, as I have shown, Panama, Ecuador, El Salvador, and Guatemala are more or less fully dollarized. Honduras, Nicaragua, and Costa Rica are seriously considering it. Once we move from small to large countries, however, it becomes more difficult to come up with clear-cut answers.

Argentina had a currency board from 1991 until the beginning of 2002, and this operated reasonably well until 1999, when Brazil was forced first to devalue the real and then allow it to sharply depreciate. With the peso rigidly tied to the dollar, Argentina suffered a huge loss of international competitiveness vis-à-vis Brazil (its largest trade partner) and plunged into recession. Besides having a grossly overvalued currency, Argentina also had an out-of-control budget deficit, and these resulted in a serious economic and financial crisis in the fall of 2001. Tightening up its public finances in order to encourage foreign investments only deepened the recession without succeeding in attracting many more foreign investors because of the fear that Argentina would abandon its currency board and devalue the peso. This left Argentina only two choices: devaluing the peso or fully dollarizing. Abandoning its currency board and devaluing the peso, however, could return Argentina to the hyperinflation of the late 1980s, and so Argentina was very reluctant to take that road. Dollarization was not without risks either. Specifically, while it would eliminate the foreign exchange risk and very probably attract more inflows of foreign investments, dollarization would not eliminate Argentina's international competitiveness problem, especially with respect to Brazil, nor would it solve Argentina's budget problems.

The ideal situation for Argentina would be if Brazil also dollarized, but this, for a country such as Brazil, which considers itself to be the leader of South America, seems to be entirely out of the question in the near future for reasons of national pride. It is inconceivable that Brazil would give up its central bank and its currency without having a strong say in the conduct of the dollar-area monetary policy—something that the United States is clearly not about to do. And a monetary policy à la EU is not even being considered in the Americas. In any event, it makes little economic sense for Brazil to dollarize, in view of its very different economic structure with respect to the United States.

One way to resolve its international competitiveness problem would be for Argentina to tie the peso to the Brazilian real. Adopting Brazil's currency, however, would expose Argentina to many of the serious monetary and financial problems that Brazil faces. The only alternative for Argentina, therefore, seems to be full dollarization. The elimination of the foreign exchange risk (that financial markets believe to exist because of the possibility that Argentina could abandon its currency board) would lead to lower interest rates, and could attract enough foreign capital to overcome the recession and improve Argentina's international competitiveness and stimulate its growth. The United States, for its part, could facilitate the official dollarization of Argentina by sharing its seigniorage with Argentina (as is done in the euro area) based on the amount of dollars actually used by Argentina. Of course, Argentina would also want access for its banks to the

discount window at the Federal Reserve System in time of crisis, cooperation on banking supervision, and possibly a seat at the Federal Reserve
Board—things that the United States (as indicated earlier) would not do.
The optimal or first best situation, of course, would be if Argentina were
able to manage its own economy efficiently and with discipline. Short of
this, however, full dollarization seems to be the only way out of its difficult
predicament. It is true that dollarization would not solve Argentina's debt
and budget problems, but it would force it to deal with those problems
quickly and forcefully—no matter how painful. At the beginning of 2002,
Argentina abandoned its currency board and allowed its currency to depreciate in the face of economic, financial, and political collapse.

Ecuador dollarized unilaterally in September 2000 in the midst of a
political and economic crisis precipitated by Brazil's devaluation of the real,
and without any assistance from the United States—not even seigniorage
sharing—and so did El Salvador at the beginning of 2001 (from a noncrisis
situation). El Salvador, however, with the support of the U.S. Treasury and
the World Bank, will probably be able to negotiate with the IMF a standby
agreement to provide it funds in case of a crisis, thus essentially replacing
its central bank as a lender of last resort.

More sensible and more feasible than that of Brazil would also be the
dollarization of Mexico, which is more integrated with the U.S. economy
and faces fewer (but by no means insignificant) political problems in dollarizing than Brazil. But even here, one can point to Canada, whose economy is much more integrated with the U.S. economy than Mexico's, and
which also has a currency that for the most part fluctuates freely vis-à-vis
the U.S. dollar and other currencies, and which, nevertheless, has been and
is doing very well economically. The question is then why should Canada,
hence Mexico, dollarize?

Although the topic is being discussed, Canada regards dollarization as
neither necessary nor desirable. Pursuing this matter further, we then need
to ask why is Canada doing so well economically without dollarization? The
answer is clear. It is because Canada is highly integrated both financially
and economically in the global economy and pursues sound economic policies. If Mexico could become as highly integrated in the world economy
and if it were able to follow economic policies as sound as those of Canada,
then dollarization would make much less sense for Mexico also. In general,
dollarization would make sense for Mexico if it would (1) speed up Mexico's
integration into the world economy; (2) encourage Mexico to follow better
economic policies; and, in the final analysis, (3) significantly stimulate economic growth. But clearly these are questions, not answers.

And when questions are asked as to why North America or all of the
Americas shouldn't have a common currency if Europe does, the answer is
that Europe created a European Central Bank and all participating nations,
no matter how small, have a voice in the making of the common monetary

policy. They all share in the seigniorage from the euro and aim for full monetary, economic, and political integration. None of these things are true for the Americas or even for North America. Thus, aside for the small open economies of Central America, the case for dollarization for North America or for all of the Americas can only be justified by an OCA analysis or by the economic discipline that it would impose on a country that is unable to effectively and efficiently manage its economy.

Since the United States is not ready to open its borders (particularly its southern border) to migrants and establish a common central bank, the American continent—and North America—are not ready for and do not need a common currency. In fact, monetary union and a common currency are not even being considered for NAFTA at this point in time (Chriszt, 2000). Thus, Canada, Mexico, Argentina, and other countries in the American continent must individually decide whether full unilateral dollarization makes economic and political sense for them. For Argentina and Mexico it may, for Canada and Brazil it may not.

▲ Benefits and Costs of Dollarization for the United States

Dollarization confers some benefits and imposes some costs on the United States also. An obvious benefit that the United States would reap from the dollarization of more Latin American and other countries is seigniorage. It has been estimated that seigniorage results in about $25 billion of gain per year to the United States government. Since from 55 to 70 percent of dollars in circulation are now held outside the United States, the U.S. seigniorage gains from abroad are about $15 billion per year. If more countries dollarized in Latin America and elsewhere, or make increasing use of the U.S. dollar, the United States would gain even more from seigniorage. Since most Latin American countries that have already dollarized or are seriously considering dollarization are rather small, however, the potential additional gains to the United States are also small. The gains would be much greater if Canada, Brazil, Mexico, or Argentina were to dollarize.

Other possible gains flowing from the dollarization of Latin American or other countries result from (1) the increase in the flow of trade between the United States and the dollarizing countries, (2) the elimination of the need to exchange dollars into the local currency by American tourists, and (3) the need to hedge the foreign exchange risk by American firms. The dollarization of more countries will also help the dollar retain its position as the most important international currency, rather than risk losing its position of preeminence to the euro as more European countries adopt the euro as their currency and as other countries make increasing use of it for their international transactions.

The United States would face two possible costs from the full and unilateral dollarization of more Latin American and other countries. One cost results from the constraint on U.S. monetary policy resulting from the fact that with so many dollars moving in and out of the United States it is difficult for the Federal Reserve Bank to fine-tune the growth of the U.S. money supply and pursue the appropriate monetary policy for the nation. Related to this problem, but potentially more serious, is the fact that if the foreign holders of dollars ever lost confidence in the stability of the dollar and undertook a massive switch in favor of the euro, this could lead to a sharp depreciation of the dollar, which, in turn, would inflict a strong inflationary shock on the U.S. economy and possibly lead to serious financial instability in the nation.

▶ References

Antinolfi, Gaetano, and Todd Keister. (2001). Dollarization as a Monetary Arrangement for Emerging Markets. *Federal Reserve Bank of St. Louis Review, 83,* 29–40.

Baliño, Tomás J. T., and Charles Enoch. (1997, August). *Currency Board Arrangements, Issues, and Experiences.* (IMF Occasional Paper 151). Washington, D.C.: International Monetary Fund.

Calvo, Guillermo A. (2001). Capital Markets and the Exchange Rate, with Special Reference to the Dollarization Debate in Latin America. *Journal of Money, Credit, and Banking, 32,* 312–34.

Calvo, Guillermo A., and Carmen A. Reinhart. (2000, November). Fixing for Your Life. (NBER Working Paper No. 8006). National Bureau of Economic Research.

Chang, Roberto. (2000). Dollarization: A Score Card. *Federal Reserve Bank of Atlanta Economic Review, 85,* 1–11.

Chriszt, Michael. (2000). Perspectives on a Potential North American Monetary Union. *Federal Reserve of Atlanta Economic Review, 85,* 29–38.

Frankel, Jeffrey. (1999). No Single Currency Regime Is Right for All Countries or at All Times. *Essays in International Finance, 215.*

International Monetary Fund. (1999). *Dollarization: Fad or Future for Latin America.* (IMF Economic Forum). Washington, D.C.: Author.

LeBaron, Blake, and Rachel McCullock. (2000). Floating, Fixed, or Super-Fixed? Dollarization Joins the Menu of Exchange-Rate Options. *American Economic Review, 90,* 32–37.

Mendoza, Enrique G. (2000, August). On the Benefits of Dollarization When Stabilization Policy Is Not Credible and Financial Markets Are Imperfect. (NBER Working Paper No. 7824). National Bureau of Economic Research.

Moreno-Villalaz, Juan Luis. (1999). Lessons from the Monetary Experience of Panama: A Dollar Economy with Financial Integration. *Cato Journal, 18,* 421–39.

Mundell, Robert. (1961). A Theory of Optimum Currency Areas. *American Economic Review, 51,* 657–65.

Murray, John. (2000). Why Canada Needs a Flexible Exchange Rate. *North American Journal of Economics and Finance, 1,* 41–60.

Posner, Adam S. (2000). *Dollarization, Currency Blocs, and U.S. Policy.* Washington, D.C.: Institute for International Economics.

U.S. Senate. (2000, July). Joint Economic Committee. *Basics of Dollarization.* Washington, D.C.: Author.

12 George M. von Furstenberg

Pressures for Currency Consolidation
in Insurance and Finance

Are the Currencies of Financially Small Countries on the

Endangered List?

The currencies of a few geographically small countries, like Switzerland, are financially big, and the currencies of some large countries, like China and Brazil, are financially small. Neither type of currency, one small and internationally fit and the other large and protected, is of interest here because the viability of each is not as yet in question. Instead the focus is on the declining usefulness of the separate currency denominations maintained by that large number of *small* open economies whose currencies play little or no role in international finance. There is a real question of whether such currencies will survive, even in domestic use, when faced with the ever-decreasing restriction of competition from the international currency dominant in the region and from those most expert at doing business in it.

As Eichengreen (1994, p. 39) anticipated, "the problem posed by deep integration is that accompanying changes in technology, politics, and market structures may render [the provision of monetary stability] possible only under a very limited set of international monetary arrangements." This chapter argues, and in small part substantiates, that e-commerce, regional economic integration, and global liberalization have eroded the monopoly of small currencies in their home markets. These developments now threaten the continued viability of a number of them over the medium run. Even partial currency consolidations, such as those afforded by currency boards, are likely to prove unsustainable in the new environment that is leading to regional monetary unions.

▶ A Glance at History and Prospects

Briefly looking both back and ahead suggests that, in matters of currency competition, we may be returning to conditions once common in many parts of the world. In British North American colonies (Schweitzer, 1997), for instance, several moneys and coinages, foreign and domestic, competed for acceptance side by side. Declaring certain notes and coins legal tender for the settlement of money debts both public and private did little to prevent contracts from being made, and settled, in other denominations or standards. Nor did something need to have legal tender status in the colonies to be accepted as payment and hence to be valuable there.

This situation changed only when strong regulatory and legal restrictions were enacted by independent states to shelter their national currency from competition by other denominations on their home turf. As with the Legal Tender Act that was adopted during the U.S. Civil War in 1862, legal tender laws were needed to introduce a national fiat money, but that did not necessarily make it more widely used than established moneys. Gresham's law could come into operation only when a new form of money was declared legal tender at an overvalued legal exchange rate for money and debt contracts denominated in some older form or substantiation of money.

Over time, many countries sought to strengthen the issuing authority's monopoly power in order to afford effective protection for the national currency. Such action led from the production of national money in monopolistic competition with other such moneys to positively reserving the domestic market for its use. To assure such exclusivity, the domestic currency may have been sheltered by capital controls and by banking regulations that strictly limited the booking of foreign currency assets and liabilities for domestic residents and gave the national denomination exclusive rights in many home-country applications.

These barriers have tended to erode over the past two dozen or more years as worldwide internal and external liberalization have taken hold. As a result, national moneys have been exposed to international competition and have to struggle for survival once again. Barriers to foreign competition have been falling first in developed and then in developing countries as they have integrated into the liberal international trade and investment regime and have extended national treatment to foreign suppliers with fewer or expiring derogations. Freer cross-border provision of financial services and a changed official attitude to foreign establishment and takeovers have encouraged foreign entry. These developments also have opened the door to more widely denominating and trading domestic claims in international denominations. Providing such foreign-currency-denominated loan, debt, and equity financing is a business in which foreign providers, domiciled in the country that issues the relevant international currency, tend to have a funding and marketing advantage.

The end result now clearly in view is that individual and corporate citizens in many small countries will be able to choose to make payments in more than one acceptable currency and to freely incur debts or acquire assets denominated in different currencies. Furthermore, using financial derivatives, they will be able to swap, alter, or hedge their currency exposure increasingly at will. However, they can do so only at considerable cost when their own currency is involved: risk premiums that are reflected in interest rates and hence cause the forward exchange rates for small currencies to exceed their expected future spot rates add to the cost of hedging. These risk premiums are almost entirely due to currency risk, in the sense that absent currency risk, very little remains of what was formerly identified as country risk, as southern members of the Euro Area can attest. It is inconceivable, for instance, that Mexico, if it dollarized completely, would face premiums as high as the 300 to 340 basis points that were observed on its sovereign dollar borrowing in 2000. This is the yield spread over comparable U.S. Treasuries that Mexico's central bank (Banco de México 2000, p. 16) has identified, quite conventionally and yet misleadingly, as pure country risk.

The question then is how many currencies will remain in wide use under arrangements that are more open to foreign currencies. Will the local currency be among the survivors? In my view, globalizing and centralizing tendencies tend to weigh against such a prospect if the country is financially small to start with and if it lacks a very large internal market in which strong network externalities from the use of the domestic money can still be obtained. This naturally leads to the search for a quantitative perspective on what is small and how much countries that lie next to an area with a dominant currency still use their own money.

▶ To What Extent Does a "Small" Open Economy, Like Mexico, Use Its Own Money?

The Federal Reserve has put forward (Leahy, 1998) a new method for estimating summary measures of the foreign exchange value of a currency. The method provides for calculating a set of weights to be applied to a country's most important bilateral exchange rates while also taking account of competition between imports and goods produced and sold in the same country, including the home country. The resulting weights are so comprehensive that they can be used for purposes other than deriving effective exchange rates, for which they were originally intended. In particular, the weights sum to unity when including the weight for the one-to-one exchange rate of a country's own currency. The latter weight provides a useful inverse measure of its foreign currency dependence or degree of monetary openness.

Application of the method to Mexico when a total of n countries are considered calls for establishing the following.

- The market shares of Mexican-produced goods in each of their $n-1$ major foreign markets, $X_{MX,j}$, as well as in Mexico itself, $X_{MX,MX}$
- The market shares of foreign-produced goods sold in Mexico, $M_{MX,j}$ as well as of Mexican goods sold in Mexico, $M_{MX,MX}$
- The market shares of goods imported by each of Mexico's major trading partners in all goods sold in the respective country j, $M_{j,k}$

where $j \neq k$, as well as the share of home-produced goods sold in the respective country, $M_{k,k}$

With these definitions, the weight on the k-currency real exchange rate with the Mexican peso would be:

$$W_{MX,k} = \Sigma_{j=1,\ldots n} \, X_{MX,j} \, M_{j,k}.$$

By setting $k = MX$ we can calculate the weight of the Mexican peso in Mexico to gauge how important the domestic currency remains in that country relative to other currencies used in its economic transactions. The United States (US), the Euro Area (E), and Japan (J) are Mexico's major trading partners, as they together accounted for 92 percent of its goods exports and 85 percent of its imports in 1999. (These import and export weights are normalized to 100 percent to represent all exports and imports.) With the market share values for 1999 calculated from data provided by the IMF (2000a, 2001), application of the above formula to obtain the weight for the Mexican peso yields:

$$W_{MX,MX} = X_{MX,MX} \, M_{MX,MX} + X_{MX,US} \, M_{US,MX} + X_{MX,E} \, M_{E,MX} + X_{MX,J} \, M_{J,MX} =$$
$$0.717(0.710) + 0.271(0.011) + 0.010(0.001) + 0.002(0.000) = 0.512.$$

In the same way the weight of the U.S. dollar for Mexico is calculated as:

$$W_{MX,US} = X_{MX,MX} \, M_{MX,US} + X_{MX,US} \, M_{US,US} + X_{MX,E} \, M_{E,US} + X_{MX,J} \, M_{J,US} =$$
$$0.717(0.252) + 0.271(0.870) + 0.010(0.022) + 0.002(0.016) = 0.417.$$

The conclusion derived from the application of this weighting scheme is that the weight of the U.S. dollar in the Mexican economy has risen to within 10 percentage points of that of its home currency. Furthermore, the Mexican peso's share is barely above 50 percent, judged merely by its trade in goods and ignoring services, workers' remittances from the United States, and asset pricing in dollars. The result is conservative also in that it ignores not only U.S. currency circulating in Mexico but also any dollarization that has already occurred inside Mexico's domestic business in order to insulate some of its cash flow from exchange rate fluctuations.

This is an important finding that suggests that small open economies in the vicinity of large countries or groups of countries with an international currency already depend importantly on a money other than their own. They are much more exposed to currency crises and exchange rate instability than the share of bilateral trade in relation to GDP ($X_{MX,US} = 27.1$ percent), or to domestic absorption ($M_{MX,US} = 25.2$ percent), would suggest.

▶ *International Portfolio Diversification Works Best in the Dominant Currency Denomination*

Economists have often deduced that, from the point of view of obtaining optimal consumption insurance through portfolio diversification, the investment portfolios of otherwise comparably positioned investors from Canada, France, and Japan should look very much alike. The failure for them to do so, because citizens strongly favor claims on their own country's obligors, has been labeled the home bias puzzle (see Lewis, 1999). Hausmann et al. (2000, pp. 142–44) have argued that for emerging market economies, all of which are financially small, there is even a presumption against investing at home from the point of view of consumption insurance. The reason is that in a currency crisis, just when income and output fall and internal and external sources of credit dry up, domestic asset values collapse. Adding a large negative wealth shock to a negative current income shock would impart a double blow to consumption for investors at home.

Had these investors instead been invested in international foreign currency claims when the sharp real depreciation of the domestic currency occurred, they would have benefited from the real appreciation of the domestic value of their foreign holdings. This would have reduced, rather than amplified, the blow to consumption from a currency and financial crisis. Hence, to obtain optimal consumption insurance, investors in small emerging market countries should invest outside their own country and currency to an extent even greater than what is fitting for the average international investor. When Uruguayans hold 85 percent of their savings in U.S. dollar-denominated accounts in their own country, they are acting to reduce this double exposure to a degree that depends on whether they deposit in domestically owned banks or in local branches of foreign banks. In Argentina about 50 percent of bank assets are held in foreign-controlled institutions by a variety of measures (IMF, 2000b, p. 153). Multinational financial institutions are almost always originating in the key-currency countries that have long been leading the development of the financial services industry and have determined its international coordination and supervision. They bring their privileged key-currency connection with them wherever they establish around the globe and make that denomination their stock in trade.

Large international currencies convey other advantages to foreign users. To protect their international standing, such currencies and their financial infrastructure tend to be consistently well managed. Emerging market economies, in particular, commonly experience real exchange rates that are both highly variable and prone to drift up between major corrections, not necessarily around a fixed mean. Hence denominating annuities and pensions and lump-sum or life insurance settlements of any kind in such currencies would provide far less calculable real-value assurance than denominating in one of the large currencies. The latter are key to international pricing in product and finance markets and reliable stores of value and of future purchasing power over a broad range of goods. The added purchasing-power risk thus detracts from the suitability of small currencies for extended use in intertemporal trades, and this contributes to the case for currency consolidation.

International financial derivatives since their inception have functioned almost exclusively in U.S. dollars and in only a few other major currencies. The reason is that the underlying debt and equity claims suitable for listing, securitization, and exchange trading in international financial markets are themselves almost exclusively denominated in dollars, and to a lesser extent in euros and yen. Countries can use only very few other currencies to borrow in international financial markets. Generally, large risk premiums and illiquidity, reflected in wide bid-ask spreads, discourage denominating in peripheral currencies. Since calculability of risk exposure and a high degree of liquidity of positions taken by major participants, including hedge funds, are essential to the functioning of the market in derivatives, standardization on a common currency is convenient in many, though not all, applications.

The dollar may "intrude" even into exchange contracts between other currencies. International Monetary Fund (1999, p. 49) explains, for instance, that nondeliverable foreign exchange forwards (NDFs) in emerging markets tend to be settled in U.S. dollars for the difference between the implied exchange rate on the contract and the prevailing spot rate on the maturity date of the contract. The IMF notes further that net settlement in domestic currency existed in many industrial countries in the 1970s and 1980s prior to the removal of exchange controls. The big currencies thus tend to get bigger when capital controls are removed.

◤ Common Currency in E-Trade and E-Commerce

Many regional and global electronic spot markets and electronic trading platforms price in U.S. dollars or, prospectively, in euros. It may be instructive to consider a simple example. Certain electronic auctions conducted in Canada are bid in U.S. dollars to encourage cross-border participation. One could, of course, reflect on the screen, second by second, what the auction price amounts to in Canadian dollars. However, little would be gained by this instant currency conversion. For instance, if the U.S. dollar price achieved at auction is final and binding, paying with a debit or credit card on a Canadian dollar account could cost an extra 2 percent commission for the exchange conversion. Uncertainty would be added for the Canadian buyer at auction because the exchange rate would be the interbank sell rate prevailing when the charge is processed by the bank.

Instead of putting up with this cost and uncertainty, the Canadian could, of course, have a U.S. dollar account with his or her Canadian bank or in the United States. But if the balance in that account must be maintained by drawing on income earned in Canadian dollars, the problem of uncertain settlement costs does not really go away. With digital signatures now having legal effect, validity, and enforceability in the United States (see *Tech Law Journal,* 2000) and in a growing list of other countries or country groups, ordering, shopping, and settling in international money anywhere in the region, indeed in the world, has become increasingly attractive. This however creates pressures not just to convert to such money but either to be paid in it or to have payments indexed to it.

In business applications, there are even stronger pressures for currency consolidation. Transnational bidding on business that should lead to standing orders is handicapped if persistent exchange rate movements keep interfering with what subcontractors or component suppliers must ask. To avoid the disruption of continuing relationships by exchange rate movements whose eventual results for competitiveness cannot be hedged, those who seek to be integrated into the regionwide supply chain try to control their costs, from parts to labor, in the same currency in which they must bid.

▲ Should Small Countries Keep Nominal Exchange Rate Flexibility?

Flexible exchange rates are often advertised as a low-cost and fast-acting compensatory mechanism for countries with nominal rigidities that are subject to either real or nominal shocks. The unspoken assumption, frequently falsified (see, for instance, Buiter, 1997; Hausmann et al., 2000) is that exchange rates can be counted on to move reliably so as to facilitate efficient adjustment rather than having a disturbing way of their own. Buiter (1999, 50) gives a sardonic example of the heroic deeds to be accomplished by monetary policy enabled by flexible rates against a supposedly unitary shock:

> There is assumed to be only one kind of shock, a national aggregate supply shock. The national monetary authority is assumed to observe the national supply shock immediately and perfectly. It then sets national monetary policy instantaneously and optimally to cope with this shock. The national authority knows the true structure of the economy and this structure of the economy makes certainty-equivalent strategies optimal.

While some Canadian (see Laidler, 1999) and Mexican (see Schwartz and Torres, 2001) economists continue to try to prove that flexible exchange rates work just fine for their countries, they have yet to include complete U.S. dollarization or other forms of monetary union among the alternatives seriously considered. In Mexico at least, such a union would preclude the very currency crises from which advocates of flexible rates get their economic "supply shock" observations. As Calvo and Reinhart (2000) have explained, in many countries there is deep and cogent doubt that floating exchange rates in fact have tended to move to facilitate adjustment in the goods and factor markets. Small open economies in emerging market countries rarely find that when things start to go badly—usually first because there is an international-portfolio or private-capital-account shock—exchange rate movements quickly reverse the tide and let conditions improve again. Instead, currency crises commonly make things much worse before they start getting better, and, contrary to once-popular belief, flexible exchange rates do not preclude such crises.

Even when real exchange rates move in textbook fashion to accommodate the needs of trade balance and production adjustment, some of the other tacit assumptions that make such movement unequivocally beneficial are less and less likely to be satisfied. One of these is that countries are homogeneous internally but heterogeneous internationally in their production structure and shock exposure. Likewise, factor mobility, particularly that of labor, often is assumed to be high internally and low internationally. Mexico's adjustment to the 1999–2000 increase in the price of crude oil shows what can be wrong with these assumptions. The oil price increase and the effect on Mexico's federal budget and current account may have encouraged increased private capital inflows that contributed to an appreciation of the Mexican peso in both nominal and real terms. But only small additional amounts of capital and labor have been attracted to oil and gas exploration and development while the real appreciation has slowed the development of the nonoil sector in the country at large.

If small countries were indeed internally homogenous and externally heterogeneous so that they had a specialized, nationally integrated production structure for final goods, shocks to both domestic supply conditions and to (mostly) foreign demand for the small country's specialized output in theory could be cushioned, and adjustment could be speeded by movement in nominal exchange rates. But for many small open economies, this picture of the production structure bears little relation to the reality they confront in a regionalizing, and to a lesser extent globalizing, economic system. Becoming a component part of international supply chains means that anything that disrupts this chain anywhere will be felt everywhere else in the region.

By the same token, if many countries in the region share in the production of final goods, such as automobiles or electronic appliances, through the production or assembly of parts, any shock to aggregate demand for the final good will affect all who contribute to its supply as well. Under these conditions, exchange rate movements among the partners in the region cannot be part of efficient adjustment. Hence in an economically interlocking world, little remains of the classical case for flexible exchange rates. Once countries are firmly committed to low inflation and do not cherish the freedom to engage in inflationary experiments, they will benefit further by irrevocably relinquishing the option to change their exchange rate with their hard-currency neighbors. Indeed, currency union would enhance the regional integration process by markedly raising trade and GDP within the union (Frankel and Rose, 2000).

▶ Is a Currency Board Arrangement Sufficient for Currency Consolidation?

A number of business and banking groups seeking some form of monetary union with the United States, for instance in Mexico, recently have come out in favor of a currency board arrangement (CBA) because they view such an arrangement as politically more acceptable than complete dollarization. This section argues quite generally that currency boards may, or may not, advance the objective of monetary union. It all depends on how appropriate the choice of the peg is to their trade and finance and what better alternatives are available in their economic neighborhood.

Currency boards in theory have a fixed reserve ratio against high-powered money and a fixed exchange rate with something "hard" in common with the gold standard. Yet while there were rules of the classical gold standard that were sufficiently widely observed to make the standard credible and speculation generally stabilizing (Eichengreen 1994, p. 43), CBAs now make their own rules. For instance, Argentina's and Hong Kong's CBAs have very little in common in the way they operate, in the extent to which they are backed by reserves and constrained by their particular status, and in the fluctuations they have experienced in their credibility. As described in Dodsworth and Mihaljek (1997) for instance, there is little that is classical or ruled out in the operation of Hong Kong's currency board since it was established in 1983. Indeed, some of its defenses against speculative attack, such as using more than 10 percent of its foreign exchange reserves in August 1998 to discourage short selling by buying shares in the local stock market, have been unprecedented.

Apart from each CBA being increasingly *sui generis* and thus requiring detailed individual assessment, there is also the question of the choice of currency peg that is appropriate for each. It is not true that any and all of the major hard currencies will do. For instance, Hong Kong, Argentina, and Lithuania, all with a U.S. dollar-based currency board, are surrounded (or will be surrounded when the renminbi starts to float against the U.S. dollar) by countries whose real exchange rates may develop very differently. Because these countries are unduly exposed to foreign-induced misalignment of their trade-weighted exchange rate, the rationale for sticking with their CBAs can become doubtful. When such a misalignment becomes acute, as between Argentina and Brazil in the aftermath of Brazil's currency crisis of January 1999, risk premiums surge. They may feed on themselves by placing the benefits of maintaining the CBA further in doubt.

Currency board arrangements that peg unnaturally to a currency from outside their major trading region are prone to stress. Singapore's switch from a sterling-based currency board in 1967 to the U.S. dollar, though precipitated by the desire to disassociate from the pound's devaluation from $2.8 to $2.4, was appropriate to its trade and finance as well. Singapore broadened its exchange rate reference further a few years later when it made the transition to managed floating. By contrast, Lithuania's perverse insistence on maintaining a dollar-based currency board in what is rapidly becoming a sea of euros has been costly. Real GDP fell over 4 percent in 1999, and little or no growth has been reported for 2000, as the strength of the dollar against the euro persisted during the year.

Thus while CBAs incorporate a strong policy commitment to fixed exchange rates that is backed up by a high level of international reserve, this commitment may still not be sustainable politically when it is perceived to be harmful to the economy and to its secure integration in the region. Only currency boards within economically and financially heavily integrated and interdependent regions are likely to provide adequate insurance against disruptive changes in real exchange rates with their main trading partner or partners. U.S. dollar-based CBAs with Mexico and Central American and Caribbean countries, and euro-based CBAs in eastern European countries, thus could qualify as useful precursors to more complete and less reversible forms of currency consolidation. Currency boards established in distant outposts far away from the "peg" country and its currency area, however, represent false starts from the point of view of currency consolidation: they are likely to lead either to floating or to new forms of monetary union in their region down the road.

Even currency boards with the dominant currency next door may not survive for long when the respective financial systems are placed in direct competition with each other. The strength of trade and finance relations, say of countries in the vicinity of the United States or of Euroland, makes the almost complete financial integration and interest rate convergence that is available upon formally adopting the U.S. dollar or euro more attractive than staying in the halfway house of a currency board. Hence if currency consolidation is to be allowed, some form of monetary union is the way to achieve it. Whether that union should take the form of unilateral dollarization or of multilateral and comanaged monetary union as in Euroland is another important matter meriting detailed analysis. I have begun to explore some of these alternative ways of achieving currency consolidation elsewhere (von Furstenberg, 2001, 2002).

◤ Conclusions

As was the case centuries ago, small open economies now make much more use of foreign money, especially the dominant currency of their region, than international trade analysis and past measures of effective exchange rates have tended to recognize. The currencies of financially small countries, in particular emerging market countries, are at a distinct disadvantage in both spot transactions in the electronic marketplace and in intertemporal trade and insurance. Even direct consumption insurance counsels residents of emerging market countries exposed to currency crises to keep away from investing in their own currency at home lest shocks to their income be compounded by shocks to their wealth. Foreign financial institutions from the key-currency countries often bring financial services that are denominated in those very same currencies that the market demands.

Idiosyncratic exchange rate behavior and country risk premiums that are due, in good part, to currency risk are the downside to keeping small countries in small countries. Doing so is more likely to discourage and disrupt their membership in international supply chains than to promote adjustment to supply shocks. Even CBAs are unlikely to prove a highly durable substitute for the more complete forms of currency consolidation provided by regional monetary union. However, they may lead the way to such union if they are established with a peg to the currency that is most suitable for intense commercial and financial relations with neighboring countries in the respective region.

▲ References

Banco de México. (2000). *Inflation Report, July-September 2000.* October.

Buiter, W. (1999). *Optimal Currency Areas: Why Does the Exchange Rate Regime Matter?* Sixth Royal Bank of Scotland/Scottish Economic Society Annual Lecture, Edinburgh.

Buiter, W. (1997). The Economic Case for Monetary Union in the European Union. *Review of International Economics, 5*(4), 10–35.

Calvo, G. A., and C. M. Reinhart. (2000). Fear of Floating. (NBER Working Paper No. 7993). National Bureau of Economic Research.

Dodsworth, J., and D. Mihaljek. (1997, August). Hong Kong, China: Growth, Structural Change, and Economic Stability During the Transition. (Occasional Paper N. 152). Washington, D.C.: International Monetary Fund.

Eichengreen, B. (1994). *International Monetary Arrangements for the 21st Century.* Washington, D.C.: Brookings Institution.

Frankel, J. A., and A. K. Rose. (2000, August). Estimating the Effect of Currency Unions on Trade and Output. (NBER Working Paper No. 7857). National Bureau of Economic Research.

Hausmann, R. et al. (2000). Financial Turmoil and the Choice of Exchange Rate Regime. In E. Fernández-Arias and R. Hausmann (Eds.), *Wanted: World Financial Stability* (pp. 131–64). Washington, D.C.: Inter-American Development Bank.

International Monetary Fund. (1999, September). *International Capital Markets: Developments, Prospects, and Key Policy Issues.*

International Monetary Fund. (2000a). *Direction of Trade Statistics Yearbook 2000.* Washington, D.C.: IMF.

International Monetary Fund. (2000b, September). *International Capital Markets: Developments, Prospects, and Key Policy Issues.* Washington, D.C.: IMF.

International Monetary Fund. (2001, January). *International Financial Statistics*. Washington, D.C.: IMF.

Laidler, D. (1999). *What Do the Fixers Want to Fix? The Debate about Canada's Exchange Rate Regime*. C. D. Howe Institute Commentary, Toronto.

Leahy, M. P. (1998). New Summary Measures of the Foreign Exchange Value of the Dollar, *Federal Reserve Bulletin, 84*, 811–18.

Lewis, K. V. (1999). Trying to Explain Home Bias in Equities and Consumption. *Journal of Economic Literature, 37*(2), 571–608.

Schwartz, M. J., and A. Torres. (2001, January). Long-term Viability of a Flexible Exchange Rate Regime in Mexico. Paper prepared at the Banco de México.

Schweitzer, M. (1997). *Should a Country Have More Than One Legal Tender?* Available online at //www.eh.net/Archives/eh.res/nov-1997/0025.html.

Tech Law Journal. (2000). *Summary of Bills Pertaining to Electronic Signatures and Authentication in the 106th Cong*. Available online at *//techlawjournal.com/cong106/digsig/Default.htm*.

von Furstenberg, G. M. (2001). The Case against U.S. Dollarization. *Challenge, 43*(4), 108–20.

von Furstenberg, G. M. (2002). Unilateral and Multilateral Currency Integration: Reflections on Western Hemispheric Monetary Union. In T. J. Courchene (Ed.), *Money Markets and Mobility: Celebrating the Ideas of Robert A. Mundell, Nobel Laureate in Economic Sciences* (pp. 253–66). Kingston, Canada: John Deutsch Institute, Queen's University, published in cooperation with McGill-Queen's University Press.

Political Economy

13 Benjamin J. Cohen

Monetary Union

The Political Dimension

Should Canada and the United States adopt a common currency? Should Mexico or other Latin American nations adopt the U.S. dollar? Suddenly, monetary union in one form or another is very much on the Hemispheric agenda. Debate focuses on the advantages and disadvantages of either merging two or more national moneys into one (currency unification) or replacing one national currency with another (dollarization). Assessments range from the highly favorable to the distinctly critical, as other contributions to this book amply demonstrate. Consensus remains elusive.

Among the reasons for discord is a tendency for most analysis to focus narrowly on just the *economic* gains and losses associated with monetary union. No discussion could be complete, however, without some consideration of the *politics* involved as well. The purpose of this chapter is to highlight the political dimension of monetary union: key domestic and international political issues implicated when sovereign states consider either currency unification or formal dollarization. The role of politics will be explored in the context of two distinct stages: first, at the time when the initial decision is made whether to *create* a monetary union (i.e., to unify separate currencies or dollarize); and second, as part of what determines the subsequent *sustainability* of such a joint endeavor. Economic factors, which figure so prominently in the other contributions to this book, are of course a necessary part of the analysis. But they are not sufficient. By highlighting the political dimension, I hope to help clarify what is really at stake today for the nations of the Western Hemisphere.

▲ Creating Monetary Union

Monetary union can be created in one of two ways. First, two or more countries can agree among themselves to merge their separate currencies into a wholly new joint money, as the members of the EMU have done with the euro. This is *currency unification*. Other examples of currency unification in the twentieth century include the Eastern Caribbean Currency Union (with the Eastern Caribbean dollar) and the now-defunct East African Community (with the East African shilling). Close variations, involving separate currencies so tightly tied together in an exchange rate union that they effectively function as one money, include two in Africa, the CFA Franc Zone, with 14 francophone countries in West and Central Africa, and the Common Monetary Area, joining together South Africa and three of its poorer neighbors (Lesotho, Namibia, and Swaziland). They also included, until recently, one in Europe, the Belgium-Luxembourg Economic Union (BLEU), now superseded by the EMU. Second, one country can unilaterally or by formal agreement replace its own currency with the already existing money of another. This approach, generically referred to as *dollarization,* is typically characteristic of tiny enclaves or microstates such as the Marshall Islands and Micronesia in the Pacific (using the U.S. greenback) or San Marino and the Vatican in Italy (using the euro). The two largest fully dollarized countries are Panama, which has used the dollar ever since gaining independence in 1903, and Ecuador, which switched to the greenback in 2000. Each of the two approaches, currency unification and dollarization, can be considered separately.

Currency Unification

First, consider the possibility of currency unification as advocated by Courchene and Harris and by Grubel (chapters 17 and 18 of this book). Since monetary union is by definition an economic matter, it seems only natural to focus attention mainly on economic considerations—the material costs and benefits associated with a merger of separate national moneys into one. Would the citizens of Canada and the United States be better off sharing a single money between them? Or would real welfare losses, whether at the microeconomic or macroeconomic level, exceed any conceivable gains that might accrue? In practical terms, however, such a narrow focus is not only incomplete but potentially misleading. A common currency is not just about economics but is quite obviously also about politics—about gains and losses that fall outside the standard cost-benefit calculus of economics. Ultimately, it is about the exercise of power and the ability of a national community to control its own affairs.

Economic Analysis

Would a common currency be good or bad policy? In the formal economics literature the decision to create a common currency is addressed as an optimization problem limited mostly to issues of general economic welfare as reflected in standard measures of macroeconomic performance. Analysis, as other contributions to this book emphasize, is based on the familiar theory of OCAs, dating back to Robert Mundell's pioneering article published nearly four decades ago (Mundell, 1961).

In its first incarnation, OCA theory was strikingly apolitical. Following Mundell's lead, most early contributors concentrated on a search for the most appropriate domain of a currency irrespective of existing national frontiers. The globe, in effect, was treated as a tabula rasa. The central issue was to find the best criterion for the organization of monetary space. But as the practical limitations of the so-called criteria approach (Tavlas, 1994, p. 213) became clear, an alternative—and, in political terms, seemingly less naïve—approach eventually prevailed, focusing instead on material gains and losses, as seen from a single country's point of view, stemming from participation in a common currency or equivalent.

On the positive side, currency unification can be expected to reduce transactions costs and increase money's underlying network externalities. The usefulness of a currency is enhanced in its standard functions as a medium of exchange, unit of account, and store of value. On the negative side, governments are assumed to consider the disadvantages of the corresponding surrender of monetary autonomy: the potential cost of having to adjust to domestic or external disturbances without the option of changing either the money supply or exchange rate. Monetary policy now becomes a matter of collective rather than unilateral decision making, limiting what the country itself can do to cope with transitory or cyclical disturbances. As Paul Krugman has neatly summarized the calculus, it "is a matter of trading off macroeconomic flexibility against microeconomic efficiency" (1993, p. 4).

A diverse range of variables is stressed in the OCA literature, including wage and price flexibility, labor and capital mobility, commodity diversification, geographic trade patterns, size and openness of economies, levels of development, inflation trends, and the nature, source, and timing of potential shocks. Each country characteristic arguably affects the magnitude of losses at the macroeconomic level by influencing either the severity of potential disturbances or the ease of consequent processes of adjustment. The explanatory power of OCA theory, however, appears to be quite limited. There are simply too many permutations possible among the many factors cited. As one source puts it, quite bluntly, "theoretical ambiguities abound" (Argy and De Grauwe, 1990, p. 2). Not all of an economy's features may point in the same direction, making forecasts difficult; nor are the variables necessarily mutually independent or easy to measure or compare for relative importance. One recent study concedes: "overall the country characteristics do not help very much to explain the countries' choice of exchange rate regime. It might be that the choices are based on some other factors, economical or political" (Honkapohja and Pikkarainen, 1994, pp. 47–48). Indeed—why should we be surprised that politics might also enter into such a critical decision?

In fact, political factors enter in two ways. First, the policy calculus is manifestly affected by domestic distributional politics: the tug and pull of organized interest groups of every kind. As political scientist Jeffry Frieden has emphasized, "domestic distributional considerations are also central to the choice of exchange rate regimes" (1993, p. 140). The critical issue is the familiar one of whose ox is gored. Who wins and who loses? The material interests of specific constituencies are systematically influenced by what a government decides to do with its currency. Producers of tradable goods, for example, as well as internationally active investors, are all apt to be favored by a currency regime that maximizes the predictability of exchange rates. Currency volatility, for such groups, is anathema. Domestically oriented sectors, by contrast, are more likely to benefit from stability at home and thus to attach higher priority to preserving as much national policy autonomy as possible. Such groups stand to lose most from a common currency insofar as their local interests are submerged in a broader monetary area. Government choices are bound to be sensitive to the interplay among such domestic political forces.

Second, even apart from distributional concerns, the policy calculus includes much more than just macroeconomic performance alone. Plainly, diverse political goals at the national level must weigh at least as heavily as economic welfare in the strategic calculations of policymakers. It is by no means unreasonable to assume that governments are sensitive to the balance between macroeconomic flexibility and microeconomic efficiency. But in considering whether to share their monetary sovereignty, states are unlikely to limit their thinking to that one trade-off alone. There must also be strong political incentives involved to persuade policymakers to make the kind of firm commitment that is demanded.

Certainly that appears to be the lesson of history, where it is impossible to find a single example of a common currency motivated exclusively, or even predominantly, by the concerns highlighted in OCA theory. As Paul De Grauwe has observed: "not a single monetary union in the past came about because of a recognition of economic benefits of the union. In all cases the integration was driven by political objectives" (1993, p. 656). Of the half-dozen currency unions that have been attempted among states of any significant size during the twentieth century, one—the Belgium-Luxembourg BLEU, founded in 1922—grew out of the security needs of a small and vulnerable ministate; and four others—the Eastern Caribbean Currency Union (ECCU), the CFA Franc Zone, the now defunct East African Community (EAC), and southern Africa's Common Monetary Area (CMA)—derived from arrangements initially imposed by colonial powers.

And what of the newly established EMU, which began in January 1999? After decades of debate, it is by now clear that the purely economic case for EMU is inconclusive at best. The real issues, most observers concur, are undoubtedly political, relating first and foremost to the EU's declared goal of an "ever closer union." To its critics as well as to its advocates, Europe's newborn currency, the euro, is seen as a harbinger of eventual political integration. In the words of one careful survey:

> Although there are surely economic benefits to be expected from a monetary union, the main driving force for [the EMU's] resurgence remains the quest for the political integration of Europe. . . . The main objections

to monetary union have also been largely political. (Fratianni, von Hagen, and Waller, 1992, pp. 1–2)

In brief: economics matters, but politics matters more.

Political Analysis

What politics? Most relevant are the direct political benefits of monetary sovereignty, all of which are likely to be compromised by the creation of a common currency. A distinct national money may not be an essential attribute of state sovereignty, but along with the raising of armies and the levying of taxes it has long been regarded as essential. As one observer has argued, with only a touch of sarcasm,

> a government that does not control money is a limited government. . . . No government likes to be limited. . . . Governments simply must monopolize money if they are to control it and they must control it if they really are to be governments. (O'Mahony, 1984, p. 127)

It is easy to see why a monetary monopoly is so highly prized. Genuine power resides in the privilege that money represents. Apart from the instrument that a monetary monopoly provides to help manage the macroeconomic performance of the economy, three direct political benefits are derived from a strictly national currency: first, a potent political symbol to promote a sense of national identity; second, a potentially powerful source of revenue to underwrite public expenditures; and third, a practical means to insulate the nation from foreign influence or constraint. All are important elements of the fundamental purpose of the state: to permit a community to live in peace and preserve its own social and cultural heritage.

At the symbolic level, a national currency is particularly useful to rulers wary of internal division or dissent. Centralization of political authority is facilitated insofar as citizens all feel themselves bound together as members of a single social unit—all part of the same "imagined community," in Benedict Anderson's apt phrase (1991). Anderson, a cultural anthropologist, stresses that states are made not just through force but also through loyalty, a voluntary commitment to a joint identity. The critical distinction between "us" and "them" can be heightened by all manner of tangible symbols: flags, anthems, postage stamps, public architecture, even national sports teams. Among the most potent of these tokens is money, as the Italian central banker Tommaso Padoa-Schioppa has noted:

> John Stuart Mill once referred to the existence of a multiplicity of national moneys as a "barbarism." . . . One could perhaps talk of a tribal system, with each tribe being attached to its own money and attributing it magical virtues . . . which no other tribe recognizes. (1993, p. 16)

Money's "magical virtues" serve to enhance a sense of national identity in two ways. First, because it is issued by the government or its central bank, a currency acts as a daily reminder to citizens of their connection to the state and oneness with it. Second, by virtue of its universal use on a daily basis, the currency underscores the fact that everyone is part of the same social entity—a role not unlike that of a single national language, which many governments also actively promote for nationalistic reasons. A common money helps to homogenize diverse and often antagonistic social groups.

A second benefit of a national currency is seigniorage—the capacity a monetary monopoly gives national governments to augment public spending at will. Technically defined as the excess of the nominal value of a currency over its cost of production, seigniorage can be understood as an alternative source of revenue for the state beyond what can be raised via taxation or by borrowing from financial markets. Public spending financed by money creation in effect appropriates real resources at the expense of the private sector, whose purchasing power is correspondingly reduced by the ensuing increase of inflation—a privilege for government if there ever was one. Because of the inflationary implications involved, the process is also known popularly as the "inflation tax."

Despite the economic disadvantages associated with inflation, the privilege of seigniorage makes sense from a political perspective as a kind of insurance policy against risk—an emergency source of revenue to cope with unexpected contingencies, up to and including war. Decades ago John Maynard Keynes wrote: "a government can live by this means when it can live by no other." Generations later another British economist, Charles Goodhart (1995, p. 452), has described seigniorage as the "revenue of last resort"—the single most flexible instrument of taxation available to mobilize resources in the event of a sudden crisis or threat to national security. It would be the exceptional government that would *not* wish to retain something like the option of an inflation tax.

Finally, an important political benefit is also derived in a negative sense—from the enhanced ability a national money gives government to avoid dependence on some other provenance for this most critical of all economic resources. A national monetary monopoly draws a clear economic boundary between the state and the rest of the world, promoting political authority. The more effectively a government is able to enforce its monopoly within its own territorial frontiers, the better it will be able to insulate itself from outside influence or constraint in formulating and implementing policy.

That sovereign states might use external monetary relations coercively, given the opportunity, should come as no surprise. As the political scientist Jonathan Kirshner has reminded us: "monetary power is a remarkably efficient component of state power . . . the most potent instrument of economic coercion available to states in a position to exercise it" (1995, pp. 29, 31). Money, after all, is simply command over real resources. If a nation can be denied access to the means needed to purchase vital goods and services, it is clearly vulnerable in political terms. The implication is simple: if you want political autonomy, don't rely on someone else's money.

Although generally ignored by OCA theory, these three political benefits are all obviously affected by a decision to create a common currency. In effect all three are diluted at the national level and recreated at the group level, to be shared and in some manner managed collectively by the partner countries involved. Though this may on balance represent net gain for the group as a whole, for each partner individually it necessarily implies a significant degree of loss of sovereign power and privilege. Money's magical virtues can no longer be relied on to enhance a unique sense of national identity. Insofar as value continues to be attached to loyalty to a distinct political community, it can no longer be promoted through the tangible symbol of a separate state-sponsored currency. Likewise, neither the revenue of last resort nor the political autonomy that a national money offers is as readily available when replaced by a common currency. Responses to crises are now subject to collective, not unilateral, decision making; joint management, in turn, leaves each country individually more open than before to overt influence or constraint by its partners. Such considerations are bound to figure prominently in the calculations of governments.

Good or bad policy, in short, is not defined by strictly economic considerations alone; nor can the value of sovereignty be measured solely by its ability to deliver higher material standards of living. What is to be optimized is welfare in a much broader sense—in political economy terms, welfare in the sense of a community's overall sense of identity and control of its own destiny. Even if the economic case for currency unification can be made, policymakers must still ask: What will be the effect on the "imagined community"? On the government's ability to handle unexpected emergencies? On the society's insulation from external coercion? To omit such key political concerns is to risk rendering analysis seriously deficient if not downright irrelevant.

Dollarization

The same point also applies to dollarization, which has become a topic of intense public debate in Mexico and several other Latin American nations since Carlos Menem of Argentina spoke out in favor of the approach in early 1999. In 2000, Ecuador actually did choose to dollarize, as did El Salvador in 2001. Should other Latin Americans follow these examples, abandoning their local currencies in favor of the greenback (or perhaps a future joint U.S.-Canadian currency)? Here too attention tends to remain misleadingly focused on technical economic considerations rather than on welfare in a broader political economy sense. Hence, here too most analysis runs the risk of being deficient if not irrelevant.

Like the decision to create a common currency, dollarization in the economics literature tends to be addressed as an optimization problem limited mainly to issues of strictly material welfare. As in OCA theory, income gains or losses are evaluated from a single country's point of view—a country that might consider replacing its own money with the money of a larger and more successful partner (such as the United States). Typically, the foreign partner's money already circulates widely, albeit unofficially, within the domestic economy as a result of a market-driven process of currency substitution (in analytical terms distinguished as *informal* dollarization). The question is: Should the government take the process to its seemingly logical conclusion by officially withdrawing all of the local money from circulation (*formal* dollarization)?

On the positive side, as in OCA theory, benefits are expected from reduced transactions costs and enhanced usefulness of money for all its standard functions, and perhaps also from lower interest rates and a more predictable exchange rate. Conversely, on the negative side, three economic costs tend to be emphasized. None of the costs is insignificant. All are likely to be greater than if the two countries mutually agree to create a new common currency.

First, there is a loss of monetary autonomy, since the dollarizing country can no longer exercise unilateral control over its money supply or exchange rate. That is true with a common currency too, of course. But as compared with currency unification, the degree of loss is greater since dollarization as such implies no direct part in the making of monetary policy. With currency unification, each country presumably has a seat at the table where joint policy is made. With dollarization, unless based on an agreement with explicit provision for power sharing, all authority is simply ceded to the partner country's central bank. The relationship is not one of parity but of hierarchy, with no promise at all that the dollarizing country's specific circumstances or needs would be taken into account when monetary decisions are made.

Admittedly, in practical terms, much of the country's monetary autonomy may already have been lost as a result of informal dollarization. The greater the degree of currency substitution that has already occurred, reflecting market pressures and preferences, the greater is the degree of constraint already imposed on a government's ability to manage macroeconomic conditions. As a recent IMF report concluded: "[informal] dollarization can complicate . . . monetary policy by introducing a foreign currency component into the money supply. . . . Dollarization may complicate stabilization and cause additional volatility" (Baliño, Bennett, and Borensztein, 1999, pp. 1, 3). But retreat is one thing, complete surrender quite another. As compared with a strategy of keeping the national currency in circulation, which enables a government to retain at least a residual degree of control, formalization of the informal does imply an extra loss. Henceforth there will be absolutely nothing that the country can do to directly influence monetary conditions within its borders.

Second, there is a loss of a steady portion of seigniorage, since the dollarizing country must finance replacement of local currency still in circulation with a new issue of the partner's money. Circulating cash represents in effect a noninterest obligation of the central bank, matched on its balance sheet by interest-bearing reserve assets that are an ongoing source of revenue. Dollarization automatically terminates that revenue unless explicitly offset by some kind of agreed formula for seigniorage sharing, as would logically be expected in the case of currency unification. In a classic contribution, Stanley Fischer (1982) divided this seigniorage loss into two parts: first the "stock cost," equal to the one-time expense of obtaining the new notes and coins needed to replace local currency in circulation; and second the "flow cost," representing the continuing flow of income forgone because the partner's money pays no interest to the local government. Both stock and flow costs will be smaller, of course, the greater is the degree of prior informal dollarization. But unless domestic circulation of local currency has already dwindled to the vanishing point, the seigniorage loss is unlikely to be trivial.

Finally, a dollarizing country is said to lose a lender of last resort, since in adopting a foreign currency it also formally gives up a central bank capable of discounting freely in times of financial crisis. Domestic banks thus are said to be more exposed to potential liquidity risks. To a large extent, however, this alleged cost is a red herring, inasmuch as the loss of a lender of last resort can be rather easily offset on a unilateral basis. Dollarization, for example, reduces the overall need for international reserves, since a share of external transactions that previously required foreign exchange can now be treated as the equivalent of domestic transactions. A portion of the central bank's assets, therefore, could be dedicated instead to a public stabilization fund to help out domestic financial institutions under stress. Alternatively, a contingency fund could be built up over time from tax revenues, or flexible credit lines with foreign banks or monetary authorities could be negotiated, using future tax revenues as collateral. These possibilities stand in stark contrast to dollarization's other economic costs— the losses of monetary autonomy and seigniorage—which require explicit sharing agreements if they are to be contained or reduced significantly.

Once again, however, the question is not whether economic considerations of these kinds matter—of course they do—but whether they are *all* that matter. Here too one can legitimately argue that politics matters at least as much to governments, if not a good deal more.

From a political point of view, the same three issues are involved here as with a common currency: losses of a symbol of national identity, a revenue of last resort, and a measure of political insulation. But in contrast to currency unification, which implies some degree of parity and sharing among the partners, dollarization is a hierarchical relationship that offers little in the way of direct compensation and no necessary role at all in decision making. The foreign partner enjoys not only all the status and prestige that goes with more extensive cross-border use of its money but also an enhanced capacity to mobilize fiscal resources when needed. What government would not factor such vital concerns into its calculus of the advantages and disadvantages of abandoning its own currency?

Perhaps most important, the foreign partner gains a powerful instrument of influence or coercion over the dependent dollarized economy. Consider, for example, the case of Panama, which since its independence has used the U.S. dollar as legal tender for most domestic monetary purposes. Panama owes its existence to the United States, which encouraged secession from Colombia to facilitate construction of a canal across the isthmus, and has always maintained a special relationship with Washington. Although a national currency, the balboa, exists in principle, only a negligible amount of balboa coins actually circulates in practice. The bulk of the money supply, including all paper notes and most bank deposits, is accounted for by the dollar. In the late 1980s, Panamanians learned just how exposed they were to external coercion under this monetary arrangement.

In economic terms, most observers have rightly had only praise for Panama's currency dependence. Reliance on the dollar has created an environment of stability that has both suppressed inflation—a bane of most of Panama's hemispheric neighbors—and helped establish the country as an important offshore financial center. But in political terms Panama has been extremely vulnerable in its relations with Washington, which of course could sour at any time.

Such a moment came in 1988, following accusations of corruption and drug smuggling against General Manuel Noriega, the country's de facto leader. In March 1988, Panamanian assets in U.S. banks were frozen, and all payments and dollar transfers to Panama were prohibited as part of the Reagan administration's determined campaign to force Noriega from power. The impact was swift. Most local banks were forced to close, and the economy was squeezed by a severe liquidity shortage. The effect on the economy was devastating, despite rushed efforts by the Panamanian authorities to create a substitute currency, mainly by issuing checks in standardized denominations that they hoped recipients would then treat as cash. The country was effectively demonetized. Over the course of the year, domestic output fell by a fifth.

As it happens, the sanctions turned out to be insufficient to dislodge Noriega on their own. Ultimately, in 1989, Washington felt it necessary to mount a military invasion that led to a temporary occupation of the country until a new, friendlier government could be installed. But there can be no doubt that the liquidity squeeze was painful and contributed greatly to Noriega's downfall. The message is obvious, as economist Lawrence Klein has prudently suggested:

> Panama . . . uses U.S. dollars for its monetary units. As long as relations remain cordial, this is not a bad arrangement. . . . But for Panama the risk price is very high for having the convenience of U.S. dollars. The small country would be in a better and more independent position if it

had not let some of its monetary actions be governed by foreigners. (1993, pp. 112–13)

No country concerned for its sovereignty is likely to ignore Klein's point.

◣ Sustaining Monetary Union

Consider now the *sustainability* of a monetary union. In principle, monetary union, whether via currency unification or dollarization, is supposed to be permanent—a formally irrevocable commitment. But if the history of world politics teaches us anything, it is that in relations between sovereign states one can never truly say never. No interstate commitment, no matter how seemingly firm, may be regarded as truly irrevocable in practice. Hence we must also look beyond the initial decision to the unfolding of subsequent events. What conditions determine whether a commitment to a currency union or dollarization, once made, can be successfully sustained over time? Again, each of the two approaches can be taken up separately.

Currency Unification

We start once more with currency unification. Some currency unions have been successfully sustained for decades, including BLEU, ECCU, CFA, and CMA among those already mentioned. (The jury is still out, of course, on the EMU.) But many others, by contrast, have gradually eroded over time or even totally failed, including not only the EAC but also the Soviet Union's ruble zone and other former federations like Czechoslovakia and Yugoslavia, which disintegrated almost as soon as their constituent members gained political independence. Much the same was also true of the nineteenth century's two major experiments in currency unification, the Latin Monetary Union (LMU) and the Scandinavian Monetary Union (SMU). Each functioned more or less effectively until World War I (a not inconsiderable achievement), yet ultimately both were formally terminated. If we look carefully at this variety of experience, we find that here too politics plays the leading role in determining final outcomes.

Economic variables offer little assistance in explaining the sustainability of monetary unions. As I have noted elsewhere (Cohen, 2000), for every one of the characteristics conventionally stressed in OCA theory, there are contradictory historical examples—cases that conform to the expectations suggested by OCA theory and others that do not. None seems sufficient to explain observed outcomes. This is not to suggest that economic factors are therefore unimportant. Clearly they do matter, insofar as they tend, through their impact on economic welfare, either to ease or exacerbate the challenge of sustaining a common currency. But equally clearly, more has gone on in each case than can be accounted for by such variables alone.

Nor is much help offered by an analysis of institutional design—that is, the legal provisions concerning issue of currency and management of monetary policy. Such organizational formalities have differed sharply in various cases. Only in three instances, apart from fragmenting federations, have members at any time relied exclusively on a true common currency—in the Eastern Caribbean and, more briefly, in East and southern Africa. In all the others, including the EAC after 1967 and the CMA after 1974, arrangements have featured national or regional currencies that were officially linked together to one extent or another. And in parallel fashion, monetary institutions have also varied greatly, ranging from a single central authority in two cases (the ECCU and, before the mid-1960s, the EAC) to two regional authorities in one case (CFA) and to separate national agencies in all the others (including the ruble zone and other such federations after their breakups). No systematic relationship is evident, however, between these organizational differences and the success or failure of various monetary alliances.

In principle, such differences might be thought to matter insofar as they affect the net costs of compliance or defection by individual states. Recent theoretical literature on transactions costs emphasizes the key role that institutional design can play in promoting credible commitments, by structuring arrangements to match anticipated incentive problems. From this perspective, creation of a single currency would appear to be superior to a formal linking of national currencies because of the higher barriers to exit involved: the greater cost of reintroducing an independent money and monetary authority.

That was also the conclusion of policy discussions of alternative strategies for EMU before its creation, which directly addressed the relative merits of full currency unification versus a simple exchange rate union (Gros and Thygesen, 1992, pp. 230–33; von Hagen and Fratianni, 1993). Most analysts express doubt that a system retaining existing currencies and central banks, no matter how solemn the political commitments involved, would be as credible as a genuine joint money, precisely because the risk of reversibility would presumably be greater. The implication is that compliance mechanisms are likely to be weaker to the extent that governments continue to exercise any control at all over either the price or quantity of their currency. Thus one might have expected to see in historical experience a direct correlation between the degree of centralization of a monetary union and its practical sustainability over time. In fact, however, no such relationship can be found. Contradictory examples abound.

The lesson of history is clear. The degree of centralization surely must matter insofar as it influences the potential cost of exit. But high barriers to exit or not, the evidence is that commitments can be—and, indeed, frequently have been—broken when governments decide it is in their interest to do so. Institutional design is probably no less important than economic characteristics. But it is equally clear that there is still something else at work here that overshadows them both. That something, of course, is politics.

From a political perspective, two characteristics stand out as crucial to the fate of monetary unions. One, suggested by traditional realist approaches to international relations theory, is the presence or absence of a powerful state that is willing and able to use its influence to keep such an arrangement functioning effectively on terms agreeable to all. The other, suggested by more institutional approaches, is the presence or absence of a broad constellation of related ties and commitments sufficient to make the loss of policy autonomy, whatever the magnitude of prospective costs, seem basically acceptable to each partner. The first, which implies a degree of subordination as well as a sharing of monetary sovereignty, calls for a locally dominant country—a "hegemon"—and is a direct reflection of the distribution of interstate power. The second calls for a well-developed set of institutional linkages, and it reflects, more amorphously, the degree to which a genuine sense of solidarity—of *community*—exists among all the countries involved. Judging from the historical record, it seems clear that one or the other of these two factors is necessary for the sustainability of monetary union among sovereign states. Where both are present, they are a sufficient condition for success. Where neither is present, unions tend to erode or fail.

In short, when it comes to sustaining currency unification, the issue is only secondarily whether countries meet the traditional criteria identified in OCA theory or whether monetary management and currency issue happen to be centralized or decentralized. The primary question is whether the necessary political conditions exist: either a local hegemon or a fabric of related ties with sufficient influence to truly neutralize the risk of exit. Sovereign governments require incentives to stick to bargains that turn out to be inconvenient. The evidence from history suggests that these incentives may derive either from side payments or sanctions supplied by a single powerful state or else from the constraints and opportunities posed by a broad network of institutional linkages. One or the other of these political factors, it appears, must be present to serve as an effective compliance mechanism.

Dollarization

With dollarization, the leading role of politics is even more nakedly obvious. Since the relationship is inherently hierarchical, the presence of a dominant state is guaranteed. The only question is what, if anything, the hegemon will do when faced with the prospect of exit by a subordinate partner. Will the hegemon actively deploy its influence to sustain use of its currency, or will it remain passive, more or less calmly acceding to its partner's altered preference? Much depends on how vital the partner is felt to be to the dominant country's political or economic interests.

Two historical examples will suffice. One involves the CMA, whose origins go back to the 1920s, when South Africa's currency, now known as the rand, became the sole legal tender in three of Britain's nearby possessions, Bechuanaland (later Botswana), British Basutoland (later Lesotho), and Swaziland, as well as in the United Nations trust territory of South West Africa, previously a German colony (now Namibia). In effect, all of South Africa's four closest neighbors were officially dollarized. Once decolonization began in the region, however, the monetary arrangement began to loosen, despite formalization first in 1974 as the Rand Monetary Area and later in 1986 as the CMA, as distinct national currencies were introduced by each of the junior partners. Diamond-rich Botswana eventually dropped out altogether, preferring to promote its own national money. Likewise Swaziland, even though remaining linked to the rand, ultimately chose to withdraw the legal tender status of South Africa's currency within its own borders. As a result, today only Lesotho and Namibia remain formally dollarized, insofar as the rand continues to circulate in each country alongside the national currency as legal tender.

Why have Lesotho and Namibia remained dollarized while the others have not? Essentially it is because South Africa has been willing to bribe them to avert defection. Side payments are provided in two forms. First is direct compensation for the seigniorage the two countries forgo by permitting circulation of an amount of rand within their domestic economies. Compensation is based on an estimate of the income that would accrue to each if they instead held reserves of equivalent amount invested in rand-denominated assets. And second is an assurance that the South African central bank will stand as lender of last resort for their domestic banking system in the event of need. Pretoria's willingness to make such critical concessions is clearly related to the importance the government attaches to good relations with its immediate neighbors. It is also the only reason why any degree of dollarization at all is still sustained in the southern African region.

The second historical example involves Liberia, which from the time of its independence in 1847 has always, like Panama, had a special relationship with the United States. During World War II, as the United States built up its military presence in the country, Liberia made the U.S. dollar sole legal tender, replacing the British West African coinage that had previously dominated the local money supply. Though supplemented, beginning in the 1960s, by a limited issue of small-denomination Liberian coins (also named the dollar), America's greenback maintained its dominant role until the mid-1980s, when political turmoil and fiscal deficits led the Liberian authorities to issue large amounts of higher-denomination coins as well as notes—a classic example of a government resorting to seigniorage as a revenue of last resort. Also true to form, Gresham's law quickly went to work, and by the end of the 1980s U.S. dollars had almost completely disappeared from circulation, though the monetary agreement with Washington remains nominally in effect. Technically, the greenback is still the principal currency of Liberia, though it no longer actively circulates much as a medium of exchange. In practice, dollarization has not been sustained, and for one simple reason—Washington has not felt particularly moved to do anything about it. Liberia simply does not rank very high among U.S. vital interests around the globe.

◣ Implications for Canada and Latin America

What are the implications of all this for Canada and Latin America? Highlighting the political dimension of monetary union suggests a paradox of sorts for both the northern and southern neighbors of the United States. Politics would appear to favor sustainability but to hinder creation. The problem is not how to preserve a common currency for Canada or dollarization for Latin Americans, once such a commitment is made. The real challenge is how to achieve the commitment in the first place—how to get from Here to There. Political barriers could prove to be insurmountable.

In the case of Canada, for instance, both political conditions needed to sustain a common currency would appear to be satisfied. Certainly there already exists a sufficiently broad constellation of institutional linkages between Canada and the United States—manifested most obviously in NAFTA—to ease the risk of possible unilateral exit by either partner. If not yet a single community, the two countries do not lack for a significant sense of solidarity. Likewise there already exists a locally dominant country, the United States, with an undoubted ability to keep an arrangement functioning effectively if it so chooses. Once a mutual commitment to currency unification is made, it should not be particularly difficult to ensure compliance on both sides.

But there, of course, is the rub. Can the necessary initial commitment be attained? For Canada, clearly, the key issue is how monetary policy would be made if North America's two dollars are merged. Will Ottawa be able to negotiate a share of power over a joint currency sufficient to compensate Canadians for the political losses involved—not least the loss of one of the most tangible symbols of their carefully guarded distinctiveness as a nation? Conversely, will the much larger United States, so accustomed to having its own way in monetary affairs, be prepared to cede much more than token influence to Canada? It is not difficult to imagine that the gap between the two countries over this issue might turn out to be simply too wide to bridge.

Similarly, in the case of Latin America, the basic condition needed to sustain dollarization—a committed hegemon—would also appear to be satisfied. Few regions of the world are seen in Washington as more vital to U.S. interests. If the U.S. and Latin governments formally agree to replace local currencies with the greenback, there seems little doubt that Washington would subsequently make every effort to keep the arrangement from failing. But again, the question is: Can the necessary initial commitment be attained? For Latin America, unlike Canada, the key issue would probably not be a direct role in decision making. As junior partners in a distinctly hierarchical relationship, Latin Americans could not realistically aspire to seats at the Federal Reserve. Rather, attention is more likely to focus on such matters as seigniorage and lender-of-last-resort facilities as a way of gaining compensation for the obvious political risks involved in becoming another Panama writ large. But will Washington be willing to play the role of South Africa, offering either a share of seigniorage revenues or a safety net to Latin American banking systems? Here too it is not difficult to imagine an unbridgeable gap between negotiating positions.

Yet these are precisely the gaps that will have to be addressed if dreams of currency unification or dollarization are to become reality. They are what is truly at stake today. Easily overlooked by strictly economic analysis, such political considerations will be decisive in determining whether monetary union is ultimately possible in the Western Hemisphere.

◣ Note

An earlier version of this chapter, in French translation, appeared in January 2000 under the title "Dollarisation: la dimension politique," in *L'Economie Politique* 5(1), 88–112.

◣ References

Anderson, Benedict. (1991). *Imagined Communities: Reflections on the Origins and Spread of Nationalism* (Rev. ed.). London: Verso.

Argy, Victor, and Paul De Grauwe (Eds.). (1990). *Choosing an Exchange-Rate Regime: The Challenge for Smaller Industrial Countries.* Washington, D.C.: International Monetary Fund.

Baliño, Tomás J. L., Adam Bennett, and Eduardo Bonrensztein. (1999). *Monetary Policy in Dollarized Economies.* Washington, D.C.: International Monetary Fund.

Cohen, Benjamin J. (2000). Beyond EMU: The Problem of Sustainability. In Barry Eichengreen and Jeffry A. Frieden (Eds.), *Political Economy of European Monetary Integration* (2nd ed.) (pp. 179–204). Boulder, Colo.: Westview Press.

De Grauwe, Paul. (1993). The Political Economy of Monetary Union in Europe. *The World Economy, 16*(6), 653–61.

Fratianni, Michele, Jurgen von Hagen, and Christopher Waller. (1992). *The Maastricht Way to EMU.* (Essays in International Finance No. 187). Princeton: International Finance Section.

Fischer, Stanley. (1982). Seigniorage and the Case for National Money. *Journal of Political Economy, 90*(2), 295–313.

Frieden, Jeffry A. (1993). The Dynamics of International Monetary Systems: International and Domestic Factors in the Rise, Reign, and Demise of the Classical Gold Standard. In Jack Snyder and Robert Jervis (Eds.), *Coping with Complexity in the International System* (pp. 137–62). Boulder, Colo.: Westview Press.

Goodhart, Charles A. E. (1995). The Political Economy of Monetary Union. In Peter B. Kenen (Ed.), *Understanding Interdependence: The Macroeconomics of the Open Economy* (pp. 448–505). Princeton, N.J.: Princeton University Press.

Gros, Daniel, and Niels Thygesen. (1992). *European Monetary Integration: From the European Monetary System to European Monetary Union.* London: Longman.

Honkapohja, Seppo, and Pentti Pikkarainen. (1994). Country Characteristics and the Choice of the Exchange Rate Regime: Are Mini-Skirts Followed by Maxis? In Johnny Akerholm and Alberto Giovannini (Eds.), *Exchange Rate Policies in the Nordic Countries* (pp. 31–53). London: Centre for Economic Policy Research.

Kirshner, Jonathan. (1995). *Currency and Coercion: The Political Economy of International Monetary Power.* Princeton: Princeton University Press.

Klein, Lawrence R. (1993). Some Second Thoughts on the European Monetary System. *Greek Economic Review, 15*(1), 105–14.

Krugman, Paul R. (1993). *What Do We Need to Know about the International Monetary System?* (Essays in International Finance No. 190). Princeton: International Finance Section.

Mundell, Robert A. (1961). A Theory of Optimum Currency Areas. *American Economic Review, 51*(3), 657–65.

O'Mahony, David (1984). Past Justifications for Public Interventions. In Pascal Salin (Ed.), *Currency Competition and Monetary Union* (pp. 127–30). The Hague: Martinus Nijhoff Publishers.

Padoa-Schioppa, Tommaso. (1993). *Tripolarism: Regional and Global Economic Cooperation.* (Occasional Papers No. 42). Washington, D.C.: Group of Thirty.

Tavlas, George S. (1994). The Theory of Monetary Integration. *Open Economies Review, 5,* 211–30.

von Hagen, Jurgen, and Michele Fratianni. (1993). The Transition to European Monetary Union and the European Monetary Institute. *Economics and Politics, 5*(2), 167–86.

14 Jürgen Schuldt

Latin American Official Dollarization
Political Economy Aspects

> *The international monetary system depends on the power configuration of the countries that make it up.*
>
> —Robert Mundell, "A Reconsideration of the Twentieth Century" (2002)

Recently, and not by chance,[1] seminars and workshops on full or official dollarization of Latin American economies have proliferated, and myriad interesting essays on this subject have emerged. Unfortunately the debates are centered almost exclusively on economic aspects, having reached a point of decreasing returns. So, in order to predict the future and the possibilities of de jure dollarization in Latin America, instead of just considering the theoretical and empirical arguments put forward by economists in favor and against it, we should approach the issue from the points of view of the *relations among the globalizing triad* (the United States, Europe, and Japan), of the *interdependencies developed recently between the United States and the subcontinental countries,* and of the *interests of certain domestic power groups* in the United States and in Latin America.

My principal hypothesis can be presented plainly. For some of the reasons I will give explicitly hereafter, the complete official dollarization of most of the subcontinental economies will become a reality before 2010. With this, these economies would become part of a tendency that is becoming more and more general in the world,[2] even though for the time being the main economic and political authorities in Washington, including the multilateral organizations, are being cautious and even reluctant regarding the complete dollarization proposals made by some Latin American governments.

▶ About the Forecasting Capabilities of Economic Theory

> *Economists rank second only to astrologers in their predictive abilities.*
>
> —Dani Rodrik, "How Far Will International Integration Go?" (1999)

Any sensible person would have concurred with the following forecast that Sebastián Edwards ventured in April 1999 of the possibilities of de jure dollarization in certain countries of Latin America: "although I am convinced that a currency board, and maybe even dollarization, is the right system for Argentina, I am equally convinced that it would be the utmost frivolity to think that, say, Ecuador, could go in that direction" (1999b, p. 39).

Curiously, the Latin American country he considered least likely to adopt an *official* dollarization process was the first one to do so, and now many economists find themselves in trouble, carrying out the most unlikely acrobatics so as to justify the measure from an economic point of view (De la Torre, 2000). But, as ever, for most orthodox economists, what cannot be explained economically is labeled as utmost frivolity, irrationality, populism, or simple stupidity.

Thanks to this apparently extreme tropical event, we should remember that it is indispensable to consider the sociopolitical dynamics of a country, the actions taken by the interest groups, and the peculiarities of the political regime, in the context of international geostrategic, technological, and sociopolitical processes, so as to improve our economic analysis and, most important, to enhance our abilities to forecast the economic tendencies and the economic policies a government will adopt.

Luckily, in recent years, various strands of the so-called new political economy have grown stronger. Interested readers may already find fascinating materials in textbooks, such as the most recent one by Allan Drazen, who has reached the marrow of a problem every economist should consider more often in his or her models, analysis, and predictions: the fact that certain economic decisions are generally taken under social and political considerations, independently from the apparently solid and coherent arguments that economists may present in opposition to or in favor of certain economic measures. In his convincing words, "positive political economy thus asks the question how political constraints may explain the choice of policies (and thus economic outcomes) that differ from optimal policies, and the outcomes those policies would imply. . . . [T]he mechanisms that societies use in choosing policies in the face of conflicts of interest will imply that the result will often be quite different than what a benign social planner would choose" (Drazen, 2000, pp. 6–7).

This is the orientation I would like to explore in this essay, so as to establish *some hypotheses concerning the possibilities of full dollarization in Latin America.* Evidently it is still too soon to develop formal political macroeconomic models so as to give a greater consistency to empirical analysis, but I do think we should take some additional informal steps in that direction. In general terms, I agree with the hypothesis that economic policies adopted (or declined) by governments generally respond to geostrategic, political, social, and even cultural factors, much more than to the hygienic automatics of rational economic logic. In practice, most economic arguments obey an a posteriori function, that of rationalizing ex post the measures that are adopted and that are at the service of specific domestic and international hegemonic interests and alliances.

From a more global conceptual perspective, dollarization will be adopted principally for political and other minor reasons that in general are far from the purely economic ones that of course also play a role.[3] From the point of view of the principal continental power, the interest in official dollarization consists in strengthening and *expanding its hemispheric hegemony and dominance,* advancing along the way the demands of its "national" international corporations and banks. As for the Latin American countries, internal political forces and the fear of losing a place in the international economy—the so-called peripherization pressure (Senghaas, 1982, 1988)—have an essential explicative character in this and many other matters. I will now show why.

▶ *United States Interests and Latin American Full Dollarization*

Dollarization by Latin America is in the enlightened self-interest of the United States.

—Michael Gavin, "Official Dollarization in Latin America" (2000)

The United States would benefit at least for the following reasons from Latin American official dollarization, as expressed in the *Economic Report of the President* (*ERP,* 1999) and some papers prepared for the Joint Economic Committee of the U.S. Senate (Stein, 1999, 2000), concerning basically the International Monetary Stability Act (IMSA) project.[4]

In the first place, "dollarization abroad would stabilize and expand export markets, thereby helping U.S. workers and businesses," as James Dean puts it, adding that "dollarization would encourage closer trade, investment and financial integration with the United States, that too would, under optimistic assumptions, be good for growth" (2000a, p. 18).

In the second instance, "it will be of great support for North American investors because the measure eliminates the 'exchange risk' " and reduces the sovereign risk. That is, the United States "benefits mainly to the extent that the policy generates deeper hemispheric integration—an avowed goal of U.S. policy . . . greater economic and financial stability, and more rapid development of our neighbors in the hemisphere" (Gavin, 2000).

Third, given the fact that dollarized countries would not have a lender of last resort, North American banks could offer the necessary "collateral" with which probably "foreign banks will come to dominate the financial sector of 'client' countries—especially banks from the country whose currency is adopted" (D'Arista, 2000, p. 5).

Then there is, of course, the "convenience for the country's residents. It is certainly more convenient for a country's exporters, importers, borrowers, and lenders to be able to deal in their own currency rather than in foreign currencies. The global use of the dollar, like the increasingly global use of the English language, is a natural advantage that American businesses may take for granted" (*ERP,* 1999).

Fifth, as is known, "seigniorage income of the United States would increase with this process of unilateral dollarization (*ERP,* 1999)."

It would also help taxpayers save a lot of money because, as Latin American economies become more sound, it would not be necessary to "bail out countries due to sudden currency-related economic problems (*ERP,* 1999)."

Other economists have found additional advantages for the United States, like for example the ones to be gained by their workers:

> As [monetary] integration proceeds, the greater stability of Latin American economies that is likely to be generated by a more accident-proof monetary regime becomes increasingly important. Monetary mishaps that lead to a collapse of wages and living standards in Latin American economies impose important collateral damage on U.S. workers, who may suddenly be forced to compete with Latin American labor that has been impoverished by currency collapse. Other than workers in Latin America, no group has more at stake in the avoidance of monetary crisis in the region than U.S. workers. (Gavin, 2000, p. 4)

Last but not least,

> having an international currency may confer power and prestige, but the benefits therefrom are somewhat nebulous. Nevertheless, historians and political scientists have sometimes regarded key currency status and international creditor status, along with such non-economic factors as colonies and military power, as among the trappings of a great power. (*ERP,* 1999, p. 301)

Therefore, if we consider all the political, economic, and sociopsychological advantages that Latin American full dollarization would bring to the United States, plus the fact that if many other countries adopt the dollar as legal tender this would generate a dollarized fort to face the euro, I conclude that the *necessary* (but not sufficient) conditions exist for official dollarization to become a reality, sooner or later. In effect, "international monetary systems . . . have to be consistent and evolve with the power configuration of the world economy" (Mundell, 2000c), mirroring in this case the ever greater importance of the United States in world hegemony.

▶ *Why Is the North American Government So Reticent toward Dollarization?*

So, I would say that the idea merits American blessings even if it can't be official blessings.

—Jeffrey Frankel, "Comments" (1999)

Given the clinching arguments in favor of official dollarization in Latin America, it is fair to ask why the North American government has so many scruples about openly encouraging official dollarization in Latin America. Although science still does not permit us to penetrate other human beings' minds (especially those of politicians), I shall try to clarify the political and cognitive interiorities of the former secretary of the Treasury of the United States, Lawrence Summers, and the different reasons that could have led him to be so disinclined toward the proposals for an official dollarization in Latin America.

To my understanding there may be several political arguments as well as personal intuitions that have led Summers to adopt a different attitude without necessarily having changed his own political and economic position since his academic days, in which he fiercely defended de jure dollarization as follows:

> In the long term, finding ways of bribing people to dollarize, or at least give back the extra currency that is earned when dollarization takes place, ought to be an international priority. For the world as a whole, the advantage of dollarization seems clear to me and I am surprised that it is not a more prominent item on the visionary agenda in this Conference. (Summers, 1992, p. 32)

I shall look at each one of Summers's probable motivations, distinguishing between those related to global foreign policy considerations—where the emergence of the euro plays an important part, those related to intrahemispheric relations, and finally those related to North American domestic policy administration.

First, as a politician Summers cannot be as emphatic in his support of dollarization as when he was an academic. His apparent estrangement from this idea is just a tactical position due to the peculiarities and manners of the political administration of the Treasury Department, the requirements of U.S. foreign policy, and the potential attitudes emerging nations might adopt in relation to the idea if it is presented too insistently by a representative of the U.S. government.[5]

Second, nor must it escape Summers's lucid mind that the

> substitution of national currencies on account of dollars especially in regions where the U.S. has direct political and economic interests might constitute an effective method to fortify the long-term fundamentals of

North American political domain. By following a similar argument the French and German governments were in favor of the euro so as to increase the international political weight of the EU in a certain way. (Isbell, 2000, p. 127)

Summers surely shares the opinion that with official dollarization "a new reason for North American leadership in the twentieth century will have been found; a much more acceptable one—nationally as well as internationally—than trying to be a world gendarme" (p. 135).

Third and most important, every treasury secretary—as well as any U.S. government—knows well that the emergence of the euro constitutes a potential threat to the U.S. dollar and with this to North American hegemony on a global scale, because

> wherever the dollar settles the euro can not. As a preventive measure towards the increasing influence of the euro that will probably continue— it has conquered great part of the international bond market and many national banks are considering the possibility of exchanging some of their dollar reserves into euros—the dollar could increase its presence in a much more formal way in a progressing world." (Isbell, 2000, pp. 127– 28)

Summers must also be conscious that it still will be a good while before the euro becomes a powerful competitor for the dollar, because "although it is likely that the euro will become an international currency, it is unlikely that the dollar will be replaced anytime soon in its role as the leading international currency" (*ERP,* 1999, p. 299), as "there is a strong inertial bias in favor of using whatever currency has been the vehicle currency in the past. . . . In the present context the inertial bias favors the continued central role of the dollar" (*ERP,* 1999, p. 304).

Fourth: thinking about the delicate official terms referred to previously, I am sure that Summers shares Paul Isbell's opinion that

> it might be of political interest for the U.S. to maintain the appearance that they oppose a possible dollarization so as to elude any potential anti- American reactions and therefore increase negotiating power in the future once the great emerging economies have lost any hope of returning to a monetary sovereignty and they show themselves more than willing to adopt the dollar in U.S. economic terms. (2000, p. 134)

Fifth, Summers must be conscious that with the end of the Cold War the "anti-American spirit" declined abruptly in most of Latin America during this new era of globalization, with which many Latin American governments will gradually attach themselves to the Northern Giant, without requiring any type of pressure from that giant. Of course, Latin American countries could be blessed with a series of preferences that have not yet been spelled out (and that will depend on their bargaining power on a case-by-case basis) but that will surely be offered to them by the United States if they dollarize (with or without the IMSA).

Sixth, certainly the U.S. government cannot officially intervene in the initial decision concerning official dollarization because of the potential difficulties—economic or political—that a dollarizing country might find in the uncertain future. If such difficulties appear, that could lead to a series of demands and accusations against the United States, which the secretary will want to avoid by all means. In this sense, it is possible that Summers is also sensing the weight of the pressure that would focus on him (or the Fed) as the result of a specific official dollarization process running into trouble. Clearly, the ancestral resentments against the IMF that persist in Latin American countries—and, of course, are absent in the minds of the conservative governments or the new power groups—would be transferred to a new scapegoat: the U.S. treasury secretary or the Fed (if the IMSA is not approved), especially if the U.S. government applies a monetary policy that does not coincide—which is very common—with the economic cycle of Latin American dollarized economies.

Seventh, referring specifically to U.S. domestic policy, every treasury secretary has to be very concerned about the "politically correct" distribution of the public budget. In this case, evidently, the government must find it more convenient to assign a budget to health and education in the United State, than to make public future payments of seigniorage to "emerging" countries if the IMSA is approved. In other words, if the IMSA were approved, then a permanent political problem would persist, related to the annual payments of seigniorage to be made to the dollarized nations. This would create difficulties, mainly for the governing politicians, because they would have to

> inject the seigniorage issue into the annual U.S. budgetary process, generating the potential of misunderstanding and political frictions down the road and exposing the dollarizing economy to the risk that some future Congress will change its mind and fail to compensate the country for lost seigniorage. (Gavin, 2000, p. 5)[6]

Finally, the U.S. government could save some foreign aid:

> In many ways, I see dollarization as an anti-poverty, pro-development policy—a policy that promises to be far more effective than foreign aid or World Bank efforts in the past. In fact, for those who see sovereignty at issue, I see dollarization as a way to decrease the dependency of some of our Latin neighbors on foreign assistance programs that, quite frankly, have been a mixed blessing. (Mack, 2000b, p. 3)

In brief, the maximum authorities of the U.S. government would use every argument they have at hand so as to demonstrate that Latin American governments had independently chosen to dollarize their economies and that the U.S. government "had nothing to do with it." In that spirit, Michael Gavin has recommended to the U.S. government that

> with respect to the decision to dollarize, the U.S. should mainly stand aside and allow individual countries to make the decision through their own democratic process. However, given that the United States has an enlightened self-interest in allowing dollarization to proceed, we should certainly remove unnecessary barriers to dollarization. The most important of these is the issue of seigniorage.

This matches with the idea that "Washington, until now, has resisted active encouragement of dollarization, mainly for fear of any compromise of Federal Reserve policy" (Cohen, 2000b, p. 19).[7]

Thus, in conclusion, I think that a complex combination of various elements of the previous arguments may explain the reluctance of my hypothetical treasury secretary with respect to the official dollarization of the Western Hemisphere economies. Therefore, I do not have the slightest doubt that deep inside of Summers's mind (and that of any future treasury secretary) persists the yearning for a complete dollarization of every Latin American country. As a faithful American, it is quite clear that he has a vision toward foreign policy that is centered in trying to strengthen and expand U.S. hemispheric leadership and in which official dollarization could become one of the main roads to accomplish this. To achieve a second "American Century" would be a quite enviable goal. We all know that dollarization is not a panacea and that it can create more problems than it solves, but from an official American political perspective it seems to be an effective mechanism to fortify their hemispheric and world hegemony.

Some Accelerating Factors

> *In the 1980s the foreign policy of the United States was dedicated to spreading freedom and democracy. Now it's time to spread sound money.*
>
> *—Senator Connie Mack, "Dollarization and Cooperation: Achieving Sound Money" (2000)*

I think that it is valid to generalize the assumed preferences and attitudes of my imaginary treasury secretary to the rest of the high bureaucracy in the American democratic (or an eventual republican) government, as well as its congresspeople. Above all, North American transnational enterprises as well as international private banks have a better disposition toward the official dollarization of most Latin American countries.[8]

On the other hand, the multilateral organisms in Washington deserve a special mention, although here things get a bit more complicated. Regarding the World Bank and the IMF, their every official declaration says that they have no unanimous opinion with respect to de jure dollarization of other countries. For example, Miguel Savastano, from the Research Department of the IMF, points out: "I don't think the IMF has an official position on the subject and I am not even sure if it will ever have one" (quoted in Du Bois and Morón, 2000, p. 43).[9]

However, if we observe the case in East Timor, we will find ourselves with a great surprise, because in that country de jure dollarization was imposed in a highly authoritative way by the IMF. As they honestly or candidly recognize:

> The most critical initial steps toward reviving the payments system were the choice of the currency that would serve as legal tender and the establishment of a monetary authority. The East Timor leadership indicated their interest in introducing their own currency at the time of independence. While receptive to their views, the IMF Staff . . . recommended the adoption of a single currency as it would help eliminate the inefficiencies and distortions already apparent by the use of multiple currencies. . . . From all the currencies that were under consideration, the U.S. dollar was the currency that best satisfied for East Timor the desirable characteristics of a legal tender, such as stable value, wide international use, and convertibility. The adoption of the U.S. dollar was also advisable because most of the international trade of East Timor is denominated in U.S. dollars. (Valdivieso et al., 2000, p. 11)

That is, they "recommended" that imposition of the North American dollar.[10]

Despite all that has been mentioned previously, Washington's position toward official dollarization is likely to change—slowly or even radically—because of the potential rise of certain political or economic circumstances in national and especially international fields. I think it is possible to see a more "dollar-friendly" attitude on the part of the United States than has traditionally been the case in recent times. I shall point out some factors in that direction.

In first place, with Republicans now in power, clearly the United States will encourage full dollarization more openly then with a Democratic government, and the possibilities of approving the IMSA will grow. A close advisor of Senator Mack told me: "I think the chances of the IMSA or a similar bill passing during the next two presidential terms (2001–2008) are poor if Gore wins the presidential election, and fair (50 percent) if Bush wins."[11] In my opinion what is most likely in the proximate future is that we will see some bilateral agreements between the United States and some strategic countries such as Argentina, Chile, or Mexico. It is quite evident that the dollarization of any of these countries would be very motivating for other nations by means of the "demonstration effect."

Second, from an economic point of view, if the United States "bubble" bursts—that is, if the "irrational exuberance" Alan Greenspan announced toward the end of 1996 finally implodes—if the inflation rate as well as the interest rates rise and the economic growth of Latin America's great northern neighbor declines, then the U.S. government will be forced to approach the Latin American dollarization program more aggressively. This would also lead to rapid approval of the IMSA, despite its impact on U.S. public finances and the probable opposition of a great percentage of U.S. population.

Third, if new regional banking and exchange crisis appeared with repercussions and contagion effects—of the magnitude of the tequila, dragon, vodka, or caipirinha crisis effects—this would clearly encourage a change of attitude toward official dollarization, in particular if U.S. economic and financial stability were endangered by them.

Fourth, the threatening advance of the euro may become a basic factor in this change of attitude, even more so if the active foreign pressure of Euroland in favor of the euroization of other countries increases:

> but what if Europe were to begin actively promoting widespread adoption of the euro?, as some observers (e.g., Rogoff, 1998) think possible, Washington's attitude could then quickly grow more conciliatory, at least on the issue of seigniorage-sharing. Support for the Mack bill would certainly grow if the euro were seen to be seriously challenging the dollar's presently dominant market share. (Cohen, 2000b, p. 19)

In the same vein, Robert Mundell assures us that

> the introduction of the euro redraws the international monetary landscape. With the euro . . . a tri-polar currency world involving the dollar, euro, and yen came into being. The exchange rates among these three islands of stability will become the most important prices in the world economy. The creation of the euro will doubtless lead to its widespread adoption in Central and Eastern Europe as well as the former CFA franc zone in Africa and along the rim of the Mediterranean. Expansion of the wider euro area . . . will eventually give it a transactions area larger than that of the United States and will, inevitably, provoke countervailing expansion of the dollar area in Latin America and parts of Asia. Other currency areas are likely to form, adapting to local needs the example of Europe. But stability for the near future will be best assured by stabilization with one of the "G-3" areas. (2000a, p. 337)

Finally, the fact that dollarized countries, such as Ecuador, El Salvador, and others that will join the "experiment" in the next few years, show important successes will be a powerful incentive for other countries to adopt the U.S. dollar and for the United States government to assume a much more favorable attitude toward it. This could happen also if the efforts to create regional currencies fail, especially in Mercosur, which is very probable.

◣ *Official Dollarization from a Latin American Perspective*

Putting it succinctly, whereas the center is made of "policy making" economies (again, with variations among them), the periphery is largely "policy taking."

—José Antonio Ocampo, "Exchange Rate Regimes and Capital Account
   Regulations for Emerging Economies" (2000)

Despite the arguments presented previously, it would be naïve to believe that dollarizing pressures will emerge only—or even principally—from the North. The Ecuadorian experience already has showed us how internal political desperation can result in a dollarizing experiment. Similarly, some other governments are already flirting with the idea, as was President Carlos Menem of Argentina during the first half of 1999. I believe that de jure dollarization will be implemented in the course of the first decade of this century, beginning quite slowly and then in an accelerating way, once the bandwagon effect and other positive network externalities start acting.

On the one hand, this will come from countries that are technically ready to dollarize, as they have already completed certain economic and political preconditions,[12] for example, Argentina—and in this particular case, it will happen faster as Argentina continues to lose competitiveness vis-à-vis Brazil. However, in the present moment, Argentine authorities will only be willing to complete the project through a monetary association with the United States, that is, if part of the seigniorage they are losing (approximately $750 million annually) is returned to them and some special additional concessions in commercial matters are given to them, although these have not been explicitly requested. But again, the *beginning* of the full dollarization experiment will only be undertaken during a dramatic political crisis caused by domestic interest conflicts and/or as a consequence of an external (economic or political) shock.[13]

On the other hand, there are other countries, especially the small and weak ones, that would have no problem in adopting the measure unilaterally even without complying with the supposed necessary economic preconditions.[14] In these cases they would substitute their national currency for the U.S. dollar for reasons that I will now explain.

Let us understand that in this second group of Latin American countries—in contrast to the case of the euro, where the political will played an essential role in the constitution of the monetary union—the political need to dollarize unilaterally will be the main propelling factor, maybe in the most unexpected moment of a politico-economic crisis. It will be a defensive, desperate move rather than a consistent, medium-term, programmed process.

In the first place, I believe that in the majority of these cases, full dollarization would be adopted by countries that find themselves in a desperate political and/or economic crisis, so as to gain "political time," roughly following the (bad) example of Ecuador. An extreme domestic political miscarriage or a potential or effective hyperinflation that could even hit together—although they seem quite remote possibilities in the present situation—would be obvious economic catalysts that would encourage a complete (and unilateral) dollarization for political motivations.

Second, and based on the last argument, dollarization could also be adopted in a crisis as a trust shock measure or as a tranquilizing hit in the middle of a great deal of insecurity. In other words, it can "help to give credibility" (*ERP,* 1999, p. 289), as was the case of the transition of some countries from a pegged exchange rate regimen to a currency board.

In the third place, there is also the real possibility that a government considers that if it does not adopt this measure, the country will "miss the train" and will be even more marginalized from the so-called globalization process. This includes the majority of cases, especially small countries—for example, the Central American ones, all of which would adopt de jure dollarization. Here is what the previous president of Argentina said recently in relation to this point:

> Currency also plays a central role in the possibility of linking countries to the global economy. In this sense, currency acquires an increasingly political dimension. This is not just a question of monetary stability or unit of account; rather, currency serves as a means of immediate global standarization. . . . [D]ollarization is, therefore, the main political instrument to consolidate the governance capacities of our countries in a historical period characterized by increasingly rapid changes. (Menem, 2000)

Let us not forget that Latin American governments and business associations constantly refer to the necessity of (passively) joining globalization, and all their worries are focused on the desperation of attracting foreign investments. That is why they need to have international goodwill by all means, basically from the U.S. government and the multilateral institutions. Progress in Latin American countries has become a synonym of this priority, whose orientation comes from outside. Consequently, official unilateral dollarization is in these countries' plans, but the political conditions are still missing and will appear only—as I have said—at very unstable political and/or economic junctures that will serve as an excuse to begin the process by imposing it "from above."

Such opportunistic behavior on the part of most of the Latin American governments could undoubtedly take some of them to the adoption of the dollar because of the unprecedented prosperity and stability that the United States has held since 1992 and up to 2001. A political approximation is intended permanently with Washington, one that would assure a fruitful association with us in many ways. This is much more important than monetary sovereignty or even national identity, which is now not under discussion by the influential groups in and outside the government. The "typically Latin American" values that would supposedly be lost, such as Latin American identity, national honor, or even patriotic pride, could be largely compensated for—at least for the few powerful domestic economic and political factions—by many commercial and financial benefits.

Fourth and most important: in some countries dollarization would be used as a cunning instrument of the government so as to force adjustments on the first or the second generation (Stiglitz, 1998) in the countries whose populations sustain a serious resistance toward them. In a confidential report, an informed analyst has told me that "one important argument for dollarization has been that it has created a context within which Ecuador's political system can carry through overdue structural reform."

In addition, if the IMSA were approved, some governments would seek the corresponding U.S. treasury secretary's certification, not necessarily because of the income from "seigniorage" they will get through it but because this would let them introduce the structural reforms required in their countries. In this case, the U.S. Treasury would play the role of judge and executor that the IMF has played in certain countries. In other words, official dollarization can also be the result of a Machiavellian political measure *that is intended* to accelerate and impose structural adjustment that is rejected by a great part of the population. This has been done in the past by many governments, using the excuse that the necessity of complying with an agreement with the IMF obligated them to adopt drastic measures. This process would emerge in highly conflictive societies where the government would use complete dollarization as an instrument of social discipline (Canitrot, 1979). Apparently in Ecuador this process has been working somewhat easily, at least for the moment; however, I am very pessimistic about the future of this experiment.

And, in general, from the perspective of Latin American countries, complete dollarization can be a very useful instrument to get away from political crisis and to impose, accelerate, or improve economic policies of adjustment and to adopt structural reforms when facing an unfriendly "civil society." In brief, "dollarization is seen as a way of jump-starting reform and restoring investor confidence" (Eichengreen, 2000a, p. 2).

In the fifth place, we can still put forth the argument that a country dollarizes because it recognizes that there exists a relatively generalized popular suspicion regarding a domestic monetary policy in Latin American countries, as Roberto Salinas-León (2000) has recognized; his argument is shared by the U.S. President's Council of Economic Advisors, who point out that currency boards—as in official dollarization—would be used because of

a desire for further close integration with a particular neighbor or trading partner; a strong need to import monetary stability, because of history of hyperinflation or an absence of credible public institutions; access to adequate foreign exchange reserves; and a strong, well-supervised, and well-regulated financial system. (*ERP,* 1999, pp. 289–90)

Finally, because in Latin America "everything is possible," other exotic motivations may arise that may drive toward full dollarization. For example, we should not be surprised that a certain misunderstood originality or economic chauvinism[15]—which were so important during the process of implanting the mandates of the Washington Consensus—could have an important function in a dollarizing country. In effect, dollarization is a rough measure for "strong men" in this subcontinent of magic realism. It is not a remote possibility that somewhere could surge the willingness to experiment with a new idea such as dollarization, advanced by an ambitious economist (as a minister or an advisor), as has happened before with other heterodox experiences (in the worst sense of the word) on the Latin American subcontinent. Instead of "putting their boots on and taking the gun out," they try dollarization as an experiment or to distract attention from an important political crisis.[16]

In all these cases in which complete and official dollarization will be adopted, the initiative would evidently come from conservative governments—that is, "neoliberal" ones, in the plain sense of the word—who still concur with the mandates settled in the Washington Consensus and by no means from governments led by social-democratic or center-left parties. For example, while Fernando Henrique Cardoso and his followers stay in power, dollarization will be politically impossible if we take into account the hegemony Brazil is still trying to acquire in the subcontinent,[17] and not only within Mercosur.[18]

To sum up, I do not have the slightest doubt that the official dollarization of most Latin American nations will basically be a response to political factors, including certain sociological, psychological, and other extraeconomic elements—although sophisticated economic arguments could help to rationalize them ex post. Obviously it is very difficult to expose ex ante the specific political and psychosocial factors that will determine the process.[19] These variables would result either from the simple desperation resulting from a social-political crisis or from the recognition that the measure gradually favors the alliance of the social factions that support the government—or finally from the action of those who think it is a necessary measure so as to avoid any greater political and economic exclusion on a global scale. So "when it comes to the choice between alternative models of currency regionalization, political linkages are likely to be far more useful than strictly economic ties as a predictor of state attitudes" (Cohen, 2000b, p. 17).

But couldn't there be massive domestic opposition to the complete dollarization of a Latin American country? I think the answer is a clear no, at least for the moment. And the reason is simple: the neoliberal economic policies adopted in the subcontinent during the last 20 or more years have not only changed the values, norms, and institutions of the Latin American countries but have destroyed the principal potential opponents to the Washington Consensus by fragmenting socially and politically the peripheral societies and by debilitating the popular groups and some powerful interests. For the moment we no longer have powerful rentist-industrialists, big labor unions, massive regional movements, great *campesino* organizations, strong government bureaucracies, leftist political parties, solid middle classes, and so on. So where could the opposition come from if the power groups decide to dollarize-from-above?

As the number of officially dollarized economies in America (or Asia) grows, the snowball effect will start to activate. Afterward, because of the network, bandwagon, or demonstration effects, the rest of the countries will follow in the same direction, and not only because the dollarizing countries show positive results. Clearly the United States will help these countries— with the support of the IMF, the World Bank, and maybe the Inter-American Development Bank—once the process has started, so as to show positive results, independently of the initial and the structural conditions of the country. Of course, as long as the U.S. economy continues on the stable road it finds itself at present time, which is not guaranteed in any way, the process could advance without obstacles. In the long run the snowball effect could involve even social-democratic or leftist governments in Latin America, as well as in other latitudes.

As an aside, it is interesting to note that the case of Panama has not served Latin American governments as an ideal paradigm to follow, precisely because of the special characteristics of its economy, although this example is still used demagogically by some academics and politicians for propagandist means. To repeat: economists use Panama's example for political reasons, despite its tremendous economic difficulties and social problems. Many evidences are hidden or ignored in the attempts that have been made to defend the supposed success of dollarization in that country.[20]

Without doubt there are a series of exogenous factors that may speed up or stop the official dollarization process in the Latin American countries. Events that would precipitate or accelerate it, to name only a few, would be: the continuous strengthening of the U.S. economy, the weakening of the euro, the multiplication of contagious international financial crises (equal or worse than the recent ones in Southeast Asia, Russia, and Argentina) inside the subcontinent, the mounting belief that dollarization would prevent these impacts, and so on. These processes would be reinforced by a well-known domestic economy factor, again as a reflex of critical politicoeconomic processes: the fact that spontaneous dollarization will keep on growing in the subcontinental economies.

▶ Conclusions and Some Research Priorities

*Like the [Rorschach] test, pronouncements about exchange rate policy
often tell you more about the speaker than they do about some objective
reality.*

—Michael Gavin, "Official Dollarization in Latin American" (2000)

I have tried to present some very general hypotheses that lead us to the
very tentative conclusion that most of the economies of the Latin American
subcontinent will dollarize officially and unilaterally in the next couple of
years. If that becomes true, we will observe two or more similar monetary
blocs, which will be configured like the so-called wild geese flock paradigm
that was foreseen by Kaname Akamatsu (1962) for the productive sphere.
That is, around some currencies ordered groups of countries will form that
will adhere to the dollar, euro, or yen, the leading currencies of the three
groups.[21] The countries that decide to fly alone, unguided by one of the
"geese-leaders," will be left aside by the dynamics of the new international
division of labor.

A second idea I tried to advance is that, in practice, the final decision
on complete dollarization will not be imposed or rejected by reason, in this
case by so-called rational economic arguments. Instead, it will respond to
the complex dynamics that derive from the global and domestic power
structures that reflect the dominant political interests of the United States
and the forces of international capital, supported by the dominant groups
of Latin American countries.[22] First the countries will dollarize as a consequence of profound political and social crises, and afterward by the bandwagon effect and the fear of falling behind in the international politico-
economic competitive game.

Thus if we do not include the political dimension in its diverse scales
(international, national, and regional), as well as its peculiar modalities (interest groups, political regimen, institutionality, social-political alliances and
collisions, interhegemonic conflicts, etc.) in the dollarization debate (unilaterally or by monetary association), we will not be able to understand *why
or when* a government will adopt it or if it will be sustainable in time.[23]
This is why it is essential to continue developing the theoretical, method-
ological, and instrumental bases of what is called political economy, following Allan Drazen's pioneering effort or some other theoretical politico-
economic approach.

In conclusion, I would like to present some areas and problems of
interest that require urgent research regarding the multiple puzzles related
to the different exchange rate regimes and the criteria to be considered in
relation to adopting one of them.

In first place we have to address the dilemma: How could we reduce
de facto dollarization of Latin American countries so as to make possible
again the adoption of (relatively) autonomous exchange rate and monetary

policies? It is quite surprising that a great majority of economists, especially the ones who are against official dollarization, have not written extensively on this matter.[24] This is true even of those who believe that there are many more economic and sociopolitical reasons to favor more flexible, mixed, or pegged exchange rate regimes in the subcontinent,[25] in which case they should give first priority to this problem, because the viability of these exchange rate systems entails the search for new "market-friendly" formulas to reduce the high spontaneous liability dollarization so that it does not exceed 30 percent of total liquidity. Contrarily, free floating would mean "harakiri-floating,"[26] implying financial collapse (and even "twin crises"), high inflation, and social unrest. Israel and some transition countries of eastern Europe could serve as good examples to determine the "market-friendly" factors and policies that have permitted the reduction of de facto dollarization.

A second important—but very complicated—research effort should be devoted to country-specific studies of the domestic political, social, and economic factions that will benefit or lose out through the official dollarization process.[27] It is premature to generalize on this theme, but it is a necessary task so as to establish the sociopolitical possibilities of officially dollarizing an economy and to calibrate its sustainability.

Third: How can we think about exchange rate regimes, if we do not have a global development conception and strategy for the twenty-first century? In this sense, we need to rethink the development strategies for Latin America after the fiasco of the Washington Consensus.[28] In this respect Dani Rodrik (2000b) has made a series of important remarks regarding the exchange rate regimes. He points out that "the discussion. . . . focuses too much on making the system safe for capital flows, and too little on the developmental needs of countries. The associated policy efforts are diverting attention from development, and distorting policy priorities" (p. 4).

He adds that "the trouble with this debate is that the evidence shows clearly that neither corner [either floating exchange rates or irrevocably fixed rates] works very well for developing countries for long periods of time" (2000b, p. 6).

He goes on to say:

> The prevailing perspective is one that says governments have got to do whatever is required to maximize the flow of trade and capital around the world. Adopting this perspective, results in viewing everything from the standpoint of the needs of foreign investors. . . . The alternative perspective is one that views globalization as a means to an end, rather than an end in itself. It is a perspective that says governments should follow developmental priorities even when it conflicts with the requirements of capital mobility. . . . It is a perspective that accepts that strategic use of international trade and capital flows is *part* of a development strategy, but appreciates that it does not substitute for it. (pp. 14–15)

All of this forces us to rethink the concept of development, both at the periphery and at the centers.[29]

In the fourth place, almost every economist has forgotten—or not even noticed—that since the early 1980s an infinity of nonofficial complementary currencies has appeared, basically as a consequence of a defensive reaction developed by certain communities and regions that were or are being marginalized by the process of "globalization." In effect, today hundreds of thousands of base communities, municipalities, ethnic groups, schools, informal enterprises, and NGOs exchange among themselves thousands of millions of goods, but with moneys called Ithaca Hours, Talents, Commitments, Tlalocs, Resources, Mountain Dollars, and so on, which are local or regional exchange mediums that are additional or complementary to official currencies.[30]

More than simple barter, these are *mutual credit systems* among people of small communities, or of the same region, in which neither official money nor interest rates play a role.[31] If that system is successful—which contemporarily seems to be a utopia—we would arrive, in the long run, at what Keynes predicted, in his *General Theory:* the *euthanasia of the rentist!* Thus a process that began in the years of crisis, the 1930s in Europe (where it was prohibited by the central banks) and the United States (where it stopped during the "Golden Years"), starts to repeat itself, although in a more sophisticated way.[32]

Last but not least, in my opinion, if we do not consider the special characteristics of the new international division of labor that is taking shape as a result of the current technological revolution; if we do not review the desperate attempts of the leading nations, at a worldwide level, regarding the design of a new international financial architecture; if we do not examine the conflicts between the leading regional economic blocs; and if we do not contemplate the conflicting interests of power groups in "emerging market" economies, we will not be able to weigh up the possibilities that "5 or 105 currencies" (Hausmann, 1999) will be established worldwide, as is intended by some economists who appeal to "technical" arguments to advance their ideological positions.

To conclude, let us consider that in the lapse of the next generation we will have about five official international moneys (and maybe five hundred thousand extraofficial local moneys[33]) as a reflection of the structure and dynamics of power at the global and national scales. That is, in the medium run, complete dollarization will gradually impose itself on many Latin American countries, as a consequence of the pressure of the governments and power groups of the Northern Hemisphere and/or because of the demands made by the Latin American governments who fear becoming even more marginalized from the so-called globalization process. Of course, economic arguments will play a role, but a posteriori.

To complicate the future world monetary panorama even more, I shall add some additional hypotheses, which today seem utopian. Consider the fact that in the future there will be a tendency to consolidate virtual and electronic money (Cohen, 2000a), so that "money production" might well be left in the hands of the private sector, in a sort of modern version of "free banking," so as to initiate the "denationalization of money" to which Friedrich von Hayek aspired (1972).

Of course, in this uncertain world it could also be possible that "gold may again serve as the ultimate hedge in chaotic conditions. Its return to its traditional role as universal money is unlikely, however, unless the time should come when the dollar, the euro, and the yen have all failed to function as acceptable means of payment across international borders" (Bernstein, 2000, p. 372). But not even Mundell (1997) is so pessimistic, although he must be praying: "let us hope that the most important event of the twenty-first century will be that the dollar and the euro learn to live together."

On the other extreme, we could go to one worldwide currency,[34] maybe using today's praised dollar or the ineffective special drawing rights or the forgotten Bancor or some other new universal money. But these are dreams (or nightmares?) that would only turn into reality toward the end of this new century, if the conditions will be ripe for the configuration of a world government, hopefully polycentric (based on Rodrik's global federalism) and not Orwellian.

And finally, going a little deeper into the future, maybe toward the middle of the twenty-second century, in a miraculous world of abundance, we won't need any kind of money . . . Fortunately, this is not a Rorschach test.

◣ Notes

The author wants to thank Alberto Acosta, José Luis Coraggio, Guillermo Runciman, and Cynthia Sanborn for their insightful comments on the original version of this chapter, which was presented at the seminar *Dollarization for the Western Hemisphere?* at the North-South Institute, Ottawa, October 4–5, 2000.

1. As a consequence of the recent financial crisis in Mexico, Southeast Asia, Russia, and Brazil and the startup of the EMU.

2. Monetary unions are fashionable today. Recently, 11 European countries have adopted a common regional currency, and in eastern Europe the possibility of adopting the euro is being considered; currency boards are in force in Bulgaria (1997), Hong Kong (1983), Estonia (1992), and Lithuania (1994), among others; and complete dollarization is an issue that is being heatedly debated in Argentina, Central America, Mexico, Chile, and Peru, while, since January 2000, East Timor and Ecuador have set out toward it in a rush, accompanying Panama and some additional tiny countries in this adventure.

3. Superficially speaking, the causes that should lead us to complete dollarization (or the adoption of currency boards) are the result of a series of economic factors, all

of which have been presented in the well-known literature of those who favor this process (such as: Barro, 1999; Calvo, 1999; Dornbusch, 1999, 2000; Hausmann, 1999; and Schuler, 1999). Some of the economists who oppose official dollarization of Latin American countries are Krugman (1999), Rojas-Suárez (2000), Sachs and Larraín (1999), Schuldt (1999), and Von Furstenberg (2000).

4. The proposed bill (sponsored by Republican Senator Connie Mack) called the International Monetary Stability Act of 2000 (U.S. Senate-House of Representatives, 2000) was designed "to promote international monetary stability and to share seigniorage with officially dollarized countries." The best-informed analysis of this act can be found in Schuler (2000a).

5. I am convinced that Summers still thinks the same as before because what apparently changes, when one travels from academy to government, are the tactics but not the strategy, the forms but not the contents, the timings but not the methods. In this way, I believe, as an economist one performs politics by camouflaging it under technical jargon, while as a politician one does economic analysis by camouflaging it under diplomatic slang.

6. Of course we cannot neglect the fact that in the presence of the "political economic cycle" the government has to avoid mentioning any sort of spiny subjects. In this sense, Summers might have chosen a tactic of strategic estrangement since the start of the electoral campaign, so as to avoid any frictions or collisions with possible anti-dollarizing domestic interests.

7. On the other hand, it has been argued that "the dollarization issue is much too important for the United States to stand by passively. If the U.S. refuses to take a position, dollarization will continue to be considered only by countries in crisis, rather than being an option they consider during relatively stable times" (Mack, 2000a).

8. On the other hand, a good argument against official dollarization could be that these international parties, especially the banks, could lose part of their benefits by this procedure because the countries couldn't devalue their national currencies any more, which always has been the "easy way" to gain competitiveness and to make sure that they could pay their foreign debt service. Maybe, because of this, the banks would not be so interested that countries with a low spontaneous dollarization go the way to official dollarization. It is not very farfetched to think that the hesitant attitude of Summers with respect to official dollarization could also have something to do with this phenomenon.

9. Even Stanley Fischer displays an elegant distancing from the subject: "I believe that if the euro succeeds—and it will succeed—that we will gradually see fewer currencies. What precisely that means for Latin America, whether the use of the dollar, or the *real,* after a long period of stability, or a regional currency, is too far off to discern. The answer depends not only on Latin America, but also on the provisions the United States might be willing to make to encourage dollarization, for instance by finding ways to remit seigniorage to countries that adopt the dollar" (2000, pp. 6–7).

10. But, contrarily to the constant pressures for an official dollarization of this country by the World Bank, the IMF, and United Nations officers, neither the society nor the market accepted it, because "many returned exiles have advocated the Portuguese escudo, and by extension the euro, in recognition of East Timor's colonial links to Portugal. The U.N. and the World Bank are pushing the American dollar. But both currencies have been losing out in the countryside to the Indonesian Rupiah: it may belong to the former oppressors, but there are a lot of notes about. In the capital, the only currency

that can compete with the Rupiah is the Australian dollar. The U.S. dollar's fans say that it has failed because there is no small change. This is not a problem with the Rupiah . . . or with the Aussie dollar. So the multilaterals have adopted a novel currency defense: bringing in huge shipments of coins" (Anonymous, 2000). Unfortunately the public, as well as many academics, know little about this case, so experts still keep on selling the idea that multilateral institutions maintain a neutral position regarding this type of exchange rate system, ignoring the intervention in East Timor (and the support of Ecuador—in which case, on the contrary, the official dollarization was "imposed" on the IMF!).

11. On the contrary, John Williamson showed himself pessimistic toward a quick approval of the IMSA, pointing out that "it would be approved in ten years in the best case" (North-South Institute Conference, Ottawa, October 2000).

12. The most important seem to be openness, transparency, and supervision of the financial system; flexibility of labor markets; concertation between the government and the principal economic and political actors; and solidly secured property rights.

13. Mexico might be another candidate to adopt this measure, for obvious reasons (as a member of NAFTA), and maybe also Chile (as it will be the first future South American member of NAFTA). These two cases would immediately stick to the measure—also due to domestic interest conflicts or to the initiative of a right-wing government—if they could get a bilateral agreement, which could be very possible because of their strong bargaining power. From a purely economic point of view, the costs of dollarization for Chile are greater than the benefits, as is argued—for Chile—by Velasco (2000), Morande and Schmidt-Hebbel (2000), and Fontaine and Vergara (2000); the preconditions seem not to be present in Mexico (Carstens and Weiner (2000).

14. The controversy between those who say that certain minimal economic and institutional conditions are needed to dollarize officially (Calvo, Hausmann, Rojas-Suarez) and those who believe that the dollarization process would automatically implant or force those reforms (Schuler, Hanke, Barro) is well known.

15. Some ministers of economy in the Latin American countries thought that they got much prestige in international circles by adopting drastic and unconsulted measures, certainly within the framework of an authoritarian government or a "delegative democracy" (O'Donnell, 1992).

16. There are many research results with respect to machismo in Latin America, but not one has applied it to the form it adopts when economic policy is decided and made public by certain governments (an interesting theme for sociological and psychiatric researchers).

17. The same happens with China, where it is—for political reasons—highly improbable to think in an association of the yuan with the yen, the euro, or the dollar. In the best case the Asian giant will try to form a bloc of "yuanized countries," maybe in 10 or 20 years.

18. On the other hand, it is evident that Argentina's currency board is an obstacle in that direction. So it is more probable that they will adopt official dollarization and not a hemispheric monetary association. The same applies to the Andean Community of Nations, where Ecuador's dollarization impedes a regional monetary association.

19. Although at first sight it could seem that the IMSA is a stimulus to dollarize, it really is not, at least at start, if we remember that the first payment of seigniorage will only be done 11 years after the official dollarization in association with the United States and, above all, the exaggerated conditions those countries have to comply with so as to reach the required "certification" of the U.S. treasury secretary.

20. Miguel Savastano (quoted in Du Bois and Morón, 2000) has also reminded us of one of the weaknesses of that most cited "ideal" case: "Panama is the Latin American economy that has celebrated the most agreements with the IMF since 1963; more than Haiti, Jamaica, Argentina and Peru. Taking this fact into consideration I think that the argument that states that the foreign crisis shall be minor in totally dollarized economies loses a great backup. And that is not all, if we revise the data of Panama of the last three decades (IMF, *International Financial Statistics,* Annuals), we will find that the fiscal deficit (as percentage of the GNP) surpassed 5% between 1969 and 1984 and was more than 10% during the years 1976, 1979 and 1982. The current account deficits exceeded 5% of GNP in 1997, 1981, 1987 and 1998–99 (in this last year it was about 14%!). Real interest rates were over 10% from 1986 to 1999. Finally, external debt was 50% or more of GNP during 1988–89 and 1996–99." That is why Sebastián Edwards (1999a) has pointed out that the IMF turned into his "lender of first resort." The most interesting studies of this particular case are the ones by Moreno-Villalaz (1999) and, especially, Goldfajn and Olivares (2000).

21. Maybe only the real and the yuan will fly loosely around the world, in their eagerness to become hegemonic regional powers.

22. As is known, neither in Panama, East Timor, or Ecuador nor in the multiple small Caribbean countries was "de jure" dollarization adopted for purely economic reasons (for example, as an anti-inflationary measure).

23. Cohen (2000b) proposes a very useful distinction the forces that take to the initial decision to dollarize from the forces that assure the sustainability of the process. In my opinion, the predominant support in the initial phase will come, as I have said, unilaterally from the initiative of the governments of the emerging countries, while the sustainability will be assumed and assured especially by the United States, as it is in their interest in the global prestige and power play.

24. Considering, as Dean (2000b, p. 3) has pointed out, that "*de facto* dollarization has already rendered monetary policy relatively impotent and active exchange rate policy downright dangerous."

25. Taking into account, also, that in the lapse of the last decade we can observe in many Latin countries an increased responsibility, technical preparation, and coherence of the monetary and political authorities; this is one of the important arguments most economists provide to promote official dollarization in emerging market economies.

26. In some cases it should even be called "kamikaze-floating" if the process not only hurts the devaluing country but also—through the contagion effect—many other countries of the region or even of other parts of the world.

27. Of course the other exchange rate regimes serve certain groups more than others, as does any economic policy measure. As Schuler (2000b) has reminded us (although he uses it as an argument for dollarizing): "A national central bank always benefits some people by giving them positions, prestige, or privileged access to credit that would not exist under other monetary arrangements. Unless a much wider group also benefits, however, monetary sovereignty is just camouflage for redistributing wealth from the public at large to a special-interest group that is often substantially richer." Does not official dollarization also benefit some interest groups vis-à-vis others?

28. See, for example, Stiglitz (1998) and the latest book by Hernando De Soto (2000).

29. Only by rebuilding our societies and economies from their foundations and political base movements will it be possible to build a more humane world, in terms of "Capabilities and Liberties" (Sen, 1989, 2000), in the hope to attain open roads for

"development on a human scale" (Max-Neef, 1993). Other interesting proposals for this "Other Development," from very different theoretical approaches, can be found in: CEPAL (1990, 2000), Rodrik (2000a), and Stiglitz (1998), among many others.

30. In Ecuador, in fact, where there were only two systems of this type, about 50 systems called *Sintrales* (better known as LETS, Local Exchange and Trade Systems) have emerged in the last eight months as a consequence of dollarization. These systems are headed by the Pestalozzi Foundation. One of the largest exchange networks of this type is developing in Argentina, unquestionably as a consequence of the convertibility law (March 1991). But I am not only talking about the proliferation of this tendency in peripheral countries. These practices have also been successfully implemented in Australia and New Zealand, and even in the heart of the most developed countries, at least from the beginning of the 1980s, both in the United States and in Great Britain. Even in countries such as Switzerland (and Austria and Germany), which has the most stable currency in the world, there are local exchange networks that are multiplying the number of unconventional moneys and that in some cases reach the regional and even the national level (this is the case of the Aarau, Switzerland, "talents").

31. Those who are experimenting with these moneys wouldn't agree with those who think "small really is not beautiful in matters of money" (Von Furstenberg, 2000).

32. Some of the contemporary authors who have written on this subject, not necessarily in Silvio Gesell's (1916[1991]) spirit, are Tom Greco (1994), Margrit Kennedy (1995), Bernard Litaer (1994), Jürgen Schuldt (1997), and Lewis Solomon (1996).

33. Certainly, these complementary and extraofficial moneys will not represent, even in the best of the cases, more than 5 percent of international liquidity.

34. Although we know that "each time the idea of a world currency comes up, it runs afoul of the ambitions of the dominant power, which is content to see its own currency elevated to monarchical status. It was Britain in the nineteenth and America in the twentieth century that rejected the idea of world currency" (Mundell, 2000b).

► References

Akamatsu, Kaname. (1962, March-August). A Historical Pattern of Economic Growth in Developing Countries. *Developing Economies,* 3–25. Preliminary Issue No. 1, Tokyo, Japan: Institute of Developing Economies.

Anonymous. (2000). East Timor's Financial Edge. *Economist, 356*(8186), 71.

Barro, Robert. (1999, May 19). Let the Dollar Reign from Seattle to Santiago. *Wall Street Journal.*

Bernstein, Peter L. (2000). *The Power of Gold: The History of an Obsession.* New York: Wiley.

Calvo, Guillermo. (1999, April 20). *On Dollarization.* University of Maryland. Available online at www.bsos.umd.edu/econ/ciecpn5.pdf.

Calvo, Guillermo. (2000, June 21). The Case for Hard Pegs in the Brave New World of Global Finance. University of Maryland. Available online at www.bsos.umd.edu/econ/ ciecpn10.pdf.

Calvo, Guillermo, and Carmen Reinhart. (2000a, November). *Fear of Floating.* (Working Paper no. 7993). National Bureau of Economic Research. Available online at papers.nber.org/papers/ W7993.pdf.

Calvo, Guillermo, and Carmen Reinhart. (2000b). *Fixing for Your Life.* (Working Paper No. 8006). National Bureau of Economic Research. Available online at www.nber.org/papers/w8006.

Canitrot, Adolfo. (1979). La disciplina como objetivo de política económica. Un ensayo sobre el programà económico argentino. *Estudios CEDES,* No. 2, Buenos Aires.

Carstens, Agestin, and Alejandro Weiner. (2000). Monetary Policy and Exchange Rate Choices for Mexico. In Cuadernos de Economia, *Latin American Journal of Economics, 37*(110), 139–75.

Comision Económica para América Latina y el Caribe (CEPAL). (2000). *Equidad, Desarrollo y Ciudadanía.* Santiago: Author. Available online at www.eclac.org/espanol/Publicaciones/lcg2071/indice.htm.

Comision Económica para América Latina y el Caribe (CEPAL). (1990). *Transformación Productiva con Equidad.* Santiago: Author.

Cohen, Benjamin. (2000a, March 18). *Electronic Money: New Day of False Dawn?* Prepared for the Annual Meeting of the International Studies Association, Los Angeles. Available online at *www.polsci.ucsb.edu/faculty/* cohen/working/emoney.html.

Cohen, Benjamin. (2000b, July). *Monetary Governance in a World of Regional Currencies.* In Miles Kahler and David A. Lake (Eds.), *Globalizing Authority: Economic Integration and Governance* (in press). Available online at www.polsci.ucsb.edu/faculty/cohen.

D'Arista, Jane. (2000, October 4–5). Dollarization: Critical U.S. Views. Presented at the conference *Dollarization in the Western Hemisphere* organized by the North-South Institute in collaboration with the Canadian Centre for Policy Alternatives, Ottawa. Available online at www.nsi-ins.ca/ensi/events/.

Dean, James. (2000a). *De Facto Dollarization in Latin America.* Simon Fraser University.

Dean, James. (2000b, October 6). *Why Ecuador is Ripe for Dollarization but Not Canada.* Prepared for the conference *The Political Economy of Monetary Integration: Lessons from Europe for Canada.* University of Ottawa.

De la Torre, Augusto. (2000, October 4–5). *Dollarization in Ecuador.* Paper presented at the conference *Dollarization in the Western Hemisphere* organized by the North-South Institute in collaboration with the Canadian Centre for Policy Alternatives, Ottawa. Available online at www.nsi-ins.ca/ensi/events/.

De Soto, Hernando. (2000). *The Mystery of Capital: Why Capitalism Triumphs in the West and Fails Everywhere Else.* New York: Basic Books.

Dornbusch, Rudiger. (1999, March 16). *The Euro: Implications for Latin America.* Paper prepared for a policy research project of the World Bank at MIT. Available online at web.mit.edu/rudi/www/PDFs/elatin.PDF.

Dornbusch, Rudiger. (2000, January 3). Millenium Resolution: No More Funny Money. *Financial Times.* Available online at http:web.mit.edu/ rudi/www/PDFs/resolution.pdf.

Drazen, Allan. (2000). *Political Economy in Macroeconomics.* Princeton, N.J: Princeton University Press.

Du Bois, Fritz, and Eduardo Morón (Eds.). (2000). *Dolarizar la economía peruana: Riesgos y oportunidades.* Universidad del Pacífico e Instituto Peruano de Economía, Lima, Peru.

Eichengreen, Barry. (2000a, May). Dollarization and Sense. Preliminary version of a note forthcoming in *Business and Strategy.*

Eichengreen, Barry. (2000b). *When to Dollarize.* University of California, Berkeley. Available online at ftp.itam.mx/~delnegro/dollar/eichen:f.pdf.

Edwards, Sebastián. (1999a, September 24). The IMF is Panama's Lender of First Resort. *Wall Street Journal.* Available online at www.anderson.ucla.edu/faculty/sebastian.edwards/panama2.pdf.

Edwards, Sebastián. (1999b, April). Interview. *Deutsche Bank Research, 38*–41. Available online at *www.anderson.ucla.edu/faculty/* sebastian.edwards/sebdb.pdf.

Economic Report of the President (ERP). (1999, February). Available online at w3. access.gpo.gov/usbudget/ fy2000/pdf/1999_erp.pdf.

Falcoff, Mark. (1999, April). Dollarization for Argentina? For Latin America? *AEI Latin American Outlook.* Washington, D.C.: American Enterprise Institute for Public Policy Research. Available online at www.aei.org/lao/lao10297.htm.

Fischer, Stanley. (2000, October 12). Latin America 2000. LACEA Conference, Rio de Janeiro. Available online at *www.imf.org/external/np/speeches/2000/101200. htm.*

Fisher, Irving. (1933). *Stamp Scrip.* New York: Adelphi.

Fontaine, Ivan Andrés, and Rodrigo Vergara. (2000). Debe Chile Dolarizar. In Iouadernos de Economia, *Latin American Journal of Economics, 37*(110), 227–40.

Frankel, Jeffrey. (1999a). Comments. In International Monetary Fund (1999).

Frankel, Jeffrey. (1999b, September). *No Single Currency Regime Is Right for All Countries or at All Times.* (Working Papers No. 7338). National Bureau of Economic Research. Available online at papers.nber.org/tmp/26910~w7338.pdf.

Friedman, Milton. (1999, May 3). Beware the Funny Money. (Interview by Peter Brimelow). *Forbes Magazine.* Available online at wysiwyg://93/http://www.forbes. com/forbes/99/0503/ 6309138a.htm.

Gavin, Michael. (2000, June 22). *Official Dollarization in Latin America.* UBS Warburg, LLC.

Gesell, Silvio. (1916[1991]). *Die Natürliche Wirtschaftsordung durch Freiland und Freigeld.* In *Gesammelte* Werke, *11.* Lütjenburg: Gauke Verlag.

Goldfajn, Ilan, and Gino Olivares. (2000). Full Dollarization: The Case of Panama. Pontificia Universidade Católica, Rio de Janeiro. Available online at wbln0018. worldbank.org/LAC/LACInfoClient.nsf/ d29684951174975c85256735007fef12/ 8579a523181fb3b685268 dc0052bf8e/$FILE/PANAMAWB5.PDF.

Greco, Thomas. (1994). *New Money for Healthy Communities.* Tucson: Greco.

Hausmann, Ricardo. (1999, July 23–24). *Currencies: Should There be Five or One Hundred and Five?* Paper prepared for the seminar *Opciones Cambiarias para la Región,* Banco Interamericano de Desarrollo, Panamá. Available online at *www. iadb.org/* OCE/exchange_rate/5curr.pdf.

Hayek, Friedrich von. (1972). *Desnacionalización de la Moneda.* Buenos Aires.

International Monetary Fund. (1999). *Dollarization: Fad or Future for Latin America?* Washington, D.C.: IMF Economic Forum. Available online at wysiwyg://103/ htttp://ads.admonitor.net/ adengine.cgi.

International Monetary Fund. (2000, November 8). *One World, One Currency: Destination or Delusion?* Economic Forum with remarks of Maurice Obstfeld, Paul Masson, and Robert Mundell. Washington, D.C.: IMF Economic Forum.

Isbell, Paul. (2000). Economía Política de la Dolarización. *Política Exterior, 14*(77), 121–35.

Kennedy, Margrit. (1995). *Interest and Inflation Free Money.* Philadelphia: New Society.

Krugman, Paul. (1999, April 15). Monomoney Mania. *Slate.* Available online at slate.msn.com/Dismal/99-04-15/Dismal.asp.

Litaer, Bernard. (1994). *The Future of Money: Beyond Greed and Scarcity.* Discussion draft.

Mack, Connie. (2000a, February 8). Dollarization Allows U.S. to Export Price Stability. (U.S. Congress Joint Economic Committee, Press Release). Available online at www.senate.gov/~jec/press54.htm.

Mack, Connie. (2000b, March 6). Dollarization and Cooperation: Achieving Sound Money. (U.S. Congress Joint Economic Committee). Available online at www.senate.gov/~jec/press59.htm.

Max-Neef, Manfred. (1993). *Desarrollo a escala humana.* Montevideo, Uruguay: Nordan Comunidad.

Menem, Carlos. (2000, March 6). Conference in the *Seminar on Dollarization.* Federal Reserve Bank, Dallas, Texas.

Morande, Felipe, and Klaus Schmidt-Hebbel. (2000). Chile's Peso: Better Than (Just) Living with the Dollar? In Cuadermos de Economia, *Latin American Journal of Economics, 37*(11), 177–226.

Moreno-Villalaz, Juan Luis. (1999). Lessons from the Monetary Experience of Panama: A Dollar Economy with Financial Integration. *CATO Journal, 18*(3), 421–39.

Mundell, Robert A. (2000a, April 17). *Currency Areas, Exchange Rate Systems and International Monetary Reform.* Paper delivered at Universidad del CEMA, Buenos Aires. Available online at www.columbia.edu/~ram15/cema2000/html.

Mundell, Robert A. (2000b, September 22). *Exchange Rates, Currency Areas and the International Financial Architecture.* Remarks delivered at an IMF Panel, Prague. Available online at *www.usagold.com/gildedopinion/mundellprague.html.*

Mundell, Robert A. (2000c). A Reconsideration of the Twentieth Century. *American Economic Review, 90*(3), 327–40.

Mundell, Robert A. (1997, March 12). The International Monetary System in the 21st Century: Could Gold Make a Comeback? Lecture delivered at St. Vincent College, Letrobe, Pennsylvania. Available online at www.columbia.edu/~ram15/LBE.htm.

Ocampo, José Antonio. (2000, October 4–5). Exchange Rate Regimes and Capital Account Regulations for Emerging Economies. Paper presented at the conference *Dollarization in the Western Hemisphere.* Organized by the North South Institute in collaboration with the Canadian Centre for Policy Alternatives, Ottawa. Available online at www.nsi-ins.ca/ensi/events/.

O'Donnell, Guillermo. (1992). ¿Democracia Delegativa? *Cuadernos de CLAEH, 17*(61), 5–20.

Rodrik, Dani. (1999, September 1). *How Far Will International Economic Integration Go?* In *Journal of Economic Perspectives, 14*(1), 177–86. Available online at www.ksg.harvard.edu/rodrik/JEPrev1. PDF.

Rodrik, Dani. (2000a, January 26–27). *Development Strategies for the Next Century.* Paper presented at the conference Developing Economics in the 21st Century. Institute for Developing Economies, Japan. Available online at www.ksg.harvard.edu/rodrik/.

Rodrik, Dani. (2000b, September). *Exchange Rate Regimes and Institutional Arrange-*

ments in the Shadow of Capital Flows. Harvard University. Available online at www.ksg.harvard.edu/rodrik/.

Rogoff, Kenneth. (1998). Blessing or Curse? Foreign and Underground Demand for Euro Notes. In David Begg, Jürgen von Hagen, Charles Wyplosz, and Klaus Zimmermann (Eds.), *EMU: Prospects and Challenges for the Euro* (pp. 261–303). Oxford: Blackwell. (Cited by Cohen, 2000b, 19.)

Rojas-Suárez, Liliana. (2000, 4–5 October). What Exchange Rate Arrangement Works Best for Latin America? *World Economic Affairs, 3*(2), 35–40. Available online at www.nsi-ins.ca/ensi/events/).

Sachs, Jeffrey y Felipe Larraín. (1999). Why Dollarization Is More Straitjacket Than Salvation, *Foreign Policy,* 116.

Salinas-León, Roberto. (2000, June 22). Testimony. U.S. House of Representatives, Committee on Banking and Financial Services. Hearing on Dollarization and Monetary Stability in Latin America. Available online at www.house.gov/banking/62200leo.htm.

Schuldt, Jurgen. (1997). *Dineros Alternativos para el DesarrolloLlocal.* Universidad del Pacífico, Lima, Peru.

Schuldt, Jurgen. (1999). *Dolarización Oficial de la Economía.* Universidad del Pacífico, Lima, Peru.

Schuler, Kurt. (1999, July). *Basics of Dollarization.* U.S. Congress, Joint Economic Committee Staff Report. Available online at www.senate.gob/jec/basics.htm.

Schuler, Kurt. (2000a, October 4–5). *The International Monetary Stability Act: An Analysis.* Paper presented at the conference *Dollarization in the Western Hemisphere.* Organizsed by the North-South Institute in collaboration with the Canadian Centre for Policy Alternatives, Ottawa. Available online at *www.nsi-ins.ca/ensi/events/.*

Schuler, Kurt. (2000b, August). What Use Is Monetary Sovereignty? Draft. Available online at users.erols.com/kurrency/monsov.htm.

Sen, Amartya. (1989). Development as Capability Expansion. *Journal of Development Planning, 19,* 41–58.

Sen, Amartya. (2000). *Development as Freedom.* New York: Anchor Books.

Senghaas, Dieter. (1982). Elements of an Export-Oriented and Autocentric Development Path. *Economics* (Germany), 7–17.

Senghaas, Dieter. (1988). *Aprender de Europa.* Barcelona: Editorial Alfa.

Solomon, Lewis. (1996). *Rethinking Our Centralized Monetary System: The Case for a System of Local Currencies.* London: Praeger.

Stein, Robert. (2000). *Dollarization: A Guide to the International Monetary Stability Act.* U.S. Congress Joint Economic Committee Staff Report, Office of the Chairman. Available online at www.senate.gov/~jec/dollaract.htm.

Stein, Robert. (1999). Citizen's Guide to Dollarization. U.S. Congress, Joint Economic Committee Staff Report, Office of the Chairman. Available online at www.senate.gov/docs/reports/dollar.htm.

Stiglitz, Joseph. (1998, October 19). Towards a New Paradigm for Development: Strategies, Policies, and Processes. Prebisch Lecture at UNCTAD, Geneva, Switzerland. Available online at www.worldbank.org/html/extdr/extme/jssp101998.htm.

Summers, Lawrence. (1992). Rules, Real Exchange Rates and Monetary Discipline. In Nissan Liviatan (Ed.), *Proceedings of a Conference on Currency Substitution and Currency Boards* (pp. 32–33). (World Bank Discussion Papers, No. 207).

United Nations Transitional Administration in East Timor. (2000, January 22). On the Establishment of a Legal Tender for East Timor. (Regulation No. 2000/7. United Nations Transitional Administration in East Timor).

U.S. Congress Joint Economic Committee Staff Report. (2000, March). *Dollarization: A Guide to the International Monetary Stability Act.* Office of the Chairman, Senator Connie Mack. Available online at *www.senate.gov/* jec/dollaract.htm.

U.S. Senate-House of Representatives. (2000). International Monetary Stability Act of 2000. 106th Congress, 2d Session, S2101 (Report No 106–354). Washington, D.C. Available online at www.senate.gov/~jec/.

Valdivieso, Luis M., Thoshihide Endo, Luis V. Mendonca, Shamsuddin Tareq, and Alejandro López-Mejía. (2000). *East Timor: Establishing the Foundations of Sound Macroeconomic Management.* Washington, D.C.: International Monetary Fund.

Velasco, Andrés. (2000). *Exchange-Rate Policies for Developing Countries: What Have We Learned? What Do We Still Not Know?* (G-24 Discussion Paper Series No. 5). New York: UNCTAD. Available online at *www.unctad.org/en/pub/pubframe. htm.*

Von Furstenberg, George. (2000). A Case Against U.S. Dollarization. *Challenge, 43*(4), 108–20.

15 Nancy Neiman Auerbach and Aldo Flores-Quiroga

The Political Economy of Dollarization in Mexico

Mexico entered the international debate over dollarization on January 28, 1999, at the annual meeting of the World Economic Forum in Davos, Switzerland, when world leaders and reporters questioned the Mexican secretary of finance about the possibility that his country would follow the Argentine example by adopting either a currency board or dollarizing. José Angel Gurría responded that neither approach was under consideration. His country's government was satisfied, he said, with the performance of the freely floating exchange rate regime adopted since the onset of the crisis of 1994.[1] This statement became the starting point of a debate in which Mexican businessmen, government officials, academics, and international analysts made periodic declarations in newspapers and domestic and international forums in support of their preferred vision for the future of the Mexican currency. The debate was almost put to rest in August 2000, when the president-elect of Mexico, Vicente Fox, left no doubt that his government would not attempt to alter the current policy of free flotation of the peso.[2] But the issue did not die, and it is likely to remain on the Mexican agenda in the years to come. After the 2001 New Year announcement that El Salvador would adopt the dollar as its official currency, observers once again began to speculate about the eventual abandonment of local currencies in favor of the dollar throughout Central America, including Mexico.[3]

Mexico's sudden jump into the dollarization debate seems puzzling, at least if viewed from the standpoint of the traditional economics literature alone. Standard arguments indicate that small open economies would be the only ones for which the extreme policy of formal dollarization would make sense (see chapter 8). For these countries the economic benefits can outweigh the significant economic and political costs of giving up the domestic currency in favor of unilateral adoption of another more dominant currency.[4] Some countries that have dollarized, like Ecuador and Panama, clearly fit the small open economy model, but others, like Argentina, do not. Nevertheless, decisions to dollarize or adopt a currency board in both countries have come about more because of extreme inflationary pressures and economic crisis conditions than theoretical considerations of the benefits under the OCA model. But Mexico is a large, open economy that has been experiencing very stable growth and relatively little exchange rate fluctuation since the peso began to float in 1994. Furthermore, as Cohen argues in chapter 13 of this book, traditional political concerns with monetary sovereignty strongly mitigate against giving up one's national currency. Such concerns were of course overridden by broader desires for political integration in Europe, and a European monetary union has been created. But no such overriding desires for regional political integration exist for Mexico. So why has such serious attention been given to official dollarization in Mexico?[5]

In this chapter we suggest that the answer involves the interaction of historical experience and the distributive struggles associated with the integration of the North American market. On the historical side, Mexico's dollarization debate can be understood as a component of a larger and ongoing discussion over alternative ways of stabilizing the Mexican economy. Dollarization can have a powerful stabilizing effect on inflation-ridden and crisis-prone economies, as underscored by the experience of Ecuador since adopting the dollar.[6] And even though Mexico is not currently experiencing a crisis, a longer-term view of the Mexican economy provides some justification for considering dollarization. Since the economic crisis of 1976—the first after 22 years of sustained economic growth—Mexicans have attempted to regain economic stability with fixed exchange rate regimes, crawling pegs, freely floating exchange rates, and managed floats. None of these arrangements have survived more than five years, all have been linked to the onset of an economic crisis, and all have collapsed at the end of a presidential term, except for the most recent transition that brought President Vicente Fox to power. A strong domestic and international demand for Mexico's adoption of sustainable and credible stabilization measures has therefore surfaced.

Our approach to explaining the dollarization debate in Mexico contrasts with standard realist analyses of the costs and benefits of dollarization. For example, Cohen (2000b) relies primarily on the state as the unit of analysis. As a result, his analysis suggests that a country seeking to maximize its power or security in the international system would be quite unlikely to relinquish the power to issue its own currency. A country's currency, like its language and territory, has historically been considered an integral aspect of national sovereignty and, by extension, national interest. On a more practical level, giving up the national currency means giving up any hope of independent monetary policy, another cornerstone of national sovereignty and a key means of maintaining political legitimacy for a regime capable of smoothing economic downturns. But once domestic politics and recurrent crises are taken into consideration, dollarization becomes a clear possibility, if not a viable option.

In the second section of this chapter we examine why Mexico fails to fit the standard mold, and we attempt to explain the political economy of dollarization in Mexico both by disaggregating interests among key domestic actors and by accounting for the policymaking context (i.e., what is the status quo). Thus our analysis draws on another international political economy approach, which focuses on domestic distributional effects of foreign economic policy (Frieden, 2000). The third section argues that the costs and benefits of dollarization must be assessed in the specific context of current Mexican politics in order to make sense of the debate. We conclude by speculating on the likelihood of Mexico adopting the dollar as its official currency in light of the political economic framework offered here.

◣ The Framework

Traditional political-economic analyses of the costs and benefits of dollarization have focused on three main issues: (1) macroeconomic policy autonomy versus microeconomic efficiency, (2) the symbolic nature of currency and nationalism, and (3) the loss of seigniorage.[7] In these analyses it is not apparent that dollarization carries substantial benefits relative to costs, especially for larger countries.

The loss of macroeconomic policymaking flexibility suggests that only through longer and deeper recessions will a country be able to achieve external balance after a negative shock to the balance of payments. Fixed exchange rates require the entire economy to adjust to external shocks because the exchange rate cannot do some of the adjusting. If a country begins running a balance of payments deficit, currency will automatically flow out of the country to pay for the extra imports. Under a flexible exchange rate regime, the exchange rate would adjust downward. The depreciated exchange rate will bring about a quicker resolution to the balance of payments crisis than would be possible under a fixed exchange by encouraging exports and discouraging imports. Under a fixed exchange rate regime, or in this case a dollarized economy, the only way to achieve external balance is through restrictive macroeconomic policies. Unless wages and prices are highly flexible, this will in turn generate domestic recession.

The case of Argentina, which through a currency board officially tied its currency to the dollar from 1991 to 2001, illustrates both the macroeconomic costs and benefits associated with dollarization. The currency board adopted a decade ago successfully ended Argentina's bouts with hyperinflation, but the inflexibility of the exchange rate is also "largely to blame for the country's inability to cope with a run of bad news," most notably the devaluation of the Brazilian cruzado.[8] The situation in Argentina became so serious in 2001 as to prompt the IMF to offer as much as $25 billion in order to avert a Latin American financial crisis, should Argentina default on its debt in 2002.[9] This guarantee proved ineffectual, as Argentina recently announced it would default on its debt, prompting the resignation of President De La Rua and ultimately leading Argentina to abandon its currency board.

The macroeconomic policymaking impotence associated with an inflexible exchange rate certainly involves significant economic and political costs. But to the extent that a country is already unofficially dollarized because of extreme inflationary conditions, as had been the case in Argentina, policymaking flexibility may already be minimal, a condition that tends to mitigate the actual costs associated with the move toward official dollarization (Savastano, 1996). Moreover, dollarization can bring significant microeconomic benefits in the form of transaction cost savings on the part of businesses that trade in both the domestic currency and the dollar, in the form of reduced uncertainty from foreign exchange risk, negating the need for currency hedging and reducing the cost of currency conversion.

Even allowing for the potential economic benefits—greater stability on the macro side and increased efficiency on the micro side—from the perspective of state policymakers, the political costs of dollarization may be prohibitively high. Short-term economic downturns cannot be smoothed with the use of an independent monetary policy, and thus they result in unemployment and reduce the popularity of incumbent governments. In addition, giving up the national currency implies giving up a potent political symbol to promote a sense of national identity (Cohen, 2000b, p. 7). As with a single language, a common currency can help smooth over differences and antagonism among diverse groups. National governments considering whether to adopt the dollar must also accept the loss of sovereignty associated with ceding monetary policy to a foreign power. That is, dollarization involves not simply giving up the policymaking flexibility that comes with central bank authority; it also involves giving the country that is home to the dominant currency real influence over the newly dollarized economy.

Seigniorage is another benefit of retaining a national currency that gets ceded to a foreign power with the decision to dollarize. Defined as the excess of the nominal value of a currency over its cost of production, seigniorage provides government with an alternative source of revenue, which can be especially important for those states that cannot collect revenue through taxes very efficiently. Certainly, the inflationary consequences of this type of public financing make printing money an inferior option. Nevertheless, simply having the option "makes sense from a political perspective as a kind of insurance policy against risk, an emergency source of revenue" (Cohen, 2000b, p. 8; see also chapter 8).

The three arguments just identified suggest that large countries would be better off maintaining their own currencies. They thus fail to explain the level of interest in dollarization among both public and private elites in Mexico. A likely reason for the weakness of the traditional approach is that it focuses on the costs and benefits of dollarization from the standpoint of the nation as a whole, much the way political realists approach policymaking. And from the perspective of the nation-state, the political costs of dollarization will, except in the rarest of situations, be too high. A clear distinction between state and market actors, together with an account of the economic or political context, would go a long way in providing a solution to this shortcoming.[10] Domestic political institutions and policymaking history affect the way state and market actors assess the costs and benefits associated with dollarization. For example, dollarization can become not only the focus of distributive struggles but also part of a broader struggle for power and policymaking discretion. As such, the economic policy mix in place when dollarization is being debated will also affect the perceived costs and benefits of the actors involved and the country. Domestic politics matter, in that policies reflect the interests and interplay between powerful state and market actors. And neither the state nor market actors are represented by a unified voice or set of interests. These interests are in turn shaped by policy context. The status quo can affect (sometimes dramatically) how a proposed new policy is viewed. Of course this is intuitive, since the benefits expected from new policies always need to be weighed against the alternative. But most of the economics literature applies the cost-benefit analysis of dollarization without reference to prevailing policies in specific countries.

For example, when the status quo is a freely flexible exchange rate regime and not a managed float, it changes the perceived costs and benefits of dollarization from the perspective of market actors. Under Mexico's pre-1994 crawling peg, financiers, together with government officials, resisted devaluing the currency at a rate that would have been more compatible with market pressures. In fact, the political pressures against increasing the rate of the crawl were so great that it did not occur until the peso had become dangerously overvalued and billions of dollars in reserves had been spent defending it. Bankers took this position in part because they stood to gain from overvaluation and lose from devaluation, given their heavily leveraged positions in terms of short-term dollar-denominated debt (Auerbach 2001). It needs to be asked, then, whether these still heavily leveraged banks stand to gain from overvaluation enough to lobby for a return to a pegged exchange rate regime. In fact, we see no evidence of a desire to return to a pegged exchange rate regime on the part of Mexican bankers. In the long run, the policy of overvaluation was not sustainable, and the banks suffered huge losses when the peso finally plunged in 1994.

But Mexican bankers were not the only group to resist devaluation. Organized labor has also sought to protect itself from the loss of purchasing power that results from inflation with inadequately indexed wages. A prime example is the National Accord for the Elevation of Productivity and Quality, sometimes referred to as the PACTO, which constituted a historical agreement between official labor and the state in which labor promised to support the reform process in exchange for certain government assurances. The PACTO represents an attempt to institutionalize an antiinflation bias, in that official labor unions agreed to a strict wage policy to help tame inflationary pressures in exchange for the Salinas administration making wage contracts contingent on exchange rate stability. In short, if the downward-crawling peg crawled faster than expected, wage contracts would be adjusted to reflect the decreased purchasing power of the peso and might impede inflation control. Thus, because a central goal of the Mexican government was to control inflation, the institutional arrangement with labor made policy officials resistant to more rapid devaluation (Auerbach, 1997).

However, the incentives to resist devaluation or even to move to floating rates from fixed are not the same in reverse. The status quo matters. One of the reasons is that once rates are market-determined, banks manage to hedge their exchange rate risk, which reduces the short-run gains from a return to pegged rates. More important, the 1994 crisis contributed significantly to the market's learning curve. The last thing financiers want is a repeat of 1994. But all this begs the question: Why not just stay with the status quo of flexible rates since they seem to be working quite well?

A public choice approach can account for the puzzle of dollarization being given serious attention despite what appears to be the overall welfare-reducing effects that fixed exchange rates would have on the Mexican economy. With regard to distributive politics, dollarization plays a dual role: it transfers purchasing power away from domestically oriented creditors and toward export-oriented sectors and debtors, and it blocks transfers of wealth from the private sector to the government in the event of a major currency crisis. The wealth transfers between economic sectors result from the incentives to exploit the uneven distribution of costs and benefits associated with the loss of monetary sovereignty. In the short run, a minority of concentrated interests, typically exporters and traders, together with debtors, saves on transaction and capital costs, while a majority of producers suffer from the absence of government support in the form of anticyclical monetary policy. In addition, dollarization can be viewed as a means of stopping transfers of wealth from the private to the public sector. This is especially true in the context of recent Mexican history, which is fraught with examples in which an unconstrained Mexican executive implemented policies to effectuate those transfers after a currency crisis. The policies have included higher taxes and expropriations of productive assets, such as the nationalization of Mexican banks. A way to avoid such wealth transfers is to avoid currency crises altogether, by removing the executive's discretionary power over monetary policy, and thus the risk of monetary mismanagement. The move to dollarize from floating exchange rates would constitute a consistent trajectory toward reducing the Mexican government's discretion in monetary affairs. Dollarization would be attractive even for actors who currently benefit from the status quo—a floating exchange rate regime—but who would be hurt if the government reverses its commitment to floating rates and reinstitutes an unsustainable (or overvalued) peg. Unless one takes this political story into account, it is difficult to see why those who benefit from the status quo would be in favor of dollarization.

In addition to the role that dollarization plays in the struggle over policymaking autonomy, we highlight the relatively concentrated nature of the benefits and the relatively widespread nature of the costs associated with dollarization. The economic benefits of dollarization, such as transactions costs savings, tend to be quite concentrated. This explains why the politics of dollarization, when viewed in the aggregate, may appear somewhat ir-rational. The transactions costs benefits of dollarization tend to be concen-trated among exporters and transnational businesses. These businesses stand to benefit from reduced exchange rate risk, as well as saving the cost of currency conversion. Moreover, these businesses stand to lose the least from prolonged recessionary adjustment at home, since their consumer base is international. In addition, as the export sector grows in relation to the rest of the economy, its ability to generate foreign exchange makes it an increas-ingly indispensable ally of the state.

Contrast these small and concentrated benefits with the large and wide-spread costs of dollarization. Under a current account deficit, as dollars begin to leave the country, the whole economy would have to be subjected to a recession in order to bring about economic equilibrium. The short-term political and economic costs can therefore be quite significant. But the question remains open: Why is there considerable interest in dollarization and other forms of fixed exchange rate regimes in relatively large countries that are not currently experiencing economic crises? Certainly one possibility is that not only are the costs so disperse that individual citizens don't weigh them very heavily when it comes to revealed preference or that few average citizens are actually aware of the underlying macroeconomic forces at play. Nonetheless, the evidence from Mexico provided in the next section sug-gests that domestic political-economic factors play a crucial role.

◣ Assessing the Costs and Benefits of Dollarization in the Context of Mexican Politics

Four main factors triggered the mobilization of Mexico's business com-munity and international experts in favor of dollarization during early 1999. The first factor was the fear of yet another economic crisis at the end of a Mexican presidential administration. President Zedillo was scheduled to leave office on December 1, 2000, and investors had fresh memories of the severe crises that engulfed the administrations of his four predecessors at the end of their terms (1976, 1982, 1987–88, 1994). These economic downturns were preceded by long periods of real exchange rate appreciation, due primarily to high inflation under a pegged exchange rate regime, and substantial losses in foreign reserves, which fostered speculation against the Mexican currency. As economic imbalances accumulated, pressure on Mex-ican authorities to take corrective or preventive actions, such as a devalua-tion and fiscal austerity, increased. But the proximity of presidential elections motivated the incumbent administration to delay implementing such poli-cies. As a consequence, once elections passed, the Mexican government had no option but to devalue and adopt severe economic stabilization measures. President Zedillo's administration differed from that of his predecessors in that it did not commit to a fixed exchange rate regime. Yet it was unclear whether the pressures of an electoral cycle would motivate his administration to intervene on exchange rate markets, or if the appreciating real exchange rate, given the high rate of inflation, would begin to affect the current account balance. Under these circumstances of low credibility, the demand for some economic measure that reduced the uncertainty was strong.

The second factor was the collapse of Mexico's domestic credit market following the peso devaluation of December 1994. Since the time of the bank privatization of 1990–92, and due to mistakes in its implementation, Mexican banks were undercapitalized, loosely supervised, unconstrained by official minimum reserve requirements, and supported by full deposit insurance.[11] The incentive structure was thus biased toward a lending boom, which the devaluation of 1994 transformed into an unprecedented amount of nonperforming loans, mainly due to the overnight increase in interest rates and the banks' unwillingness to refinance these loans. The high cost of capital led business representatives to suggest an opening of Mexico's capital markets as a way of solving the problem. Dollarization would be especially helpful, many argued, because small and medium-sized Mexican firms that did not have access to international capital markets could gain access to low-cost credits denominated in a relatively more stable currency.

The third factor was the negative impact that events in international financial and commodity markets were having on the demand for the Mexican currency. Mexico was affected by the financial turbulence and drop in commodity prices that followed the 1997 Asian financial crises. It was also affected by the speculation associated with the "samba" and "tango" effects, the financial fallout from the Brazilian and Argentine currency crises. Since Mexico's debt service payments depended on the conditions of international financial markets and its fiscal deficit was strongly sensitive to the movement in oil prices (the oil industry is state owned), the sustainability of Mexico's economic adjustment program was put into doubt. Then came the statement by President Carlos Menem in late 1998 in support of dollarization of the Argentine economy, as a way to both shield Argentina from the samba effect and carry the mechanism of the currency board to its logical conclusion. Economists and investors thus began to ponder whether dollarization also made sense for the Mexican economy.

The fourth factor was Mexico's growing integration into the North American market. Since the implementation of NAFTA, Mexico has become the United States' second-largest trade partner, after Canada, and 80 percent of its trade is directed to the United States. The growing importance of the export sector as an engine of Mexico's economic growth, together with the fact that many internationally integrated sectors already work in an informal dollar economy, has prompted demands for a currency arrangement that reduces transaction costs in exchanges between the United States and Mexico. With these four factors, the stage was set for an open debate around the dollarization issue in Mexico. Its main actors and positions are the subject of the following subsections.

The Politics of State versus Market in Mexico

The first component of Mexico's dollarization debate concerns the economic role of the state. There is a widespread perception that domestic mistakes in the management of macroeconomic policy are largely to blame for the cyclic and severe economic crises Mexico experienced between 1976 and 1994.[12] Ambitious development goals led Mexican authorities to spend beyond the government's means, expand the money supply to unhealthy levels, and commit to unsustainable exchange rate pegs.

To a large extent, these mistakes originated in the extreme discretionary power that Mexican presidents had during this period. The ruling party's predominance in every branch of power and in every level of government provided Mexican presidents with direct control over virtually every aspect of economic policymaking, from fiscal and monetary policies to specific trade or credit regulations. As a consequence, presidents could attempt to accomplish an ambitious development agenda in only six years (Mexico's presidential term) or to create mini-economic booms prior to elections to shore up support for their handpicked successors. Presidential discretion reached a peak during the crises of 1976 and 1982. In 1976, as President Luis Echeverría devalued the Mexican peso for the first time in 22 years, he also increased trade barriers and tried to regain political clout by nationalizing land holdings in the northwestern state of Sonora. In 1982 President José López Portillo responded to the economic crisis, in less than 20 days, by nationalizing the banking industry, imposing exchange controls, expropriating dollar-denominated savings deposited in Mexico, and restricting imports of goods and services not deemed necessary. Such an extreme use of executive discretion—both a cause and a consequence of these crises—persuaded some Mexicans that it was no longer in their interest for a single individual to control Mexico's economic affairs. Business leaders, opposition political parties, and recently formed NGOs therefore engaged in an intense campaign for domestic institutional reform, aimed at reducing presidential discretion. The campaign resulted in the gradual adoption of institutional structures that reduced the president's discretion over the management of trade, fiscal, and monetary policy.

Some examples are illustrative. Mexico formalized its trade liberalization with adhesion to GATT (1986) and the signing of NAFTA (1993). In so doing, it increased the costs of unilaterally closing Mexico's economy, as presidents Echeverría and López Portillo had done. The autonomy granted to Mexico's central bank in 1994 promised to improve the credibility and quality of monetary policy. Electoral reforms enacted in 1993 and 1997 permitted the absence of a majority party in Congress and forced the Mexican president to negotiate every fiscal package with opposition parties in order to get approval.

Viewed from this perspective of institutional reform, the demand for dollarization is yet another expression of the private sector's persistent 20-year campaign to impose constraints on the Mexican government's policymaking discretion. Regarding monetary policy, the first step was to take it away from the president's direct control. The last step would be to take away that instrument entirely from the Mexican government's hands by adopting another country's currency.

This threat to their discretionary power explains why officials in the Mexican government were not (and have not been) enthusiastic about dollarization in the short term. Their assessment is that the credibility gains from dollarization are low, perhaps negligible, because of the Mexican banking sector's current weaknesses and high internal debt rollover frequency; while the costs are high, since the conditions for an optimum currency area between the United States and Mexico are not satisfied. They point to the lack of harmonization between the Mexican and U.S. business cycles, the low labor mobility across the U.S. and Mexican border, and the absence of a fiscal compensation mechanism between both countries.[13] With variations, such is the position shared by Mexico's presidents Ernesto Zedillo and Vicente Fox, by the central bank governor Guillermo Ortiz, by the finance ministers José Angel Gurría (Zedillo administration) and Francisco Gil Díaz (Fox administration), and by the trade ministers Herminio Blanco (Zedillo administration) and Ernesto Derbez (Fox administration).[14] All prominent members of the Mexican government, in fact, have expressed similar arguments, ruling out short-term dollarization.[15]

Distributive Politics

As argued earlier, the benefits of dollarization are concentrated, at least in the short term, whereas the costs are widespread. That, in and of itself, is likely to lead to rent-seeking behavior on the part of those who benefit from the formal adoption of the dollar. This will be the case even if the general welfare benefits for the economy as a whole do not outweigh the costs. Whereas the harsher macroeconomic adjustment costs associated with dollarization are borne disproportionately by the service industry and other domestically oriented firms and by the domestic population more broadly, there is a high likelihood that export-oriented industrialists would capture a large share of the concentrated benefits from dollarization. In the context of the macro economy, the transaction costs savings associated with not having to engage in currency conversion are relatively small. But from the perspective of the firms involved, the savings are potentially large. Indeed, as this analysis predicts, northern industrialists took the lead in advocating dollarization for Mexico. Their views are well summarized by the leader of the Mexican Council of Businessmen (CMHN), Eugenio Clariond Reyes, an industrialist from Mexico's northern region with core business interests in the steel and machinery industry, who suggested that substantial gains, including more trade, more savings, and cheap loans, were available to Mexico if it formally adopted the dollar. His position was close to those of other northern manufacturers. As he put it, "except for our payroll, all of our transactions are already denominated in dollars."[16] Another prominent northern businessman, Alfonso Romo, with interests in the North American market, has expressed virtually the same view and has even organized a high-visibility conference in support of dollarization, with the participation of U.S. and Mexican academics.[17]

Support for dollarization extends as well to the leadership of some peak business associations, such as the head of the Coordinating Business Council (Consejo Coordinador Empresarial, CCE), the business association to which all other chambers in the country belong, or that of the National Confederation of Industrial Chambers (Confederación Nacional de Cámaras Industriales, CONCAMIN).[18] It must be noted, however, that this support has been expressed as a matter of personal conviction and not as the official position of these chambers. The fact that these chambers represent such a broad array of sectors may explain why they have been unable to reach a consensus on the dollarization question.

The issue of credit expansion is also a potential focal point for popular mobilization in favor of a scheme for currency stability, probably including dollarization. The highly visible members of El Barzon, Mexico's powerful grassroots debtors' movement, who suffered direly from the rise in interest rates that followed the devaluation of 1994, want the government to nationalize over three hundred thousand mortgages and force banks to forgive much of the debt owed to banks by small farmers, small firms, and average citizens. El Barzon has even negotiated with transnational corporations, U.S. portfolio investors, international financial institutions, and the U.S. government to put pressure on Mexican banks (Barkin, Ortiz, and Rosen, 1997, p. 14). This suggests that regardless of the actual size of credit expansion that can be expected from dollarization, and because of their similarity of interests, a coalition between exporters and debtors is likely.

The ranks of the undecided and the antidollarizers are more diverse, not to mention dispersed. They include interests from manufacturing regions less reliant on international trade, executives in the financial sector, business leaders with a diversified portfolio oriented toward the domestic market, academics, labor union leaders, and politicians. One prominent argument they use against dollarization is that convergence with U.S. inflation rates, fiscal performance, and other macroeconomic parameters is a prerequisite for either dollarization or monetary integration. The representatives of Mexico's employers' union (Confederación Patronal de la República Mexicana, COPARMEX), a broad-based interest group, and of Mexico's largest manufacturers' chamber (Cámara Nacional de la Industria de la Transformación, CANACINTRA), an association composed mostly of inward-oriented firms, have repeatedly observed that too little is known about the potential costs and benefits of dollarization, and much more convergence is required between the U.S. and Mexican economies before adopting the dollar.[19] Their view is shared by Mexico's wealthiest entrepreneur, Carlos Slim, who controls a diversified portfolio that includes Mexico's telephone giant, Telmex, and large stakes in various retail, manufacturing, and trading sectors.[20] He has also criticized the current state of the discussion because it is framed in simplistic terms (or proposes "magical" solutions) and does not give enough weight to the preservation of national sovereignty.[21]

A majority of Mexican bankers and financial executives also estimate that the absence of macroeconomic convergence makes dollarization unwise in the short term.[22] The presidents of Mexico's Bank Association (Asociación Mexicana de Bancos, ABM) and Institute of Finance Executives (Instituto Mexicano de Ejecutivos de Finanzas, IMEF) emphasized this theme during the high point of the debate and insisted that it is necessary to build a national consensus in favor of dollarization.[23]

The opposition of Mexican bankers may seem odd at first, given that the financial sector in Mexico has become increasingly internationalized with the introduction of NAFTA. Mexican banks would be expected to gain in terms of reduced transactions costs just as northern manufacturing firms would. Moreover, this was the sector that was hurt the most as a result of the economic crisis of 1994, and it may therefore be wary of returning to monetary mismanagement under pegged exchange rates.

Three answers might explain the bankers' position. The first is that such a measure would introduce or intensify direct competition with foreign banks. As mentioned earlier, Mexican manufacturers repeatedly mentioned the need for access to low-cost capital as a reason for supporting dollarization, and foreign banks would be in a better position to provide those low-cost loans than Mexican banks struggling to reorganize after the crisis of 1994. A second answer is that Mexican banks lend mostly to inward-oriented Mexican firms, and should the government renounce the use of anticyclical monetary policy, the likelihood of encountering nonperforming loans in a downturn would increase. This is consistent with the perspectives advanced by Alan Greenspan, chairman of the U.S. Federal Reserve, and by Robert Rubin, treasury secretary under President Clinton, during the initial stages of the dollarization debate. Both warned that monetary policy in the United States would not be designed to stabilize other economies, even if they are dollarized.[24]

Yet another answer is that due to bankers' close ties to Mexico's financial authorities, the costs of dissenting from their positions could be high. Mexican private bankers have tended to hold similar policy preferences, at least in public, to those of Mexican economic authorities, except in times of extreme macroeconomic mismanagement (Maxfield, 1990). To the chorus of dollarization dissenters one can add a vocal group of Mexican congressmen, union leaders, and academics. It is not necessary to review their arguments here, for they share the reasoning of other participants in the debate. Suffice it to say that they are divided along the usual lines: the left tends to be more nationalistic and therefore less inclined to support dollarization, while the right is more open to the idea.[25] On the academic front, the spectrum of positions parallels that of U.S. academic circles, with one group focusing on the transaction costs savings and discipline-inducing benefits of dollarization and the other concentrating on macroeconomic costs and the problem of convergence.[26]

A number of economists from prominent international financial institutions have, surprisingly, endorsed the idea of a fixed exchange rate regime for Mexico but have stopped short of either endorsing or opposing dollarization. Michel Camdessus and Stanley Fisher argued during the early months of Mexico's dollarization debate in favor of fixed exchange rates.[27] Michael Mussa of the IMF declared around the same time that a currency board would best serve Mexico's stabilization goal.[28] The chief economist of the International Development Bank, Ricardo Hausmann, has articulated the popular view that since Mexico's macroeconomic policy is already reactive to the policies of the Federal Reserve, the aspiration of a truly independent monetary policy is nothing more than an illusion.[29] But this view has not been uncontroversial among economists, and some prominent economists clearly disagree with this assessment (Willett, 2001).

In summary, the political landscape of the dollarization debate in Mexico conforms to standard sectoral analysis, with a few outliers. Concentrated export-oriented groups and debtors either support, or are open to the idea of, dollarization, as one would expect. Dispersed groups have ambiguous positions on the issue, as one would also expect. Politicians tend to incline in favor of nationalistic statements and policy regimes that protect their discretionary power, though surprisingly few politicians have been willing to reject out of hand the long-run possibility of dollarization. Another surprise is the group of Mexican bankers who hesitate to relinquish their control over the Mexican lending market. We have presented some hypotheses to account for their position, but at this stage there is little information to confirm or disprove them.

▶ Conclusion: Wither Dollarization in Mexico?

President-elect Vicente Fox tried to put an end to the dollarization debate during his visit to Argentina in August 2000. He said at a joint press conference with Argentina's President De La Rua that he would continue to support the flexible exchange rate policy during his six-year mandate. The favorable performance by the Mexican economy during 1999 and 2000 lent support to his position. Later in January 2001, as he took over the reigns of the Mexican presidency, Fox reiterated his commitment to a freely floating peso at the meeting of the World Economic Forum.

Notwithstanding President Fox's declarations, it is unlikely that the debate over dollarization in Mexico will die. As the previous discussion underscores, dollarization is about more than economic efficiency or national sovereignty. Distributive politics matter, and the Mexican case suggests an ongoing debate kept alive in part by those who stand to reap concentrated benefits should dollarization become a reality. Moreover, one should not discount a powerful demonstration effect from other Central and South American countries that have either dollarized or are considering doing so. Each new announcement of dollarization seems to act as a trigger to renew the debate in Mexico, as the most recent decision of El Salvador did. But the demonstration effect is unlikely to have any real impact on Mexican actors' assessment of the costs and benefits associated with dollarization unless, or until, another relatively large and economically more advanced country like Argentina dollarizes.

In an international climate of volatile capital markets and financial contagion, debates in favor of some type of currency fixing are likely to continue. Since a North American version of the euro is a remote possibility, the only options left for countries unwilling to cede exchange rate management to the vagaries of the currency markets are a currency board or dollarization. Now that Argentina's currency board has collapsed, the debate over dollarization will most likely reemerge with the next wave of financial crises, not only in Mexico but also in other unlikely spots where dollarization might produce significant concentrated benefits.

◣ Notes

1. For a report of these declarations, see *La Jornada,* January 29, 1999.

2. President-elect Fox's statements were published in *Excelsior,* August 8 and 25, 2000.

3. Luhnow, David, "The Outlook," *Wall Street Journal,* January 15, 2001.

4. On the basis of an assessment of costs and benefits, we should expect some small open economies to show interest in unilateral dollarization, but few countries even among these are likely to adopt formal dollarization. Microstates like the Marshall Islands (dollar), Micronesia (dollar), and the Vatican (lira) certainly fit the model most clearly. See Cohen (2000b, p. 1).

5. Or in Latin America, for that matter? Recent Latin American interest in full dollarization does not necessarily conform to the small open economy model. Ecuador, which chose to unilaterally dollarize in 2000, might arguably qualify as small by world standards, but it has not been a particularly open economy either with respect to low trade barriers or percentage of GNP generated by international trade. Argentina formally tied its currency to the more stable U.S. dollar through a currency board arrangement in 1992, and it has more recently actively pursued the alternative option of dollarization.

The Argentine case is particularly puzzling, given that it is neither small nor the most open of economies.

6. Ecuador's president, Gustavo Noboa, described the move toward dollarization as "a rabbit pulled out of a hat to save the economy from ruin," referring to the fact that inflation has slowed to 2.5 percent a month compared with 14.3 percent a year earlier, and that the banking system has made a remarkable recovery, thanks to the significant fall in domestic interest rates. David Luhnow, "The Outlook," *Wall Street Journal,* January 15, 2001.

7. See for example Berg and Borensztein (2000); Cohen (2000a).

8. Norris, F. "Argentina's Woes: With the Peso Overvalued, It Can't Compete," *New York Times,* December 8, 2000. See also DePalma, Anthony. "Argentina and Canada: Two Sides of Uncertainty," *New York Times,* November 26, 2000.

9. Kraul, "Argentina to Get IMF Bailout of up to $25 Billion: The Agency Steps in Early to Avert a Latin American Financial Crisis as a Nation Is Poised to Default on Debt Next Year," *Los Angeles Times,* December 7, 2000.

10. Two analyses that do distinguish between the policy preferences of state and market actors with respect to dollarization are: Frieden (2000) and Frieden and Stein (2000).

11. For details on this crisis, see Edwards and Naim (1998), Tornell and Krueger (1998), and Flores-Quiroga (2000).

12. See, for example: Del Negro and Obiols (2001); Weintraub (1999); Gruben (1996); Little et al. (1993); Rojas (1992); Taylor (1985).

13. This view is articulated in the numerous statements of the Central Bank governor and in the presentations of officials at the ministries of finance and foreign trade and industry, Ministry of Finance and Public Credit, and Sistemade Información Empresarial Mexicano, respectively, collected in their web sites, www.shcp.gob.mx and www.secofi.gob.mx.

14. This is a position he has expressed repeatedly. Examples can be found in the Central Bank's web site or in *El Economista,* March 17, 1999.

15. Note that even President Fox's new finance minister, Francisco Gil Díaz, a well-known supporter of dollarization, has defended the current float, until better conditions emerge for discussing the issue. See the *Wall Street Journal,* January 15, 2001.

16. *La Jornada* and *El Economista,* March 16, 1999.

17. See *El Economista,* March 16, 1999, for his statements. See also the report on this conference—largely in favor of dollarization—by Judy Shelton, in *El Economista,* May 10, 1999.

18. *El Norte,* March 16, 1999.

19. Ibid.

20. In a long interview with *La Jornada* he expressed his opposition to any measure that implies the loss of sovereignty or relies on "magic" solutions to Mexico's economic problem.

21. A focus on Slim's portfolio exposure provides a clue to his position. If the Mexican and U.S. business cycles are not synchronized, and if Mexico renounces control over monetary policy, Mexican authorities would not be in a position to apply countercyclical policies, and the value of his portfolio will be affected adversely.

22. Fifty-four out of 60 bankers and financial experts, in response to a survey made by the newspaper *El Economista* during the annual meeting of the AMB, said that they were against dollarization. *El Economista,* April 13, 1999.

23. See, for example, *El Economista,* May 31, 1999.

24. *Excélsior,* April 17, 1999.

25. See, for example, the positions against dollarization of the Institutional Revolutionary Party senator Rodolfo Becerril Sraffon, who is president of the senate's treasury committee, or the party of the Democratic Revolution senator Juan José Moisés Calleja, who is international relations coordinator of his party's congressional group.

26. Economic consulting firms such as GEA emphasize the need for convergence, as do some economists from the academic units of Centro de Investigación y Docencia Economicas (CIDE), Autonomous Technological Institute of Mexico (ITAM), National Autonomous University (UNAM), and El Colegio de Mexico (COLMEX). Examples of their reasoning can be found in *El Economista,* May 5 or October 19, 1999,

27. *Excélsior,* April 22, 1999.

28. At the Inter-American Dialogue. See *La Jornada,* May 20, 1999.

29. Statements made at the annual meeting of the International Development Bank in Paris. See *La Jornada,* April 17, 1999.

◣ References

Auerbach, Nancy N. (1997, December). *The Mexican Peso Crisis: Constituent Pressure and Exchange Rate Policy.* Lowe Policy Brief.

Auerbach, Nancy N. (2001). *States, Banks, and Markets: Mexico's Path to Financial Liberalization in Comparative Perspective.* Boulder, Colo.: Westview Press.

Barkin, David, Renato Ortiz, and Fred Rosen. (1997). Globalization and Resistance: The Remaking of Mexico. *NACLA Report on the Americas, 30*(4).

Berg, Andrew, and Eduardo Borensztein. (2000). *The Pros and Cons of Full Dollarization.* (IMF Working Paper 00/50). International Monetary Fund.

Cohen, Benjamin. (2000a). Monetary Governance in a World of Regional Currencies. Unpublished manuscript.

Cohen, Benjamin. (2000b). *Monetary Union: The Political Dimension.* Unpublished manuscript.

Del Negro, Marco, and Francesc Obiols-Homs. (2001). Has Monetary Policy Been so Bad That It Is Better to Get Rid of It? The Case of Mexico. *Journal of Money, Credit, and Banking, 33*(2), 404–33.

Frieden, Jeffry. (2000, May). The Political Economy of Dollarization: Domestic and International Factors. Unpublished manuscript.

Frieden, Jeffry, and Stein. (2000). *The Political Economy of Exchange Rate Policy in Latin America: An Analytical Overview.* (Research Network Working Paper No. R-420). Inter-American Development Bank.

Gruben, William. (1996). Policy Priorities and the Mexican Exchange Rate Crisis. *Federal Reserve Bank of Dallas Economic Review,* 19–29.

Kalter, Eliot, and Armando Ribas. (1999). *The 1994 Mexican Economic Crisis: The Role of Government Expenditure and Relative Prices.* (IMF Working Paper, WP/99/160.) International Monetary Fund.

Little, Ian, Richard Cooper, Max Corden, and Sarath Rajapatirana. (1993). *Boom, Crisis, and Adjustment: The Macroeconomic Experience of Developing Countries.* Oxford: Oxford University Press for the World Bank.

Maxfield, Sylvia. (1990). *Governing Capital: International Finance and Mexican Politics*. Ithaca, N.Y.: Cornell University Press.

Rojas, Raul. (1992). *From the Debt Crisis toward Economic Stability: An Analysis of the Consistency of Macroeconomic Policies in Mexico*. (IMF Working Paper, WP/92/17). International Monetary Fund.

Savastano, Miguel. (1996). *Dollarization in Latin America: Recent Evidence and Some Policy Issues*. (IMF Working Paper 96/4). International Monetary Fund.

Taylor, Lance. (1985). The Crisis and Thereafter: Macroeconomic Policy Problems in Mexico. In Peggy Musgrave (Ed.), *Mexico and the United States: Studies in Economic Interaction* (pp. 147–70). Boulder, Colo.: Westview Press.

Weintraub, Sidney. (2000). *Financial Decisionmaking in Mexico: To Bet a Nation*. Pittsburgh: University of Pittsburgh Press.

Willett, Thomas. (2001). Truth in Advertising and the Great Dollarization Debate. *Journal of Policy Modeling, 23,* 279–89.

16 Harris Dellas and George S. Tavlas

Lessons of the Euro for Dollarization
Analytic and Political Economy Perspectives

I think that there is a real, though very slow-moving, tendency for national interests to overrule provincial interests, and international interests to over-rule national, and I think the time will come when it will be thought as un-reasonable for any country to regulate its currency without reference to other countries, as it will be to have signaling codes at sea which took no account of the signaling codes at sea of other countries.

—Alfred Marshall, Evidence before the Gold and Silver Commission, 1887

The view that the only viable exchange rate options in today's world of high capital mobility are the corner solutions of flexible exchange rates and rigidly fixed exchange rates (including such options as official dollarization and currency boards) has appropriated the high ground of international economic policy discourse (e.g., Eichengreen, 1994; Summers, 2000). In-termediate exchange rate regimes, such as crawling pegs and target zones, have been in steady retreat.[1] One logical implication of this progressive drumbeat toward corner solutions is the notion that countries will become increasingly grouped into expanding currency blocs, including the euro bloc in Europe and the dollar bloc in the Western Hemisphere, whose common currencies will float against each other (LeBaron and McCulloch, 2000; Salvatore, 2000).

Several factors underlie the view that the viability of intermediate re-gimes has become problematic. First, in recent years increases in the size and speed of capital movements have proved especially detrimental to coun-tries that adhered to pegged exchange rates and whose economic policies were considered misaligned. Successive speculative attacks against EMS cur-rencies in 1992–93,[2] the Mexican peso in 1994–95, the Thai baht in 1997, the Russian ruble in 1998, the Brazilian real in 1999, and the Turkish lira in 2001 were all associated (to varying degrees) with pegged rates and un-sustainable policy mixes. In and of itself, however, the role of misaligned fundamentals is not sufficient to warrant the retreat from pegged exchange rates. After all, if collapses of exchange rate pegs have been due to misaligned policies, the solution is to align the policies. This argument leads to a second factor that has contributed to the demise of the intermediate regime option. Recent currency crises have apparently also claimed in their wake innocent bystanders, countries whose economic fundamentals were seemingly sound but whose only wrongdoings were the pursuit of pegged exchange rates and their geographical proximity to the country of original sin. Countries with floating exchange rates and hard pegs (such as currency boards), while not unaffected by this process of contagion, have escaped without the collapse of their currencies.[3] An implication of recent currency crises, therefore, is that it may not be enough for a smaller, open economy to have its economic policy structure in order; that structure needs to be fortified by one of the corner solutions.

A third factor contributing to the popularity of the corner solution hypothesis has been the demonstration effect of the EU's effort toward monetary union, culminating in the adoption of the euro by 11 EU members on January 1, 1999.[4] This experiment has supported the view that countries of varying sizes and diverse economic structures can successfully pursue a common monetary policy and forgo the exchange rate option, and it has contributed to calls for countries in Latin America to pursue a similar course by adopting the U.S. dollar as their common currency (Barro, 1999; LeBaron and McCulloch, 2000).

This article assesses the implications of the euro experiment for dollarization in Latin America. The remainder of the article is divided into four sections. The second section draws out the implications of the OCA criteria for European monetary union. As discussed, one implication of the "new" theory of OCAs is that high-inflation countries can enhance the credibility of their monetary policy by tying the monetary policy of the high-inflation country to that of a low-inflation country. This section also describes the political element that has underpinned the euro experiment. The third section appraises the successive target zone experiments adopted by the EU against the backdrop of the credibility literature. An inference drawn from the discussion is that exchange-rate/nominal-anchor regimes contain internal dynamics that render them especially fragile. The fourth section applies the lessons of the euro experiment to Latin America. The fifth section concludes.

◣ The Relevance of the Theory of OCAs

An OCA is a region for which it is optimal to have a single monetary policy and a single currency (Frankel, 1999, p. 11). Two broad approaches have been formulated in the literature to assess whether countries should form an OCA.[5] One approach assesses the conditions under which nations should adopt a common currency (or rigidly fix their exchange rate to the value of another currency). A second approach evaluates the costs and benefits of a common currency. In what follows, each of these approaches is discussed in turn.

Country Characteristics

The following characteristics have been proposed as relevant for choosing which countries are best suited to form an OCA.

1. Labor mobility. Regions between which there is a high degree of labor mobility are viewed as better candidates for currency-area membership because such mobility provides a substitute for exchange rate flexibility in promoting external adjustment (Mundell, 1961). Alternatively, because external adjustment can also be accomplished by a change in labor costs denominated in domestic currency, a high degree of real wage flexibility is viewed as a precondition for currency area participation.

2. Fiscal integration. The higher the level of fiscal integration between two areas, the greater their ability to smooth out diverse shocks through endogenous fiscal transfers from a low-unemployment region to a high-unemployment region.

3. The degree of commodity diversification. Highly diversified economies are viewed as better candidates for currency areas than less diversified economies since the diversification provides some insulation against a variety of shocks, forestalling the necessity of frequent changes in the terms of trade via the exchange rate (Kenen, 1969).

4. Trade integration. The more concentrated a country's trade is with a subset of partner countries, the greater the saving in transactions costs associated with the use of single currency (Eichengreen, 1994, p. 80).

5. The openness and size of an economy. Highly open economies tend to prefer fixed exchange rate arrangements since nominal exchange rate changes in such economies are not likely to be accompanied by significant effects on real competitiveness (McKinnon, 1963). Moreover, in open economies frequent exchange rate adjustments diminish price stability since the overall price index would vary more than in relatively closed economies (McKinnon, 1963). As a corollary to this criterion, the smaller the size of the economy, the more open it is likely to be and thus the more inclined to join in a currency area.

6. The degree of goods market integration. Countries that possess similar production structures are prone to symmetric terms-of-trade shocks, negating the effectiveness of the exchange rate tool between the countries. Consequently, countries with similar production structures are deemed to be better candidates for currency areas than are countries whose production structures are markedly different (Mundell, 1961).

On the whole, the EU countries do not satisfy the OCA criteria. Compared with the United States monetary union, the degree of labor mobility, wage/price flexibility, fiscal integration, and commodity diversification are low in the EU.[6]

Recent work dealing with the OCA criteria has stressed the endogeneity of the criteria, implying that, although the necessary characteristics may not be satisfied ex ante, they may be satisfied ex post. For example, the elimination of currency-transactions costs and exchange rate uncertainty is said to stimulate trade among participants in a monetary union. Higher trade integration can lead to increased income correlation (Frankel, 1999). In addition, countries with nondiversified export structures can join together to form a monetary union that is more diversified than its individual components (Tavlas, 1997). If country A is a commodity exporter (to countries other than country B), for example, and country B an exporter of industrial goods (to countries other than country A), then currency union A plus B is an exporter of both commodities and industrial products. Moreover, although monetary unification in the EU has not led to fiscal integration, it has resulted in enhanced fiscal coordination and consolidation. These considerations underscore the difficulty of ascertaining whether countries should form a monetary union ex ante on the basis of a static analysis of the traditional criteria.[7]

Benefits and Costs of an OCA

Traditionally, the basic case in favor of an OCA has rested on the desirability of exchange rate certainty. Floating rates, so the argument goes, may reflect nonfundamental noise so that they create variability, uncertainty, and misalignment of currencies, inhibiting international trade and investment.[8] The adoption of a common currency also eliminates the transactions costs of exchanging currencies and the information costs of processing and storing information about multiple currencies.[9] The main costs traditionally associated with an OCA are the inability to use monetary policy for domestic objectives and the loss of the exchange rate tool in the event of differentiated terms-of-trade shocks.

In addition to the foregoing factors, in recent years the arguments used to assess the benefits and costs of an OCA have been extended to include credibility effects and political factors.

The credibility hypothesis. This hypothesis emphasizes that, if credible, the use of the exchange rate as a nominal anchor could discipline both the policy makers and private agents.[10] By changing the expectations of the latter, the costs of attaining a low inflation equilibrium are lessened. The hypothesis leads to the view that the stronger the commitment to a fixed exchange rate, the greater the credibility. While the hard options of dollarization and a currency board provide the most credibility to a country seeking to enhance its reputation by tying its hands to the monetary policy of a low-inflation country, during the late 1980s and early 1990s the credibility hypothesis was used in support of looser arrangements, including that of the EMS (as discussed hereafter).

Political factors. Historically, political factors have dominated economic criteria in explaining successful currency unions. The political element can include both benefits and costs. In the case of the euro area, the main benefits are said to be: (1) the creation of a currency to compete with the U.S. dollar in private markets and as a reserve asset, and to enhance Europe's bargaining position and power in intergovernmental monetary negotiations; (2) the desire of Germany's partner countries to regain some influence in monetary affairs, having ceded their sovereignty in the EMS to the Bundesbank (De Grauwe, 1993, p. 655);[11] and (3) the creation of an important symbol (the euro) for eventual merger at the political level. In the case of the euro area, the main political cost of adopting a common currency appears to have been the loss of symbols of national identity (i.e., the national currency).

The political element has been a key force underlying the move to European monetary union. The European monetary experiment, however, differs fundamentally from the process of dollarization, whereby a particular country unilaterally adopts the currency of another country (e.g., the United States) as its own currency. As discussed hereafter, the benefits a country derives from dollarization appear to be smaller, and the costs greater, than when countries mutually agree to adopt a new currency and to create a common central bank.

▲ *Importing Credibility and the EMS*

The credibility hypothesis contains the following institutional implications. First, a single currency peg to the currency of a low-inflation country is preferable to a trade-weighted peg, although fluctuations in the anchor currency imply fluctuations in the trade-weighted exchange rate of the currency in question. A single currency peg is a more visible, verifiable, and easily understood barometer of the policymakers' behavior than a basket peg, which may not be easily understood (or closely monitored) by private agents. Second, devaluation is an option that cannot be effected very often because the more it is used, the more it undermines credibility. Third, credibility is strengthened if there are bands around the central rate that are narrow and visible (i.e., publicly announced). Put differently, wide and quiet (i.e., not publicly announced) bands are unlikely to provide a strong and reliable anchor because they will not sufficiently narrow expectations about the future exchange rate. Fourth, a systems peg is preferable to a unilateral peg because international agreements are considered to be more constraining than unilateral actions (Giavazzi and Giovannini, 1989). Under a systems peg, if the policymakers want to change the central rate, they are obliged to negotiate a new central rate and explain to the other participants in the system why a new rate is appropriate, thus interjecting peer pressure into policy formation (Frenkel and Goldstein, 1986).

The seductive appeal of decreased adjustment costs on the path to low inflation provided a strong inducement for high inflation countries in the

EU to peg their currencies against the deutsche mark in a systems arrangement with narrow (mostly +2¼ percent) bands. With the EMS increasingly viewed as a regime change that improved credibility, the "new" EMS began to take shape in 1987, whereby, in a determination to show their commitment to pegging, policymakers eliminated exchange rate realignments altogether until the EMS crisis beginning in 1992.[12]

With the lifting of the remaining capital controls in EU countries, in the early 1990s, the EMS became vulnerable to speculative attack. Increases in the size and speed of capital movements have proved especially detrimental to the sustainability of nominal exchange rate anchor pegs, since a basis of these pegs, at least in their initial stages, is a peripheral country with relatively high inflation. In the interim, the relatively high interest rates in the peripheral country attract capital inflows and distort market signals for a number of reasons, as follows.

1. The inflows (if unsterilized) increase the monetary base and push down nominal interest rates. With a given level of inflation expectations, real interest rates decline. Both the increase in the monetary base and the decline in real interest rates imply an expansionary monetary policy, contrary to the tightening needed to disinflate. An increase in inflows can be used to finance widening current account deficits, reinforcing the unsustainability of the peg.

2. Sterilization of such inflows produces quasi-fiscal costs, which add to the budget deficit (or reduce the surplus). Moreover, to the extent that sterilization causes domestic interest rates to be higher than they would be otherwise, capital inflows will tend to be higher than they would be in the absence of sterilization.

3. In the early stages of the peg, the weak (i.e., high-inflation) currency can be at the bottom of its band (expressed in terms of domestic currency units per unit of foreign currency), having appreciated, and the anchor currency at the top, with the implication that the weak currency is a candidate for appreciation.

4. A "new" EMS type of regime, involving a numeraire anchor currency, relatively narrow bands, wide inflation differentials between some of the members, and a bilateral parity grid, provides a further layer of distortion of market signals, since official interventions are governed by attempts to preserve the bilateral parity grids. As Pill (1995) pointed out with regard to the EMS, any country with a relatively low inflation rate (say, the United Kingdom) that wanted to use the deutsche mark as an anchor continuously found itself being bound by its bilateral obligations to member countries other than Germany.

5. The increase in reserves arising in situations in which net capital inflows exceed the current account deficit makes the use of reserves as a leading indicator of currency crises inappropriate.

6. The high domestic interest rates provide incentive for domestic firms and financial institutions to borrow in foreign currencies that carry low

interest rates, laying the foundation for a financial crisis that amplifies an exchange rate crisis. During an exchange rate crisis, the (unhedged) debt burden of domestic foreign currency borrowers increases because of the devaluation of the domestic currency. Often the foreign currency debt is short term. Consequently, the rise in domestic interest rates in the wake of the exchange rate crisis leads to higher interest rate payments, compounding both the exchange rate and financial crises.

Magnification and Other Effects

The operating domain of the EMS was a mixed international monetary system comprising both floating rates and pegged rates. A mixed system can magnify the effects of asymmetric shocks on exchange rates, compared with those of a pure float or a fixed rate regime (Dellas and Tavlas, 2000). To demonstrate, consider the implications of the German reunification shock of 1990 within a portfolio-balance framework. Beginning in 1990, Germany undertook a massive fiscal expansion to finance investment in infrastructure and unemployment benefits to the former East Germany. To keep a lid on inflation, the Bundesbank reacted by progressively tightening monetary policy. The fiscal expansion and monetary tightening put upward pressure on interest rates, causing a net capital inflow and appreciation of the real equilibrium value of the mark. In this framework, the fiscal shift causes a shift in Germany's international net investment position. If it began in a position of current account balance, Germany would need to run a current account deficit (in the short run) as its net investment position fell. The fiscal expansion decreased the relative demand for German goods versus those from the rest of the world, and for nontraded goods versus traded goods in Germany, also requiring a real appreciation to restore equilibrium.

In a mixed floating and pegged monetary system, the effects of this kind of an asymmetric shock on the center country can be compounded. This result occurs because the needed current account adjustment operating through the change in the real exchange rate is not allowed to work through usual channels. Since the German reunification shock was asymmetric, an appreciation of the deutsche mark against the currencies of Germany's trading partners was required, but many of Germany's main trading partners pegged their currencies to the mark. Consequently, the necessary relative-price adjustment through the current account initially had to operate primarily through currencies that did not peg to the mark. The implication for the EMS is that the exchange rate pegs against the mark meant that the mark had to appreciate in the short run even more against third currencies than it would have done otherwise.[13]

Several other problems weighted on the "new" EMS, inhibiting its performance. First, all nominal anchor pegs are saddled with a transition problem because the currencies of peripheral countries typically become overvalued (relative to their equilibrium values) during the move to a low-inflation regime. The resulting increase in the price of nontraded goods relative to traded goods encourages producers to shift production toward the former and consumers to shift demand toward the latter, causing the current account position to worsen. Second, a pegged exchange rate rule may be time-inconsistent, hence economically infeasible (Dellas, 1988). If a policy rule is not known to be optimal over the entire future path and if the monetary authorities can abandon it without costs, agents will assume that the authorities will change it, even if the authorities have announced that they would not do this. Hence unless any attempt to use surprise inflation is punished with retaliation from other countries, agents may have the incentive to speculate against a currency when the economy is shocked into a disequilibrium in the current account, since they know that an adjustment of the exchange rate might improve welfare compared with a policy that excludes a change of parities. Third, in a system comprising both floating and pegged exchange rates, the purported disciplining effects of pegged rates are lessened. A devaluation under the Bretton Woods system, for example, made newspaper headlines, but an adjustment of a currency pegged to a nominal anchor may not (Collins, 1996), and even if it does, it may be ascribed to market contagion that is divorced from the fundamentals.

The speculative attacks against the currencies of the EMS in late 1992 and in 1993 eventuated in a widening of the fluctuation bands to ± 15 percent (in August 1993) and a suspension of the pound sterling and the Italian lira from the system.[14] The regime that replaced the 1987–92 regime was a less rigid system; it permitted adjustments in central rates to avoid misalignments and to restore external equilibrium. The wide fluctuation bands provided a degree of monetary policy autonomy, which allowed high-inflation countries to keep their real interest rates at high levels in order to reduce inflation. In contrast to the 1987–92 regime, the regime that followed used convergence of key economic magnitudes—inflation, long-term nominal interest rates, budget deficits, and the government debt-to-GDP ratio—to gradually attain nominal exchange rate stability. In other words, the regime that began in August 1993 and lasted until the adoption of the euro stood the credibility hypothesis on its head. The collapse of the 1987–92 regime and the relative success of the regime that followed contain a number of implications for the dollarization debate, as I will now discuss.

▶ Euro Lessons

Both economic and political considerations have figured in the decision by 12 EU countries to adopt the euro. With regard to the economic considerations, although the OCA criteria have played a role in the process of the EMU, they have not been of overriding importance. With the exception of the criterion of trade integration, EU countries do not generally satisfy the characteristics that have been prescribed for an OCA. This fact, and the consideration that some of the criteria are endogenous over time, indicate that the differences that exist between the Latin American countries and the United States are not sufficient to hinder a dollar monetary union in the Western Hemisphere.

The euro experiment also provides one piece of evidence that exchange rate nominal anchor pegs are especially fragile when capital is mobile. Nominal anchor pegs contain internal dynamics, including magnification effects and transition effects that make such regimes especially fragile. Further, such regimes can be time-inconsistent. While the EMS regime that began in August 1993 provides some evidence that target zones may be viable if the economic fundamentals are aligned and if supported by a systems arrangement, mutual intervention facilities, and political will, these factors do not seem to be applicable for Latin American countries.

For the purpose of garnering credibility through an external commitment while at the same time addressing the challenge posed by speculative flows, a hard currency option provides a greater commitment technology and higher credibility than a peg. This fact suggests that if the attainment of anti-inflation credibility through an external commitment is of paramount importance, dollarization or a currency board are the routes to take. There is little reason to believe, however, that the hard options are more credible than a regime of floating exchange rates accompanied by such institutional arrangements as independent central banks and congressional requirements for central banks' performance.

The failure of EU countries to adequately fulfil the OCA criteria adequately and the demise of the credibility hypothesis underscore the importance of the political economy aspect of monetary union. Here the calculus of the costs and benefits is not so favorable to dollarization as it is to EMU. As noted earlier, the euro area countries share common goals in having adopted the euro. Foremost is that as a newly created common currency, the euro will allow each of the participating countries to share in the prestige of having an international currency. Countries such as Greece and Ireland, for example, will continue to reap the seigniorage benefits that go along with having a national currency through a sharing arrangement with the ECB. In addition, such countries will be able to partake, for the first time, in the further seigniorage that derives from having an international currency. The main cost to the euro area countries was the loss of national symbols. In some cases, however, these national symbols were primarily associated with the bygone days of inflationary finance.

The situation of dollarization is very different from that of the EMU. Latin American countries that opt for the U.S. dollar do not get common currency. Instead they get someone else's currency. As Klein (1993) has pointed out, the Constitution of the United States (article I, section 8) assigns the power to coin money and to regulate the value of money to the U.S. Congress. Therefore, it would seem to be unconstitutional for any other nation to play a significant role in issuing money or in regulating its value for the United States.

The decision to dollarize is not based on common consent but on unilateral action. Unlike the situation in the euro area, where each participating country has a voice on the ECB board, Latin American countries would not, in present circumstances, have a say in the conduct of monetary policy or in the sharing of seigniorage. In contrast to the ECB, which has recently reached a common understanding with participating national central banks that lender-of-last-resort facilities will be provided in cases of liquidity (but not solvency) crises, Latin American countries that dollarize will not have recourse to such facilities in times of liquidity crises.

Because dollarization entails forfeiting monetary sovereignty to a foreign country, it also opens up other avenues of political costs. As was the case in Panama in 1988 when the United States froze Panama's U.S. dollar assets, a country that dollarizes its economy can be subject to economic warfare. The political costs are not, however, all on one side. Consider an oil-importing economy that dollarizes its economy and undergoes a negative terms-of-trade shock (due to an oil price hike). The residents (including the politicians) of that country would have a natural culprit—symbolized by their currency, the U.S. dollar. Dollarization, in other words, is not necessarily in the foreign policy interests of the United States.

For the foregoing reasons, if a country is to consider a hard currency option, a currency board seems a preferable option to dollarization. A currency board retains seigniorage (in terms of the interest earnings from the foreign assets that back the monetary base) and can provide some scope for lender-of-last-resort facilities. Above all, a currency board does not forfeit national currency symbolism to a foreign currency, with all the implications that official dollarization can imply, implications that extend beyond symbolism. Alternatively, floating exchange rates, accompanied by institutional arrangements such as constitutional requirements for central-bank actions, retain seigniorage, lender-of-last-resort capabilities, and political independence.

◣ Conclusion

In sum, the euro experiment provides evidence in favor of the corner solution hypothesis. Intermediate regimes (such as the 1987–92 EMS) that seek to align relative prices through a credibility mechanism contain internal dynamics that lead to the collapse of such regimes. While the OCA criteria were of some relevance in the euro experiment, they were not of paramount importance. For the euro experiment, the OCA approach, which assesses the costs and benefits of a single currency, was crucial in determining the decision to adopt the euro. In turn, the calculus of costs and benefits centered on political economy considerations. For the euro-area countries, a new currency and a common central bank were judged (by the participant countries) to provide higher political benefits than political costs. For Latin American countries, the potential political benefits appear to be less than for euro-area countries. Dollarization appears to involve greater political costs than either a currency board or a regime of floating exchange rates.

▶ **Notes**

We thank Michael Ulan for helpful comments. The views expressed are those of the authors and should not be interpreted as those of their respective institutions.

1. This is not to say, however, that there have not been areas of resistance. For recent, well-articulated proposals for intermediate regimes, see McKinnon and Ohno (1997), Bergsten (1998), Wolf (1999), and Williamson (2000). Frankel (1999) argues that intermediate solutions are more likely to be appropriate for many countries than are corner solutions. Calvo and Reinhart (2000) provide evidence showing that many countries that have been classified as having floating exchange rates by the IMF have, in fact, pegged their exchange rates, thus casting doubt on evidence used to support the notion that there has been a generalized move to floating (one of the corner solutions).

2. Throughout, references to the European Monetary System (EMS) should be taken to refer to the countries participating in the exchange rate mechanism (ERM) of the EMS.

3. For example, the Australian dollar and the Hong Kong dollar weathered the East Asian crisis of 1997–98 under floating exchange rates and a currency board, respectively. The case of the Australian dollar is discussed by Tavlas (2000), and the case of the Hong Kong dollar is discussed by Hanke (2000).

4. On January 1, 2000, Greece became the twelfth country to participate in the euro area.

5. For recent surveys see Tavlas (1993, 1994), Corden (1994), and De Grauwe (2000).

6. Comparisons of the degree of labor mobility in the United States and EU countries include those of Eichengreen (1992) and Blanchard and Katz (1992). Tobin (1998) compares fiscal integration in the EU and the United States. Tavlas (1997) provides evidence on export diversification in larger EU countries and in the United States.

7. Other problems plague the criteria approach. The criteria are difficult to measure and cannot be weighed against each other. In addition, the criteria need not point in the same direction; for example, an economy might be open but possess a low degree of labor mobility with adjoining areas. For further discussion, see Tavlas (1994).

8. A counterargument is that financial markets provide financial instruments that allow firms the opportunity to hedge exchange rate (and other) risks. Such opportunities are not available for hedging the risks of speculative attacks and devaluations under pegged exchange rate systems (Stockman, 2000).

9. However, as Stockman (2000, p. 117) aptly puts it, "these costs do not appear to be particularly large in comparison with . . . the costs of adding sales taxes (in the United States) or determining the relative merits of the 32-oz size at $4.29 or the 20-oz size at $2.98."

10. For an evaluation of the credibility hypothesis, see Tavlas (2000).

11. In return for the sharing arrangement in the conduct of monetary policy at the

euro-area level, Germany is said to have received agreement by other EU countries for German reunification.

12. In January 1990 there was an implicit devaluation of the Italian lira as the currency moved from the wide (± 6 percent) band to the narrow ($\pm 2\frac{1}{4}$ percent) band. Realignments were a prominent feature of the EMS prior to 1987.

13. Dellas and Tavlas (2000) provide evidence of magnification effects.

14. The Italian lira subsequently rejoined the EMS.

◣ References

Barro, R. (1999, March 9). Let the Dollar Reign from Seattle to Santiago. *Wall Street Journal Europe.*

Bergsten, F. C. (1998, Nov. 20). How to Target Exchange Rates. *Financial Times.*

Blanchard, O., and L. Katz. (1992). *Regional Evolutions.* Brookings Papers on Economic Activity, No. 1, 1–61. Washington, D.C.: Brookings.

Calvo, G., and C. Reinhart (2000). *Fear of Floating.* University of Maryland.

Cohen, B. (1993). Beyond EMU: The Problem of Sustainability. *Economics and Politics, 5,* 187–202.

Cohen, B. (1996). *The Geography of Money.* Ithaca, N.Y.: Cornell University Press.

Collins, S. (1996). On Becoming More Flexible: Exchange Rate Regimes in Latin America and the Caribbean. *Journal of Development Economics, 51,* 117–38.

Corden, W. M. (1994). *Economic Policy, Exchange Rates and the International System.* Chicago: University of Chicago Press.

Dellas, H. (1988). Time Consistency and the Feasibility of Alternative Exchange Rate Regimes. *Journal of Monetary Economics, 22,* 461–72.

Dellas, H., and G. S. Tavlas. (2000). *Mixed Exchange Rate Systems.* Bern: University of Bern.

De Grauwe, P. (1993). The Political Economy of Monetary Union in Europe. *World Economy, 16,* 653–62.

De Grauwe, P. (2000). *The Economics of Monetary Union.* Oxford: Oxford University Press.

Eichengreen, B. (1992). *Should the Maastricht Treaty Be Saved?* Princeton: Studies in International Finance No. 74. Princeton: Princeton University Press.

Eichengreen, B. (1994). *International Monetary Arrangements for the Twenty-First Century.* Washington, D.C.: Brookings.

Frankel, J. (1999). No Single Currency Regime Is Right for All countries or at All Times. Essays in International Finance No. 215. Princeton: Princeton University Press.

Frenkel, J., and M. Goldstein. (1986). *A Guide to Target Zones.* IMF Staff Papers, 33, 633–73.

Giavazzi, F., and A. Giovannini. (1989). *Limiting Exchange Rate Flexibility: The European Monetary System.* Cambridge, Mass.: MIT Press.

Hanke, S. (2000). The Disregard for Currency Board Realities. *Cato Journal, 20,* 49–60.

Kenen, P. (1969). The Theory of Optimum Currency Areas: An Eclectic View. In *Monetary Problems of the International Economy,* edited by R. Mundell and A. Swoboda. Chicago: University of Chicago Press.

Klein, L. R. (1993). Some Second Thoughts on the European Monetary System. *Greek Economic Review, 15,* 105–114.

LeBaron, B., and R. McCulloch. (2000). Floating, Fixed, or Super-fixed? Dollarization Joins the Menu of Exchange-Rate Options. *American Economic Review, 90,* 32–37.

McKinnon, R. (1963). Optimum Currency Areas. *American Economic Review, 53,* 717–25.

McKinnon, R., and K. Ohno. (1997). *Dollar and Yen: Resolving Economic Conflict between the United States and Japan.* Cambridge, Mass.: MIT Press.

Mundell, R. A. (1961). A Theory of Optimum Currency Areas. *American Economic Review, 51,* 657–65.

Pill, H. (1995). *Target Zones and the European Monetary System: A Reconciliation.* Stanford University.

Salvatore, D. (2000). The Present International Monetary System: Problems, Complications and Reforms. *Open Economies Review, 11,* Supplement, 133–48.

Stockman, A. (1999). Choosing an Exchange Rate System. *Journal of Banking and Finance, 23,* 1483–98.

Stockman, A. (2000). Exchange Rate Systems in Perspective. *Cato Journal, 20,* 115–22.

Summers, L. (2000). International Financial Crises: Causes, Prevention, Cures. *American Economic Review, 90,* 1–16.

Tavlas, G. S. (1993). The "New" Theory of Optimum Currency Areas. *World Economy, 16,* 663–86.

Tavlas, G. S. (1994). The Theory of Monetary Integration. *Open Economies Review, 5,* 211–30.

Tavlas, G. S. (1997). The International Use of the U.S. Dollar: An Optimum Currency Area Perspective. *World Economy, 20,* 709–48.

Tavlas, G. S. (2000). On Exchange Rate as a Nominal Anchor: The Rise and Fall of the Credibility Hypothesis. *Economic Record, 76,* 183–201.

Tobin, J. (1998). *Currency Unions: American versus European.* Yale University.

Williamson, J. (2000). *Exchange Rate Regimes for Emerging Market Economies.* Washington, D.C.: Institute for International Economies.

Wolf, M. (1999, February 3). Off Target. *Financial Times.*

North America

17 Thomas J. Courchene and Richard G. Harris

North American Currency Integration

A Canadian Perspective

The advent of the euro in January 1999 represents a watershed in the annals of economic and monetary history. At one level, the euro signals the denationalization of national currency regimes. At another and related level, the euro is also signaling that in a progressively integrated global economy, currency arrangements are emerging as a supranational public good, one that is fully consistent with the twenty-first-century notion of what national sovereignty will be about. The purpose of this chapter is to establish the case that a North American monetary union also makes eminent sense for this side of the Atlantic, and in particular from the Canadian point of view.

Understandably, perhaps, this is not the view of Canada's macro officials. As the governor of Bank of Canada, Gordon Thiessen, noted in a recent speech "the Euro is not a blueprint for North America. The political objectives that motivated monetary union in Europe do not have a parallel in North America" (1999, p. 6). We grant that NAFTA is largely a trade and economic blueprint, whereas EU integration does incorporate, in addition, aspects of a confederal and, in some areas, a federal overarching structure. But to link the euro only to the potential political evolution of Europe is to ignore the emerging and compelling economic rationales for a supranational currency. For example, it is highly unlikely that the British will ever buy into the overarching European political project, but it is highly likely that they will ultimately embrace the euro. Even Switzerland, not a member of the EU, is embracing "market Eurorization." As Tagliabue noted:

> The reasons for this [Swiss] enthusiasm for the Euro are clear. Switzerland, with just seven million people and an area a little larger than Maryland's, is surrounded by four Euro nations—Germany, France, Italy and Austria—and conducts about 70 percent of its trade with the 15 nations of the European Union. (1999)

But with roughly 82 percent of its exports destined for U.S. markets, Canada is more deeply integrated with the U.S. economy than is Switzerland with Europe: indeed, as noted hereafter, no euro country has this high a share of its exports destined to the other 10 euro countries. Not surprisingly, this enhanced degree of North American integration will feature prominently in terms of making an analytical case for a North American monetary union (henceforth NAMU).

In more detail, the chapter will focus on three interrelated issues:

- Canada's floating exchange rate is not serving the nation well
- There are persuasive arguments for greater exchange rate fixity
- The longer-term objective of exchange rate fixity should be a NAMU

While a NAMU is not on the immediate horizon (hence the reference to "longer-term" here), there is nonetheless an urgency in terms of placing NAMU on both the Canadian and North American policy agenda. As will be detailed later, this is because policy developments elsewhere in NAFTA, and the Americas generally, appear to be moving rather quickly in the direction of "dollarizaton," that is, using the greenback as the national currency. Given, on the one hand, the earlier assumption, or assertion, that currency arrangements will progressively take the form of a supranational public good and therefore that some form of North American currency integration is probably inevitable, and given also, on the other, that we shall argue that dollarization is much inferior to a NAMU, it thus becomes important from a Canadian perspective that the incipient spread of dollarization does not preclude evolution toward a NAMU.

The Downsides of Canada's Floating Dollar

The following propositions have varying merit in terms of the overall objective of arguing that the current flexible exchange rate regime in Canada is seriously flawed.

Falling Living Standards

In 1974 (i.e., shortly after Canada abandoned the 1960s experiment with fixed exchange rates), the Canadian dollar was worth U.S.$1.04. Now it is worth roughly 68 cents, dipping as low as 63 cents in the currency crisis of the late summer of 1998. This represents an enormous fall in Canadians' living standards vis-à-vis those of Americans. Beyond this, the low dollar not only puts Canadian asset prices at bargain basement levels for American investors but also provides significant incentives for skilled Canadians to ply their human capital south of the border, as they are doing in increasing numbers. A reasonable question is why a high-income industrial country would pursue or validate such a policy. The traditional argument is that Canadian monetary independence and a floating dollar enhances policy sovereignty and economic flexibility, the former because it allows for a made-in-Canada inflation and nominal interest rate policy and the latter because a floating rate can isolate Canada from unwanted global policy and price shocks. Apart from noting that Fortin (1994, 1996) has effectively countered the supposed virtues of Bank of Canada monetary independence, it is instructive to emphasize that the loss of Canadian assets, both physical and human, arising from a value of the Canadian dollar roughly two-thirds of what it was 25 years ago represents a powerful counter to the sovereignty argument.

Exchange Rate Volatility

The Canadian dollar has not only fallen: it has, en route, also departed significantly, both upward and downward, from underlying fundamentals for long periods of time. In the literature, this is typically referred to as the "misalignment" problem or, in popular parlance, the volatility issue. The Canadian dollar went from 104 cents in 1974 to 71 cents in 1986, to 89 cents in 1991, to the low 70 cent range for most of the 1990s, and then to 63.5 cents in the summer of 1998, rebounding to the 67–69 cent range recently. The problem here is that within the integrating NAFTA context, "floating exchange rates provide inherently volatile and unpredictable cost structures" whereas "stable and predictable rates of international exchange and cost calculations to support the volumes of trade and degree of specialization associated with [this trade]" are increasingly required (Harris, 1993, pp. 40 and 39). This is especially the case as Canada moves from a resource-based economy to an economy based on human capital, since this is a move away from organized commodity spot markets priced in U.S. dollars and toward a regime where (generally unhedgeable) long-term bilateral contracts loom large within an economy with a substantial import-competing manufacturing sector. On both the latter counts, exchange rate volatility is bound to be problematic.

In our Howe Commentary (1999) we note that the asymmetric nature of these upside and downside misalignments is economically very troubling. On the upside (a substantially overvalued currency), the degree of overvaluation swamps any possible role for productivity improvements to regain competitiveness. Hence downsizing, outsourcing, and exit become viable avenues for adjustment, especially if the overvaluation is deemed to be permanent. On the downside (i.e., substantial undervaluation), exports certainly do increase. However, other factors also come into play. First, undervaluation is a double-edged sword—productivity improvements (assuming that they are based on U.S. imports or on intermediate goods priced in U.S. dollars) become more expensive as the value of the Canadian dollar falls.

Second, the immediate impact of a depreciation is to shift relative incomes from wages to profits. Third, and relatedly, real wages in the United States rise sharply relative to those in Canada and, as already noted, skilled labor begins to migrate in response to these higher-paying jobs abroad. Thus, many firms will resist raising wages in the short run, and would rather use the depreciation to cut prices and build market share. If the low exchange rate persists, most firms will ultimately come to realize that over the longer term the situation is unsustainable—either they are going to have to raise real wages for their skilled workers or follow them to the United States. The longer-term legacy of repeated bouts of misalignment is likely to result in Canadian comparative advantage shifting toward industries that are resource based and/or capital intensive, and with an employment base that is both less diversified and less human-capital-intensive than would be the case with exchange rate stability. This is not an appealing future in a world where economic growth is driven by knowledge and human capital formation.

Flexible Rates and Productivity

Consistent with the foregoing reflections on the relationship between a weak currency and low productivity is John McCallum's "lazy dollar" hypothesis. (For the record, one should probably note that McCallum is one of the most ardent defenders of Canada's floating rate). Writing in the *Current Analysis* series of the Royal Bank, he notes:

> The idea that a weak currency induces "laziness" on the part of the manufacturing sector is not one that appeals to this author, but it seems to be broadly consistent with the data, [which] suggests a "double dip" in Canada's relative manufacturing productivity or the first half of the 1980s and then in the period 1994–97. Both of these periods correspond roughly to times of weak currency. Indeed, there is a positive and significant correlation (R = .45) between the Canada-minus-U.S. productivity growth gap and the lagged value of Canadian unit labor costs in manufacturing relative to the United States (expressed in the same currency). So it may be that a weak currency has been a *cause* rather than a *consequence* of poor productivity growth in our manufacturing sector. (1988, pp. 3–4; our italics)

In his more recent article, McCallum (1999) quantifies this relationship—as a 10 percent reduction in the Canadian currency is associated, two years later, with a 7 percent reduction in the ratio of Canadian to U.S. productivity in manufacturing. Since Canada's future living standards depend on productivity growth, this is an ominous finding indeed.

Admittedly, productivity measurement is immensely complicated (Harris, 1998, 1999), so that this evidence is probably best viewed in the nature of a hypothesis that merits further research. Nonetheless, it does accord well with anecdotal evidence within Canadian manufacturing.

The Exchange Rate as an Economic Buffer

Those who defend the floating Canadian dollar always (and too often *only*) point to the potential safety valve or "buffer" role of the exchange rate in addressing the asymmetric shocks that hit Canada and the United States. There is, of course, some merit in this argument. Later, however, we shall argue that there is a better way to address Canadian-U.S. adjustment issues. In this subsection, we want to address what has become a principal issue in the assessment of the Canadian exchange rate regime: just what is the exchange rate "buffering" as it tracks the trend decline in commodity prices.

The first point to note in this context is that Canada's total terms of trade (the ratio of export prices to import prices) over the 1990s have fallen only about 3 percent. To allow the exchange rate to mirror only the commodity price decreases is to *exacerbate the internal Canadian (i.e., east-west) terms of trade,* an issue that will be dealt with in more detail later.

The second point relates to some recent evidence offered by Grady and Macmillan (1998). They note that over the first four years of the Canada-U.S. Free Trade Agreement (FTA) period (1989–93) the top five export sectors in terms of recording increases as a percent of GDP were (in order): transport equipment (including autos); machinery and equipment; electrical and communications products; lumber and wood; and chemical and chemical products, followed by several service categories. The five export groups that contracted most as a share of GDP were (again in order): grains; utilities; metallic ores and concentrates; nonmetallic minerals; and petroleum and coal products. Only one of the former group falls in the commodity category, whereas four out of the latter five do. These data heighten the earlier concern that exchange rate buffering is tilting Canada's comparative advantage in perverse directions. Herb Grubel (1999) is far more direct about the consequences: by allowing the dollar to track the downward trend in commodity prices, "the declining dollar has retarded the move of labor and capital out of commodity-producing and into high-tech industries because it signaled the wrong price trends to producers."

Relatedly, one might well ask whether Canada's exchange rate policy has, inadvertently or otherwise, become the latest version of regional development policy. There are few economists who would argue that the exchange rate is the appropriate instrument to deal with inequalities in regional development.

All of the analysis in this section has focused on the impact of asymmetric shocks on producers. What about the effects on consumers? In a recent paper, McKinnon counters the idea that asymmetric shocks undermine the case for a common currency. Specifically, the international portfolio diversification and risk sharing that would accompany a common currency would mitigate the impact of asymmetric shocks:

> A country suffering an adverse shock can better share the loss with a trading partner because both countries hold claims on each other's output in a common currency. Whereas, under a flexible exchange rate without such portfolio diversification, a country facing an adverse shock and devaluing finds that its domestic-currency assets buy less on world

markets. The cost of the shock is now more bottled up in the country where the shock originated. (McKinnon, 2000, p. 4)

Intriguingly, therefore, it is a common currency, not a flexible rate, that buffers asymmetric shocks for consumers. To be sure, this common currency could be the U.S. dollar (i.e., dollarization) as well as some version of a NAMU. We shall make the case for NAMU rather than dollarization later.

▲ The Case for Exchange Rate Fixity

We now direct attention to some of the benefits that will be associated with greater exchange rate fixity.

North-South Integration

The greater the degree of integration between two economies, the greater will be the benefits, other things equal, of a common currency or a permanently fixed exchange rate. This is a standard argument of OCA theory. And dramatically enhanced north-south integration of Canada and the United States has been the FTA/NAFTA experience:

- In 1996, all but two provinces exported more to the rest of the world (international exports) than they did to their sister provinces (interprovincial exports) (Courchene, 1999).
- For each dollar of interprovincial exports in 1996, international exports were running at $1.83. In the early 1980s, the opposite was the case: interprovincial exports were running above international exports (Courchene and Telmer, 1999). More recent data (Grady and Macmillan, 1998) indicate that international exports are now running at more than twice the level of interprovincial exports.
- Since over 80 percent of Canada's international exports are destined for the United States, it is clearly the case that, in the aggregate, north-south trade exceeds east-west trade, that is, exports to the United States exceed interprovincial exports.
- Ontario is an interesting case. In 1981, Ontario's interprovincial exports were running at roughly the same level as international exports. By 1996, international exports were roughly 2 ½ times interprovincial exports and growing nearly a magnitude faster. The most recent data for Ontario indicate that about 90 percent of Ontario's international exports are destined for the U.S. market. Indeed, the value of Ontario's shipments to the United States represents roughly 45 percent of Ontario's GDP.

As an aside, it is instructive to note that Canada is integrated, tradewise, with the United States to a much larger degree than the average euro country is integrated with its fellow euro countries. Hence, on *economic integra-*

tion grounds, the argument for a common currency or exchange rate fixity with the United States is at least as compelling as euro membership is for the average European nation. Admittedly, other factors are at play in Europe.

In addition to this trend toward sharply increased north-south trade integration, one should note that Canada's regions not only are quite different industrially but also appear to be marching at times to quite different cyclical rhythms. For example, the early 1980s recession was short-lived for central Canada, as it latched on to the U.S. recovery, triggered by the rebound in the North American auto industry and Reagan's "military Keynesianism," whereas the Western and Prairie provinces languished in the face of the energy and commodity price collapse. The 1990s recession was quite different. British Columbia skated through it largely unscathed, whereas the impacts on central Canada were near-draconian. Even prior to the FTA, and the subsequent shifts in trading patterns that it induced, eastern and western Canada displayed a cyclical pattern in marked contrast to one another. When one eliminates common demand shocks due to similar fiscal and monetary policies, the pattern of correlation of supply shocks is instructive—1966–86 data from a study by Bayoumi and Eichengreen (1994) confirm the inherent asymmetry in supply shocks hitting eastern and western Canada yet indicate relatively strong correlations between western Canada and the southern and western regions of the United States and Mexico.

As Courchene has argued elsewhere (1999), progressively Canada is less and less a single national economy and more and more a series of regionally differentiated, cross-border economies. This leads to an entirely different view of Canada-U.S. adjustment, based, in turn, on a different view of the asymmetry issue. Specifically, we shall parse asymmetry into its "regional" component and its "national" component and then make a case that exchange rate fixity can adequately address this overall asymmetry challenge.

Exchange Rate Fixity and Asymmetry

We focus first on "regional" asymmetry, where the proposition (perhaps hypothesis is better) is that there is little Canada-U.S. cross-border asymmetry. Consider the following thought experiment. British Columbia aligns its policies to become competitive in the American Northwest and the Pacific Rim. Likewise, suppose Alberta sets its domestic cost and tax parameters so that they are on par with its competitors in the Texas Gulf. And Ontario and Quebec gear their economic policies to match those of the U.S. Great Lakes states. Ditto for the Canadian and American breadbaskets and also for Atlantic Canada as it pursues its more complicated economic future with respect to the New England states and the Atlantic rim. In any event, the scenario assumes that each province or region has aligned itself to be competitive with its cross-border counterpart.

Now comes a commodity price shock (say a positive shock from western Canada's vantage point). *Initially, this affects each side of the regional cross-border economies similarly,* that is, there is no cross-border regional asymmetry. British Columbia lumber is affected in the same way as northwest U.S. lumber. Alberta oil faces the same price change as Texas Gulf oil. Oshawa and Windsor are still in step with Detroit in terms of autos, and so on. However, if the commodity shock results in terms of an appreciation of the Canadian exchange rate (vis-à-vis the U.S. dollar), *then all of the Canadian provincial/regional economies are now offside with respect to their American counterparts.* This is inappropriate policy, especially if this exchange rate "buffering" is also associated with volatility. Arguably, each Canadian trading region would prefer to maintain exchange rate and transactions certainly with *both* east-west and north-south trading partners. This necessarily implies exchange rate fixity relative to the U.S. dollar.

But there may still be aggregate consequences of this shock, and thus there is still the issue of "national" asymmetry. There are two components to what we refer to as this national asymmetry. One is a north-south component, since any change in, say, commodity prices will have a larger overall impact on Canada because commodity-based goods and services are a larger component of Canadian GDP than U.S. GDP. The second component relates to "east-west" asymmetry. Both require some "buffering," to use the bank's term, but not necessarily of the exchange rate variety. How is buffering accomplished with a fixed exchange rate?

The answer is at least threefold. The first mechanism is, of course, the internal adjustment of prices. Note that this is not as significant a challenge as might at first be imagined, because the terms-of-trade shocks affect both of the cross-border sides of the regional economies in a similar fashion, that is, it is the exchange rate response, not the commodity price shock, that triggers the cross-border disequilibrium for Canada's regional economies. Phrased differently, we allow Canadian regions (e.g., Ontario) to adapt in the same way that their regional U.S. counterparts do (e.g., Michigan).

Second, if there is a significant commodity price shock, fiscal stabilization will have to play a role. But this has always been an integral part of the philosophy underpinning fixed rates. Moreover, it is probably important that individual provinces/regions become involved in the fiscal stabilization of the exchange rate. In particular, and as argued in Courchene and Telmer (1999), one would expect that economies that are beneficially affected by a favorable terms-of-trade shock to their own region would use their fiscal levers to temper their booms. Had Canada been under fixed exchange rates in the late 1980s, the pressure on Ontario to temper (rather than *fuel*) its boom would have been much more transparent and intense, since one and all would have understood the implications for the fixed exchange rate.

The third adjustment mechanism is arguably the most important, since it addresses the east-west or internal asymmetry within Canada. In the case of regional-specific shocks, there are already *national policy mechanisms to deal with this*—the national tax transfer system, unemployment insurance, federal-provincial equalization payments, internal migration, and the like. And apart from internal migration, all of the rest are triggered automatically, that is, they operate as automatic stabilizers.

Hence it is simply not the case that adjustment to external price shocks requires a floating exchange rate. Indeed, the adjustment mechanisms underpinning exchange rate fixity are, arguably, more appropriate for an integrating North America. At the very least, this distinction between "regional" and "national" asymmetry merits further research.

The Analytical Case for Exchange Rate Fixity

While the economic and transactions gains from exchange rate fixity will depend on the nature of the "fix," so to speak (with more benefits accruing to a currency union than to fixed exchange rates), the benefits will be substantial. The estimates of currency conversion costs are typically on the order of 0.5 percent of GDP. However, there is a much broader range of potential benefits. For example, Canadian firms operating in the North American market could eliminate the accounting costs that arise from using two currencies. Companies that currently hedge exchange rate risk would no longer find it necessary to do so, and most of the costs associated with providing exchange-rate-related derivatives would no longer be necessary. Menu costs associated with providing price information and invoicing in two currencies would be eliminated, which might prove particularly important to the development of "e-commerce" in Canada. Capital markets would be deeper and interest rate spreads on government and corporate debt would be reduced, thereby improving the efficiency of financial intermediation and reducing borrowing costs in Canada. Canadian issuers of new equity offerings would find a larger market in the absence of exchange rate risk. In product markets, price discrimination by national market would be less prevalent, given better price comparison information on the part of consumers.

Beyond these transactions-related benefits, there are a host of other efficiency and operational gains for exchange rate fixity (Courchene and Harris, 1999).

▶ Exchange Rate Fixity: From Fixed Rates to NAMU

Thus far, we have used "exchange rate fixity" as a generic term to encompass a broad range of alternatives—fixed exchange rates, currency boards, dollarization, and a NAMU. We now turn to an evaluation of some of these alternatives.

Fixed Exchange Rates

There is a widely held view, certainly in the corridors of power but also in the economics profession and the media, that there are only two viable currency options for Canada—floating rates on the one hand and irrevocable fixity on the other (i.e., dollarization or NAMU). This is a convenient myth for central bankers and other floating rate advocates. All they have to do is emphasize that dollarization is unacceptable and NAMU is unattainable, et voilà! Floating rates become optimal, by default as it were. In the Canadian case, there is the often associated claim that Canadian social policy can only be sustained with a flexible exchange rate. Apart from the analytical deficiencies of this argument, this assertion ignores much of postwar currency history, including Canada's fixed rate period in the 1960s. Specifically, the fixed-exchange-rate 1960s represented a veritable flowering of creative Canadian social programs—for Medicare, for postsecondary education, for welfare, for equalization payments to provinces, for public pensions, and so on. And at the more global level, the Bretton Woods fixed rate regime facilitated the evolution of "embedded liberalism"—the magnificent accomplishment of combining increasing international integration with the evolution of national welfare states. These are hardly black marks against fixed exchange rates.

The fact that a lot of highly industrialized and successful small countries have rejected flexible rates ought to weigh in favor of the case for fixed exchange rates. Yet this evidence is typically viewed as lending strength to arrangements like dollarization and a common currency rather than as favorable to fixed rates. When obvious fixed-exchange-rate success stories are emphasized, such as the Austria-Germany and Netherlands-Germany fixes, these often tend to be viewed as special cases, for example:

> The Netherlands guilder, which might seem an exception since it shadows the German mark within an explicit tight band, is to all practical intents fixed, rather than adjustable. This is because successive Dutch governments have made attachments to the mark a keystone of national economic policy within the broader framework of strong support for the political goal of European Union. Austria and Belgium are close to being in the same camp as the Netherlands because of their overriding political commitment to shadowing the mark. (Crow, 1996, p. 17, n. 2)

But surely this is exactly the manner in which Canada ought to approach fixed exchange rates—the attachment to the U.S. dollar would have to be a keystone of the overall macro strategy as part of the NAFTA-oriented framework. Austria and the Netherlands are excellent examples in this context since the transactions case for a Canadian exchange rate link with the U.S. currency is even more compelling than it is for these two countries' link with the deutsche mark. A political commitment by Canadian macro authorities to "shadow" the U.S. dollar, backed up by a full understanding of what this means on the fiscal front and by increasing north-south integration of trade and investment, could make a Canada-U.S. fixed exchange rate among the most stable in the world. This does not mean that it could not be toppled by unforeseen events. The European exchange rate mechanism became unstuck for a time when Germany integrated the former East German länder. And, arguably, *any* Canadian exchange rate regime would probably be in trouble were Quebec to become an independent country.

While we regard a fixed rate regime as an eminently feasible option for Canada, there are a number of transition issues that deserve mention, only one of which is aired here, namely the issue of how one would get to a fixed rate. It seems obvious, and the Dutch example is useful in this context, that one cannot go into a genuine fix without first demonstrating some policy commitment to greater exchange rate stability. That is, the monetary authorities must first demonstrate they are willing to use monetary policy as an instrument to deliver on exchange rate goals, most likely in the form of a target band for the exchange rate, rather than simply intervention in the foreign exchange rate market. Once this credibility is established with respect to the exchange rate goal, foreign exchange speculation will tend to be stabilizing, and interest rates between the two countries should tend to converge. Over time, the exchange target band can be narrowed, and limited intervention will be necessary. This is the "shadow" policy referred to by John Crow. In short, credibility has to be earned, and therefore it would be unwise to move suddenly to a fixed exchange rate. How long would such a transition take? No one can know for sure, but it took the Dutch about three years from their initial shift to "fixed rates" before they achieved interest rate convergence with Germany.

Dollarization

In a sense, dollarization is the ultimate fix. In Canada's case it would mean abandoning the Canadian dollar and using the U.S. dollar. However, it would also mean abandoning most of the domestic monetary and financial institutional framework, the Bank of Canada included. It is convenient to distinguish between "market dollarization" and "policy dollarization." Policy dollarization in Canada is highly unlikely, since it implies a conscious decision by the authorities to opt for the U.S. dollar as the official currency. On the other hand, market dollarization—use of the dollar by the private sector—is alive and well. We already noted that the British (and to a lesser but still significant extent, the Swiss) are well launched on the EU-equivalent path of "market Euroization." Similar developments are evident within Canada.

A willy-nilly drift into dollarization, triggered by an unstable Canadian exchange rate, would be enormously costly to the country. In this context, we disagree with the position of many economists and financial analysts that, during the summer 1998 currency crisis, Canadian macro authorities should have allowed the value of the dollar to be determined by the whims of international capital. In this context, the uncertainty associated with, and the expressed indifference of those policy authorities toward, the movements of the dollar were especially inappropriate. While it is no doubt the case that the 1 percent interest rate hike in the then economic environment was problematical, it was far more important to stem the flight from Canadian-dollar-denominated assets. The international capital markets and domestic asset holders had clearly lost confidence in the Canadian currency. Not to put too fine a point on this, Canada was effectively veering in the direction of market dollarization. Hence we support fully the Bank of Canada's 1 percent interest rate hike in the "scary" situation (McCallum, 1998) that was associated with the dollar's free fall in the late summer of 1998. The larger message is that private agents, whether domestic or international, *will* act in their self-interest to protect their investments. If the volatility of the exchange rate places these interests at risk, rational agents will shift to more certain transactions and store-of-value alternatives. In the Canadian context this means using the U.S. dollar. It would be an enormous mistake on the part of analysts and authorities alike to assign this scenario a zero probability.

While dollarization may well end up as a default option, there is a much more preferable longer-term alternative from Canada's perspective—a NAMU.

NAMU

A North American monetary union would be the North-American equivalent of the euro. In the case of the euro, this means an overarching (supranational) central bank with a board of directors selected in part from the still-existing national banks. Hence the Bank of Canada would have a role (at a minimum one-fourteenth, complementing the 12 Federal Reserve Banks and the Mexican central bank), in designing North American monetary policy. Since the U.S. dollar is already the world's foremost reserve currency, the Americans would maintain their greenback. But European experience suggests that the other partners in the arrangement, Canada and Mexico, would have some flexibility in terms of currency symbolism. One side of the Canadian part of the NAMU currency (say the $5 bill) would proclaim that this is North American legal tender and a perfect substitute for a U.S. $5 bill (or words to this effect) while the other side (the Europeans call this the "landscape" side) could be emblazoned with Canadian symbolism. (Note that this approach to the EU currency—a common side and a country-specific side—was only abandoned at the eleventh hour. Now all bills will be identical. But the euro coins will differ on one side.) Since the national currencies would be perfect substitutes, there would be no exchange rate.

Implicit in all of this is an *internal revaluation* of Canadian wages and prices in order that one new Canadian (NAMU) dollar will exchange for one U.S. dollar. But this process of currency conversion is exactly the same process that all 11 European countries underwent in preparation for the launch of the new euro currency.

The process toward locking in the precise exchange rates at which old Canadian dollars would be swapped for the new NAMU dollar would presumably follow the European approach to the euro.

What is the possible interest of the U.S. government in a NAMU? We do not know the answer to this. However, with the euro currency reach now exceeding the formal U.S. dollar reach, the United States would presumably be in favor of a larger formal U.S. dollar area, especially given their proclivity to run current account deficits. Moreover, from the perspective of U.S. foreign policy objectives, and in particular security in the Western Hemisphere, the U.S. government is obviously concerned with the repeated currency implosions in Latin and South America and their political consequences. But it is probably the case that the U.S. government cannot initiate a move to a NAMU, given political sensitivities in Canada and Mexico. Canada's role will be crucial. Canadians initiated the FTA negotiations and then, with Mexico, spearheaded NAFTA. The same will have to be true for a NAMU.

However, to the extent that the Americans are in favor of a larger U.S. dollar area, surely the way to do this is via dollarization, not a NAMU, or so the typical argument would go. Indeed, there already are various proposals, some at the quasi-official level, that argue for a return of some seigniorage if countries opt for the U.S. dollar as legal tender, for example, the bill recently introduced by Senator Connie Mack. Yet, even if this occurs, the fact of the matter is that when a significant number of countries in the Americas adopt the dollar as legal tender, some influence over monetary matters will begin to flow to them as well. Thus the Americans may well want to "expand" the Fed, informally at first, in order to internalize some of these monetary interdependencies. Think, for example, of the implications of, say, a dozen already dollarized countries then contemplating the creation of a common currency to be pegged to the U.S. dollar (and the resulting excess supply of U.S. dollars) if they do not get access to some representation on the Federal Reserve Board. The key message here is that while dollarization has substantial initial appeal to many countries in the Americas, over the longer term these countries will surely prefer some version of NAMU (or rather AMU) to dollarization.

Would Canadians, if asked, be in favor of a NAMU? Again, we do not know the answer to this. But the issue is wrongly posed. If currency integration of some sort is highly likely in North America, the question for Canadians is whether they would prefer a NAMU to dollarization. Here, the answer is clear and positive, as recent polls attest: Canadians would prefer a NAMU.

Nonetheless, there is one important issue relating to a NAMU that remains a stumbling block for many Canadians, namely that the governance of North American monetary policy will remain in the hands of the U.S. Federal Reserve, since it will probably have a dominating influence on the board of directors of the North American Federal Reserve Board, as it were. Hence North American monetary policy will, for all intents and purposes, be U.S. monetary policy. At one level, this is, of course, correct and desirable—moving to a fixed exchange rate means that Canada would adopt U.S. policy with respect to inflation and interest rates. At another level, however, the issue becomes one of pointing out the inherent difference between multipolar Europe and the euro on the one hand and the hegemonic United States and the NAMU on the other. The European Central Bank (ECB) is a federation of 11 central banks, whereas a NAMU would be a federation of three, with the United States probably having the overwhelming voting power. Actually, it is probably more correct to say that a NAMU will have 14 constituent banks, if one counts the 12 U.S. federal reserve banks.

While this is surely the NAMU reality (although less so if the common currency eventually extends to all the Americas), there is another way to approach the comparison between a NAMU and the euro. The first point to be made here is that a comparison between Canada and Germany or Canada and Italy is not fully appropriate. The Europeans needed to join together to form a currency that could compete in global portfolios with the U.S. dollar. In other words, the appropriate comparison is not between the euro and a NAMU but between the euro and the U.S. dollar. In this light, consider the currency choices facing Canada and Britain. Both countries have to weigh the economic benefits and costs of maintaining a separate currency or adopting the common currency. In Canada's case, this means sharing a voting membership on a North American Federal Reserve with the 12 existing U.S. Federal Reserve banks and, say, the Mexican central bank. In Britain's case, this means joining the euro with a similarly small voting role—one vote in the face of the 11 existing central banks (with many more participants soon to join the euro). It is probably the case that the 11 European central banks are likely to exercise more policy independence than are the 12 U.S. Federal Reserve banks. However, we would hazard a guess that Canada would be more likely than Britain to garner a seat on any executive council. In any event, it is likely not only that the mandate of these supranational central banks will be driven by price stability but also that these supranational banks themselves will appoint a further number of "independent" directors to the board (as in the ECB).

To be sure, this does not counter the concern that policy under a NAMU would be U.S. driven. But it does provide an alternative vantage point for viewing the euro-NAMU comparison.

▶ *NAMU: Operational Considerations*

As already noted, the transition to a NAMU would presumably follow the euro model. Canada, Mexico, and the U.S. would, having agreed to a NAMU in principle, engage in a transitional EU-type exchange rate mechanism that would set their currencies on a convergence path for entry into NAMU. We have already noted aspects of this convergence in terms of the Dutch example, that is, gradually calibrating policy to embrace the common exchange rate. Presumably, there will exist some "convergence" criteria, along euro lines. In any event, Canada will presumably want, as a runup to establishing a NAMU "entry point," to bring its debt/GDP ratio down to U.S. levels. This will ensure that Canada has similar degrees of freedom on the fiscal side under a NAMU as will the United States. One can view this as the NAMU equivalent to the Maastricht fiscal guidelines. More important, as the Canadian debt/GDP ratio declines, the Canada-U.S. exchange rate will presumably appreciate (along the lines of McCallum's [1998] exchange rate equation, where the value of the Canadian dollar is negatively related to the debt/GDP ratio). In other words, part of the NAMU conversion process will be to generate an appropriate equilibrium entry point for the common currency. Of course, similar issues must be addressed for Mexico's convergence and ultimate entry to a NAMU.

Unlike dollarization, which would mean the disappearance of the Bank of Canada and the likely integration of the Canadian financial infrastructure into the American institutional environment, NAMU will allow for preservation of Canada's domestic financial institutions and regulatory structure. The Bank of Canada will remain. So will the existing clearing system, since the North American equivalent to the European "Target" system would serve to provide crossnational clearings. In principle, at least, it should be possible to extend NAFTA's governing principle, namely "national treatment," to the operations of financial institutions and regulation. In other words, Canada could and would maintain its existing approach to its financial sector (e.g., branch banking and ownership rules). Under the euro the national banks will still be responsible for, among other things, monitoring and research functions. This will also carry over to a NAMU: indeed under the existing U.S. system, the 12 Federal Reserve banks already play an important research and advisory role. Seignorage would be shared across the member banks of the NAMU. And on and on.

The key macroeconomic difference once a NAMU is in place will be in terms of how Canada and Mexico adjust to any shocks to the system. Obviously, the exchange rate would no longer exist as a policy instrument, so that adjustment must take place in other ways. As noted earlier, this means that Canada will have to adjust to exogenous shocks in much the same way California and New York will have to adjust, that is, via changes in prices and wages, and internal migration among other avenues. And for shocks that have different impacts across Canada's regions, the east-west tax and transfer system (income taxes, equalization, and employment insurance [EI]) will provide some "buffering." At the aggregate level, there is still scope for national stabilization policy, especially if in the convergence to a NAMU Canada succeeds in bringing the debt/GDP ratio down to U.S. levels.

Will a common currency require policy harmonization elsewhere as well? At first blush, the answer might appear to be yes. But this answer must be conditioned by the following consideration. First, and as noted earlier, it was during the 1960s fixed exchange rate regime that Canada initiated the constellation of policies that, to this day, make Canada distinct socially within North America. Second, there are a whole host of areas where further harmonization is necessary and probably regardless of the exchange rate regime. For example, there is an ongoing public debate within Canada about the appropriate competitive level of marginal tax rates on corporate and personal income, a debate that is likely to continue independently of the exchange rate regime. Third, neither exchange rate regime, fixed or flexible, allows Canada to avoid the implications of, say, U.S. monetary policy changes. Under a common currency, Canadian interest rates are of course tied directly to the decisions of the North American "Fed." But a flexible exchange rate clearly does not insulate Canada from a change in U.S. interest rates, for example.

▲ Conclusions: The Geopolitical Reality

By way of a concluding comment, we want to signal a note of urgency in terms of addressing the NAMU issue. A NAMU itself may well take the better part of a decade to come to fruition. But the march of events rolls relentlessly forward. In particular, pressures toward policy dollarization in Latin America seem to be accelerating. Argentina's former president, Carlos Menem, proposed that his country move from its currency board arrangement to full dollarization. In January 1999, the head of the Mexican Bankers Association called for a North American common currency. A prominent Mexican business group called for full dollarization of the Mexican economy. While the Mexican government has not embraced dollarization, this issue is likely to surface in the upcoming Mexican presidential election. In February 2000, the government of Ecuador officially dollarized. It is unclear as of this writing where all this is headed, but certainly there has been substantial official interest in dollarization both in Latin and South America and in the United States.

Intriguingly, the U.S. economist Robert Barro (writing in the *Wall Street Journal,* March 8, 1999) suggested that the United States would (and should) find creative ways to support these dollarization initiatives. For example, Barro suggested that the U.S. Federal Reserve could simply "give" the Argentine Central Bank a one-time allotment ($16 billion) of newly issued U.S. currency. In return, the Fed would get $16 billion of non-interest-bearing pesos (the peso and the U.S. dollar already exchange on a one-to-one basis), which the Fed would hold as collateral. This transfer of U.S. dollars to Argentina would cost nothing (except paper and ink) and the longer-term return would be the seigniorage arising from an expanding supply of U.S. dollars in Argentina. Barro then goes beyond this to note that one of the problems with dollarization is that it would remove the existence of a lender-of-last-resort facility. He argues the United States could become a lender of last resort for its dollar-zone clients. He even suggests that the United States should take the lead in promoting this monetary integration. As noted earlier, some of these ideas have surfaced more recently in a formal proposal by Senator Connie Mack of Florida.

Part of the U.S. geopolitical reality is that as economic growth in Latin and South America proceeds, it will surely put pressure on the United States for further economic and institutional integration. This implies that the United States will progressively be pulled or drawn "south" even as Canada is drawn closer to the United States. In other words, a NAMU is probably destined to eventually become an AMU (American Monetary Union). Indeed, AMU offers a concrete example of hemispheric policy beyond trade issues that is potentially a win-win situation for all parties. Arguably, there will be few, if any, visible losers from an AMU, and this will become increasingly evident as the potential problems and challenges associated with "dollarization" become apparent. This stands in sharp contrast, for example, to further deals on trade or the environment where there are likely to be clear winners and losers within these countries. From the perspective of the region as a whole, a NAMU on the way to an AMU presents itself as a deal with limited downside risks on the political side.

In terms of this chapter, one implication of the larger issue is that the United States, in the interests of stabilizing the region, will almost certainly be forced to explore the monetary integration option. Canada as the northern partner in such an arrangement will have some leverage, as was the case in NAFTA. However, there has been an official reluctance within Canada to discuss either a NAMU, an AMU, or dollarization. But we should be clear that a Canadian failure to participate in these discussions will not slow down the forces pushing toward either AMU or dollarization. This would be a strategic mistake on the part of Canada, especially if, as a result, it will tend to preclude NAMU as an option. In the case of free trade within the continent, Canadians took the initiative both on the policy and research front. There is a need for Canadian officials and policy analysts to likewise embark on a NAMU research agenda with regard to both policy and implementation in the likelihood that currency integration becomes an integral feature of the global economic order in the millennium. In turn, this harkens back to our introductory comments, namely that to view the emergence of the euro as linked primarily to the potential political evolution of Europe may well be to misinterpret one of the watersheds in monetary and economic history. Arguably, the euro is signaling not only the denationalization of national currency regimes but also the emergence of currency arrangements as a supranational public good. Thus, a NAMU must assume some pride of place in Canada' s policy and research agenda.

◤ Note

This chapter was originally presented at the conference *Should Canada and the U.S. Adopt a Common Currency?* at Western Washington University, Bellingham, Washington, April 30, 1999. The authors are grateful to conference participants for comments. An earlier version was published in the *North American Journal of Economics and Finance* (Courchene and Harris, 2000).

◤ References

Barro, Robert. (1999, March 8). Let the Dollar Reign from Seattle to Santiago. *Wall Street Journal.*

Bayoumi, Tamim, and Barry Eichengreen. (1994). Monetary and Exchange Rate Arrangements for NAFTA. *Journal of Development Economics, 43,* 125–65.

Courchene, Thomas J. (1999). Towards a North American Common Currency: An Optimal Currency Area Analysis. In Thomas J. Courchene (Ed.), *Room to Manoeuvre? Globalization and Policy Convergence* (pp. 271–334). Kingston, Ontario: John Deutsch Institute, Queen's University.

Courchene, Thomas J., and Richard G. Harris. (1999). *From Fixing to Monetary Union: Options for North American Currency Integration.* (C. D. Howe Institute Commentary). Toronto: C. D. Howe Institute.

Courchene, Thomas J., and Richard G. Harris. (2000). North American Monetary Union: Analytical Principles and Operational Guidelines. *The North American Journal of Economics and Finance.*

Courchene, Thomas J., and Colin R. Telmer. (1999). *From Heartland to North American Region State: The Social, Fiscal and Federal Evolution of Ontario.* Toronto: Faculty of Management, University of Toronto.

Crow, John. (1996). The Floating Canadian Dollar in our Future. In Thomas J. Courchene (Ed.), *Policy Frameworks for a Knowledge Economy* (pp. 11–36). (Bell Canada Papers on Economic and Public Policy). Kingston, Ontario: John Deutsch Institute, Queen's University.

Fortin, Pierre. (1994). Slow Growth, Unemployment and Debt: What Happened? What Can Be Done? In Thomas J. Courchene (Ed.), *Stabilization, Growth and Distribution: Linkages in the Knowledge Era* (pp. 67–108). (Bell Papers on Economic and Public Policy). Kingston, Ontario: John Deutsch Institute, Queen's University.

Fortin, Pierre. (1996, November). The Great Canadian Slump. *Canadian Journal of Economics, 29,* 761–87.

Grady, Patrick, and Kathleen Macmillan. (1998). Why Is Interprovincial Trade Down and International Trade Up? *Canadian Business Economics, 6*(4), 26–35.

Grubel, Herbert G. (1999). *The Case for the Amero: The Merit of Creating a North American Monetary Union.* Vancouver: Fraser Institute.

Harris, Richard G. (1993). *Trade, Money and Wealth in the Canadian Economy.* (Benefactors' Lecture). Toronto: C. D. Howe Institute.

Harris, Richard G. (1998). Long Term Productivity Issues. In Thomas J. Courchene and Thomas A. Wilson (Eds.), *Fiscal Targets and Economic Growth* (pp. 67–90). Kingston, Ontario: John Deutsch Institute, Queen's University.

Harris, Richard G. (1999.) *Determinants of Canadian Productivity and Growth: Issues and Prospects.* (Industry Canada Discussion Paper No. 8). Ottawa: Industry Canada.

McCallum, John. (1998, September). Government Debt and the Canadian Dollar. *Current Analysis, 2*(10).

McCallum, John. (1999). Canada, the Euro and Exchange Rate Fixity. *Current Analysis.*

McKinnon, Ronald I. (1997). Monetary Regimes, Government Borrowing Constraints and Market-Preserving Federalism: Implications for EMU. In Thomas J. Courchene (Ed.), *The Nation State in a Global/Information Era: Policy Challenges* (pp. 101–42). (Bell Canada Papers on Economic and Public Policy, Vol. 5). Kingston, Ontario: John Deutsch Institute, Queen's University.

McKinnon, Ronald I. (2000). Mundell, the Euro, and Optimum Currency Areas. In Thomas J. Courchene (Ed.), *Money, Markets and Mobility: Celebrating the Ideas and Influence of the 1999 Nobel Laureate, Robert A. Mundell.* Kingston, Ontario: John Deutsch Institute, Queen's University.

Tagliabue, John. (1999, February 24). Switzerland's Enthusiasm for Euro Grows. *New York Times.*

Thiessen, Governor Gordon G. (1999, January 20). The Euro: Its Economic Implications for Canada. Remarks to the Canadian Club of Ottawa, Ottawa.

18 Herbert G. Grubel

The Merit of a North American Monetary Union

The successful launch of the euro at the beginning of 1999,[1] the prospect of official dollarization in Argentina and Mexico, and the poor performance of the Canadian economy in recent years have prompted a growing interest in monetary union in North America. This chapter considers first how a common currency would be created, then analyzes the economic benefits and costs of such an arrangement for Canada, the United States, and Mexico. The chapter concludes with some speculation about the political feasibility of monetary union between the two countries.[2]

▶ *The Mechanics and Institutions of a Common Currency*

The process of establishing a North American Monetary Union involves the following steps. On January 1, 20*xx*, the public in Canada, Mexico, and the United States will surrender their current banknotes and coins in return for new ones, which might be called ameros.[3] At the same time, all prices in the three countries are converted to ameros. The North American Central Bank will be created and will determine monetary policy for the continent. The three member states are represented on the executive board and staff in proportions that reflect their economic importance.

One crucial issue is the rate at which the national currencies are exchanged for ameros. To minimize the cost of conversion, one U.S. dollar will be equal to one amero. The exchange of the Canadian and Mexican currencies for ameros will take place at a rate that leaves unchanged the international competitiveness of these countries. To minimize opposition to the monetary union by nationalists, one side of notes and coins circulating in each country will show appropriate national symbols, the other will exhibit abstract designs and writing that identifies them as amero notes or coins. To keep the circulation of national currencies dominant in each country, commercial banks will return foreign amero notes to their home country in exchange for their own country's notes. The currency circulating in each country can be produced locally so that each country can continue to earn the seigniorage profits from that activity and the mints remain in place.

The introduction of the amero at the appropriate rates of exchange

318

leaves unchanged the real income and wealth of individuals in all three countries. Incomes, prices of goods, services, and assets all change in the same proportion. The process of creating a common currency involves only what in practice are accounting changes. The public in all countries is likely to get quickly used to the new unit of account. So what are the benefits from monetary union? The following analysis discusses a number of different sources of welfare gains, the assessment of which is facilitated by a brief review of OCA theory.

Optimum Currency Area Theory

After 1945 the international monetary system relied on a system of fixed exchange rates. This system was introduced to prevent the competitive devaluations that had aggravated the depression of the 1930s. However, during the 1960s this fixed exchange rate system came under criticism based in Keynesian economic theory. This theory suggested that countries could lower unemployment permanently by expansionary monetary and fiscal policies at the expense of only relatively small and constant inflation. The fixed exchange rate system was seen as the main obstacle to the pursuit of such policies, and the move to flexible exchange rates gained great momentum.

During this period academics and politicians also gave much attention to Milton Friedman (1953) arguing the merit of freely floating exchange rates. His arguments were powerful and influential because he equated the exchange rate to the price of foreign exchange. He then developed the universally accepted idea that price flexibility assures the efficient allocation of resources and thus leads to the maximization of income. The confluence of Keynesian and Friedman's criticism of fixed rates ultimately resulted in the abandonment of fixed exchange rates.

However, important for the present purposes of analysis is the fact that during this period of growing support for exchange rate flexibility, Robert Mundell (1961) published a seminal article in which he introduced the world to the concept of what he called optimum currency areas. He questioned the merit of Friedman's generalized recommendation for freely floating rates by asking the following question. If flexible exchange rates are such a good system, why is their introduction limited to existing nation-states? Why don't regions within countries adopt them?

Mundell's answer is that the exchange rate is different from any other price, much the way money is not just a commodity. He argued that large currency areas tend to have more stable prices and economies than small areas simply because within a larger region random shocks tend to average out more than they do in a smaller one. As a result, a country that joins a larger currency area enjoys important microeconomic benefits. In addition, it no longer has to pay the risk premium existing in capital markets of countries with unstable exchange rates. The usefulness of money is increased. The costs of currency trading and measures to deal with exchange rate uncertainty are diminished. All of these benefits translate into higher productivity and living standards through both the more efficient allocation of resources and stimuli to economic growth.

Mundell concluded therefore that the adoption of freely floating rates or the permanent linking of its currency to another requires each country to consider a trade-off between microeconomic benefits and the losses in macroeconomic flexibility, which is at the heart of the case for flexible exchange rates made by Keynesians.

Keynesians dominated the economics literature on optimum currency areas that developed in response to Mundell's original article. The focus of their articles was the specification of economic conditions that determined the costs associated with countries' losses due to their reduced ability to deal with economic shocks through monetary, fiscal, and exchange rate policies. Mundell's call for an examination of the microeconomic costs of flexible rates went largely unheeded.[4] The Delors Commission Report redirected the focus from Keynesian macro to Mundellian micro effects by estimating the size of the microeconomic benefits of fixing exchange rates permanently through the creation of a monetary union in Europe.

However, while the new emphasis on the micro- and macroeconomic costs and benefits is a step forward, no economist until now has spelled out one of the main conclusions I reach hereafter: flexible exchange may well not have brought macroeconomic benefits but mostly costs.

◣ The Microeconomic Benefits

The benefits from monetary union consist of gains from lower costs of exchange dealings, reduced risk premiums on financial assets, increased labor market discipline, fewer monetary and fiscal policy adventures, and having a direct influence on the formulation of monetary policy in the union.

Reduced Costs of Foreign Exchange Dealings

All trade in goods, services, and securities among the countries of North America requires one party in the transaction to buy or sell foreign exchange. In addition, financial derivatives like forward and future contracts are used to reduce the exchange risk associated with this trade. Speculation takes place in currency contracts. Exchange rate developments need to be forecast. International travelers require foreign currencies to pay for transactions abroad. All of these currency-related activities absorb labor and capital in banks and other firms.

It is difficult to estimate the savings from the elimination of the need to engage in such activities in North America. The gross values of trade, capital flows and travel—for which good data are available—are an imperfect measure of the potential savings. Thus, much of the recorded trade takes place between divisions of the same firm and does not require foreign exchange transactions. Recorded net changes in the holdings of foreign securities are accompanied by much intraperiod buying and selling, and the time cost and hassle facing international travelers are not recorded anywhere.

The Delors Commission Report (Commission of the European Communities, 1990) assessed the merit of forming the EMU by commissioning special surveys of banks and other private agents. It concluded that savings might be as large as one half of a percent of national income of the average European country. Other, more recent estimates suggest that the foreign exchange departments of European banks will shrink by two-thirds.[5]

Without special surveys it is impossible to come up with an equivalent estimate of savings for Canada, Mexico, and the United States. However, given that Canada is one of the most open economies in the world and the bulk of its trade is with the United States, potential savings may be as large as the 0.5 percent estimated for the average European country. It might well be in the same range for Mexico.

Lower Interest Rates and Exchange Risk

Figure 18.1 shows that Canadian interest rates on long-term government bonds exceeded those on U.S. bonds, averaging 1.17 percentage points during the postwar period. However, there were some periods during the 1970s and early 1980s when the turbulence of international exchange and capital markets created a spread much larger than one point. The year 1983 saw the record spread of 3.5 points. Since 1998 the Canadian rates have been lower than the U.S. rates.

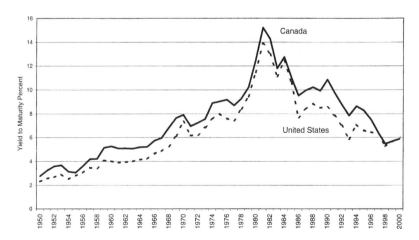

Figure 18.1. Long-term Government Bond Yields: Canada and United States. *Source*: IMF, International Financial Statistics, Country Tables, line 61.

The difference in the two interest rates is due to four factors: first, the risk of depreciation of the Canadian against the U.S. dollar; second, the fluctuations in the exchange rate around a trend (called the exchange risk); third, a difference between the two countries in the risk of default on their debts (called the sovereign risk); and fourth, the lower liquidity of Canadian government bonds (called the liquidity risk).

Clinton (1998), an economist at the Bank of Canada, attributes most of the interest rate gap to the risk of currency depreciation. He estimates the other causes of the difference to be relatively minor, though the threat of Quebec separation has undoubtedly increased the sovereign risk component of the spread during the 1990s.

Not covered in Clinton's article is the period since 1998 when the Canadian interest rates were below the U.S. interest rates and Canada's inflation rate was below that of the United States. These recent conditions suggest that estimates of the possible lowering of interest rates from monetary union should be based on differences in real rather than nominal interest rates. Clinton deflated nominal interest rates by the consumer price index and found for the period 1961–98 a spread in real yields of 0.97 points and in nominal rates of 1.17 points. We may therefore expect that the present lower Canadian rates probably will turn out to be in nominal terms only and that the real interest differential will favor U.S. rates.

A common currency in Canada and the United States will eliminate the historic interest rate differentials caused by the exchange risk. A small difference due to the sovereign and liquidity risks may remain but is difficult to forecast. Chances are that it will be about the same size as exists between the federal and provincial debt obligations presently prevailing in Canada. The gap between Mexican and U.S. securities is much larger. At times it has reached 30 percent, even when inflation rates in the two countries differed by much less. The interest rate differentials reflect a risk premium that is based on past experiences and fears about future development. A monetary union would shrink this historic interest rate gap, though it may require some time before capital markets will have gained sufficient confidence in Mexico's commitment to the union.

There will be several important, beneficial effects of lower interest rates in the two countries. In the case of Canada, first, the cost of serving government debts will fall. The federal government alone, with a debt of $600 billion, will enjoy savings of $6 billion annually if the nominal and real interest rates drop by one percentage point. Second, the annual fixed interest obligations of other Canadian governments, agencies, private companies, and individuals will be reduced by many billions of dollars. Third, the yield on common shares required by investors will fall, and stock market values will rise correspondingly. The gains for Mexico would be correspondingly larger.

The stimulation in consumer spending by such lower borrowing costs will in large part be offset by lower interest incomes of lenders. However, the lower interest rates will encourage higher investment by business, which in turn will increase labor productivity and raise living standards. Mortgage rates will fall and cause a higher demand for housing stock. This demand will stimulate the building industry and the producers of furnishings. The increase in the value of stock market holding will stimulate consumer spending and lower unemployment. Cumulatively and through time, all of these effects will be large.

Expansion of Trade

Lower transactions costs in the foreign exchange market are equivalent to lower tariffs and transportation costs. In traditional international trade theory, the relatively small reductions in the costs of trade due to these factors were considered not to have had much impact on the level of trade. However, new theories of international trade have changed these conclusions. Reduced costs encourage trade in differentiated products that can be manufactured under conditions of increasing returns.

The experience after the introduction of NAFTA suggests the correctness of this new theory. Canada enjoyed an unprecedented expansion of exports, and individual industries had very few adjustment problems. These developments validated the essence of an econometric study by Harris and Cox (1983) that used the new trade theory to predict that the dynamic gains from free trade would equal 5 to 10 percent of national income in the longer run. We may expect similar increases in trade between members of the monetary union to be much larger than is suggested by the relatively small savings due to the elimination of exchange rates on intraunion trade.

More Efficient Price Structure

Studies have shown that in Europe the prices of identical products on two sides of national borders often are quite different. Why do consumers let these price differences persist? Geographic distances are not great, and language differences in most regions are not a serious obstacle to consumer arbitrage. Free trade has existed in Europe for some time, and consumers are able to bring goods across borders without hassle and the payment of tariffs.

The answer to the puzzle has been found to lie in the fact that prices in the two countries are in different currencies. As a result, consumers find price comparison cumbersome. The technical term used in this context is that prices are not "transparent." In addition, the currency conversion adds extra costs to cross-border shopping. These barriers to the equalization of consumer prices in Europe will disappear with the adoption of the euro.

As a result of the equalization of consumer prices, retailers will be forced to become more efficient or go out of business. There will be a growth in community-wide retailers that will charge the same retail prices everywhere.

Consumers will gain from the increased efficiencies and enjoy higher living standards. Under the proposed North American monetary union we can expect analogous benefits to accrue to consumers in all three member countries.

Increased Labor Market Discipline

The Delors Commission Report (Commission of the European Communities, 1990, p. 47) noted that one of the expected benefits from the creation of the euro area would be "increased labor market discipline." This result stems from the fact that excessive wage settlements, often caused by strong labor union actions, can no longer be offset by currency depreciation to keep the offending industries in business and prevent increases in unemployment. The permanently fixed exchange rate will force unions to either accept wages in line with productivity increases or accept higher unemployment among its members.

In Canada, wage increases in excess of productivity gains are not caused by direct union demands. They arise instead from a more subtle process that tends to be ignited by a fall in the world price of commodities. Figure 18.2 shows that during the postwar years this price has been on a consistent and pronounced downward trend.[6] Figure 18.2 also shows that there is a strong correlation between these commodity prices and the exchange rate. The correlation coefficient (r-squared) is 0.7 for the period 1955–98). However, the correlation is far from perfect. Between 1955 and 1971 commodity prices fell nearly 30 percent while the exchange rate remained unchanged. Between 1972 and 1980 commodity prices remained unchanged, and the real exchange rate dropped nearly 20 percent. Only in recent years did the exchange rate and commodity prices have a trend downward simultaneously around minor coincident cycles.

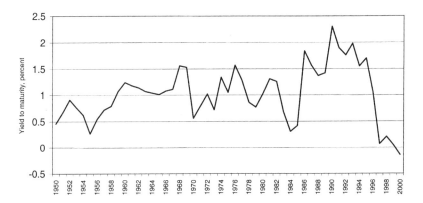

Figure 18.2. Spread on Canada-U.S. long-term government bond yields.
Source: IMF, International Financial Statistics, Country Tables, line 61.

Why is this correlation so imperfect, and why does the recovery of commodity prices not prompt the return of the exchange rate to its correspondingly high level? The answer lies in the operation of a Canadian process equivalent to that existing in Europe. The depreciated exchange rate raises profits in other industries, in particular the heavily export-oriented large automobile sector but also in import-competing industries. Higher profits in turn induce wage demands, which spread throughout the economy. When commodity prices recover to their previous level, the exchange rate does not return to its old level because the higher costs of production in export and import-competing industries make them noncompetitive at the higher exchange rates.

It is for this reason that the Canadian dollar has been on the secular downward trend apparent from figure 18.2. There is no doubt that future fluctuations in commodity prices will lead to a continuation of this process and that in 30 years the value of the Canadian dollar will drop the same 30 percent that it did in the preceding three decades.

There is a fundamental reason for this process, which was argued by Hayek (1937), addressing the fact that during the Great Depression competitive devaluations were used widely to deal with economic troubles. In an economy otherwise on an even path, if for whatever reason one industry is disequilibrated, then using an exchange rate adjustment to remedy the problems of that industry by definition disequilibrates other industries, which in turn tend to bring about further adjustments like changes in labor costs.

A common currency will prevent Canadian industries other than the commodity-producing sector from suffering such disequilibria induced by temporarily lower commodity prices and exchange rates. Unions will be unable to negotiate higher wages based on their employers' profits. In effect, labor market discipline will be increased. Canada will enjoy the same benefits that the Delors Commission Report predicted would accrue in the euro zone.

No More Monetary Policy Adventures

Much of the world inflation and currency instability of the postwar years in Canada and other countries can be explained by experiments in macroeconomic policies based on Keynesian economic models and the belief that inflation could be used to lower unemployment through the famous Phillips curve trade-off. It is now well understood that these models do not reflect reality. Unemployment rates and economic growth cannot be improved by inflation but tend to become worse. But this lesson was won at great costs in terms of economic turmoil, inflation, unemployment, and reduced economic growth.

The constitution of the European Central Bank reflects this new thinking on the merit of inflation. Its prime mandate is the maintenance of price stability. It is not responsible for full employment, as many central banks of industrial countries still are. I suggested earlier that the proposed North American Central Bank be given the same constitutional mandate. If that happens, Canada will be protected from future monetary policy misadventures that could be stimulated by Canadian politicians in pursuit of self-interest or by new generations of economic advisers equipped with new models and amnesia about the lessons of the postwar years.

Imposing Fiscal Responsibility

Membership in the euro system imposes on governments the requirement to keep government deficits to less than 3 percent of national income. This rule was created because large deficits by member countries put upward pressures on interest and exchange rates in the entire euro zone if they lead to foreign borrowing. These higher interest and exchange rates resemble a classical economic externality since they affect all countries in the union. The limits on deficits are designed to prevent these spillover effects.

I believe that the concern of Europeans over the effects of national government deficits is exaggerated. In federal states like the United States and Canada the ability of junior governments to borrow and impose externalities on others is strictly limited because of sanctions that private capital markets impose on transgressors. Higher debt service costs tend to prompt legislators to mend their ways, even if they do so often at an undesirably slow rate.

However, I believe that limits on spending deficits are meritorious whether they originate in constitutional clauses, legislation, or international agreements. I therefore believe that Canadians will benefit from any possible limits on deficits that are enshrined in an agreement for a North American monetary union.

Having a Voice in Policy Formulation

National monetary sovereignty under the present regime of managed exchange rates is supposed to give countries maximum freedom to use interest rates for domestic purposes. In fact, however, monetary policy and exchange rates are closely linked through the capital flows induced by interest rate changes. Canada has a very open economy and cannot afford to disregard its exchange rate, except in rare circumstances when fundamental changes in policy objectives are adopted, as they were in the early 1990s with the adoption of a zero inflation target.

As a result, interest rate changes in the United States in recent years tend to have been accompanied by corresponding changes in Canada even when the lagging Canadian economy would have benefited from the maintenance of lower interest rates. The need to follow U.S. interest rate policies will increase even more in the future as the elasticity of capital flows between the two countries rises even more and goods markets become more integrated.[7]

Under present conditions Canada has no direct input into the formulation of U.S. monetary policy. The proposed organization of the North American Central Bank board of management will have Canadian representatives. While these and Mexican directors will always be in a minority, they will have systematic opportunities to present their countries' views on interest rates in the union. Their privilege and the limit of their influence are no different from those of directors from U.S. reserve districts. Having some input and voice is superior to having none.

◣ *Macroeconomic Costs*

The macroeconomic costs of currency union are considered to arise from the lost opportunity to use the exchange rate as a shock absorber. This shock absorber is needed to minimize the impact of such disturbances as lower commodity prices for exports, harvest failures, civil unrest, large-scale strikes, shifts in demand, inflation at home and abroad, and other such events. Disturbances of this nature tend to lead to lower domestic demand and higher unemployment. The adjustable exchange rate allows the impact of temporary disturbances to be reduced. It also facilitates the redeployment of resources between industries and permits the pursuit of inflationary policies that differ from those in the rest of the world.

In the Keynesian literature on OCAs, concern about the macroeconomic cost of monetary union focuses on the effects of real disturbances, like lower export prices and shifts in demand. In Canada, the lower export prices have been given much play. In Europe, a hypothetical example used by the defenders of flexible exchange rates is a shift in demand away from Irish lace and the simultaneous increase in the demand for Italian shoes. Under the Keynesian recipe for dealing with such shifts in demand, Ireland requires lower and Italy higher interest rates. A common interest rate for all of Europe prevents this national policy response.

It has long been recognized that the need of Ireland and Greece for separate interest rates depends greatly on the flexibility of labor markets in the two countries. It also depends on the mobility of labor into and out of the affected countries and the availability of low-cost credit to facilitate the creation of new industries. Eichengreen (1992) and Bayoumi and Eichengreen (1994) have added the argument that it also depends on external assistance from a central government.

These authors contrasted the extent to which these facilities existed in the United States and Europe. They found that U.S. states experiencing an economic decline adjusted easily because of large central government transfers and the emigration of workers. European countries do not have the benefit of such transfers and emigration, so they have to rely on flexible exchange rates to deal with economic declines. For this reason Bayoumi and Eichengreen predict that the European monetary system will fail. They conclude that individual countries of the union do not represent an OCA. These views are held by a number of economists, who are known as euro-pessimists.[8]

However, an increasing number of economists—the so-called euro-optimists—challenge the views of the euro-pessimists. Mundell (1998), in a series of articles in the *Wall Street Journal,* argues that the macroeconomic losses will be small. The Delors Commission Report, after a long and complicated assessment of the process of adjustment to disturbances under flexible exchange rates, concluded that "the fixing of exchange rates within the Community represents, at worst, only a very limited loss" (Commission of the European Communities, 1990, 136). Swoboda (1991) in a prestigious lecture echoes this view. Belke and Gros (1999) find no evidence that in fact external disturbances in Europe have been correlated with unemployment.

The euro-pessimists tend to be Keynesians and preoccupied with aggregate demand conditions and inflexible labor markets. In my view, the emphasis on macroeconomic variables is misplaced. McKinnon (1963) already argued that flexible exchange rates facilitate adjustment only on the assumption that workers have money illusion, that they will accept lower wages through a rise in prices induced by the currency depreciation but not otherwise. The postwar experience has shown that workers do not suffer from money illusion. When exchange rate depreciations bring inflation, workers insist on the indexation of wages and real wages remain inflexible.

The key to the efficient adjustment to economic shocks is the flexibility of labor markets. If the demand for Irish lace decreases, the duration and depth of unemployment depends on the willingness of workers to retrain and accept lower wages if necessary. In California, when the Cold War ended, the defense industries went into a severe tailspin. However, unemployment was relatively small and short-lived because the workers were quickly absorbed by new industries that were attracted to the availability of a skilled and flexible labor force and the existence of a superb infrastructure.

In my view, the flexibility of labor markets and the ability of other institutions in the economy to deal with economic shocks are determined by the exchange rate regime itself. If Canada had experienced a decrease in demand for an industry as important as the defence industry in California, the exchange rate would have depreciated. As a result, these industries could have lowered their prices abroad while maintaining their Canadian dollar income. They would have gained market share at the expense of competing industries in other countries. Unemployment would have been less. Unions would have seen the experience as further evidence of the fact that they need not be flexible in their demands for wages and job guarantees.

But earlier I already noted how the depreciation of the currency disequilibrates other industries and causes lower real incomes. More important is the fact that the economy retains labor and resources in the defense industry, which suffers from a permanent global reduction in demand. New, modern industries are deterred from moving into the country because there is no pool of unemployed labor willing and able to retrain. By keeping resources in the declining industry, overall productivity and living standards are lowered.

In a recent article Eichengreen (2000) has shifted his emphasis from the analysis of historic events shaped by the existing currency regime to questions about the ability of fixed exchange rates to bring about greater labor market flexibility. He notes that during the 1990s Argentina made all of its markets more competitive. Its adoption of a fixed exchange rate through a currency board represents a capstone for these reforms, and he is optimistic that its economy will be able to deal efficiently with external shocks. On the other hand he notes that such market reforms have not taken place in Ecuador, which also has indicated its determination to adopt a currency board. The important empirical question is whether such a commitment to a fixed exchange rate can bring about the needed market reforms or whether the present rigidities lead to economic and social turmoil.

I agree with Eichengreen's diagnosis of the issues. However, I am confident about Argentina's and Ecuador's experiments with fixed exchange rates because of indications that the EMU has the desired effects. There have been no disequilibria in any of the members' labor market. The *Economist* (2000, April 29 and June 10) published a series of reports the contents of which are summarized by the headline of the cover: "Europe Limbers Up." The main message of the articles is that the monetary union has already imposed greater flexibility on European economies and labor markets.

In sum, the preceding analysis implies that the use of flexible exchange rates to absorb external shocks is costly. It also suggests that the labor market flexibility needed to deal with such shocks is endogenous to currency regimes. I conclude, therefore, that the loss of flexible exchange rate and monetary sovereignty does not lead to macroeconomic costs of higher unemployment and adjustment costs. To the contrary, it induces greater labor market flexibility and makes adjustment to shocks more efficient. This conclusion has an important implication for the traditional theory of OCA. A country considering membership in a currency area does not have to consider microeconomic benefits and macroeconomic costs. Such a membership brings only benefits in both the micro and macro areas.

◤ Cultural Sovereignty and Political Independence

Many Canadians will oppose a North American monetary union in the expectation that it will interfere with national cultural sovereignty and that it represents a further step in a process that will ultimately lead to the political absorption of Canada by the United States.[9] Cultural and political nationalists have opposed the Canada-U.S. agreement and NAFTA on these grounds. Their fears have not been realized. Free trade has not brought the predicted loss of Canada's freedom to have an independent foreign policy, a wide range of cultural policies, and a uniquely Canadian program of medical and social insurance.[10]

Canada's foreign policy under free trade has been as independent as it ever was. Lloyd Axworthy, the minister of foreign affairs, had his Moosehead beer and Cuban cigar during a 1999 chat with Fidel Castro in Cuba, in spite of strong opposition by the U.S. government. Prime Minister Chretien advocated a revision of NATO's nuclear policies without regard for U.S. government views on the subject. Sheila Copps, the minister for Cultural Affairs, continued to advance policies in support of Canadian cultural industries. Canada's Medicare system has not been hijacked by U.S. business and is in as much trouble as it was before free trade. Canadian provinces prohibit the export of bottled water. Supply management for the dairy and other agricultural industries continues to thrive and make some farmers into millionaires.

The basic fact is that the introduction of the amero will do nothing to the existing national border and the ability of Canadian governments to pursue nationalistic foreign and cultural policies to get themselves reelected.

▚ *The Interests of the United States*

The benefits and costs to the United States from a North American monetary union in principle are the same as those of Canada just discussed. However, since the U.S. economy is very large, the benefits in terms of greater price stability, incentives for adjustment, lower interest rates, and other factors are much less than they are for Canada and Mexico. United States economic performance in these indicators will improve somewhat if there is a monetary union with Canada alone. It will increase more if Mexico will join that union and even more if countries in the Caribbean and Central America join.

One of the main reasons the United States should be interested in a North American monetary union is that the development of the euro zone diminishes the position, power, and usefulness of the U.S. dollar in international portfolios and transactions and as a unit of account. Thus, table 18.1 shows that the 11 countries that presently make up the euro zone have a population greater than that of the United States and a national income slightly smaller.

However, there are strong indications that the euro zone will soon be enlarged as Group 1 countries join. There is also a strong possibility that

Table 18.1
Comparing Actual and Potential Euro- and Amero-Zones

	GDP	Population		GDP	Population
Euro 11	6,890	290	USA	7340	265
Group 1	1,693	83	Canada	579	30
Euro 11 + Group 1	8,583	373	USA + Canada	7919	295
Group 2	239	60	Mexico	335	93
Super Euro	8,822	433	Amero N. America	8254	388

Notes: GDP is for 1996 in billions of US dollars at market exchange rates. Population is in millions in 1996.

Group 1 countries: UK, Sweden, Denmark, Greece (in European Union but not Monetary Union)

Group 2 countries: Poland, Hungary, Czech Republic, Estonia (applied for European Union membership)

Source: *World Devleopment Indicators*, CD-ROM, Washington: World Bank.

the Group 2 countries in central Europe will join the euro zone if and when their promised accession to the EMU is approved. Table 18.1 shows that the size of national income and population in what I call the super-euro zone will be considerably greater than those of the United States. It also shows that a North American monetary union that includes Canada, the United States, and Mexico will nearly equal in size the super-euro zone.

The comparisons of the size of the economic unions made in table 18.1 are important for the United States because they reveal a real threat to the current status and power of the U.S. dollar and the benefits U.S. citizens derive from it. The use of dollars in the reserve portfolios of the central banks of all countries will shrink as they diversify into holding euros as well as dollars. In Europe, U.S. dollar holdings will shrink even more as countries pool and reduce their reserves in the hands of the European Central Bank. The U.S. dollar serves as the unit of account in many international financial transactions, including the issuance of private and government bonds. It also is used to establish crosscurrencies of smaller nations. In international tourism and business U.S. dollar notes and travelers' checks are used widely. The underground economies of many countries rely heavily on the use of U.S. dollar notes.

All of these uses of the U.S. dollar provide benefits to the U.S. economy. The reserves held by central banks abroad allow the financing of U.S. trade deficits or the purchase of equities and real assets in foreign countries. The use of dollar notes and travelers' checks generates substantial seigniorage for the government and private U.S. firms.[11] Investment banking in dollars provides U.S. firms with a competitive edge. American nationalists appreciate the symbolism of a "powerful" and widely used U.S. dollar.

The euro threatens these benefits, though it is difficult to know how big the losses will be. Nevertheless, the United States should consider that the creation of a North American monetary union will reduce the size of these losses.

The Prosperity of Neighbors

The United States has a great stake in the prosperity of its neighbors to the north and south. Such prosperity increases the opportunity to trade and to enjoy the real income gains it brings. Greater prosperity in Mexico also will increase political stability and, most important, will reduce the incentives for illegal migration to the United States through the porous southern border.

Mundell opposes the creation of a North American monetary union on the grounds that it threatens the current prestige and uses of the U.S. dollar. He argues that these characteristics were acquired through many years of economic leadership and stability, that the U.S. dollar's status is a national asset, provides useful services to the rest of the world, and therefore should not be endangered. I disagree with Mundell's judgment on this issue because I do not understand how the proposed arrangements for the union would endanger the current prestige and uses of the U.S. dollar. Monetary policy in the union would continue to be made through an unchanged system in which the United States would always have the majority of votes. If anything, the amero would be stronger and more widely used than the U.S. dollar, and Americans, along with Canadians and Mexicans, would gain correspondingly.

◤ Miscellaneous Issues

The proposal for the creation of a North American monetary union raises a number of important issues that I cannot develop fully here because of space limitations. Therefore, the following short summaries must suffice; readers interested in more details may wish to turn to Grubel (1999).

Why Not Fixed Rates, a Currency Board, or Dollarization?

Most of the benefits from a North American currency union noted earlier could be achieved by some alternative currency arrangements that have been discussed widely in recent years. The advantages and disadvantages of these arrangements are as follows. Canada and Mexico could permanently fix their exchange rates to the U.S. dollar by appropriate monetary policies and exchange market intervention. Such policies would be simple to carry out, but they bring great risks. History has shown that periodically economic shocks and political crises raise doubt about the government's ability to maintain the fixed rate. Speculative expectations are one-sided, and capital flight has no downside risk. The resultant massive sales of the suspect currency cannot be offset by interest rate changes and exchange market intervention, and eventually devaluation takes place. The economic turmoil accompanying such events is very costly.

Currency boards establish a firm link between a country's money supply and interest rates to the dollar or another currency like the deutsche mark.[12] They can be adopted unilaterally. However, currency boards still retain national central banks and currencies. As a result, under extreme economic distress caused by other factors, speculators can take positions against the domestic currency. Their withdrawal of possibly massive funds drives domestic interest rates to intolerably high levels and severely tests the political resolve of the government. Risk premiums on domestic currency obligations remain. And the government forgoes the seigniorage gains from the issuance of its currency.

Official dollarization removes a country's central bank and currency.[13] It can be undertaken unilaterally and removes forever any risk of currency fluctuations and the accompanying risk premiums on interest rates. There are three disadvantages of dollarization. First, the circulation of U.S. dollar notes and coins, with all of their nationalist symbols, may not be acceptable to nationalists in large countries with proud histories like Mexico and Canada. Second, the dollarized country loses the seigniorage, and finally, it has no vote or advice on the determination of monetary policy and the interest rate. All of these disadvantages are particularly large if the dollarized country is geographically and culturally as far removed from the United States as is Argentina or Ecuador.

Accountability and Dispute Settlement

The basic independence of the North American Central Bank postulated earlier and deemed essential to the achievement of the goals of monetary union raises an important problem of accountability. Accountability will become an issue if and when the monetary authority engages in policies that are seen widely to involve economic and social costs and that cannot be remedied by the intervention of democratic legislatures.[14]

This issue surrounds all international organizations, including the World Trade Organization (WTO), the IMF, and UN agencies, and it has been dealt with by allowing countries to opt out. This is done through well-defined escape clauses built into the original agreements to create the institutions. I am certain that such escape clauses will also constrain the freedom of the proposed North American Central Bank and assure that there exists some ultimate measure of democratic accountability.

It is also possible that member countries will feel disadvantaged by certain operations of the proposed monetary authorities or that countries will have disagreements over the legality of certain domestic policies affecting the functioning of the monetary system. Undoubtedly, the proposed

North American Central Bank will have in its charter a dispute resolution mechanism, modeled after that of other international organizations like the WTO and IMF.

Lender of Last Resort, Clearing Mechanisms, and Deposit Insurance

Liquidity crises in the monetary union will be dealt with by the injection of liquidity by the North American Central Bank. Such liquidity operations by national central banks in recent decades have been required very rarely. When they were needed, financial costs were minimal because once a crisis of confidence has passed, liquid loans are repaid quickly. If there are costs, they can be allocated among member countries according to a formula that reflects their relative economic importance.

Clearing mechanisms for bank balances can remain the primary responsibility of national organizations, and international links presently in operation among central banks and financial institutions like the Visa system can be expanded to keep up with growing volumes.

The regulation of financial institutions can also remain a national responsibility, since the costs of failure will also fall on national deposit insurance systems for banks and the equivalent private but publicly regulated cooperative mechanisms for insurance companies and securities dealers. The looser such national regulatory systems, the higher will be the rate of failure and the premiums needed to keep the systems operative. Competition among the national systems will cause them to become efficient and to converge. Financial institutions from one member country operating in another will have to adhere to the regulations of the country in which they do business. Regulations will have to be adopted to prevent bankruptcies in one country from affecting owned subsidiaries in other countries and thus triggering insurance provisions based on a different regulatory regime. These regulations can be modeled after those existing in international financial centers like London.

Why Not a World Monetary Union?

If the preceding analysis of the merit of the European and North American monetary unions is correct, it is possible to turn Mundell's rhetorical question on its head. If fixed exchange rates are so good for individual countries, why is this not for all? Why is it not optimal to have only one world currency? Mundell has dealt with these questions implicitly by his consistent recommendation of a world gold or commodity standard. As a compromise or intermediate step he recommended in the *Wall Street Journal* (2000) that the three major industrial regions of the world, the European Community, the United States, and Japan, adopt a formal cooperative system for fixing exchange rates among themselves.

My own views are that a world currency is a long-run goal but in the shorter run regional monetary unions are a compromise that has two important benefits. First, it unites countries with similar cultures, political traditions, and incomes. These affinities will make it easier to reach agreement on difficult issues requiring trust and compromise. Second, there is merit in having competition among regional monetary unions. Innovative policies adopted by some will be shown to be good or bad because of the relative performance of those that do not adopt them. Good innovations will thus be adopted universally, and bad ones will be discarded. As Hayek noted, there are no substitutes for competition as a process for discovery of successful innovations in markets and, by extension, in economic policies.

◣ The Politics of Monetary Union

Public choice theory has alerted economists to the fact that good economic proposals require support from the general public or interest groups to get legislatures to adopt them. Public interest in a monetary union is quite strong. After some publications proposing such a policy, the media reported on it, and my colleagues Courchene and Harris and I defended our ideas on radio talk shows and before live audiences. My experience suggests that about one-third of Canadians support the idea, one-third oppose it, and the other third reserves judgment and wants to know more about the consequences.

The minister of finance and governor of the Bank of Canada[15] opposed the creation of a monetary union. Internal experts who still, for the most part, work with the traditional Keynesian models advised them. The article by John Murray in this book (chapter 18) is typical of the bureaucrats' point of view. Some politicians in Canada have begun to explore the public appeal of the proposal. In 1999, the Senate held hearings[16] and a group of members of parliament from three different parties asked the prime minister to form a committee of Parliament to study the subject. In 2000 the House of Commons Standing Committee on Finance discussed the issue with me and a number of other experts.

Hefeker (1997) concludes that the interest group of domestic producers is the most likely to take up the cause for monetary union. The reason is that industry likes exchange rate stability, which facilitates long-range planning and lowers the costs of doing business abroad. In addition, Canadian business should support monetary union because it promises to bring lower interest rates, for reasons discussed earlier.

Using Hefeker's argument, it is clear that the interest of the general public and industry in monetary union will not lead to a political movement if the Canadian dollar remains stable and avoids extreme highs and lows. However, significant lowering of the exchange rate in a short period will affect many Canadians' income and wealth directly, and they may be goaded into action. Ironically, a high value of the Canadian dollar will mobilize business and organized labor, since it lowers profitability and employment. Such events will raise public interest in the causes of exchange rate fluctuations and the reaching of new highs and lows.

The idea for a North American monetary union will receive the needed attention from the general public only if and when one or more political parties and their leaders adopt the policy as their own and make it an issue in a national election. Such a process will produce a broad public debate, and I am convinced that the arguments made in this chapter will lead to the appropriate support from voters.

◤ Concluding Comment

The postwar years saw the development of Keynesian economic theories and policies. The theories were based on the notion that market economies failed to deal automatically with the unemployment brought on by business cycles and economic shocks, pointing to the tragedy of the Great Depression of the 1930s as the outstanding example for this need. The failure of market economies was attributed primarily to rigidities in labor markets, especially the willingness of workers to accept lower nominal wages. The policies enacted to deal with these problems were inflation, spending deficits, and flexible exchange rates.

After several decades of inflation and deficits, it is now understood that they cause higher rather than lower unemployment. As a result, almost all industrial countries during the 1990s adopted price stability and balanced budgets as primary policy objectives. However, the same countries remain committed to flexible exchange rates to deal with labor market inflexibility as the main obstacle to prompt adjustment to economic disturbances.

I believe that this last remnant of Keynesianism will go the way of inflation and deficits. The experience of the EMU and countries like Argentina shows that labor market flexibility will increase as exchange rate adjustments are no longer available to absorb the consequences of rigidities. Canada and Mexico would be well advised to heed these lessons and take the leadership in demanding the creation of a North American monetary union.

◤ Notes

This is the revised version of a paper prepared for the symposium *Should Canada and the United States Adopt a Common Currency?* held on April 30, 1999, at Western Washington University in Bellingham, Washington. The revision has benefited from comments made by participants at the symposium, a note by Steve Globerman, and discussions at other academic meetings concerning the merit of fixed exchange rates.

1. For an excellent explanation of the economics and institutions of the European monetary system, see the articles in the *Economist* (1998).

2. This chapter draws heavily on Grubel (1999) and other publications in this field, spanning 30 years (Grubel, 1970, 1973, 1984, 1993). Recent articles covering the same material as this chapter and reaching much the same conclusions are Courchene (1999), Harris (1998), Courchene and Harris (1999a), and Beddoes (1999). To the best of my knowledge I was the first economist (Grubel, 1992) to propose the creation of monetary union for North America.

3. Gregg Haymes, who was my legislative assistant in Parliament, has suggested this name to me.

4. For Mundell's assessment of the way in which the discussion in the economics literature involved a misrepresentation of his views, see Mundell (1998).

5. In considering these savings, it is important to remember that monetary union eliminates these costs only on transaction among members of the union. Dealings with the rest of the world continue to absorb some resources. Similarly, a Canada-U.S. monetary union would not eliminate the need to maintain foreign exchange activities in the currencies of the rest of the world. However, with the creation of the euro, the need to deal in the many former European currencies will reduce costs as well.

6. The CRB index used here excludes energy, is produced by the Commodities Research Bureau of Chicago, and is used widely in empirical economic analysis. It is based on U.S. dollar prices, and I deflated it by the U.S. consumer price index. For ease of interpretation, the index is plotted as a two-year moving average. I also set the commodity prices equal to 1 in 1955, when the nominal and real exchange rate were also very close to 1. As a result it is possible to see readily the relative rates of decline of the two variables.

7. It is interesting to note that even U.S. monetary policy is not free from external constraints. During the Asian crisis in the 1990s U.S. interest rates were lowered to assist Asian countries' efforts to reduce capital outflows and keep their interest rates low.

8. An articulate representative of this view in Canada is Brenner (1999a, 1999b).

9. Readers interested in the arguments presented by nationalists can find them on the website of the organization headed by David Orchard called Citizens Concerned about Free Trade at www.davidorchard.com and web.idirect.com/~ccaft.

10. For an overview of the predictions made by nationalists and a study of the actual results, see Law and Mihlar (1998).

11. For an estimate of the seigniorage from the use of dollar notes in the underground economy, see Feige (1997). There has been speculation that this economy will favor euro notes because they will be issued in denominations of E200, which are more convenient than the $100 U.S. notes.

12. For an explanation of the nature of currency boards, see Hanke and Schuler (1994, 1996).

13. The economics and politics of dollarization are explained in Schuler (1999a, 1999b).

14. See Berman and McNamara (1999) for views held by political scientists who retain great faith in the ability of governments to fine-tune economies and the willingness of legislatures to act in the public interest.

15. For the governor's views see Thiessen (1999).

16. See Carr et al. (1999) for a transcript of the discussion.

► References

Bayoumi, Tamim, and Barry Eichengreen. (1994). Monetary and Exchange Rate Arrangements for NAFTA. *Journal of Development Economics, 43,* 125–65.

Beddoes, Zanny Minton. (1999). From EMU to AMU? The Case for Regional Currencies. *Foreign Affairs,* July/August, 8–13.

Belke, Ansgar, and Daniel Gros. (1999). Estimating the Costs and Benefits of EMU: The Impact of External Shocks on Labour Markets. *Weltwirtschaftliches Archiv, 145*(1), 1–47.

Berman, Sheri, and Kathleen R. NcNamara. (1999). Bank of Democracy: Why Central Banks Need Public Oversight. *Foreign Affairs,* March/April, 2–8.

Brenner, Reuven. (1999a). Dollar Debate Is Off Track. *Financial Post,* June 26, D5.

Brenner, Reuven. (1999b). The Trouble with the Euro. *Financial Post,* June 15, C7.

Carr, Jack, Thomas Courchenes, John Crow, Herbert Grubel, and Bernard Wolf. (1999). Round Table on a North American Currency. *Canadian Parliamentary Review, 22*(2), 5–13.

Clinton, Kevin. (1998). *Bank of Canada Review,* Spring, 17–38.

Commission of the European Communities. (1990). *European Economy: One Market, One Money.* (Known as the Delors Commission Report). Brussels: Commission of the European Communities.

Courchene, Thomas J. (1999). Towards a North American Currency: An Optimal Currency Area Analysis. In *Room to Manoeuver? Globalization and Policy Convergence.* (Bell Canada Papers on Economic and Public Policy, Vol. 6). Kingston, Ontario: John Deutsch Institute, Queen's University.

Courchene, Thomas J., and Richard G. Harris. (1999a, June). From Fixing to Monetary Union: Options for North American Currency Integration. (C. D. Howe Commentary). Toronto: C. D. Howe Institute.

Delors Commission Report: see Commission of the European Communities (1990).

Economist. (2000, June 10). Lurking Behind the Continuing Fall in Europe's Unemployment Rate Are Some Surprisingly Radical Changes to the Nature of the Job Market.

Economist. (2000, April 29). Change at Last, in the Continent's Economies.

Economist, Euro-Briefs. Oct. 17, 1998, p. 81; Oct. 24, 1998, p. 85; Oct. 31, 1998, p. 85; Nov. 7, 1998, p. 83; Nov. 14, 1998, p. 89; Nov. 21, 1998, p. 71; Nov. 28, 1998, p. 83; Dec. 5, 1998, p. 97.

Eichengreen, Barry. (1992). Is Europe an Optimum Currency Area? In Borner, Sylvio and Herbert Grubel (Eds.), *The European Community after 1992.* London: Macmillan.

Eichengreen, Barry. (2000, May). Dollarization and Sense: More than the Big Mac, Coca Cola, or Levi. *Strategy and Business.* Available online at www.strategy-business.com.

Feige, Edward. (1997). Revised Estimates of the Underground Economy: Implications of U.S. Currency Held Abroad. In Owen Lippert and Michael Walker (Eds.), *The Underground Economy: Global Evidence of its Size and Impact* (pp. 151–208). Vancouver, BC: Fraser Institute.

Friedman, Milton. (1953). The Case for Flexible Exchange Rates. In *Essays in Positive Economics* (pp. 157–203). Chicago: University of Chicago Press.

Grubel, Herbert. (1970). The Theory of Optimum Currency Areas. *Canadian Journal of Economics, 318*(24).

Grubel, Herbert. (1973). A Theory of Optimum Regional Associations. In Harry G. Johnson and Alexander Swoboda (Eds.), *The Economics of Common Currencies* (pp. 99–113). London: Allen and Unwin.

Grubel, Herbert. (1984). *The International Monetary System: Efficiency and Practical Alternatives* (4th ed.). Middlesex, U.K.: Penguin Books.

Grubel, Herbert. (1990). Some Thoughts on the Future of the European Monetary Union: Comments on a Paper by Niels Thygesen. In Herbert Giersch (Ed.), *The Consequences of European Unification 199.* Tübingen: Mohr.

Grubel, Herbert. (1992, May 19–22). A Common Currency for North America. Paper presented at the conference Liberating the Hemisphere: Free Trade and Beyond in Mexico City, sponsored by the Cato Institute of Washington in conjunction with the Centro de Investigaciones Sobre la Libre Empresea and the Instituto Cultural Ludwig von Mises.

Grubel, Herbert. (1993, April 30). Looking Ahead: A Common Currency for North America. Paper presented at a conference NAFTA: Issues and Assessment, Cormier Center of International Economics, Bishops University, Lennoxville, Quebec.

Grubel, Herbert. (1999). *The Case for the Amero: The Economics and Politics of a North American Monetary Union.* (Critical Issues Bulletin). Vancouver, BC: Fraser Institute.

Hanke, Steven H., and K. Schuler. (1994). *Currency Boards for Developing Countries: A Handbook.* San Francisco: ICS Press.

Hanke, Steven H., and K. Schuler. (1996). Monetary Systems and Inflation in Developing Countries. In James A. Dorn and Roberto Salinas-Leon (Eds.), *Money and Markets in the Americas: New Challenges for Hemispheric Integration* (pp. 235–60). Vancouver, BC: Fraser Institute.

Harris, Richard G. (1998, November). Fix the Loonie by Fixing the Exchange Rate. *National Post.*

Harris, Richard G., with David Cox. (1983). *Trade, Industrial Policy and Canadian Manufacturing.* Toronto: Ontario Economic Council.

Hayek, Friedrich A. (1937). *Monetary Nationalism and International Stability.* London: Longmans Green.

Hefeker, Carsten. (1997). *Interest Groups and Monetary Integration: The Political Economy of Exchange Rate Choice.* Boulder, Colo.: Westview Press.

Law, Marc T., and Fazil Mihlar. (1998). *Debunking the Myths: A Review of the Canada-U.S. Free Trade Agreement and the North American Free Trade Agreement.* (Public Policy Sources 11). Vancouver, BC: Fraser Institute.

McKinnon, Ronald. (1963). Optimum Currency Areas. *American Economic Review, 53,* 717–25.

Mundell, Robert. (1961). A Theory of Optimum Currency Areas. *American Economic Review, 51*(4), 657–65.

Mundell, Robert. (1998, March 24–April 30). The Case for the Euro—I. The Case for the Euro—II. Making the Euro Work. *Wall Street Journal.*

Murray, John. (1999, April 30). Why Canada Needs a Flexible Exchange Rate. *The North American Journal of Economics and Finance, 11*(1), 41–60.

Schuler, Kurt. (1999a, July), Basics of Dollarization. (U.S. Joint Economic Committee Staff Report). Washington, D.C.: Office of the Chairman, U.S. Senator Connie Mack.

Schuler, Kurt. (1999b, April). *Encouraging Official Dollarization in Emerging Markets.*

(U.S. Joint Economic Committee Staff Report). Washington, D.C: Office of the Chairman, U.S. Senator Connie Mack.

Swoboda, Alexander. (1991). *The Road to European Monetary Union.* Washington, D.C.: Per Jacobsson Foundation Lectures.

Thiessen, Gordon. (1999, January 20). The Euro: Its Economic Implications and Its Lessons for Canada. Remarks to the Canadian Club of Ottawa. Reprinted in *Bank of Canada Review,* Winter, 117–23.

19 John D. Murray

Why Canada Needs a Flexible Exchange Rate

Canada has operated under a flexible exchange rate for all but 10 of the last 50 years. This makes us very unusual; indeed, no other country during the postwar period has been as devoted to the flexible exchange rate system. Most countries have preferred to tie their currencies to that of another trading partner and to operate under some form of fixed exchange rate arrangement.

This global predisposition toward a fixed exchange rate is understandable. Any movement in the exchange rate, whether up or down, usually has political repercussions. Some important constituent will almost invariably be made unhappy. From a businessperson's perspective, it is also a mixed blessing. If the exchange rate appreciates, exporters will complain about their lost competitiveness in international markets. If the exchange rate depreciates, importers will complain about their lost competitiveness in domestic markets (and consumers will complain about higher prices). For the public at large, the exchange rate is often a symbol of national pride, a sort of international report card. Exchange rate depreciations from the public's perspective are invariably bad—a sign of national inferiority. Given these harsh political realities, why would any country risk potential embarrassment by choosing a flexible exchange rate?

One of the few friends that the flexible exchange rate has had during the past 50 years has been the academic economist. This more sympathetic regard has not been shared by all members of the profession, however; nor has it remained constant over time. The painful experience of the Great Depression convinced many economists that flexible exchange rates were inherently unstable. The competitive depreciations and "beggar-thy-neighbor" trade policies that characterized this period were blamed for much of the chaos in the world economy. Subsequent disappointment with the system of pegged exchange rates that was established after World War II, however, soon caused them to reconsider the virtues of a more flexible exchange rate regime. In the early 1970s, the Bretton Woods system finally collapsed, and the major industrial powers once again found themselves operating under a de facto float. Some countries, such as Canada, embraced the new reality with greater enthusiasm than did others and were wary of any attempts to resurrect the old fixed exchange rate system or create a new one.

The performance of international financial markets since the collapse of the Bretton Woods system has been mixed but, on balance, supportive of the more flexible arrangements that have existed among the major industrial economies. Repeated crises in Latin America during the 1980s—and more recent difficulties in emerging countries like Mexico, Korea, Russia, and Brazil—have been useful reminders of the problems associated with more rigid currency arrangements.

Given this disappointing experience with fixed exchange rates, the renewed interest that some Canadians have shown in a common currency with the United States might seem surprising. It can probably be credited to three factors. The first concerns Europe and the interest surrounding the introduction of the euro in January 1999. If Europeans can have a common currency, Canadians asked, why can't we? The second is linked to the record lows that the Canadian dollar reached in 1998 in response to the Asian crisis and the dramatic decline in world commodity prices. Many Canadians believe that a fixed exchange rate could have prevented the depreciation and the loss in income associated with Canada's "northern peso." The third is the official interest shown by countries such as Argentina and Mexico in establishing a common currency in the Americas. Do they know something that we don't? Is there a risk that Canada will be left behind?[1,2]

The purpose of this article is to explore these issues and to reexamine the case for a flexible exchange rate in Canada. One of the fundamental lessons of the OCA literature is that no single currency arrangement is likely to be best for all countries at all times. Conditions change, and so should the currency arrangements under which a country operates. Is Canada at such a turning point?

▶ *Advantages of a Flexible Exchange Rate*

Flexible exchange rates provide a country with two principal advantages. The first is monetary policy independence. In a world where capital is completely mobile and free to move across international borders, it is impossible to have both a fixed exchange rate and an independent monetary policy. Policymakers must choose between maintaining a stable exchange rate and pursuing domestic monetary policy objectives such as price stability. The two can seldom coexist for a sustained period of time. Flexible exchange rates are the only way of preserving monetary policy autonomy.

The second advantage is the automatic buffer or cushion that flexible exchange rates can provide against economic shocks. Though this protection is seldom complete, movements in the nominal exchange rate can work to offset some of the effects of a temporary shock and facilitate the transition to a new steady state if the shock proves to be permanent.

Some Important Conditions

Different Monetary Policy Objectives and Policymaking Ability

The desirability and effectiveness of the exchange rate adjustment mechanism will depend on several factors. These include the monetary policy objectives of the country, the ability of the domestic monetary policy authority to attain these objectives, and the underlying structure of the economy. If the prospective partner in a fixed exchange rate system shares the same monetary policy objectives as the home country and has shown the same skill in the conduct of monetary policy, the policy independence allowed under flexible exchange rates will be largely irrelevant—except for political considerations and the sense of sovereignty that it might convey. If the prospective partner has a history of superior policy performance, and the citizens of the home country think that the performance of their own officials is unlikely to improve, the lack of independence associated with a fixed exchange rate system might be viewed as an important advantage.

Institutional and Structural Differences

The institutional and structural characteristics of a country are also likely to play a critical role in the decision to fix or float the exchange rate. If two countries have similar economic structures and are subject to the same external shocks, not much will be gained by having separate and floating currencies. Both economies will need to respond to the shocks in a similar manner, and their currencies will presumably move more or less in tandem. Little would be lost, therefore, in terms of insulation or policy effectiveness if their currencies were linked.

Nominal Wage-Price Stickiness and Immobile Factors of Production

Different policy objectives, different economic structures, susceptibility to different shocks, and a (presumed) home country advantage in the conduct of monetary policy are all factors that favor the adoption of a flexible exchange rate. They are not sufficient, however, to guarantee that it will dominate other fixed exchange rate alternatives. Certain other conditions must also be satisfied. The first of these is that domestic prices and wages must show some stickiness or downward rigidity. If this is not the case, and domestic prices and wages are relatively flexible, there is no need for a flexible exchange rate. The economy can adjust to any internal or external shock with little difficulty and, in the limit, always be at full employment. Therefore, a flexible exchange rate would offer no advantage in terms of facilitating the adjustment process. A similar situation would arise if factors of production, such as capital and labor, were perfectly mobile within (or across) countries. Resources could be effortlessly reallocated across regions and industries following a shock, reducing the need for domestic or external price adjustment. Regrettably for those proposing a return to the fixed exchange rate system, none of these conditions appears to be met in the real world.

Real Wage-Price Stickiness

Another necessary condition for flexible exchange rates to be both desirable and effective is that real prices and wages in the economy not be fixed or completely rigid. Flexible exchange rates help stabilize an economy by overcoming the stickiness that is assumed to exist in nominal prices and wages, thereby allowing real prices and wages to reequilibrate. If the latter cannot move for some reason, such as fixed real wage contracts, excessive union power, or other institutional rigidity, the extra degree of freedom provided by the flexible exchange rate will not be effective in restoring equilibrium.

A Shortage of Policy Tools

In an ideal world, flexible exchange rates can be made redundant or unhelpful if the country already has a surfeit of macro instruments at its disposal and does not require any additional tools to help stabilize the economy. An example of this might be a system of generous fiscal transfers that could be activated whenever a region or industry was hit by an external shock. Industries faced with a temporary downturn in prices or world demand could receive government subsidies to continue their operations; workers who found themselves out of a job could receive special social assistance until conditions improved. It is possible that private capital markets might also perform this function, lending money to industries and individuals in bad times and being repaid in good times. The additional room to maneuver provided by flexible exchange rates would once again be unnecessary.[3]

In the real world, of course, policymakers seldom find themselves with too many policy levers. Existing tools are typically overcommitted, and any additional help that policymakers can receive is readily accepted. Discretionary fiscal measures often lack the necessary speed and focus to serve as effective stabilization tools and are difficult to reverse once the shock has passed. Additional problems arise if the shock is permanent and the fiscal expenditures inhibit necessary long-run economic adjustments. There is also a risk that trading partners might complain about the subsidies offered to certain industries under these schemes and retaliate with countervailing duties and other antidumping measures. In short, discretionary fiscal measures and other government actions are unlikely to be a perfect substitute for flexible exchange rates. Experience with them in Canada and elsewhere has not been very encouraging.[4]

Assuming that all the previous conditions have been satisfied, and a credible case can be made for a flexible exchange rate on macroeconomic grounds, what other benefits might a country such as Canada have to forgo by choosing this alternative? What extra costs might it have to bear by having a flexible exchange rate rather than a fixed exchange rate? Casual observation suggests that a fixed exchange rate must offer some important advantages; otherwise, it would not be so popular. Of the 181 countries that are currently members of the IMF, fewer than 20 can be said to operate under a truly flexible exchange rate. Indeed, logic suggests that, if there were not some offsetting disadvantages, every individual would find it in his or her interest to issue his or her own currency and to operate under a flexible exchange rate. Since we do not observe this phenomenon in everyday life, there must be a point at which the microeconomic advantages of a fixed currency arrangement (in this case a common currency) exceed the macroeconomic benefits of increased flexibility.

◣ *Advantages of a Fixed Exchange Rate*

The advantages of a fixed exchange rate, as suggested earlier, are largely microeconomic. Some of them are evident and easily measured, such as the reduced transactions costs associated with converting and hedging currencies. Others are less obvious but potentially more important. They are linked to the improved efficiency and increased welfare that can result from reduced uncertainty and better economic decision making. In this regard, they are much like the advantages that central banks often cite in support of domestic price stability.

By extending the domain over which a given currency operates, fixed exchange rates can improve the operation of the price system and enhance the usefulness of money as a medium of exchange, unit of account, and store of value. Fixed exchange rates facilitate price comparisons across currencies, thereby promoting increased competition and a more efficient allocation of resources. They also tend to reduce the cost of cross-border transactions and can eliminate (or at least reduce) the risk of holding assets denominated in different currencies.

Were it not for one important caveat, therefore, it would clearly be optimal for everyone in the world to operate under a fixed exchange rate system and, in the limit, to use the same currency. (Fixed exchange rates alone are not sufficient to maximize the microeconomic benefits, since they would still involve converting one currency into another for transactions purposes and their parity values could always be changed, thereby introducing some exchange rate uncertainty.)

The one complication that has been discussed earlier is the difficulty that an economy might experience trying to reequilibrate after a macroeconomic shock. If an economy is subject to serious and frequent macroeconomic disturbances, and the nominal exchange rate is not allowed to adjust to help offset them, the resulting economic pressures are typically shifted onto other variables. Since prices and wages in most real-world economies are relatively sticky, and factors of production have difficulty moving between countries, the result is often greater variability in output and employment than would have been the case if the exchange rate had been allowed to move. The exchange rate uncertainty and destabilizing economic forces that one had hoped to eliminate by fixing the currency may simply manifest themselves elsewhere—in a less obvious but potentially more damaging form.

▶ *All Fixed Exchange Rates Are Not Alike*

Much of the previous discussion has implicitly assumed that all fixed exchange rate systems are alike. In reality, of course, they can take many different forms, ranging from softer, more pliant systems (such as adjustable pegs) to harder, more rigid systems (such as currency boards and common currencies). The practical differences between them can be significant.

Common currencies and currency boards involve a more serious commitment on the part of the government. This is their strength as well as their weakness. Because they are harder to unwind, they are also more credible. Uncertainty is thereby reduced and transactions costs are minimized. Unfortunately, this frequently implies a complete loss of monetary policy independence or, at best, a sharing of this responsibility with another sovereign state. This awkward political feature has proved difficult for many countries to accept, as has been the implied inability of the monetary authority to change exchange rate parities in response to serious shocks. There is a natural tension between a country's desire to maximize the benefits of a fixed exchange rate system via the adoption of a common currency or currency board and the need to preserve some degree of policy autonomy and self-determination.[5]

The Bretton Woods system, established after World War II, tried to effect a Solomon-type compromise to overcome this problem. Under the new system, countries were obliged to declare a parity value for each of their currencies in terms of gold and U.S. dollars. A narrow band was also established to either side of parity, so that currencies could move in response to minor and transient shocks. If the exchange rate pressures continued, however, and threatened to push a currency outside the bands, countries were obliged to resist them through active exchange market intervention and appropriate adjustments to their domestic policy settings. In the event of a serious and permanent shock that could not be accommodated through exchange market intervention or acceptable domestic policy adjustments, the country would be allowed to change the parity value of its currency.[6] The multilateral nature of this decision was designed to prevent capricious and self-interested actions that might destabilize the system. While some exchange rate uncertainty would still exist owing to these periodic devaluations, it was hoped that the risks and transactions costs associated with the Bretton Woods system would be relatively modest and that the resulting stability would promote world trade and development.

History has shown that, instead of combining the best features of the fixed and flexible exchange rate systems, the Bretton Woods system managed to deliver the worst of both worlds. The system was neither flexible enough to prevent periodic crises nor strong enough to prevent its own collapse. Necessary adjustments to exchange rate parities proved difficult to negotiate and were always delayed until it was too late. In the interim, countries were required to sacrifice their domestic economic objectives in the interest of short-run exchange rate stability. In the end, however, market forces inevitably prevailed and eventually triggered an exchange rate crisis. The continuous, and at times disquieting, movements of a flexible exchange rate system had simply been replaced by periods of artificial calm, punctuated every two or three years by a major currency collapse.

Experience since the end of the Bretton Woods system has only confirmed the view that an adjustable peg is the least sustainable of all exchange rate systems. Countries are forced to choose, therefore, between two extreme solutions—a completely free exchange rate system and a common currency (or its close cousin, a currency board). There would appear to be no viable middle ground.

◣ *What System Would Be Best for Canada?*

In many respects, Canada and the United States would seem to be well suited to a common currency. The two economies are highly integrated and share many important characteristics. They are in close geographic proximity; their citizens travel extensively between the two countries; and they share similar values, culture, and history. Exports account for 45 percent of Canada's GDP, and over 80 percent of its exports go to the United States. Indeed, as we are often reminded, most Canadian provinces have more trade with the United States than they do with one another. Few of the countries entering into the EMU in 1999 were as open as Canada or as dependent on any one trading partner. Surely, it is argued, two countries that are so inexorably bound, and growing ever more integrated, should be natural candidates for a common currency.

The gains to Canada from a common currency in terms of reduced transactions costs and the elimination of currency risk could be substantial. Conservative estimates of the savings, focusing only on the transactions costs that are incurred in the Canadian foreign exchange market, are approximately $3.0 billion annually. Discounted at a 4 percent real rate of interest, the implied present value of the foreign exchange savings alone would be $75.0 billion dollars, or roughly one-tenth of Canada's current GDP. (This

348 NORTH AMERICA

does not include any savings that might be realized in the form of lower
borrowing costs, improved economic efficiency, increased competition, and
better investment decisions.)[7] Are the benefits of monetary policy independence and increased macroeconomic stability worth the cost?

With regard to monetary policy independence, the evidence is at best
ambiguous (see fig. 19.1). The United States has enjoyed slightly better
inflation performance than Canada over the last 30 years, but by a very
small margin (a cumulative difference of 3 percent, or roughly 0.1 percent
per annum). Moreover, there is no guarantee that this superior performance
will continue. Unlike many of the countries that entered into the EMU,
Canada could not expect to trade on the reputation of a North American
"Bundesbank." Neither has Canada's inflation record been as disappointing
as that of Italy, Portugal, or Spain. In short, it is unlikely that a common
currency would ever be viewed as a necessary defense against bad domestic
monetary policy.[8]

While the inflation objectives of the monetary authorities in Canada
and the United States appear to be similar, only those of Canada have been
made explicit in the form of announced inflation targets. There is no equivalent and convincing commitment to price stability on the part of U.S.
authorities.[9] To the extent that enhanced accountability and transparency
improve monetary policy outcomes, one might expect superior inflation
performance in Canada in the future.

One thing is absolutely clear: Canadians would have very little say over
the conduct of monetary policy under a currency union with the United
States. If the United Kingdom were to join the EMU, it would be one of

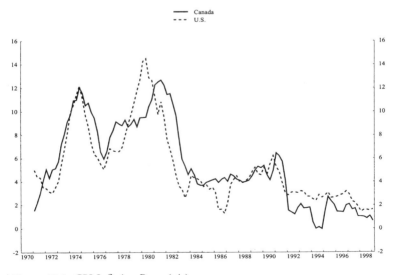

Figure 19.1. CPI Inflation Rates (y/y)

13 countries setting monetary policy, all with roughly equivalent voting power. In addition, the GDP weights of the major participants would not be as seriously unbalanced as those of Canada and the United States. It is unrealistic to think that Canadians would ever have anything more than a token voice in a Canada-U.S. currency union. Expanding the size of the currency block to include all of the Americas would improve the situation, but not by enough to counterbalance the importance of the world's largest economy. Whether the United States would see any advantage in such an arrangement, and be willing to cede any of its economic power, is another question. Whether Canadians would ever accept such a "colonial" relationship is also unclear.[10]

The strongest case for monetary policy independence and a flexible exchange rate, however, rests with the different structures of the Canadian and U.S. economies, not with the political forces that might be at play under a currency union. Despite the highly integrated nature of the two economies, empirical work suggests that important structural differences remain. Canada is more exposed to external shocks than the United States and often sees its terms of trade improve in response to a sudden increase in world commodity prices.[11] The United States, in contrast, typically experiences a deterioration in its terms of trade whenever there is such an increase.

Although Canada's terms of trade, taken on their own, tend to be relatively stable, they always move in the opposite direction to those of the United States in response to commodity price shocks (see the last two rows in table 19.1). As a result, movements in the relative terms of trade between Canada and the United States tend to be more exaggerated than movements in their individual or absolute terms of trade (see the first and third rows of table 19.1). They also move in different directions vis-à-vis other G-10

Table 19.1
Absolute and Relative Terms of Trade for Canada and the United States

	Canada	United States
Absolute terms of trade variability[a]	7.7	12.1
Absolute terms of trade correlation with G-10[b]	−0.85	0.63
Relative terms of trade variability[c]	17.5	9.1
Absolute terms of trade correlation with oil price	0.85	−0.89
Absolute terms of trade correlation with nonoil commodity price	0.87	−0.92

Note: From Roger (1991).

[a]Standard deviation of the terms of trade for each country.

[b]Calculated as the correlation against the trade-weighted average terms of trade of the other G-10 countries plus Switzerland.

[c]Terms of trade relative to a trade-weighted average of the other G-10 countries plus Switzerland.

countries. While the terms of trade for the United States are positively correlated with those of the G-10, the terms of trade for Canada display a large negative correlation.

Although Canada has become much less reliant on natural resources during the postwar period, commodities still account for more than 10 percent of its GDP (roughly the same percentage as in 1971) and 35 percent of its merchandise exports. These are not small numbers.

Other econometric research published over the last few years provides even more convincing evidence of the deep structural differences separating the two economies. Structural vector autoregressions (VARs) and variance decomposition techniques have been applied to Canadian and U.S. data by several outside academics, such as Bayoumi and Eichengreen (1994), as well as a number of economists within the Bank of Canada, such as DeSerres and Lalonde (1994).[12] Their results have shown that Canada and the United States are subject to significant asymmetric shocks. As a consequence, it is unlikely that they would form an optimum (or perhaps even viable) currency area. Interesting extensions of this work have applied the same VAR methodology to other regions and countries, in the expectation that their experiences might serve as useful benchmarks for the situation in Canada and the United States. These areas included Mexico, the major countries in Europe, and a number of different regions within Canada and the United States. The objective in each case was to see which of the regions or countries might form an OCA. The principal results are summarized here.

1. The structural shocks hitting Canada, Mexico, and the United States share very few common characteristics (see table 19.2). The common components in the VAR analyses conducted by Lalonde and St-Amant (1995) for the three North American economies seldom exceeded 10 percent. This suggests that the monetary authorities in each country need to respond to domestic and external shocks in a very different manner and that a flexible exchange should help the adjustment process.[13] They are not, therefore, obvious candidates for a common currency.

2. The structural shocks hitting the nine regions of the United States are all very similar. The common components reported by Lalonde and St-Amant for the nine regions comprising the United States were all quite large (varying between 50 and 99 percent). The sole exception is New England. Macroeconomic stability across the regions should not be significantly affected, therefore, by the fact that the regions are forced to operate under a common currency and under a common monetary policy directed by the Federal Reserve. The United States, in other words, is a natural currency area.[14]

3. The structural shocks hitting the six regions of Canada also share a strong common component with one another, but their contemporaneous correlation with U.S. shocks is very small (see table 19.3).

Table 19.2

Decomposition of the Structural Shocks Hitting Canada, Mexico, and Various Regions of the United States: Relative Contribution of Common Component (%)

Regions and countries	Demand shocks	Supply shocks	Monetary shocks
Mexico	6[a]	2[a]	0[a]
Canada	13	3[a]	5[a]
New England	56	0[a]	71
Middle Atlantic	86	59	97
Northeast Central	83	76	93
Northwest Central	85	71	94
South Atlantic	85	89	99
Southeast Central	95	89	96
Southwest Central	50	64	95
Northwest Pacific	66	62	80
Southwest Pacific	76	67	92

Note: From Lalonde and St-Amant (1995).

[a]Shocks that are not statistically related to the common component (5 percent significance level).

While the common components shared by the six regions in Canada are smaller than those reported for the nine regions in the United States, they are still much higher than the common components between any one of the Canadian regions and the U.S. economy taken as a whole. A common currency seems to be a viable arrangement for Canada, therefore, even if the relationships linking the different regions are not as strong as those for the United States.

4. The structural shocks hitting many of the countries participating in the EMU have smaller common components than the six regions in Canada (see table 19.4). Many of the countries participating in the EMU, particularly those on the periphery, bear a far weaker relationship with France, Germany, and Italy than do the outlining regions of Canada with Ontario and Quebec. This would suggest that macroeconomic stabilization and the conduct of monetary policy within the EMU may prove difficult. It is important to note, however, that they have larger common components with one another than Canada does with the United States and therefore represent a more viable currency area than would Canada and the United States.

The main message that one should take from all of this is that the present currency arrangements in Canada and the United States make a great deal of sense, and that attempts to create a currency union similar to the EMU might pose a serious problem.

Robert Mundell, the originator of the OCA concept, together with

Table 19.3
Decomposition of Structural Shocks in Canada

Supply shocks: Relative contribution of three components (%)			
Regions and countries	Exogenous American shocks	Common Canadian shocks	Specific shocks
Atlantic	0[a]	49	50
Quebec	2[a]	56	42
Ontario	8	48	43
Prairies	1[a]	16	82
Alberta	0[a]	23	76
British Columbia	1[a]	20	78

Real demand shocks: Relative contribution of three components (%)			
Regions and countries	Exogenous American shocks	Common Canadian shocks	Specific shocks
Atlantic	2[a]	41	56
Quebec	1[a]	11	88
Ontario	5	10	84
Prairies	0[a]	61	38
Alberta	4	57	39
British Columbia	0[a]	1	98

Monetary shocks: Relative contribution of three components (%)			
Regions and countries	Exogenous American shocks	Common Canadian shocks	Specific shocks
Atlantic	4	76	20
Quebec	5	83	11
Ontario	6	81	12
Prairies	4	81	14
Alberta	3[a]	51	46
British Columbia	8	83	8

[a]Shocks that are not statistically related to the common component (5 percent significance level).

various other proponents of a currency union, has observed that the current political boundaries between Canada and the United States bear little resemblance to those that economists might draw if they were asked to construct an OCA in North America. The dividing line between the two currency areas would in all likelihood run north-south, as opposed to east-west, recognizing that the western provinces of Canada probably have more in common with their counterparts in the western United States than with their partners in the east. While this might be true, it is also largely irrel-

Table 19.4
Decomposition of Structural Shocks in Europe

Countries	Relative contribution of common components (%) Real demand shocks	Supply shocks
Germany	51	51
France	22	12
United Kingdom	13	18
Italy	5[a]	5[a]
Spain	12	25
Netherlands	26	13
Belgium	20	14
Switzerland	37	44
Austria	11	12
Sweden	4	1[a]
Norway	0[a]	0[a]
Portugal	28	5[a]
Greece	0[a]	7[a]

Source: Chamie, DeSerres, and Lalonde (1994).
[a]Shocks that are not statistically related to the common component (5 percent significance level).

evant. The political boundaries of the two countries are not likely to be redrawn in the near future (at least in the manner suggested earlier). The real issue, therefore, is whether the Canadian economy, taken as a whole, responds differently from the U.S. economy to common external shocks. The answer, based on the evidence presented earlier, appears to be yes.

◣ Some Potential Problems

Many of the economists who advocate a currency union with the United States do so not because of the microeconomic advantages that might be realized or because they disagree with the macroeconomic analysis presented earlier but because they believe that flexible exchange rates cannot be trusted. More specifically, they do not believe that flexible exchange rates help reequilibrate economies following a shock. They also claim that flexible exchange rates encourage bad behavior and undermine economic efficiency. The validity of these concerns is reviewed in the next section.

Concerns That Exchange Rate Movements Are Dominated by Destabilizing Speculation

Critics of flexible exchange rates often claim that they are subject to excessive volatility and rarely move in response to market fundamentals. Instead they are driven by destabilizing speculators, whose tremendous resources allow them to push currencies up or down in response to the latest rumors and market whim.

A different and more positive story, however, is suggested by the econometric evidence drawn from the experience of the Canadian dollar over the last 25 years. Using an equation that was first developed in the early 1990s, two Bank of Canada economists, Robert Amano and Simon van Norden (1993), have shown that it is possible to explain most of the long-run movements of the Can\$/U.S.\$ exchange rate with a simple error-correction model and three fundamental variables: the Canadian-U.S. inflation differential, the relative price of energy, and the relative price of nonenergy commodities. (A fourth variable, the difference between short-term interest rates in Canada and the United States, is added to the equation to help it track higher-frequency movements in the exchange rate.)

$$\Delta \ln (rpfx) = \alpha(\ln(rpfx)_{t-1} - \beta_0 - \beta_c \, comtot_{t-1} - \beta_e \, entot_{t-1}) + \gamma(rdiff)_{t-1}$$

where:
$rpfx$ = real bilateral exchange rate
$comtot$ = commodity terms of trade
$entot$ = energy terms of trade
$rdiff$ = Canada-U.S. short-term interest rate differential

Not only does the equation fit the data with surprising accuracy, it is also remarkably robust (see table 19.5).

A dynamic simulation, based on parameters estimated over the

Table 19.5
Real Bilateral Exchange Rate

Variable	Estimation period 1973Q2–86Q1	1973Q2–91Q4	1973Q2–94Q4	1973Q2–97Q2ç
α	−0.192	−0.149	−0.1497	−0.134
	(−3.10)[a]	(−3.67)	(−4.05)	(−4.14)
β_0	2.415	1.602	2.483	2.700
	(3.98)	(4.06)	(6.86)	(7.58)
β_c	−0.498	−0.384	−0.525	−0.561
	(−4.67)	(−5.22)	(−6.72)	(−6.99)
β_e	0.059	0.141	0.079	0.070
	(1.25)	(2.83)	(2.01)	(1.64)
^	−0.528	−0.470	−0.574	−0.570
	(−2.28)	(−2.75)	(−3.36)	(−3.77)
R^2	0.276	0.251	0.239	0.228
$D - W$	1.265	1.217	1.249	1.319

[a]t-statistic.

1973Q2–1997Q2 period and projected out to 1999Q1, is shown in figure 19.2. As the reader can see, all the major movements in the exchange rate appear to be driven by these few fundamental variables, not by destabilizing speculation. While there are periods—such as the present (1998Q3 to 1999Q1)—where the exchange rate seems to be over- or undervalued relative to its predicted value, these differences are seldom large and usually disappear after a short period of time. Additional research conducted at the Bank has shown that episodes of increased volatility in the exchange rate are often characterized by *stabilizing* speculative activity, which pushes the exchange rate back toward its equilibrium level and helps to stabilize the macroeconomy. Destabilizing noise trading tends to dominate the market during more tranquil periods and lends a sort of inertia momentum to the exchange rate. This in turn causes the exchange rate to gradually drift away from its fundamentals. At a certain point, however, the discrepancy between the actual and equilibrium rates becomes large enough that stabilizing traders enter the market and push the Canadian dollar back to where it should be (see Murray, van Norden, and Vigfusson, 1996). Authorities should be wary, therefore, of resisting exchange rate movements.

It is one thing to show that Canada experiences asymmetric shocks creating a potential role for a flexible exchange rate and that exchange rate movements appear to be driven by two or three fundamental variables. But do these movements actually help stabilize the economy? Figure 19.3 shows the response of the nominal exchange rate and domestic prices to a one-standard-deviation shock in aggregate demand. As the graph indicates, both the exchange rate and the price level have tended to rise (appreciate) in the

Figure 19.2. U.S.-Canada Exchange Rate

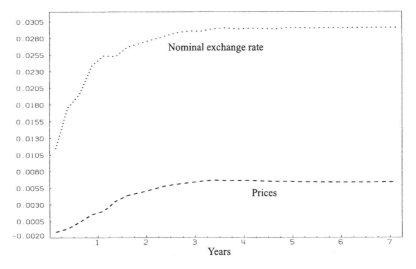

Figure 19.3. Response of Nominal Exchange Rate and Prices to a Real Demand Shock

wake of a demand shock. However, the response of the exchange rate has typically been much larger and faster than that of domestic prices, suggesting that it speeds the adjustment process. It would be costly, therefore, for Canada to move to a fixed exchange rate regime.

Concerns That Flexible Exchange Rates Lead to Loose Fiscal Policy

It is often argued that flexible exchange rates lead to loose fiscal policies—undisciplined governments can finance their spending simply by printing money and letting the exchange rate depreciate to preserve their country's international competitiveness. While the freedom provided by flexible exchange rates can easily be abused, empirical evidence concerning the assumed disciplinary effect of fixed exchange rates is not very strong. Casual inspection of the fiscal policies of several Latin American countries just prior to the debt crisis of the 1980s, or of certain European countries throughout most of the postwar period, does not suggest that fixed exchange rates have served as much of a fiscal deterrent. Italy and Belgium, for example, managed to accumulate two of the highest debt-to-GDP ratios in the industrialized world under a fixed exchange rate. It is also difficult to explain the recent improvement in Canada's fiscal position, if one believes that flexible exchange rates invariably lead to excessive spending. Binding governments in a currency union, as opposed to an adjustable peg arrangement, might provide more effective discipline. It is interesting to note, however, that the architects of EMU still found it necessary to impose additional fiscal constraints on their governments in the form of the Stability and Growth Pact.

Concerns That Flexible Exchange Rates Reduce World Trade and Investment

A third common criticism of flexible exchange rates is that their uncertain movements discourage world trade and investment activity. While the argument has a certain intuitive appeal, the theoretical and practical support for such a claim is also very weak. In theory, an increase in price variability has an ambiguous effect on economic behavior. As with many price changes, there is both an income and a substitution effect. Depending on an agent's utility function, therefore, an increase in price variability can lead to more or less of a risky activity being undertaken.

As a practical matter, the empirical evidence reported to date has been unable to uncover any significant or consistent relationship between the variability of exchange rates and the volume of world trade (see Côté, 1994). The evidence on investment activity is more limited but suggests a similar conclusion. The recent growth in world trade and investment flows certainly does not indicate that this has been a serious problem. In fact, some academics and policymakers have called for the introduction of Tobin taxes and other restrictive measures to limit international capital flows because they believe that there is too much investment activity—at least of a certain type.

Concerns That Flexible Exchange Rates Hurt Productivity

The latest, and potentially most serious, charge leveled at flexible exchange rates concerns their effect on productivity. Although the argument can take various forms, the most recent version starts with the presumption that Canadian firms, unlike their U.S. counterparts, are "satisficers" rather than profit maximizers and are content to earn just enough money to stay in business. Since flexible exchange rates automatically adjust to preserve international competitiveness, Canadian firms do not have to invest in the latest labor-saving technology or production techniques to realize their limited business objectives. Moreover, they have no incentive to get out of declining industries, such as natural resources, and into more profitable areas, such as computers. Canadians, as a result, have seen their standard of living decline, both in absolute terms and relative to the United States, and are likely to fall even further behind their southern neighbors unless they move to a common currency.

What the critics fail to realize is that exchange rate depreciations are not the cause of Canada's declining economic welfare but simply the symptom. Moreover, currency depreciations never offset all of the decline in world commodity prices or other external shock that the country might have experienced. As a consequence, capital and labor still have an incentive to move into other sectors, like manufacturing, which not only benefit from the depreciation but have experienced an increase in the relative price of the goods and services that they produce.[15] In short, all the relevant price signals are still operative and pushing the economy in the right direction.

Two other problems with the productivity argument are (1) the assumption that a common currency would suddenly force Canadian firms to become more efficient, and (2) the assumption that declining commodity prices necessarily imply declining profits. If Canadian firms are inherently lazy and undermotivated, a flexible exchange rate is the least of their concerns. Under these circumstances, a common currency is unlikely to have much curative effect; the problems would be more fundamental in nature. More important, it is a mistake to assume that the road to prosperity is paved with computers, and that natural resource industries are intrinsically unproductive and unprofitable. Indeed, the trend decline that we have witnessed in commodity prices over the past 25 years is largely a reflection of the sharp productivity increases that the resource industries in Canada and elsewhere have enjoyed during this period, not declining demand. Neither do declining prices necessarily denote declining profits. If they did, computers would be the last area that one would want to enter.

The biggest flaw in the productivity debate, however, is the presumption that productivity growth in Canada has fallen behind that of the United States. While earlier data painted a rather grim picture, more recent evidence suggests that Canadian performance has been roughly equal to that of the United States, and perhaps superior. This is especially true if one focuses on multifactor productivity, as opposed to labor productivity, and includes the entire business sector in the sample, as opposed to just the manufacturing sector. Even if one believed that Canadian productivity performance had been deficient, it is doubtful that the variability of the Canadian dollar would be the culprit. Deeper policy problems and institutional biases, such as the level and structure of taxes and onerous government regulations, would be more likely suspects.

More detailed analysis of Canada's economic performance at the two-digit industry level indicates that any slippage in Canada's productivity has been specific to two manufacturing industries—computers and electronic equipment. Even then, the story is more one of U.S. success than Canadian failure. These industries appear to have achieved remarkably high rates of productivity growth in the United States and account for a much larger share of manufacturing output in the United States than they do in Canada. (It is also worth noting that there is some question about the reliability of the hedonic price indices that the U.S. authorities use to calculate productivity and output in these sectors.) If a flexible exchange rate were the source of the productivity problem, it would be surprising if it affected only two industries and left all the other manufacturers in Canada unaffected.

McCallum (1998a, 1998b) has published some work showing that there is a high positive correlation between lagged movements in the Canadian dollar and changes in Canadian productivity relative to that of the United States. He is careful to note, however, that correlation does not imply causation, and that movements in both variables were likely driven by other, omitted variables. Granger-causality tests recently completed by David Dupuis and David Tessier at the Bank of Canada show that, once cyclical factors are controlled for, the causality runs from changes in productivity to changes in the exchange rate rather than the reverse.

◣ Looking Ahead

The evidence that I have reviewed so far tends to support Canada's decision to operate under a flexible exchange rate. Contrary to the fears expressed by many observers, the flexible exchange rate does not appear to have misbehaved or subverted Canada's economic performance. Indeed, it is hard to imagine how certain sectors of the economy would have coped with the Asian crisis and the dramatic decline in world commodity prices without a depreciating Canadian dollar. It is unlikely that Canada would have recorded the strong growth rates that it did in 1997 and 1998, and again in 2002, without this assistance.

Still, it must be admitted that the microeconomic benefits related to a common currency have not been as thoroughly investigated as those on the macro side. The bold experiment launched by the 12 countries participating in the EMU may have a great deal to teach us in this regard. Although it was initiated more for political reasons than for any expected economic benefits, its economic effects will still warrant close attention.

It is also possible that the Canadian economy will change in ways that make a common currency more attractive in the future. As Canada becomes more closely integrated with the U.S. economy, and the importance of trade continues to expand, the advantages of a common currency should also increase.[16] If prices and wages become more flexible, or labor begins to move more freely across national borders, the need for a flexible exchange rate will also decline. If the U.S. government continues to implement sound monetary policies and were to announce inflation targets consistent with our own, the case for an independent monetary policy would also be weakened.

Unfortunately, it is doubtful that many of these conditions will be met in the foreseeable future. In the meantime, we will have to closely monitor developments in Canada and elsewhere, and take comfort from the fact that a flexible exchange rate is at least a workable, if not optimal, policy option.

◣ Notes

1. See Courchene and Harris (1999) and Laidler (1999).
2. Interest in a common currency seems to take different forms in Argentina, Mexico, and Canada. Whereas Grubel (1999) and Courchene and Harris (1999) favor the

introduction of a new currency that would be used jointly by Canada, the United States, and any other partner in the currency union, proponents in Argentina and Mexico appear willing to adopt the U.S. dollar.

3. The low correlations observed between savings and investment rates within countries suggest that capital markets play an important stabilizing role in most domestic economies. The opposite tends to be observed between countries where, despite the much-vaunted globalization process, savings and investment rates still tend to be highly correlated. See Feldstein and Horioka (1980). Greater capital market integration between Canada and the United States would presumably reduce the costs of a monetary union. See Sorensen and Yosha (1998) and Antia, Djoudad, and St-Amant (1999).

4. A similar skeptical view on the usefulness of fiscal transfers as an adjustment mechanism is provided by Obstfeld and Peri (1998).

5. Laidler (1999) considers these and other related issues in greater detail and highlights the importance of accountability, as distinct from independence, in the conduct of monetary policy.

6. In theory, the adjustment process was supposed to be symmetric, with both surplus and deficit countries contributing. But, in practice, only devaluations occurred.

7. It is important to note, however, that the potential loss of seigniorage could reduce these savings by 50 percent or more. For the United States, of course, this would represent an additional advantage, unless some sort of sharing arrangement were worked out with Canada.

8. Indeed, Canada has managed to achieve a lower inflation rate than the United States for the past ten years.

9. The Fed has an explicit mandate to pursue growth and employment, as well as price stability. The latter has never been defined, however, or couched in terms of an explicit inflation target. Neither is there any suggestion as to what weights the Fed should attach to different, and possibly conflicting, objectives in the short run.

10. The implications for Canadian policy independence and accountability are explored in Laidler (1999).

11. See Roger (1991).

12. See also Lalonde and St-Amant (1995); Dupasquier, Lalonde, and St-Amant (1997).

13. The common components obtained from the VAR analyses measure the extent to which the shocks in different regions are contemporaneous, correlated, and determined by a shared, underlying factor.

14. Some authors have suggested that operating under a common currency forces regions to become more similar (see Frankel and Rose, 1996). As a result, their suitability for an OCA is impossible to determine ex ante. Krugman (1993), on the other hand, has suggested that monetary union might lead to greater specialization and make asymmetric shocks more likely.

15. Indeed, owing to the change in relative prices, capital and labor would have an incentive to move out of the commodity sector even if the exchange rate offset all of the decline in commodity prices.

16. Care must to be taken with this argument, however, as more trade could also lead to greater specialization, thereby increasing the need for a flexible exchange rate to help deal with asymmetric shocks (see Krugman, 1993).

◣ *References*

Amano, R., and S. van Norden. (1993). A Forecasting Equation for the Canada-U.S. Dollar Exchange Rate. In *The Exchange Rate and the Economy* (pp. 207–65). Proceedings of a Conference held at the Bank of Canada, June 22–23, 1992. Ottawa: Bank of Canada.

Antia, Z., R. Djoudad, and P. St-Amant. (1999). Inter-provincial and International Risk Sharing in Canada. Photocopy. Bank of Canada.

Bayoumi, T., and B. Eichengreen. (1994). *One Country or Many Analysing the Prospects for Monetary Unification in Various Parts of the World.* (Princeton Studies on International Finance, No. 76). Princeton University.

Chamie, N., A. DeSerres, and R. Lalonde. (1994). *Optimum Currency Areas and Shock Asymmetry: A Comparison of Europe and the United States.* (Bank of Canada Working Paper No. 94–1). Bank of Canada.

Côté, A. (1994). *Exchange Rate Volatility and Trade: A Survey.* (Working Paper No. 94–5). Bank of Canada.

Courchene, T., and R. Harris. (1999). From Fixing to NAMU: Redressing Canada's Sinking Float. (Queen's University Working Paper). Queen's University.

Crow, J. (1999). *Any Sense in a Canadian Dollar?* (Policy and Economic Analysis Program Policy Study 99–1A). University of Toronto.

DeSerres, A., and R. Lalonde. (1994). Symétrie des chocs touchant les régions canadiennes et choix d'un régime de change. (Bank of Canada Working Paper No. 94–9). Bank of Canada.

Dupasquier, C., R. Lalonde, and P. St-Amant. (1997). Optimum Currency Areas as Applied to Canada and the United States. In *Exchange Rates and Monetary Policy* (pp. 131–70). Proceedings of a Conference held by the Bank of Canada, October 1996. Ottawa: Bank of Canada.

Dupuis, D., and D. Tessier. (1999). *Analyse empirique du lien entre la productivité et le taux de change.* (Bank of Canada Working Paper No. 2000–22). Bank of Canada.

Feldstein, M., and C. Horioka. (1980). Domestic Savings and International Capital Flows. *Economic Journal, 90,* 369–79.

Fenton, P., and J. Murray. (1993). Optimum Currency Areas: A Cautionary Tale. In *The Exchange Rate and the Economy* (pp. 485–531). Proceedings of a Conference held at the Bank of Canada, June 22–23, 1992. Ottawa: Bank of Canada.

Fortin, P. (1999, March 15). Imiter l'Europe . . . de la bonne manière. *L'actualité.*

Frankel, J., and A. Rose. (1996). The Endogeneity of the Optimum Currency Area Criteria. (NBER Working Paper No. 5700). National Bureau of Economic Research.

Grubel, H. (1999). The Case for the Amero: The Merit of Creating a North American Monetary Union. Photocopy. Simon Fraser University.

Kenen, P. (1969). The Theory of Optimum Currency Areas: An Eclectic View. In R. Mundell and A. Swoboda (Eds.), *Monetary Problems of the International Economy* (pp. 41–60). Chicago: University of Chicago Press.

Krugman, P. (1993). Lessons of Massachusetts for EMU. In F. Torres and F. Giavazzi (Eds.), *Adjustment and Growth in the European Monetary Union* (pp. 241–61). New York: Cambridge University Press.

Laidler, D. (1999). The Exchange Rate Regime and Canada's Monetary Order. (Bank of Canada Working Paper No. 99–7). Bank of Canada.

Lalonde, R., and P. St-Amant. (1995). Optimum Currency Areas; The Case of Mexico and the United States. (Centre for Latin American Studies). *Money Affairs*, 93–128.

McCallum, J. (1998a). Drivers of the Canadian Dollar and Policy Implications. *Current Analysis, 2*(9), 1–5.

McCallum, J. (1998b). Government Debt and the Canadian Dollar. *Current Analysis, 2*(10), 1–5.

McKinnon, R. (1963). Optimum Currency Areas. *American Economic Review, 53,* 717–25.

Mundell, R. (1961). The Theory of Optimum Currency Areas. *American Economic Review, 51,* 657–65.

Murray, J., and L. Schembri. (1999). Commentary on "Towards a North American Common Currency: An Optimal Currency Area Analysis," by T. Courchene. Photocopy. Bank of Canada.

Murray, J., S. van Norden, and R. Vigfusson. (1996). *Excess Volatility and Speculative Bubbles in the Canadian Dollar: Real or Imagined?* (Technical Report No. 76). Bank of Canada.

Obstfeld, M., and G. Peri. (1998). Regional Non-adjustment and Fiscal Policy: Lessons for EMU. (Center for International and Development Economics Research, Working Paper 98–096). University of California, Berkeley.

Powell, J. (1999). *A History of the Canadian Dollar.* Bank of Canada.

Roger, S. (1991). *Terms of Trade Movements in Major Industrial Countries.* (Working Paper No. 91–2). Bank of Canada.

Sorensen, B., and O. Yosha. (1998). International Risk Sharing and European Monetary Unification. *Journal of International Economics, 45,* 211–38.

Thiessen, G. (1999, January 20). The Euro: Its Economic Implications and Its Lessons for Canada. Remarks to the Canadian Club of Ottawa, Ottawa. Reprinted in *Bank of Canada Review,* 117–23.

Latin America

IV

20 James W. Dean

Should Latin America's Common-Law Marriage to the U.S. Dollar Be Legalized? Should Canada's?

In Ecuador, inflation—which threatened to spiral out of control 18 months ago—slowed to a monthly rate of 2.5 percent in December [after dollarization] from 14.3 percent in January 2000 [before dollarization]. Interest rates are plummeting and banks are out of intensive care. President Gustavo Noboa described the move as a rabbit pulled from a magician's hat to save the economy from ruin.

El Salvador needed no such rabbit. It has long been a star pupil of Washington's free-trade gospel and enjoyed a steady currency and low inflation. But the country wanted to grow faster and believed that adopting the dollar would eliminate foreign-exchange risk and allow interest rates in the country to fall. That, in turn, would make it possible for businesses to expand faster and would make buying a home affordable for more consumers. Even before the dollar officially made its debut at the start of January, interest rates fell.

—Asian Wall Street Journal, January 16, 2001

As this newspaper extract illustrates, official, "de jure" dollarization was recently implemented in Ecuador and El Salvador, two of Latin America's smallest and poorest countries. With the exception of Panama, which has used the U.S. dollar as its sole official currency since 1904, and a few minor territories of the United States, these two countries were the first in the world to dollarize officially. But they will not be the last. Guatemala undertook official dollarization in mid-2001, and Costa Rica, Honduras, and Nicaragua are seriously discussing the possibility. In Mexico, where it was a hot topic in 2000 surrounding President Fox's election, popular opinion has swung *contra*, but some form of monetary cooperation with the United States is still in the air. Even Argentina may emerge from its morass dollarized.

Informal or "de facto" dollarization is already well established all over Latin America, not least in some of its largest and richest countries. According to data compiled by Feige et al. (see fig. 2.1 in chapter 2 herein), the most highly de facto dollarized Latin American countries are Bolivia, Nicaragua, Argentina, Peru, Venezuela, and Costa Rica. This chapter will argue that de facto dollarization may be irreversible. It will also report evidence and arguments that in many Latin American countries de facto dollarization has rendered monetary policy relatively impotent and active exchange rate policy downright dangerous. Hence full, de jure dollarization might be the only sensible course left to such countries, whatever the putative benefits of alternative regimes might have been were de facto dollarization not already in place.

These arguments are not conclusive, nor do they necessarily apply to all Latin American economies.[1] For example, the largest of them all, Brazil, is not heavily dollarized in terms of cash or bank deposits, although it does have large dollar liabilities. But in Argentina, Bolivia, Nicaragua, Peru, and Uruguay, the value of dollar cash plus dollar-denominated bank deposits is higher than that in local currency. Citizens and firms in all Latin American countries also hold huge dollar deposits offshore. And in all Latin American countries, governments, firms, and banks have huge dollar liabilities. Not one Latin American country is able to issue external debt in its own currency. In fact, as Eichengreen and Hausmann (1999) point out, virtually no non-OECD countries can borrow abroad in their own currency: part of a pervasive developing-country problem of mismatched balanced sheets they call "orginal sin."

Hausmann (1999) studied 11 Latin American countries during the troubled period between October 1997 and April 1998. Three "stylized facts" emerge. In response to negative external shocks:

- Most countries lowered their exchange rates very sparingly
- Most countries raised their interest rates very aggressively to defend their exchange rates
- Interest rates were hiked least in countries with fixed exchange rate regimes

These results seem to run against conventional theory and merit closer attention.

Over and above the much-debated costs associated with fixed exchange rates (notably, loss of monetary sovereignty), the two main costs of full dollarization would be loss of seigniorage revenue and loss of the option to "exit" to domestic currency in case devaluation (or revaluation) became desirable. Loss of seigniorage can cost a country upward of 1 percent of its annual GDP. However, the additional loss associated with fully dollarizing countries that are already partially dollarized would be proportionately less. Moreover, the United States *might* agree to share seigniorage with countries that officially dollarize. A U.S. Senate bill to facilitate seigniorage sharing failed in 1999 but could be revived. Recently, various plans for how this might work in practice have been proposed (see for example Hanke and Schuler, 1999; Hausmann and Powell, 2000).

► *Causes of De Facto Dollarization*

When you get right down to it, the benefits of having your own currency are much smaller than we used to think, especially for countries that already to a considerable extent are using the dollar.

—*Stanley Fischer, speaking in the context of Ecuador's dollarization (quoted in the* Wall Street Journal, *May 17, 2000)*

If individuals and firms in one country choose to use the dollar without any requirement or even authorization to do so by law, the phenomenon can be called "de facto dollarization." De facto dollarization is by private rather than public choice; the latter, where use of the foreign currency is legislated, is called "official" or "de jure" dollarization.

De facto dollarization has typically occurred in response to high inflation and, relatedly, a rapidly depreciating exchange rate.[2] A secondary motive has been to hedge against losses in the event of a banking crisis. Whereas losses of purchasing power due to inflation or losses of exchange value due to depreciation can be averted by holding either foreign currency bank deposits or foreign cash, losses from a domestic banking collapse can be averted only by holding foreign cash or bank deposits in a foreign bank. In short, de facto dollarization has typically been a response to actual or expected financial turmoil (Hausmann, 1999).

But while financial turmoil typically explains an initial flight to foreign currency, it cannot explain the *persistence* of dollarization after turmoil ceases. Such persistence is documented by Kamin and Ericsson (1993). Although the flight to foreign currency was substantially reversed in, for example, Israel and the transition countries of eastern Europe after their macroeconomies were to some extent stabilized, dollarization has persisted in the Americas despite stabilization (Sahay and Vegh, 1995).

Whereas initial dollarization is typically motivated by asset substitution so as to preserve value, persistent dollarization is motivated by sufficient currency substitution that foreign currency is in widespread use as a medium of exchange. The most cogent explanation for persistence is that once foreign currency comes to be widely used as a medium of exchange, so-called network effects begin to raise the cost of reverting to the domestic currency.[3] At some point, de facto dollarization may become irreversible, except by de jure means.

► *The Case for De Jure Dollarization*

Perhaps the most prominent advocate of de jure dollarization for Latin America has been Ricardo Hausmann, notably when he was chief economist of the Inter-American Development Bank (Fernando-Arias and Hausmann,

2000; Hausmann, 1999; Hausmann, 1999).[4] The argument has several strands, as follows.

Dangers of Liability Dollarization

According to Hausmann, nominal exchange rate depreciation has become too dangerous to permit because of de facto liability dollarization. When a country's firms, banks, and government have borrowed in a foreign currency such as the United States dollar, sharp depreciation of the domestic currency leads to an equally sharp increase in the domestic currency value of foreign currency debt obligations. This in turn sharply increases the demand for foreign currency and can lead to a downward spiral in the price of domestic currency. And not only does an x percent depreciation increase the local currency debt burden by an equal x percent, it increases the likelihood of default on such debt. Hence banks, which are both borrowers and lenders, are exposed doubly, to currency risk as well as default risk.

Episodes such as Mexico's attempt at a moderate devaluation in 1994 led to uncontrolled depreciation that had to be countered by crippling increases in interest rates. Recently, most Latin American countries have, in practice, ruled out any exchange rate policy other than nominal targeting, and monetary policy has in effect become passive. In other words, liability dollarization has become a strong deterrent to depreciation, a phenomenon that Calvo and Reinhart (2000) term "fear of floating."

Currency and Default Risk Premiums on Interest Rates

De facto liability dollarization acts to increase the currency risk premium on Latin American interest rates, because of the dangers alluded to earlier. It also acts to increase default risk. De jure dollarization would eliminate currency risk premiums, and probably reduce country (default) risk premiums as well. This would be likely to stimulate investment and growth. Even Argentina, which enforces a rigidly fixed rate against the U.S. dollar under its currency board arrangements, may be well advised to dollarize because of the currency risk premium on peso-denominated debt that persists because of the perceived risk that the currency board may be compromised or collapse (Berg and Borenzstein, 2000b).

Less Predictable Control of the Domestic Money Supply

De facto substitution of the U.S. dollar for local currencies has reinforced the impotence of monetary policy because on the margin it weakens the ability of central banks to control the stock of domestic money predictably (Baliño et al., 1999).

Stronger Monetary Than Real Shocks

Currency substitution also increases the relative importance of the monetary as against real shocks that buffet an economy and hence reduces the relative desirability of a flexible exchange rate as a buffer against such shocks (Berg and Borenzstein, 2000a).

Irreversibility

Informal use of U.S. cash—currency substitution—has now become so widespread in Latin America that it may be irreversible because of exponentially growing network externalities. This conjecture is untested and probably untestable, but models of network externalities in currency use, such as Dowd and Greenaway (1993), identify indicative parameters that, for Latin America, are within ranges that suggest irreversibility.

Impotence

Although most of Latin America operates under putatively flexible exchange rate regimes, real exchange rate depreciation is difficult to achieve because of the high pass-through to domestic prices that is a lingering legacy of recent high inflation. Hence exchange rate policy has become impotent (Hausmann, 1999).

▲ Though Ecuador Was Ripe for Dollarization, Canada Is Not

De facto dollarization is also well under way in Canada. Over the last three years, the case for de jure dollarization has been made in both government and academic circles (see, for example, Courchene and Harris, 1999, chapter 16 herein), and lively debate has ensued. But the case for Canada is not as strong as the case for Latin America. In fact I am on record against dollarizing Canada (Dean, 1999). Here I will contrast the Canadian case with the Latin American.

The case for dollarizing Latin America rests on six grounds: dangerous exposure of both banks' and firms' balance sheets to currency risk, related currency and country risk premiums on Latin American interest rates, weakened monetary control due to substitution of U.S. for domestic currency, probable dominance of nominal over real external shocks, high pass-through from exchange rates to wages and domestic prices, and probable irreversibility of currency substitution.

The case for dollarizing Canada fails on all six of these grounds. Consider each in turn, as follows.

Dangers of Liability Dollarization

Unlike Latin America, Canada is capable of issuing debt, both domestic and foreign, in its own currency. While Canadian banks and firms do issue U.S. dollar debt, only about 9 percent of Canadian bank deposits booked by residents are in U.S. dollars; moreover, banks also hold substantial U. S. dollar assets, and firms enjoy extensive U.S. dollar revenues. And while on balance the net liability exposure of both banks and firms is still in U.S. dollars, the extent of the exposure is not nearly as large as in most Latin American countries. Equally important, Canadian banks, unlike many in Latin America, are prudentially sound, with adequate loan loss reserves to cover any likely currency losses. It is simply not plausible to argue that Canada should dollarize because rapid depreciation of the Canadian dollar might cause a banking crisis.

Currency and Default Risk Premiums on Interest Rates

Not only are currency risk premiums against the U.S. dollar absent in Canada, but they have been apparently negative for most of the past few years! Canadian interest rates, both short- and long-term, have been well below American. The easy explanation for this is that the markets have generally expected the Canadian dollar to rise against the American, due to lower inflation and inflationary expectations in Canada, notwithstanding that this expectation has been consistently and palpably wrong. A more paranoiac explanation—one to which I do not subscribe—is that the Bank of Canada in conspiracy with the Department of Finance deliberately held Canadian rates lower than American in order to depreciate the Canadian dollar and hence the external value of Canadian-dollar-denominated debt. Given that the bulk of Canada's external debt, except for the federal government's, is U.S. dollar denominated, this implies a fantastic conspiracy of the Finance Department against provincial and local and municipal, not to mention corporate, debtors, as well as Canadian travelers and consumers of all other imports. But the bottom line is that for whatever reason, Canadian interest rates have been lower than American, not higher, and it is hard to argue they would have been even lower had Canada adopted the U.S. dollar.

Less Predictable Control of the Domestic Money Supply

Does currency substitution weaken Canada's control over its money supply? In Latin America, currency substitution—holding U.S. cash—is, at bottom, motivated by store-of-value considerations: the need to hedge against inflation, exchange rate depreciation, or banking crises. Asset substitution— holding U.S. dollar-denominated bank deposits—is even more directly motivated by such considerations.[5] As a result, major injections or withdrawals of domestic money by Latin American central banks often prompt large and unpredictable movements into or out of U.S. dollars.

Currency substitution in Canada, by contrast, is relatively minor and stable, motivated largely by tourist transactions. Asset substitution in Canada is admittedly more substantial and is motivated by a mixture of hedging as well as transactions motives. But asset substitution in Canada is also more *predicable* than in Latin America, simply because inflation and (even!) exchange rate movements are more predictable. This relative predictability extends to marginal movements in response to money supply management by the Bank of Canada. Hence currency and asset substitution are not serious impediments to monetary control.

Stronger Monetary Than Real Shocks

Other things equal, an economy is better buffered from monetary shocks by a fixed rate and from real shocks by a flexible rate. In Latin America, currency substitution is sufficiently substantial that monetary shocks are likely to dominate, due to unpredictable *internal* shifts between domestic and foreign cash. Moreover, Latin America is vulnerable to substantial shocks on its *external* capital account: capital inflows and outflows are volatile. And finally, unless these external shocks are sterilized, they translate into internal monetary shocks because exchange rates are, in practice, heavily managed. Canada, by contrast, has relatively little currency substitution: U.S. cash in circulation is low by Latin American standards, and (as in Latin America) U.S. dollar bank checks are not legal tender. Furthermore, Canada is not subject to as sharp shocks to its external capital account as is Latin America, and when capital does flow in or out, the exchange rate is usually permitted to respond sufficiently that the domestic money supply is not forced to respond.

Canada still *is*, however, dependent on resource exports relative to the United States; hence its flexible nominal exchange rate does provide a useful buffer against real terms-of-trade shocks. This flexibility proved particularly valuable in 1997–98, when resource prices plummeted in the wake of East Asia's financial crisis.[6]

Irreversibility

Some suggest that currency substitution in Latin America may now be irreversible, short of draconian legislation and its enforcement. According to the Dowd and Greenaway (1993) model of network externalities, whether domestic monetary expansion induces currency substitution depends on the sensitivity of the exchange rate to money, the sensitivity to exchange rate changes of the number of people using foreign currency, and the extent to which the broad money supply is not covered by foreign exchange reserves. In Latin America, these two sensitivities are relatively high, and the coverage ratio is typically low. Moreover, the monetary "slippage" effect increases exponentially as levels of cash dollarization increase, due to network externalities in the use of foreign currency. In Canada, the two sensitivities are relatively low, the coverage ratio is relatively high, and the level of cash dollarization is relatively low. Hence the case for de jure dollarization is correspondingly weaker.

Impotence

In Latin America, exchange rate depreciation is often quickly matched by domestic wage and price inflation, leaving the real exchange rate unchanged. Hence depreciation or devaluation as a tactic to stimulate real output is bound to prove futile. Latin America's pervasive and persistent wage indexation and short-period contracting is a legacy of its recent rampant inflation. Canada does not have such a legacy. More fundamentally, Canada has a long history of responsible—some would say excessively restrictive—monetary growth. Particularly over the past 12 years, the Bank of Canada has earned a reputation as a consistent inflation fighter. No central bank in Latin America—with the exception of Argentina's, which is bound by a currency board, and possibly Chile's, which has worked the inflation rate down—can match this reputation. As a result, Canada's real exchange rate can and does depreciate markedly, and as a further result, nominal exchange rate targeting is not at all necessary to control inflationary expectations or to discipline the central bank.

A final reason for dollarizing Latin America—one I have not emphasized here but is emphasized by many advocates—is to promote tighter trade and investment ties with the United States, presumably because both exchange rate uncertainty and currency conversion costs would be eliminated. But surely explicit free trade and investment pacts are a more straightforward way to go about this, and indeed NAFTA has been accompanied by a burgeoning cross-border trade and investment between both Mexico and the United States and Canada and the United States. While it may be that direct investment into Mexico would be further encouraged by dollarizing, it is not at all clear that cross-border trade needs such encouragement. It is even less clear for Canada, which now sends some 85 percent of its exports to the United States.

◣ Notes

This chapter was originally published in 2001 in *Journal of Policy Modeling, 23,* 291–300.

1. For strong counterarguments, see Willett (2001) and Williamson (2000, 2001, chapter 9 herein).

2. Ize and Levy-Yeyati (1998) present a model of bank dollarization in which currencies are chosen on the basis of hedging decisions. For a broad sample of countries, they are able to approximate actual dollarization closely as a result of minimum variance portfolio allocations. Moreover, they show that dollarization hysteresis (irreversibility) occurs when the expected volatility of the inflation rate is high relative to that of the real exchange rate.

3. As the transactions use of foreign currency increases, its utility value rises nonlinearly with the number of users. This phenomenon has been captured by Dowd and Greenaway (1993) in a model of network externalities: for a secondary exposition, see Dean (2000) and Feige et al. (chapter 2 herein).

4. For elaborations of the arguments outlined in this section, see Dean (2000). An excellent critique of Hausmann's (1999, 2000) arguments and evidence in favor of de jure dollarization can be found in Willett (2001). Interestingly, Hausmann's strong advocacy of dollarization was disavowed by the bank's resident, and even more interestingly, Hausmann resigned from the bank in mid-2000 to take up a professorship at Harvard.

5. Following Feige et al. (chapter 2), a *currency substitution index*, CSI, can be defined as the fraction of a country's total currency supply that is made up of foreign currency: CSI = FCC/(FCC + LCC), where FCC is foreign currency in circulation and LCC is local. An *asset substitution index*, ASI, can be defined (for bank deposits) as the ratio of foreign currency-denominated monetary deposits to domestic-plus-foreign-currency-denominated deposits: ASI = FCD/(DCD + FCD).

6. According to the Bank of Canada's amazing econometric model, which consistently "explains" movements in the Canada/U. S. exchange rate, Canada's continued low dollar is due to continued low resource prices—of agricultural products, including pulp and paper, and of nonoil and gas mineral products. Surprisingly to some, Canada is a net *importer* of oil and petroleum products, when intermediate goods are taken into account.

◤ References

Baliño, T. J. T., A. Bennett, and E. Borensztein. (1999). Monetary Policy in Dollarized Economies. (IMF Occasional Paper 171). International Monetary Fund.

Berg, Andrew, and Eduardo Borensztein. (2000a, February). The Choice of Exchange Rate Regime and Monetary Target in Highly Dollarized Economies. (IMF Working Paper WP/00/29). International Monetary Fund.

Berg, Andrew, and Eduardo Borensztein. (2000b, March). The Pros and Cons of Full Dollarization. (IMF Working Paper). International Monetary Fund.

Calvo, G. A., and C. A. Végh. (1992). Currency Substitution in Developing Countries: An Introduction. (IMF Working Paper WP/92/40). International Monetary Fund.

Calvo, Guillermo, and Eduardo Fernandez-Arias. (2000). The New Features of Financial Crises in Emerging Markets. In Eduardo Fernando-Arias and Ricardo Hausmann (Eds.). *Wanted: World Financial Stability*. Washington, D.C.: Inter-American Development Bank.

Calvo, Guillermo, and Carmen M. Reinhaert. (2000). Fear of Floating. (NBER Working Paper No. 7993). National Bureau of Economic Research.

Dean, James W. (1997). Is the European Common Currency Worth It? *Challenge*, 40(3), 57–74.

Dean, James W. (1999, September). Our Money or Theirs? *National Post Magazine.*

Dean, James W. (2000, October 4–5). *De Facto Dollarization in Latin America.* Prepared for conference To Dollarize or Not to Dollarize: Exchange-Rate Choices for the Western Hemisphere, sponsored by the North-South Institute, Ottawa.

Dowd, Kevin, and David Greenaway. (1993). Currency Competition, Network Externalities and Switching Costs: Towards an Alternative View of Optimum Currency Areas. *Economic Journal, 103,* 1180–89.

Eichengreen, Barry, and Ricardo Hausmann. (1999, November). Exchange Rates and Financial Fragility. (NBER Working Paper 7418). National Bureau of Economic Research.

Fernando-Arias, Eduardo, and Ricardo Hausmann (Eds.). (2000). *Wanted: World Financial Stability.* Washington, D.C.: Inter-American Development Bank.

Hausmann, Ricardo. (1999). Should There Be Five Currencies or One Hundred and Five? *Foreign Policy, 11,* 65–78.

Hausmann, Ricardo, Michael Gavin, Carmen Pages-Serra, and Ernesto Stein. (1999). Financial Turmoil and the Choice of Exchange Rate Regime. In Eduardo Fernanco-Arias and Ricardo Hausmann (Eds.), *Wanted: World Financial Stability.* Washington, D.C.: Inter-American Development Bank.

Hausmann, Ricardo, and Andrew Powell. (2000). *Dollarization: How to Go about It.* (Working Paper). Inter-American Development Bank.

Hanke, Steve H., and Kurt Schuler. (1999). A Monetary Constitution for Argentina: Rules for Dollarization. *Cato Journal, 18*(3), 405–19.

Ize, Alain, and Eduardo Levy-Yeyati. (1998). Dollarization of Financial Intermediation: Causes and Policy Implications. (IMF Working Paper WP/98/28). International Monetary Fund.

Kamin, Steven B., and Neil R. Ericsson. (1993, November). Dollarization in Argentina. (International Finance Discussion Paper No. 460). Board of Governors of the Federal Reserve System.

Sahay, R., and C. A. Végh. (1995). Dollarization in Transition Economies: Evidence and Policy Implications. (IMF Working Paper WP/95/96). International Monetary Fund.

Willett, Thomas D. (2001). Truth in Advertising and the Great Dollarization Scam. *Journal of Policy Modeling, 23.*

Williamson, John. (2000). *Exchange Rate Regimes for Emerging Markets: Reviving the Intermediate Option.* Washington, D.C.: Institute for International Economics.

21 Liliana Rojas-Suarez

What Exchange Rate Arrangement Works Best for Latin America?

Crisis periods are fertile ground for the development of reform proposals both at the national and international level. In the midst of economic disruption and social pain, it is only natural that policymakers, members of multilateral organizations, academics, and representatives from the private sector reexamine what went wrong and what could be done to prevent the emergence of future crises.

Latin America exemplifies this process. The region has spawned numerous reform proposals, some that have worked well and others that have not. But in most cases of success, the solution involved actions from both national authorities and the international community. For example, the debt crisis of the early 1980s, perhaps the deepest and most costly for the region in recent times, took a number of attempts at resolution until, finally, the implementation of the Brady Plan laid the groundwork for recovery. At the domestic level, exchange-rate-based stabilization programs proved to be the effective remedy for containing hyperinflation.

However, when the next crisis, the so-called tequila crisis, erupted at the end of 1994, the sustainability of fixed exchange rate regimes began to be questioned, and Mexico opted for a flexible exchange rate. Because the connection between banking crisis and exchange rate crisis was identified, an overhaul of the regulatory and supervisory framework of domestic financial institutions was commonly agreed on as a needed reform.

Not surprisingly, the emerging market crisis that began in East Asia in 1997 brought about heated discussions of reform proposals. Because the crisis hit emerging economies in all regions of the world, this time around the proposals focused on reforms to the architecture of the international financial system and, particularly, to the role of multilateral organizations in containing financial risks. The outcome of this debate remains to be seen. In Latin America, several countries joined Mexico (and Peru) in the choice of more flexibility in their exchange rate systems, notably Brazil, Chile, Colombia, and Venezuela. But while most policymakers in the region have seemed to favor flexibility, a number of small countries have chosen the opposite extreme: full dollarization. To date, Ecuador and El Salvador have joined Panama in dollarizing their economies. Interestingly enough, the heated debate on dollarization that has been the central topic of debate in a large number of academic and policy forums did not emerge from these small countries. Instead, the debate originated as a proposal to deal with the mounting economic and financial problems in Argentina since the late 1990s. However, following a debt default in late 2001, the Argentinean authorities abandoned convertibility, discarded the proposal of dollarization, and moved to a managed flexible exchange rate system. In the eyes of supporters of dollarization, Argentina could have avoided its financial turmoil if it had chosen to fully dollarize.

Is dollarization what the region needs now? Has a fair chance been given to the recently implemented flexible exchange rate regimes? This chapter addresses these questions. My conclusion is that, while I fully recognize the long-term benefits of convergence toward a single currency (with dollarization being only one of the alternatives among the "hard peg" choices), the current features of most Latin American countries do not warrant an immediate implementation of such a regime. Indeed, given current conditions in international capital markets, the severe constraints facing Latin American countries call for the use of increased flexibility in exchange rates as a tool for dealing with the trade and financial shocks that continue to plague the region. But one tool is not enough when facing multiple constraints. An appropriate provision of liquidity, as well as an effective use of monetary instruments, must complement exchange rate flexibility.[1]

Rather than focusing on how to quickly implement dollarization, the policy debate needs to be redirected toward how to eliminate the constraints that render currency unification ineffective.

▲ Why Does Dollarization Sound Attractive?

I believe there are two primary interrelated arguments that make dollarization appealing. First is disillusionment with the performance of the region over the last few decades. If, on the basis of a history of hyperinflation and currency crises, an analyst concludes that Latin American countries are not capable of running sound monetary and exchange rate policies, the seemingly straightforward solution is to take the privilege of printing money away from the hands of domestic monetary authorities. Furthermore, given that a significantly large component of Latin American trade is with the United States, most reserve holdings are in U.S. dollars, and the financial systems of several countries in the region are already partially dollarized, the apparently obvious choice is dollarization.

The second argument for dollarization is that it addresses the high costs stemming from the lack of a hard currency to undertake international transactions. Latin American countries, and for that matter almost all emerging economies, can neither trade nor borrow internationally in their own currencies. Proponents of dollarization argue that this has a fundamentally adverse impact on growth and development. First, concerned by Latin America's history of significant exchange rate instability, foreign investors limit the amount of flows into the region and reverse inflows at the first sign of trouble, preventing Latin America from taking full advantage of the benefits of globalization. Second, moved by the same concerns, domestic investors are willing only to lend long term if the contracts are denominated in U.S. dollars. Since many of the long-term projects take the form of goods and services directed to the domestic market, where transactions take place in local currency, there is a structural currency mismatch between the liabilities (dollars) and the assets (local currency) of the private sector. The risks associated with this mismatch, in turn, increase financial instability and discourage the development of domestic financial markets.[2]

Proponents of dollarization claim that their system addresses these problems. A dollarized system promises to both reduce risk and increase the return on investing in local economies by bringing down domestic real interest rates. With the reduction of the probability of an exchange rate depreciation to zero, lenders will demand a lower return and will be willing to engage in long-term financing. A fixed exchange rate system is not sufficient to accomplish this goal because the promise of exchange rate stability can be broken at any time. Even if countries maintain cautious monetary policies, the presumption is that at the first sign of trouble, which could arise from a domestic or external shock, a large depreciation of the exchange rate will eventually follow (either through the abandonment of the fixed exchange rate system or through a large depreciation of the currency under a more flexible arrangement). It is the probability of large changes in the exchange rate that keeps domestic real interest rates high and, as such, is an important constraint on sustained economic growth.

With such strong arguments, why then has dollarization not become the obvious choice for policymakers in Latin America? Why is there still a heated debate in academic circles? Why do multilateral organizations not include dollarization as part of their conditionality for external support? In my view, the reason is that the preceding arguments tell only part of the story. While they are correct in emphasizing the efficiency gains that can be derived from dollarization, they ignore other serious constraints facing Latin America in today's complex international financial system. As such, their arguments miss a basic point, namely, that the region needs more, rather than fewer, tools to manage financial risks. At the current turning point in Latin America's economic history, dollarization, or even a less restrictive fixed exchange rate system or currency board, would further limit the region's ability to achieve sustainable growth and may even compromise its efforts toward stability.

▶ *The Deficiencies of the Dollarization Proposal*

The main deficiency of the dollarization proposal is its extreme (and practically sole) focus on exchange rate volatility as a source of financial instability. In contrast to the proponents of dollarization, I would argue that the main and immediate risk facing Latin America is the so-called country or default risk, which has to do more with the current features of international capital markets, as well as the underlying fundamentals in each country, than with a specific exchange rate regime. I will argue that it is this "default" risk that keeps real interest rates high in the region and that, by itself, dollarization can do very little to tackle the problem.

The Nature of International Capital Markets, Default Risk, and Domestic Real Interest Rates

It has, of course, always been true that investors' perceptions of emerging economies' capacity and willingness to pay their debt are instrumental in determining the size and cost of financial resources available to those economies. What has changed in recent times, however, is that emerging markets have found it increasingly convenient to meet some of their financing needs in the international bond markets.

There are two basic distinctions between bank loans and bonds that are relevant to emerging markets. First, in contrast to unsecuritized bank lending, the existence of a well-developed secondary market for international bonds implies that any change in country risk perceptions is quickly translated into the market price of bonds. Second, contrary to bank loans, which can often be assembled through syndication and other concerted arrangements among creditors, bondholders are too spread out to make any coordinated arrangement simple. It is, therefore, not surprising that any economic policy or political news affecting investors' perceptions of a country's capacity or willingness to service its debt is reflected immediately in the spread between the yield from bonds issued by that country and the yield from U.S. Treasury bonds of corresponding maturity. As both yields are expressed in U.S. dollars, the spread is free of exchange rate risk and is considered a typical measure of the "country" or "default" risk.

As reflected by higher spreads, the deterioration of investors' risk perceptions raises that country's external financing costs. This increase, in turn, translates into higher domestic interest rates, as existing financing needs press against the limited supply of domestic financial funds.

Proponents of dollarization argue that "default" and exchange rate risk are correlated. I agree, but I also believe that the causality effect runs in the opposite direction than that suggested by defenders of dollarization. From the perspective of dollarizers, an increase in the risk of large exchange depreciations leads to higher default risk. The argument is that the structural currency mismatch between the assets and liabilities of the private sector causes extended corporate bankruptcies when the exchange rate depreciates significantly (see earlier). As investors are aware of this effect, their perceptions of default risk increase. The problem with this argument is that it ignores the initial source of the problem, which I would argue rests on the presence of domestic policy inconsistencies. In a number of recent emerging market crises, large and increasing stocks of short-term debt (either domestic or external), fueled by equally large and increasing fiscal deficits, raised doubts about the capacity of these countries to service their debt. As perceptions of default risk deteriorated, countries found it more difficult to roll over maturing external debt. Net external amortization payments and the consequent reduction in international reserves followed, putting in question the sustainability of the exchange rate.

Dollarization would not have prevented the deterioration in country risk arising from these policy inconsistencies. Indeed, in some cases, such as those of Mexico in 1994 and Korea in 1997, depreciating the exchange rate was part of the solution, as improved competitiveness allowed for an increase in needed resources. But while exchange rate depreciation was essential, it was certainly not enough. A crucial component of crisis resolution was the large financial packages that were made available to these countries by multilateral organizations. The immediate availability of liquidity provided assurances to external investors that debt obligations could be met on a timely basis. Perceptions of default risk were, therefore, contained.

Figures 21.1–3 show the importance of default risk in the behavior of domestic real interest rates in Argentina, Brazil, and Mexico.

The graphs suggest a key feature of the relationship between these two variables, namely, that in all three countries, during the period under consideration, domestic real interest rates (RIR) and yields on sovereign external

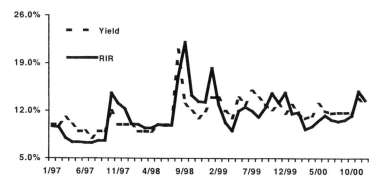

Figure 21.1. Argentina

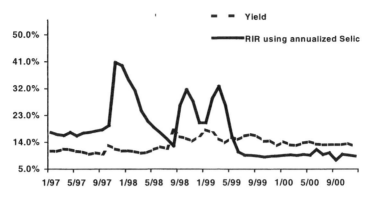

Figure 21.2. Brazil

debt tended to converge. While, the domestic real interest rate "jumped" at times of speculative attacks on the exchange rate, these deviations were transitory. In other words, drastic changes in the perception of exchange rate risk do affect domestic real interest rates and, at times, may become the dominant explanatory variable; but these effects are of a temporary nature. In contrast, perceptions of default risk appear to maintain a more stable and permanent relationship with domestic real interest rates.[3] Brazil and Mexico clearly exemplify this observation.

Argentina's case is particularly telling, as the convertibility law was in effect during the period considered in the graph (fig. 21.1). Notice that at all times (even at times of strong doubts about the capacity of this country to maintain the convertibility law) domestic real interest rates remained very close to yields on external sovereign obligations. That is, default clearly dominated the behavior of domestic real interest rates in Argentina.

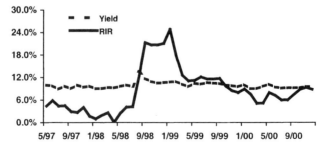

Figure 21.3. Mexico

Additional Features of Latin America That
Do Not Support Dollarization

Having identified default risk as investors' central criterion for assessing emerging markets, one needs to ask what features specific to Latin America contribute to current perceptions of country risk and how relevant the choice of exchange rate regime is in dealing with these perceptions. Here I identify two features of the region that call for more, rather than less, flexibility in the exchange rate.

The first feature is that the region is subject to large terms-of-trade shocks that are partly explained in some countries by a dependence on commodity exports. Large terms-of-trade shocks represent a sudden reduction in the net transfer of real resources from abroad. As such, a large terms-of-trade shock requires an adjustment in relative prices, implying a reduction in the price of nontradable goods relative to the price of tradable goods; namely, a depreciation of the real exchange rate. This needed adjustment simply reflects changes in supply and demand and, therefore, can be characterized as a "real," as opposed to a "monetary," phenomenon.

Dollarization cannot prevent this adjustment but can influence the form in which it takes place. If the exchange rate cannot adjust, by the mere definition of dollarization, the adjustment will need to take place by contractions in output growth and employment and/or reductions in real wages. Moreover, as the relative prices of nontradable goods decline, so do the real revenues of producers in that sector, and therefore their capacity to service their debt obligations falls. Consistent with my view that country risk is the most important factor determining investors' attitudes toward emerging markets, long and deep recessions do nothing but exacerbate the perception of a country's reduced capacity to service its debt.

By contrast, in a more flexible exchange rate system, the needed adjustment following the shock can take place through a nominal depreciation of the exchange rate. This could, at least partly, compensate for the loss of competitiveness, mitigating the negative impact on output and employment. This is the well-known "shock-absorber" advantage of flexible exchange rates.[4]

Theory came into practice after the emerging market crisis that started after the Russian debt default. Argentina, a country that kept a very restrictive exchange rate system in the form of a currency board, for a decade displayed a dramatic slowdown in economic activity, especially relative to those countries in the region with more flexible exchange rate regimes. Indeed, Mexico and Peru, the two countries that had a floating system before the eruption of the Russian crisis, experienced the least recessionary impacts from the crisis. As recession was associated with a decreased capacity to service debt, sovereign spreads remained extremely high in Argentina all the way through the country's debt moratorium in late 2001.

The second feature that calls for more flexible arrangements in the region is the presence of what I will call "stock problems." These manifest in either a large stock of debt and/or a weak banking system, implying contingent liabilities to the government, that is, future government debt. If the country is not fully dollarized but under a fixed rate arrangement, speculators would perceive a "one-side bet" when pressures on the exchange rate develop. The bet is that governments will eventually choose to abandon the fixed exchange rate rather than defend the parity by keeping interest rates very high for a prolonged period of time. This is because the defense would aggravate existing fragilities in the banking sector or increase the fiscal cost of servicing the existing large stock of debt. As a result, speculators exacerbate the attack on the exchange rate when governments attempt to defend the parity.

What if the economy is fully dollarized? While no bets against the parity are possible here, the country would lack mechanisms needed to generate resources to deal with an exacerbation of the stock problems. If an unexpected shock (domestic or foreign) severely reduces a government's capacity to service its debt, the perception of default will increase immediately as investors assume that the government cannot adjust the exchange rate to generate additional real resources. This increased default risk will also translate quickly into domestic real interest rates that, in turn, exacerbate the debt problem.[5]

If the problem is one of a weak banking system, the situation is even more complicated by the lack of a lender of last resort in a dollarized economy.[6] To elucidate my point: imagine that Mexico attempted to dollarize its system in 1995 in the middle of its severe banking crisis. At that time, a run on deposits was contained, partly because of the presence of full deposit insurance in pesos. While this problem caused significant fiscal costs, and its problems are by now well known, a sudden dollarization when banks were facing loan problems would have caused bank runs, as depositors would have realized that neither the banks nor the authorities had a sufficient amount of dollars to back the value of their deposits. This problem could, of course, be avoided if dollarization were to occur in conjunction with a monetary agreement with the U.S. Federal Reserve or with massive inflows of capital from foreign banks (through access to the discount window of the Fed and to the FDIC). But I would argue that even the strongest defenders of dollarization would agree that neither foreign banks nor the Fed would open deposit insurance to a country facing a severe banking crisis.[7]

▲ *What Works Best for Latin America?*

On the basis of the discussion just presented, I clearly favor more, rather than less, flexibility in exchange rate management, but I do not believe that that is enough. The same constraints that render fixed exchange rates inappropriate also call for complementing flexibility with a large stock of foreign holdings. Indeed, this combination has served well those countries facing large external shocks. While the flexibility of the exchange rate allows countries to compensate for the loss of competitiveness following the shock, the abundance of foreign exchange liquidity, both in banks and in the central bank, helps provide investors with assurance that debt obligations will be met on time even if a large, unanticipated shock hits the system.

Some analysts argue that the call for large international reserves in the context of flexible exchange rates defeats the purpose of flexible rates: Is it not the claim of flexible rates that shocks are absorbed through changes in the exchange rate with little or no variation in the stock of international reserves? Are not flexible exchange rates supposed to ensure monetary policy independence? Yes, if the country faces continuous access to international capital markets, which is a central assumption in the traditional models of exchange rates. However, this assumption does not hold for Latin America. Because country risk dominates investors' perceptions of the region, a bad signal not only increases a country's cost of funding but, if concerns are large enough, drastically reduces available financing. It is this constraint on access to international capital markets that keeps flexible exchange rates alone from doing the full job. Curtailing financial resources in the middle of economic projects (public or private) would certainly affect growth, further deteriorating investors' perception of default risk. Only the availability of significant foreign exchange liquidity in the hands of both the private and the public sector can contain the perception of default. While countries may lose international reserves immediately after the shock, the offsetting effect of a depreciated exchange rate would, in due time, allow for the accumulation of resources that would restore international reserves.

There is an important issue related to the required accumulation of reserves, namely that it imposes significant opportunity costs on countries. Notice, however, that this problem would be exacerbated if the economy were under either a fixed or dollarized exchange rate regime, since the country could not use the exchange rate mechanism to restore reserve losses. Nonetheless, because I believe that the issue of creditworthiness cannot be solved in the near future, I support a central role for multilateral organizations in facilitating access to liquidity in cases where the assessment of a country's difficulties lies in liquidity as opposed to solvency problems. The role of multilateral organization does not necessarily have to take the form of public funds available to countries. It could very well involve preventive contracts with the private sector where the role of multilateral organizations entails providing guarantees or ensuring the transfer of credible collateral. This crucial topic is at the center of current discussions about reforms to the architecture of the international financial system.

What about the use of interest rate policy in a more flexible exchange rate regime? Critics of flexibility argue that central banks do not let the exchange rate fully float following a shock and that, instead, the interest rate policy is used to contain sharp fluctuations of the exchange rate.[8] I certainly agree that there is evidence of central bank intervention in countries claiming to have a flexible exchange rate regime. But this evidence only lets me conclude that "pure" flexibility has not been the policy choice. Does that mean that I advocate "limited flexibility" in the form, say, of exchange rate bands? Certainly not! Does it then mean that I favor "discretion" rather than "rules" in the operation of exchange rate policies? No way; discretion is another word for "lack of transparency," and that can only deteriorate perceptions of country risk. What I believe is that the optimal exchange rate rule may be an active rule taking into account the constraints facing the region. Indeed, although still far from being fully implemented, the choice of "inflation targeting" in a number of Latin American countries (notably Brazil, Mexico, and Chile) is a step in the right direction. Under this policy arrangement, central banks are allowed to intervene in the foreign exchange market, but only under very clearly specified rules.

I have already stressed the constraints imposed by a limited access to international capital markets and by existing "stock" fragilities. I will point out one more constraint, namely, the adverse impact on inflationary expectations of sharp movements in the exchange rate. This comes from a long history, in a number of countries, of wage indexation to changes in the exchange rate. Latin American central bankers in the more flexible exchange rate systems, under an inflation-targeting scheme, intervene by increasing interest rates when they perceive that their target on inflation, the main policy objective of the central bank, may be compromised. While inflation targeting is a new policy in the region, the experience so far seems to indicate that this mechanism has served countries well at times of turmoil in international capital markets.

In spite of the complexity of the issues at hand, the message is straightforward: Latin America needs more tools because it faces more constraints than industrial countries. On its own, the exchange rate policy (or the absence of it through dollarization) cannot handle all these restrictions. The region needs a combination of policies that allows for movements in both the exchange rate and interest rates. Moreover, it needs the cooperation of the international community to deal with the sudden shortages of liquidity that have characterized the region's recent history.

▲ Conclusion

While the goal of moving toward a single currency, be it the U.S. dollar or a new currency in the region, is a good one, its time has not yet come. I strongly believe that Latin America faces an important trade-off between efficiency and stability. Full dollarization deals with some of the inefficiencies but cannot yet contribute to stability. Indeed, it runs the risk of exacerbating a financial crisis if necessary preconditions are not in place.

The main policy conclusion of this chapter is twofold. First, facing severe constraints in terms of a lack of access to international capital markets coupled with what I called "stock problems," policymakers need the flexibility of the exchange rate to act as an absorber of adverse shocks. Second, the medium-term focus needs to be on removing the constraints that prevent a successful move toward currency unification. Issues to tackle include the large stock of debt and remaining fragilities in the financial sector. Efforts in the area of trade diversification and improvements in competitiveness, such as labor reform and the removal of tax distortions, should also be in the agenda of policy reform. At the top of the list is the depoliticization of economic policies. As long as concerns remain that governments may change the "rules of the game" either to benefit certain groups, to gain popularity, or to delay costly solutions, perceptions of country risk will remain high in the region and real interest rates will reflect it. Last but not least, a better role for multilateral organizations aimed at facilitating access to resources from the international private sector needs to be defined.

I recognize that this is a difficult agenda and that it may take a long time to implement, but experience is full of many great ideas ending in failure only because insufficient attention was given to the preconditions for success. Financial liberalization is certainly a case in point. In the 1980s, nobody would have argued for the efficiency gains of this policy, but few paid attention to the preconditions for success. We are all very aware of the severe banking crisis that followed. Only ex post was full recognition given to the need to have appropriate banking supervision and entry-exit rules for financial institutions to exploit the benefits of a liberalized financial system while minimizing the risks to stability. It is my view that the dollarization proposal faces similar challenges.

◣ Notes

An earlier version of this chapter was published in 2000 with the same title in *World Economic Affairs, 3*(2), 35–40.

1. Some of the issues discussed in this chapter are contained in Rojas-Suarez (1999).
2. It is also argued that the lack of a "hard" currency brings about a structural maturity mismatch in local markets. As long-term domestic capital markets are underdeveloped, long-term projects often need to rely on short-term financing, increasing the vulnerability of the financial system to sudden shortages of liquidity. See Hausmann (1999).
3. Of course, these are casual observations derived only from a graphic relationship. Definite conclusions would need more strict empirical analysis, such as the use of co-integration techniques.
4. For further discussion of this issue, see Sachs and Larrain (1999).
5. This is true for either domestic or external debt. If the government liability is mostly floating domestic debt, increases in interest rates have an immediate impact on

servicing costs. If the debt is mostly external, the increase in real interest rates leads to reduced economic activity, aggravating the risk of default.

6. The problem of a lack of lender of last resort is fully recognized by proponents of dollarization. For a response to this criticism, see Calvo (1999).

7. Ecuador dollarized in the middle of a banking crisis but also after it had defaulted on its external obligations. While the final assessment on this dollarization experiment remains to be determined, sovereign spreads on Ecuadorian debt have remained extremely high after dollarization. Indeed, the Ecuadorian spreads are among the highest in the region, reflecting investors' continued perceptions of high risk. What dollarization can certainly do is to serve as an effective anchor for inflation. Basically, dollarization is playing a similar role to that of the exchange-rate-based stabilization programs implemented in other Latin American countries in the late 1980s and early 1990s.

8. See for example Hausmann et al. (2000) and Calvo and Reinhart (2000).

▶ References

Calvo, G. (1999). Testimony on Full Dollarization. Website, U.S. Senate.

Calvo G., and C. Reinhart. (2000). Fear of Floating. Photocopy. University of Maryland.

Hausmann, R. (1999). Should there be Five Currencies or One Hundred and Five? *Foreign Policy, 116.*

Hausmann, R., M. Gavin, C. Pages, and E. Stein. (2000). Financial Turmoil and the Choice of Exchange Rate Regime. In E. Fernandez-Arias and R. Hausmann (Eds.), *Wanted: World Financial Stability.* Washington, D.C.: Inter-American Development Bank.

Rojas-Suarez, L. (1999). Dollarization in Latin America? Website, U.S. Senate.

Sachs J., and F. Larrain. (1999). Why Dollarization Is More Straitjacket than Salvation. *Foreign Policy, 116.*

22 Steve H. Hanke

A Dollarization/Free-Banking Blueprint for Argentina

To put an end to monetary mischief and rein in hyperinflation, Argentina established an unorthodox currency board system on April 1, 1991. Argentines called the system "convertibility," an uncommon term for an unusual system. Like all currency board arrangements, convertibility maintained a fixed exchange rate on the spot market between the peso and its anchor currency, the U.S. dollar. That nominal anchor checked inflation: the consumer price index at the end of 2001 was about where it was in 1994.

Convertibility was not trouble-free, however. Indeed, its deviations from currency board orthodoxy allowed it to behave more like a central bank than a true currency board in some important respects.[1] Under currency board orthodoxy, a floor and a ceiling of 100 percent and 110 percent, respectively, are typically mandated for the foreign reserve cover of a board's monetary liabilities. Furthermore, a board's net domestic assets are frozen. Accordingly, an orthodox currency board has no latitude to sterilize foreign currency inflows or offset outflows and it cannot engage in discretionary monetary policies. However, with the convertibility system there was a floor under the foreign reserve cover but no ceiling. Moreover, the central bank's net domestic assets were not frozen. Consequently, the convertibility system had the ability to sterilize inflows of foreign currency and offset outflows. These powers were used liberally. Indeed, in virtually every month of its existence, the central bank under the convertibility system sterilized or offset changes in its foreign reserves, and in most months after 1994, these powers were used aggressively. For example, foreign reserves fell by 12 billion dollars over the course of 2001, and 122 percent of those foreign reserve outflows were offset by increases in the central bank's net domestic assets. Contrary to the musings of most observers, the convertibility system engaged in superactivist monetary policies, particularly after 1994. In that time period, the net domestic asset position of Argentina's central bank under convertibility was over six times more volatile than that of Chile's central bank, which has an independent monetary policy and is operating under a floating-exchange-rate regime.

The problems created by convertibility's deviations from orthodoxy, as well as those associated with rigidities in Argentina's economy, became particularly apparent during the Mexican tequila crisis of 1995 (Hanke, 1999, pp. 341–66). The same problems arose in January 1999, after Brazil devalued, and in 2001, when Argentina sought to renegotiate its external and internal debt, moved from a unified to a multiple exchange-rate regime, and passed legislation that would have eventually changed the peso's anchor from the dollar to a dollar-euro basket. In all cases, the peso traded at a deep discount to the dollar on the forward markets, even though the peso traded at parity with the dollar on the spot market. The discount reflected perceived currency risk, and implied that markets viewed the peso as inferior to the dollar.

To eliminate the currency risk and lower interest rates in Argentina, former president Carlos Menem suggested, in January 1999, the possibility of officially replacing the peso with the dollar. By unilaterally dollarizing the economy, monetary policy would become "looser" because the exchange-rate risk with the dollar would be eliminated, interest rates would be lower, and credit would be more readily available. An Argentine government study estimated that official dollarization would increase the trend rate of GDP growth by two percentage points a year at a cost of lost seigniorage of only 25 basis points.[2] However, as Rudi Dornbusch stressed, the modest seigniorage costs of unilateral dollarization would be more than offset by the reduced cost of servicing public debt under a dollarized regime (Dornbusch, 2001). Kurt Schuler and I supported Menem's initiative with a proposal explaining in detail how to achieve official dollarization (Hanke and Schuler, 1999).

The lost opportunity to dollarize officially in 1999 left Argentina with a confidence deficit that became pronounced after the de la Rúa government was installed in December of 1999. Not surprisingly, the economy slumped[3] and the peso came under intense speculative pressure in 2001, as Argentina's economic czar Domingo Cavallo began to push the convertibility system further from orthodoxy. Instead of ending the 2001 speculative attack by dollarizing, President Eduardo Duhalde chose to abandon the convertibility system by decree on January 6, 2002, pesofy the economy and bank balance sheets asymmetrically, and eventually float the peso on February 12, 2002. It is important to stress that the Duhalde devaluation was more than a garden-variety devaluation because convertibility's redemption pledge—the government's legal obligation to redeem one peso for one dollar—was broken. Even though the Argentine courts subsequently ruled (September 2002) that the pesofication of the economy and devaluation were illegal, a confiscation of peso holders' property ($17.8 billion) occurred in January 2002, and economic chaos ensued.

The IMF, and especially first managing director Anne Krueger, likewise rejected dollarization as an option for Argentina. When asked about the dollarization option for Argentina at a press briefing on January 11, 2002, Krueger responded, "Well, my understanding at the moment is that [dollarization] is technically unfeasible. So I don't think the authorities are thinking about it; I don't think we are thinking about it." With that statement, the IMF dismissed the possibility of dollarization. This meddling in the internal affairs of Argentina also made a sham of the IMF's campaign to foster local ownership of economic policies (Boughton and Mourmouras, 2002).

If that was not bad enough, the facts did not support the IMF's position. On January 10 the central bank had "pure" foreign reserves equal to $14.75 billion and 3.93 billion pesos in overdrafts and rediscounts to banks which were fully collateralized by publicly traded securities assessed at market value. Unless the central bank was cooking the books—or the IMF knows something that we don't—those two categories of assets would have been more than adequate to cover the central bank's 17.92 billion in outstanding peso liabilities at a one peso–one dollar exchange rate (Hanke, 2002a, 2002b).

The case for dollarization is stronger today than ever. There is more than one way for Argentina to use the dollar, though. It would be particularly advantageous for Argentina to combine use of the dollar as its unit of account with issue of dollar-denominated notes (paper money) by banks.[4] Competitive note issue by banks has a long history and is known to economists as free banking (in Spanish, *banca libre*).[5] By doing so, Argentina would both eliminate devaluation risk from the peso and capture seigniorage—the profit from issuing notes, which otherwise would accrue to the U.S. government.[6] And to protect note-issuing banks from an Argentine government which is prone to abuses of the law and expropriation of property, banks should be permitted to move offshore.

Prior to the suspension of internal convertibility (the so-called corralito) and the asymmetric pesofication of bank balance sheets, the Argentine banking system was robust. Extensive foreign ownership, regulations that required a high level of capital, and prompt action to close insolvent banks made the banking system much stronger than it was when the tequila crisis hit in 1995. The Duhalde administration, however, reversed several years of progress when it decreed the asymmetric pesofication of bank balance sheets. Under the terms of pesofication, dollar reserves were seized from banks and converted into pesos at the rate of 1.4 pesos per dollar. Bank loans made in dollars were converted into pesos at one peso per dollar in a populist move to reduce consumers' personal debt service cost. Finally, bank deposits made in dollars were converted into dollars at the 1.4 peso per dollar rate. Unable to withdraw their deposits, Argentines have seen their savings disappear as the peso-dollar exchange rate has depreciated roughly 70 percent since the beginning of the year. The impact of these measures on the banking sector was considerable. The windfall loss from the measures immediately following their implementation exceeded the capital of the consolidated banking system.

The banking system remains under considerable stress. Table 22.1 shows statistics of the Argentine financial system as of August 30. All the key figures have deteriorated since the convertibility system was abandoned. Bank deposits, which amounted to roughly $70 billion in dollar terms in mid-November 2001, now stand at 66.3 billion pesos, or $18.31 billion in

Table 22.1
Key Statistics of the Argentine Financial System, August 30, 2002

Central bank (BCRA)—amounts in billions of pesos			
Assets		Liabilities	
"Pure" foreign reserves	32.949	Peso notes and coins held by public*	13.270
Argentine government bonds	NA**	Peso notes and coins held by banks*	1.646
Reserves against government deposits	.324	Peso deposits of customers*	6.367
Rediscounts to banks	16.971	Dollar deposits of customers*	.189
Net of repurchase agreements*	4.131	Government deposits	.324

*Items comprising monetary base (liability items − asset items = 17.341 billion pesos).

Foreign reserve coverage of monetary base = 52.5% (Foreign reserves converted at August 30 exchange rate of 3.62; this coverage ratio implies dollarization would be possible at an exchange rate of 1.91 pesos per dollar).

**Data on Argentine government bonds ends on February 11, 2002. On that date the value of bonds held by the BCRA was 8.721 billion.

Financial institutions—amounts in billions of pesos			
Assets		Liabilities	
Loans to private sector in pesos	64.376	Peso deposits	65.271
Loans to private sector in dollars	4.861	Dollar deposits	1.013
Peso vault cash***	1.646		
Dollar vault cash***	.396		
Peso deposits at central bank***	6.367		
Dollar deposits at central bank***	.189		

***Items comprising bank reserves (8.598 billion pesos).
Ratio of bank reserves to deposits = 13.0%.

Interest rates	Percentage
Overnight interbank rate	39.1%
Prime rate	90.5%

Note: Some assets and liabilities are unlisted, hence assets may not equal liabilities.

Source: Banco Central de la República Argentina, Boletín Estadístico del Banco Central de la República Argentina available at www.bcra.gov.ar.

dollar terms. Bank reserves (technically known as liquidity requirements) have fallen from 12.7 to 8.6 billion pesos (from 18.1 to 13.0 percent of deposits).

The decline in bank deposits and reserves has put pressure on the banks to reduce their lending. Loans, which peaked at $77.8 billion in dollar terms in December 2000, now stand at 69.2 billion pesos, or $19.1 billion in dollar terms. As a result of this decline, interest rates are very high. The overnight interest rate was 39.1 percent per annum at the end of August, and the prime rate was a stiflingly high 90.5 percent at the same time.

Dollarization coupled with free banking, based off-shore, would put an end to monetary chaos, deliver a much-needed confidence shock and reverse Argentina's life-threatening credit crunch. Banks rely on reserves as a signal to judge whether they should expand or contract credit. When banks think their reserves are too low, they contract credit. When they think their reserves are higher than necessary, they expand credit. Provided that banks have any confidence in the future, reversing Argentina's recent trend of declining bank reserves would therefore lead to an expansion of bank credit and lower interest rates, enabling businesses to undertake projects that are not profitable in today's very high-interest rate environment. More business activity would create jobs and spur economic growth.

As reserves, banks use the local monetary base. In the monetary system of most countries, the monetary base (also known as "high powered money") consists only of monetary liabilities of the local central bank. In Argentina the situation is somewhat different. Unofficially, Argentina has a "bimonetary" financial system, in which the dollar circulates alongside the peso and the value of the dollars in circulation is 5.8 times larger than the peso monetary base at the current exchange rate of 3.6 pesos per dollar. So, besides the peso monetary base, dollar notes (paper money) in circulation are in effect a potential supplementary monetary base. For reasons discussed hereafter, the central bank's (as well as all other Argentine governmental entities') power to issue currency should be repealed. In the resulting fully dollarized monetary system, the peso monetary base would be replaced with components of the dollar monetary base—quite feasible, since the central bank has foreign reserves exceeding the peso monetary base. Indeed, given the central bank's foreign reserves, the peso monetary base could be liquidated at a rate of 1.91 pesos per dollar. If that liquidation was implemented, then the monetary base would consist solely of notes and other monetary liabilities issued by the U.S. Federal Reserve System.

As of August 30, 2002, the peso monetary base was 17.3 billion pesos, of which the public held 13.3 billion in the form of notes and coins. Since dollar notes circulate from hand to hand without being traced, it is impossible to know precisely how many dollar notes Argentines hold. However, the available evidence from Instituto Nacional de Estadistica y Censos (or INDEC—Argentina's national statistical agency) suggests that holdings of dollar notes are substantial. INDEC estimated in December 2001 that holdings of dollar notes in Argentina were perhaps 28 billion dollars or more.

Adding the known amount of peso notes (which would be replaced by dollar notes in a dollarized system) plus the estimated amount of dollar notes held by the Argentine public gives the total monetary base held by the public outside of banks. That amount is about 116.3 billion pesos (= 32.1 billion dollars at the current exchange rate), more than thirteen times the current level of bank reserves. There is ample room for banks to gain increased reserves, if they can persuade the public to move the monetary base from outside banks to inside banks. Doing so changes the monetary base into bank reserves.

One way of moving the monetary base from outside banks to inside them is to encourage the public to deposit its Federal Reserve-issued dollar notes. The public would use fewer notes and more deposit transfers, such as checks, in payment.

Another way of moving the monetary base from outside banks to inside them would be to *allow banks in Argentina to issue their own notes (paper money), denominated in dollars.* Bank-issued notes would be denominated in dollars, not pesos. Denominating notes in dollars would eliminate fears of a devaluation. At the demand of people holding bank-issued dollar notes, the notes would be payable in notes issued by the U.S. Federal Reserve or in an electronic form acceptable to note holders, such as Fed funds. Bank-issued notes would be much like bank-issued traveler's checks. People would accept the notes if they had confidence in the issuer and reject them if they lacked confidence. They would always have the option of continuing to use dollar notes issued by the U.S. Federal Reserve.

To the extent that the public was willing to accept bank-issued notes in exchange for Federal Reserve–issued notes, banks would increase their *supply* of reserves on hand. Bank-issued notes would also reduce banks' *demand* for reserves. In a monetary system that uses the dollar but where banks are not allowed to issue notes, when depositors wish to exchange deposits for notes, banks must give them Federal Reserve notes. Banks call these reserves vault cash. When a depositor wishes to convert a 100-dollar deposit into 100 pesos of notes, his bank loses 100 dollars of reserves. If depositors were willing to accept bank-issued notes, converting deposits into notes would not result in any loss of reserves, any more than switching funds from a checking account to a certificate of deposit within the same bank results in a loss of reserves.

Banks would accumulate Federal Reserve dollar notes when people came to deposit them. Banks would put their own notes into circulation by paying out their own notes instead of Federal Reserve notes when depositors wished to convert deposits into notes. Again, depositors would always have the option of demanding Federal Reserve notes rather than bank-issued notes if they desired. If there were sufficient confidence in bank-issued notes, gradually the supply of Federal Reserve notes would be replaced by bank-issued dollar notes.

The central bank's power to issue currency should be repealed. Argentina has never had a stable central bank-issued currency. Consequently, Argentines do not trust the peso (della Paolera and Taylor 2001). To eliminate the possibility of more Argentine monetary mischief and restore confidence, the central bank should be liquidated and its power to issue currency should be repealed.

The central bank can cease issuing pesos at any time by an administrative decision. It can simply call in all its peso monetary liabilities and give everyone who holds them the equivalent value in dollars. The foreign reserves that the central bank holds are adequate to do so at an exchange rate of 1.91 pesos per dollar. This would be a form of dollarization.

To discourage future governments from reintroducing the peso, it should be abolished as legal tender, all contracts in pesos should be redenominated in dollars at the chosen exchange rate, and the central bank's (or any other Argentine governmental entities') power to issue currency should be repealed.[7]

The Argentine government earns a seigniorage profit from note issuance. While its seigniorage earnings during the convertibility episode were simply investment returns on the foreign reserve assets of the central bank, the government now earns seigniorage through the inflation tax—a time-honored tradition in Argentine central banking. Under a system of note issue by banks, seigniorage would accrue to commercial banks rather than to the government. Ultimately, the profits from issuing notes would tend to be competed away and passed along to customers in the form of lower costs or better services. The great advantage of dollarization under free banking, in contrast to conventional dollarization, is that the seigniorage would stay in Argentina and not be lost to the Federal Reserve.

Allowing banks to issue dollar-denominated notes and repealing the central bank's power to issue pesos would have a powerful effect in making monetary policy "looser," by reducing interest rates. Monetary policy is much "looser" in the United States, Panama, and Ecuador than in Argentina because the perceived risk of devaluation is absent. In Argentina, the measures proposed here would make monetary policy "looser" through the following channels:

- Eliminating the peso would eliminate currency risk.
- Allowing banks to issue dollar-denominated notes would help them increase their supply of reserves on hand by "capturing" some of the Federal Reserve notes now held by Argentines and replacing them with bank-issued notes.
- Allowing banks to issue dollar-denominated notes would reduce banks' demand for reserves by reducing their need for Federal Reserve notes as vault cash.

• The boost to confidence that would result from eliminating the peso and allowing note-issuing banks to operate offshore could lead depositors to bring back the deposits that have flowed out of Argentina's banking system in recent months. A similar thing happened in Ecuador after it dollarized in 2000.

The incentive for banks to issue notes is apparent: supplying notes to the public changes from being a cost, as it is now, to a source of profits. But what incentive would the public have to use bank-issued notes?

In contrast to peso notes issued by the Argentine central bank, a great advantage of bank-issued notes would be lower perceived risk. Bank-issued notes denominated in dollars would be much less subject to fears about depreciation than those issued by the central banks. For one thing, commercial banks operating offshore are not protected by sovereign immunity as are central banks. Consequently, if a commercial bank broke its promise to redeem one of its dollars for a U.S. dollar, the holder of the commercial bank note could sue the bank. In addition, competitive market forces would push banks to maintain their redemption pledge. After all, if people thought there was a possibility of one bank not fulfilling its redemption pledge, they would switch to another brand of dollar-denominated bank notes. Consequently, incentives in the market and legal system would make the quality of the redemption pledge under free banking even stronger than under a currency board system.

In contrast to Federal Reserve notes, dollar-denominated notes issued by banks could offer three features that would make them more attractive for the public to use. One is a higher-quality supply. Federal Reserve notes in circulation in Argentina are often more worn than usual, and small denominations are scarce. The second thing bank-issued notes could offer is design features, such as Spanish words and local symbols, that would appeal to Argentines more readily than the design features of Federal Reserve notes. The third thing bank-issued notes could offer is a lottery payment feature. The idea, which has been suggested but never put into practice, is that bank notes would be like permanent lottery tickets. Now and then, banks would announce that whoever held a note with a winning serial number, drawn at random, would receive a special payment (McCulloch, 1986). The lottery payment feature would be a kind of substitute for payment of interest on notes, which is impractical because, unlike deposits, a note issuer does not know how long a particular person has held a note.

Bank-issued notes are nothing new. Allowing banks to issue their own notes might seem far-fetched or at least novel, but it is neither. Many financial firms already issue paper travelers checks, which resemble currency although they cannot pass from hand to hand without having to be endorsed. Also, casinos issue chips that are accompanied by a redemption pledge. Before the 20th century, commercial banks issued their own notes in most financially advanced countries of the time—nearly 60 countries in all. Multiple brands of notes did not confuse people any more than multiple brands of traveler's checks now do. Governments took over note issuance from commercial banks not because the private sector was doing a bad job but because governments wanted the profits for themselves. The record of private issuance of notes was generally good (Dowd, 1992).[8] In some countries bank failures caused losses to note holders, but the losses were small compared to the losses inflicted by the central banks that later took over note issuance.

Argentina was one of the countries that had note issuance by commercial banks, in the 1880s. Argentina had a rather unhappy experience because it made a number of mistakes. One was that bank notes were redeemable in government-issued pesos, a depreciated fiat currency, rather than in an international unit such as gold or the pound sterling. Another mistake was that as a condition for issuing notes, banks were required to hold specified Argentine government bonds. Argentina's default on its foreign debt in 1890 triggered a currency and banking crisis. It was not the banks, but the government that created the crisis—something that can be avoided with off-shore banking. Even so, the government responded by ending note issuance by banks and establishing the Caja de Conversión in 1891. In 1902 the Caja began to operate as a currency board, and continued to do so, providing Argentina with one of its few periods of monetary stability, until the First World War broke out in 1914.

The United States was another country where restrictions on banks gave note issuance by banks an undeserved black eye. U.S. banks were prohibited from establishing branches across state lines or in most cases even within states. As a result, the banking system consisted of thousands of small and often weak banks, rather than the small number of larger, stronger banks that existed in Canada and other countries that did not restrict branch banking. Thousands of banks meant thousands of varieties of bank note brands and greater proportional losses to note holders from bank failures than occurred in Canada. In addition, banks chartered by states were often required to back the dollar notes they issued with low-quality bonds issued by the states. This was a formula for problems with banking and currency quality. Countries that did not make the regulatory mistakes that Argentina and the United States did had much happier experience.

Would it work? Extensive historical experience indicates allowing Argentine banks to issue notes would not cause any particular problems. Again, people now accept multiple brands of traveler's checks and bank debit and credit cards in payment. Allowing banks to issue their own notes would simply be an extension of the competition that already exists in other spheres.

The workings of a system of note issuance by banks have been the subject of considerable theoretical and historical research.[9] There is no need to repeat the findings of that research here, except to reply briefly to a few commonly asked questions.

How stable would the system be? The large-scale changes resulting from the tequila crisis in 1995 made Argentina's banking system much more stable by closing weak government-owned banks and a few small privately owned banks not well suited to the changing times. Until pesofication, which confiscated banks' property, the system had withstood stresses that would have made many banking systems elsewhere crack. However, banks such as Citibank, Deutsche Bank, and HSBC are in better financial condition and have considerably more "brand name" capital than the Argentine government, so the public would be likely to find them more trustworthy than the government as issuers of currency, particularly if those banks were allowed to operate off-shore, beyond the long arm of Argentine law. Were banks allowed to issue their own notes, changes in the public's demand to hold notes as opposed to deposits could be satisfied by increasing the supply of bank-issued notes. Bank reserves would remain unchanged. In contrast, under the current system, a change in the public's demand to hold notes changes bank reserves because notes are "high-powered money." The current system is less stable in that sense than a system of bank-issued notes would be.

What would happen to note holders if banks failed? Bank notes, like bank deposits, would be a general claim on the assets of failed banks. In some countries where banks have issued their own notes, local laws have required banks to hold special reserves against notes or have given notes priority over deposits as claims to the assets of a failed bank. There is no particular reason why notes should have priority. Should people not trust bank-issued notes, they will have the option of using Federal Reserve-issued notes.

Historically, bank failures that caused big losses to note holders and depositors were infrequent in monetary systems where banks issued their own notes and did not face burdensome regulatory restrictions.[10] One of the supposed advantages of central banking is that a central bank can act as a "lender of last resort" to rescue commercial banks. But central bank rescues are not free, and in practice, they have encouraged bad banking practices and have been enormously costly for taxpayers around the world. Argentina holds the record for the costliest banking system failure on record, as a percentage of GDP: failures from 1980–82 caused losses of an estimated 55 percent of GDP, much of which was paid by taxpayers. In contrast, under the convertibility scheme, which greatly reduced the central bank's capacity to rescue commercial banks, Argentina's 1995 banking problems are estimated to have cost only 1.6 percent of GDP (Caprio and Klingebiel (1999, October). By creating an open-ended liability for taxpayers, the capability of central banks to act as lender of last resort has generally led to less stable rather than more stable banking.

Would fraud and counterfeiting be big problems? By fraud, I mean banks established with the intent of swindling the public, by issuing notes and then running away with the assets. Counterfeiting does not appear to be a big problem now in Argentina. If banks issued their own notes, it would likely be even less of a problem, because bank-issued notes tend to return to the counter of the issuer for inspection more often than central bank-issued notes (particularly Federal Reserve notes, in Argentina's case, since Argentina is a long distance from the United States). Counterfeits are more readily traced to the source the shorter the time they circulate before passing through the hands of a bank teller or a bank note-sorting machine.

What would limit the system's ability to inflate? Some people think that bank-issued notes would enable banks to create inflation without limit. This misconception arises because people are unaware of the difference between notes issued in monopoly fashion by a central bank and notes issued competitively by commercial banks. Notes issued by a central bank are forced tender, that is, people in the country that has the central bank are required to accept them in payment. Forced tender laws deprive people of the choice of using better currencies, requiring use of the local currency no matter how much inflation it suffers. Moreover, central banks cannot be sued for devaluing. Notes issued by commercial banks would not be forced tender, so if banks did not keep their promise to redeem them in dollars they would be subject both to loss of market share and lawsuits. The means by which banks would be held to their promise is the clearing system. Banks would present the notes of rival banks for payment through the clearing system, just as they now do with checks and as they have done historically in systems of note issue by banks.[11]

Would an influx of bank reserves cause a burst of high inflation? If bank-issued notes were to increase bank reserves substantially by displacing Federal Reserve-issued notes from circulation in Argentina, increased reserves would encourage banks to expand credit. Inflation should remain well in single digits, though, because the dollar is a low-inflation currency and Argentina is substantially though not perfectly integrated into world financial markets. The foreign banks that play a large role in the Argentine banking system seek the most profitable opportunities worldwide. They can easily lend anywhere, not just in Argentina, so a doubling of their reserves in Argentina would not mean they would double loans there. Even for Argentine banks, lending opportunities in the domestic market compete with lending opportunities abroad, such as buying foreign bonds.[12]

There are no constitutional barriers. Unlike the case in some other countries, nothing in Argentina's constitution stipulates that it must have a central bank or a nationally issued currency. In fact, because the constitution has roots in the nineteenth century, when note issue by multiple banks was widespread around the world, the constitution contemplates the possibility of multiple issuers. Article 75, paragraph 6 of the constitution gives the

Argentine Congress the right to "Establecer y reglamentar un banco federal con facultad de emitir moneda, así como otros bancos nacionales" (establish and regulate both a federal bank with the ability to issue money, and other national [that is, federally chartered] banks). However, the constitution explicitly contemplates the possibility of multiple note issuers in article 126, which states that "Las provincias. . . . [n]o pueden . . . acuñar moneda; ni establecer bancos con facultades de emitir billetes, sin autorizacion del Congreso Federal" (provinces may not coin money or establish note-issuing banks without the authorization of the federal Congress).[13] By implication, the federal government may itself authorize banks to issue notes, or it may authorize the provinces to charter private banks or government-owned banks that issue notes. The federal government could likewise authorize only banks domiciled off-shore to issue notes.

Argentina's Law on Financial Institutions does not mention note issuance as a permitted power of commercial banks or other financial institutions. The Organic Law of the Central Bank gives the central bank power to issue notes but does not state that the power is a monopoly. It may be possible to give offshore commercial banks the freedom to issue notes through administrative decisions, without changing any existing laws. As was mentioned above, though, it would be desirable to eliminate any role for the central bank as an issuer of currency, which would require amending the Organic Law of the Central Bank.[14]

◣ Conclusion

Replacing the peso issued by the central bank with dollar-denominated notes issued by commercial banks operating off-shore would eliminate the perceived risk of depreciation of the peso, increase the supply of bank reserves, reduce banks' demand for reserves, and promote a return of deposits into the banking system. The result would be much lower interest rates and a boost to Argentina's lagging economy. There is nothing novel about such a system. It is technically feasible and can begin to operate as soon as banks can get notes printed.

Eleven years ago the Argentine government ended a recession and launched the economy onto a path of growth by establishing the convertibility system. The convertibility system was a vast improvement over the monetary policy it replaced, but over time its weaknesses became more and more apparent. Its elimination has been disastrous. The steps proposed here will abolish the present monetary chaos and help launch Argentina on a new path of growth. Monetary policy alone cannot sustain growth, however. To accomplish that goal, Argentina will have to implement fiscal and legal reforms that increase the level of transparency and reduce corruption. In addition, the economy remains too inflexible and desperately needs a supply-side overhaul.

▲ Notes

1. An early diagnosis of these problems was made in Hanke, Jonung and Schuler (1993, pp. 72–76).

2. The government expressed its ideas in Banco Central de la República Argentina (1999) and Castro (1999).

3. For analyses of causes of this evolution, see Steve H. Hanke, "The Confidence Question," *Forbes,* September 18, 2000; "Argentina's Boom and Bust," *Forbes,* April 16, 2001; "An Exit Strategy for Argentina," *Forbes,* August 20, 2001; and "The Hoodwinkers," *Forbes,* November 26, 2001. These are available online at <www.forbes.com/hanke>.

4. A similar suggestion has been made by George Selgin, "Let Private Money Spark a Recovery in Argentina," *Wall Street Journal,* August 17, 2001, p. A9.

5. A free banking system in the general sense means one largely devoid of special regulations that prevent banks from doing things that other businesses commonly can. Free banking in this sense must be distinguished from some historical systems that were called "free banking" because they were less restrictive in some respects than the systems they replaced, but which required banks to hold specified government bonds as a condition for issuing notes, prohibited branch banking, or imposed other regulations that did not generally apply to other businesses. "Free banking" systems of that type existed in a number of U.S. states in the mid 1800s.

6. For simplicity, Argentina could at least initially use U.S. coins. The seigniorage generated by coins is small compared to that from notes.

7. An alternative course would be to allow the central bank to continue issuing notes in competition with commercial banks. However, if Argentina's history is a guide, the government will be more tempted to meddle with the monetary system in ways that are harmful to the economy, as long as the central bank continues to exist.

8. Kevin Dowd, ed., *The Experience of Free Banking,* London: Routledge, 1992.

9. For a guide to research on free banking, see Selgin White (1994, pp. 1718–49). Selgin has proposed that banks in Hong Kong, whose monetary system is somewhat like that of Argentina, be allowed to issue notes (Selgin 1988a, pp. 14–24).

10. See the essays in Dowd (1992).

11. For an explanation of how the money supply works under a system of bank-issued notes, see Selgin (1988b).

12. For more on the behavior of bank credit in a dollarized system, see Hanke (2002d).

13. Federally chartered banks in the United States have had the capacity to issue notes since 1994 (for the first time since 1935). One reason they have not issued notes is that they have been unaware the law allowed them to do so. See Schuler (2001, pp. 453–65).

14. Selected laws concerning the Argentine financial system are available on the Web site of the central bank at <http://www.bcra.gov.ar/publica/epub0001.asp>.

▲ References

Banco Central de la República Argentina. (1999, January 21). *Tratado de asociación monetaria. Produndizar la convertibilidad: un camino havia la Unión Monétaria Americana.* Mimeograph.

Boughton, James M., and Alex Mourmouras. (2002, April). Is Policy Ownership an Operational Concept? IMF Working Paper 02/72.

Caprio, Gerard, Jr., and Daniela Klingebiel. (1999, October). Episodes of Systemic and Borderline Financial Crises. (World Bank Paper). World Bank.

Castro, Jorge. (1999, April 15). *Global Currencies as a Central Contemporary Trend: Basis of the Dollarization Strategy and a Treaty of Monetary Association.* (Working paper submitted to the Presidential Cabinet of the Argentine Republic). (Unofficial translation.)

Della Paolera, Gerardo, and Alan M. Taylor. (2001). *Straining at the Anchor: The Argentine Currency Board and the Search for Macroeconomic Stability, 1880–1935.* Chicago: University of Chicago Press.

Dornbusch, Rudi. (2001, May). Fewer Monies, Better Monies. *American Economic Review, 91,* 2, 238–42.

Dowd, Kevin. (Ed.). (1992). *The Experience of Free Banking.* London: Routledge.

Hanke, Steve H., Lars Jonung, and Kurt Schuler. (1993). *Russian Currency and Finance: A Currency Board Approach to Reform.* London: Routledge.

Hanke, Steve H. (1999). Some Reflections on Currency Boards. In Mario I. Blejer and Marko Skreb (Eds.), *Central Banking, Monetary Policies, and the Implications for Transition Economies* (pp. 341–66). Boston: Kluwer Academic.

Hanke, Steve H., and Kurt Schuler. (1999, February 1). A Dollarization Blueprint for Argentina. Friedberg's Commodity and Currency Comments Experts' Report. Also available as Cato Institute Foreign Policy Briefing No. 52, March 11, 1999. Available online at www.cato.org/pubs/fpbriefs/fpb52.pdf.

Hanke, Steve H. (2002a). Questions the IMF Is Obliged to Answer. *Financial Times,* 17 January.

Hanke, Steve H. (2002b). Questions Remain Unanswered. *Financial Times,* 6 February.

Hanke, Steve H. (2002c). Putting the Banks in Charge. *Latin Finance,* June: 39–41.

Hanke, Steve H. (2002d). El Novedoso Sistema Monetario Y Bancario Panameño. In Nicolas Ardito Barleta (Ed.), *Panama Financiero.* Bogota, Colombia: Ediciones Gamma.

McCulloch, J. Huston. (1986). Beyond the Historical Gold Standard. In Colin D. Campbell and William R. Dougan (Eds.), *Alternative Monetary Regimes* (pp. 74–75). Baltimore: Johns Hopkins University Press.

Schuler, Kurt. (2001). Note Issue by Banks: A Step toward Free Banking in the United States? *Cato Journal, 20*(3), 453–65. Available online at www.cato.org/pubs/journal/cj20n3-8.pdf.

Selgin, George A., and Lawrence H. White. (1994, December). How Would the Invisible Hand Handle Money? *Journal of Economic Literature, 32*(4), 1718–49. Available online at the web sites of Selgin, *www.terry.uga.edu/~selgin/,* and White, *www.umsl.edu/~whitelh/links.html.*

Selgin, George A. (1988). A Free Banking Approach to Reforming Hong Kong's Monetary System. *Asian Monetary Monitor, 12*(1), 14–24.

Selgin, George A. (1988). *The Theory of Free Banking: Money Supply Under Competitive Note Issue.* Totowa, NJ: Rowman and Littlefield.

23 José María Fanelli

Argentina's Currency Board and the Case for Macroeconomic Policy Coordination in Mercosur

In the last 10 years, the Argentine economy has changed significantly. Three sets of policies played a crucial role. First were the market-oriented structural reforms. These reforms began to be implemented in 1990 along the lines of the so-called Washington Consensus. The trade and capital accounts were opened; the financial system was deregulated; state-owned firms were privatized; and a new scheme of prudential regulations inspired in the Basle Accord was implemented. Second, the "convertibility law" put in force a currency-board-like regime in 1991. Under the convertibility plan, the peso was pegged to the U.S. dollar and the parity was fixed at one peso per dollar. It was established that the Central Bank would hold an amount of international reserves that would at least be equal to the currency in circulation. Third, in March 1991 the Treaty of Asunción was signed. This treaty created Mercosur and established that Argentina, Brazil, Paraguay, and Uruguay would form a customs union within a few years. Today these four countries form an imperfect customs union that has introduced significant changes in both their level and pattern of trade.

The results observed after the implementation of these reforms have been mixed. One of the most remarkable outcomes was the reduction in the inflation rate. Under the Convertibility Plan Argentina ceased to be a high-inflation country. Today the rate of inflation is well below international standards. Another important fact is that the average rate of growth of the economy was considerable in the nineties (4.1 percent per year) while there have been marked efficiency gains in specific sectors. In spite of these encouraging results, however, sustainable growth is far from ensured. The aforementioned average growth rate is the result of two completely different periods, separated by the tequila effect in 1995. In the first years of the reform, the increase in GDP was strong. But, after 1995, the evolution of the economy showed several disappointing features: The activity level followed a stop-and-go pattern; the average increase in GDP was low; and the unemployment rate soared. Likewise, the fiscal deficit and the stock of the external debt experienced an upward trend. In such a context, Argentina faced increasing difficulties in meeting its external obligations. Ultimately, at the end of 2000, the country was forced to resort to the

IMF. The financial agreement (the so-called *blindaje*) was reached in December 2000.

The widening of macroeconomic disequilibrium and the increasing financial fragility from mid-1998 on have given rise to a vivid debate on the causes of the discouraging evolution of the economy and on the issue of whether Argentina should keep its currency board. Three features of the current situation deserve to be highlighted for a better grasp of why the exchange rate regime is playing such an important role in the debate.

The first is that, at present, the economy is being suffocated by a recession that has lasted for almost three years and there are no clear signals that the situation will improve significantly in the near future. It has been argued that the economy is experiencing a depression rather than a recession and that the currency board is one important factor behind this. Some analysts claim the country is now overindebted, hence there should be an upward correction in the real exchange rate. But such a correction is very difficult to achieve under a currency board. In fact, via deflation, the real exchange rate has shown a slight tendency to move in the correct direction in recent years, but the lack of sufficient downward flexibility in prices in the context of a fixed nominal exchange rate made the correction of the real exchange rate slow and painful in terms of unemployment.

Second, the evolution of the international situation since the Asian crisis has not helped to correct the misalignment in domestic relative prices. On the one hand, the American dollar has tended to appreciate in the last years. On the other, in January 1999 Brazil changed its exchange rate regime for one of free floating combined with inflation targeting, resulting in a sharp depreciation in the Brazilian currency. This generated a debate over the issue of macroeconomic policy coordination within Mercosur so as to avoid unilateral initiatives that could hamper the deepening of the integration process.

Third, the Argentine economy was hit by several external financial shocks, the most severe being the Russian crisis in August 1998. Many economists believed the dollarization of the economy would greatly help to shelter the economy from these kinds of financial shocks.

There is no consensus on the most suitable alternative before the convertibility scheme was abandoned. The main proposals under analysis were: (1) to peg the peso to a basket of currencies reflecting Argentina's trade structure; (2) full dollarization; and (3) a higher degree of macroeconomic policy coordination in Mercosur, including, eventually, the creation of a monetary union in the future.

While many interesting analyses of dollarization in Argentina have been produced recently, the issue of macroeconomic policy coordination has attracted less attention. Taking this fact into account, the main purpose of the chapter is to evaluate the pros and cons of macroeconomic policy coordination (and, eventually, a monetary union in Mercosur) vis-à-vis the maintenance of the currency board and dollarization.

The chapter has two sections. In the first section I review the macroeconomic functioning of the Argentine economy under convertibility. In the second I examine several features characterizing the exchange regimes and the trade structure of the Mercosur countries and evaluate the conditions for macroeconomic policy coordination in the region. The issues are selected on the basis of the questions raised in the literature on optimum currency areas and on the evaluation of exchange regimes.[1]

▲ Argentina's Currency Board: Ten Years After

The Convertibility Plan and Its Stages

When the plan was launched, its main purpose was to achieve a rapid disinflation. In 1989 and 1990 there where two hyperinflation episodes and, in the first quarter of 1991, the inflation rate increased rapidly, fueled by the depreciation of the currency. The stabilization plan had two main elements. First was the use of the nominal exchange rate as a nominal anchor for prices. As I mentioned before, the convertibility law fixed the nominal exchange rate between the peso and the dollar at one. Second, a new monetary regime was established. In addition to the requirement of a 100 percent backing of the monetary base with international reserves, in 1992 Congress passed a new law establishing the independence of the Central Bank. The law (the Ley de Carta Orgánica) prohibited the monetization of the fiscal deficit and severely restricted the capacity of the Central Bank to act as lender of last resort. This regime implies that the money supply is endogenously determined by the evolution of the domestic demand for money, as is, to a large extent, the credit supply. Under these conditions there is not much room for independent monetary actions.

It is worth mentioning, nonetheless, that the restrictions on the capacity of the Central Bank to support the banking system via rediscounts were relaxed after the tequila effect of 1995. Under the pressure of the crisis, the authorities reviewed the strict limits that had been imposed on rediscounts to allow the Central Bank to act as lender of last resort. The results were very positive. Countercyclical actions by the Central Bank preserved the stability of the financial system in 1995 and helped to reverse the fall in the demand for deposits that the external shock had caused. In order to reduce the probability of a new financial crisis, the Central Bank authorities took decisive steps to improve prudential regulations. A new set of norms in line with the Basle Accord's recommendations were gradually introduced. The most important changes were: the imposition of capital requirements (11.5 percent); the need for financial institutions showing severe liquidity or solvency difficulties to implement a "Regularization Plan" under the surveillance of the Central Bank; and higher liquidity requirements (over 20 percent). The new scheme was very successful at improving the stability of the financial system, but it had its costs. The new regulations induced important changes in both the microenomic structure of the banking system and the macroeconomic dynamics. I will return to this later.

The evolution of the economy under the convertibility plan showed four well-differentiated phases: a period of high growth (by quarter: 2:1991–4:94); the recession triggered by the tequila effect (1:1995–3:95); vigorous recovery (4:95–2:98); and, finally, a long period of recession (from 3:98 on). Figure 23.1 shows the quarterly evolution of the activity level under convertibility.

The beginning and duration of these phases have been closely associated with the developments in emerging capital markets. Two extremely important ones were, first, the Mexican devaluation in December, 1994 and, second, the period of financial turmoil between the Russian crisis (August 1998) and the Brazilian devaluation (January 1999). Indeed, this is only natural in an economy that adopted a currency-board–like regime and is extremely open to international capital flows. In what follows I will analyze the macroeconomic functioning of the economy under convertibility in more detail, focusing, first, on prices and quantities and, afterward, on the monetary and financial aspects. I selected these issues because they are crucial to understanding my arguments about macroeconomic policy coordination in the section that follows.

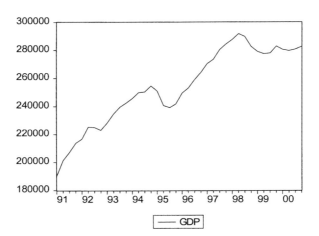

Figure 23.1. Evolution of Seasonally Adjusted GDP
Quarterly, Millions at 1993 prices

From Disinflation to Deflation: Prices and Quantities under the Convertibility Regime

The convertibility plan proved to be a highly effective instrument for the disinflation of the economy. Figure 23.2 shows the evolution of the inflation rate as measured by consumer prices.

As can be seen, since 1995, the Argentine inflation rate has either been in line with or has fallen below international standards. In order to fully assess the importance of this achievement, it is useful to take into account that in only 2 out of the 15 preconvertibility years was the inflation rate lower than 100 percent per year. In spite of this success, nonetheless, the process has had two important weaknesses. First, disinflation was not instantaneous and, as a consequence, misalignments in some key relative prices occurred that did not completely disappear afterward. Second, the ultimate outcome of the process was not price stability. Since 1999 the economy had been suffering from deflation.

The transition period from the old high-inflation setting to the new regime lasted around four years (1991–94). During this period, domestic inflation showed a systematic downward trend but was much higher than the international one. It must be taken into account, in addition, that the speed of adjustment differed markedly among price indices. The speed of convergence toward international inflation of wholesale and industrial prices was much higher than the one corresponding to consumer and services prices. The cumulative inflation rate between March 1991 and December 1996 in terms of consumer and wholesale prices was 61 percent and 21 percent, respectively. Wages followed an intermediate path between con-

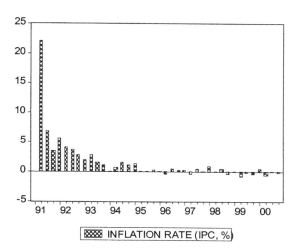

Figure 23.2. Disinflation in Consumer Prices

sumer and wholesale prices. This price dynamics resulted in a lagging real exchange rate that weakened the competitiveness of the economy. Taking the wholesale inflation rate in the USA as a proxy for international inflation, table 23.1 shows that there was a significant fall in the real exchange rate (a higher value of this variable means depreciation) in the convergence period.

Disinflation in the 1991–94 period occurred together with a strong growth in aggregate demand. The components of aggregate demand that showed a greater expansion were those that depended more on the increase in the credit conditions: investment and consumer durables. This behavior of prices and quantities during the transition is typical of stabilization plans based on the nominal exchange rate as an anchor for absolute prices. In Argentina, a similar pattern of lagging-exchange-rate-cum-raising-activity-level was observed in the case of the Tablita (1978/80) and the Austral Plan (1986/88). The most remarkable difference between these programs and convertibility, nonetheless, is that the former collapsed during the period of convergence between the domestic and international inflation rates while the latter succeeded completely. Three factors that contributed heavily to curbing inflation in the case of the convertibility plan were the opening of the economy that exerted a significant downward pressure on tradables; the strong path of productivity, fueled by the significant recovery in the investment rate; and the increase in the unemployment rate induced by structural reforms (see table 23.1).

The expansion of the economy and the lagging real exchange rate induced a boom in the demand for imported goods that, in turn, resulted in a mounting current account deficit. The external imbalance grew from $672 million in 1991 to $11,159 million three years later (table 23.1). The higher deficit increased the external vulnerability of the economy. When the tequila crisis erupted, the capital inflows that were financing the external gap reversed, and the expansion that commenced in 1991 came to a halt in 1995. Although the 1996–97 current account deficit almost halved, the tendency for the country to generate excessive current account imbalances became a permanent feature of the economy after 1998. To a great extent, this new feature reflected the steady increase in both the interest and dividend payments abroad.

The way the economy adjusted to the tequila crisis and the dynamics of prices and quantities in the fluctuations that have occurred since then show that the new convertibility regime was operating in full after 1995. There are many features that suggest this. First, from the point of view of economic policy, one important difference with Argentina's postwar experience was that neither in 1995 nor in 1998 did the country resort to currency devaluation as a way to face balance of payments difficulties. In both cases, the support of the IMF was essential to sustaining the fixed parity. In 1995 and 2000 the IMF-led rescue financial packages significantly contributed to closing the external gap. In this regard, the IMF acted as a

Table 23.1
Macroeconomic Indicators (1991–2000)

Year	Unempl. Rate (percent)	Real Exchange Rate 1991=100	Growth Rate of GDP and the Components of Aggregate Demand (percent)					Inflation Rate		Current Account Millions ($)	Fiscal Deficit Millions ($)
			GDP	Imports	Consumpt.	Investment	Exports	CPI (percent)	WPI (percent)		
1991	6.9	100.0	10.6	80.0	14.8	29.9	-3.6	84.0	56.7	-672	-675
1992	6.9	94.6	9.6	65.7	13.2	32.6	-1.0	17.5	3.2	-5715	3030
1993	9.6	95.2	4.7	8.3	4.0	13.1	0.5	7.4	0.1	-8158	2731
1994	10.7	95.8	5.8	21.1	5.0	13.7	15.1	3.9	5.8	-11158	-286
1995	18.4	92.1	-2.8	-10.0	-3.6	-13.1	22.6	1.6	6.0	-5191	-1373
1996	17.1	90.9	5.5	17.4	5.9	8.9	7.8	0.1	2.1	-6843	-5264
1997	16.1	90.8	8.1	26.6	7.9	17.7	12.0	0.3	-0.9	-12328	-4277
1998	13.2	91.5	3.9	8.4	3.1	6.6	10.1	0.7	-6.3	-14603	-4074
1999	14.5	95.9	-3.0	-11.1	-3.4	-7.6	-1.1	-1.2	-2.5	-12312	-4768
2000	15.4	96.7	0.5	-0.1	1.9	-7.8	4.6	-0.7	2.4	11000 (e)	6200 (e)

kind of international lender of last resort. Second, the effects of macroeconomic disequilibrium on the unemployment rate were much stronger. After the tequila crisis the rate of unemployment jumped to a new level that had never before been observed. Although the unemployment rate fell together with economic recovery in 1996, the rate did not return to the pretequila level and, until the end of 2001, the unemployment rate fluctuated around 15 percent. A third characteristic of the new regime was to much greater downward flexibility of nominal prices than in the past. In fact, the recession that began in 1998 created severe deflationary pressures, and the economy showed negative inflation indices in 1999 and 2000. This lack of price stability created new problems for the Argentine economy because deflation affected fiscal revenues and the burden of both private and public debt. For a better understanding of these issues it is necessary to take a look at the evolution of financial variables.

Credit, Dollarization, and Capital Movements

High inflation, frequent maxidevaluations, and uncertainty were the rule rather than the exception during the so-called lost decade that followed the debt crisis in 1982. In such a context, the domestic demand for financial assets fell systematically in the eighties. As a result, in 1991, the degree of financial deepening of the economy was very low. Total deposits amounted to around 5 percent of GDP. The changes induced by the convertibility plan in this financial scenario, a legacy of the lost decade, were as significant as those in the price dynamics. The stabilization of the exchange rate and disinflation greatly favored the recovery in the demand for domestic assets. Nonetheless, this recovery benefited in addition from the substantial improvement in the conditions of the capital markets for emerging countries in the first part of the nineties.

Figure 23.3 shows the continuous improvement in financial deepening in the 1991–94 period as measured by the increase in the demand for deposits and total credit. These developments not only softened the tight credit rationing of the eighties but also opened up new opportunities for the firms to innovate in the form of financing capital projects.

The process of increasing financial deepening under convertibility, however, has certain features that are very important for assessing whether a currency board regime best suits Argentina. In the first place, there has been an increasing dollarization of portfolios. Figure 23.4 shows the evolution of the stock of dollar-denominated credit and deposits in the domestic financial system as a proportion of the total stock of credit and deposits.

As can be seen, the proportion of dollar-denominated instruments grew continuously. At the end of 2000 more than 60 percent of credits and deposits were denominated in dollars. However, the proportion of dollarized credit was greater than the proportion of deposits. This implied that, in fact, banks were more than hedged against a devaluation of the currency.

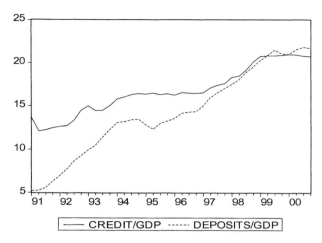

Figure 23.3. Evolution of Deposits and Credit

A second feature was that the evolution of the demand for domestic assets proved to be highly dependent on external conditions. As can be seen in figure 23.3, external shocks impacted rapidly on the demand for domestic assets and the credit supply. The Mexican crisis interrupted the upward trend in deposits and credit. After the recovery in 1996–97, the Russian crisis had the same effect. Note that the speed of the recovery in deposits

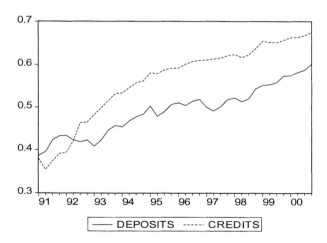

Figure 23.4. Dollarization of Credit and Deposits (Proportion of dollar-denominated over total, %)

and credit was very different after the tequila and the Russian shocks. While the recovery was very rapid in the former case, credits and deposits showed a much more sluggish evolution in the latter.

External shocks, both positive and negative, also influenced the cost of domestic credit. In this regard, the main link between external and domestic credit markets is the country risk premium. Changes in the conditions in emerging countries' capital markets and/or in the domestic macroeconomic scenario are reflected immediately in changes in the country risk premium. The volatility of both domestic and external conditions is echoed in the evolution of the country risk. Via its influence on the cost of credit, this volatility increased the variance of aggregate demand. Figure 23.5 shows the evolution of the country risk premium and compares it with the economy's quarterly rate of growth. Both variables show high volatility, and there is a marked and negative association between changes in the country risk premium and changes in the growth rate of quarterly GDP.

The third feature is, precisely, the close association between the supply of credit and the activity level. Indeed, given that Argentina's capital markets are far from perfect, it seems plausible that changes in the availability of credit do matter to the macroeconomic evolution of the economy.[2] I can present some evidence that is consistent with this hypothesis. Equations 1 through 3 present an error correction quarterly model that represents the relationship between credit and GDP in the short and long run. The model assumes that, in a context of pervasive imperfections in financial markets (rationing), the availability of real credit in the banking system (crd) influences the activity level (gdp) in the short run, while there is a long-run relationship between the stock of real credit and the activity level. Taking into account the effects of capital inflows, assume that the country risk premium (r) has a negative effect on activity and available credit.

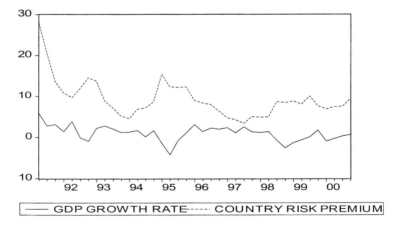

Figure 23.5. Country Risk Premium and Growth Rate (%)

[1] $loggdp_t = \delta_1 + \delta_2\, logcrd_t + s_t$

[2] $\Delta\, loggdp_t = \delta_3\, (loggdp_{t-1} - \delta_1 - \delta_2\, logcrd_{t-1})$
$\qquad\qquad + \delta_4\, \Delta loggdp_{t-1} + \delta_5\, \Delta logcrd_{t-1} + \delta_6 r_t + z_{1t}$

[3] $\Delta\, logcrdt_t = \delta_7\, (loggdp_{t-1} - \delta_1 - \delta_2\, logcrd_{t-1})$
$\qquad\qquad + \delta_8\, \Delta loggdp_{t-1} + \delta_9\, \Delta logcrd_{t-1} + \delta_{10}\, r_t + z_{2t}$

The results obtained using quarterly data for the convertibility period (1991: 2/2000:4) were as shown in table 23.2.

The coefficient of credit in the long-run equation (δ_2) is positive and significant at the 5 percent level, and so it seems that credit and GDP are cointegrated. As coefficient δ_3 is also significant, it can be hypothesized that deviations of GDP from its long-run relationship with credit are relevant in the short run. The coefficient corresponding to risk premium is negative and significant in the case of GDP. These results are consistent with the hypotheses of a relevant influence of credit on output in the short run and of a negative correlation between the country risk premium and the evolution of the macroeconomy.

In sum, the features analyzed suggest that, under convertibility and free capital movements, there is a close association between capital flows, the generation of credit, and the activity level because the money and credit supplies are to a great extent passively determined by the evolution of the demand for domestic assets. This is an important potential source of macroeconomic and financial uncertainty, as international capital flows into "emerging" countries are far from stable.

It must be taken into account, nonetheless, that the economic author-

Table 23.2
Credit, Risk and Activity Level

Coefficient	Estimated value	t-statistic
δ_1	8.9	—
δ_2	0.33	13.2
δ_3	−0.38	−4.0
δ_4	0.50	4.5
δ_5	0.10	0.9
δ_6	−0.20	−3.1
δ_7	0.10	0.6
δ_8	0.40	2.1
δ_9	0.40	2.6
δ_{10}	0.08	0.6

Included observations = 38; sample period: 1991:2/2000:4

ities' degrees of freedom under convertibility are not equal to zero. In fact, it seems that the depth of the recession after 1998 was not independent of some policy actions on the financial and fiscal sides. In order to see this, notice that there has been a persistent tendency for the rate of growth of credit to lag behind the rate of growth of deposits since 1995. In fact, in 1999 the line representing deposits crosses the credit line (fig. 23.3). The tightening in prudential and liquidity regulations of the Central Bank in the second part of the nineties is closely associated with this result.

But, in fact, the credit squeeze in the private sector since 1998 has been stronger than what is suggested in figure 23.3. The figure clearly shows that the aggregate stock of credit as a proportion of GDP has stagnated since 1998. But the aggregate conceals the fall in the stock of private credit that was offset by an increase in the amount of public sector credit demand. The increase in the fiscal deficit from 1998 (which was associated with the political cycle) raised the public sector's borrowing needs, and as a consequence the government crowded out the private sector. The private/public credit ratio fell from 7.7 when the Russian crisis hit the economy in 1998 to 4.4 at the end of 2000. The tightening of credit conditions for the private sector was, undoubtedly, one major factor that deepened the recession. The funds available for financing the private sector suffered, simultaneously, from the pressure exerted by the fall in capital inflows, the tightening in prudential regulations, and a mounting public demand for credit. In such a context, it is not surprising that the demand for investment and consumer durables, which is a major factor behind the stagnation of aggregate demand, plummeted.

▲ The Exchange Regime, Trade, and the Problem of Macroeconomic Policy Coordination

The problem of macroeconomic policy coordination is very complex. It has many aspects and involves a considerable number of variables, structural parameters, and policy determinants. In addition, the literature on the issue is ample and rather dispersed. It embraces a wide spectrum of articles, starting with those aimed at evaluating the advantages and disadvantages of alternative exchange rate regimes to studies on OCAs that analyze the convenience and consequences of monetary unions. The problem is no less complex from the economic policy point of view because the different alternatives to coordination imply degrees of international commitment that differ significantly (De Grauwe, 1994; Mundell, 1961, 2000). Given this complexity, I do not intend to embrace all aspects of the problem. I will focus, first, on the issues associated with the exchange regime and, second, on the role trade variables play. This selection of issues arises from having based my discussion on the results of a research project that concentrated on them.[3] A central hypothesis of the project was that, in a world of imperfect markets, the choice of the exchange rate regime is rigorously limited by the specific structural features of both international trade and each country's macroeconomy and that different regimes may have distinct and nonneutral effects on the evolution of the real side of the economy. My main purpose here is to draw some lessons for Argentina, taking into account the stylized facts of the convertibility regime I analyzed in the previous section.

The Exchange Rate Regime and Policy Coordination

In choosing an exchange rate regime, the authorities must decide on three key elements: first, the desired degree of autonomy of the monetary policy; second, the degree of openness of the capital account, which will contribute decisively to determining the intensity of capital mobility; and third, the degree of nominal exchange rate flexibility. If there are no restrictions on choice, the authorities might assign monetary policy to domestic targets (inflation/unemployment), ensure free capital mobility to facilitate the intertemporal allocation of resources and of risk, and set a stable nominal exchange rate to favor the stability of the private sector's expectation formation. The number of "free" parameters and variables in the authorities' opportunity set, however, is too limited. The lack of degrees of freedom determines the appearance of a trilemma: it is not possible, simultaneously, to achieve nominal exchange rate stability, free capital mobility, and an autonomous monetary policy (Frankel, 1999). Two of these objectives can, at most, be consistently pursued.

In principle, when choosing objectives and instruments, one should assume that a country's preferences reveal an optimal choice, given the economic and political restrictions. Under this assumption, the choices regarding the exchange rate regime of the four regional partners in Mercosur reveal a wide disparity in preferences and/or restrictions limiting the opportunity set. The two principal economies are in rather asymmetric situations. As I have shown, Argentina has a currency board and free capital mobility. In facing the trilemma, its choice reveals that according to the country's scale preferences, it is worth renouncing an autonomous monetary policy in order to secure nominal exchange rate stability and free capital flows. Brazil, to the contrary, has chosen a floating exchange rate and free capital mobility and has thereby obtained the necessary degree of freedom to assign the monetary policy to domestic targets (inflation). With Brazil's scale it pays off to accept a higher nominal exchange rate volatility.

This asymmetry in the order of preferences is, for many analysts, a serious obstacle to future attempts at coordinating the macroeconomic policy between the partners and to intraregional trade as well. Although the argument seems to be compelling at first sight, it is, indeed, much more complex than intuition suggests. In the first place, *ceteris paribus,* if the election of the exchange rate regime is "optimal" for each country, given the constraints, it will contribute significantly to ensuring macroeconomic stability. This is very important in a region in which stability has been a permanent source of concern in the recent past. It is unlikely that the regional bloc would consolidate in an unstable environment. The econometric studies show that income effects are much stronger than price effects in explaining the level of the intrabloc trade flows (Heyman and Navajas, 1998). Therefore, the best exchange rate regime is one that is more suitable to the steady and rapid growth of the effective demand of each of the partners. If Brazil grows steadily, the Argentine exports will receive a strong incentive. In the second place, it is necessary to consider the endogenous consequences of a regime change on macroeconomic stability. For example, an extemporaneous attempt at establishing a monetary union or at accelerating the path toward policy coordination could result in strong macroeconomic disequilibria. Such disequilibria, in turn, could jeopardize credibility and depress animal spirits and capital accumulation. In the end, this could be very harmful to trade and the overall process of regional integration.

One can sensibly hypothesize, obviously, that the observed choice of the exchange rate regime is not optimal. Under this assumption, the countries are not on the "efficiency frontier," hence there is room to improve the design of the existing exchange rate regimes. This view is implicit in some of the policy proposals that are being discussed in the region. A notable case is dollarization. This alternative was discussed basically in Argentina, where dollarization would have to be a unilateral decision of the authorities. Consequently, it should not be assessed on exclusively economic grounds because it would certainly have political consequences, too. Specifically, it could harm the spirit of cooperation within the regional bloc. There is another proposal that also implicitly assumes the lack of optimality of the existing exchange rate arrangements. It proposes that the two countries define a priori a band to limit the acceptable range of variation of the bilateral real exchange rate around its "equilibrium" level. If the observed value of the real exchange rate falls outside the band, the countries would automatically put into practice compensatory changes in their tariffs on intraregional trade flows in order to make up for the difference.

If one assumes that a given exchange rate regime is optimal, taking into account short-run restrictions, the best short-run choice for Brazil seems to be a flexible exchange rate regime and for Argentina a currency board. But insofar as the restrictions change in the long run, the existing regimes should be changed accordingly. This approach means that the authorities will have to work on two issues. First, it is necessary to identify the short-run restrictions that impede the authorities from reaching the efficiency frontier regarding the regime choice and design a plan to eliminate such restrictions. This implies taking into account not only fundamental economic variables but also the political conditions and dynamics in each country. The second issue has to do with the factors that are endogenous to the integration process. These are critical to the design and the timing in implementing the macroeconomic policy coordination. This approach to the problem comprises all those proposals that imply a gradual development of the institutions and of the necessary instruments to be coordinated. Given that these proposals assign a primary role to the short-run restrictions imposed by the fundamentals, their advocates favor a gradual harmonization of such fundamentals. They usually propose first building a consensus on the value of key domestic variables, such as the inflation rate, the fiscal deficit, and the evolution of the public debt. These proposals, nonetheless, are compatible with different goals for the long run, including a monetary union.

The evidence analyzed in Fanelli (2001) and the stylized facts on convertibility that I presented earlier suggest that the proposals under discussion will not necessarily have similar effects. There are three features of the macroeconomy that will probably have an important bearing on the final outcome regarding macroeconomic policy coordination: the degree of price flexibility, the volatility of the environment, and financial deepening.

The literature assigns a role of major importance to price and wage flexibility, as in the works on OCAs, exchange regimes, and economic cycles. The more flexible prices and wages are, the less relevant the exchange rate arrangement is. When the prices of goods, services, and factors are flexible, a deviation of the real exchange rate from its equilibrium value will generate demand and supply excesses that will induce the appropriate changes in nominal prices so as to rapidly move the economy and, particularly, the market for foreign exchange, toward an equilibrium. Under these circumstances, the costs of renouncing monetary policy autonomy will be minimal.[4]

When prices and wages are not fully flexible, the literature highlights three facts:

1. There is a high correlation between nominal and real changes in the exchange rate, and this should not occur if nominal values were irrelevant to real magnitudes (Froot and Rogoff, 1995; Rogoff, 1996).
2. The purchasing power parity (PPP) does not hold in the short run, and the period of adjustment toward equilibrium is longer than one would expect, given the observed short-run variability of both the real and nominal exchange rate. In developed countries the PPP seems to hold in the very long run, but there is no evidence of this in developing countries because of the lack of data (Edwards and Savastano, 1999).
3. Under a floating exchange rate regime, the observed variance of the real exchange rate and domestic prices is higher (Basu and Taylor, 1999).

The evidence in Fanelli (2001) strongly suggests that the economies in the regional bloc show important rigidities, and I have shown the difficulties that Argentina is facing to correct the real exchange rate via deflation in the first section. Consequently, in the Mercosur area I should be prepared to observe a correlation between nominal and real fluctuations in the exchange rate, lengthy departures from the PPP rule, and significant deviations of the real exchange rate from its equilibrium value, as suggested by Edwards and Savastano (1999). Under such circumstances, the excesses of supply and demand will induce adjustments not only in price but also in quantities, and consequently the activity level and employment will be affected by a transitory deviation in the real exchange rate. This means that the trilemma is a true source of concern to the Mercosur countries and that renouncing capital controls or the monetary policy may entail a real cost.

The recent evolution of Mercosur's two biggest countries makes it clear how significant the lack of flexibility is. Brazil changed its regime and let the exchange rate float in order to induce an adjustment in the real exchange rate, while Argentina is experiencing a prolonged deflationary period in a context of fixed parity. Under these conditions the authorities face difficult policy trade-offs and are obliged to take stressful decisions. Very often, such decisions have substantial costs in terms of both financial fragility and employment. The facts on the Argentine experience under convertibility I presented previously clearly illustrate this situation.

Given the existence of these policy trade-offs, if the countries under consideration show similar policy preferences, coordination will be easier. Likewise, the more ambitious the coordination goals are, the more restrictive the constraints will become. For example, a monetary union supposes a similarity in the preferences related to the inflation/unemployment trade-off. Such a similarity is not necessary in the case of milder coordination initiatives, such as a gradual convergence in the inflation rates, fiscal deficits, and levels of public indebtedness.

The literature stresses that free labor mobility across national boundaries helps greatly to limit the effects of price rigidities on unemployment and market disequilibrium in general. The authorities, nonetheless, show no interest in attaining a rapid unification of labor markets in Mercosur. Besides, the existence of a marked disparity in the regional unemployment rates within each country suggests that labor mobility may be too sluggish to eliminate macroeconomic disequilibria with the required speed. In this regard, it is very important to take into account that there is a marked duality in the economies of the region.

Some authors suggest that the existence of nominal rigidities calls for fiscal policy as a means to manage problems of employment or regional disparities. Fiscal policy hence is the third element on the list. The fiscal instruments utilized often take the form of direct transfers. Regrettably, the country studies in Fanelli (2001) suggest that, at present, the authorities do not have too much room for maneuver. On the one hand, the fiscal systems are fragile and inefficient and are experiencing structural problems. For example, they are facing serious difficulties to finance the social security system, and the allocation of both expenditures and taxes to different levels are not clearly defined, which gives rise to recurrent conflicts between the central and federal governments. Likewise, the constraints on the ability to perform anticyclical fiscal policies are tight. One important restriction is that capital flows are not only volatile but also show a procyclical behavior, and therefore the financial conditions the government faces tend to become tighter just when the authorities require a softer financial constraint. In fact, the weak financial position of the public sector in Brazil and Argentina has determined that the main fiscal objective in the two countries is to strengthen the budget in order to ensure solvency. The strong increase in the country risk following the crisis in Russia gives priority to this objective and other objectives, such as anticyclical policies, were subordinated to it.

One relevant characteristic of the two main economies in Mercosur is the volatility of the macroeconomic environment. In fact this is not surprising, since a stylized fact of developing economies is that they are more volatile (Fanelli, 2000; Inter-American Development Bank, 1995). This has implications for both macroeconomic policy coordination and the choice of exchange rate regimes. Fanelli (2001) examined the stochastic properties of the time series associated with the real exchange. They used generalized autoregressive conditional heteroskedastic (GARCH) models and identified two stylized facts. First, high volatility is, in effect, a characteristic of the time series corresponding to prices in Brazil and Argentina, and second, regime changes have a substantial influence on volatility. This is very clear regarding the launching of convertibility in Argentina in 1991 and the implementation of a floating regime in Brazil in 1999.

Given that the evolution of the real exchange rate will be critical in determining the success or failure of macroeconomic policy coordination exercises, ideally it would be optimal to know two things: first, the average duration of deviations from equilibrium; and second, the volatility of the series. It is not an easy task, though. The evolution of the real exchange rate is the result of the interaction of each country's nominal prices and the nominal bilateral exchange rate. Therefore, it is necessary to take into account the process of domestic pricing. All the economies in Mercosur have experienced long periods of high inflation. As a consequence, the average duration of contracts tends to be very short compared to other developing countries, not to mention developed ones. In spite of the stabilization efforts in the nineties, this characteristic was only partially reversed. This introduced a difference in the findings in the literature on developed countries. In Argentina and Brazil there is less inertia, and this affects the duration of the adjustment period, which seems to be shorter than in the developed world. The greater flexibility in the contract structure implies that when a certain deviation from the equilibrium exchange rate as determined by fundamentals occurs, the speed of adjustment toward equilibrium is higher. The cost of less inertia is more volatility. That is, the econometric evidence shows a greater variance around the equilibrium values but a shorter mean duration of deviations. From this point of view, higher volatility and low duration of deviations are not incompatible. In fact, I have found that it is easier to reject the hypothesis of the presence of a unit root in the bilateral real exchange rate (between Brazil and Argentina) compared to the case of developed countries. I think this must be considered when designing the coordination policy.

The economies in Mercosur area show a market structure that is more incomplete than that in the developed world. This is particularly true regarding the financial side of the economy. Some markets that are key to the monetary and exchange rate policies are either too thin or missing. There are practically no markets to hedge from exchange rate risks. I have shown that, in the case of Argentina, the level of financial deepening is low and volatile and that there is a systematic increase in the degree of dollarization of financial instruments. The low degree of monetization did not allow for more or less aggressive sterilization policies. There is ample evidence, especially in the nineties, that the attempts at sterilizing the monetary effects of capital inflows in Latin American countries induced strong increases and a higher variability in the domestic interest rates. The costs of sterilization policies are often extremely high.

The previous argument made it clear that I have been using the image of the trilemma because it is very useful for illustrating synthetically the policy options. But to a certain extent the image may be somewhat misleading in the case of Mercosur. It could give too optimistic a view of the degrees of freedom when undertaking economic policy in the region. In effect, on the one hand, the trilemma assumes that the countries have the ability to engage in monetary policy actions and to impose controls on capital flows. This is not always true. In the Uruguayan case, for example, unrestricted capital movements are part and parcel of its development strategy, oriented to becoming a regional financial center. In the case of Argentina it is a critical ingredient in its strategy to gain international credibility. The only country to show a certain willingness to impose (mild) capital controls in the recent past is Brazil. We should not lose sight of the fact that the ability to implement an independent monetary policy without resorting to capital controls is a function of the degree of financial deepening achieved.

Trade Structure and the Macroeconomy

In the OCA literature trade variables play a significant role in defining an OCA. The approach has recently been extended in two directions. In the first place, Bayoumi and Eichengreen (1997) argue that the two main factors in the OCA theory are the symmetry of cyclical movements and the trade features. And if they are relevant to determining the boundaries of the currency area, they must also influence the functioning of other exchange rate arrangements. The authors conclude that these factors explain the extent of intervention and/or flexibility of the nominal rate allowed by the monetary authorities. The second extension is the introduction of endogeneity by Frankel and Rose (1996). They say the OCA theory has correctly identified the key factors. However, the theory tends to ignore the fact that causality does not run in only one direction. These authors advance evidence that suggests that trade integration affects the pattern of comovement of key macrovariables and, so, affects cyclical correlation.

I believe that the role of the transformations in the trade structure is particularly important in relation to macroeconomic policy coordination in the Mercosur area. Mercosur is a young regional agreement, and therefore deep transformations in the magnitude and the pattern of trade should be expected. If the two extensions of the OCA theory are correct, this should impact the macroeconomic dynamic. This, in turn, should change the set of restrictions and opportunities the authorities face in the process of coordinating macroeconomic policies in the region. The dimensions I would like to analyze briefly here are: country size, the degree of openness, the specialization pattern, and the level of intraindustrial trade.

According to theory, the smaller and the more open the country is, the more beneficial the stability of the exchange rate will be. In an open economy, the participation of tradable goods and services is higher. Therefore, the benefits of the exchange rate stability in terms of reduction in transaction costs will be higher. Likewise, the role of nominal anchor played by the nominal exchange rate will be more important. On the other hand, a small economy open to capital flows has a rather limited capability to conduct an independent monetary policy. Hence the costs of renouncing autonomy are lower. In the case of Mercosur, two additional features I have already mentioned need to be considered: weak financial deepening and high portfolio dollarization. Both factors represent further constraints on the possibility of conducting an autonomous monetary policy. Furthermore, dollarization reinforces the effects of the volatility of the exchange rate on financial risks.

In the Mercosur area, Uruguay represents the paradigm of a small country open to capital flows. In line with the predictions of the theory, in the nineties the country did not use monetary policy as an anticyclical device. The aim of stabilizing the nominal exchange rate was privileged. Given the characteristics of the stochastic processes, the election of a stable nominal exchange rate did not imply the fixation of the nominal exchange rate. The choice, instead, was to establish a pattern for the fluctuation of the nominal rate within a band.

Brazil and Argentina show a markedly low degree of openness and share a past of high inflation. In the case of Argentina, its reduced openness is a priori a reason against the fixation of the nominal exchange rate. However, its history of instability, together with the firm determination to lower the level and volatility of the inflation rate, led the country to establish a currency board arrangement to gain credibility and to anchor nominal magnitudes. The examination of the stochastic properties of the price series in

Fanelli (2001) clearly shows that the change in regime in 1991 induced a structural transformation. Thus, the Argentine case strongly suggests the nonneutrality of the exchange rate regime. In addition, it should be highlighted that dollarization contributed to locking in the system. Given the elevated proportion of dollar-denominated debt, an unexpected change in regime (i.e., a devaluation) would set in motion strong destabilizing forces on the financial side. This severely limits the probability of an unexpected modification in the nominal parity.

In contrast with the Argentine and Uruguayan cases in the nineties, Brazil has shown a certain propensity to modify the exchange rate regime. After the failure of the Real Plan, based on the use of the nominal exchange rate as an anti-inflationary device, the authorities have chosen a free-floating regime. In this way, Brazil acts as if it were a large, closed, and nondollarized country. The Brazilian study shows that the Central Bank conducts the monetary policy with autonomy at the cost of increased real and nominal exchange rate volatility. This fact is consistent with the existence of imperfections that determine the nonneutrality of the nominal fluctuations in the value of the currency. There are two factors that suggest that an inconsistency could appear between the new exchange rate regime and the long-run evolution of trade and macroeconomic fundamentals. They are, on the one hand, the increasing interdependency within the bloc and the active trade liberalization policies in general and, on the other, a certain tendency for the private sector to dollarize its portfolio in a context of crisis. The move in the exchange rate regime until the end of 2001, however, showed a difference with the past: the low inflation rates observed after the modification in the exchange rate arrangement in January 1999. This contrasts with the explosive inflation rates that usually followed devaluation. From the point of view of coordination, this new fact was encouraging because it could have made the harmonization of economic policies with Argentina easier. Argentina already had a very low inflation rate, and in fact, as I have shown, was experiencing deflation.

In fact, regarding size, Mercosur is a rather singular experience. It represents a small portion of the world economy, around 4 percent, and within the bloc no country is big enough and/or has sufficient credibility to be a leader in the context of a monetary union. Hence Mercosur is much smaller than the EU, and a country like Germany is not a member. This fact, together with the disparity of exchange rate arrangements, calls for a flexible coordination scheme and does not favor a rigid one, such as a monetary union. This situation, nonetheless, could change endogenously in the future. An increasing regional integration accompanied by an upward trend in the relative size of the bloc as compared to the world economy (because of catching up) could make a more rigid intrabloc exchange arrangement more attractive. Such an arrangement does not necessarily imply a fixed exchange rate but rather a gradual convergence to a situation of less real and nominal volatility in the bilateral rates.

In the literature, it is assumed that the mutations in the specialization pattern and the structure of trade contribute to determining the way shocks affect the economy. However, there is no firm consensus on the way regional agreements affect the trade specialization pattern. There are two contrasting hypotheses. According to Eichengreen (1992) and Krugman (1993), integration accentuates specialization. Each country will have an increased incentive to exploit its comparative advantage. This should increase the asymmetry of cycles, insofar as the shocks that affect specific industries are idiosyncratic. Frankel and Rose (1996) suggest, instead, that increasing integration means more synchrony in the cycles. Two arguments support this conclusion. First, if there is an augmentation in the intensity of trade between two economies, the demand shock that occurs in one will affect the other. Second, a good part of modern trade is intraindustrial. Under these circumstances, productivity and demand shocks will affect the economies on both sides of the frontier.

In the Mercosur area, the regional agreement induced increases in openness and intraindustrial trade, and the countries were able to better exploit their comparative advantages. This generated a greater interdependence (Fanelli 2001; World Bank, 1999), and evidence shows that changes in global demand tend to generate spillover effects (Heyman and Navajas, 1998).

Under the hypothesis of increasing interindustrial specialization, integration makes the fixation of the bilateral exchange rate or a monetary union less convenient. When shocks are asymmetric, monetary autonomy is more valuable. The conclusion is the opposite if integration increases symmetry. This does not imply, at least in the context of Mercosur, that more symmetry of the cycles facilitates macroeconomic policy coordination in general. More symmetry makes coordination based on a fixed exchange rate easier, not coordination in general. The OCA literature implicitly assumes that each country can, in fact, conduct an independent monetary policy. I have already shown, however, that in the Mercosur area, the lack of financial deepening and dollarization severely reduces the monetary authorities' room for maneuver. Besides, correlated cyclical movements do not necessarily make coordination easier. For example, suppose an exogenous shock impacts two partners of a bloc in the same way and one of them decides to increase trade barriers and impose capital controls. In a crisis situation, the other country will not be inclined to tolerate such deviations. But, perhaps, the reaction would have been much more benevolent and tolerant if the second country had not received the impact of the shock.

Indeed, when the obsession of the literature with monetary policy is eliminated, other interesting opportunities for coordination appear for countries experiencing asymmetric shocks. Assume that there are two highly specialized countries with perfect asymmetry in their shocks and living in a world of imperfect capital markets. Under such circumstances, those countries would experience high volatility. Idiosyncratic shocks would affect the industries in which each country is specialized, and market imperfections would impede the diversification of risk in the international markets. Macroeconomic coordination between the two countries should be Pareto-improving under these circumstances, even though a currency union would not be a good solution. The two countries could design a common compensatory fiscal policy. Given the negative correlation of shocks, good times for the budget in one country would coincide with bad times in the other. It would be possible to offset the cycles in the two countries by means of an intertemporal reallocation of fiscal deficits and surpluses. This coordination scheme would help to soften the effects of market failures in the international capital markets, insofar as it would allow for risk diversification. In fact, this example is very realistic. On the one hand, international capital markets are highly imperfect; on the other, at the domestic level the fiscal policy is frequently utilized to offset the effects of idiosyncratic shocks to particular industries in specific regions within the country. In the cases of Argentina and Brazil, these kinds of proposals would encounter two obstacles. First, there is the fragility and inefficiency of fiscal institutions. Second, there are important exogenous shocks that affect the two economies symmetrically. My research showed that intraindustrial trade is increasing rapidly and that shocks originating in external capital markets tend to affect the two economies in a similar way.

In sum, the countries in the Mercosur area showed much less volatility and instability now than in the recent past. But there is still much work to be done. So these countries could reap substantial benefits if they found a way to gradually advance in macro coordination. They should aim, in the first place, to reduce the remaining volatility in the evolution of nominal and relative prices within the bloc. Nonetheless, under the present circumstances, to set ambitious goals of coordination such as a monetary union would neither be beneficial for macroeconomic stability nor for the regional agreement In this regard, "Declaración de Buenos Aires," which established the gradual harmonization of inflation rates, fiscal deficits, and public indebtedness, seems to be a step in the right direction.

◣ Notes

This chapter was elaborated for presentation at the seminar *Dollarization in the Western Hemisphere,* Ottawa, October 4–5, 2000. I gratefully acknowledge the financial support of the International Development Research Center and the North-South Institute.

1. The analysis in the second section of this chapter is based on the results of a research project undertaken by CEDES (Buenos Aires), CINVE (Montevideo), and the Economics Department of the Federal University (Rio de Janeiro). Each of these institutions elaborated a country study and analyzed the macroeconomic regime from the perspective of the regional agreement. The results are presented in Fanelli (2001).

2. It can also be assumed that finance also matters at the microeconomic level for both the results of the restructuring process launched in the nineties and the strategies specific firms chose. See Fanelli (2000).

3. For these results, see the country studies corresponding to Argentina, Brazil, and Uruguay in Fanelli (2001).

4. Under a complete market structure, the choice of a specific exchange rate regime is neutral. It has no real effects (Obstfeld and Rogoff, 1996). In a setting characterized by full price flexibility without restrictions on the intertemporal allocation of resources and on risk management, the information on the characteristics of the existing exchange rate regime would be irrelevant. The rules specified by the authorities to buy and sell different currencies and to manage the monetary supply would only be relevant to the equilibrium value of the nominal variables. The real world of markets, nonetheless, is far from complete, hence the exchange rate regime matters to the real variables because the nominal magnitudes may affect real ones.

▲ References

Basu, S., and A. M. Taylor. (1999). Business Cycles in International Historical Perspective. *Journal of Economic Perspectives, 13* (Spring), 45–68.

Bayoumi, T., and B. Eichengreen. (1997, August). Exchange Rate Volatility and Intervention: Implications of the Theory of Optimum Currency Areas. International Monetary Fund and CEPR, University of California, Berkeley.

De Grauwe, P. (1994). *The Economics of Monetary Integration.* Oxford: Oxford University Press.

Edwards, S., and M. A. Savastano. (1999, July). Exchange Rates in Emerging Economies: What Do We Need to Know? (NBER Working Paper 7228). NBER Working Paper Series, Cambridge, Mass.

Eichengreen, Barry. (1992). Should the Maastricht Treaty Be Saved? *Princeton Studies in International Finance, 74.* Princeton University: International Finance Section.

Fanelli, J. M. (2000, June). Macroeconomic Regimes and the Trade Agenda in Latin America. Latin American Trade Network, Buenos Aires.

Fanelli, J. M. (Ed.). (2001). *La Coordinación Macroeconómica en el Mercosur,* Siglo 21, Madrid.

Frankel, J. A. (1999). No Single Currency Regime is Right for All Countries or at All Times. (NBER Working Paper 7338). NBER Working Paper Series.

Frankel, J. A., and A. K. Rose. (1996, August). The Endogeneity of the Optimum Currency Area Criteria. (Working Paper 5700). NBER Working Paper Series, Cambridge, Mass.

Froot, K. A., and K. Rogoff. (1995). Perspectives on PPP and Long-run Real Exchange Rate. In G. Grossman and K. Rogoff (Eds), *Handbook of International Economics, Vol. III* (pp. 1647–88). Amsterdam: Elsevier.

Heyman, D., and F. Navajas. (1998). Coordinación de Políticas Macroeconómicas en Mercosur: Algunas Reflexiones. In Ensayos sobre la inserción regional de la Argentina, *Documento de Trabajo* No. 81. Comisión Económica para América Latina y el Caribe—CEPAL, Buenos Aires.

Inter-American Development Bank. (1995). *Economic and Social Progress in Latin-America.* Washington D.C.: Inter-American Development Bank.

Krugman, Paul. (1993). Lessons of Massachsetts for EMU. In Giavazzi and F. Torres (Eds.), *The Transition to Economic and Monetary Union in Europe* (pp. 241–61). New York: Cambridge University Press.

Mundell, Robert. (1961, November). A Theory of Optimum Currency Areas. *American Economic Review,* 509–17.

Mundell, Robert. (2000). *Currency Areas, Volatility and Intervention.* Mimeograph. Columbia University.

Obstfeld, M., and K. Rogoff. (1996). *Foundations of International Macroeconomics.* Cambridge, Mass.: MIT Press.

Rogoff, K. (1996). The Purchasing Power Parity Puzzle. In *Journal of Economic Literature, 34*(2), 647–68.

World Bank. (1999, October). *Trade Blocs and Beyond: Political Dreams and Practical Decisions.* Draft Policy Research Report.

24 Archibald R. M. Ritter and Nicholas Rowe

Cuba

"Dollarization" and "Dedollarization"

> Cuba is the only country where people earn one currency—pesos—from their work, but must have another—the dollar—to survive.
>
> —Popular Cuban saying

> I believe that in the future, it will never be necessary again to ban the possession of dollars or other foreign currencies, but its [the dollar's] free circulation for the payment of many goods and services will only last for as long as the interests of the Revolution make it advisable. Therefore we are not concerned about the famous phrase "the dollarization of the economy." We know very well what we are doing.
>
> —President Fidel Castro (June 2000)

In August 1993, the government of Cuba "depenalized" the possession of U.S. dollars by Cuban citizens, following more than three decades in which holding U.S. dollars was illegal. It also permitted family remittances to be sent to Cuba from relatives in the "diaspora" and to be received by family members in Cuba. This resurrected the former underground market for dollar exchange, opened the floodgates for dollars from Cubans in exile, and rapidly expanded the dollar economy.

These changes, in turn, generated some indispensable positive effects on the economy in general, such as large increases in available foreign exchange from remittances and from tourism earnings. They also, however, contributed to a number of harmful economic and social consequences, which have not yet been managed effectively. Instead of confronting the difficult task of strengthening the use of the Cuban peso in the domestic economy, the government appears ready to continue with the U.S. dollar, after flirting with the idea of replacing it with the more politically acceptable euro.

The objective of this chapter is to analyze the process of dollarization in the Cuban economy, focusing on the forces that have propelled it, its economic and social impact, and the official policy response so far. It assesses the desirability of substituting the euro for the dollar. Its basic argument is that a forced switch to the euro from the dollar would probably generate more problems than it would resolve, regardless of its political attractiveness to the Cuban leadership. A preferable objective would be to reestablish and reconsolidate the position of the peso in the Cuban economy. This study suggests a basic approach to that process.

The Cuban economy is "dollarized" in an informal but also quasi-official manner. The country's stock of U.S. dollars is undoubtedly high, although its true magnitude is unknown. The dollar is a major "medium of exchange" and "unit of account." It also is probably the principal "store of value" for Cuban citizens, a refuge for financial savings amid the country's economic meltdown and the peso's loss of purchasing power. Dollars are required for some transactions by Cuban citizens with the government itself (exit permits, passports, medical tests for exit permits) and is the currency in which some taxes are levied. State enterprises, moreover, pay income supplements in U.S. dollars to approximately 1.08 million workers in a number of sectors of the Cuban economy (United Nations, 2000a, p. 8).

Most Cubans hold dollars, along with pesos, for use in day-to-day transactions. Many individuals use one or the other interchangeably. The use of the dollar is therefore definitely more than informal. Also in circulation is a so-called convertible peso, issued by the Central Bank, which is also used interchangeably with the U.S. dollar. It is an attempt by the government, successful so far, to capture some of the seigniorage associated with the circulation of the U.S. dollar and accruing to the U.S. government. (In the mid-1990s, coupons, or *bonos,* also were distributed to workers in some sectors, such as sugar, permitting them to purchase imported products at prices below those in the dollar stores. The coupons therefore had a quasi-monetary function, though they were not part of the formal money supply.)

Cuba thus has, in effect, two general economies, a dollar economy and a peso economy, with significant segmentation and overlap between them. There are two exchange rates between the dollar and the peso, both essentially "official," but for different purposes and types of transactions. The "official" rate, mainly for international trade, is fixed at par: U.S.$1.00 = Cuban peso(CUP) 1.00. The quasi-official or "extraofficial" rate, which is the relevant rate for Cuban citizens, varied around U.S.$1 = CUP 20–22 during the period 1998–2001.

This dual system makes an accurate analysis of the Cuban monetary system, and indeed the Cuban economy in general, all but impossible. The dual currency and double exchange rate complications apparently are not treated transparently in information presented publicly on inflation, the value of the money supply, the government budget, or the national accounts.[1] Information is presented only in pesos, with any conversion of dollars done at an unspecified exchange rate (see, for example, Banco Central de Cuba, 2000). The Central Bank undoubtedly tracks carefully the circulation of dollars; the Ministry of Finance officially taxes dollar expenditures and some dollar incomes. Individual enterprises and some institutions, such as universities, arbitrage between the two currencies and keep two budgets and sets of books, one in dollars and the other in pesos.

▲ *Antecedents to Dollarization*

The use of the dollar in Cuba has long and strong precedents in the twentieth century. Following the War of Independence, the dollar was proclaimed the sole currency in 1898, replacing the Spanish and other currencies previously in use. This situation lasted until 1914, when the Cuban government acquired the right to mint coins, though still relying on U.S. paper currency. In 1934, the Cuban government began issuing paper currency, which circulated with the U.S. dollar (Comisión de Asuntos Cubanos, 1935, ch. 14).

In time the peso came to predominate, but the U.S. dollar continued to have a strong presence. For example, the "Truslow Mission" of the International Bank for Reconstruction and Development estimated (1951, p. 545) that the public's holdings of U.S. dollars in 1950 amounted to 86.6 percent of the total peso currency in circulation. Dollar holdings were also estimated at 28.0 percent of the total peso money supply, defined to include demand and savings deposits. Despite these large dollar holdings, however, the peso predominated in the domestic economy.

Following the radicalization of the revolution and the diplomatic and economic rupture with the United States, private ownership and circulation of the U.S. dollar was prohibited, and it continued to be illegal until 1993; dollars were held, nevertheless, and circulated clandestinely from 1960 to 1993. The market was thin, at least until the late 1980s. The early sources of dollars were probably the small flow of Western businesspeople visiting the island, the dollar supply that predated 1960, some payments to Cuban workers at the U.S. military base at Guantanamo, and some Cuban citizens traveling abroad. The demand for dollars was probably generated by Cubans traveling abroad wishing to make major purchases, by some who saw the dollar as a more secure store of value, and by Cubans leaving the country illegally who wished to convert their assets into a transferable medium, as the peso was totally inconvertible. Some observers suggest that another motive to hold liquid assets in U.S. dollars was the expectation that the Castro regime would be overthrown and a transition would eventually occur.

The dollar's value waxed and waned on the black market, but it stayed generally in the area of 3 to 5 pesos, in relation to the official rates of U.S.$1.00 = CUP 1.00. Transaction costs were exceedingly high. People caught holding dollars could be jailed; some remained incarcerated even after decriminalization of dollar holding. In the 1980s, the supply of available dollars increased as tourism slowly expanded and as more Cubans traveled abroad.

The major expansion of dollar usage in the Cuban economy followed the end of the special trade, credit, and aid relationship with the former Soviet Union in the 1988 to 1990 period, together with the loss of a proportion of the export markets in eastern Europe. The loss of the hidden Soviet subsidization embedded in Cuban-Soviet export and import prices led to an approximate 67 percent reduction in imports, a 34 percent reduction in GDP per capita, an energy crisis, and an agricultural and food crisis (United Nations, 2000b, fig. A.1).

Particularly important was the increase in the fiscal deficit to about 29 percent of GDP in 1993, resulting from the coverage of burgeoning state enterprise losses, from continuing expenditures for social programs, and from covering the deficits of the rationing system in the context of large reductions in tax revenues. This fiscal deficit was immediately monetized, generating large increases in the peso money supply in the hands of the public, from 20.0 percent of gross national product in 1989 to 66.5 percent in 1994 (United Nations, 2000b). With supplies of available goods and services declining and with fixed prices for many products in the rationing system, however, inflationary pressures intensified.

The rationing system plus price controls in such areas as housing, automobiles, and interenterprise transactions suppressed much of the inflationary pressure. But those pressures leaked into the expanding black market prices for goods and services and into the market for dollars. In this unofficial peso market, the price of the U.S. dollar reached as high as 150 pesos for a short period in 1994, averaging 95 pesos per dollar throughout that year (see table 24.1).[2]

For these reasons, the demand for dollars intensified sharply from 1989 to 1994. The supplies of dollars coming into Cuba after 1989 also began to expand, for a number of reasons. Tourism began to increase, and the government began to reemphasize tourism in its development strategy after many years of deemphasis. Business travel from Western countries also increased, as Western enterprises and countries tried to move into the vacuum left by the departure of the Soviet Union. Cubans quickly adapted their activities to tap Western tourism and business in order to acquire some foreign exchange. What's more, family remittances found their way through various channels into the country to support families and relatives facing destitution.

By 1993, the Cuban government was confronting a multidimensional economic crisis to which the old remedies—intensifying controls and regulations or mounting state-led campaigns and programs—seemed irrelevant. Under these circumstances, the government announced in August 1993 that the possession of dollars would no longer be a criminal activity and legalized the open transfer of family remittances from abroad to Cuban citizens.

▲ The Dollarization Process since 1993

Since then, the process of informal and quasi-official dollarization has expanded and consolidated significantly. It is worth emphasizing that this growth has occurred naturally and spontaneously, even though the Cuban government would clearly prefer that it had not taken place. However,

Table 24.1
Cuba: Balance of Payments (Millions of U.S. dollars)

	1991	1992	1993	1994	1995	1996	1997[b]	1998[b]	1999[b]	2000	2001
Balance on Current Account	-1,454	-420	-372	-260	-518	-167	-437	-396	-176	n.a.	—
Commercial balance	-1,138	-215	-371	-308	-639	-419	-746	-617	-426	-780	-3,309
Merchandise trade Balance	-1,254	-536	-847	-971	-1,374	-1,703	-2,168	-2,669	-2,867	-3,124	1,708
Exports of Goods and Services	3,563	2,522	1,968	2,542	2,926	3,707	3,882	4,182	4,521	4,807	
Goods[c]	2,980	1,779	1,137	1,381	1,507	1,866	2,059	2,738	3,149	3,124	
Services	584	742	832	1,160	1,419	1,841	1,823	1,444	1,372	1,692	
Imports of Goods and Services	4,702	2,737	2,339	2,849	3,565	4,125	4,628	4,800	4,947	5,587	5,125
Goods[d]	4,234	2,315	1,984	2,353	2,883	3,569	3,996	4,182	4,307	4,816	
Services	468	422	355	497	683	556	632	618	640	771	
Income	-334	-248	-264	-423	-525	-493	-483	-599	-600	-670	
Current Net Transfers	18	43	263	470	646	744	792	820	850	850	
Remittances[e]	...	...	...	...	537	630	670	700	725	720	
Donations[e]	...	...	...	...	109	88	92	48	50	n.a.	
Other transfers[e]	...	419	356	262	596	174	458	413	486	640	

(continued)

429

Table 24.1 (continued)

Cuba: Balance of Payments (Millions of U.S. dollars)

	1991	1992	1993	1994	1995	1996	1997[b]	1998[b]	1999[b]	2000	2001
Factor Services	1.421	...	54	563	5						
Balance on Capital Account[f]		−1	−16	2	78	82	442	207	205	n.a.	
of which direct foreign investment	−33					7	21	17	24	n.a.	
Global balance											

Note. From UN ECLAC, on the basis of official statistics from the *Oficina Nacional de Estadísticas* (ONE) and the Central Bank of Cuba, as well as their own estimates.

[a] Foreign merchandise trade statistics may diverge from other sources due to differences in sources and methodologies, especially for 1993 to 1998.

[b] Preliminary estimates.

[c] 1989–92: merchandise exports (without donations); source: ONE, FOB valuation. 1997–1998: *Informe economico* 1998, Central Bank of Cuba, April 1999.

[d] 1989–1992: merchandise imports (without donations); source: ONE, valuation according to the conditions of purchase and CIF. 1997–98: source: *Informe economico* 1998, Central Bank of Cuba, April 1999.

[e] Estimates of ECLAC.

[f] Includes errors and omissions.

430

Table 24.2
Cuba: Exchange Rates 1990–2000 (Pesos per dollars)

Year	Official exchange rates		Quasi-official exchange rate (Annual average)
	Commercial rate[a]	Tourist rate[a]	
1989	0.74	1.0	5.0
1990	0.74	1.0	7.0
1991	0.74	1.0	20.0
1992	0.74	1.0	35.0
1993	0.74	1.0	78.0
1994	0.74	1.0	95.0
1995	1.0		32.1
1996	1.0		19.2
1997	1.0		23.0
1998	1.0		21.0
1999	1.0		20.0
2000[b]	1.0		21.0
2001[b]	1.0		22.0
2002[a]	1.0		26.0

Note: From United Nations (2000a, table A.1), on the basis on statistics from the Central Bank of Cuba and their own estimates.

[a]The commercial and tourist rates were unified at the parity rate of $US 1.00 = CU. Peso 1.00 by 1995.

[b]Preliminary estimates.

fundamental economic circumstances and the decisions of numerous actors, including the citizenry of Cuba, the Government, tourists, Cubans abroad, and foreign businesses, have produced this situation.

Initially, legalizing the circulation of the U.S. dollar was intended to permit a more effective "capture" of foreign exchange through expansion of sales at the dollar stores, where tax rates were high.[3] The introduction of the "convertible peso" was also a means of replacing a portion of the circulating dollars, thereby capturing the seigniorage. In a second phase, enterprises and some institutions were encouraged to become self-sufficient in dollars and to turn over some of their dollar acquisitions to the treasury. Then the state itself imposed fees and taxes on citizens in dollars.

The two major continuing forces underlying the dollarization process since 1993 have been the increase in the supply of dollars flowing into Cuba and the increase in the opportunities to spend them, hence the growth in demand. Clearly, the more dollars that are available to Cuban people and enterprises, the more likely these consumers are to use dollars as a medium of exchange and store of value; and the greater the opportunities to spend dollars, the greater the likelihood that dollars will be accepted in exchange for goods and services.

The most important source of dollars for monetary circulation is undoubtedly family remittances. Members of the Cuban diaspora, principally those in South Florida and other parts of the United States, send income supplements in the form of dollars to their relatives in Cuba through a variety of mechanisms. These dollars flow directly to the citizens to whom they are sent and become part of the stock of money.[4] These inflows have increased from very low levels, from under U.S.$18 million in 1991 to perhaps $725 million in 1999, as estimated by the Economic Commission for Latin America and the Caribbean (ECLAC; see table 24.1). Other estimates are somewhat lower, however. Monreal (2000, p. 2), for example, estimates them very roughly at $500 million.

A variety of other transfers are probably lumped together with family remittances in some official estimates, but they are actually different. Most important of these would be purchases of goods and services, by tourists and other visitors, from unreported nonstate sectors (such as the underground economy) or from the legal self-employment sector, where transactions may be underreported or even not directly recorded.[5] Subsequently, however, a portion of these may be "caught" and officially recorded, in sales at the dollar stores, for example. Transfers to Cuban citizens from the same sources may also follow the same path. There is no way to distinguish these types of expenditures and transfers from family remittances, so the estimates of the latter probably include some proportion of the former.

A third source of dollar inflows is the unofficial but tolerated additional income payments to Cuban employees by foreign enterprises operating in joint ventures with state firms, by foreign embassies, and by international organizations. Such payments in cash or kind are again impossible to estimate but apparently widely used. They are considered necessary income supplements to provide a work incentive and to enable employees to concentrate on their work rather than their next meal.

Perhaps a lesser source of dollar inflows includes the funds saved from per diem allowances by Cubans who can travel abroad, a widely known and valuable income supplement. Those able to transfer dollars into Cuba this way would include government officials, academics, sports figures, business managers, artists, musicians, and anyone attending an overseas conference or meeting. Though impossible to measure accurately, unrecorded dollar inflows of this type have also undoubtedly increased in the 1990s, as more Cubans have been able to work or travel abroad for official purposes.[6] The amounts of these dollar inflows become clear only when expended at dollar stores.

The sum of the inflow of dollars through the four aforementioned channels is probably higher that the sum of "remittances" and "other" transfers listed under "current net transfers" in table 24.1. This is because the dollar inflows from these sources are not only expended at the dollar stores and official tourist facilities, which are, in effect, surrogate measures for these inflows, but they also contribute to the expanding dollar money supply held by Cuban citizens.

Yet another important source of U.S. dollars or, often, "convertible pesos" backed by dollars for Cuban citizens (though not the nation) is the incentive payment in dollars made by some domestic enterprises, as well as some joint ventures to workers in key sectors, such as mining or construction. Presumably these dollars come through the government tax office, which acquires them through taxation on dollar transactions. Some 1.08 million workers were receiving such payments in 1999 (United Nations, 2000b, p. 8). One source estimates the payments at an average $19 per month per worker, for an annual value of U.S.$246.24 million (Triana Cordovi, 2000, p. 5).[7] This large relative magnitude equals 34 percent of remittances or 18 percent of merchandise exports.

In terms of demand, the predominant transaction demand for U.S. dollars is for the purchase of imported goods and some domestic foodstuffs sold in state "dollar stores," or *tiendas para la recaudación de divisas* (stores for the collection of foreign exchange). The chains of retail stores for dollars include convenience stores, grocery stores, and retailers of clothing, footwear, household gadgetry, major electronic products, and a broad range of consumer products. The volume of sales at these outlets is enormous, if the value of their dollar sales is translated into pesos at the quasi-official exchange rate, which is actually the relevant rate for Cuban citizens. In 1997, for example, the volume of retail sales at the dollar stores was equivalent to 3.2 percent of GDP, if the parity rate of U.S.$1.00 = CUP 1.00 were used. But at the rate relevant for Cuban citizens, which averaged U.S.$1.00 = CUP 23.00 in 1997, the value of retail sales at these stores constituted 73.6 percent of GDP (calculations derived from Sánchez Egozcue [1999, table 1]).

The Cuban government applies a sales tax of 140 percent for most of the products in the dollar stores, though for large items, such as imported televisions, the rate is a lower 100 percent. Cuban-produced foodstuffs and other items are increasingly sold in the dollar stores rather than through the rationing system in the traditional peso economy. Most of these dollars make a one-way journey from family in Miami to Cuban citizen to dollar store to the tax office (ONAT, the Oficina Nacional de Administración Tributaria [ONAT]) and the government (which then imports other goods and services), or to the importing enterprise. They then exit the country again to finance the imported goods sold by the retailer or other products imported by the government. As noted, some dollars are paid out again to workers in key sectors.

United States dollars are also required for some official payments of fees to the government. For example, in 1996, a Cuban citizen wishing to leave Cuba as a private tourist had to pay U.S.$200 to the Consultoria Jurídica Internacional for the legalization of the letter of invitation from a foreign friend, U.S.$150 for the exit permit, and U.S.$50 for a passport. These magnitudes might not appear unreasonable until compared with the average monthly income in Cuba of 223 pesos, or about U.S.$11 at the quasi-official (relevant) exchange rate (United Nations, 2000a, p. 8).

Cuba's stock of U.S. dollars has probably increased as transaction demands have risen. The volume of goods and services available for dollars has increased steadily compared to those available for pesos. Even in the dollar stores, the proportion of domestically produced goods that were previously available for pesos but are now for sale for dollars has been increasing noticeably. It is also estimated that the portion of the population that has access to dollars through various channels reached 62 percent in 1999, up from 56.3 percent in 1998 (United Nations, 2000a, p. 9).

Another major type of demand for U.S. dollars is for "store of value" purposes. Solid quantitative evidence on the magnitude of savings held in U.S. dollars and outside the banking system is not available. Anecdotal evidence, however, would suggest that much if not most of the savings of Cuban citizens is in the form of dollars rather than pesos and generally is not kept in the banks. Indeed, this was the response of almost every Cuban the authors asked about the form of individual savings. These people also said that many of their acquaintances and Cubans generally did the same, although those with access only to pesos and not dollars might save in pesos if they were indeed able to save at all.

The dollar deposit interest rate is rather low, moreover, and thus would not seem to provide much of an incentive for holding savings in the formal banking system. The interest rate paid by the banks for U.S. dollar deposits is 0.5 percent annually for deposits of more than U.S.$200, while the rate for peso deposits is 1.75 percent for deposits exceeding 200 pesos. Popular memories of confiscation of various types of assets and some recent discussion of confiscatory conversion of bank deposits in a monetary reform process also contribute to an aversion to saving, especially dollars, through the banks (Gutiérrez Urdaneta, Monreal, and Carranza, 1996). The magnitude of the money supply in U.S. dollars maintained for store-of-value purposes and outside the formal banking system is therefore likely to be large, even if not known with accuracy.

Cubans save U.S. dollars partly because of their recent experience of severe inflation and fears of future inflation. In the 1990–95 period, for example, open inflation of the peso was rapid, although this may not be evident from official estimates. Using an "implicit deflator for private consumption," ECLAC calculated a time series for "real average monthly wages." The estimate of this price deflator indicated an estimated inflation rate of 93.1 percent from 1989 to 1995 (United Nations, 2000b, fig. A.1). This rate has probably declined since, given the successful implementation of fiscal policies that have reduced the fiscal deficit from around 29 percent to 2 to 4 percent of GDP recently (United Nations, 1997, pp. 50–72).

The true purchasing power of the peso for citizens has continued to decline nevertheless, driven by the reduced volumes of rationed goods available in the old peso economy and the need to purchase ever larger proportions of basic goods, including foodstuffs produced in Cuba, in the high-priced dollar stores. If the true rate of inflation is therefore high, then the store-of-value incentive to hold dollars also is probably high and perhaps intensifying. Any uncertainty concerning the future course of economic policy and political events in Cuba, furthermore, would contribute to the decision to hold U.S. dollars, which appear to have international stature relative to the peso.

Unfortunately, it appears impossible to know accurately what the volume of the dollar money supply might be. Undoubtedly the Central Bank has made its own estimates, but no information is available on these. Official monetary figures basically ignore the circulation and stock of dollars in the economy.

In its analysis of the Cuban economy, ECLAC (United Nations, 1997, p. 92) estimates "conservatively" the value of dollar holdings at U.S.$650 million at 1996 year end. At the quasi-official or "free" exchange rate, ECLAC estimates, this would amount to 130 percent of peso liquidity or 49 percent of GDP. This estimate may be unduly high because the stock of dollars for purchases in the dollar stores undoubtedly circulates rapidly. It may be plausible, on the other hand, if large volumes of dollars are held as a store of value and circulate slowly.

A second estimate was made by two researchers in Cuba's Institute of Research on Finance and Prices (Alvarez Hernández and Chaviano, 1998). Their approach was to calculate the sum of the total value of sales in the dollar stores plus sales of dollars in the state exchange (CADECA), then to multiply this by the quasi-official exchange rate and compare the result to the total value of current peso expenditures in the economy. For 1996, this yielded an estimate of the value of dollars (U.S.$639 million) equivalent to 13,209 million pesos (at a quasi-official exchange rate of U.S.$1.00 = CUP 20.12), compared to 13,133 million pesos for national peso expenditures). According to this approach, the value of U.S. dollars in circulation would have exceeded the value of pesos in circulation. If this conclusion were correct, it is likely that in the years since 1996, the degree of dollarization has increased significantly in view of the increases in tourism, foreign travel by Cubans, and payments of dollar wage supplements to workers.

◣ Consequences of Dollarization

The dollarization phenomenon is tied to, and often blamed for, a number of serious problems currently facing the Cuban economy. Yet the sources of these problems rest mainly in other aspects of public policy (see Ritter, 1995).

The most serious consequence of the bifurcation between the dollar and peso economies concerns income distribution and the general structure of incentives. In the state sector in general, average monthly wages and salaries in 1999, in real or purchasing power terms, amounted to only 54.8 percent of their level in 1989, according to ECLAC estimates (United Nations, 2000b, fig. A.1). In 1999, the average Cuban worker earned 223 pesos per month in the socialist economy (United Nations, 2000a, p. 8), and in 2000 the average pensioner received 104 pesos per month (Espinosa Chepe, 2001). Doctors, teachers, engineers, and professors earned in the range of 200 to 450 pesos monthly, which, at the exchange rate of relevance for citizens (say 20 CUP = U.S.$1), amounts to about U.S.$10.00–$22.50. On the other hand, those in the tourist sector or providing auxiliary services or those receiving remittances might receive a very large multiple of these amounts.

This situation gives people a powerful incentive to leave the state peso economy and switch to the dollar economy; for example, teachers becoming sellers of artisanal products, chemists becoming self-employed shoemakers, professors becoming hotel receptionists or security guards, engineers driving taxis. People may also forsake the state or peso economy for work in the underground economy. The result for society generally is that those who perform vital functions in health, education, agriculture, or industry receive much less for their efforts than those with access to dollar sources of income.

Essential public services, notably education, health, public administration generally, and social security, which are provided in the peso economy, have experienced severe reductions in the real purchasing power of their budgetary allocations. In nominal peso terms, for example, Cuba's total education budget fell from 1,620 million pesos in 1990 to 1,585 million pesos in 1999 (United Nations, 2000a, fig. A.21). The total value of salary payments in the education sector also declined in this period. This means that, including the effects of inflation in the peso economy together with citizens' need to purchase from the high-priced agricultural markets and the dollar stores, the real value of the education budget would have declined seriously. This has affected the quality of these services, as well as the availability of supplies, maintenance, and replacement investment. The real living standards of employees in the educational and health systems, whose incomes are restricted to pesos, have also declined with their purchasing power. The costs of Cuba's "structural adjustment" therefore have been borne by the employees in the education and health sectors, and by pensioners or those on social security.

Another general impact is on the pattern of trade. Some sectors, such as tourism, receive part of their revenues in dollars and are entitled to purchase their needed imported inputs in dollars at the official parity rate. Other sectors, such as sugar, or potential new export producers, receive pesos from their export products at the official parity rate but are not themselves entitled to acquire their imported inputs at the same parity rate. Instead, the foreign exchange goes into a central fund, which then allots it to all the sectors.

The sugar sector, for example, earns pesos from its exports at a rate of 1 peso per dollar's worth of sugar exported, not 20 pesos (the "extraofficial" or other official rate). It has only limited access to the foreign exchange it earns, although the imported inputs it is able to acquire come at a rate of U.S.$1.00 = CUP 1.00. The sector therefore appears to be perennially unprofitable and economically unviable. At an exchange rate of 20 pesos to the dollar and with access to its own foreign exchange earnings for input purchase, on the other hand, sugar would probably be exceedingly profitable and viable.

Similarly, at what might be a reasonable market-determined exchange rate for the country, perhaps 5 to 10 pesos per U.S.$1.00, the sugar sector would earn roughly 300–900 percent more pesos for each pound of sugar exported. It would be able to cover its domestic currency costs with ease. If also permitted access to its own foreign exchange earnings, it could import the inputs and capital equipment it needed. It would therefore probably be commercially profitable and economically viable.

This general situation arising from the exchange rate policy impedes the expansion of traditional exports and creates a major monetary disincentive or barrier to the development of new export activities.

◤ The Prospects for Euroization

Discussions took place in 1999–2001 in Cuba concerning the possibility of switching from the U.S. dollar to the euro (e.g., Hidalgo et al., 2002, p. 36). Indeed, the issue seems to have been opened up for general academic discussion as well as raised in the government—a somewhat uncommon situation. The reasons can be surmised.

One of the disadvantages of dollarization in the Cuban government's eyes is that the seigniorage goes to its "historic enemy," the U.S. government. For every dollar that stays in Cuba as part of the stock of money, the U.S. Federal Reserve can issue one more dollar for domestic circulation without causing domestic inflation, so that $1 worth of goods and services gets transferred from Cuba to the U.S. government. The overwhelming portion of the dollars coming to Cuba, however, arrives as a free gift through family remittances from Cubans abroad and mainly in the United States. In that case, the resources are transferred from the individual foreign donor to the U.S. government. (Even if the dollar eventually leaves Cuba, and if it were then to be withdrawn from circulation by the Federal Reserve, Cubans have made an interest-free loan to the U.S. government for the whole time the dollar stayed in Cuba.) Naturally, this is a strong reason for the Cuban government to prefer "euroization" to dollarization, for then the seigniorage would go to the EU rather than the United States.

A second possible factor is the dollar's fluctuation relative to the euro. The U.S. dollar was riding high in 2000–2001, appreciating sharply against the euro and most other currencies; but that rise is not likely to last forever. Uncertainties regarding the euro, moreover, along with worries about the quality of economic policy formulation in Europe and a perception of greater technological dynamism and growth prospects in the United States, have encouraged large financial outflows from Europe to the United States. If and when that uncertainty diminishes, or if the euro is perceived to have been seriously undervalued in 1999 and 2000, central banks, enterprises, and individuals may shift into the euro from the dollar, again putting downward pressure on the dollar.

Indeed, if there were a "hard landing" in the near future for the U.S. economy as it faces up to its severe current account imbalances (about 4 percent of GDP in 2001, as reported in the *Economist,* February 16, 2002, p. 71), a major realignment of the dollar and the euro could be expected; namely, a dollar depreciation (IMF, 2000, p. 55).

By shifting dramatically and totally from the dollar to the euro or by threatening to do so, the Cuban government might hope to weaken the U.S. dollar as an international currency. In principle, the Cuban government could effect this through two channels: by selling Cuba's stock of dollars and buying euros, causing the dollar to depreciate against the euro, or by abandoning the dollar and adopting the euro as its international currency, making the dollar less attractive and the euro more attractive for other countries to use and creating a network externality against the dollar and in favor of the euro.

In both channels, however, the impact is likely to be small, because the Cuban economy is itself small relative to that of the United States and the rest of the dollar zone. The world supply of U.S. dollar currency is more than $500 billion. A high estimate of U.S. dollars in Cuba would be $1 billion, which is a mere 0.2 percent of the total world supply. And Cuban transactions in U.S. dollars, as a percentage of world transactions in U.S. dollars, would be smaller still. Compared to the recent full dollarization of Ecuador and El Salvador (toward which the U.S. government seemed to be largely indifferent), Cuban dedollarization or euroization would be a small backward step in dollarization in Latin America.

The Cuban government nevertheless might overestimate its power, or else simply want to make a symbolic shift away from the dollar for political reasons, as did Saddam Hussein of Iraq, who recently tried to demand payment for petroleum exports in euros instead of dollars (*National Post,* 2000).

A frequently mentioned justification for replacing the dollar with the euro is that a large share of Cuba's trade and tourism comes from Europe.

In 1998, for example, about 30 percent of total trade was with Canada and the Western Hemisphere while 36.3 percent was with western Europe. (Russia, China, and Japan were also major trade partners, with about 15.6 percent of Cuba's total exports plus imports; [CIA, 2000, tables 2 and 3]). A switch to the euro would lower the transaction costs of trading with western Europe and perhaps save Cuba a small percentage of transaction costs.

With respect to tourism, in 1999, 20.9 percent of Cuba's tourists came from the United States (an estimated 60,000) and Canada, and 9.2 percent from larger Latin American countries (Argentina, Brazil, Mexico, and Venezuela), while 41.2 percent came from the larger European countries (United Nations, 2000a, p. 38). The proeuro argument is that because more tourists came from western Europe, Cuba's use of the euro asf its currency for the tourist sector would attract them in greater numbers and induce them to spend more. In this case, European tourists would be saved the transaction costs of converting their euros to dollars; Cuba perhaps could raise prices accordingly and earn more revenue. On the other hand, the reverse impact would occur for tourists from North America and probably from Latin America as well, who stand more or less within the dollar's sphere of influence.

The actual impact of switching from the dollar to the euro is likely to be insignificantly positive in the short run and substantially negative in the long run. In the short run, in terms of tourism, based on the percentages noted, the gain to Cuba could be on the order of about 1 percent of its gross receipts from eurozone tourists. This would be roughly U.S.$9.2 million on gross receipts of U.S.$2,220 million for 1999 (United Nations, 2000b, p. 510) but in contrast to a loss of U.S.$6.7 million for Western Hemisphere tourism. This net gain—U.S.$2.5 million—does not appear significant compared to the probable transitional and administrative costs of switching to the euro.

What would be the impact on family remittance payments, most of which come from the Cuban American community? It is hard to predict how the volume of those remittances would be affected if either the donors or the recipients had first to convert their U.S. dollars into euros. Presumably they would bear some of the increased transaction costs, and the net amount of foreign exchange available to be spent in Cuba would fall. This "nuisance factor," moreover, might induce donors to reduce their gifts. More significant for the government, however, would be the possible loss of foreign exchange represented by those remittances (as expressed in the eventual tax revenues from the dollar stores). If that loss exceeded the earnings from actual European tourists, it might make the Cuban government prefer dollarization to euroization.

In the longer term (which might be 10 years or more), normalization of economic and political relations with the United States will inevitably occur. In that context, it seems obvious that U.S.-Cuban trade, as well as tourism, will expand quickly and overwhelm Cuba's interactions with other countries and regions. To adopt the euro in that context would not make sense. Change to the euro might be virtually impossible to police unless extremely intrusive controls were placed on the transactions. Such intrusiveness would be counterproductive and impractical and would incur high administrative costs and ultimately high economic costs.

Finally, the U.S. dollar has a long history of acceptance in Cuba, while the euro, as a new currency, obviously does not. Cubans know the dollar's worth and trust its value. The mere availability of an alternative foreign currency will not necessarily drive the dollar out of circulation.

Therefore, if the Cuban government were to attempt to introduce the euro, it might only convert a two-currency economy into a three-currency economy and raise transaction costs further. The U.S. dollar has been accepted by Cuban citizens spontaneously and naturally over the years. If the euro were similarly accepted, then an official switch might be reasonable; but an attempt to force a switch would simply add a third currency to Cuba's monetary system.

While euroization as an alternative to dollarization may not be feasible except at prohibitive cost, to hold the euro as part of the foreign exchange reserve portfolio would be reasonable and cost-effective for financial transactions with the EU and other countries that may use the euro in future. Presumably Cuba now holds European currencies in its foreign exchange reserves, so adding or switching to the euro cannot be seen as particularly newsworthy.

▶ *Strengthening the Role of the Peso*

The other monetary alternative is to strengthen the use of the Cuban peso in the Cuban economy so that in time it replaces the U.S. dollar through the same natural process of choice among Cuban citizens and businesses that the dollar has experienced. This is such a difficult task, however, that the Cuban government is essentially ignoring it at the moment, at least in terms of implementing relevant policy measures, presumably because the costs of reversing the dollarization process exceed the benefits. A variety of Cuban analysts, whose works have been summarized by Sánchez Egozcue, agree that it would be desirable to reduce dollarization by strengthening the use of the peso but also conclude that to do so is unrealistic under current circumstances (Sánchez Egozcue, 1999, pp. 18–19).

In its 1999 annual report, the Central Bank of Cuba (Banco Central de Cuba, 2000) makes no mention of policy measures designed specifically to unify the exchange rates, the monetary systems, or the peso and dollar economies. By 2000, however, the monetary duality issue apparently had become a focus of research in the Central Bank, the Ministry of Finance, and possibly other agencies.

A number of advantages would arise from a successful strengthening of the peso, that is, making it a freely convertible currency, circulating domestically by popular choice and not as a result of coercive controls and regulations, with its value sustainable freely in international currency markets.

The first advantage is that a convertible and stable currency could permit the Central Bank of Cuba to pursue an effective and independent monetary policy. This would be desirable as a way to contribute to domestic economic stabilization in the face of external or internal shocks in aggregate demand. This would also require a more market-oriented economy, however, in which price signals were allowed to operate more comprehensively and more effectively, as well as an internal bond market, so that monetary policy could actually function. A second advantage is that Cuba would capture the seigniorage that currently is transferred ultimately to the U.S. government. Although the value of this is not now known with accuracy, it is likely to be significant.

A strengthened peso and convertibility would facilitate the unification of the current two exchange rates and the two corresponding areas of the economy. Indeed, this is probably a necessary condition for the unification of the domestic economy. This would resolve the ubiquitous and profound problems arising from the deformities of the general structure of incentives.

To strengthen the place of the peso requires nothing less than a unification of the general dollar-peso bifurcation of the economy, which is not only monetary in character but also institutional, structural, behavioral, and rooted in the government's dual exchange rate policy. Such a unification will require a unification of the official and quasi-official exchange rates for the dollar. This will necessitate a major devaluation of the official dollar-peso parity rate, which will increase the cost of some important imported products, such as cereals and other food products currently provided at low prices to citizens through the rationing system.

The devaluation of parity, in turn, would necessitate a restructuring of the wage and salary scale, which ranged, in 2000, from about 100 pesos per month for a pensioner to around 550 for high officials. This is because with higher prices of basic imported necessities, current wage levels would not permit the purchase of the essential "basket" of food necessary for survival. (Indeed, it is surprising that anyone could survive on peso wages and salaries in the 2000–2001 period without access to dollars.) The task of reconfiguring the whole system of prices and incomes in a socially equitable manner is immense.

What types of policy measures would be necessary in order to unify the two exchange rates and indeed the peso and dollar economies? While a detailed plan of action, is beyond the scope of this chapter, the relevant policy areas and a few of the relevant types of policies can be considered.

Exchange Rate Policy

It would be necessary and desirable to begin a gradual, market-driven process of devaluation of the official rate of the old peso. This would also imply eliminating the spread between the official rate (U.S.$1.00 = CUP 1.00) and the quasi-official rate (U.S.$1.00 = CUP 22.00 in 2001) and, in effect, unifying the old peso and the U.S. dollar (and also the "convertible" peso).

The mechanics of the devaluation of the official rate and the unification of the "official" and "extraofficial" rates can be illustrated with a graphic analysis of Cuba's foreign exchange market; that is, the market for U.S. dollars from Cuba's perspective (fig. 24.1). In figure 24.1, which is the standard framework for a simple analysis of a foreign exchange market, the peso price of the dollar, or the exchange rate, is shown on the vertical axis, and the volume of U.S. dollars demanded and supplied by Cuba is shown on the horizontal axis. The supply (*S*) of U.S. dollars that would be earned or acquired at different exchange rates slopes upward to the right. This shows that as the value of the U.S. dollar increases (or as the value of the peso declines), Cuba's exports of goods and services become relatively cheaper, so that the volume of U.S. dollars earned increases. The demand (*D*) for U.S. dollars curves downward, showing that as the value of the dollar declines (and the peso increases), larger volumes of imported goods and services would be demanded, as such imports would be relatively cheaper.

In this illustration, with no intervention in the foreign exchange market, the exchange rate would settle at 5 pesos per U.S. dollar, with foreign exchange receipts equaling foreign exchange expenditures at $7 billion. If, however, the exchange rate were to be fixed at parity (as is actually the case)

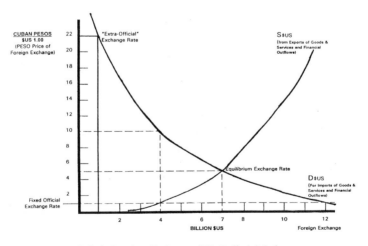

Figure 24.1. Cuba's Foreign Exchange (US Dollar) Markets

or CUP 1.00 = U.S.$1.00, the foreign exchange acquired is shown here at U.S.$4 billion. At the parity exchange rate, the volume of foreign exchange that would be demanded for imports of goods and services would be very large indeed, in the absence of bureaucratic controls on imports, as such imports would be very inexpensive for Cuban citizens at that exchange rate. In figure 24.1, the volume of imports is shown to be U.S.$12 billion. If all of the $4 billion of foreign exchange were to be made available to the general public via auction, the auction-determined exchange rate would be 10 pesos to the U.S. dollar in this illustration.

Assuming that $3 billion of the $4 billion of foreign exchange available is expended by the government or authorized agencies for the purchase of imports, the remaining $1 billion then would be available to the public through remittances, tourist purchases, circulation outside official channels, and other means. This scenario is not far from current realities. The exchange rate for this market would be determined by supply and demand, not by edict. It is this "extraofficial" exchange rate that rises to the currently observed level of 22 pesos to the U.S. dollar in reality as well as in the diagram.

To make the peso convertible and to consolidate its place in the domestic Cuban economy, the Cuban monetary authorities would have to do two things. First, they would need to permit the exchange rate to move steadily, though perhaps slowly, to a market-determined level, which, in effect, is to permit a gradual devaluation of the peso. Second, they would have to make the foreign exchange freely available to the public in increasing volumes.

For example, a devaluation of the official exchange rate to 3 pesos per U.S. dollar would increase foreign exchange available to U.S.$6 billion in the diagram, while the total amount of U.S. dollars demanded for the purchase of imports would decline from $12 billion to around $8.5 billion. If the amount of U.S. dollars made available to the public were increased substantially, the extraofficial exchange rate for the peso would "appreciate"; that is, the price of the U.S. dollar would decline in the extraofficial market from the original 22 pesos to around 7 pesos.

Over time, a series of devaluations of the official rate, together with increases in the amounts of foreign exchange made available for general public use, would lead to a convergence of the official and the extraofficial exchange rates. In figure 24.1, this would occur at 5 pesos per U.S. dollar, and with perhaps U.S.$7 billion of foreign exchange acquired and expended for both current and capital account purposes.

Monetary Policy

With respect to monetary policy, one policy already successfully implemented has been to reduce the so-called monetary overhang of the old peso; that is, the number of pesos in circulation that had no real monetary function and were surplus to the public's transactions and precautionary demand for money. Monetary "liquidity" was actually reduced from 66.5 percent of GDP to 37.5 percent from 1993 to 1998 (United Nations, 2000b, fig. A.1).

This was achieved by various fiscal austerity measures (higher taxes on tobacco products, for example), higher prices for some state-provided goods and services, reduced subsidies to state enterprises, and tight limits on any increases in the money supply. Further measures that would increase the use and demand for the "old peso" would be to establish legal domestic markets for major assets, such as cars, housing, capital goods, and intermediate inputs for individuals, enterprises, and governments. These products have been undervalued in official exchange circuits (but not unofficial exchange circuits). Liberalizing their prices would absorb the purchasing power of the peso and increase the demand for pesos relative to the dollar.

Another helpful policy would be to reduce the large volume of interenterprise debt, which, in effect, adds to the volume of peso credit in the system. (The aforementioned measures of monetary liquidity do not include interenterprise credit). Furthermore, some decontrol of prices in the peso economy may be appropriate. The rise in prices in the short run would provide additional uses for the peso and increase the demand for it relative to the dollar. Finally, tourists might be permitted to use pesos as freely as dollars, obtaining them at the market-determined rate, thereby increasing the demand for pesos. This would also mean permitting tourists to convert their dollars back into pesos at the market-determined rate.

Fiscal Policy

Fiscal policy has been operating with considerable success in maintaining the basic fiscal balances, and it should continue on course. In 1999, the fiscal deficit was reduced to 2.4 percent of GDP, a quite acceptable level (Banco Central de Cuba, 2000, p. 11). There are still significant deficits in some state enterprises that might be further reduced and the fiscal savings redirected to other uses, such as, perhaps, well-targeted income support measures.

Incomes, Social Security, and Prices

These exchange rate and monetary policies would have the effect of increasing the prices of those imported goods that are now imported at the parity exchange rate and made available through the rationing system. (Imports available in the dollar stores, however, at the international price plus 140 percent tax for basic foodstuffs or 100 percent for electronic products, and for which the extraofficial exchange rate is the relevant rate, would actually be cheaper.) Still, many people without access to U.S. dollars would face serious increases in their cost of living as prices rose for imported goods available through the rationing system.

This means that the structure of wages and salaries would have to be adjusted in step with any devaluation of the official rate of the peso. Basically this would involve a redesign and gradual phase-in of modifications to the general structure of incomes and prices to permit prices to move to market-determined levels. This measure is particularly dangerous because the increases could launch an inflationary spiral. Appropriate monetary and fiscal policy would be necessary to contain such a tendency. As the official and extraofficial exchange rates converged, the official wage and salary scales would recover their purchasing power in terms of foreign exchange in the extraofficial dollar economy. Perhaps the increases in the nominal wage and salary scale therefore would not have to be extreme.

As the real incomes of workers in the peso economy recovered, the major inequities between those with access to dollars and those earning only pesos would shrink and ultimately disappear. Moreover, the perverse character of the general structure of incentives, which currently deforms people's and enterprises' economic behavior, would also vanish. These two effects would have immense value in terms of both equality and efficiency.

A system of income support measures for lower-income receivers rather than universal untargeted subsidization of everyone through the rationing system could also be considered. This process generally would certainly benefit from the support of the international community and the international financial institutions (IFIs). Indeed, because Cuba has no debt to the IMF, the World Bank, or the Inter-American Development Bank, a good deal of unconditional credit would be available, conditionality being a feature of such borrowing that the Cuban government has criticized in the past. Unfortunately, Cuba is not a member of the major IFIs at this time and is ineligible for such support. In time, this will change.

This type of policy package would be difficult to implement and would create much public uncertainty. It would require careful implementation and explanation. Cuban citizens, however, are well aware of the difficulties, irrationalities, and injustices of the current system. It is probable that many or most Cubans would be receptive to a well-designed and well-executed strategy aimed at unifying the two parts of the economy and restoring the peso to its place as a strong convertible currency.

▶ Conclusions

Today the dollar may be a more significant component of Cuba's overall money supply than the old peso. This study has argued that attempting to adopt the euro as an alternative would be unviable, except at high cost. This apparently is also the conclusion of the Central Bank of Cuba, for it does not appear to be pursuing the euroization option.

Nor does the Cuban government appear to be planning to restore the Cuban peso as a strong and convertible national currency, possibly a more advantageous objective. Other objectives continue to be more urgent. In time, however, it is to be hoped that "putting the Cuban economy in order" will lead to a full rehabilitation of the Cuban peso.

Cuba's near-term monetary future will probably be much the same as its recent monetary past. The Cuban government will not deliberately abandon the peso; symbolic reasons aside, it simply cannot afford the loss of seigniorage. But neither will the government eliminate the use of the U.S. dollar. Its past attempts to do this have failed; and forcing foreign tourists to use the inconvertible peso would seriously damage Cuba's tourist revenues and family remittances. Introducing the euro would only further complicate an already complicated monetary system. The euro would not drive out the dollar.

In the longer term, probably well post-Castro, some radical changes to Cuba's monetary system are possible. If Cuba were to become a market economy that responded to price incentives, it would see a definite advantage in having an independent and strong national currency, freely convertible under flexible exchange rates. An independent central bank could then use monetary policy to pursue macroeconomic stabilization. But this is feasible only if budgetary discipline is accepted and a market in government bonds reestablished, so that the central bank is not simply forced to monetize government budget deficits. A more pessimistic scenario is also possible, of course, in which a governmental, budgetary, and economic crisis causes the collapse of the peso and leads to full official dollarization by default.

◣ Notes

We acknowledge useful comments from Jorge Mario Sánchez and Orlando Gutiérrez of the University of Havana; Ana María Nieto, director, Financial Studies, Central Bank of Cuba; and the anonymous referees for Oxford University Press. None of these persons, of course, bears any responsibility for the views, interpretations, or analyses presented in this chapter, which are the responsibility of the authors alone.

1. Official estimates of inflation are likely to be particularly inaccurate, as they do not take the changing "basket" of consumer goods into account in the latter part of the 1990s. Cuban citizens must spend steadily increasing proportions of their incomes on food and other purchases from the dollar stores, where prices are a very large multiple of those in the peso economy and also include a 140 percent tax. Citizens must purchase food in these stores because their rationed foodstuffs do not last for the month-long ration period. Cuban-produced foodstuffs are increasingly sold in the dollar stores as well. This represents a large increase in the monthly food bill for many Cubans and a high rate of authentic inflation.

2. The extreme "spiking" of the unofficial exchange rate for the dollar in 1994 also came from the extraordinarily large demand for dollars by the *balseros* fleeing Cuba by

boat or homemade raft in August of that year. The *balseros* were trying to convert their assets into dollars before departure, in the context of a very thin dollar market.

3. The early estimates of Mesa-Lago (1995, p. 62) for remittance payments and other similar inflows of U.S. dollars are surprisingly close to the actual volumes of the later 1990s.

4. As is well known, tourism has increased rapidly in Cuba. By 1999, tourist arrivals reached 1.6 million persons. Gross revenues from tourism amounted to U.S.$1.9 billion that year. If import leakages in the sector actually diminished from 70 percent to reported levels of 50 percent or 46 percent, then net tourist revenues would have figured between $950 million and $1.05 billion that year (United Nations, 2000a, p. 6; Gancedo Gaspar and Gutiérrez Castillo, 2000, citing Figueres, 2000). Tourist purchases of goods and services and transfers to Cuban citizens outside official circuits probably have increased as gross tourism expenditures have expanded.

5. Some of those working abroad also transfer a proportion of their earnings to their home institution. University professors, for example, pay their university 75 percent of their dollar earnings from courses taught abroad.

6. The large amount of U.S. dollars held outside the banking system for purposes of savings constitutes a major untapped resource for the Cuban economy. Access to such savings by society at large, if they could be shifted to the banking system and made available for investment and for the importation of investible goods, would benefit society in general.

7. It is useful to recall that opening the agricultural markets in 1994—where Cubans could spend marginal pesos, albeit at high prices—immediately caused the peso to appreciate to about 40 pesos per dollar from a low of about 120. Allowing the legal exchange of old pesos for dollars and "convertible pesos" increased the demand still further, and the peso appreciated to about 20 per dollar. These steps, coupled with attempts to control the budget deficit and reduce the stock of pesos in circulation, helped to prevent the peso's collapse as a store of value and medium of exchange. Permitting additional uses for the peso would have a similar result.

▶ References

Alvarez Hernández, J. E., and N. Chaviano. (1998). La circulación monetaria de la población en Cuba. Unpublished manuscript. Havana: Instituto de Investigaciones de Finanzas y Precios.

Banco Central de Cuba. (1999, April). *Informe económico, 1998.* Havana: Author.

Banco Central de Cuba. (2000, April). *Informe económico, 1999.* Havana: Author.

Comisión de Asuntos Cubanos. (1935). *Problemas de la nueva Cuba.* New York: Foreign Policy Association.

Espinosa Chepe, Oscar. (2001, June 25). Dismal Future. Cubanet. Available online at www.cubanet.org/Cnews/y01.

Castro, Fidel. (2000, June 22). Interview by Federico Mayor Zaragoza, January 28, 2000. *Granma* (Havana). Available online at www.cuba.cu/gobierno/discursos/2000/ing/f220600i.html.

Figueres, Miguel. (2000, May 16). El turismo en Cuba. Paper presented at the conference *La administración pública en los umbrales del siglo XXI.* Havana.

Gancedo Gaspar, Nélida, and Orlando Gutiérrez Castillo. (2000). Cuba's Development Strategy for Tourism: Results, Challenges, and Perspectives. Unpublished manuscript. Havana.

Gutiérrez Urdaneta, Luis, Pedro Monreal, and Julio Carranza. (1996). La desmonetización de la economía Cubana: una revisión de las alternativas. In *Cuba: La reestrucluracion de la economia.* FESCARIBE—Nueva Sociedad, Caracas, Venezuela. Reprinted in Ditmar Dirmoser and Jorge Estay (Eds.), *Economía y reforma económica en Cuba* (pp. 313–33). Caracas: Nueva Sociedad.

Hidalgo, Vilma, Lourdes Tabares, and Yaima Doimeadios. (2002). El Debate sobre regímines cambiarias en economias dolarizadas: el caso de Cuba. Unpublished paper. University of Havana.

International Bank of Reconstruction and Development (IBRD). (1951). *Report on Cuba: Findings and Recommendations of an Economic and Technical Mission.* Washington, D.C.: Author.

International Monetary Fund. (2000, September). *World Economic Outlook.* Washington, D.C.: Author.

Mesa-Lago, Carmelo. (1995). Prospective Dollar Remittances and the Cuban Economy. In Archibald R. M. Ritter and John Kirk (Eds.), *Cuba in the International System: Normalization and Integration* (pp. 58–69). London: Macmillan.

Monreal, Pedro. (2000). Migraciones y remesas familiares: veinte hipótesis sobre el caso de Cuba. Unpublished manuscript.

Ritter, Archibald R. M. (1995). The Dual Currency Bifurcation of the Cuban Economy in the 1990s: Causes, Consequences and Cures. *CEPAL Review, 57,* 113–32.

Sánchez Egozcue, J. M. (1999, September). La dualidad monetaria en Cuba: problemas y perspectivas. Unpublished manuscript. University of Havana.

Triana Cordovi, Juan. (2000, April). La economía cubana en 1999: coyuntura, reflexiones, y oportunidades. Havana: Centro de Estudios de la Economía Cubana.

United Nations. Comisión Económica para América Latina y el Caribe (CEPAL). (2000a). *La economía cubana: reformas estructurales y desempeño en los noventa.* Mexico City: Fondo de Cultura Económica.

United Nations. (2000b). *Cuba: Evolución económica durante 1999.* Mexico City: CEPAL.

United Nations. (1997, August). Economic Commission for Latin America and the Caribbean (ECLAC). *The Cuban Economy in the Nineties: Structural Reform and Economic Performance.* Santiago de Chile: Author.

Index

EMU. *See* European Monetary Union
England. *See* Great Britain
English language, 241
ENM. *See* effective narrow money supply
enterprise theft, 47
Ericsson, Neil R., 61, 367
ERM. *See* exchange rate mechanism
ESCB, 40, 41
escudo (Portugal), 257–58n.10
Estonia, 159, 165
  currency board, 4, 130, 150–51, 256n.2
e-trade, 211–12, 216
EU. *See* European Union
euro, 35, 221, 248, 256, 257n.9, 342
  adoption of, 3, 4, 35, 37, 156, 167n.9,
    181, 247
  APEC monetary fund creation and, 29
  critics' view of, 224–25, 328
  currency board arrangements and, 215
  currency design, 310
  as dollar rival, 17–18, 145, 177, 179, 181,
    203, 243, 247, 287, 311, 330–32
  Eastern European adoption of, 69n.1, 247,
    256n.2
  exchange rate volatility and, 37–38, 39
  fixed exchange rates and, 41, 44–45n.15
  as free-floating currency, 177, 186
  Great Britain and, 299, 309, 312
  inflation targeting and, 27
  international financial derivatives and, 211
  lessons of for dollarization, 283–93
  monetary union benefits, 202–3, 324, 325,
    326
  in multiple-currency monetary unions, 41–
    42
  North American Monetary Union
    compared with, 312
  significance of introduction of, 21, 299,
    315–16
  special drawing rights and, 29
  stability of, 30, 39
  trade invoicing and, 179, 180
  wild geese flock paradigm and, 253
  world currency considerations and, 40, 41
  See also euroization
Eurobonds, 76–78, 82
euroization, 247, 299, 309
  Cuba and, 14, 425, 437–40, 445, 446
  emerging economies and, 11, 69n.1
  San Marino and, 222
  Vatican and, 222
Europe
  bond market, 186
  labor reform issues, 134

Maastricht Treaty conditions, 36–37, 133,
    137n.16
  multiple-currency monetary unions and, 41
  optimal currency area theory and, 163–64
  post-World War II economy, 19, 181
  trade issues, 28
  See also Central Europe; Eastern Europe;
    Western Europe; *specific countries*
European Central Bank
  emergency loans from, 105, 137n.16
  lender-of-last-resort facilities, 292
  monetary sovereignty issues, 143
  organization of, 35, 202–3, 312
  price stability mandate, 133, 325–26
  reserve holdings, 331
  seigniorage issues, 203, 291
  world currency and, 41, 42
European Community. *See* European Union
European Monetary System, 79, 286–90
  crisis (1992), 28, 38, 98n.4, 283, 288, 290
European Monetary Union, 29, 222, 347,
    359
  British entry into, 21, 28, 299, 348–49
  capital control issues, 27
  central bank. *See* European Central Bank
  economic costs of, 166, 166n.5
  export invoicing and, 179
  financial market growth and, 132
  foreign exchange savings and, 321
  future membership growth, 21
  labor market issues, 329, 336
  optimal currency area criteria and, 154, 290–
    91, 292
  political considerations in formation of,
    155, 224–25, 232, 267
  predicted failure of, 328
  Stability and Growth Pact, 133, 356
  structural shock analyses, 351
  as world currency guide, 40, 41
  See also euro
European Union, 137–38n.19, 288, 299
  Cuba and, 438, 440
  international bonds and, 179
  lira (Italy) depreciation and, 28
  monetary union, 22, 40, 224. *See also*
    European Monetary Union
  new entrant common currency adoption,
    156
  optimal currency area criteria and, 285,
    286, 290–91
  target zone experiments, 284, 291
  trade with Mexico, 209
  world currency implementation and, 334
Eurostat, 42

Ichimura, H., 121, 122
Ickes, Barry W., 154, 163
identity. *See* national identity
IFIs. *See* international financial institutions
imagined community, 225, 227
IMF. *See* International Monetary Fund
IMF International Financial Statistics, 25
IMSA. *See* International Monetary Stability
    Act of 2000
income tax rates, U.S., 19–20
INDEC (Argentina). *See* Instituto Nacional de
    Estadistica y Censos
Indonesia, 3, 183, 184, 186, 191
    Asian crisis (1990s) and, 38, 193
    See also rupiah
industrial structure, optimal currency area
    theory and, 159
inflation
    Argentina and, 9, 14, 25, 27, 91, 98n.11,
        268, 372, 401, 403, 405–8, 419, 420
    bank-issued notes and, 397
    Brazil and, 29, 91, 164, 419, 420
    Canada and, 33, 182, 348, 372
    Cuba and, 426, 428, 434–35, 446n.1
    currency area considerations and, 28
    de facto dollarization and, 47, 196, 367
    dollarization and, 8, 34, 35, 46, 73, 112,
        114, 115, 124, 132, 133, 137n.15,
        138n.20, 197–98, 249
    Ecuador and, 280n.6
    emerging economies and, 3, 10
    exchange rate and, 88
    fixed vs. flexible exchange rates and, 6,
        103
    gold standard collapse and, 19, 30
    Hong Kong and, 31
    Italy and, 37, 348
    Keynesian approach to, 319, 325, 336
    Latin America and, 13, 164, 183, 369,
        372, 417
    Mexico and, 164, 270–71, 272–73
    monetary sovereignty and, 150, 226
    optimal currency area theory and, 162,
        163, 164, 223, 284
    Panama and, 115, 118, 198, 230
    Portugal and, 348
    real interest rates decline and, 288
    Russia and, 165
    seigniorage considerations and, 144, 226
    Spain and, 348
    stabilization programs, 72, 375, 403, 406,
        417
    United States and, 19, 30, 178, 348
    See also hyperinflation

inflation rate
    fixed exchange rate systems and, 25, 26
    gold and, 45n.17
    inflation vs. monetary targeting and, 26–27
    multiple-currency monetary unions and, 41
    optimum, 44n.11
    past peak, 70n.16
    world currency implementation issues and,
        40
inflation targeting, 26–27, 38, 103, 107, 182
    Brazil and, 384, 402, 413
    Canada and, 348, 359
    in Latin America, 27, 372, 384
    in multiple-currency monetary unions, 42
inflation tax, 132, 133, 137n.15, 144, 192,
    226, 393
informal dollarization, 228. *See also* de facto
    dollarization
information technology, 18, 20, 104
Institute of Finance Executives (Instituto
    Mexicano de Ejecutivos de Finanzas),
    277
Institute of Research on Finance and Prices
    (Cuba), 435
institutional design, monetary unions and,
    232
Instituto Nacional de Estadistica y Censos
    (Argentina), 391–92
integration, economic and financial. *See*
    economic integration; financial
    integration
Inter-American Development Bank, 252, 445
interest rates, 288–89
    in Argentina, 74–75, 78–82, 388, 391,
        393, 398
    credibility as factor in, 22
    currency board implementation and, 105
    deflation and, 87
    dollarization appropriateness and, 172–76,
        368, 370
    dollarization impact on, 9, 10, 35, 46, 79,
        97, 111, 132, 172, 197–98, 228, 377
    Latin American concerns and, 13, 14, 201,
        366, 368, 377–80, 382–84
    monetary union benefits and, 321–23, 326–
        27
    multiple-currency baskets and, 30
    multiple-currency monetary unions and, 41,
        45n.18
    North American Monetary Union and,
        314, 321–23, 326–27, 335
    risk premiums and, 184–85, 186, 196–97,
        207–8, 214, 368, 370
    speculative attacks and, 72, 104, 192, 380